Security Opportunities in Nano Devices and Emerging Technologies

Security Opportunities in Nano Devices and Emerging Technologies

Edited and Contributed by

Mark Tehranipoor
Domenic Forte
Garrett S. Rose
Swarup Bhunia

CRC Press
Taylor & Francis Group
Boca Raton London New York

CRC Press is an imprint of the
Taylor & Francis Group, an **informa** business

CRC Press
Taylor & Francis Group
6000 Broken Sound Parkway NW, Suite 300
Boca Raton, FL 33487-2742

First issued in paperback 2020

ISBN 13: 978-0-367-57262-4 (pbk)
ISBN 13: 978-1-138-03577-5 (hbk)

This book contains information obtained from authentic and highly regarded sources. Reasonable efforts have been made to publish reliable data and information, but the author and publisher cannot assume responsibility for the validity of all materials or the consequences of their use. The authors and publishers have attempted to trace the copyright holders of all material reproduced in this publication and apologize to copyright holders if permission to publish in this form has not been obtained. If any copyright material has not been acknowledged please write and let us know so we may rectify in any future reprint.

**Visit the Taylor & Francis Web site at
http://www.taylorandfrancis.com**

**and the CRC Press Web site at
http://www.crcpress.com**

To my family.

Mark Tehranipoor

To my family.

Domenic Forte

To my wife Betsy and daughter Lilly for their constant support and encouragement.

Garrett S. Rose

To my students.

Swarup Bhunia

Contents

SECTION I   NANO AND EMERGING DEVICES

SECTION II EMERGING TECHNOLOGIES AND ARCHITECTURES

Preface

Over the past three decades, the semiconductor industry and research community have devoted considerable effort toward developing new nano devices, analyzing their fundamental properties, and evaluating their viability for life after CMOS. Phase change memories (PCMs), memristors, nanowires, carbon nanotubes (CNTs), and graphene are just a few examples of such technologies. As the search for a successor continues, CMOS has remained a viable technology despite nanoscale integration challenges through the emergence of FinFET, fully depleted silicon on insulator (FD-SOI), and other technologies contributing to its staying power. In all these developments, the emphasis has always been placed on conventional metrics such as scalability (to smaller technology nodes), performance, power, reliability, and endurance. Little if any attention has been given to the properties, opportunities, and challenges that nano devices may offer to the security community, manufacturers, system integrators, and end users.

Research in CMOS technology-based hardware security at higher levels of abstraction (e.g., circuit and architecture) has seen consistent growth over the past decade, but the past several years have seen an uptick in research on the security of nano devices.

To date, any discovery identifying certain devices or features in some devices to be suitable for improving security has been based on an understanding of the individual primitives or properties of those devices. The research community currently lacks both the capability to fully explain the effectiveness of existing techniques and the metrics to predict the security properties and vulnerabilities of the next generation of nano devices and systems. No standards exist in government and industry to theoretically or experimentally evaluate any new devices against a set of known metrics and examine their strengths and weaknesses against known attacks. Further, since security is not considered a primary objective during device development and modeling, today, most security techniques are developed after devices have reached a certain level of maturity. Thus, obtaining a high level of security in that stage can be extremely challenging and expensive.

The objective of this book is to address these gaps in the fundamental knowledge base by bringing active researchers in hardware security and nanoelectronics areas together to provide an in-depth analysis of various security issues and to explain how nano devices and their unique properties can address them. This book includes contributions from experts in logic and memory devices like resistive memory elements, PCM, and silicon nanowire devices, as well as emerging architectures and systems like 2.5/3D architectures and memory architectures for neuromorphic computing. This book is composed of two major sections and a brief outline is provided below:

1. Section I focuses on nano devices and building security primitives from them. The target devices include nano CMOS, CNTs, nanowires, PCMs, resistive RAM, and memristors.
   - Chapter 1 provides a brief background on conventional CMOS and examples of emerging nanoscale CMOS transistors as our first foray into the nano regime. The cornucopia

of emerging nanoelectronic device technologies, including CNTs, spintronics, and memristors, and how such technologies come together in the form of nanoelectronic circuits and systems is discussed, including a perspective on how such technologies are changing the landscape of computing.

■ Chapter 2 begins by introducing the most popular hardware security primitives and countermeasures. The state-of-the-art nanoelectronic CMOS devices and their potential features are highlighted with emphasis on the trade-off between the underlying performance of these new features and security. Further, security primitives like physical unclonable function (PUF) and true random number generators (TRNGs), corresponding attacks, and countermeasures are presented in detail.

■ Chapter 3 considers security primitives based on memory cells. In particular, this chapter presents PUF and TRNG design with SRAM and DRAM, practical issues surrounding their reliability and need for error correction, security analysis, and attacks. In addition, novel PUF schemes based on data retention voltage, flip-flops, and flash memory are briefly discussed.

■ Chapter 4 discusses current efforts in memristor-based security primitive design. Common models describing the underlying physics and principles of operation are provided first, followed by the progress and development in hardware security primitive design using them. The chapter also describes the common performance and operational issues that demand attention before integrating memristive designs into existing hardware platforms.

■ Chapter 5 focuses on one of the emerging nonvolatile memories (NVMs) called resistive random access memory (RRAM) and RRAM-based hardware security primitives. RRAM has very special intrinsic randomness features, such as probabilistic switching, resistance variability, and random telegraph noise. The benefits of using these features to construct PUFs and TRNGs are discussed in detail.

■ Chapter 6 introduces another emerging resistive NVM technology called phase change memory (PCM). Similar to previous chapters, the basic operation of PCM is introduced first. This includes cell structure, materials, and modeling of PCM physics. Then the unique characteristics of PCM and how they can be used in hardware security applications are discussed.

■ Chapter 7 reviews the security properties offered by spintronics as well as their security vulnerabilities. In particular, different spintronic elements, including magnetic tunnel junctions and magnetic nanowire in domain wall memory, are introduced, and security primitives like PUFs, encryption engines, and TRNGs based on these elements are discussed.

■ Chapter 8 proposes the use of silicon nanowire (SiNW) FETs to assist in intellectual property (IP) protection. SiNW FETs, with their unique polarity-controllable feature, are used as a case study. Two security primitives, camouflaging layout and polymorphic gates, are investigated and implemented with SiNW FETs.

■ Chapter 9 introduces carbon-based emerging nano devices, including graphene and CNT. It describes novel graphene and CNT materials, and highlights their noteworthy features for security applications. Several hardware designs based on graphene and CNTs are described.

2. Section II focuses on emerging technologies and integrations that include 2.5D structures, 3D structures, biochips, and neuromorphic computing.

- Chapter 10 highlights the state-of-the-art nanoelectronic devices and their interesting properties for designing unique and robust PUFs. In-depth discussion on how to leverage CMOS logic devices and different compositions for PUF quality enhancement and thwarting different PUF-related attacks and vulnerabilities are presented in detail. This chapter also highlights the composition of PUFs in the emerging nanoelectronic memory domain.

- Chapter 11 consists of two parts. The first describes how double patterning lithography (DPL) can help thwart attacks from an untrusted employee in a foundry. The fundamentals of DPL and employing a customized DPL flow to defend the untrusted employee attacks are reviewed. In the second part, the security opportunities and challenges in 3D integration are surveyed.

- Chapter 12 demonstrates how an attacker can learn and replicate a proprietary algorithm. A secure neuromorphic computing system (MNCS) design is proposed to thwart replication attacks by leveraging memristor obsolescence effect. In addition, device-, circuit-, and architectural-level techniques to balance security and performance overhead are developed. Experimental results show that the proposed MNCS provides better usability as well as resilience to replication attacks, without introducing considerable calibration overhead.

- Chapter 13 presents a circuit edit-based design obfuscation. The key idea behind it is to fabricate and test an obfuscated design at the untrusted foundry, and then use circuit edit techniques to recover the original design functionality at a trusted facility. This chapter highlights the potential applications for such a technique, explains several gate-level techniques that can be used to obscure the logic structure of the design, and describes the challenges associated with FIB-based circuit edit.

- Chapter 14 outlines the basic properties of TRNGs and PUFs along with their implementations and standard tests for their evaluation. The methodologies to evaluate the desired properties of TRNGs and PUFs and architecture of the built-in-self-test (BIST) scheme are also discussed. This chapter also proposes the first BIST scheme for comprehensive online assessment of TRNGs and PUFs in hardware.

- Chapter 15 describes several emerging security threats and countermeasures for digital microfluidic systems. The high-level design flows, synthesis, and integration of cyberphysical digital microfluidic biochips (DMFBs) are discussed, followed by threats to DMFBs like denial-of-service, reading forgery, and design theft. Toward the end of this chapter, key properties of DMFBs are summarized, and their potential security challenges and opportunities are given as a guide for future research.

- Chapter 16 is focused on discussing the overview, feasibilities, and perspectives of engineering possible powerful security primitives, by exploiting the unique properties of fundamentally different state variables, in new, unconventional devices, namely, nanoelectromechanical systems (NEMS) featuring intrinsic electromechanical coupling effects that enable programmable state variables.

- Chapter 17 provides an overview of chaos-based computing, the parameterized chaogate model, and an analysis of its probabilistic behavior. It then describes how chaogates can be incorporated with static logic gates to create chaotic logic (CL) circuits. Deterministic and metaheuristic design approaches for CL circuits with tunable probability distributions are discussed with the perspective of providing code obfuscation and potentially other security benefits.

- Chapter 18 explores the possibilities for new computing architecture where the computer memory serves the purpose of both a storage and processing unit. Specifically, it discusses security applications of sneak paths in crossbar memory architecture, including sneak path-based encryption for memory data, memory testing based on sneak path currents, and tag generation from memory data for integrity checking.

We hope this book serves as an invaluable reference for students, researchers, and practitioners in the area of nanoelectronics and hardware security.

Mark Tehranipoor
Domenic Forte
Garrett S. Rose
Swarup Bhunia

Acknowledgments

We would like to acknowledge the tremendous effort of all the contributors of this book. We would also like to thank the Air Force Office of Scientific Research (AFOSR) for supporting MURI-2014 project on exploring security opportunities by nano devices and emerging technologies. Our special thanks to Dr. Xiaolin Xu, postdoctoral fellow at the University of Florida, for his contribution to Chapter 13 as well as his great assistance with the organizing and proofreading of this book. Finally, thanks to Richard O'Hanley and Stephanie Place of CRC Press/Taylor & Francis Group for proofreading and publishing this book.

Editors

Mark Tehranipoor earned his PhD from the University of Texas at Dallas in 2004. He is currently the Intel Charles E. Young Preeminence Endowed Professor in Cybersecurity at the University of Florida (UF). His current research projects include: hardware security and trust, supply chain security, VLSI (very-large-scale integration) design, and test and reliability. Dr. Tehranipoor has published more than 300 journal articles and refereed conference papers and has delivered more than 150 invited talks and keynote addresses. He has published 6 books and 11 book chapters. He is a recipient of several best paper awards as well as the 2008 IEEE Computer Society (CS) Meritorious Service Award, the 2012 IEEE CS Outstanding Contribution, the 2009 NSF CAREER Award, and the 2014 MURI award. He serves on the program committee of more than a dozen leading conferences and workshops. Dr. Tehranipoor served as program chair of the 2007 IEEE Defect-Based Testing (DBT) workshop, program chair of the 2008 IEEE Defect and Data Driven Testing (D3T) workshop, co-program chair of the 2008 International Symposium on Defect and Fault Tolerance in VLSI Systems (DFTS), general chair for D3T-2009 and DFTS-2009, and vice-general chair for NATW-2011 (IEEE North Atlantic Test Workshop). He cofounded the IEEE International Symposium on Hardware-Oriented Security and Trust (HOST) and served as general chair for HOST-2008 and HOST-2009. He is currently an associate editor for JETTA (*Journal of Electronic Testing: Theory and Applications*), JOLPE (*Journal of Low-Power Electronics*), IEEE TVLSI (*IEEE Transactions on Very Large Scale Integration Systems*), and ACM TODAES (ACM *Transactions on Design Automation for Electronic Systems*). Prior to joining UF, Dr. Tehranipoor served as the founding director for CHASE (Center for Hardware Assurance, Security, and Engineering) and CSI (Center of Excellence for Security Innovation) centers at the University of Connecticut. He is currently the codirector of the Florida Institute for Cybersecurity Research (FICS). Dr. Tehranipoor is a senior member of IEEE, a Golden Core member of IEEE, and a member of ACM and ACM SIGDA (ACM Special Interest Group on Design Automation).

Domenic Forte earned a BS in electrical engineering from Manhattan College, Riverdale, New York, USA, in 2006, and an MS and a PhD in electrical engineering from the University of Maryland, College Park, Maryland, USA, in 2010 and 2013, respectively. He is currently an assistant professor with the Electrical and Computer Engineering Department, University of Florida, Gainesville, Florida, USA. His research is primarily focused on the domain of hardware security and includes investigation of hardware security primitives, hardware Trojan detection and prevention, electronics supply chain security, and anti-reverse engineering. Dr. Forte was a recipient of the Young Investigator Award by Army Research Office (ARO) and the George Corcoran Memorial Outstanding Teaching Award by the Electrical and Computer Engineering Department at the University of Maryland. His work has also been recognized through several best paper awards and nominations from venues such as International Symposium on Hardware Oriented Security and

Trust (HOST), Design Automation Conference (DAC), and Adaptive Hardware Systems (AHS). He is a coauthor of the book *Counterfeit Integrated Circuits—Detection and Avoidance*, (Springer, 2015) and coeditor of the book *Hardware Protection through Obfuscation*, (Springer, 2017). He is currently serving as an associate editor for the *Journal of Hardware and Systems Security* (HaSS) and was previously guest editor of the *IEEE Computer Special Issue on Supply Chain Security for Cyber-Infrastructure*. He is also serving on the organizing committees of HOST and AsianHOST as well as the technical program committee of several other top conferences.

Garrett S. Rose earned a BS in computer engineering from Virginia Polytechnic Institute and State University (Virginia Tech), Blacksburg, Virginia, USA, in 2001 and an MS and a PhD in electrical engineering from the University of Virginia, Charlottesville, Virginia, in 2003 and 2006, respectively. His PhD dissertation was on the circuit design methodologies for molecular electronic circuits and computing architectures. He is currently an associate professor in the Department of Electrical Engineering and Computer Science, University of Tennessee, Knoxville, Tennessee, USA, where his research interests include the areas of nanoelectronic circuit design, neuromorphic computing, and hardware security. Prior to that, from June 2011 to July 2014, he was with the Air Force Research Laboratory, Information Directorate, Rome, New York. From August 2006 to May 2011, he was an assistant professor in the Department of Electrical and Computer Engineering, Polytechnic Institute of New York University, Brooklyn, New York. From May 2004 to August 2005, he was with the MITRE Corporation, McLean, Virginia, involved in the design and simulation of nanoscale circuits and systems. His research interests include low-power circuits, system-on-chip design, trusted hardware, and developing VLSI design methodologies for novel nanoelectronic technologies. Dr. Rose is a member of the Association of Computing Machinery, the IEEE Circuits and Systems Society, and IEEE Computer Society. He serves and has served on Technical Program Committees for several IEEE conferences (including ISVLSI, GLSVLSI, NANOARCH) and workshops in VLSI design. In 2010, he was a guest editor for a special issue of the *ACM Journal of Emerging Technologies in Computing Systems* that presented key papers from the IEEE/ACM International Symposium on Nanoscale Architectures (NANOARCH'09). Since April 2014, he is an associate editor for the *IEEE Transactions on Nanotechnology*.

Swarup Bhunia earned a BE (Hons.) from Jadavpur University, Kolkata, India and an MTech from the Indian Institute of Technology (IIT), Kharagpur, India. He earned a PhD from Purdue University, in 2005. Currently he is a professor of electrical and computer engineering, University of Florida. Earlier he was the T. and A. Schroeder associate professor of electrical engineering and computer science with Case Western Reserve University, Cleveland, Ohio. He has more than 15 years of research and development experience with more than 200 publications in peer-reviewed journals and premier conferences in integrated circuit and system design, computer-aided design tools and test techniques. His research interests include hardware security and trust, adaptive nanocomputing with emerging technologies, computing at extreme, and implantable/wearable microsystems. He has worked in the semiconductor industry on synthesis, verification, and low-power design for about three years. He was conferred the IBM Faculty Award, National Science Foundation (NSF) Career Development Award, Semiconductor Research Corporation (SRC) Technical Excellence Award as a team member, several best paper awards and best paper nominations, and SRC Inventor Recognition Award. He has been serving as an associate editor of the *IEEE Transactions on CAD*, the *IEEE Transactions on Multi-Scale Computing Systems*, the *ACM Journal of Emerging Technologies*, and the *Journal of Low Power Electronics*; served as guest editor of the *IEEE Design & Test of Computers* (2010, 2013), and the *IEEE Journal on Emerging and Selected Topics in Circuits and Systems* (2014). He has served as co-program chair of IEEE IMS3TW 2011, IEEE NANOARCH 2013, IEEE VDAT 2014, and IEEE HOST 2015, and in the program committee of many IEEE/ACM conferences.

Contributors

Md Tanvir Arafin
Department of Electrical and Computer
  Engineering
University of Maryland
College Park, Maryland

Navid Asadizanjani
Department of Electrical and Computer
  Engineering
University of Florida
Gainesville, Florida

Swarup Bhunia
Department of Electrical and Computer
  Engineering
University of Florida
Gainesville, Florida

Yu Bi
AMD
Orlando, Florida

Krishnendu Chakrabarty
Department of Electrical and Computer
  Engineering
Duke University
Durham, North Carolina

An Chen
IBM Research
Almaden and Semiconductor Research
  Corporation
Almaden, California

Yiran Chen
Department of Electrical and Computer
  Engineering
Duke University
Durham, North Carolina

Aaron Ciardullo
Department of Electrical and Computer
  Engineering
University of Connecticut
Storrs, Connecticut

Philip X.-L. Feng
Department of Electrical and Computer
  Engineering
Case Western Reserve University
Cleveland, Ohio

Domenic Forte
Department of Electrical and Computer
  Engineering
University of Florida
Gainesville, Florida

Pierre-Emmanuel Gaillardon
Department of Electrical and Computer
  Engineering
University of Utah
Salt Lake City, Utah

Bin Gao
Institute of Microelectronics
Tsinghua University
Beijing, China

Swaroop Ghosh
Electrical Engineering and Computer Science
  Department
Pennsylvania State University
State College, Pennsylvania

Ali Gokirmak
Department of Electrical and Computer
  Engineering
University of Connecticut
Storrs, Connecticut

Rekha Govindaraj
Department of Computer Science and
  Engineering
University of South Florida
Tampa, Florida

Daniel E. Holcomb
Department of Electrical and Computer
  Engineering
University of Massachusetts
Amherst, Massachusetts

X. Sharon Hu
Department of Computer Science and
  Engineering
University of Notre Dame
Notre Dame, Indiana

Siam U. Hussain
Department of Electrical and Computer
  Engineering
University of California
San Diego, California

Mohamed Ibrahim
Department of Electrical and Computer
  Engineering
Duke University
Durham, North Carolina

Chenglu Jin
Department of Electrical and Computer
  Engineering
University of Connecticut
Storrs, Connecticut

Yier Jin
Department of Electrical and Computer
  Engineering
University of Florida
Gainesville, Florida

Ramesh Karri
Department of Electrical and Computer
  Engineering
New York University
New York City, New York

Mohammad Nasim Imtiaz Khan
Electrical Engineering and Computer Science
  Department
Pennsylvania State University
State College, Pennsylvania

Raihan Sayeed Khan
Department of Electrical and Computer
  Engineering
University of Connecticut
Storrs, Connecticut

Farinaz Koushanfar
Department of Electrical and Computer
  Engineering
University of California
San Diego, California

Hai Li
Department of Electrical and Computer
  Engineering
Duke University
Durham, North Carolina

Rui Liu
School of Electrical Computer and Energy
  Engineering
Arizona State University
Tempe, Arizona

Yuntao Liu
Department of Electrical and Computer
  Engineering
University of Maryland
College Park, Maryland

Md. Badruddoja Majumder
Department of Electrical Engineering and
  Computer Science
University of Tennessee
Knoxville, Tennessee

Mehrdad Majzoobi
Mesh Motion Inc
Kensington, California

Cory Merkel
Air Force Research Lab
Rome, New York

Sadid Muneer
Department of Electrical and Computer
    Engineering
University of Connecticut
Storrs, Connecticut

Atul Prasad Deb Nath
Department of Electrical and Computer
    Engineering
University of Florida
Gainesville, Florida

Phuong Ha Nguyen
Department of Electrical and Computer
    Engineering
University of Connecticut
Storrs, Connecticut

Michael Niemier
Department of Computer Science and
    Engineering
University of Notre Dame
Notre Dame, Indiana

Nafisa Noor
Department of Electrical and Computer
    Engineering
University of Connecticut
Storrs, Connecticut

Yachuan Pang
Institute of Microelectronics
Tsinghua University
Beijing, China

He Qian
Institute of Microelectronics
Tsinghua University
Beijing, China

Gang Qu
Department of Electrical and Computer
    Engineering
University of Maryland
College Park, Maryland

Fahim Rahman
Department of Electrical and Computer
    Engineering
University of Florida
Gainesville, Florida

Garrett S. Rose
Department of Electrical Engineering and
    Computer Science
University of Tennessee
Knoxville, Tennessee

Jake Scoggin
Department of Electrical and Computer
    Engineering
University of Connecticut
Storrs, Connecticut

Bicky Shakya
Department of Electrical and Computer
    Engineering
University of Florida
Gainesville, Florida

Haoting Shen
Department of Electrical and Computer
    Engineering
University of Florida
Gainesville, Florida

Helena Silva
Department of Electrical and Computer
    Engineering
University of Connecticut
Storrs, Connecticut

Ankur Srivastava
Department of Electrical and Computer
    Engineering
University of Maryland
College Park, Maryland

Xiaoyu Sun
School of Electrical Computer and Energy
    Engineering
Arizona State University
Tempe, Arizona

Jack Tang
Department of Electrical and Computer
Engineering
New York University
New York City, New York

Mark Tehranipoor
Department of Electrical and Computer
Engineering
University of Florida
Gainesville, Florida

Mesbah Uddin
Department of Electrical Engineering and
Computer Science
University of Tennessee
Knoxville, Tennessee

Marten van Dijk
Department of Electrical and Computer
Engineering
University of Connecticut
Storrs, Connecticut

Zachary Woods
Department of Electrical and Computer
Engineering
University of Connecticut
Storrs, Connecticut

Huaqiang Wu
Institute of Microelectronics
Tsinghua University
Beijing, China

Yang Xie
Department of Electrical and Computer
Engineering
University of Maryland
College Park, Maryland

Xiaolin Xu
Department of Electrical and Computer
Engineering
University of Florida
Gainesville, Florida

Chaofei Yang
Department of Electrical and Computer
Engineering
University of Pittsburgh
Pittsburgh, Pennsylvania

Shimeng Yu
School of Electrical Computer and Energy
Engineering
Arizona State University
Tempe, Arizona

Jiann-Shiun Yuan
Department of Electrical and Computer
Engineering
University of Central Florida
Orlando, Florida

NANO AND EMERGING DEVICES

Chapter 1

Introduction: Overview of VLSI, Nanoelectronics, and Hardware Security

Garrett S. Rose

Contents

Computing in the twenty-first century has become pervasive. What was once the domain only of scientists and engineers has now become commonly available in almost every corner of the globe. We now have dozens of computer processors in our cars, we wear computers in the form of fitness trackers, and we carry in our pockets powerful computers that sometimes double as phones. In short, computers are everywhere and many people today depend on them for even the most basic tasks.

The very pervasiveness of modern computing is a direct result of constant advancements in solid-state integrated circuit (IC) technology over the past half century. We can trace the history of computing back to machines such as Charles Babbage's difference engine [1] or the ENIAC of the late 1940s [2]. However, computing as we know it today is a direct result of the advent of the transistor, first realized in the form of the point-contact transistor fabricated by Bardeen, Shockley, and Brattain at Bell Laboratories in 1947 [3]. The point-contact transistor was relatively bulky and constructed from germanium. Later, other semiconductor materials, notably silicon, would be used to realize bipolar transistors and eventually field-effect transistors (FETs) in the 1960s [3].

In 1965, Gordan Moore of Intel famously observed that the number of transistors integrated per square inch doubled every two years [3]. This observation, known as "Moore's law," became something of a self-fulfilling prophesy as transistor density, along with switching speeds, indeed continued to double every 18–24 months for the next 5 decades. Figure 1.1 illustrates increases in transistor density from the early 1970s through the latest generation of processors in 2016 [4,5]. While the continued increase into the early 2000s is quite impressive, it is also worth pointing out that transistor scaling has already begun to slow down, as illustrated by the flattening of the curve in Figure 1.1. Thus, we are now entering an interesting period where alternative nanoscale technologies are actively pursued for future computing applications.

With the slowdown of transistor scaling, often pointed to as a sign of the looming end of Moore's law, many researchers have begun to consider "Beyond Moore" or "More than Moore" technology alternatives [5]. One underlying goal of such research into novel nanoelectronic devices is to find technologies that allow for a continuation of the performance scaling that has been enjoyed over the past several decades. However, many novel nanoelectronic technologies are often not, in and of themselves, more robust than silicon-based CMOS transistors. Instead, these emerging devices are more often found to offer new opportunities for novel applications or to provide performance improvements through hybrid integration with CMOS [6–8]. Thus, "More than Moore" advocates would argue that nanoelectronic technologies should be considered for the novel applications they are likely to enable, as opposed to simply enhancing the performance of existing computer architectures. Regardless, the landscape of IC technology is beginning to change right at the moment that computing has become commonplace.

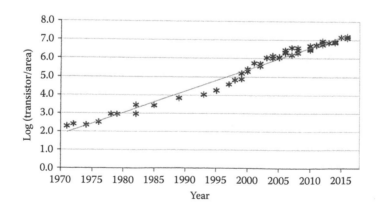

Figure 1.1 **Illustration of Moore's law, showing a biannual doubling of the number of transistors per unit area since Intel's first microprocessor in 1971.**

This chapter first provides some brief background on computer engineering and conventional CMOS. From there, examples of already-emerging nanoscale CMOS transistors are discussed as our first foray into the nano regime. While the cutting edge of silicon transistor technology is nanoscale, many in the research community use the terms "nanotechnology" and "nanoelectronics" to refer to nonsilicon nanoscale electronic devices. Thus, we next discuss the cornucopia of emerging nanoelectronic device technologies, including carbon nanotubes, spintronics, and memristors, to name a few. How such technologies come together in the form of nanoelectronic circuits and systems is also discussed, including some perspective on how such technologies are changing the landscape of computing.

Finally, given the very pervasiveness of computing, it is important that we also consider the security implications of these systems that have become so common in everyday life. As people continue to become more connected and leverage information systems more often, it is clear that they also become more willing to use such systems to store and communicate sensitive information. Thus, the design of modern computer systems, including emerging nanoelectronic computer architectures, must consider security as a first-order design criterion.

1.1 Nanoscale Transistor Technologies

Nanotechnology is most often defined as the field of study associated with the synthesis and integration of structures with defining feature sizes less than 100 nm [9]. Given the fact that gate lengths for silicon CMOS transistors have been below 100 nm (now at 14 nm) for more than a decade now, modern electronics is already dominated by nanotechnology. To differentiate conventional CMOS from non-CMOS nanotechnologies, terms such as "nanoscale CMOS" and "deep submicron" are often used. That said, several novel forms of semiconductor transistor technology have emerged that are certainly worth considering in the context of "Beyond Moore" nanoelectronics.

1.1.1 Silicon-on-Insulator

Silicon-on-insulator (SOI) technology has emerged in recent years as a way to improve the performance of semiconductor devices. Specifically, SOI refers to a fabrication technique where a semiconductor, typically silicon, is layered on top of an insulator, typically silicon dioxide. Since the top semiconductor layer can be very thin, it becomes possible to implement doped diffusion regions that extend all the way through to the insulator underneath. Further, some SOI transistors fall into the category of "fully depleted," meaning when the device is "on," the entire channel is inverted. In short, the SOI structure leads to reduced parasitic capacitance and other nonideal effects such that the performance is drastically improved relative to conventional, non-SOI approaches.

Manufacturing SOI devices and circuits can be challenging depending on how the top semiconductor layer is fabricated on top of the insulator. Ideally, the top semiconductor would be grown via epitaxial techniques such that the resulting layer is very thin. However, the crystallinity of the oxide/insulator layer typically does not match that of the desired semiconductor, meaning epitaxial growth leads to nonideal behavior. A more common technique for SOI is the use of a "handle" wafer—a thick wafer of the same material as the top semiconductor that is flipped and essentially glued onto the insulator. Since the top semiconductor is manufactured independent of the insulator, it will have the necessary crystallinity required for the desired electronic devices and circuits. However, the process of flipping, "glueing," and thinning that top layer tends to be expensive.

1.1.2 FinFETs

Another approach to yielding "nanoscale" FET is to go vertical. At the device level, going vertical could be used to refer to the advent of "FinFET" transistors, meaning transistors whose semiconductor channels are fabricated vertically as fin structures. The so-called fin allows a gate to be wrapped around the channel on three sides, leaving only the bottom of the fin/channel open to the underlying bulk substrate. As is the case with SOI, the wrapped gate leads to a more fully depleted channel and thus reduced parasitic effects. The reduction of parasitic capacitance and other nonideal characteristics leads to improved performance. Further, since the fins are fabricated from an existing semiconductor substrate, as opposed to layered on top of an insulator, FinFET technology does not suffer from the same manufacturing challenges common to SOI. It is worth pointing out that FinFET technology has become the common approach for sub-20 nm CMOS technology, with companies such as Intel, Samsung, Taiwan Semiconductor, and Global Foundries all offering technology nodes defined by 14 nm and soon even 10 and 7 nm gate lengths [10,11].

1.1.3 Three-Dimensional Integrated Circuits

At feature sizes of only 10 nm and possibly smaller, CMOS transistor technology has been scaled down about as far as possible in terms of lateral dimensions. In order to continue to gain density improvements in modern semiconductor electronics, vertical dimensions must be better exploited. This is the primary motivation of three-dimensional integrated circuit (3DIC) technology. Specifically, 3DIC refers to a layered approach to manufacturing where multiple semiconductor substrates are stacked on top of one another in order to implement circuits vertically as well as laterally. There are several approaches to 3DIC, including face-to-face, front-to-back, and SOI-based approaches. Examples of both the face-to-face and front-to-back arrangements can be seen in Figure 1.2.

The face-to-face approach to 3DIC is perhaps the simplest in that no additional structures need to be implemented in silicon. Instead, the top metal layers of two die or wafers would include contact points or landing pads for connecting the two layers together. One layer is then flipped and oriented on top of the other such that connections are made at the predefined contact points. Thus, the resulting 3DIC consists of two semiconductor layers oriented in a "face-to-face" arrangement. One challenge with the face-to-face approach comes when trying to construct a 3DIC with more than two layers. In this case, either off-chip connections are needed to connect to other pairs or a

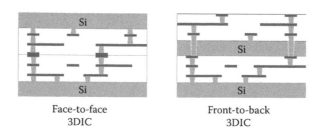

Face-to-face
3DIC

Front-to-back
3DIC

Figure 1.2 Example illustrations of two-tier 3DIC arrangements, showing face-to-face (left) and front-to-back (right) integration.

second form of 3DIC is required that utilizes through silicon vias (TSVs) to connect layers oriented in a "back-to-back" arrangement.

Many 3DIC implementations are constructed from some form of a back-to-front arrangement where each semiconductor layer is oriented with metal layers to the top. In this case, connections across layers require the use of TSVs. Each TSV tends to be larger in the cross-sectional area relative to conventional vias, limiting the number of total TSVs one could integrate onto a single die. However, such 3DIC technologies enable drastic reductions in total wire lengths, thereby reducing delay and interconnect power consumption. Further, the ability to stack transistors vertically enables a form of scaling where the number of transistors per unit area continues to rise with an increase in the number of layers.

1.1.4 Bulk-Silicon Electronics and Limits to Moore's Law

Bulk silicon CMOS continues to be the major workhorse in modern electronics. While novel "Beyond CMOS" nanotechnologies are emerging, many in the community see CMOS as playing a significant role for some time to come. This has led to hybrid CMOS–nanoelectronic approaches where CMOS is used for functions such as I/O and gain while a nanoscale technology is used for dense memory and/or logic implementations [6]. The major advantage nanotechnology brings is increased density and the ability to squeeze functionality into regular crossbar structures. Further, nanoelectronic materials are continually being explored as extreme low-power alternatives to their CMOS counterparts. This is particularly important for 3DIC-based architectures where heat across upper layers becomes a major concern [12,13]. While nanoscale CMOS continues to have its place, emerging systems and application domains such as digital microfluidics, Internet of things (IoT), and neuromorphic computing bring new and exciting design challenges. Thus, the future for ICs consist of a mixed bag of technologies, including many niche devices constructed from novel nanoscale materials.

1.2 Beyond CMOS Nanoelectronics

1.2.1 Molecular and Organic Electronics

In 1974, Aviram and Ratner presented a "molecular rectifier" designed as a single organic molecule with both donor and acceptor regions built into the molecular structure itself [14]. This seminal work marks the beginning of the field of molecular electronics where carbon-based structures are designed and synthesized to realize a variety of useful electronic devices and circuits. By the late 1990s, several research groups had even experimentally demonstrated electrical conduction through single molecules. A famous example was conductance through a benzene ring connected between two gold electrodes, also known as a "break junction" (Figure 1.3) [15]. These advances drew interest to the field of molecular electronics for two primary reasons: (1) molecular scale meant a form of "deep" nanoscale suggesting ultimate advances in terms of scaling and (2) molecular structures could be tailored in such a way that they "self-assemble" into complex structures, in this case electronic circuits. Self-assembly became a hallmark of nanotechnology more generally as fabrication costs for more traditional, solid-state electronics began to skyrocket. Indeed, modern semiconductor fabrication facilities easily cost billions of U.S. dollars to maintain, leaving only a handful of companies able to provide advanced manufacturing capabilities at the bleeding edge. With self-assembly, fueled in part by the rise of molecular electronics, comes the possibility for significant reductions in IC manufacturing costs.

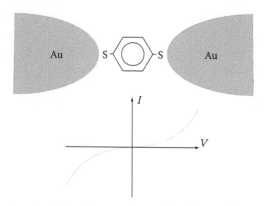

Figure 1.3 Example of a benzene ring electrically connected via thiol groups to two gold electrodes within a "break junction." This technique was pioneered by Mark Reed et al. Conductance of a molecular junction. *Science,* **278(5336):252–254, 1997.**

Along with the advent of molecular electronics came considerations for the use of DNA as a means to self-assemble nanoscale structures, including electronic devices and circuits. As the basic building block of life, a strand of DNA can be thought of as a program, defined by patterns of base pairs, used to construct proteins and other complex structures. Depending on the programming, DNA fragments can also be made to self-assemble into a variety of complex nanoscale structures. Various methods have emerged to harness DNA programming, including DNA tiles, lattices [16], and DNA origami [17]. These DNA-based self-assembly techniques have also been used to organize materials such as gold nanoparticles [18] and carbon nanotubes [19] into small electronic devices. While this research is ongoing, DNA provides an interesting example of how molecular-scale electronics can enable self-assembly techniques for future cost-effective IC fabrication.

Also related to molecular electronics is the field of polymer-based organic electronics, including organic light-emitting diode (OLED) and organic field-effect transistor (OFET) technologies [20,21]. Similar to their smaller molecular electronic counterparts, structures such as OLEDs utilize semiconducting properties in molecular compounds, specifically polymers, to realize electronic systems. OLED technology has already proven successful in some commercial domains, including in the form of high-definition OLED-based televisions. An interesting aspect of polymer-based electronics is that circuits can literally be printed onto flexible substrates. Such capability is already leading to interesting applications of flexible electronics not previously feasible using solid-state electronic technologies alone.

While polymer-based electronics has proven to be a successful example of molecular electronic technology, the field representing device technologies such as the molecular rectifier has faced many challenges and setbacks. For starters, molecular electronic devices, especially those synthesized from "short" molecules, must be low power such that operating temperatures also remain low. Temperature constraints also present fabrication challenges, particularly for molecular devices that might be integrated alongside bulk silicon CMOS. Such challenges notwithstanding, molecular electronics led to a variety of interesting nanoscale electronic devices, including the molecular switching devices constructed from self-assembled monolayers (SAMs) of molecules such as Tour wires [22,23] and rotaxane [24,25]. Early investigations into molecular electronics included several circuit and system proposals that leveraged such molecular switches, mainly as dense memory arrays and programmable logic systems [26,27].

1.2.2 Memristors and Memristive Systems

While investigating molecular electronic switches, researchers discovered that a variety of materials could be leveraged to implement nanoscale hysteretic switching devices. Specifically, in 2008, HP Labs first associated behavior they had observed for nanoscale titanium oxide materials with a property known as "memristance," a concatenation of memory and resistance [28]. This TiO_2 electronic switch, or "memristor," behaved in many ways like the molecular electronic switches fervently studied earlier in the same decade. However, the memristors presented by HP were based on solid-state transition metal-oxide (TMO) materials that are much more robust than their molecular counterparts. Hysteretic switching in this case refers to the pinched *I–V* curve indicative of resistance changes upon the application of an electric field. Typically, the devices are also nonvolatile, meaning the last-known resistance state is maintained even when powered down. Memristive and related switching devices have been studied extensively as potential high-density successors to other nonvolatile memory technologies such as Flash.

The theory behind the memristor, and even the term itself, actually dates back to the early 1970s when Leon Chua first proposed the memristor as the fourth fundamental electronic circuit element [29,30]. Chua's insight was that all fundamental electronic devices (resistors, capacitors, and inductors) relate two out of four parameters: voltage, current, charge (the integral of current), and flux linkage (the integral of voltage). Resistance is due to a direct relationship between current and voltage, capacitance relates charge and voltage, while inductance relates flux linkage with current. At the time Chua first presented his memristor theory, nothing yet related charge with flux linkage. Figure 1.4 illustrates the memristor symbol along with the other fundamental electronic devices. According to the theory, this very relationship between charge and flux linkage also leads to a "pinched hysteresis" signifying changing resistance as a function of the applied voltage. This very property has been observed for a variety of nanoscale materials, including TiO_2, TaO_2, HfO_2, chalcogenides, and spintronic materials, to name a few.

1.2.3 Carbon Nanotubes and Graphene

Two-dimensional (2D) materials, including sheets of carbon or graphene, have also emerged as interesting materials for potential beyond CMOS device technologies [31]. Owing to several

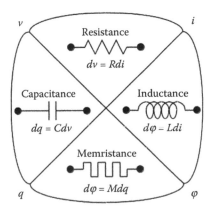

Figure 1.4 The four fundamental electronic devices, including the memristor, and their associated relationships with parameters current *i*, voltage *v*, charge *q*, and flux linkage *ϕ*.

important mechanical and electrical properties, graphene has attracted a lot of attention from the research community. On the mechanical front, a single sheet of graphene (one carbon atom thick) is considered one of the strongest materials in the world. In terms of electrical properties, graphene can be used as either a metal or a semiconductor depending on the size of the sheet and the orientation of the carbon lattice relative to the flow of current. Further, electron transport through graphene is often considered ballistic, meaning the sheet resistance of graphene is negligible. Thus, graphene and carbon nanotubes are often considered for emerging interconnect technologies.

A carbon nanotube or CNT [32] can be thought of as a rolled-up graphene sheet capped by half-spheres of carbon on each end. Many of the same properties evident in graphene, strength, ballistic transport, semiconducting, and metallic behaviors, are also present in CNTs. An electron transported through a CNT will tend to travel along the length of the tube. Thus, the orientation of the sheet, as it is "wrapped" to form the CNT, will determine whether the CNT is semiconducting or metallic. Put another way, some CNTs, depending on how they are wrapped, will come in semiconductor flavors while others come as metallic. In order to use a single CNT as part of a circuit, it must first be sorted according to its wrapping and then assembled. Sorting CNTs for metallic versus semiconducting behavior has proven to be one of the great challenges for implementing CNT-based electronics.

Graphene and CNTs, along with other 2D and 1D materials, have gained attention as successors to bulk silicon. Since these materials come in both semiconducting and metallic forms, they are naturally suited to implementing transistors, diodes, and other semiconductor-based electronic devices. Further, ballistic transport properties lead to the potential for vast speed improvements relative to their bulk silicon counterparts. In short, where technologies such as memristors bring new behavior, graphene and CNTs offer possibilities to implement extreme scale versions of more conventional electronic devices. As promising as these materials are, challenges in assembling already-formed tubes and sheets, in addition to sorting, present significant impediments to near-term commercial realizations.

1.3 Nanoelectronic Circuits and Systems

Along with novel materials and device technologies come new opportunities for circuit design. Common to many nanoelectronic circuits considered in the literature is the crossbar structure (illustrated in Figure 1.5), consisting of two sets of nanoscale wires organized perpendicular to one another. The crossbar became popular with molecular electronic technologies where researchers proposed dense arrays of molecular switches at the crosspoints. Addressing the vertical and horizontal wires of the crossbar could most naturally be used to select individual crosspoints as memory elements. Depending on the relative strength of an individual crosspoint or switch, such crossbar arrays could also be used as programmable logic arrays. Many memristor-based systems also leverage the crossbar array as a fundamental structure in memory and logic architectures.

The upside of the crossbar array is the increased density gained by using two-terminal devices (e.g., memristors) as memory elements. As a point of comparison, traditional static RAM (SRAM) memory cells consist of at least six transistors each. Even dynamic RAM (DRAM) consists of both a transistor and a capacitor that either takes up a significant area or must be implemented as a "trench." Circuits built from floating gate transistors (e.g., Flash) are also larger than a single crosspoint in a crossbar architecture. Thus, at the extreme, memristor-based crossbars provide the potential for significant device density improvements.

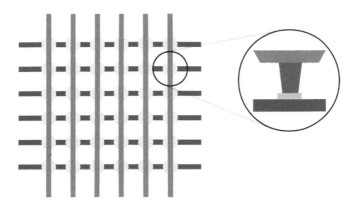

Figure 1.5 Illustration of a crossbar array with a transition metal-oxide memristor fabricated at each crosspoint (right). Self-assembled monolayers of molecular electronic switches have also been considered for the reconfigurable crosspoints of crossbar-based architectures.

One major challenge for memristor-based (or for that matter molecular electronic) crossbar memory architectures is that each memory element is resistive. More specifically, regardless of what resistance state is stored onto a particular memristor, current is allowed to flow in both directions. This leads to parasitic sneak path currents, such that the output current measured for a selected memory cell is also a function of unselected cells. To eliminate such sneak paths, most resistive RAM (RRAM or ReRAM) structures include a select transistor alongside each resistive or memristive memory element—an arrangement referred to as 1-transistor, 1-resistor (1T1R). Even with the added transistor, an individual RRAM memory cell tends to be smaller, and hence more dense, than its CMOS counterparts [33].

Novel nanoelectronic technologies also offer opportunities to implement more analog circuits at smaller scales. In the case of memristors, for example, many materials exhibit a range of possible resistance states. For memory, this leads to the possibility of storing multiple bits of information for every two-terminal memristive memory cell, leading to even further density improvements. Further, since the resistance of a memristor changes with the applied voltage signal (essentially becoming more or less conductive with use), the device is very similar in operation to a biological synapse. Thus, many in the research community have explored memristors, including memristor-based crossbars, for implementing nanoelectronic brain-inspired or neuromorphic circuits [34,35]. Nanoelectronic neuromorphic systems make for an interesting example of how novel nanoelectronic device behavior (e.g., memristance) can lead to novel circuits and applications (e.g., neuromorphic computing).

1.4 Modern Computing Landscape

Whether nanoscale CMOS, molecular electronics, carbon nanotubes, or memristors, nanoelectronic technologies are already reshaping computer technology and the way we must approach design. A prime example of this changing landscape is the emerging IoT paradigm (see Figure 1.6) where small, low-power electronics, often enabled by nanotechnology, is integrated into everyday systems. Once "unintelligent" devices, such as toasters, thermostats, and food dispensers, are now equipped with computing power equivalent to something only available to governments and large

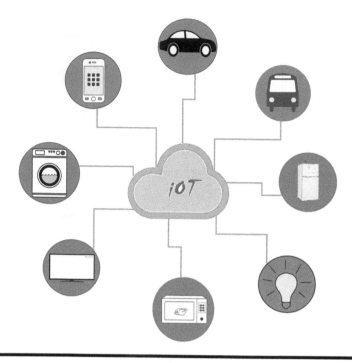

Figure 1.6 The Internet-of-things (IoT) paradigm.

corporations not much more than a generation ago. With such computing power, these simple devices are now part of an ever-growing information ecosystem whereby nearly every corner of our lives can be connected to the Internet. This is IoT and, in many ways, it has arrived.

As nanoelectronic technologies, such as memristor-based memory, become more commonplace, IoT devices will continue to become more "intelligent" in terms of the information they are able to gather, process, and communicate. Dense, persistent memory technology, of which memristive RRAM is an example, enables this continued improvement in computational power for IoT. However, as these systems emerge, designers must also be cognizant of the security challenges associated with such technology. Persistent memory, for example, presents many security and privacy challenges necessitating robust techniques that offer assurances that sensitive information is protected.

Modern computing also intersects with sensitive application domains such as medicine. While medical information stored in large data centers presents privacy concerns that must be addressed, so do small wearable devices used for a whole host of medical applications, from monitoring vital statistics to regulating insulin injections. Further, as these wearable devices are often now part of the IoT ecosystem, patients are now vulnerable to computer security threats that may even impact their safety. It goes without question that safeguarding such systems becomes a critical design decision that must be met head-on from the very start of the design process itself. No longer can security be left as a second-class design consideration.

In addition to the growing IoT landscape, novel nanotechnologies are also enabling novel forms of computing. In fact, this is what "Beyond Moore" computing is all about—leveraging the unique attributes of beyond CMOS nanoelectronics. Here, the aim is not to use nanotechnology to continue constructing classic systems for which CMOS is particularly well suited. Instead, novel nanotechnology should be leveraged for enabling application domains in which CMOS has historically struggled.

An example of how nanoelectronics enable novel computing is the ever-emerging area of brain-inspired neuromorphic computing. The field of neuromorphic computing is not new. In fact, early brain-inspired computing models date back to the earliest days of modern computing. Further, the term "neuromorphic" was coined by Carver Mead in the late 1980s to describe analog CMOS circuits he was then investigating to model biological neural systems [36]. More recently, neuromorphic computing has been reinvigorated in part by the advent of the memristor, which in many ways naturally behaves as an artificial synapse [34]. Given the density advantages of memristive technology, memristors are expected by many to provide key advances to implementing complex neuromorphic computing sytems in ways that have proven impractical for standalone CMOS.

Neuromorphic computing enabled by nanotechnology offers an example of how we must be prepared to rethink the way we approach emerging technologies. What are the security challenges for systems that are trained instead of programmed? What further challenges, or even opportunities, exist for computer systems that learn continuously? While the ever-growing area of machine learning, including deep learning technologies, may offer some clues, it is worth pointing out that nanoelectronic neuromorphic computing may one day be used for IoT, bringing new meaning to the concept of enabling intelligence to ordinary household appliances.

1.5 Hardware Security and Nanoelectronics: A Primer

Traditionally, computer security has primarily been concerned with the encryption and decryption of sensitive data. Cryptographic algorithms are continually being developed and improved for the purpose of providing provably secure encrypted ciphertext that can be communicated over unsecured channels with little concern that an attacker would be likely to recover the original plaintext. These cryptographic approaches are often based on the assumption that the complex algorithm (RSA, AES, etc.) used for encryption/decryption is executed in a secure environment with little to no expectation that information can leak during execution. However, no system is truly ideal and some information can be expected to leak, especially when vulnerabilities such as side-channel attacks are ignored. Thus, not only must the cryptographic algorithm be strong, but also the algorithm must be implemented with care, whether in hardware or software.

Hardware security is concerned with, among other things, the robustness of the implementation of security protocols in a real-world environment. This is particularly important for paradigms such as embedded systems and nano-enabled IoT. Here, computer systems are deployed in a real-world environment where attackers have increased opportunities to gain direct access and potentially exploit side-channel vulnerabilities. For example, power analysis on an embedded system running the AES block cipher can be used to extract secret keys within a matter of hours [37,38]. Of course, mitigation schemes exist to limit these threats but must be incorporated into the cipher implementation during design. Often, this includes careful design of the underlying hardware executing the algorithm.

While encryption of sensitive data constitutes a traditional view of computer security, serious vulnerabilities also exist for the hardware and underlying logic design. For example, IC design relies on a global supply chain to realize most bleeding-edge computer systems on the market today. This means systems designed on one continent comprise intellectual property (IP) blocks provided by vendors on a second continent. Further, the final system design itself is fabricated by

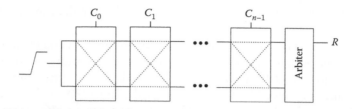

Figure 1.7 A delay-based arbiter PUF constructed from 2×2 switches, each path yielding an independent delay based on process variations. Two unique paths are selected to race one another using an N bit challenge C. The path with the fastest delay determines the state of the resulting response bit R for the challenge provided.

yet another corporation, often with fabrication facilities located on yet a third continent. In short, an IC design passes through many hands from inception to assembly, hands that original IP owners and designers must learn to trust.

Given the nature of the global supply chain, much vulnerability exist for modern ICs, including counterfeiting, reverse engineering, design piracy, and cloning. While many of these threats are concerned with IP protection, more aggressive threats are also possible via malicious design modifications or Hardware Trojan Horses [39,40]. In order to mitigate such threats, a variety of hardware security primitives have been devised that help track valid ICs through their life cycle and, in some cases, provide active management.

A common example of a hardware security primitive is the physical unclonable function or PUF [41]. A PUF essentially works as a sort of unique identifier where unique fingerprints are generated for each IC implementation or chip. This is made possible by extracting information from the inherent process variations of an IC chip itself. Process variations are stochastic in nature and each variability profile is thus unique to each individual chip coming off a fabrication line. For example, Figure 1.7 depicts a delay-based PUF that leverages subtle delay differences between any two delay paths selected out of a large number of possible combinations [42]. These various combinations are selected via a challenge that is supplied to produce a response unique to the particular chip in question. Thus, a PUF can be a powerful tool for a variety of authentication protocols [43].

Nanoelectronic technologies, including both nanoscale CMOS and beyond CMOS devices, tend to exhibit process variations. Thus, early work in the area where nanoelectronics and security meet has been focused on the implementation of nanoelectronic security primitives that leverage such variability as a feature. This includes a variety of nanoelectronic PUF circuits, some of which offer advantages over their CMOS counterparts [44,45]. For example, nanoelectronic technologies such as memristors are inherently very dense and often consume very little power. As such, security primitives implemented from nanoelectronic technologies tend to be more energy and area efficient relative to CMOS only alternatives. This can be particularly useful for emerging computing domains such as IoT where resources such as power tend to be very scarce [46]. Thus, novel nanotechnologies offer possibilities for more energy-efficient security primitive implementations.

Threats related to reverse engineering and cloning are often best addressed via obfuscation techniques that hide logic design and execution detail. From a device perspective, obfuscation could potentially be achieved by leveraging the low power consumption of emerging technologies (relative to CMOS) to hide information loss through side-channels [47]. In terms of emerging architectures, neuromorphic and other approaches can also inherently provide the equivalent of code obfuscation where instructions executed become difficult to reverse engineer [48]. It should also be noted that such obfuscation techniques work by adding a degree of complexity that confuses the would-be attacker. This complexity will inevitably also complicate the authenticated user experience. Thus, a balance must be found between the confused attacker experience and any subsequent added complexity for authorized users. After all, security-aware design can be thought of as a form of user-aware design.

1.6 Conclusion

The objective of this chapter is to provide an overview of nanoelectronics, including both nanoscale CMOS and beyond CMOS technologies, and how such technologies impact hardware security. Several examples of emerging nanotechnologies have been discussed, including molecular electronics, memristors, graphene, and carbon nanotubes. These technologies are examples of a wide spectrum of novel nanoelectronic materials and devices that are beginning to reshape computing. In the following chapters, other examples of emerging device technologies are discussed. For example, magnetic RAM or spintronic devices are very similar to metal-oxide memristors in terms of their potential for memory technology disruption. Such technologies, spintronics and memristors, provide important opportunities for increased memory density and improved performance. Further, these and other related technologies offer opportunities for efficient security primitive design, as is discussed in depth in the following chapters.

A secondary goal of this introduction has been to motivate the emerging landscape of novel computer architectures and application domains. Neuromorphic computing is one such architecture used as an example of just how different emerging design paradigms can be relative to conventional von Neumann architectures. A more in-depth discussion on nano-enabled neuromorphic computing is provided later in this book, with particular emphasis placed on corresponding security challenges and opportunities. As another example of beyond von Neumann computing, chaos-based computing that leverages the large state space of chaotic oscillators can provide new opportunities for code and logic obfuscation. These and other examples of emerging nano-enabled computer architectures provide useful insight into how security concerns can and should be addressed in the twenty-first century.

Finally, with novel device technologies and disruptive computer architectures come new application domains. As part of this introduction, IoT has specifically been called out as an example of how modern computing has entered nearly every facet of daily life. With such an abundance of computing power come real challenges for privacy, security, and in some cases even safety. While other application domains are certainly emerging (biomedical, machine learning, etc.), all of these examples show that the ever-changing computing landscape is both challenging and exciting. As computer scientists and engineers continue forward with these new technologies and applications, they must do so with the mindset that security is now a first-class design paradigm.

Acknowledgments

The author would like to thank Mesbah Uddin and Md. Badruddoja Majumder of the University of Tennessee for useful discussion about these topics and for help with organizing some of the figures and references included in this chapter.

References

1. D. Harris and S. Harris. *Digital Design and Computer Architecture* (2nd edition). Morgan Kaufmann, Boston, 7, 2012.
2. W. Stallings. *Computer Organization and Architecture: Designing for Performance* (7th edition). Prentice-Hall, Inc., Upper Saddle River, NJ, 2005.
3. N. Weste and D. Harris. *CMOS VLSI Design: A Circuits and Systems Perspective* (4th edition). Addison-Wesley Publishing Company, Boston, MA, 2010.
4. G. E. Moore. Cramming more components onto integrated circuits. *Electronics*, **38**(8):114–117, 1965.
5. M. M. Waldrop. More than Moore. *Nature*, **530**(7589):144–147, 2016.
6. M. M. Ziegler and M. R. Stan. A case for CMOS/nano co-design. In *IEEE/ACM International Conference on Computer Aided Design*, San Jose, CA, USA, pages 348–352, November 2002.
7. K. K. Likharev and D. B. Strukov. *CMOL: Devices, Circuits, and Architectures*, pages 447–477. Springer, Berlin, 2005.
8. G. S. Rose, Y. Yao, J. M. Tour, A. C. Cabe, N. Gergel-Hackett, N. Majumdar, J. C. Bean, L. R. Harriott, and M. R. Stan. Designing CMOS/molecular memories while considering device parameter variations. *Journal on Emerging Technologies in Computing Systems*, **3**(1):24, 2007.
9. V. Parihar, R. Singh, and K. F. Poole. Silicon nanoelectronics: 100 nm barriers and potential solutions. In *IEEE/SEMI Advanced Semiconductor Manufacturing Conference and Workshop*, Boston, MA, USA, pages 427–433, September 1998.
10. T. Song, H. Kim, W. Rim, Y. Kim, S. Park, C. Park, M. Hong, G. Yang, J. Do, J. Lim et al. 12.2 a 7 nm FinFET SRAM macro using EUV lithography for peripheral repair analysis. In *IEEE International Solid-State Circuits Conference (ISSCC)*, San Francisco, CA, USA, pages 208–209, February 2017.
11. J. Chang, Y. H. Chen, W. M. Chan, S. P. Singh, H. Cheng, H. Fujiwara, J. Y. Lin, K. C. Lin, J. Hung, R. Lee et al. 12.1 a 7 nm 256Mb SRAM in high-k metal-gate FinFET technology with write-assist circuitry for low-VMIN applications. In *IEEE International Solid-State Circuits Conference (ISSCC)*, San Francisco, CA, USA, pages 206–207, February 2017.
12. J. H. Lau and T. G. Yue. Thermal management of 3D IC integration with TSV (through silicon via). In *59th Electronic Components and Technology Conference*, San Diego, CA, USA, pages 635–640, May 2009.
13. K. Tu. Reliability challenges in 3D IC packaging technology. *Microelectronics Reliability*, **51**(3):517–523, 2011.
14. A. Aviram and M. A. Ratner. Molecular rectifiers. *Chemical Physics Letters*, **29**(2):277–283, 1974.
15. M. A. Reed, C. Zhou, C. J. Muller, T. P. Burgin, and J. M. Tour. Conductance of a molecular junction. *Science*, **278**(5336):252–254, 1997.
16. P. J. Paukstelis, J. Nowakowski, J. J. Birktoft, and N. C. Seeman. Crystal structure of a continuous three-dimensional DNA lattice. *Chemistry & Biology*, **11**(8):1119–1126, 2004.
17. S. M. Douglas, A. H. Marblestone, S. Teerapittayanon, A. Vazquez, G. M. Church, and W. M. Shih. Rapid prototyping of 3D DNA-origami shapes with caDNAno. *Nucleic Acids Research*, **37**(15):5001, 2009.
18. N. C. Seeman. Nanomaterials based on DNA. *Annual Review of Biochemistry*, **79**:65–87, 2010.
19. H. T. Maunel, S. Ping Han, R. D. Barish, M. Bockrath, W. A. Goddard III, P. W. K. Rothemund, and E. Winfree. Self-assembly of carbon nanotubes into two-dimensional geometries using DNA origami templates. *Nature Nanotechnology*, **5**(1):61–66, 2010.
20. W. Helfrich and W. G. Schneider. Recombination radiation in anthracene crystals. *Physical Review Letters*, **14**:229–231, 1965.
21. M. Pope and C. Swenberg. *Electronic Processes in Organic Crystals and Polymers. Monographs on the Physics and Chemistry of Materials*. Oxford University Press, Oxford, UK, 1999.
22. J. Chen, M. A. Reed, A. M. Rawlett, and J. M. Tour. Large on-off ratios and negative differential resistance in a molecular electronic device. *Science*, **286**(5444):1550–1552, 1999.
23. J. M. Tour. Molecular electronics. synthesis and testing of components. *Accounts of Chemical Research*, **33**(11):791–804, 2000.

24. P. L. Anelli, N. Spencer, and J. F. Stoddart. A molecular shuttle. *Journal of the American Chemical Society*, **113**(13):5131–5133, 1991.

25. A. R. Pease, J. O. Jeppesen, J. F. Stoddart, Y. Luo, C. P. Collier, and J. R. Heath. Switching devices based on interlocked molecules. *Accounts of Chemical Research*, **34**(6):433–444, 2001.

26. G. Cuniberti, G. Fagas, and K. Richter. *Introducing Molecular Electronics*. Lecture Notes in Physics. Springer Berlin Heidelberg, 2006.

27. J. C. Ellenbogen and J. C. Love. Architectures for molecular electronic computers. i. logic structures and an adder designed from molecular electronic diodes. *Proceedings of the IEEE*, **88**(3):386–426, 2000.

28. D. B. Strukov, G. S. Snider, D. R. Stewart, and R. S. Williams. The missing memristor found. *Nature*, **453**(7191):80–83, 2008.

29. L. Chua. Memristor—The missing circuit element. *IEEE Transactions on Circuit Theory*, **18**(5):507–519, 1971.

30. L. O. Chua and S. M. Kang. Memristive devices and systems. *Proceedings of the IEEE*, **64**(2):209–223, 1976.

31. M. C. Lemme, T. J. Echtermeyer, M. Baus, and H. Kurz. A graphene field-effect device. *IEEE Electron Device Letters*, **28**(4):282–284, 2007.

32. P. L. McEuen, M. S. Fuhrer, and H. Park. Single-walled carbon nanotube electronics. *IEEE Transactions on Nanotechnology*, **99**(1):78–85, 2002.

33. H. Manem, J. Rajendran, and G. S. Rose. Design considerations for multilevel CMOS/nano memristive memory. *Journal on Emerging Technologies in Computing Systems*, **8**(1):6:1–6:22, 2012.

34. M. Hu, H. Li, Y. Chen, Q. Wu, G. S. Rose, and R. W. Linderman. Memristor crossbar-based neuro-morphic computing system: A case study. *IEEE Transactions on Neural Networks and Learning Systems*, **25**(10):1864–1878, 2014.

35. T. E. Potok, C. D. Schuman, S. R. Young, R. M. Patton, F. Spedalieri, J. Liu, K.-T. Yao, G. Rose, and G. Chakma. A study of complex deep learning networks on high performance, neuromorphic, and quantum computers. In *Proceedings of the Workshop on Machine Learning in High Performance Computing Environments*, Salt Lake City, UT, USA, pages 47–55, 2016.

36. C. Mead. *Analog VLSI and Neural Systems*. Addison-Wesley Longman Publishing Co., Inc., Boston, MA, 1989.

37. P. Kocher, J. Jaffe, B. Jun, and P. Rohatgi. Introduction to differential power analysis. *Journal of Cryptographic Engineering*, **1**(1):5–27, 2011.

38. S. B. Ors, F. Gurkaynak, E. Oswald, and B. Preneel. Power-analysis attack on an ASIC AES implementation. In *Information Technology: Coding and Computing, 2004. Proceedings. ITCC 2004. International Conference on*, Vol. **2**, 546–552, IEEE, New York, NY, 2004.

39. S. Bhasin, J.-L. Danger, S. Guilley, X. T. Ngo, and L. Sauvage. Hardware trojan horses in cryptographic IP cores. In *Fault Diagnosis and Tolerance in Cryptography (FDTC), 2013 Workshop on*, pages 15–29, IEEE, New York, NY, 2013.

40. R. S. Chakraborty, S. Narasimhan, and S. Bhunia. Hardware trojan: Threats and emerging solutions. In *High Level Design Validation and Test Workshop, 2009. HLDVT 2009. IEEE International*, pages 166–171, IEEE, New York, NY, 2009.

41. B. Gassend, D. Clarke, M. Van Dijk, and S. Devadas. Silicon physical random functions. In *Proceedings of the 9th ACM Conference on Computer and Communications Security*, pages 148–160, ACM, New York City, New York, 2002.

42. G. E. Suh, C. W. O'Donnell, I. Sachdev, and S. Devadas. Design and implementation of the AEGIS single-chip secure processor using physical random functions. In *Proceedings of the 32nd Annual International Symposium on Computer Architecture*, Madison, WI, USA, pages 25–36, 2005.

43. G. Suh and S. Devadas. Physical unclonable functions for device authentication and secret key generation. In *44th ACM/EDAC/IEEE Design Automation Conference (DAC)*, San Diego, CA, USA, pages 9–14, June 2007.

44. G. Rose and C. Meade. Performance analysis of a memristive crossbar PUF design. In *52nd ACM/EDAC/IEEE Design Automation Conference (DAC)*, San Francisco, CA, USA, pages 1–6, June 2015.

45. M. Uddin, M. B. Majumder, and G. S. Rose. Robustness analysis of a memristive crossbar PUF against modeling attacks. *IEEE Transactions on Nanotechnology*, **16**(3):396–405, 2017.
46. S. Senni, L. Torres, G. Sassatelli, and A. Gamatie. Non-volatile processor based on MRAM for ultra-low-power IoT devices. *ACM Journal on Emerging Technologies in Computing Systems (JETC)*, **13**(2):17, 2016.
47. G. Khedkar, D. Kudithipudi, and G. S. Rose. Power profile obfuscation using nanoscale memristive devices to counter DPA attacks. *IEEE Transactions on Nanotechnology*, **14**(1):26–35, 2015.
48. G. S. Rose. A chaos-based arithmetic logic unit and implications for obfuscation. In *VLSI (ISVLSI), 2014 IEEE Computer Society Annual Symposium on*, pages 54–58. IEEE, New York, NY, 2014.

Chapter 2

Nano CMOS Logic-Based Security Primitive Design

Fahim Rahman, Atul Prasad Deb Nath, Domenic Forte, Swarup Bhunia, and Mark Tehranipoor

Contents

Gone are the days when computer system security issues would encompass software and information vulnerabilities only. The advent of novel security threats like hardware Trojans, counterfeit electronic products, and various physical attacks have nullified the underlying notion of hardware as the root of trust over the years. In addition, the prevalence of mobile and embedded systems devices mandates secure and reliable hardware platforms capable of authenticating users and devices, generating keys, conducting secure operations, and storing sensitive information. As a result, the domain of hardware-oriented security has seen tremendous growth over the past decade [1]. Today, most of the hardware security applications and primitives heavily rely on CMOS platforms due to the maturity of the technology and a solid understanding of the device behavior. Interestingly, many of them seek to leverage the device variability and reliability phenomena that designers often suppress for the sake of performance. Among common hardware security primitives, *physical unclonable functions* (PUFs) and *true random number generators* (TRNGs) leverage inherent process variation and noise of the device to extract entropy [2–4]. In addition, novel designs and countermeasures like *combating die and integrated circuit (IC) recycling* (CDIR) circuitries used for detecting counterfeit (recycled-)ICs in electronic supply chain exploit CMOS aging and wear-out mechanisms [5]. Nevertheless, with the rise of emerging threats and vulnerabilities, and long-standing attacks becoming more practical, we constantly seek novel primitives and countermeasures that utilize the device's inherent properties to enhance security.

In this chapter, we provide a brief overview on some of the existing nanoelectronic CMOS logic-based security primitives and countermeasures that exploit inherent device properties for security and trust. First, we introduce some common hardware security primitives and countermeasures to the readers. Next, we highlight the state-of-the-art nano-CMOS devices and their interesting properties that are key to designing various hardware security primitives. We discuss the underlying performance versus security trade-offs as well, followed by detailed descriptions, analysis, and applications of some crucial security primitives and countermeasures.

2.1 Common Hardware Security Primitives and Countermeasures

Researchers have proposed several hardware security primitives and countermeasures that offer safeguards to various potential threats and vulnerabilities arising at different phases of the IC life cycle or device operation. In this section, we introduce common security primitives and countermeasures, namely, PUF, TRNG, and design for anticounterfeit (DfAC), to the reader and explain their common properties and quality metrics.

2.1.1 Physical Unclonable Function

A PUF is a cryptographically secure one-way function that generates a digital output (response) for a given digital input (challenge) without revealing any predictable mapping between the challenge and response [2,3]. As the name suggests, a PUF can generate keys by leveraging *inherent physical variations from manufacturing processes*. Therefore, identical (by design and lithography) ICs manufactured by the same fabrication facility and process can generate different challenge–response pairs (CRPs) (or cryptographic keys) as there always exist small but nondeterministic variations in the manufacturing process.

To date, several security applications and protocols based on PUFs have been proposed, such as key generation for encryption, IC identification, authentication, and hardware metering

[6–8]. However, these applications mostly require an ideal PUF assuming that the PUF itself is attack-resilient, that is, cannot generate a deterministic response to external attacks, or cannot be replaced with a software model to replicate the intrinsic hardware behavior. The most popular quality metrics of PUF include *uniqueness, randomness* or *uniformity,* and *reliability. Uniqueness* measures the distinctive CRP generation quality of a PUF with respect to other instances. An inter-chip hamming distance (inter-HD) of 50% produces the maximum ideal uniqueness, producing a maximum difference of responses between any two PUFs. *Randomness* or *uniformity* stands for the unpredictability of a PUF showing if it has any measurable trend in the generated key since an ideal PUF should be free from bias and maintain a good diffusive property. *Reliability* assesses the PUF's performance in terms of reproducibility to measure its capability to generate same CRPs across different environmental conditions and over time. Ideally, a PUF should always maintain the same CRP over different operating conditions and/or times resulting in a zero bit error rate (i.e., 0% intrachip Hamming distance). Such properties are crucial as a qualitatively poor PUF may be prone to different modeling and machine learning attacks [9–12].

2.1.2 True Random Number Generator

A TRNG is a security primitive widely used in security and cryptographic applications to generate session keys, one-time pads, random seeds, nonces, challenges to PUFs, etc., and these applications are growing in number with time [4,13,14]. It typically generates a random digital bitstream with high uncertainty, or *entropy*, where the sequence of producing 0's and 1's are equal and completely independent of its previous value or any other external control. To generate an output that is "truly" random, a TRNG must rely on *device intrinsic electrical and/or thermal noise* that is inherently nondeterministic and uncontrollable.

A typical TRNG consists of an entropy source, entropy extraction/sampling unit, and, in most cases, a cryptographic conditioning unit. The entropy source is the focal point of a TRNG, as the quality of the TRNG system highly depends on the raw entropy coming from this entropy source. For a TRNG, such sources are analog in nature and include random telegraph noise (RTN) found in scaled transistors, power supply noise, radioactive decay, latch metastability, jitter in ring oscillators, and so on [14]. One problem with entropy sources is that although they might be "intuitively random," statistical tests run on the output of the TRNG show a certain level of bias and predictability, especially under conditions such as environmental and process variations. To combat this, cryptographic hash functions, a von Neumann corrector, and stream ciphers are employed to manipulate the raw output of the TRNGs to ensure the uniformity and statistical randomness. Also, additional tuners and processing blocks may be employed to control the TRNG quality and throughput [15]. In order to assess the *randomness* of the bits produced by a TRNG, statistical test suites such as the NIST Test Suite [16], DieHARD [17], etc. are commonly used, and are usually the first (and the easiest) step to analyze the randomness and uniformity of a TRNG.

In addition to TRNGs, software-based random number generators, mostly known as pseudo-random number generators (PRNGs), rely on algorithms and tend to produce high throughput with lightweight implementations, although with deterministic outputs. Despite being fast and lightweight, PRNGs are not secure because their next state can be predicted from the current state if someone gains access to the design and can expose the sensitive data to the adversary.

It should be noted that the operating condition of the TRNG is also a key factor for generating "truly" random numbers, as power supply variation, temperature deviation, clock frequency, added noise, external signal, etc. can impact the intrinsic entropy source and extracted features. Hence, the *reliability* of the TRNG is also crucial in the sense that the TRNG itself needs to maintain the randomness throughout the operational lifetime and, additionally, show resiliency against attacks tailored with operational condition variation [15].

2.1.3 Design for Anticounterfeit

A global electronic supply chain experiences different types of counterfeits, such as recycled, remarked, cloned, overproduced, and out-of-spec/defective ICs [18]. Recycled and remarked ICs contribute to most of the counterfeit ICs present in the supply chain today. Counterfeit electronics pose a significant challenge due to the lack of efficient, robust, and low-cost detection and avoidance techniques. However, developing a comprehensive solution for different ICs (ranging from microprocessors to analog ICs) from different vendors is a challenging task. Moreover, this issue becomes more serious for legacy parts used in critical applications and commercial-off-the-shelf (COTS) products that do not have proper documentation and/or a supply chain history. Physical inspection and imaging-based counterfeit detections have been quite successful to date since they can detect the physical aspects of aging and wear-out mechanisms. However, such techniques are extremely costly, slow, often destructive, and not suitable for large-scale automated detection [19]. Hence, investigation of electrical and parametric tests and embedded anticounterfeit designs are growing in popularity as fast and low-cost alternatives for detection and prevention of counterfeit electronics. However, the choice of a particular electrical characteristic and/or design is crucial for such applications since it may be largely affected by the process and environmental variations [18]. Hence, the research community has come up with several characteristics-based detection techniques as well as novel sensors and structures for counterfeit detection, that is, DfAC, using CMOS logic devices. Details on such DfAC structures are discussed in Section 2.5.

2.2 Nano-CMOS Logic Devices for Security

Even after five decades, Moore's law is still considered the guiding principle in the semiconductor industry [20,21]. As technology scaling continued over the years, researchers from both academia and industry have come up with different CMOS-based device architectures—from regular planar bulk-CMOS devices to high-k/metal-gate transistors and tri-gate/FinFET devices—to make the devices smaller, faster, and cheaper than the predecessor technology nodes. However, in advanced nodes, the industry faces major manufacturing and reliability issues [22,23]. In particular, CMOS devices are now experiencing greater process variations and more aggressive degradation due to aging and runtime variations. Such degradation mechanisms can have drastic negative effects on IC performance and reliability [24]. Nevertheless, many such properties and phenomena play a key role in devising hardware security applications and primitives.

2.2.1 Security Properties of CMOS Devices

To have a better understanding of the relationship of these state-of-the-art CMOS devices and various hardware security primitives, we first take a look at these device structures and some of their interesting properties that can be leveraged for different security-oriented applications (other than the trivial performance-oriented logic or volatile memory applications).

■ *Bulk CMOS devices:* A planar bulk CMOS transistor is the most traditional of all, as shown in Figure 2.1a. Although it has dominated the logic domain for the past several decades as

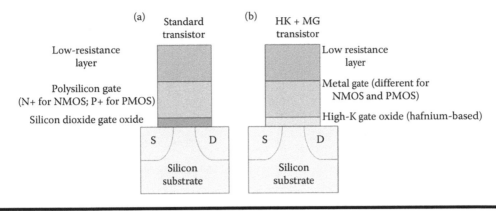

Figure 2.1 Schematic view of the (a) standard planar transistor and (b) HK/MG transistor.

the most mature technology, the lithographic limitations have caused a potential hit in the performance wall for this simplest structure in the advanced node, especially regarding low current density and excessive leakage current with high interdevice variations. To combat this, ultrathin body silicon-on-insulator (SOI) or fully depleted (FD) SOI devices have been developed where the bulk silicon of the traditional planar CMOS is replaced by a thin layer of silicon placed on an insulating layer for low-leakage applications [26].

■ *High-k/metal-gate devices:* With the scaling of the transistor feature size, the quantum mechanical tunneling becomes more prominent due to the thinner gate thickness, eventually increasing the leakage current of the device. One way to combat this is to physically increase the thickness of the gate, without increasing the effective "electrical" oxide thickness, by using high-k (i.e., high-dielectric coefficient) materials. It also allows the usage of low-resistance metal for transistor gates, further increasing the device performance, as shown in Figure 2.1 [25].

■ *Tri-gate/FinFET devices:* At advanced nodes from 22 nm and below, the trigate-fin FETs (FinFETs) have become an efficient novel architecture. It is often called a 3D device as its channel is turned on to its sides elevating from the transistor surface [27]. The transistor gate forms an upside U-shaped draping over the channels of the device as shown in Figure 2.2. A three-sided gate over the channel improves the controllability of the current flow. In addition, the SOI-FinFETs offer an enhanced electrostatic integrity, reducing the leakage and statistical variability [28,29].

All these devices are originally intended to offer high performance with high speed and low leakage, and provide better reliability. However, with the technology nodes getting more advanced with smaller feature sizes, the variability in the performance increases mostly due to manufacturing process variation, runtime conditions, and aging. In Figure 2.3, we list some key physical parameters and runtime/reliability factors that may alleviate the variation in performance from device to device and architecture to architecture. As stated previously, these factors play a key role in logic performance as well as security-oriented applications.

■ *Process variations:* The IC manufacturing process has numerous sources of systematic and random variations that play a critical role for yield and performance. CMOS front-end of the line (FEOL) variation sources are most notably patterning (proximity) effects, line-edge

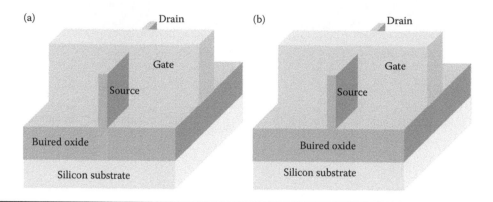

Figure 2.2   Schematic view of the (a) bulk and (b) SOI FinFETs.

roughness (LER), and gate dielectrics such as oxide thickness variations, defects, and traps. Variations due to random dopant fluctuations and gate material granularity (poly-si or metal gate) are also becoming significant in advanced nodes [22,23]. These phenomena directly impact the electrostatic integrity of the channel and affect the strength of the device. Back end of the line (BEOL) sources, such as metal interconnect and dielectric variations, also have a significant impact [30]. All such variations holistically cause deviations in device characteristics making every single transistor slightly different from each other with a shift from the nominal performance. Such manufacturing process variations are undesirable for performance-oriented logic applications, yet unavoidable and even prominent in the advanced nodes.

■ *Runtime/environmental variations:* Similar to manufacturing process variations, runtime/environmental variations, such as temperature and power supply noise, also have

	Phenomena	Electrical manifestation	Security applications
Process variation	• Geometric variation (patterning—W, L) • Random dopant fluctuation (RDF) • Line edge roughness (LER) • Oxide thickness (T_{ox}) fluctuation • Interface defect and traps (ITC) • Polysilicon/metal gate granularity (MGG)	• Threshold voltage deviation (ΔV_{TH}) • Carrier mobility degradation ($\Delta \mu_n$) • Drain current variation (ΔI_{ON}) • Off-state leakage current variation (ΔI_{Leak}) • Drain induced barrier lowering (DIBL)	PUF	• Arbiter • RO • Leakage current • Bistable ring • Hybrid Delay/cross-coupled PUF
Runtime variation	• Power supply noise • Temperature variation		TRNG	• Thermal/power supply noise • Clock jitter • Metastability • Oxide soft-breakdown
Aging and wear-out mechanism	• Bias temperature instability (NBTI/PBTI) • Hot carrier injection (HCI) • Time dependent dielectric breakdown (TDDB) • Electromigration (EM)		Anti-counterfeit design	• Recycling—aging (CDIR) • Cloning—process variation

Figure 2.3   CMOS bulk, HK+MG, and FinFET device properties for security applications.

a direct impact on the transistor electrical characteristics. An increase in the operating temperature decreases both carrier mobility (μ) and threshold voltage (V_{th}) of the transistor, and thus impacts the speed (delay) of the device since they cause an opposing impact on the drain saturation current (I_{DS}) and leakage current (I_{Leak}). However, technology nodes also play a crucial role. For example, technology nodes from 45 nm and below show an increase in device speed with temperature, whereas it is opposite in older technologies. In addition, global and local power supply noise have an adverse impact on performance, since such variations also cause a shift in V_{th} and I_{DS} from the nominal value [31]. Hence, for both cases, a system is less robust. However, unlike a permanent shift in performance resulting from the manufacturing process variation or aging, a variation in the environmental condition causes a temporary change, and thus it is compensated once the device returns to its nominal operating state.

■ *Aging and wear-out mechanisms:* Aging degradation and wear-out mechanisms, such as *bias temperature instability* (BTI), *hot carrier injection* (HCI), *electromigration* (EM), and *time-dependent dielectric breakdown* (TDDB), lead to poor device and circuit performance. The magnitude of such degradation largely depends on the device workload, active bias, and inherent random defects, and technology nodes under consideration [32]. BTI and HCI are considered key aging mechanisms that directly impact the speed of CMOS devices. BTI slows down transistors as traps are generated at the SiO_2-Si interface, resulting in an increase in V_{th} over time. Typically, negative (N)-BTI occurring in PMOS transistors is dominant compared to positive (P)-BTI occurring in NMOS transistors beyond 65 nm technology nodes. However, the latter is eventually getting prominent for high-k metal-gate devices [33]. In addition, HCI also slows down a device by generating charged defects in gate oxide and interface to increase V_{th} as well as by reducing the mobility of a device. HCI is more prominent in NMOS with a smaller feature size. However, HCI-induced degradation can be recovered to a certain limit [34] and is affected by voltage, temperature, and device workload. Both these mechanisms greatly decrease the device's reliability and eventually shorten the chip's lifetime, increasing the possible failure rate. Although such mechanisms are quite slow, and the degradation magnitude is relatively hard to predict being statistical in nature, in most cases, an accelerated aging (i.e., running the chip at a higher voltage and/or temperature than the nominal condition) allows us to determine the possible impact and lifetime, and deploy compensating mechanisms if possible.

2.2.2 *Performance and Reliability versus Security*

We see that the CMOS device performance deviates from its nominal one due to process variation, environmental condition, and aging. Therefore, solutions must be developed to minimize process variations and other degradation phenomena for designing high-performance circuits. However, we also note that these variations and degradation mechanisms do not necessarily have adverse impacts on hardware-oriented security primitives and applications. In fact, some of these variations and degradation mechanisms can be effectively leveraged for ensuring hardware-based security. For example, PUFs and TRNGs rely on the manufacturing process variations, and an increase in such physical variations can potentially increase the PUF/TRNG outcome quality. In addition, the detection process of some types of counterfeit electronics can benefit from inherent aging and wear-out mechanisms. This is especially beneficial for recycled ICs since the presence of signs of prior usage can potentially lead to the detection of recycled chips.

Table 2.1   Design and Technology Characteristics versus Security Trade-Off

Application/ Primitive	Process Variation	Temperature	Power Supply Noise	Aging (BTI/HCI)	Wear-Out (EM)
Logic/memory design	Ugly	Bad	Bad	Bad	Bad
PUF	Good	Bad	Bad	Bad	Bad
TRNG	Good	Bad	Bad	Bad	Bad
Recycled IC detection	Ugly	Bad	Bad	Good	Good

However, all these mechanisms are not always beneficial to all the security applications either. Hence, we would like to use the terms—*good*, *bad*, and *ugly*—to qualitatively state the relationship between process variations, reliability degradation, and various hardware-based security mechanisms, as shown in Table 2.1. The first column of Table 2.1 shows some conventional and security-based applications and primitives, and the respective rows refer to how process variation, temperature, power supply noise, aging, and wear-out mechanisms affect the quality of operation. Here, the *good* indicates that the given variation or degradation mechanism is actually desirable and beneficial to a security application or primitive; the *bad* means that it should be avoided if possible, and the *ugly* means that it is highly undesirable for a reliable operation. For example, in logic/memory applications, manufacturing "process variation" is highly undesirable (*ugly*) to ensure better performance, whereas it is one of the key requirements (*good*) for PUF and TRNG applications. "Aging" and "wear-out" mechanisms are *bad* for both regular logic/memory applications and PUFs; however, they can be leveraged (*good*) for detecting recycled electronics [35].

In light of the above discussion, it is crucial that we find a sweet spot between performance, reliability, and security. Therefore, rather than building security primitives using logic/memory application-oriented designs, and vice versa, the designers should make a balance of performance, reliability, and security to obtain the best trade-off depending on their target application.

2.3 Physical Unclonable Function

As discussed in Section 2.1.1, each PUF can be considered as a black box with a set of CRPs since it exploits the inherent physical variation. Depending on the volume of the CPR set, PUFs can be generally categorized into two classes: (i) strong PUFs and (ii) weak PUFs. A strong PUF can maintain a very large set of CRPs. Ideally, it is suitable for identification and authentication protocols. Weak PUFs, on the other hand, maintain a small number of CRPs (only one in most cases) and are useful for cryptographic key generation. However, PUFs that do not maintain ideal reliability or robustness need to employ necessary error-correcting schemes because, for example, a small error (not taken care of) in the generated response used as a crypto-key can cause a failure in the encryption/decryption procedure [6,36,37].

To date, researchers have proposed numerous architectures and compositions for PUFs utilizing traditional CMOS devices and on-chip circuits, emerging nanoelectronic logic and memory devices, or even physical materials (such as the optical PUF [2]). In this section, we confine our discussion to some common CMOS-based PUF architectures.

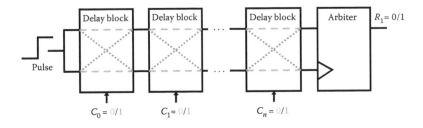

Figure 2.4 Standard structure of the arbiter PUF.

2.3.1 Arbiter PUF

Arbiter PUF is one of the most common CMOS logic-based PUF architectures that exploits the randomness of path delay due to uncontrollable process variation. Figure 2.4 shows the generic design of an arbiter PUF [38]. Each of the building blocks is an individual delay unit with path-switching capability controlled by the challenge bit (denoted by b_i). Given a pulse at the input of a delay stage, it can traverse through two design-wise identical but different paths and reach the final arbiter (or decision-making) component. If the signal in the upper path reaches first, the arbiter generates "1" (and vice versa). Ideally, in the absence of any manufacturing process variation, the delay through both the paths would be the same and the signal would reach the arbiter at the exact same time. However, there will always be some process variation-induced delay difference between these two identical paths and one of the signals would reach the arbiter faster than the other. Since the paths do not have any systematic or extrinsic delay difference, the shortest/longest path is not deterministic and only depends on the individual transistor strength and interconnects. As we see from Section 2.2, any random deviation in physical or electrical properties would cause this nondeterministic variation. In an arbiter PUF, the delay stages are cascaded in series (one after one) that exponentially increases the number of possible path pairs. Hence, it is can generate a large number of CRPs and acts as a strong PUF.

However, the arbiter PUF has some major drawbacks, one of them being the bias induced at the arbiter itself due to the finite delay-difference resolution for the setup and hold time. Also, this requires symmetric design and routing which may not be readily available for lightweight and FPGA applications. In addition, the arbiter PUF has been shown to be vulnerable to modeling attack since it can be represented as a linear delay model.

2.3.2 Ring Oscillator PUF

The schematic of a typical ring oscillator-based PUF (RO-PUF) is shown in Figure 2.5. It does not require rigorous design and can be easily implemented in both ASIC and reconfigurable platforms such as FPGAs [6]. An RO-PUF is composed of N identical ring oscillators (ROs), two multiplexers, two counters, and one comparator. Each of the ROs oscillates at a slightly different frequency due to process variations. A challenge is applied to select one pair of ROs and the number of oscillations of each of the ROs in the selected pair is counted and compared to generate a "0" or "1" based on which oscillator from the selected RO pair is faster.

Compared to an arbiter PUF, the RO-PUF is larger and slower for generating the same number of response bits. While the arbiter PUF can generate the response bits in one system clock, the RO-PUF requires a significant number of counts of the oscillatory signals to obtain a reliable value.

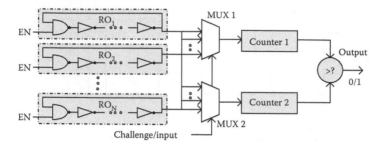

Figure 2.5 Conventional RO-PUF.

The oscillatory switching of the components makes it slightly power-hungry too. Since all the components of RO go through significant usage, it suffers from runtime power and temperature variations and aging. It makes the RO-PUF prone to generating erroneous output.

2.3.3 Butterfly PUF

The design of the butterfly PUF is inspired by the notion of creating a circuit structure with metastable properties in the FPGA matrix [39]. Similar to the SRAM PUF, the floating state of the butterfly PUF can be exploited to obtain a random state at the startup phase of a pair of cross-coupled latches in the FPGA. The latches form a combinational loop that can be excited to an unstable state through a proper signal, that is, challenge as depicted in Figure 2.6. Although conceived for FPGA implementations, similar implementation can be done utilizing the metastability of any latch or flip-flop-based architecture.

2.3.4 Lightweight PUF

Lightweight PUF, as shown in Figure 2.7 [40], utilizes the traditional arbiter PUF with nontrivial wiring between arbiter stages. Rather than directly feeding the challenges to the PUFs, it creates a networked scheme that breaks down the challenge set into several blocks and uses them on multiple PUFs. The output network then combines all the individual PUF responses to create a global response, making it relatively resilient against machine learning attacks [10].

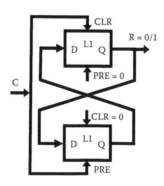

Figure 2.6 Typical butterfly PUF schematic.

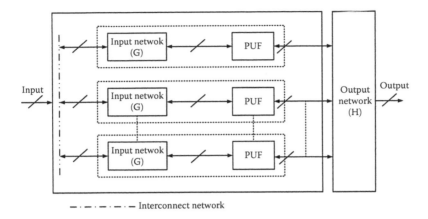

Figure 2.7   Generic structure of a lightweight PUF.

2.3.5 *Bistable Ring PUF*

The notion of a bistable ring PUF is inspired by the fact that an even number of inverters forming a ring can only have two possible options as the outcome. However, the bistable ring goes through a set of complex transitions before converging to a stable state due to the manufacturing process variation that results in mismatches in the threshold voltage and carrier mobility of the associated transistors. The meta-stability of this nature can be exploited for hardware security applications. In Reference 41, a novel bistable ring PUF structure is proposed that can generate an exponential number of CRPs. In addition to the regular architecture of a bistable ring, the authors replaced the inverters with 2-input NOR or NAND gates to mimic the inverter operation, and added a pair of multiplexers and demultiplexers in each stage to create all possible bistable ring combinations based on the input challenge as illustrated in Figure 2.8. However, the experimental results presented in References 41 and 42 make it evident that, although the design is operational, it requires additional symmetric layout constraints. Nevertheless, this strong PUF offers a relatively high resiliency against modeling attacks due to its complex and nonlinear nature, and thereby can be incorporated into emerging PUF applications such as virtual proofs of reality [43].

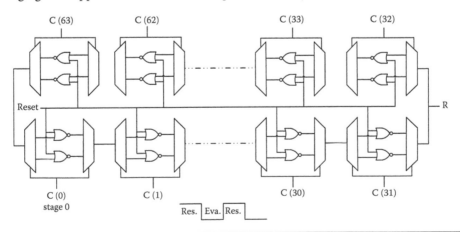

Figure 2.8   A 64-stage bistable ring PUF. Res. = reset phase; Eva. = evaluation phase.

2.4 True Random Number Generator

Typically, CMOS-logic-based random numbers are generated by comparing two symmetric systems (or even devices) that possess some process variation and random inner noise to serve as an inherent entropy source. On the basis of the sources of randomness and system architecture, TRNGs can be categorized into the device's inherent noise-based TRNGs, jitter and metastability-based TRNGs (i.e., free-running oscillator-based TRNGs), chaos TRNGs, and quantum TRNGs [14]. However, not all TRNGs proposed in the literature are entirely CMOS-based and may require external optical/laser sources for excitation of the entropy sources. In this section, we focus our discussion on CMOS-logic-based TRNGs only.

2.4.1 Noise-Based TRNGs

Device-inherent noise is typically random and can be harnessed for the generation of true random numbers. Common noise sources used as TRNG entropy sources are RTN, Zener noise (in semiconductor Zener diodes), Flicker or $1/f$-noise, Johnson's noise, etc. [14].

The basic idea of noise-based TRNG is as follows: the random analog voltage, caused by the noise source, is sampled periodically and compared to a certain predefined threshold to produce a "1" or "0" as shown in Figure 2.9. The threshold can be fine-tuned to produce an ideally equal probability of "1's" and "0's." However, setting up a proper threshold may be a rigorous process and may need resetting based on runtime conditions.

The earlier version of Intel TRNG was developed leveraging Johnson's noise where the source of randomness is the random thermal motion of charged carriers [44]. However, a more efficient, faster, extremely simple, and lightweight TRNG was put in place in 2011 as shown in Figure 2.10 [4]. This TRNG design uses a pair of cross-coupled transistors (or a trimmed RS-type flip-flop), without any analog parts making it extremely suitable for integrating with the logic chip. Ideally, the design is completely symmetric and both "set" and "reset" inputs are tied together and driven at the same time. Given any random mismatch due to noise, the nodes would be forced to settle to the stable output of either "1" or "0." However, the design is still not entirely free from bias as any systematic asymmetry would produce a highly biased output. Hence, additional current injecting mechanism and postprocessing techniques (such as raw bit conditioner and PRNG) are employed on the top of the design [4,14].

The biggest problem with different noise sources is that not all noise can always be measured, characterized, or controlled during the manufacturing phase for proper utilization. In addition, with the maturity of the process technology, some noise mechanisms that can be considered as entropy sources get more controlled and eventually are suppressed adequately to not produce a reliable measurement (i.e., voltage or current) of the entropy source. Hence, the extractor unit

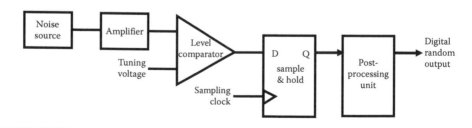

Figure 2.9   General schematic of noise-based TRNG.

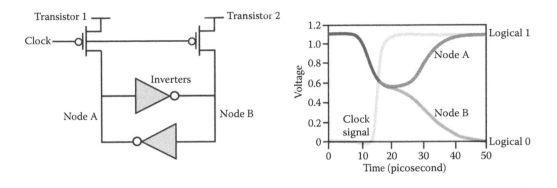

Figure 2.10   Intel TRNG. (Adapted from G. Taylor and G. Cox. *IEEE Spectrum*, 24: 2011.)

needs to be quite sophisticated with the capability of strong amplification and sampling for converting the analog noise value to the digital bitstream. This introduces further deviations from generated data being "true" random due to amplifier bandwidth and nonlinear gain limitations. Also, as it is seen, the fast electrical switching of RNG circuitry produces strong electromagnetic interference creating synchronization among nearby RNGs causing a drop in overall entropy. Hence, there is a lack of provability of the randomness since the leveraged noise source cannot be ensured as truly random because of the effect of the extractor unit and other necessary deterministic postprocessing.

2.4.2 Oscillator-Based TRNGs

Another common approach to produce random numbers in the digital domain is to use oscillators, and leverage associated jitter and metastability. Odd numbers of back-to-back connected inverters with a feedback loop act as a free running oscillator (FRO) as, even without an external input, the oscillator output is capable of driving itself as long as the power is on [45]. Figure 2.11 shows a common design of an RO-TRNG. Random electrical noise in the feedback loop causes the frequency and phase of the oscillation to have a jitter, that is, the exact time of the signal reaching

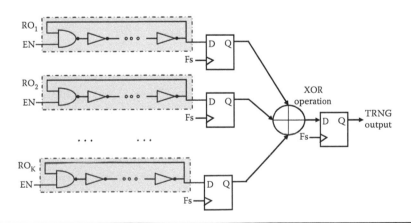

Figure 2.11   Ring oscillator-based TRNG.

the extraction point is not deterministic [46]. The entropy is further improved by proper sampling and XOR-ing each FRO output.

One problem with jitter-based TRNG architecture is that the semiconductor industry is constantly working toward the minimization of jitters and noise. In cases when the randomness of output is too weak compared to the load it is driving, the effect of the oscillator sampling may be muffled. As possible solutions, the Fibonacci ring oscillator and Galois ring oscillator have been proposed [14].

2.4.3 TRNG Reliability and Attacks

A TRNG is affected by limited process variations, especially in the older and mature technologies. Consequently, the inherent entropy sources are not sufficient for harvesting true randomness and obtaining maximum throughput. Further, the randomness of TRNGs can become even worse under environmental variations and different aging mechanisms. This opens up a variety of hardware-based attacks on TRNGs. For example, an attacker can vary V_{dd} and temperature beyond the nominal condition, and intentionally bias the output to extract the "predictable" bit-stream [15]. A frequency injection attack on RO-based TRNGs can affect the clock jitter working as the entropy source and can guess the key, for example from a smart card, with minimal effort [47]. In addition, electromagnetic attacks can leak this information without physically destroying the chip [48].

To achieve more uniformity and statistical randomness in spite of low inherent entropy, researchers have proposed cryptographic hash functions, a von Neumann corrector, and stream ciphers to be employed at the TRNG outputs. However, the modification reduces the throughput, and increases area and power overhead. Further, a vendor agnostic TRNG design for FPGA is proposed in Reference 49. Rahman et al. [15] proposed a technology-independent (TI) TRNG to combat the security issues arising from such various runtime/environmental condition-based degradations. It uses a "tunable"-RO architecture to leverage power supply noise along with clock jitter as the entropy source and can overcome environmental variation and aging-induced bias by controlling jitter, and adjusting RO delay by monitoring the runtime condition. A proposed power supply noise enhancement and tuning block, and a self-calibration scheme on bias detection further improve the performance and serve as countermeasures against the hardware-based attack [50]. The TRNG model presented by Robson et al. [51] utilizes multiple threshold-crossing methods to increase timing jitters.

2.5 Design for Anticounterfeit

In today's complex electronic component supply chain, it is very challenging to detect and prevent the infiltration of counterfeit chips and FPGAs. As mentioned in Section 2.1.3, a proper exploitation of electrical characteristics can lead to a cheaper, faster, and more successful detection of counterfeit electronics. Since aging and wear-out mechanisms generally make a chip slower over time, one can estimate aging degradation of a circuit under test (CUT) by measuring its speed and comparing it with a reference speed from original unused (golden) chips. However, acquiring such reference (golden) measurements is not always feasible. In addition, manufacturing process variation and defects cause deviation in speed/delay or other electrical measurements even for golden chips. Hence, it requires a large pool of golden data to maintain statistical significance. These issues are more prominent for legacy chips and COTS [18]. By exploiting such aging issues, researchers have proposed several techniques, such as embedding DfAC structures into the chip, or measuring degradation due to accelerated aging, for recycled IC detection.

A CDIR scheme utilizes novel DfAC architectures. It takes aging into account to determine whether a chip has gone through a prior use. It is a lightweight and low-cost DfAC sensor with an RO pair for self-referencing that eliminates the need for golden data [5,52]. The concept behind the RO-CDIR scheme is to put additional circuits or architectures, that is, ring oscillator structures, into new electronic chips in a way that the RO frequency tends to degrade more with aging, that is, the transistors in the RO get slower with time. The key points here are to employ a very lightweight design that would not practically impact the area, power, and cost requirement of the original chip, and the implemented design should produce readily available data that can reliably predict the aging (if any) or the freshness of the chip, that is, it must age rapidly and must not be affected during the testing and validation phases. Also, the impact of process variations and temperature must be minimized, and path delay deviation due to process variation and aging degradation must be satisfactorily separable.

One key point to measure aging-induced delay degradation is that the RO frequencies are needed to be compared with the golden (fresh) or reference data. The typical RO-CDIR sensor performs a self-referencing scheme to reliably measure delay degradation by comparing the frequencies of two equal length ROs, named the reference-RO and stressed-RO, respectively. The reference-RO is designed to age slowly, whereas the stressed-RO is designed to age at a much faster rate. When in operation mode, the stressed-RO's rapid aging reduces its speed (frequency), while the reference-RO's speed (frequency) largely remains the same. Thus, a large difference between the RO-frequencies implies that the chip has been used. A close physical placement of the ROs further reduces global and local process variations and environmental variations to give a finer measurement of the usage time. However, a limitation of this approach is that only half of the PMOS transistors experience DC NBTI stress, hence experiencing a limited degradation, due to the oscillatory nature of the scheme as shown in Figure 2.12.

Figure 2.13 shows an NBTI-aware RO-CDIR sensor that exploits NBTI-induced degradation for an improved detection scheme [53]. While in operation mode, it gives maximum NBTI (DC) stress to the stressed-RO by breaking the RO chain and connecting all inverter inputs to the ground so that they do not get a chance to recover from aging. However, a partial recovery may occur when the chip is completely powered off. The stressed-RO's structure is mimicked by the reference-RO to avoid parametric variations. However, during operation, the reference-RO is kept

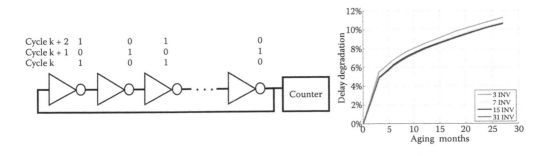

Figure 2.12 **Stressed RO in the RO-CDIR sensor in stress mode. Faster (shorter) ROs show more aging-induced delay degradation. (Adapted from X. Zhang and M. Tehranipoor.** *IEEE Transactions on Very Large Scale Integration (VLSI) Systems,* **22(5):1016–1029, 2014.)**

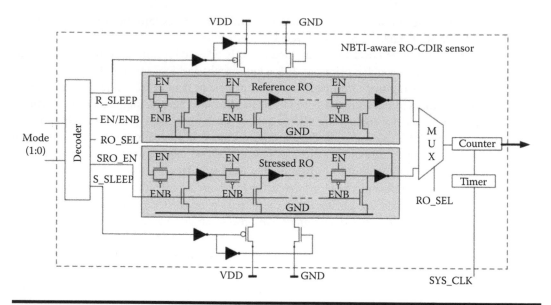

Figure 2.13   NBTI-aware RO-CDIR sensor. (Adapted from U. Guin et al. *Proceedings of the 51st Annual Design Automation Conference*, pages 1–6. ACM, New York City, NY, 2014.)

disconnected from the power and ground line to minimize aging. Since the two ROs have different aging stresses, their frequencies continue to deviate over time. A higher frequency increases the accuracy of detection.

2.6 Conclusion

A brief overview of nano-CMOS logic-based security primitives and countermeasures is covered in the chapter. The analysis of presented hardware security primitives makes it evident that the notions of PUFs, TRNGs, or countermeasures such as CDIRs are not rigorously defined by a strict set of principles; rather, they try to exploit the potential security features. Uniqueness, physical unclonability, randomness, tamper resistance, or abundant entropy are identifiable qualities that can arise from a varied number of sources ranging from intrinsic process variation to inherent noises and aging. A comprehensive study of the security properties of nano-CMOS logic devices leads to a subset of necessary requirements for hardware security applications. This study also uncovers some blind spots and unanswered questions pointing toward the unexplored areas of security primitive design aspects. We also see that performance versus security trade-off plays a key role in advanced technology node. Hence, there is no one solution that works efficiently for all objectives; rather, we need to consider them in a holistic way to find a sweet spot between performance, reliability, and security.

Acknowledgment

This project was supported in part by an Air Force Office of Scientific Research (AFOSR) MURI Grant under award number FA9550-14-1-0351 and by the National Science Foundation under Grant 1603475, Grant 1603483, and Grant 1603483.

References

1. M. Tehranipoor and C. Wang. *Introduction to Hardware Security and Trust.* Springer Science & Business Media, Berlin, Germany, 2011.
2. R. Pappu, B. Recht, J. Taylor, and N. Gershenfeld. Physical one-way functions. *Science,* **297**(5589):2026–2030, 2002.
3. B. Gassend, D. Clarke, M. Van Dijk, and S. Devadas. Silicon physical random functions. In *Proceedings of the 9th ACM Conference on Computer and Communications Security,* pages 148–160. ACM, New York City, NY, 2002.
4. G. Taylor and G. Cox. Behind Intel's new random-number generator. 2011. [online] Available at: http://spectrum.ieee.org/computing/hardware/behind-intels-new-randomnumber-generator
5. X. Zhang and M. Tehranipoor. Design of on-chip lightweight sensors for effective detection of recycled ICs. *IEEE Transactions on Very Large Scale Integration (VLSI) Systems,* **22**(5):1016–1029, 2014.
6. G. E. Suh and S. Devadas. Physical unclonable functions for device authentication and secret key generation. In *Proceedings of the 44th Annual Design Automation Conference,* pages 9–14. ACM, New York City, NY, 2007.
7. M. Majzoobi, A. Elnably, and F. Koushanfar. FPGA time-bounded unclonable authentication. In *International Workshop on Information Hiding,* pages 1–16. Springer, Berlin, 2010.
8. J. Guajardo, B. Škorić, P. Tuyls, S. S. Kumar, T. Bel, A. H. Blom, and G.-J. Schrijen. Anti-counterfeiting, key distribution, and key storage in an ambient world via physical unclonable functions. *Information Systems Frontiers,* **11**(1):19–41, 2009.
9. C. Helfmeier, C. Boit, D. Nedospasov, and J.-P. Seifert. Cloning physically unclonable functions. In *Hardware-Oriented Security and Trust (HOST), 2013 IEEE International Symposium on,* pages 1–6. IEEE, New York, NY, 2013.
10. U. Rührmair, J. Sölter, F. Sehnke, X. Xu, A. Mahmoud, V. Stoyanova, G. Dror, J. Schmidhuber, W. Burleson, and S. Devadas. PUF modeling attacks on simulated and silicon data. *IEEE Transactions on Information Forensics and Security,* **8**(11):1876–1891, 2013.
11. X. Xu and W. Burleson. Hybrid side-channel/machine-learning attacks on PUFs: A new threat?, 2014 Design, Automation & Test in Europe Conference & Exhibition (DATE), Dresden, 2014, pp. 1–6.
12. U. Rührmair, X. Xu, J. Sölter, A. Mahmoud, M. Majzoobi, F. Koushanfar, and W. Burleson. Efficient power and timing side channels for physical unclonable functions. In *International Workshop on Cryptographic Hardware and Embedded Systems,* pages 476–492. Springer, Berlin, 2014.
13. B. Sunar, W. J. Martin, and D. R. Stinson. A provably secure true random number generator with built-in tolerance to active attacks. *IEEE Transactions on Computers,* **56**(1):109–119, 2007.
14. M. Stipčević and C. K. Koç. True random number generators. In *Open Problems in Mathematics and Computational Science,* pages 275–315. Springer, Berlin, 2014.
15. M. T. Rahman, K. Xiao, D. Forte, X. Zhang, J. Shi, and M. Tehranipoor. Ti-TRNG: Technology independent true random number generator. In *Proceedings of the 51st Annual Design Automation Conference,* pages 1–6. ACM, New York City, NY, 2014.
16. A. Rukhin, J. Soto, J. Nechvatal, M. Smid, and E. Barker, A statistical test suite for random and pseudorandom number generators for cryptographic applications. Technical Report, DTIC Document, 2001.
17. G. Marsaglia, Diehard: A battery of tests of randomness. See http://stat.fsu.edu/geo/diehard.html, 1996.
18. M. M. Tehranipoor, U. Guin, and D. Forte. Counterfeit integrated circuits. In *Counterfeit Integrated Circuits,* pages 15–36. Springer, Berlin, 2015.
19. S. Shahbazmohamadi, D. Forte, and M. Tehranipoor. Advanced physical inspection methods for counterfeit IC detection. In *40th International Symposium for Testing and Failure Analysis,* pages 55–64, 2014.
20. G. Moore. Cramming more components onto integrated circuits. *Electronics,* **38**(19):114–117, 1965.
21. S. Datta. Recent advances in high performance CMOS transistors: From planar to non-planar. *The Electrochemical Society Interface,* **22**(1):41–46, 2013.

22. K. Kuhn, C. Kenyon, A. Kornfeld, M. Liu, A. Maheshwari, W.-K. Shih, S. Sivakumar, G. Taylor, P. VanDerVoorn, and K. Zawadzki. Managing process variation in Intel's 45 nm CMOS technology. *Intel Technology Journal*, **12**(2):93–109, 2008.

23. K. J. Kuhn, M. D. Giles, D. Becher, P. Kolar, A. Kornfeld, R. Kotlyar, S. T. Ma, A. Maheshwari. and S. Mudanai. Process technology variation. *IEEE Transactions on Electron Devices*, **58**(8):2197–2208, 2011.

24. M. Alam. Reliability-and process-variation aware design of integrated circuits. *Microelectronics Reliability*, **48**(8):1114–1122, 2008.

25. S. Natarajan, M. Armstrong, M. Bost, R. Brain, M. Brazier, C.-H. Chang, V. Chikarmane, M. Childs, H. Deshpande, K. Dev et al. A 32 nm logic technology featuring 2nd-generation high-k+ metal-gate transistors, enhanced channel strain and 0.171 µm 2 SRAM cell size in a 291 Mb array. In *Electron Devices Meeting, 2008. IEDM 2008. IEEE International*, pages 1–3. IEEE, New York, NY, 2008.

26. K. Ahmed and K. Schuegraf. Transistor wars. *IEEE Spectrum*, **48**(11):44–49, 2011.

27. C. Auth, C. Allen, A. Blattner, D. Bergstrom, M. Brazier, M. Bost, M. Buehler, V. Chikarmane, T. Ghani, T. Glassman et al. A 22 nm high performance and low-power CMOS technology featuring fully-depleted tri-gate transistors, self-aligned contacts and high density MIM capacitors. In *VLSI Technology (VLSIT), 2012 Symposium on*, pages 131–132. IEEE, New York, NY, 2012.

28. J. Mazurier, O. Weber, F. Andrieu, F. Allain, L. Tosti, L. Brévard, O. Rozeau, M. Jaud, P. Perreau, C. Fenouillet-Beranger et al. Drain current variability and MOSFET parameters correlations in planar FDSOI technology. In *Electron Devices Meeting (IEDM), 2011 IEEE International*, pages 25–5. IEEE, New York, NY, 2011.

29. A. R. Brown, N. Daval, K. K. Bourdelle, B.-Y. Nguyen, and A. Asenov. Comparative simulation analysis of process-induced variability in nanoscale SOI and bulk trigate FinFETs. *IEEE Transactions on Electron Devices*, **60**(11):3611–3617, 2013.

30. R. Kumar. Interconnect and noise immunity design for the Pentium 4 processor. In *Proceedings of the 40th Annual Design Automation Conference*, pages 938–943. ACM, New York City, NY, 2003.

31. R. Kumar and V. Kursun. Reversed temperature-dependent propagation delay characteristics in nanometer CMOS circuits. *IEEE Transactions on Circuits and Systems II: Express Briefs*, **53**(10):1078–1082, 2006.

32. E. Maricau and G. Gielen. *Analog IC Reliability in Nanometer CMOS*. Springer Science & Business Media, Berlin, Germany, 2013.

33. S. Zafar, Y. Kim, V. Narayanan, C. Cabral, V. Paruchuri, B. Doris, J. Stathis, A. Callegari, and M. Chudzik. A comparative study of NBTI and PBTI (charge trapping) in SiO2/HfO2 stacks with FUSI, TiN, Re gates. In *VLSI Technology, 2006. Digest of Technical Papers. 2006 Symposium on*, pages 23–25. IEEE, New York, NY, 2006.

34. D. Saha, D. Varghese, and S. Mahapatra. On the generation and recovery of hot carrier induced interface traps: A critical examination of the 2-d RD model. *IEEE Electron Device Letters*, **27**(3):188–190, 2006.

35. F. Rahman, D. Forte, and M. M. Tehranipoor. Reliability vs. security: Challenges and opportunities for developing reliable and secure integrated circuits. In *Reliability Physics Symposium (IRPS), 2016 IEEE International*, pages 4C–6. IEEE, New York, NY, 2016.

36. X. Xu and D. Holcomb. A clockless sequential PUF with autonomous majority voting. In *Great Lakes Symposium on VLSI, 2016 International*, pages 27–32. IEEE, New York, NY, 2016.

37. X. Xu, W. Burleson, and D. E. Holcomb. Using statistical models to improve the reliability of delay-based PUFs. In *VLSI (ISVLSI), 2016 IEEE Computer Society Annual Symposium on*, pages 547–552. IEEE, New York, NY, 2016.

38. D. Lim, J. W. Lee, B. Gassend, G. E. Suh, M. Van Dijk, and S. Devadas. Extracting secret keys from integrated circuits. *IEEE Transactions on Very Large Scale Integration (VLSI) Systems*, **13**(10):1200–1205, 2005.

39. S. S. Kumar, J. Guajardo, R. Maes, G.-J. Schrijen, and P. Tuyls. The butterfly PUF protecting IP on every FPGA. In *Hardware-Oriented Security and Trust, 2008. HOST 2008. IEEE International Workshop on*, pages 67–70. IEEE, New York, NY, 2008.

40. M. Majzoobi, F. Koushanfar, and M. Potkonjak. Lightweight secure PUFs. In *Computer-Aided Design, 2008. ICCAD 2008. IEEE/ACM International Conference on*, pages 670–673. IEEE, New York, NY, 2008.

41. Q. Chen, G. Csaba, P. Lugli, U. Schlichtmann, and U. Rührmair. The bistable ring PUF: A new architecture for strong physical unclonable functions. In *Hardware-Oriented Security and Trust (HOST), 2011 IEEE International Symposium on*, pages 134–141. IEEE, New York, NY, 2011.

42. X. Xu, U. Rührmair, D. E. Holcomb, and W. Burleson. Security evaluation and enhancement of bistable ring PUFs. In *International Workshop on Radio Frequency Identification: Security and Privacy Issues*, pages 3–16. Springer, Berlin, 2015.

43. U. Rührmair, J. Martinez-Hurtado, X. Xu, C. Kraeh, C. Hilgers, D. Kononchuk, J. J. Finley, and W. P. Burleson. Virtual proofs of reality and their physical implementation. In *Security and Privacy (SP), 2015 IEEE Symposium on*, pages 70–85. IEEE, New York, NY, 2015.

44. B. Jun and P. Kocher, The Intel random number generator. *Cryptography Research Inc. White Paper*, 1999.

45. N. Stefanou and S. R. Sonkusale. High speed array of oscillator-based truly binary random number generators. In *Circuits and Systems, 2004. ISCAS'04. Proceedings of the 2004 International Symposium on*, Vol. 1, I–505. IEEE, New York, NY, 2004.

46. T. Amaki, M. Hashimoto, and T. Onoye. An oscillator-based true random number generator with jitter amplifier. In *Circuits and Systems (ISCAS), 2011 IEEE International Symposium on*, pages 725–728. IEEE, New York, NY, 2011.

47. A. T. Markettos and S. W. Moore. The frequency injection attack on ring-oscillator-based true random number generators. In *Cryptographic Hardware and Embedded Systems—CHES 2009*, pages 317–331. Springer, Berlin, 2009.

48. P. Bayon, L. Bossuet, A. Aubert, V. Fischer, F. Poucheret, B. Robisson, and P. Maurine. Contactless electromagnetic active attack on ring oscillator based true random number generator. In *International Workshop on Constructive Side-Channel Analysis and Secure Design*, pages 151–166. Springer, Berlin, 2012.

49. D. Schellekens, B. Preneel, and I. Verbauwhede. FPGA vendor agnostic true random number generator. In *Field Programmable Logic and Applications, 2006. FPL'06. International Conference on*, pages 1–6. IEEE, New York, NY, 2006.

50. X. Xu, V. Suresh, R. Kumar, and W. Burleson. Post-silicon validation and calibration of hardware security primitives. In *VLSI (ISVLSI), 2014 IEEE Computer Society Annual Symposium on*, pages 29–34. IEEE, New York, NY, 2014.

51. S. Robson, B. Leung, and G. Gong. Truly random number generator based on a ring oscillator utilizing last passage time. *IEEE Transactions on Circuits and Systems II: Express Briefs*, **61**(12):937–941, 2014.

52. X. Zhang, N. Tuzzio, and M. Tehranipoor. Identification of recovered ICs using fingerprints from a light-weight on-chip sensor. In *Proceedings of the 49th Annual Design Automation Conference*, pages 703–708. ACM, New York City, NY, 2012.

53. U. Guin, X. Zhang, D. Forte, and M. Tehranipoor. Low-cost on-chip structures for combating die and IC recycling. In *Proceedings of the 51st Annual Design Automation Conference*, pages 1–6. ACM, New York City, NY, 2014.

Chapter 3

Nanoscale CMOS Memory-Based Security Primitive Design

Daniel E. Holcomb

Contents

In the digital domain, memory cells can be considered as identical across chip instances and deterministic across time. This notion of memory is an abstraction, and holds only under certain operating conditions. If we peel back the abstraction and operate outside of the typical conditions, then we find a wealth of interesting information that can be used in security. Specifically, we can find information that is unique to each chip, information about the historical operation of that chip, or information that is to some extent random. These types of information have different causes, and different applications. Chip-specific information results from process variations, and can be used for authentication or secure key storage. Historical information results from circuit aging, and can be used for anti-counterfeiting. Randomness results from noise, and can be used for generating the random numbers that are needed in cryptography.

3.1 Memory as Basis for Security Primitives

In this chapter, we consider security primitives based on memory cells. There are many ways to store state, and memory is an essential component of any computing device. In particular, we focus on devices that can be considered traditional at the time when this book is written, and primarily on static random-access memory (SRAM) and dynamic random-access memory (DRAM). SRAM is widely used as memory on microcontrollers and as caches on microprocessors, and can be found in RAM blocks on field-programmable gate arrays (FPGAs) and in standalone chips for embedded systems. DRAM is used in larger memories, such as off-chip main memory on microprocessors, or as embedded DRAM when integrated on die with a microprocessor. Toward the end of the chapter, other memories such as flip-flops and flash memory are briefly discussed. This chapter does not address the security applications of emerging or exotic technologies such as resistive RAM or phase change memory, but these memories also have important uses as security primitives.

Security primitives based on memory will often use memory as a basic information source, but the application of the primitive will require some additional circuitry around the memory to postprocess its data, or to stimulate the memory in a nonstandard way. This is to be expected, as memories are designed with the intent of being mere containers, and memory-based security primitives require them to take on a role different from their intended purpose. Even with supporting circuitry required, there are advantages to using memory cells instead of custom cells as the basis for security primitives. Memory cells are well understood, and well characterized in any technology process that a designer may chose for implementing their system. This ubiquity provides a clear path to deployment. A second benefit of memory-based primitives is that these primitives can be prototyped using commercial memory chips, with supporting circuitry implemented in off-chip logic or software during the prototyping stage.

3.1.1 Process Variations and Noise in Memories

As memories continue to scale near the end of the CMOS roadmap, they become increasingly sensitive to process variations and noise. Yet, normal operation of memory demands that variations and noise do not impact circuit behavior at higher levels of abstraction. Variation and noise are suppressed by operating the circuits under conservative conditions, such as higher than necessary supply voltages, or shorter than necessary refresh intervals in DRAM. Conservative operation with guard bands leaves some amount of energy or performance on the table in exchange for not having to worry about unpredictable behaviors.

Consider the relationship that exists between process variations, aging, and noise. If a circuit is operated in a way that makes its observable runtime behavior sensitive to the relatively small effects of process variations or aging, then the operation of that circuit will inherently also be sensitive to noise. Modifying memory operation to capture any of these influences will open up a circuit to the effects of all of these influences, even if only one is desirable. In physical unclonable functions (PUFs), the variations are desirable, while noise and aging are deleterious and must be mitigated. In random number generation, noise is desirable, but process variations and aging are deleterious and must be mitigated. In detecting recycled integrated circuits (ICs), aging is desirable, but noise and process variations can be deleterious.

3.1.2 Applications to Physical Unclonable Functions

One security primitive that can be based on memory cells is the PUF. Silicon PUFs are circuits that produce outputs according to the process variation of each chip instance. PUFs based on memory cells generally belong to the class of PUFs that are denoted "weak" PUFs; weak PUFs generate device-tied values that are analogous to physical fingerprints of a chip. The name weak is to distinguish this PUF from a second class of PUFs, termed "strong" PUFs, that maps digital inputs to digital outputs in a way that depends on process variations.

A typical application of weak PUFs is the derivation of a PUF-entangled key. Creating a perfectly reliable key from an imperfectly reliable PUF requires some amount of error correction and helper data, and the details of this are addressed later when specific PUF styles are discussed. Because the key is entangled with the volatile PUF, it only exists when the circuit is operating, and thus cannot be attacked invasively at rest. The volatility of PUF-based keys distinguishes them from keys stored in nonvolatile storage such as on-chip fuses or flash memory; values stored in these cells remain present in the cell when the chip is unpowered, and might be readable through invasive attack.

The PUF-based key may or may not be known to trusted parties external to the PUF. In the usage model where the key is known externally, a manufacturer enrolls the key before deployment, and learns the key before disabling direct access to read the key in the future. Once the PUF is enrolled, it is assumed that adversaries can no longer access the PUF's outputs or the secret key derived from them. Instead, the PUF output is only used to regenerate the key in the field, and the key will be used in a way that retains its secrecy, for example, as the key to a keyed hash function that generates message authentication codes. A weak PUF could also be used to generate a key that is unknown to any external party for use in memory encryption.

3.1.3 Applications to Random Number Generation

A second security primitive that can be based on memory cells is random number generation. Cryptographically secure random numbers are generated either by a true random number generator (TRNG) alone or by a deterministic random bit generator (DRBG) that is seeded by a TRNG. An entropy source is required in each type of random number generator, but the two approaches differ in the amount of required entropy, and in the security claim made about the generated bits.

TRNGs use fresh entropy whenever random bits are generated, and thus require a source that continually generates new entropy. Because memories are imperfect sources of entropy, postprocessing of the source is needed to extract the randomness. In this scenario of partial-entropy bits, the min-entropy of the source must be estimated and a conditioner is used to concentrate the entropy and produce random bits. NIST 800-90A [1] specifies a suite of tests for partial-entropy sources, and specifies recommended conditioners based on hash functions (HMAC) and block ciphers (CMAC and CBC-MAC). When using low-cost conditioning algorithms that are not explicitly NIST-recommended, NIST 800-90A requires testing on both the inputs to and outputs from the conditioner.

DRBGs require entropy only as a seed, and then generate future bits deterministically from that seed. Knowing the internal state of the DRBG allows prediction of all future outputs, so DRBG algorithms are designed such that learning the internal state requires computing the preimage of a one-way function. Therefore, it is important to use appropriately secure components in a

DRBG algorithm; NIST 800-90B [2] specifies recommended DRBG algorithms based on hashes (HMAC_DRBG and Hash_DRBG) and block ciphers (CTR_DRBG).

3.2 SRAM-Based Primitives

SRAM is a common building block of ICs. Single very-large-scale integration (VLSI) circuits commonly contain millions of bits of SRAM storage in caches, register files, and buffers. Each SRAM bit is typically implemented by a 6-transistor cell as shown at right in Figure 3.1. Each cell has two stable states, and in each stable state, node A or B is pulled high through transistor p1 or p2 while the other is pulled low through n1 or n2. The cell is read and written using complementary bitlines (BL and BLB) through two access transistors n3 and n4. The two access transistors of a cell are controlled by a single wordline (WL).

The SRAM cells in a memory are arranged in a matrix of rows and columns. Cells in the same column share common bitlines and hence only one cell per column is accessed at any time. A cell is written by setting one bitline high and the other low and then asserting the wordline to transfer the bitline values to the cell. In an SRAM read operation, both bitlines are first charged and equalized by the column's precharge circuit. Next, the wordline for the desired row is asserted to connect the cell to the precharged bitlines. Depending on the stored value in the cell, transistor n1 or n2 will begin to discharge one of the bitlines through the corresponding access transistor. The discharge rate of the bitline varies depending on the random variation of the transistors that are discharging it, but these variations are masked because the time allowed for bitline discharge is conservative. After discharge, the column's sense amplifier is activated to detect the difference in voltage across the two bitlines and generate from it a digital 0 or 1 value that can be read out from the SRAM.

3.2.1 SRAM Power-Up PUFs

A vast majority of SRAM PUFs are based on fingerprints extracted from the power-up state of SRAM. SRAM fingerprinting is first proposed in the security research community concurrently in

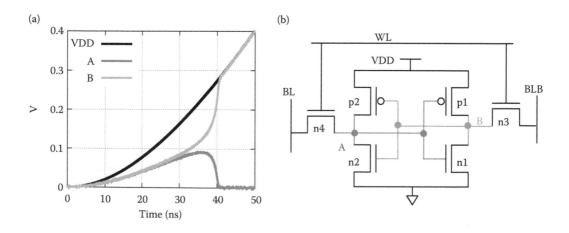

Figure 3.1   As the supply voltage of an SRAM cell increases at power-up, one state node stabilizes to the high state and the other stabilizes to the low state. The choice between the two states depends on process variation. (a) The waveforms of state nodes A and B during a power up trial and (b) the state nodes A and B within the SRAM cell schematic.

2007 by Guajardo et al. [3] and Holcomb et al. [4]; unbeknownst at that time, the idea of SRAM fingerprinting was previously investigated by Paul Layman et al. [5] for IC tracking. Guajardo's original work on SRAM PUFs is FPGA based, while Holcomb explored fingerprints from microcontroller memories and standalone SRAM chips. On more recent FPGA models from Altera and Xilinx, RAM blocks are always initialized at startup, making it difficult to now implement SRAM PUFs on arbitrary RAM blocks from FPGAs [6].

At logic level, the initial state of SRAM at power-up is undefined. However, at power-up, the SRAM cell will unavoidably transition from having both state nodes discharged to a stable state in which one of the cross-coupled nodes is charged and the other is discharged. The state that each cell takes at power-up depends on the properties of the transistors in the cell, and especially on the PMOS pull-up transistors. The waveforms at left in Figure 3.1 show a SPICE simulation of SRAM power-up. As the supply voltage begins to climb, both nodes A and B start to pull up weakly. When the supply voltage is sufficiently high, one PMOS devices wins over the other to pull up a state node and stabilize the cell. At all supply voltages above this point, the cell will continue to hold its stabilized state reliably.

SRAM cells will tend to power-up to the same state in each trial because the relative strengths of the PMOS transistors are largely persistent over the life of the chip. The dominant mode of variation within SRAM cells is threshold voltage due to random dopant fluctuations, which has very little spatial correlation and ensures that the power-up states of neighboring cells are not highly correlated, although other work finds spatial correlation in cell reliability [7]. Figure 3.2 depicts the initial states of a number of SRAM cells, and uses shading to denote propensity toward initializing to the 0 state. Ideally, a PUF will show good uniformity, meaning that it produces an approximately equal number of 0 and 1 bits. Most SRAM cells are symmetric and do show good uniformity, but even a cell that is biased toward the 0 state or the 1 state is still suitable as a PUF as long as the bits are independent and identically distributed [8].

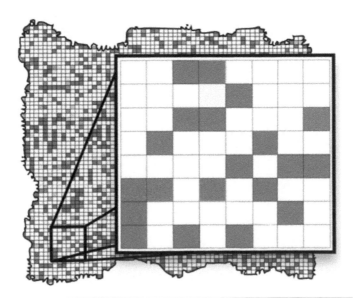

Figure 3.2   Fingerprint taken from an SRAM chip. The degree to which a cell is shaded indicates the propensity of that cell to power up to the 0 state.

The power-up of SRAM cells can be viewed as a differential circuit, and some environmental noise sources can be viewed as common mode to the two PMOS transistors that compete to determine the initial state of the cell. Temperature, for example, should impact the two devices in a common fashion. Temperature changes usually increase within-class Hamming distance by only a few percent [9,10], but some works find a much larger temperature sensitivity at extreme temperatures and even a wide variation in temperature sensitivity across instances of the same SRAM chip model [11].

SRAM cells used in a PUF are often not also used as storage, to avoid aging effects that can occur if a value is stored in the cell for long periods of time. If the cell in Figure 3.1 remains for a long time in the state having A pulled low and B pulled high, then transistor p1 will experience the aging effect of negative bias temperature instability (NBTI). NBTI causes the threshold voltage of the aged transistor to increase in magnitude. After the aging, transistor p1 is weakened in its ability to pull up node B during the next power-up trial, and the aging therefore increases the cell's probability of powering up to the state opposite to the state stored during aging [10]. Based on this principle, directed aging can be used as an attack to destroy the reliability of a cell [12], or used constructively to enhance the reliability [13].

3.2.1.1 Reliability and Error Correction

Cryptographic keys must be repeatable, but PUFs are noisy. Since a weak PUF is used to generate a secret key internally within the chip, error correction must be performed internally to eliminate the effects of noise. Deriving keys from noisy sources is a known problem in biometrics, and variety of approaches have been developed for this task in PUFs [14–17]. Key generation from a PUF will always involve some sort of error correction, and the designer must choose the parameters of error correction according the number of bits that may differ across two trials of the same PUF cells; this distance between bitstrings from two power-up trials of the same cells is the within-class Hamming distance. More robust error correction will improve reliability, but requires a larger number of bits from the PUF and has a higher hardware cost. The within-class Hamming distance distribution of Figure 3.3 shows the number of bits that differ between trials of 255-bit SRAM blocks, which is a common block size for BCH codes. Informally, from this plot, one could infer that a BCH

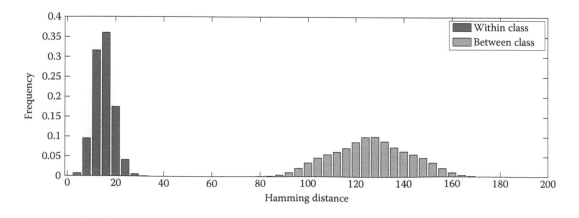

Figure 3.3   Between-class and within-class distributions of Hamming distance in 255-bit blocks from SRAM chip model number 23LC1024 from Microchip Technology Inc.

code should be chosen that can correct at least 30 bits per block, and probably significantly more to allow some margin. Making a calculated decision about error correction capacity requires a statistical model of the reliability of PUF cells.

The power-up state of SRAM cells exist on a spectrum in which some cells reliably produce 0 or 1, and some cells are more or less random (Figure 3.4). This heterogeneity of cell tendencies must be accounted for in calculations of reliability under different error correction parameters. Early works on PUFs tended to use a homogeneous error model, in which all cells are assumed to have an error rate that is equal to the average error rate over all cells. Roel Maes [18] later shows the inaccuracies of the homogeneous error model, and proposes a more accurate error probability calculation that fits a two-parameter model to the distribution of cell outcomes, and uses the model to calculate accurate reliability statistics of PUF-based keys.

3.2.1.2 Security Analysis and Attacks

At the start of this section, it is mentioned that PUF-based keys aspire to be difficult to attack while the chip is unpowered. We now revisit the security of SRAM PUFs. After de-packaging and thinning the substrate of a chip while keeping it functional, an attacker can use photonic emissions to observe values being read out of SRAM cells [19]. The emissions occur when the NMOS transistors of the cell are discharging the bitline during read-out. When the value being read in the SRAM is the power-up value, this lets an attacker learn the secret power-up values of the SRAM cell. Once the initial state is known, the attacker will be able to learn the key, and can even use a focused ion beam to perform circuit edit so that another SRAM instance can be made to act like the cloned one [19]. This very impressive attack requires a high level of expertise, and is demonstrated only on an outdated 600 nm technology process; the extent to which the same attacks would succeed against a modern SRAM is unclear.

SRAM bit values are not erased immediately once the power is turned off, and some time must elapse for the stored state to leak off of the cells and allow the next power-up to be independent of the previous state [20]. This principle of data remanence in SRAM has been used to induce faults into SRAM for the purpose of noninvasively learning the secret key [21]. While possible attacks on SRAM PUFs should continue to be monitored closely by the research community, the security assumptions of SRAM PUFs seem to have held up well thus far in the decade since their introduction, and SRAM PUFs are today available commercially from Intrinsic ID and in products by MicroSemi and NXP.

3.2.2 Other SRAM-Based PUFs

Aside from SRAM PUFs based on power-up state, a number of other SRAM-based PUFs have been proposed. One such PUF uses the minimum data retention voltage (DRV) [22] of each cell as a signature. DRV fingerprints can provide more than 1 bit of information per cell, but extracting the DRV fingerprint is more complicated than merely reading out the power-up state of SRAM. DRV of each cell is also sensitive to temperature, but the ordering of failure points across cells is largely invariant to temperature, and this allows for using a type of index-based coding to generate keys from the DRV fingerprints [23]. Retention failure signatures at reduced voltages can also be extracted via the error correction logic of caches [24]. To induce low-voltage retention failures without precise voltage control, time-based control of a power-gating signal can be used [25]. A PUF can also be created from failure signatures of attempted writes at low voltages [26], from the location of errors under varied wordline duty cycles [27], or from the resolution of SRAM cells under a nonstandard metastable write [28] or multiple concurrent reads [29]. Even current measurements from SRAM cells can be used as the basis for a promising PUF [30].

3.2.3 Random Number Generation from SRAM

Given that SRAM power-up states are noisy, they can be used as an entropy source in a TRNG [10]. Specifically, the cells with unreliable power-up states are the ones that provide entropy that can be extracted by postprocessing to derive the random numbers. In fact, SRAM cells exhibit some similarities with metastability-based TRNGs, which also use cross-coupled elements to amplify noise and generate random bits. In a metastability-based TRNG, bits are generated by repeatedly biasing a single cross-coupled element precisely to the point of metastability, and then allowing the metastability to resolve in a way that is determined by noise. SRAM-based TRNG has no mechanism to ensure that any one cell hits metastability during power-up and instead relies on the fact that, given a large enough SRAM array, some fraction of cells will have their power-up states determined by noise. What SRAM-based TRNG lacks in quality, it makes up for in quantity. Figure 3.5 shows the spatial distribution of per-cell entropy in an SRAM. The cells that are unshaded have reliable 0 or reliable 1 values. These cells have no entropy. The cells that are shaded gray are the cells that sometimes produce 0 and sometimes produce 1 in each trial.

To extract the randomness from the SRAM source after power-up, the SRAM bits are processed by an extractor (i.e., HMAC). Out of 1Mb of SRAM, roughly 1% of cells are observed to power up to the 1 state between 55 and 65 times in 120 trials (Figure 3.4), showing a high degree of randomness. A further share of cells are less random, but still provide usable entropy. The cells that produce reliable 0 or 1 values serve no purpose in random number generation, but will have no detrimental effects if fed into the randomness extractor, and there is therefore no need to separate out the random bits from the reliable ones.

Temperature is a potential threat to SRAM-based TRNG. Randomness in ICs is, at least partially, coming from physically random thermal noise. The magnitude of this noise depends upon the temperature, and lower temperatures may reduce noise. An attacker might try to exploit this by reducing temperature to decrease the entropy of the SRAM source. The plot in Figure 3.6 shows how the within-class Hamming distance changes between power-up trials of 4k-bit blocks of SRAM across temperatures from 0°C to 50°C. Each distribution shows within-class distances between trials taken from the same block at the same temperature. The higher temperatures make the power-up state more random, and the lower temperatures make it less random. To guard

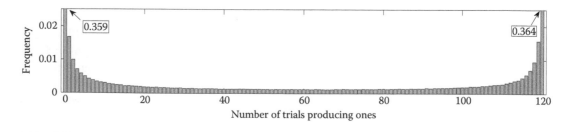

Figure 3.4   Distribution of cell power-up probabilities at 20°C on SRAM chip model 23LC1024 from Microchip Technology Inc. A majority of cells produce a 1 outcome in no trials or all trials; these cells reliably power-up to the 0 state and 1 state, respectively. A smaller number of cells produce a mixture of 0 and 1 values across trials.

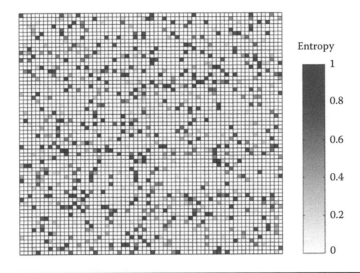

Figure 3.5 Distribution of entropy in SRAM cells. Entropy is from cells that take unpredictable power-up values in each trial. Data are collected at room temperature from 4096 bits of SRAM chip model IS61LV25616AL from ISSI Inc.

against cooling attacks on a TRNG, a design should be conservative in estimating the entropy of the source.

Validating that a particular source is sufficiently random is a nontrivial task, especially when the randomness is extracted from memory cells that may be biased. When cells are purportedly unbiased and random, one can run a battery of statistical tests to check for different statistical biases. Yet, in the case of biased bits, one should estimate the entropy of the source. Min-entropy, when treating the initial state of an SRAM as a random variable X, describes the information learned from observing the most likely outcome of that variable (Equation 3.1). Min-entropy is

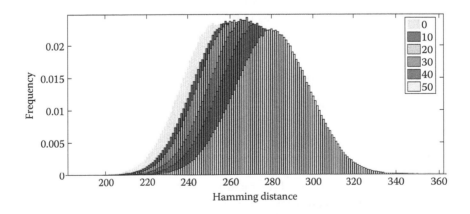

Figure 3.6 Distribution of Hamming distances between two same-temperature power-up trials from the same 4096-bit blocks from SRAM chip model 23LC1024 from Microchip Technology Inc. As the temperature is increased from 0°C to 50°C, the initial state becomes more random.

an important measure because it bounds the success rate of an adversary that knows the exact distribution of initial states of the SRAM. When using a hash function or other deterministic extractor, the attacker will achieve the highest chance of success by always guessing that the input to the extractor is the most likely valuation of X. In simple terms, if a source has at least 128 bits of min-entropy, then no initial state occurs with a probability of more than 2^{-128}, and an attacker that always guesses that the source produces its most likely value will not be correct in this guess with probability exceeding 2^{-128}. To illustrate the amount of randomness that can be extracted from SRAM power-up state, one previous work calculates that 2k bytes [31] of SRAM are needed to generate a 256-bit random number, and another calculates that 4k bits are needed to generate a 128-bit random number [10].

$$H_\infty(X) = -\log_2(\max(p(x_i))) \tag{3.1}$$

3.2.4 SRAM for Detection of Recycled ICs

Owing to the globalization of the IC supply chain, counterfeit parts are a significant and increasing threat to the reliability of electronic systems. A large share of so-called counterfeit ICs are chips that are removed from improperly recycled circuit boards [32]. These parts can be removed from their original boards, cleaned up, and resold back into the supply chain. Adding this type of recycled IC to a design is a risky proposition, because the quality of the chip is unknown, and the chip may be worn, have been damaged during disassembly or remarked before resale. One approach for mitigating the threat of counterfeit ICs is to use aging sensors that can distinguish a new chip from one that has had previous use.

SRAM can be used as an aging sensor to combat counterfeiting. Given that the stored values in the SRAM cells are not known, one must be clever in deciding how to find evidence of aging in the SRAM of recycled ICs. The Current Analysis based Counterfeit chip Identification (CACI) approach of Zheng et al. [33] exploits the observation that that more significant bits of words tend to store more 0 values than 1 values in normal usage. The asymmetry of stored states leads to an asymmetry in aging that can be detected via current measurement. If a chip shows signs of asymmetric aging, then one may conclude that the chip is recycled. Another approach to the same problem is to identify cells that initially have a reliable power-up state, which then becomes unreliable as the chip ages during its lifetime [34].

3.3 DRAM-Based Primitives

DRAM is a dense memory in which bits are stored capacitively. A basic 1-transistor 1-capacitor DRAM cell is shown in Figure 3.7; the state of the cell is determined to be 0 or 1 depending on whether the charge on the capacitor exceeds some threshold that suffices for reading. DRAM is typically organized such that some rows use the charged state to represent 0 values while other rows of the same DRAM use the charged state to represent 1 values [35]. Because stored charge on the capacitor leaks away over time, bits stored in a DRAM must be periodically refreshed by reading the cell and writing its value back. The refresh procedure restores a partially decayed value back to full strength.

The refresh interval of DRAM is chosen conservatively to ensure the state is retained in all cells across a range of temperatures. The nominal refresh interval for DDR2 SDRAM is 64 ms at low temperatures according to the JEDEC standard [36]. Beyond 64 ms refresh interval, if

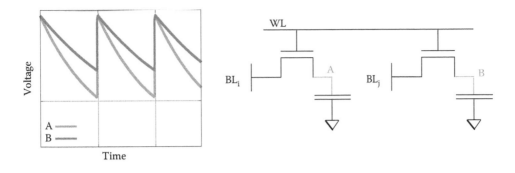

Figure 3.7 DRAM cells store value capacitively and must be refreshed periodically.

not refreshed, most cells will actually retain their state for hundreds [37,38] or thousands [39] of seconds at room temperature. If cooled in liquid nitrogen, a majority of cells will retain the state for hours [35], even if removed from its power source. Even at high temperature, only the leakiest cells fail quickly. The leakage current of each cell depends on process variation, and this makes retention failure points of each cell a unique fingerprint of the chip that can be used as a PUF. Additionally, uncertainty across trials about whether or not a cell will fail can be used as a source of randomness.

Much of the work that explores operating DRAM outside of its reliable refresh intervals comes from the architecture community, where relaxing or customizing refresh intervals provides a way to reduce the energy cost of performing the refresh [40–42], often in approximate computing scenarios that tolerate errors at the application level. Later work connects approximate DRAM to security by showing that the failure patterns in approximate DRAM serve as a fingerprint that can compromise the privacy of the device user [43].

3.3.1 DRAM-Based PUFs

DRAM PUFs seek to extract a usable signature from retention failures which are unique to each cell. The straightforward way to cause retention failures in DRAM is to lengthen the refresh interval. Because retention time is highly sensitive to temperature, the techniques used here are somewhat different from those used on SRAM. While the exact failure times are sensitive to temperature, the ordering of failures across cells is not. When a temperature increase causes a large number of cells to fail, the failing cells at the higher temperature are generally a superset of the failing cells at the lower temperature if they are from the same chip. Metrics based on Jaccard distance are more appropriate measures of dissimilarity than Hamming distance in this context [37,43].

To compensate for temperature changes, a feedback mechanism can be used to steer the DRAM to an operating point that produces a desired number of failures. When the operating point is controlled to produce a consistent number of failures, then a Hamming distance is an appropriate metric of similarity as it was in SRAM. One such feedback mechanism is to tune the wordline voltage to adjust the leakage upward or downward to increase or decrease the number of failures without changing the refresh interval [44,45] in embedded DRAM. Embedded DRAM has a much shorter refresh interval that external DRAM, and this has a benefit for PUFs of making retention failures more timely. Hashemian et al. [46] propose extracting a PUF signature from the pattern of write failures that occur when attempting to write cells under modified duty cycles. To enable retention failure-based DRAM PUFs on existing devices, Xiong et al. [37] show that it is possible to adjust refresh interval on commodity devices without hardware changes by modifying a processor's firmware or a kernel module.

3.3.2 DRAM-Based TRNG

In the same manner that DRAM can be used as a PUF, it can also be used as a basis for random number generation. Keller et al. [39] allow DDR3 DRAM to decay for 320 seconds without any refresh, and then read and extract randomness from the retention failures that occur; they are able to extract 512 bits of entropy from each 4Mb of DRAM, and use this to create a 256-bit random number. Owing to the temperature sensitivity of DRAM decay, the number of retention failures that occur after 320 seconds changes by 40% over just 2°C of temperature change (from 33.5°C to 35.5°C). This implies that reducing temperature could destroy their randomness, but a reasonable countermeasure against temperature attacks could be to adaptively adjust the decay time to target a consistent number of failures. A later work explores extracting random numbers from retention failures of a DDR2 SDRAM on Xilinx Spartan-6 FPGA boards [47]; this work observes a majority of retention failures to occur within 1 second of not refreshing. The much shorter retention time in this work appears to be caused by powering off the DRAM between refreshes, and turning off the power was also observed to reduce retention in another work [38].

3.4 Other Memory-Based PUFs

Memory structures are inherently well suited to be used in weak PUFs, and there are many memory-based PUFs beyond the SRAM and DRAM works mentioned in the preceding parts of this chapter. The cross-coupled resettable NOR-gate latches of Su et al. [48] were published shortly before the earliest works on SRAM PUFs. This design functions similar to an SRAM cell at power-up, but has control inputs that allow the cell to be discharged and evaluated at any time, and not just at power-up as in the case of SRAM. The butterfly PUF is based on cross-coupled latches [49] on FPGAs, but can be highly sensitive to routing skew which is difficult to avoid in FPGA implementations [50]. PUFs based on flip-flops [51,52] or sense amplifiers [53] have been demonstrated. Yamamoto et al. [54] propose a PUF based on RS latches with their inputs tied together, and this basic circuit can be efficiently embedded within an oscillator structure to perform a sort of autonomous majority voting [55]. Even flash memory can be used as the basis for a PUF [56].

3.5 Future of Memory-Based Security Primitives

As memory technologies change, and new memory architectures are developed, memory designers will continue to spend effort on preserving the abstraction of memories as perfect storage elements. Yet, with each new memory comes an opportunity to violate that abstraction and reveal a massively parallel structure that captures plentiful information about process variations and noise. Because the security applications of these memories are an inevitable by-product of their storage functionality, memory-based PUFs and random number generators should continue to be a fruitful area of exploration through the foreseeable future.

References

1. E. Barker and J. Kelsey. Recommendation for the entropy sources used for random bit generation. *NIST DRAFT Special Publication 800-90B*, 2012.

2. E. Barker and J. Kelsey. Recommendation for random number generation using deterministic random bit generators. *NIST Special Publication 800-90A*, 2012.
3. J. Guajardo, S. Kumar, G. Schrijen, and P. Tuyls. FPGA intrinsic PUFs and their use for IP protection. In *Cryptographic Hardware and Embedded Systems—CHES 2007: 9th International Workshop*, Paillier, P. and Verbauwhede, I. (eds), Proceedings, pages 63–80. Springer Berlin Heidelberg, September 10–13, 2007.
4. D. E. Holcomb, W. P. Burleson, and K. Fu. Initial SRAM state as a fingerprint and source of true random numbers for RFID tags. In *Proceedings of the Conference on RFID Security*, Malaga, Spain, July, 2007.
5. P. Layman, S. Chaudhry, J. G. Norman, and J. R. Thomson. Electronic fingerprinting of semiconductor integrated circuits. US6738294 B2, September 2002.
6. A. Wild and T. Güneysu. Enabling SRAM-PUFs on xilinx FPGAs. In *2014 24th International Conference on Field Programmable Logic and Applications (FPL)*, pages 1–4. Munich, Germany, September 2014.
7. K. Xiao, M. T. Rahman, D. Forte, Y. Huang, M. Su, and M. Tehranipoor. Bit selection algorithm suitable for high-volume production of SRAM-PUF. In *Hardware-Oriented Security and Trust (HOST), 2014 IEEE International Symposium on*, pages 101–106. IEEE, New York, NY, 2014.
8. R. Maes, V. van der Leest, E. van der Sluis, and F. Willems. Secure key generation from biased PUFs. In *International Workshop on Cryptographic Hardware and Embedded Systems*, pages 517–534. Springer, Berlin, 2015.
9. R. Maes, V. Rozic, I. Verbauwhede, P. Koeberl, E. Van der Sluis, and V. van der Leest. Experimental evaluation of physically unclonable functions in 65 nm CMOS. In *ESSCIRC (ESSCIRC), 2012 Proceedings of the*, pages 486–489. IEEE, New York, NY, 2012.
10. D. E. Holcomb, W. P. Burleson, and K. Fu. Power-up SRAM state as an identifying fingerprint and source of true random numbers. *IEEE Transactions on Computers*, **58**(9):1198–1210, 2009.
11. G. J. Schrijen and V. van der Leest. Comparative analysis of SRAM memories used as PUF primitives. In *2012 Design, Automation Test in Europe Conference Exhibition (DATE)*, pages 1319–1324. Dresden, Germany, March 2012.
12. A. Roelke and M. R. Stan. Attacking an SRAM-based PUF through wearout. In *2016 IEEE Computer Society Annual Symposium on VLSI (ISVLSI)*, pages 206–211. Pittsburgh, Pennsylvania, July 2016.
13. M. Bhargava, C. Cakir, and K. Mai. Reliability enhancement of bi-stable PUFs in 65 nm bulk CMOS. In *Hardware-Oriented Security and Trust (HOST), 2012 IEEE International Symposium on*, pages 25–30. San Francisco, CA, 2012.
14. M. Hiller, D. Merli, F. Stumpf, and G. Sigl. Complementary IBS: Application specific error correction for PUFs. In *Hardware-Oriented Security and Trust (HOST), 2012 IEEE International Symposium on*, pages 1–6. IEEE, New York, NY, 2012.
15. C. Bösch, J. Guajardo, A.-R. Sadeghi, J. Shokrollahi, and P. Tuyls. Efficient helper data key extractor on FPGAs. In *International Workshop on Cryptographic Hardware and Embedded Systems*, pages 181–197. Springer, Berlin, 2008.
16. M.-D. M. Yu, D. MRaihi, R. Sowell, and S. Devadas. Lightweight and secure PUF key storage using limits of machine learning. In *International Workshop on Cryptographic Hardware and Embedded Systems*, pages 358–373. Springer, Berlin, 2011.
17. R. Maes, P. Tuyls, and I. Verbauwhede. Low-overhead implementation of a soft decision helper data algorithm for SRAM PUFs. In *Cryptographic Hardware and Embedded Systems—CHES 2009*, pages 332–347. Springer, Berlin, 2009.
18. R. Maes. An accurate probabilistic reliability model for silicon PUFs. In *Proceedings of the 15th International Conference on Cryptographic Hardware and Embedded Systems, CHES'13*, pages 73–89. Springer-Verlag, Berlin, 2013.
19. C. Helfmeier, C. Boit, D. Nedospasov, and J.-P. Seifert. Cloning physically unclonable functions. In *Hardware-Oriented Security and Trust (HOST), 2013 IEEE International Symposium on*, pages 1–6. IEEE, New York, NY, 2013.

20. A. Rahmati, M. Salajegheh, D. Holcomb, J. Sorber, W. P. Burleson, and K. Fu. Tardis: Time and remanence decay in SRAM to implement secure protocols on embedded devices without clocks. In *Proceedings of the 21st USENIX Conference on Security Symposium*, pages 36–36. Bellevue, WA, USENIX Association, 2012.

21. Y. Oren, A.-R. Sadeghi, and C. Wachsmann. On the effectiveness of the remanence decay side-channel to clone memory-based PUFs. In *International Workshop on Cryptographic Hardware and Embedded Systems*, pages 107–125. Springer, Berlin, 2013.

22. D. E. Holcomb, A. Rahmati, M. Salajegheh, W. P. Burleson, and K. Fu. DRV-Fingerprinting: Using data retention voltage of SRAM cells for chip identification. In *RFIDSec'12: Proceedings of the 8th International Conference on Radio Frequency Identification: Security and Privacy Issues*. Springer-Verlag, Berlin, 2012.

23. X. Xu, A. Rahmati, D. Holcomb, K. Fu, and W. Burleson. Reliable physical unclonable functions using data retention voltage of SRAM cells. *IEEE Transactions on Computer-Aided Design of Integrated Circuits and Systems*, **34**(6):903–914, 2015.

24. A. Bacha and R. Teodorescu. Authenticache: Harnessing cache ECC for system authentication. In *Proceedings of the 48th International Symposium on Microarchitecture, MICRO-48*, pages 128–140. ACM, New York, NY, 2015.

25. X. Xu and D. E. Holcomb. Reliable PUF design using failure patterns from time-controlled power gating. In *2016 IEEE International Symposium on Defect and Fault Tolerance in VLSI and Nanotechnology Systems (DFT)*, pages 135–140. Storrs, CT, September 2016.

26. Y. Zheng, M. S. Hashemian, and S. Bhunia. RESP: A robust physical unclonable function retrofitted into embedded SRAM array. In *DAC'13: Proceedings of the 50th Annual Design Automation Conference*, Austin, TX, 2013.

27. A. R. Krishna, S. Narasimhan, X. Wang, and S. Bhunia. MECCA: A robust low-overhead PUF using embedded memory array. In *Cryptographic Hardware and Embedded Systems*, pages 407–420. Springer, Berlin, 2011.

28. S. Okumura, S. Yoshimoto, H. Kawaguchi, and M. Yoshimoto. A 128-bit chip identification generating scheme exploiting SRAM bitcells with failure rate of 4.45×10^{-19}. In *Proceedings of the 37th European Solid-State Circuits Conference*, pages 527–530. Helsinki, Finland, 2011.

29. D. E. Holcomb and K. Fu. Bitline PUF: Building native challenge-response PUF capability into any SRAM. In L. Batina and M. Robshaw, editors, *Cryptographic Hardware and Embedded Systems (CHES 2014), Volume 8731 of Lecture Notes in Computer Science*, pages 510–526. Springer-Verlag New York, Inc., New York, NY, September 2014.

30. F. Zhang, S. Yang, J. Plusquellic, and S. Bhunia. Current based PUF exploiting random variations in SRAM cells. In *2016 Design, Automation Test in Europe Conference Exhibition (DATE)*, pages 277–280. Dresden, Germany, March 2016.

31. V. van der Leest, E. van der Sluis, G.-J. Schrijen, P. Tuyls, and H. Handschuh. Efficient implementation of true random number generator based on SRAM PUFs. In *Cryptography and Security: From Theory to Applications*, pages 300–318. Springer, Berlin, 2012.

32. U. Guin, D. DiMase, and M. Tehranipoor. Counterfeit integrated circuits: Detection, avoidance, and the challenges ahead. *Journal of Electronic Testing*, **30**(1):9–23, 2014.

33. Y. Zheng, A. Basak, and S. Bhunia. CACI: Dynamic current analysis towards robust recycled chip identification. In *Proceedings of the 51st Annual Design Automation Conference, DAC'14*, pages 88:1–88:6. ACM, New York, NY, 2014.

34. Z. Guo, M. T. Rahman, M. M. Tehranipoor, and D. Forte. A zero-cost approach to detect recycled SoC chips using embedded SRAM. In *Hardware Oriented Security and Trust (HOST), 2016 IEEE International Symposium on*, pages 191–196. IEEE, New York, NY, 2016.

35. J. A. Halderman, S. D. Schoen, N. Heninger, W. Clarkson, W. Paul, J. A. Calandrino, A. J. Feldman, J. Appelbaum, and E. W. Felten. Lest we remember: Cold-boot attacks on encryption keys. *Communications of the ACM*, **52**(5):91–98, 2009.

36. DDR2 SDRAM Specification. Standard, JEDEC Solid State Technology Association, January 2005.

37. W. Xiong, A. Schaller, N. A. Anagnostopoulos, M. U. Saleem, S. Gabmeyer, S. Katzenbeisser, and J. Szefer. Run-time accessible DRAM PUFs in commodity devices. In *International Conference on Cryptographic Hardware and Embedded Systems*, pages 432–453. Springer, Berlin, 2016.

38. A. Rahmati, M. Hicks, D. Holcomb, and K. Fu. Refreshing thoughts on DRAM: Power saving vs. data integrity. In *Workshop on Approximate Computing across the System Stack (WACAS)*, Salt Lake City, Utah, 2014.

39. C. Keller, F. Gurkaynak, H. Kaeslin, and N. Felber. Dynamic memory-based physically unclonable function for the generation of unique identifiers and true random numbers. In *Circuits and Systems (ISCAS), 2014 IEEE International Symposium on*, pages 2740–2743. IEEE, New York, NY, 2014.

40. J. Liu, B. Jaiyen, R. Veras, and O. Mutlu. Raidr: Retention-aware intelligent DRAM refresh. In *ACM SIGARCH Computer Architecture News*, Vol. **40**, 1–12. IEEE Computer Society, ACM, New York, NY, 2012.

41. S. Liu, B. Leung, A. Neckar, S. O. Memik, G. Memik, and N. Hardavellas. Hardware/software techniques for DRAM thermal management. In *High Performance Computer Architecture (HPCA), 2011 IEEE 17th International Symposium on*, pages 515–525. IEEE, New York, NY, 2011.

42. R. K. Venkatesan, S. Herr, and E. Rotenberg. Retention-aware placement in DRAM (rapid): Software methods for quasi-non-volatile dram. In *The Twelfth International Symposium on High-Performance Computer Architecture, 2006*, pages 155–165. Austin, TX, February 2006.

43. A. Rahmati, M. Hicks, D. E. Holcomb, and K. Fu. Probable cause: The deanonymizing effects of approximate dram. In *Proceedings of the 42nd Annual International Symposium on Computer Architecture, ISCA'15*, pp. 604–615. ACM, New York, NY, 2015.

44. S. Rosenblatt, D. Fainstein, A. Cestero, J. Safran, N. Robson, T. Kirihata, and S. S. Iyer. Field tolerant dynamic intrinsic chip ID using 32 nm high-k/metal gate SOI embedded DRAM. *IEEE Journal of Solid-State Circuits*, **48**(4):940–947, 2013.

45. S. Rosenblatt, S. Chellappa, A. Cestero, N. Robson, T. Kirihata, and S. S. Iyer. A self-authenticating chip architecture using an intrinsic fingerprint of embedded dram. *IEEE Journal of Solid-State Circuits*, **48**(11):2934–2943, 2013.

46. M. S. Hashemian, B. Singh, F. Wolff, D. Weyer, S. Clay, and C. Papachristou. A robust authentication methodology using physically unclonable functions in DRAM arrays. In *Proceedings of the 2015 Design, Automation & Test in Europe Conference & Exhibition, DATE '15*, pages 647–652. EDA Consortium, San Jose, CA, 2015.

47. F. Tehranipoor, W. Yan, and J. A. Chandy. Robust hardware true random number generators using DRAM remanence effects. In *2016 IEEE International Symposium on Hardware Oriented Security and Trust (HOST)*, pages 79–84. McLean, VA, May 2016.

48. Y. Su, J. Holleman, and B. Otis. A 1.6 pj/bit 96% stable chip-ID generating circuit using process variations. In *International Solid State Circuits Conference*, San Francisco, CA, 2007.

49. S. S. Kumar, J. Guajardo, R. Maes, G. J. Schrijen, and P. Tuyls. The butterfly PUF protecting IP on every FPGA. In *Hardware-Oriented Security and Trust, 2008. HOST 2008. IEEE International Workshop on*, pages 67–70. Anaheim, CA, 2008.

50. S. Morozov, A. Maiti, and P. Schaumont. An analysis of delay based PUF implementations on FPGA. In *International Symposium on Applied Reconfigurable Computing*, pages 382–387. Springer, Berlin, 2010.

51. R. Maes, P. Tuyls, and I. Verbauwhede. Intrinsic PUFs from flip-flops on reconfigurable devices. In *3rd Benelux Workshop on Information and System Security (WISSec 2008)*, Vol. **17**, Eindhoven, The Netherlands, 2008.

52. J. H. Anderson. A PUF design for secure FPGA-based embedded systems. In *Proceedings of the 2010 Asia and South Pacific Design Automation Conference*, pages 1–6. IEEE Press, New York, NY, 2010.

53. M. Bhargava, C. Cakir, and K. Mai. Attack resistant sense amplifier based PUFs (SA-PUF) with deterministic and controllable reliability of PUF responses. In *Hardware-Oriented Security and Trust (HOST), 2010 IEEE International Symposium on*, Anaheim, CA, 2010.

54. D. Yamamoto, K. Sakiyama, M. Iwamoto, K. Ohta, T. Ochiai, M. Takenaka, and K. Itoh. Uniqueness enhancement of PUF responses based on the locations of random outputting RS latches. In *Cryptographic Hardware and Embedded Systems–CHES 2011*, pages 390–406. Springer, Berlin, 2011.

55. X. Xu and D. Holcomb. A clockless sequential PUF with autonomous majority voting. In *2016 International Great Lakes Symposium on VLSI (GLSVLSI)*, pages 27–32. Boston, MA, May 2016.

56. P. Prabhu, A. Akel, L. M. Grupp, S. Y. Wing-Kei, G. E. Suh, E. Kan, and S. Swanson. Extracting device fingerprints from flash memory by exploiting physical variations. In *International Conference on Trust and Trustworthy Computing*, pages 188–201. Springer, Berlin, 2011.

Chapter 4

Memristor-Based Security

Md Tanvir Arafin and Gang Qu

Contents

4.1 Introduction

In this chapter, we discuss memristors and memristor-based hardware security primitives. A memristor is a two-terminal nonvolatile memory component. The word "memristor" is coined from the words "memory" and "resistor" by circuit theorist Leon Chua [1]. In 1971, Chua first predicted the existence of the fourth basic circuit element that fundamentally relates electric charge (q) and flux-linkage (ϕ) [1]. The electrical properties of this *missing circuit element* were explored in detail by Chua and Kang [2]. However, the physical realization of memristor remained elusive.

In 2008, researchers from Hewlett-Packard (HP) Labs announced the *discovery* of memristors [3]. Their analysis on titanium dioxide (TiO$_2$) thin films in metal/oxide/metal (MIM) cross-point nano devices revealed memristive properties similar to the ones predicted by Chua [3]. This discovery leads to a renewed interest in memristive circuit and system. Numerous implementations of thin-film-based MIM systems have been designed since this breakthrough.

Memristive properties of thin-film-based cross-point nano devices were not investigated before 2008; however, these systems were actively researched for decades for designing resistive memory components. These devices are commonly denoted as resistive random access memories (RRAMs or ReRAMs). Chua has argued that such resistive-switching systems can be generalized as memristors [4]; however, there is a debate on this claim [5]. A common trend of using memristors and RRAMs in an analogous fashion exists in circuit and systems design research. Hence, in this chapter, we will use *memristor* as a general term for branding common variations of resistive switching memories, that is, memristors, RRAMs, ReRAMs, etc.

Progress in memristor-based systems research has poised memristors as a promising solution for low-power and high-density nonvolatile storage. Unique electronic properties of memristors have attracted several research directions such as memory applications, neuromorphic computation, and hardware security. As memristors gradually become a commodity component/product in computing systems, security issues related to the design and implementation of memristor-based hardware should be studied in detail. Moreover, memristors can be used for designing novel security primitives, which will employ unique intrinsic properties of these devices for security and cryptographic applications. In the next section, we introduce the basic device physics for modeling memristor and memristive system to explore and understand current research efforts in detail.

4.2 Basics of Memristor

According to the classical definition by Leon Chua, instantaneous resistance of a charge-controlled memristor can be written as [1]

$$M(q) = \frac{d\phi(q)}{dq} \equiv \frac{v(t)}{i(t)} \tag{4.1}$$

where $q = \int_{-\infty}^{t} i(\tau)d\tau$ is the electric charge, $\phi(q)$ is the magnetic flux, $v(t)$ is the voltage across the device, and $i(t)$ is the electric current flowing in the device at time t [1]. Therefore, from Equation 4.1, we can see that the resistance (also known as memristance $M(q)$) of an ideal memristor is dependent on the current that has previously passed through the device.

Chua and Kang generalized the concept of memristors and memristive system in Reference 2. It was theoretically argued that the dynamic properties of a current-controlled memristive system can be expressed with the help of an internal state variable w as

$$\frac{dw}{dt} = f(w, i) \tag{4.2}$$

$$v(t) = M(w, i) \times i(t) \tag{4.3}$$

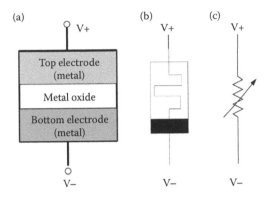

Figure 4.1 **(a) Simplified view of MIM structure for memristors. (b) and (c) Common circuit symbols used for memristors in circuit design.**

where $M(w,i)$ is the generalized resistance of the memristive system and $f(w,i)$ is a function that captures the boundary behavior and various nonlinear dynamical effects. From these equations, it can be seen that for zero input current, there will be a zero output voltage, irrespective of the state variable w. Hence, this dynamic system has a zero-crossing Lissajous figure-like input–output relationship [2]. This input–output characteristic in the $v - i$ plane is also known as pinched hysteresis loop of memristors, and it is considered to be a signature property of this circuit element [4,6]. As the frequency of the signal along the memristor increases, this zero-crossing pinched hysteresis loop shrinks in size, and it becomes a straight line when the frequency approaches infinity [6].

This fundamental circuit theoretic model was first realized in an MIM-based device structure at HP Labs [3]. The memristor discovered by HP Labs consists of a thin film (5 nm) of insulating TiO_2 sandwiched between platinum contacts in the simple metal–insulator–metal (MIM) structure [3]. Several transport models have been proposed to explain the electronic properties of this memristor and devices of similar construction. These models primarily attempt to relate the carrier transport mechanism in the thin films with the system of Equations 4.1 through 4.3. Each model provides a definition of the generalized resistance/memristance $M(w,i)$ and the function $f(w,i)$, which encapsulates the memristive nature of these devices. We discuss some of these memristor models below. Before going into the details, we introduce common circuit symbols used for memristors in Figure 4.1.

4.2.1 Linear and Nonlinear Ion-Drift Models

The simplest model that relates the resistivity of the HP devices with memristors is the linear ion-drift model proposed by Strukov et al. [3]. In this model, the governing carrier transport in the thin film of the memristor is described by linear drift of oxygen vacancies. Assume $w(t)$ as the thickness of the doped region in the thin film which is created by the linear drift of charged oxygen vacancies (dopants) at a given applied bias. Then, considering a linear ion-drift model, one can write the state equation for the state variable $w(t)$ as

$$\frac{dw}{dt} = f(w, i) = \frac{\mu_v R_{on} i(t)}{D} \tag{4.4}$$

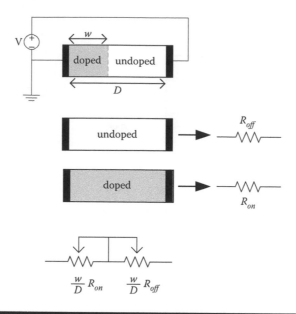

Figure 4.2 Strukov model of a Pt − TiO$_{2-x}$ − Pt device. (Adapted from D. B. Strukov et al. *Nature*, 453(7191):80–83, 2008.)

where D is the film thickness of the memristor, μ_v is the average ion mobility of oxygen vacancies in TiO$_2$, $(D-w)$ is the size of the undoped region, R_{on} is the resistance of the memristor when it is completely doped (i.e., $w=D$), and R_{off} is the resistance when it is completely undoped (i.e., $w=0$) as shown in Figure 4.2. The current–voltage relationship for a memristor in this model is defined as [3]

$$v(t) = \left(\frac{w(t)}{D} R_{on} + \left(1 - \frac{w(t)}{D} \right) R_{off} \right) i(t) \tag{4.5}$$

Overall, the effective memristance of this structure can be expressed as

$$M(w) = \frac{w(t)}{D} R_{on} + \left(1 - \frac{w(t)}{D} \right) R_{off} \tag{4.6}$$

The linear ion-drift model provides a simple explanation of the transport mechanism in a memristor. It does not consider boundary effects and nonlinear dopant kinetics. To implement boundary behaviors, Equation 4.4 can be modified as

$$\frac{dw}{dt} = \frac{\mu_v R_{on} i(t)}{D} g(w, i) \tag{4.7}$$

where $g(w,i)$ is a window function that captures the physics near the device boundary. Several approximations for the window function can be found in the literature [7–10]. These window functions are listed in Table 4.1.

Note that, for these window functions, p is a positive integer that controls the rate of change of w near the device boundary, $u(i)$ is the step function, and j controls the maximum value of

Table 4.1 Common Window Functions to Capture Physics near Device Boundary in Memristors

Author	Window Function
Joglekar et al. [8]	$g(w, i) = 1 - \left(\frac{2w}{D} - 1 \right)^{2p}$
Biolek et al. [7]	$g(w, i) = 1 - \left(\frac{w}{D} - u(-i) \right)^{2p}$
Prodromakis et al. [9]	$g(w, i) = j\left(1 - \left[\left(\frac{w}{D} - 0.5 \right)^2 + 0.75 \right]^p \right)$

$g(w)$. Although the models described above capture basic device properties, they are insufficient to describe the underlying higher-order nonlinearity of actual devices.

To simulate these models for VLSI designs, simple SPICE representations are presented in References 7, 10, 11, etc. The SPICE model proposed by Biolek et al. in Reference 7 and its derivatives are widely used in the literature for simulating HP memristors. In this circuit, the window function is incorporated using user-defined function $f()$ and the memory effects are incorporated using a feedback-controlled integrator. The circuit diagram for the model is given in Figure 4.3.

All of the discussed linear and nonlinear drift models assume that electron transport in memristors is due to the drift of carriers under electric field in the doped and undoped regions. However, quantum mechanical effects need to be considered for accurately describing carrier transport in these nano devices. Pickett et al. first incorporated the quantum mechanical effects in the basic memristor model to give a detailed description of the complex carrier dynamics in memristors [12] as discussed next.

4.2.2 *Quantum Mechanical Models*

Pickett et al. explain the observed complex carrier dynamics in TiO_2-based memristors using Simmons tunneling theory [13] and drift mechanisms of the carriers. A tunnel barrier is considered between the conducting channel and the platinum electrode of the device. An ohmic resistor in

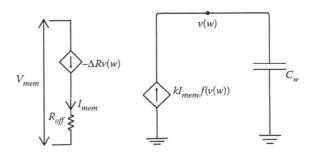

Figure 4.3 SPICE model of a memristor proposed in Reference 7. Here, V_{mem} and I_{mem} are the voltage and current across the memristor, $k = (\mu_v R_{on})/D^2$, $\Delta R = R_{on} - R_{off}$, C_w represents the doped layer of width w, and $v(w)$ is the voltage across the layer.

series with this tunnel barrier is used to explain the device characteristics. The state variable in this model is represented by the width of the tunnel barrier. This model is called the Pickett's model or Simmons tunnel barrier model. The state equation for Pickett's model is written as [12]

$$\frac{dw}{dt} = \begin{cases} f_{off} \sinh\left(\frac{|i|}{i_{off}}\right) \exp\left[-\exp\left(\frac{w - a_{off}}{w_c} - \frac{|i|}{b}\right) - \frac{w}{w_c}\right], & i > 0 \\ -f_{on} \sinh\left(\frac{|i|}{i_{on}}\right) \exp\left[-\exp\left(-\frac{w - a_{on}}{w_c} - \frac{|i|}{b}\right) - \frac{w}{w_c}\right], & i < 0 \end{cases} \tag{4.8}$$

where f_{off}, f_{on}, i_{off}, i_{on}, a_{off}, a_{on}, w_c, and b are fitting parameters. The current i through the device is given by [14]

$$i = \frac{qA}{2\pi h(\Delta w)^2}\left\{\phi_I e^{-B\sqrt{\phi_I}} - (\phi_I + q|v_g|)e^{-B\sqrt{\phi_I + q|v_g|}}\right\} \tag{4.9}$$

Here, q is the elementary electronic charge, A is the average channel area, ϕ_I is the modified barrier height, h is Planck constant, m is the average effective mass of the carrier, and

$$B = 4\pi \Delta w \frac{\sqrt{2m}}{h} \tag{4.10}$$

If we consider R_s as the series resistance of the channel and v_g is the voltage across the tunnel barrier, then the voltage across the device v can be written as

$$v = v_g + v_R = v_g + iR_s \tag{4.11}$$

To incorporate this model in circuit simulation, Abdalla et al. provided a SPICE model based on Equations 4.8 through 4.11 in Reference 14 as given in Figure 4.4. This circuit is derived from Equations 4.8 through 4.11 and uses experimental values to define its parameters. Although this model tries to accurately represent the device physics, simulating this model overestimates the current by around 20% and causes the simulated memristor to switch faster than the experimental memristor.

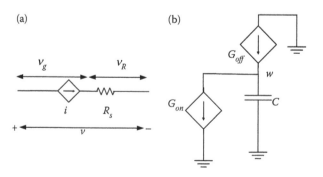

Figure 4.4   (a) SPICE model of a memristor proposed by Abdalla et al. [14]. Here, the current and voltages are given by Equations 4.9 through 4.11. Figure 4.4b represents the state-space model of the device represented by Figure 4.4a, where C is the width of the tunnel barrier, w is the voltage across the barrier, and $dw/dt = (1/C)(G_{off} - G_{on})$ where G_{off} and G_{on} are the right-hand side of Equation 4.8 for $i > 0$ and $i < 0$, respectively.

Pickett's model provides a good insight of the carrier dynamics and considers a near accurate physical model. However, this model is computationally expensive. For device simulation, Kvatinsky et al. proposed a simplified version known as the *threshold adaptive memristor (TEAM) model* to reduce the computational complexity of Pickett's model [15]. There exist similar models such as the Boundary Condition Memristor (BCM) model presented in Reference 16, which are based on the simplified versions of Equations 4.8 through 4.11. Overall, Pickett's model and the subsequently simplified models of memristors provides a good starting point for understanding basic carrier dynamics in a physical memristor.

Equations 4.4 through 4.11 are specifically derived for the TiO_2-based memristive devices. For other metal-oxide thin-film-based memristors, the characteristic equation of the device follows a similar pattern. For example, HfO_x-based memristors (also known as RRAMs) have the state equation as [17]

$$\frac{dw}{dt} = v_0 e^{-E_{a,m}/kT} \sinh\left(\frac{q a \gamma v}{DkT}\right) \tag{4.12}$$

where w is the state variable for the device as before which represents the spatial distance between the conductive filament in the oxide and the metal boundary, q is the electron charge, D is the device filament thickness, v is the applied voltage, T is the device temperature, and $E_{a,m}$, γ, v_0 are all device-dependent physical parameters. The current–voltage relationship in the device is given in the following equation [17]:

$$i = i_0 e^{-\frac{w}{w_0}} \sinh\frac{v}{v_0} \tag{4.13}$$

where i_0, v_0, w_0 are device-dependent physical parameters.

4.3 Memristor-Based Security Application

Memristors have some unique properties useful for security applications such as nonvolatility, bias-dependent write-time, fabrication variations in a filament, and nonlinearity in the current–voltage relationship [18].

1. *Nonvolatility*: Memristors are nonvolatile, that is, a memristor can retain its resistive state even without power. For single-level memory application, a memristor is used as a binary storage: the resistance remains in a higher resistive state (HRS) or lower resistive state (LRS). During state transition (i.e., moving from low to high resistive state), a significant amount of current needs to pass through the device. Moreover, after fabrication, memristor can have random initial state and this can be used for generating secure random keys.

2. *Bias-dependent write-time*: The state transition of a memristor requires the memristor to be kept under a certain bias (V_{bias}) for a given amount of time. This time is usually referred to as the write-time (t_{wr}) of the memristor. Write-time is highly dependent on the voltage bias and by adjusting the bias voltage, one can manipulate the write-time required for a given state transition [19].

3. *Fabrication variation in filament thickness*: The physical properties of a memristor vary significantly with the fabrication variation in the filament thickness. For example, Equations 4.7 through 4.9 show that the change in memristive state is nonlinearly dependent on the filament thickness w. Therefore, a small change in film thickness can lead to a significant measurable difference in the memristance of the device. Such random variability

resulting from fabrication variations can be exploited to design security features such as device authentication.

4. *Nonlinearity*: From the basic equations presented in the previous sections, it can be seen that memristors are highly nonlinear in nature. Device nonlinearity is a sought-after property for secure hardware design, and therefore, harnessing this property will provide a novel implementation of common hardware security protocols such as Physically Unclonable Functions (PUFs).

There have been many reported efforts on memristors related to security. In this chapter, we present several of these security primitives. First, we introduce our reader to the memristor PUFs that are emerging as an important hardware security component. We also discuss memristor-based true random number generators (TRNGs), encryption schemes that leverage the chaotic behavior of the memristor circuit, etc.

4.3.1 Memristor-Based PUF Design

PUFs are hardware-dependent security primitives that harness physical variation of a silicon chip to generate unique chip-dependent challenge–response pairs (CRPs). PUF CRPs can be used for secret key generation, for seeding of random number generators, and in CRP-based authentication and attestation. Physical dependence of PUF primitives has opened up new avenues for implementing hardware intrinsic security and trust.

Physical variation in the thin film of memristors has a pronounced effect on their device characteristics such as the random variation in write-time for different devices, random distribution of measured resistance after the device-forming step during fabrication, and a random resistive path between higher and lower resistive states. These fundamental properties provide an ideal situation to build memristor-based PUFs.

There have been several potential memristor-based PUF designs in the current literature with different use case and attack models. Since PUFs are inherently related to hardware-based authentication, we will assume a simple example scenario where an entity Alice wants to authenticate another entity, Bob. Malice plays the role of an attacker who subverts the authentication mechanism. Below, we have summarized the basics of operation of these PUFs.

4.3.1.1 Nano-PPUF

Memristor-based crossbars are used for designing one of the first memristor-based PUFs called nano-PPUF [20]. A simulation model of the physical design of a public PUF is publicly available; however, simulation complexity can create a time-bound authentication protocol. The attack model assumes a computationally bounded adversary unable to simulate the exact output for a given PUF design. The nonlinear equations governing the current–voltage relationship of memristors and the viability of fabricating large memristive crossbars provide the simulation complexity required by this PUF model.

In this PUF design, a public registry contains the simulation model for a given user's (Bob's) memristive PUF. When Alice wants to authenticate Bob, she first sends a random challenge vector $\mathbf{V_C} = \{v_1, v_2, \ldots, v_n\}$, where v_i represents a physical input. For the given PPUF at Reference 20, $\mathbf{V_C}$ is the voltage applied to an $n \times n$ memristor crossbar. Since Bob has the physical memristor, he can correctly respond to Alice's challenge. He sends the correct response vector $\mathbf{V_R}$. For a computationally bounded attacker Malice, completing this step would require simulating the complete crossbar, which would be computationally prohibitive. For completing the authentication, Alice then picks a subsection of Bob's crossbar (a polyomino) and requests the voltages at the boundaries of this polyomino. Bob sends the measurement and simulation results. Alice can accurately simulate the smaller polyomino using V_C and V_R, and verify Bob's results. Thus, Alice can authenticate Bob.

This initial PUF design suffers from several crucial drawbacks. The crossbar simulation and the results from the physical crossbar would only match if the physical conditions that affect the current in a memristor (such as temperature, history of current flow, aging) remain the same. This is a difficult condition to fulfill for such design. Moreover, Malice can try machine learning and model building attacks on passively obtained challenge responses to breaking the authentication scheme. Additional improvements considering these physical effects on this PUF design are discussed in References 21 and 22.

4.3.1.2 CMOS-Memristive PUF

Nano-PPUF uses memristive crossbars to generate unique challenge–response pairs. Unique device properties of single memristor cells are also used for designing other PUFs and authentication system discussed in References 18 and 23–26. Most of these works depend on the bias-dependent write-time and fabrication variations of memristors. For example, memory-based PUF cells proposed in Reference 23 uses the fabrication variation-dependent write-time differences as an entropy source. The circuit design for this PUF is shown in Figure 4.5.

The principle of operation for this PUF is simple. First, a RESET signal is applied using $NEG = 1$ and $\bar{R}/W = 1$. This puts the memristor M in an HRS. Then, a SET operation is performed with a write pulse $t_{wr,min}$ applied at V_{WR} and $NEG = 0$. The write pulse $t_{wr,min}$ is selected in a way that the likelihood of state transition is 50%. Since the write-time of memristors are random for a given voltage due to the physical randomness in their construction, the circuit (Figure 4.5) can harness 1 bit of entropy from the memristor. With a read operation $\bar{R}/W = 0$ and a challenge bit, one can receive a 1-bit response from this PUF circuit.

Similar weaknesses such as the effect of aging and noise at the supply voltage as discussed for the nano-PPUF exist for this design also. An improvement of this design can be made by dividing

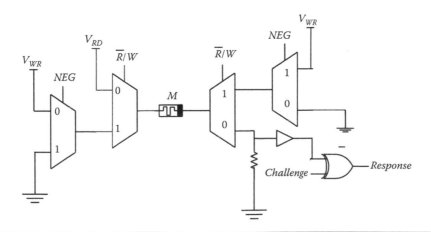

Figure 4.5 1-Bit memristive memory-based PUF cell proposed in Reference 23.

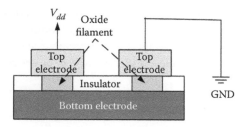

Figure 4.6 Laterally connected memristors for designing PUF cell. (Adapted from G. S. Rose et al. *IEEE/ACM International Symposium on Nanoscale Architectures (NANOARCH)*, pages 52–57. IEEE, New York, NY, 2013.)

the $t_{wr,min}$ into smaller pulses and use the number of pulses as a challenge vector as described in Reference 18. Improved PUF design with proper SET time determination for the cell shown in Figure 4.5 is also reported by Rose et al. in Reference 25. Mazady et al. [27] have experimentally verified the design proposed.

The second PUF design proposed in Reference 23 is dependent on the stochastic nature of filament formation of memristors during fabrication. Two memristors connected laterally (i.e., they share the same bottom electrode) is used for a PUF cell in this design. The top electrodes of these two memristors are connected to V_{DD} and GND, respectively, as shown in Figure 4.6. The operation for bit generation is simple. Experimental results have suggested that a lateral SET operation can SET both of the devices; however, a lateral RESET puts one of the devices to HRS and the other remains in LRS. This switching is dependent on the difference in the stochastic variation of these two laterally connected device. By comparing which one of the device has state transition, a single bit of entropy can be generated. The circuit schematics for the bit extraction is given in detail in Reference 23.

4.3.1.3 Memristive Super-High Information Content-PUF

The high packing density of memristive crossbar is useful for creating large memories with small area footprints. Passive crossbar arrays for memristors can hold a large amount of information content, which can be used for designing Super-High Information Content (SHIC)-PUFs discussed in Reference 28. SHIC-PUFs have two fundamental components: a high-density memory with random information content and a slow readout technique for this memory. It should be noted that the common memory designs are focused on fast readout circuitry for memristors due to the requirement of faster data processing and storage. However, this leads to fast leaking of the random information stored in an SHIC-PUF. Therefore, this PUF requires special readout mechanism to reduce the information leakage. These are strong PUFs with linear CRPs.

The high density of the memristor crossbars makes memristors an ideal candidate for an SHIC-PUF. Some memristor designs require an initial programming step (also known as the *forming* step) after fabrication, where the device is *formed* (i.e., becomes a memristive device instead of a common resistor). Memory contents in a memristive memory are found to be random after a forming step. This random startup resistive state can be the entropy source for such PUFs. Furthermore, probing attack on compact memristive crossbar is difficult, which makes such design secure against probing attacks.

4.3.1.4 Memristive Ring Oscillator PUF

Initial programming variation of memristors is also used in mrPUF, which integrates a memristor device into the conventional ring oscillator PUF (RO-PUF) [26]. This design uses the randomness in state distribution in a memristive crossbar as a source of entropy and uses these random resistances on the delay paths of the ring oscillators. In this design, memristors can be viewed as an entropy enhancer to the original RO-PUF designs. These designs enjoy a higher degree of stability since the scheme does not require reprogramming of the memristors.

Memristive PUF is a new concept in PUF design. Other memory-based PUFs (such as SRAM PUFs) is studied thoroughly in the literature with fabricated prototypes. However, fabrication requirements of nanoelectronic devices are demanding, and therefore, recent advances in memristive PUF design depends on the existing device model discussed in Section 4.2. Therefore, the designs and the reported results for memristive PUFs still need to be verified on fabricated designs against known modeling, learning, and side-channel attacks.

4.3.2 Memristor-Based Secret Sharing

One of the most fundamental applications of memristive PUFs is in authentication where Alice tries to authenticate Bob. Password-based authentication can be viewed as a simple case of secret sharing. Common memristor-based PUFs uses simple CRP mechanism for authentication solution. However, nonvolatility and multilevel operation of memristor can be useful in generalized secret sharing protocols. Recent works by Arafin and Qu [18,24] details a device-dependent secret sharing mechanism that uses the bias-dependent write-time properties of the memristors to provide authentication and secret sharing solutions for single and multiple users.

Secret sharing is a well-studied problem in cryptography, which can be defined as follows:

> For a given secret S, construct and distribute pieces of this secret $(S_1, S_2, \ldots, S_n)$ to n parties in a way such that the knowledge of k or more pieces would be sufficient to reconstruct the secret. However, when knowledge of any $k-1$ pieces or less is available, it would be impossible to reconstruct the secret.

One of the key solutions for this problem is given by Shamir's secret sharing algorithm [29]. This solution requires a number of theoretic calculations and might be infeasible for resource-constrained systems. Naor et al. provided another solution to this problem using visual cryptography [30]. This solution requires printing of the secret shares $(S_1, S_2, \ldots, S_n)$ on plastic transparencies and when k of these transparencies are placed on top of each other, the secret is revealed. However, for $k-1$ transparencies, no information is leaked to the participants. This is known as a *k-out-of-n* visual secret sharing.

Visual cryptography remained a solution on transparencies for the last several decades. However, multilevel memory designs and distributed key sharing schemes can harness this idea in hardware. Arafin et al. have demonstrated that multilevel memristors can be used for solving secret sharing problem in memory hardware [24]. The scheme proposed in Reference 24 uses basic visual cryptographic construct to create the secret shares $(S_1, S_2, \ldots, S_n)$. For programming the memristors, the authors used smaller write voltage, which elongated the write-time of the device. Also, instead of a (single) longer write pulse, the authors used multiple short-duration write pulses to write the memristors. It has been shown that the number of pulses required for such write is dependent on the write voltage and the fabrication variation of memristors. Hence, this number can be used as a source of entropy.

For secret sharing, the proposed solution requires not only valid users but also a valid authenticator. Assume that Alice wants to authenticate k-users simultaneously. To do so, she generates a secret to share with them according to the hardware she possesses. For sharing a 1-secret bit with k-users, first, Alice uses the following protocol to generate k-shares. This protocol for a k-out-of-k scheme is given below [31]:

- Consider a ground set G consisting of k elements $g_1, g_2, \ldots, g_k$; subsets of G with even cardinality are $p_1, p_2, \ldots, p_{2(k-1)}$ and the subsets with odd cardinality are $q_1, q_2, \ldots, q_{2(k-1)}$.
- Define $S_0[i,j] = 1$ iff $g_i \in p_j$ and $S_1[i,j] = 1$ iff $g_i \in q_j$. The resulting Boolean metrics S_0 and S_1 will have dimensions $k \times 2^{(k-1)}$.
- Permute all the column of S_0 and S_1 metrics to derive matrices C_0 and C_1, respectively.
- If the ith bit of the secret is 0, distribute the rows of C_0 to the participants.
- If the ith bit of the key is 1, distribute the rows of C_1 to the participants.

Using the techniques discussed in Reference 31, this k-out-of-k scheme can easily be converted into a k-out-of-n scheme. For sharing 1 bit of secret, Alice gives out $2^{(k-1)}$ bits to all the users. In visual cryptography, to reconstruct the secret, the users need to print these bits (a dark pixel for a 1 and a transparent pixel for a zero) on a transparency, and all of these transparencies need to be stacked up. If the stack looks darker than a given threshold ϕ (i.e., there are ϕ or more 1s in the combined share), the bit is a 1; otherwise, it is a 0.

Memristive hardware can offer a simpler way of bit reconstruction. First, assume Alice possesses a memristor for which she can set the voltage V_{read} such that it requires exactly ϕ pulses for a write operation. Alice saves the value of V_{read} for later bit reconstruction.

To reconstruct the bit, all the users put their share as a bit-stream to their respective ports (i.e., $U_1, U_2, \ldots, U_k$ of the circuit in Figure 4.7). Once the bits (related to the ith bit of the secret) for k shares are superimposed by logical OR, the bit-string consists of x number of 1s. If x is greater than the number of write pulses required for state transition in Alice's memristor (i.e., ϕ), the secret bit is reconstructed as a 1; otherwise, the bit is decoded as a 0. Here, Alice requires the knowledge of the required V_{read} that correctly reconstruct the share. If used in authentication, Alice can authenticate k-users simultaneously using this technique.

4.3.3 Random Number Generation and Memristors

Random number generators are an essential primitive of common security protocols. Entropy sources for the true random number are scarce in practice, and a proper entropy extraction mechanism is required for generating *true* random numbers. One of the preliminary designs of TRNGs using resistive memories can be found in Reference 32. This random number generator uses random trapping and detrapping of carriers in the defects of the oxide thin film in a contact-resistive random access memory (CRRAM). This trapping process results in random fluctuations of the resistance of the device, and this fluctuation is captured using a comparator and flip-flops to generate random bit-streams. The fabricated design satisfies several statistical randomness standards and tests set by National Institute of Standards and Technology (NIST).

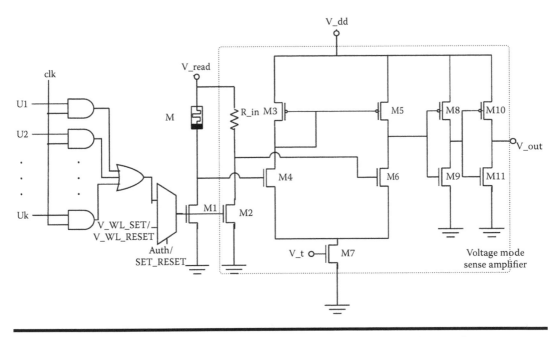

Figure 4.7 **Share commitment circuits for *k* users. At each clock cycle, all of the *k* users commit 1 bit of their secret synchronously to the $U_1, U_2, \ldots, U_i$ ports. Logical OR of this signal is applied to the memristor R_x. Since 1 bit of the secret is deconstructed into several bits, it needs multiple cycles for reconstructing the bit.**

4.3.4 *Memristor-Based Chaotic Circuits in Secure Communication*

Memristor-based circuits are an interesting primitive in chaos theory. The fundamental equations governing the memristive–RL circuit can be translated into state equations governing a chaotic system. This memristor–resistor–capacitor circuit (as shown in Figure 4.8) is known as a Chua circuit. This circuit provides new ways of chaos generation and experimentation. The absence of a "true" memristor impeded research progress in using memristive circuits for chaos generation. However, after the discovery of HP memristors, there is a renewed interest in memristive chaos circuits and networks.

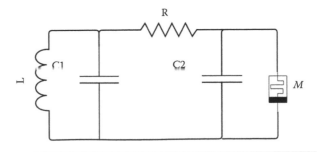

Figure 4.8 **Chua circuit for chaos generation. (Adapted from L. Chua. *The Genesis of Chua's Circuit*. Electronics Research Laboratory, College of Engineering, University of California, 1992.)**

The chaotic memristive system is used for implementing an image encryption technique in Reference 34. The authors used a modified Chua circuit for generating chaotic sequences and use these sequences as keys for image scrambling (or pixel replacement)-based encryption. The image can be unscrambled using the same sequences. The authors claimed that such techniques would be resistive toward brute-force and tampering attacks.

Researchers have also proposed chaotic sequences for stream cipher-based encryptions. Since memristor provides hardware-generated chaos, studies on active and passive memristive circuits for chaos-based encrypted communication can be found in the recent literature. One of the common examples can be found in Reference 35 where a secure communication protocol is proposed using memristive Van der Pol oscillator. In this protocol, both the communicating parties (the transmitter and the receiver) have matched Van der Pol oscillators. The message to be transmitted is used for driving this chaotic oscillator, which generates a chaotic signal. This signal is transmitted over an untrusted channel. The security model assumes that since it is difficult for an attacker to have an exactly matched oscillator, it will be impossible for an attacker to decode the message. Only a valid receiver with a matched oscillator will be able to recover the message.

Chaotic circuits are sensitive to noise. Therefore, small device mismatch or shift in the operating conditions can thwart synchronization between valid transmitter and receiver. Therefore, an adaptive synchronization feedback protocol for reconstructing the message from received chaotic signals is proposed in Reference 35. An advanced secure multiparty (up to four parties) communication using four memristive chaotic circuits is proposed in Reference 36.

Security analysis of chaos-based secure communication protocols needs to be properly addressed by the cryptographic community before validating their application. Hence, new research initiative is required for merging these two branches of technological progress.

4.4 Performance Issues of a Memristive Circuit

In this section, we discuss the common performance issues in a memristive system. Environmental variations such as temperature, and noise in the supply voltage can affect reliable performance of a memristive system. Moreover, crossbar implementation of memristors without control devices suffers from sneak path issues. Bias-dependent write-time of memristors also make them susceptible to unbalanced SET–RESET problem, which can aggravate system performance over time. We have discussed these issues in detail below:

1. *Sneak path current*: In a crossbar memory array, a memristor unit can contain a single memristor (1 M configuration) as shown in Figure 4.9 or a transistor and the memristor (1T1M configuration). Memristors can have high packing density if fabricated as a 1 M crossbar. This simple yet powerful design can lead to unprecedented storage density; however, this design faces issues with controlling the current during operation. As there is no direct access control dedicated for each memory cell, when accessing one memristor, current can flow in the adjacent memristors sharing the same row or column. This current is known as sneak path current and it can create severe performance issues in a crossbar array. Therefore, for better control and reliability, some current control mechanism is usually deployed. A simple solution is to use a transistor to control the flow of current in each device. Thus, 1T1M configuration has immunity to sneak path currents and can deliver more reliable performance. However, transistors are larger than memristors and require elaborate fabrication techniques, which make crossbar-based designs less appealing.

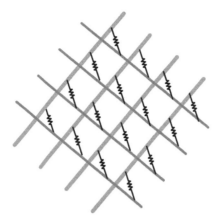

Figure 4.9 Simple view of a 4×4 memristor crossbar. The lightly shaded wires denote the top metal electrode, and the darker wires depict the bottom metal electrodes. Resistance symbols are used to represent the memristors. Applying voltage (+V) on any of the top wire and (−V) on any bottom wire with the other wires grounded creates sneak paths (from ±V to ground) involving the memristors sharing the top electrode with the lightly shaded wire and the bottom electrode with the corresponding bottom wire.

2. *SET–RESET unbalance*: Some security application may require multiple read-write on the same memristor. However, as if the bias voltage varies in between the SET–RESET cycle, then the output of the circuit used for secure hardware design may become completely unreliable. An example of this is given by Arafin and Qu in Reference 18. Moreover, the resistance of an ideal memristor depends on the history of current that has passed through the device before. As a result, inaccurate operation using wrong bias can create a cascade of failures for a number of subsequent SET–RESET cycles as shown in Figure 4.10. Therefore, proper balancing must be met when designing sensitive security protocol depending on the analog properties of a memristor.

3. *Variations in operating conditions*: Fault injection attacks on common hardware platforms depend on the voltage glitches, synchronization mismatches, and temperature manipulations for inducing a fault in cryptographic circuits. Hence, memristor-based security primitives must be designed keeping the attacks in check. Furthermore, if changes in the operating condition make the output of a security primitive unstable, then proper error correction measures need to be in place to prevent these unwanted errors. Therefore, memristor-based secure designs must meet common operating corner points in terms of operating voltage, temperature, and process variation.

   Dependence on the bias-voltage stability for state transition is discussed before. The stability of memristor's resistive switching is also dependent on temperature variations. For example, the closed-form Equations 4.12 and 4.13 for HfO_x-based memristors show a nonlinear dependence of the state variable (w) on the operating temperature T. Hence, memristor-based security designs should either experiment their prototype in different operating temperature points or consider proper device model that accounts temperature variations during operation.

4. *Aging*: Aging model for memristors is still under investigation. There are two known temporal effects in memristors: (a) short-term variation due to filament development and (b) long-term

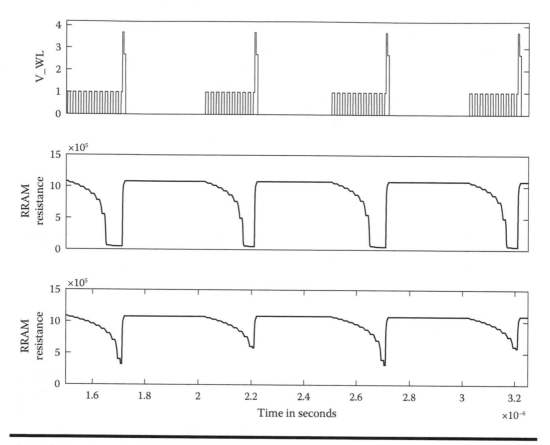

Figure 4.10 Example of SET–RESET unbalance [24] for the circuit given in Figure 4.7. The top plot shows the typical pulsed programming for a memristive device. The second figure (middle one) shows the changes in a memristor resistance for a balanced SET–RESET condition. The plot at the bottom shows the effect of unbalanced biasing where the SET voltage is lowered by 12 mV than the previous balanced condition and the RESET voltage is kept the same as before.

read-out effects. Random filament formation during operation and spatial variation of filament development in different write cycles can create cycle-to-cycle variation in low and high resistive state values within a shorter period. This is a short-term variation and can occur in random [18]. Moreover, for reading the state information of a memristor, a read/sense current must pass the through the device. Although this read current does not change the resistive state of the device dramatically, it can degrade the resistance value of a given state over time. The PUFs based on the initial programming variations may experience a wide range of errors as the device ages due to such state degradation. Furthermore, aging can change the SET–RESET dynamics and internal state transitions over time. A detailed recommendation for the designers on developing memristor-based security primitives can be found in Reference 37.

4.5 Conclusions

In this chapter, we discuss the current efforts in memristor-based security primitive design. For our readers, we first present common models describing the underlying physics and principles of operation, then we discuss the recent progress and development in hardware security primitive design using memristors, and finally, we provide the common performance and operational issues that must be properly investigated before integrating memristive designs in existing hardware platform.

Acknowledgments

This work was supported in part by the Air Force Research Laboratory under agreement number FA8750-13-2-0115 and by an Air Force Office of Scientific Research Office MURI under award number FA9550-14-1-0351.

References

1. L. Chua. Memristor—The missing circuit element. *IEEE Transactions on Circuit Theory*, **18**(5): 507–519, 1971.
2. L. Chua and S. M. Kang. Memristive devices and systems. *Proceedings of the IEEE*, **64**(2):209–223, 1976.
3. D. B. Strukov, G. S. Snider, D. R. Stewart, and R. S. Williams. The missing memristor found. *Nature*, **453**(7191):80–83, 2008.
4. L. Chua. Resistance switching memories are memristors. In *Memristor Networks*, A. Adamatzky and L. Chua (eds.), pages 21–51. Springer, Berlin, 2014.
5. S. Vongehr and X. Meng. The missing memristor has not been found. *Scientific Reports*, **5**: 2015.
6. L. Chua. The fourth element. *Proceedings of the IEEE*, **100**(6):1920–1927, 2012.
7. D. Biolek, V. Biolkova, and Z. Biolek. SPICE model of memristor with nonlinear dopant drift. *Radioengineering*, **18**(2):210–214, 2009.
8. Y. N. Joglekar and S. J. Wolf. The elusive memristor: Properties of basic electrical circuits. *European Journal of Physics*, **30**(4):661, 2009.
9. T. Prodromakis, B. P. Peh, C. Papavassiliou, and C. Toumazou. A versatile memristor model with nonlinear dopant kinetics. *IEEE Transactions on Electron Devices*, **58**(9):3099–3105, 2011.
10. S. Benderli and T. Wey. On SPICE macromodelling of TiO_2 memristors. *Electronics Letters*, **45**(7): 377–379, 2009.
11. E. Lehtonen and M. Laiho. CNN using memristors for neighborhood connections. In *12th International Workshop on Cellular Nanoscale Networks and Their Applications (CNNA)*, pages 1–4. IEEE, New York, NY, 2010.
12. M. D. Pickett, D. B. Strukov, J. L. Borghetti, J. J. Yang, G. S. Snider, D. R. Stewart, and R. S. Williams. Switching dynamics in titanium dioxide memristive devices. *Journal of Applied Physics*, **106**(7):074508, 2009.
13. J. G. Simmons. Generalized formula for the electric tunnel effect between similar electrodes separated by a thin insulating film. *Journal of Applied Physics*, **34**(6):1793–1803, 1963.
14. H. Abdalla and M. D. Pickett. SPICE modeling of memristors. In *International Symposium on Circuits and Systems (ISCAS)*, pages 1832–1835. IEEE, New York, NY, 2011.
15. S. Kvatinsky, E. G. Friedman, A. Kolodny, and U. C. Weiser. Team: Threshold adaptive memristor model. *IEEE Transactions on Circuits and Systems I: Regular Papers*, **60**(1):211–221, 2013.
16. A. Ascoli, R. Tetzlaff, F. Corinto, and M. Gilli. PSpice switch-based versatile memristor model. In *International Symposium on Circuits and Systems (ISCAS)*, pages 205–208. IEEE, New York, NY, 2013.
17. X. Guan, S. Yu, and H.-S. P. Wong. A SPICE compact model of metal oxide resistive switching memory with variations. *IEEE Electron Device Letters*, **33**(10):1405–1407, 2012.

18. M. T. Arafin and G. Qu. RRAM based lightweight user authentication. In *Proceedings of the IEEE/ACM International Conference on Computer-Aided Design, ICCAD'15*, pages 139–145. IEEE Press, Austin, TX, 2015.

19. H.-S. P. Wong, H.-Y. Lee, S. Yu, Y.-S. Chen, Y. Wu, P.-S. Chen, B. Lee, F. T. Chen, and M.-J. Tsai. Metal–oxide RRAM. *Proceedings of the IEEE*, **100**(6):1951–1970, 2012.

20. J. Rajendran, G. S. Rose, R. Karri, and M. Potkonjak. Nano-PPUF: A memristor-based security primitive. In *Computer Society Annual Symposium on VLSI (ISVLSI)*, pages 84–87. IEEE, New York, NY, 2012.

21. J. B. Wendt and M. Potkonjak. The bidirectional polyomino partitioned PPUF as a hardware security primitive. In *Global Conference on Signal and Information Processing (GlobalSIP)*, pages 257–260. IEEE, New York, NY, 2013.

22. J. Rajendran, R. Karri, J. B. Wendt, M. Potkonjak, N. R. McDonald, G. S. Rose, and B. T. Wysocki. Nanoelectronic solutions for hardware security. *IACR Cryptology ePrint Archive*, **2012**:575, 2012.

23. G. S. Rose, N. McDonald, L.-K. Yan, B. Wysocki, and K. Xu. Foundations of memristor based PUF architectures. In *IEEE/ACM International Symposium on Nanoscale Architectures (NANOARCH)*, pages 52–57. IEEE, New York, NY, 2013.

24. M. T. Arafin and G. Qu. Secret sharing and multi-user authentication: From visual cryptography to RRAM circuits. In *Proceedings of the 26th Edition on Great Lakes Symposium on VLSI*, pages 169–174. ACM, New York, NY, 2016.

25. G. S. Rose, N. McDonald, L.-K. Yan, and B. Wysocki. A write-time based memristive PUF for hardware security applications. In *Proceedings of the International Conference on Computer-Aided Design*, pages 830–833. IEEE Press, San Jose, CA, 2013.

26. O. Kavehei, C. Hosung, D. Ranasinghe, and S. Skafidas. mrPUF: A Memristive Device Based Physical Unclonable Function. *arXiv preprint arXiv:1302.2191*, 2013.

27. A. Mazady, M. T. Rahman, D. Forte, and M. Anwar. Memristor PUFa security primitive: Theory and experiment. *IEEE Journal on Emerging and Selected Topics in Circuits and Systems*, **5**(2):222–229. 2015.

28. U. Rührmair, C. Jaeger, M. Bator, M. Stutzmann, P. Lugli, and G. Csaba. Applications of high-capacity crossbar memories in cryptography. *IEEE Transactions on Nanotechnology*, **10**(3):489–498, 2011.

29. A. Shamir. How to share a secret. *Communications of the ACM*, **22**(11):612–613, 1979.

30. M. Naor and B. Pinkas. Visual authentication and identification. In *Annual International Cryptology Conference*, pages 322–336. Springer, Berlin, 1997.

31. M. Naor and A. Shamir. Visual cryptography. In *Workshop on the Theory and Application of Cryptographic Techniques*, pages 1–12. Springer, Berlin, 1994.

32. M. Hu, H. Li, Y. Chen, Q. Wu, and G. S. Rose. BSB training scheme implementation on memristor-based circuit. In *IEEE Symposium on Computational Intelligence for Security and Defense Applications (CISDA), 2013*, pages 80–87. IEEE, New York, NY, 2013.

33. L. Chua. *The Genesis of Chua's Circuit*. Electronics Research Laboratory, College of Engineering, University of California, Berkeley, 1992.

34. Z.-H. Lin and H.-X. Wang. Image encryption based on chaos with PWL memristor in Chua's circuit. In *International Conference on Communications, Circuits and Systems (ICCCAS)*, pages 964–968. IEEE, New York, NY, 2009.

35. E. M. Ngouonkadi, H. Fotsin, and P. L. Fotso. Implementing a memristive Van Der Pol oscillator coupled to a linear oscillator: Synchronization and application to secure communication. *Physica Scripta*, **89**(3):035201, 2014.

36. J. Sun, Y. Shen, Q. Yin, and C. Xu. Compound synchronization of four memristor chaotic oscillator systems and secure communication. *Chaos: An Interdisciplinary Journal of Nonlinear Science*, **23**(1):013140, 2013.

37. M. T. Arafin, C. Dunbar, G. Qu, N. McDonald, and L. Yan. A survey on memristor modeling and security applications. In *Sixteenth International Symposium on Quality Electronic Design*, pages 440–447. Santa Clara, CA, March 2015.

Chapter 5

RRAM-Based Hardware Security Primitives

Shimeng Yu, Xiaoyu Sun, Rui Liu, Huaqiang Wu,
Yachuan Pang, Bin Gao, He Qian, and An Chen

Contents

Our society has become increasingly dependent on electronic information exchange between personal devices and network servers. New ways of buying and paying, such as electronic-commerce and mobile-banking, have become popular. Unfortunately, the security of such transactions is constantly being challenged. In spite of the recent advances in network and cloud security, there have been several identity and secure information leaks in Target, Home Depot, Apple and Sony Pictures Entertainment, etc. [1]. Many of the security breaches are due to insecure access channels to the cloud. An adversary can obtain user credentials through a counterfeited device and access the

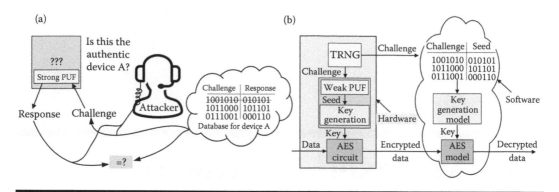

Figure 5.1 **(a) PUF-based authentication protocol. (b) PUF-based encryption protocol.**

cloud from anywhere. The security problem is likely to be exacerbated in the Internet-of-things (IoT) era where millions of devices in our homes, offices, and cars are digitally connected. It is estimated that the number of connected devices will reach 50 billion in 2020 [2]. Every connected IoT device provides more attack possibilities and adds to the potential risk. Thus, security has to be built into all layers of the system from network and cloud layers to the IoT hardware layer. Adding to the complexity is the fact that the integrated circuit (IC)'s global and distributed supply chain has introduced hardware-based security issues, such as hardware Trojans, intellectual property (IP) piracy and IC overbuilding, reverse engineering, counterfeiting, etc. [3]. Thus, hardware trustworthiness is even more important in the IoT era. Each IoT device should be equipped with a unique device signature that can be used for authentication by the cloud [4].

Physical unclonable function (PUF) has been proposed to serve as the unique device signature [5]. Figure 5.1a shows the PUF-based protocol for device authentication by the cloud. Owing to the potential man-in-the-middle attack in the communication channel, the PUF's challenge and response pair (CRP) is deleted from the database once it is used; thus, a large CRP space (or strong PUF) is needed for the device authentication. After the device is authenticated, the communication between the device and the cloud is encrypted by cryptographic algorithms such as Advanced Encryption Standard (AES) [6]. For cryptographic operations, a "root of trust" in hardware is required, and the current solution is typically to place the cryptographic keys in a nonvolatile electrically erasable programmable read-only memory (EEPROM) or battery-backed static random access memory (SRAM). This approach is expensive both in terms of chip area and power consumption, and thus not suitable for IoT devices. In addition, both the EEPROM and SRAM are often vulnerable to semi-invasive attacks such as laser or x-ray photon emission attack [7,8]. Instead, a PUF can generate the cryptographic keys only when inquired as proposed in Reference 5. For key generation in encryption, the PUF's CRP space does not need to be large; thus, a weak PUF is typically used. In addition, the responses from the weak PUF are directly sent to the on-chip cryptographic modules such as AES circuits. Thus, the responses are never exposed to the communication channel, minimizing the threat of the man-in-the-middle attack. Figure 5.1b shows a PUF-based protocol for data encryption/decryption and communication to the cloud. A true random number generator (TRNG) is also needed for generating the challenges as inputs to the PUF. Thus, the next generation of IoT devices have to support hardware security primitives such as strong PUFs, weak PUFs, and TRNG for device authentication and data encryption/decryption.

There are several implementations of silicon PUFs with complementary-metal-oxide-semiconductor (CMOS) technology, the most common being delay-based PUFs and memory-based PUFs. The arbiter PUF [5] is a delay-based PUF where the difference in the delay of the two paths is used to determine whether the output is "0" or "1." While this PUF is easy to be implemented using standard CMOS logic circuits, it can be characterized by a linear delay model and the output response can be predicted by modeling attacks (e.g., the machine learning algorithms) [9–11] or side-channel attacks [12–15]. To make the delay model nonlinear, XOR arbiter PUF and lightweight arbiter PUF [16] have been introduced. Nevertheless, these variants of the delay-based PUFs (including the ring oscillator PUF [5]) are not inherently immune to modeling attacks or side-channel attacks. Memory-based PUFs are typically based on SRAM. Here, the output response of the PUF depends upon the startup values of the cross-coupled inverters of a SRAM cell [17]. The SRAM PUFs and its variants such as latch or flip-flops [18] suffer from semi-invasive or invasive tampering attacks. For example, the SRAM PUF has been characterized by photon emission analysis and cloned by focused ion beam (FIB) circuit edit [8]. In addition, many of the aforementioned PUFs responses are not robust under environmental variations such as supply voltage or temperature variations. Therefore, additional units such as error correction [5] or fuzzy extractors [19] are needed to stabilize the PUF's response. Unfortunately, the use of helper data in these units may leak sensitive information in the PUF's response as demonstrated in Reference 20. Therefore, developing new PUFs is demanding.

The aforementioned hardware security primitives based on CMOS integrate circuits generally leverage the randomness (e.g., threshold voltage variation of transistors) originated from semiconductor manufacturing process. Such kind of randomness are closely related to the spatial location within a wafer. Some regions have more process defects than other regions which could bring uneven randomness to those regions. On the other hand, many emerging nonvolatile memory (NVM) devices [21] have exhibited randomness in their characteristics caused not only by manufacturing process variation, but also by the intrinsic stochastic mechanisms, for example, the phase transition in phase change memory (PCM), the conductive filament formation/rupture process in resistive random access memory (RRAM), and the probabilistic switching in spin transfer torque magnetic random access memory (STT-MRAM). Those randomness features are undesired properties for memory application, but could be leveraged as advantages in hardware security applications. This chapter will focus on the hardware security primitives based on RRAM technology.

5.1 RRAM Basics

RRAM is one of the emerging NVMs (note: RRAM is also referred to as memristor [22] in some papers). The typical RRAM device structure is a metal/oxide/metal stack (shown in Figure 5.2a), which can be integrated in the contact vias between interconnect layers on top of the CMOS circuits. The operation principle of RRAM device is the reversible switching between a high resistance state (HRS, off-state, "0") and a low resistance states (LRS, on-state, "1") by voltage stimulus. Nominally, the oxide is insulating; however, with the application of voltage, defects (i.e., oxygen vacancies) are created in the oxide and the oxide becomes conducting. The physical mechanism of RRAM relies on the formation and rupture of conductive filament that consists of defects in the oxide layer between two metal electrodes [23]. Figure 5.2b shows the typical $I–V$ characteristics of an RRAM cell. The switching event from HRS to LRS is called the SET process. Conversely, the switching event from LRS to HRS is called the RESET process. RRAM devices are typically integrated in the contact vias on top of CMOS circuits at back-end-of-line process,

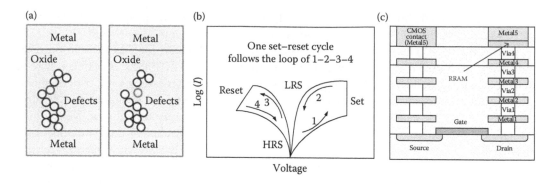

Figure 5.2 **(a) Schematic of metal/oxide/metal stack for RRAM device, showing one RRAM cell in two programming cycles with atomic change in the defect's location. (b) Typical *I–V* characteristics of the RRAM switching in a 1-transistor-1-resistor (1T1R) configuration. One SET–RESET cycle follows the loop of 1–2–3–4. (c) Cross section view of the RRAM chip. The RRAM cells integrated on top of CMOS circuits at the interconnect level by back-end-of-line process. The RRAM contact via is similar as the normal contact via. The only difference is that there is very thin (<10 nm) RRAM oxide layer in RRAM contact via.**

as shown in Figure 5.2c. RRAM technology has shown attractive attributes for NVM applications due to its low programming voltage (<3 V), fast switching speed (<10 ns), excellent scalability (<10 nm), and good programming endurance (>106 cycles) and data retention (>10 years at 85°C by extrapolation), as well as the compatibility with silicon CMOS fabrication [20]. In the recent years, 4 Mb to 32 Gb RRAM prototype chips have been demonstrated by various companies (e.g., ITRI/TSMC [24], Micron/Sony [25], SanDisk/Toshiba [26]), and embedded RRAM has been adopted for microcontroller commercial products (e.g., by Panasonic [27]). Therefore, RRAM technology is attractive for the design of hardware security primitives, as it is expected that RRAM will be widely used as embedded NVMs in IoT devices owing to its low-cost, nonvolatility, and silicon CMOS compatibility [14].

5.2 RRAM Characteristics for Hardware Security

RRAM has intrinsic stochastic characteristics, such as probabilistic switching, resistance variability, random telegraph noise (RTN), etc., which could be leveraged to design hardware security primitives.

5.2.1 Probabilistic Switching

Owing to the stochastic nature of the conductive filament formation and rupture, RRAM shows probabilistic switching behaviors under weak programming conditions. For memory application, strong programming conditions are typically applied to ensure the success of data written into the RRAM cell. However, the success rate of switching operation is closely related to the applied voltage pulse width and amplitude. In S. Yu's study [28], HfO_x-based RRAM showed probabilistic switching phenomenon during the SET process. In A. Chen's study [29], CuO_x-based RRAM with one-transistor-one-resistor (1T1R) structure showed probabilistic switching phenomenon during

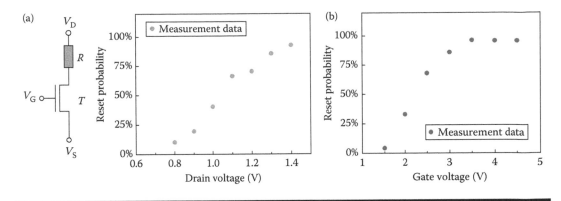

Figure 5.3 **Reset probability of CuO$_x$-based RRAM devices. (a) Consecutive voltage pulses applied on the drain of the 1T1R cell. (b) Consecutive voltage pulses applied on the gate of the 1T1R cell. (Adapted from A. Chen. *IET Electronics Letters*, 51(8): 615–617, 2015.)**

the RESET process. Figure 5.3a and b shows the effects of drain voltage/gate voltage on the RESET probability, respectively. RRAM probability switching property is a type of intrinsic randomness that could be applied on PUF and/or TRNG designs.

5.2.2 Resistance Variability

Owing to the randomness of the defect generation and annihilation in oxide, the shape of the conductive filament varies from device to device, and even from cycle to cycle within one device [30] even with the same programming conditions. Since the I–V characteristics of the RRAM device strongly depends on the conductive filament shape, any small variations in the atomic change of the filament result in significant variations in the resistances of the device. Figure 5.2a shows the schematic of the filament shape of one RRAM cell in two programming cycles that differ by the atomic displacement of a few defects. The variation of the HRS is typically larger than that of the LRS due to the tunneling nature of the HRS current. The resistance variability is remarkable in many reported RRAM devices. Figure 5.4 shows the experimental data of measured (a) device-to-device variation and (b) cycle-to-cycle variation in HfO$_x$-based RRAM [31]. The cycle-to-cycle variation suggests that the RRAM's variability is inherently caused by the stochastic nature of its atomistic dynamics, instead of the purely manufacturing process variation. In addition, the cycle-to-cycle variation can be used to generate a new set of CRPs in the runtime when necessary, thereby making PUFs reconfigurable and thus more resilient to attacks.

5.2.3 Random Telegraph Noise

In RRAM read-out current measurements, noise or RTN is often observed and attributed to the charge trapping/detrapping process, which contributes to read current fluctuation over time. In this work [32], D. Veksler et al. found that read instability could be caused not only by a repeatable capture/emission of an electron in the preexisting defect that introduces RTN, but also by irreversible random structural changes eliminating/creating an atomic defect in/near the filament. However, the irreversible random structural changes only occur occasionally and RTN plays the leading role to read instability. RTN has adverse effects for memory sense amplifier design. However, for

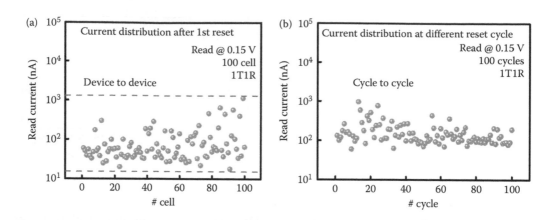

Figure 5.4 **Resistance variability measured in HfO$_x$-based RRAM 1T1R array fabricated in Tsinghua University: (a) Device-to-device variation across the array. (b) Cycle-to-cycle variation within one device. The same programming condition is applied 3 V/50 ns for RESET operation.**

hardware security applications, RTN is an important entropy source for randomness. The large amplitude of RRAM RTN signal may benefit the TRNG circuit design.

5.3 RRAM-Based PUFs

PUF is a hardware security primitive that leverages the inherent randomness in the physical systems to produce unique responses (outputs) upon the inquiry of challenges (inputs) [33]. It provides a unique characteristic to a specific device and can be used for its authentication. Depending on the number of possible CRPs, PUFs can be classified into weak PUFs (small number of CRPs) and strong PUFs (large number of CRPs). PUFs have to satisfy two important properties: (1) uniqueness and (2) reproducibility. Uniqueness means that the responses resulting from evaluating the same challenge on different PUF instances should not be similar, that is, the inter-Hamming distance (inter-HD) of the outputs for different PUF instances should ideally be 50%. Reproducibility means that response resulting from evaluating the same challenge on the same PUF instance should be similar, that is, the intra-Hamming distance (intra-HD) between the PUF responses should ideally be 0%. Besides uniqueness and reproducibility, additional metrics to evaluate PUF performance include the uniformity of the response bit stream (ideally 50% of "0" and "1") and the collision (or diffusiveness) of the responses (ideally 50% HD among all the responses within one PUF instance). On top of these performance metrics, PUFs should also be resistant to different attack models, for example, machine learning attack, physical tampering attack, etc.

RRAM-based PUF design could exploit either the probabilistic switching or the resistance variability as discussed above. The key idea of the PUF design is to generate a random data pattern in the RRAM array in the PUF construction phase, then in the PUF operation phase, only read operation is applied to the RRAM array given the input challenge (typically translated to the memory address). To read out the RRAM resistance states, L. Zhang et al. proposed two sensing modes single-ended mode (SE) and differential mode (DI) [34]. Figure 5.5a shows the circuit of SE mode. To generate a response bit, one memory cell is selected according to the challenge and compared with the fixed reference in the sense amplifier. Figure 5.5b shows the circuit of DI mode.

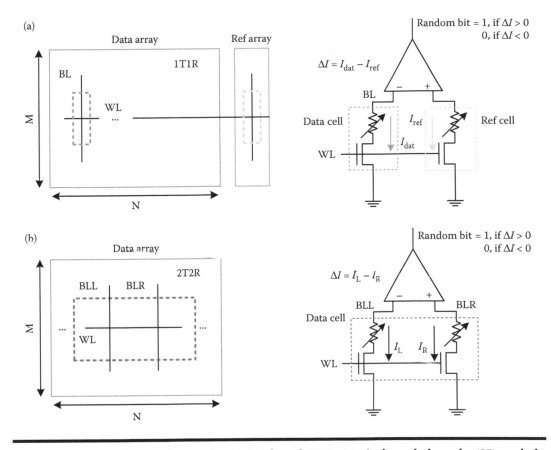

Figure 5.5 **Two sensing schemes for RRAM-based PUF: (a) single-ended mode (SE) and (b) differential mode (DI). (Adapted from L. Zhang et al. *IEEE International Memory Workshop*, pp. 1–4, Taipei, Taiwan, 2014.)**

In this mode, two memory cells are selected according to the challenge at the same time to generate a response bit, and resistance mismatch between the two cells is taken as the response bit.

5.3.1 RRAM PUF Based on Probabilistic Switching

A. Chen et al. proposed a reconfigurable PUF based on RRAMs switching probability [26]. The basic design idea is by setting a programming condition to make the switching probability of RRAM cell to 50% to form a random and unpredictable data pattern for CRP generation. Figure 5.6a shows the designed circuit for realizing the proposed RRAM PUF. The circuit is designed based on 256 kb 1T1R RRAM arrays. Initially, all the cells are written to LRS or "1." Then, a RESET voltage of 50% switching probability is applied to all the RRAM cells, resulting in a random distributed "0" and "1" data pattern in the entire RRAM array since half of the cells could be switched from "1" to "0." After the construction of the PUF data pattern, SE mode is used to generate CRPs. It should be noticed that this PUF is reconfigurable through rewriting all the RRAM cells based on the above scheme, as illustrated in Figure 5.6b. The simulated ideal distribution (line resistance RL = 0 Ω) of inter-Hamming distance (inter-HD) among 100 PUF instances centers at about 50% with a standard deviation (σ) of 3.1%. Owing to the influence of the parasitic effects

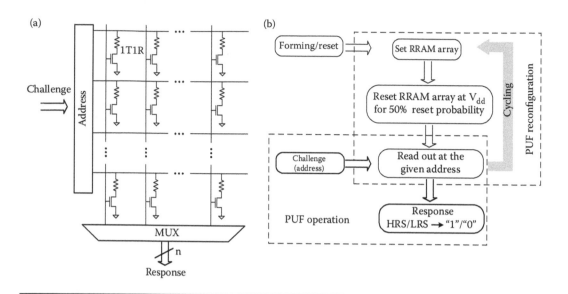

Figure 5.6   Proposal of RRAM PUF design based on probabilistic switching. (a) Schematic of 1T1R RRAM array, with challenges defined as row addresses of n-bit data and responses as memory data pattern read out by column address. The data pattern is prepared with 50% RESET probability. (b) Operation flowchart proposed PUF for reconfiguration. (Adapted from A. Chen. *IET Electronics Letters*, 51(8):615–617, 2015.)

such as voltage drop on the interconnect, the actual distribution after considering interconnect resistance (line resistance RL = 1 Ω) degrades slightly. The distribution center of the inter-HD becomes about 47%, and the standard deviation (σ) is still 3.1%.

5.3.2 RRAM PUF Based on Resistance Variability with Single-Ended Read-Out

For the first time, R. Liu et al. experimentally demonstrated the RRAM PUF based on 1 kb 1T1R array [35]. The PUF characteristics, including uniqueness and reproducibility, have been measured on 1 kb (128 rows × 8 columns) 1T1R arrays based on HfO$_x$ RRAM. Figure 5.7a shows the microscopic top view image of the fabricated 1 kb array with a built-in decoder. The RRAM device structure is TiN/TaO$_x$/HfO$_2$/TiN stack as shown in the transmission electron microscopic image (inset of Figure 5.7a), which is integrated between the interconnect layers on top of the CMOS transistors. Figure 5.7b shows the proposed circuit diagram for the PUF construction phase and the PUF operation phase.

To implement the RRAM PUF, a pulse forming process is performed row by row to set the devices to on-state in the first cycle. Then the same pulse programming condition is applied to all the cells in an attempt to reset to the off-state. The variation that occurs in the first-time RESET process is used as the entropy source. Then a read voltage is applied across each RRAM cell and the read current is measured. The measured read current distribution of the 1 kb array is shown in Figure 5.7c. This variation of the read current can be directly employed to generate the response bit of the PUF, for example, by comparing two read current from two columns as proposed in Reference 36. However, owing to the RRAM resistance temporal fluctuation and read-out noise,

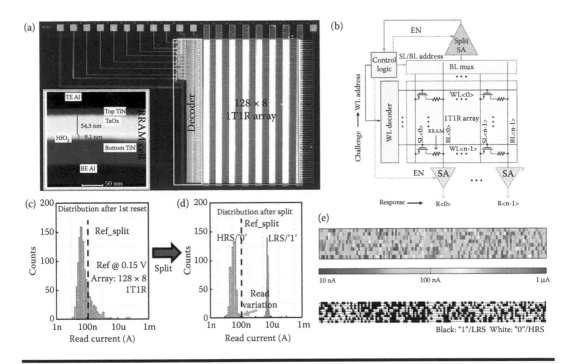

Figure 5.7 **(a) Top view of the fabricated 1 kb 1T1R RRAM array with a built-in decoder under the microscope. The inset is cross-sectional microscopic image of TiN/TaO$_x$/HfO$_2$/TiN RRAM device. (b) Proposed RRAM PUF circuit macro for the PUF construction phase and PUF operation phase. (c) Distribution of read current after the first reset operation in an RRAM array. (d) Distribution of read current after a part of cells are programmed into "1" state according to the split reference. (e) Analog data pattern before the split process. (f) Digital data pattern after the split process. (Adapted from R. Liu et al. *IEEE Electron Device Letters*, 36(12):1380–1383, 2015.)**

the response bit may not be stable. To address this problem and improve the RRAM PUFs robustness against the read-out noise, a split reference current is chosen within the distribution in the array as suggested in Reference 37 and the cells with currents above the reference are programmed to "1," and the remaining cells are kept as "0." Figure 5.7d shows the measured read current distribution in on and off states after the split process. To illustrate the effect of the split process, Figure 5.7e shows the analog data pattern before the split and Figure 5.7f shows the digital data pattern after the split. After this split process and the enrollment of CRPs in the database, the RRAM PUF construction is complete. During deployment in the field, only read operations are performed on the PUF: the row address is given as the challenge bit, then the column current through the sense amplifier generates the response bit by single-ended read-out mode. As proof of concept, 40 RRAM PUF instances are constructed using this approach. The inter-HD of the 128-bit responses is measured at around 49.8% with a small σ of 4.92%.

The key to achieve good uniqueness of the RRAM PUF is to have an ideal split reference that ensures ~50% of the distribution has a probability of "1" and the rest has a probability of "0" after the split. In order to obtain this ideal split reference on chip, a RRAM dummy column or array is needed to average out the cell variations. More dummy columns or arrays would help achieve the ideal 50% split reference but at the expense of area and power overhead. Another factor that affects the uniqueness of the RRAM PUF is the offset of the sense amplifier (S/A) used in the split process.

If the S/A's offset is significantly skewed toward either "0" or "1," the inter-HD will deviate from 50%. A commonly used voltage-mode S/A's offset voltage (3σ) is estimated to be $\sim$26 mV (by Monte Carlo simulations using TSMC 65 nm PDK). In order to minimize S/A's impact on inter-HD, further reduction of offset voltage (3σ) is needed. Possible solutions are: (1) using mirrored layout for the differential pair and increasing the W/L of the transistors of the S/A to reduce the process variation, with an overhead of more area and power; (2) exploiting more sophisticated S/A designs to minimize the offset, for example, swing-sample-and-couple S/A [38].

After the split process, RRAM PUF's responses should be robust against temporal read-out noise due to a sufficiently high on/off resistance ratio $\sim$10X. However, RRAM still suffers from aging issue: the data retention degradation (drift of resistance over a long time). Although a small percentage of response bit errors can be compensated by fuzzy extractors when the RRAM-based PUF is used for authentication, even a single bit error is unacceptable when the RRAM-based PUF is used for key generation as the output is usually hashed. In order to achieve a reproducible output, error correction codes (ECC) along with helper data is generally used. However, helper data partially leaks the secure information and the PUF is thus prone to attacks [17]. Therefore, it is desirable to design a super reliable RRAM PUF that does not require ECC within its lifetime.

To evaluate RRAM's data retention, high temperature (150°C) is used to accelerate the failure in our measurement. Figure 5.8a shows the 1 kb RRAM array's read current degradation without voltage bias at 150°C where a single RRAM cell represents a PUF response bit. The experimental result shows that the tail of on-states and off-states cross-over (resulting in errors in the PUF response) in less than 2 hours. To improve the retention properties, using multiple cells to represent a PUF response bit is proposed. The concept behind it is that if multiple RRAM cells are grouped, the read-out current will be added up and so even when some cells fail earlier than others due to inherent device-to-device variations, the redundancy can minimize the probability of early lifetime failure for the whole group. Figure 5.8b shows that with more cell as one bit, the measured data retention time increases as expected. Figure 5.8c shows when 8 parallel RRAM cells represent 1 response bit, the on/off resistance ratio can be sustained for more than 50 hours at 150°C. The equivalent lifetime using the 1/kT extrapolation gives an estimated 0% intra-HD for 10 years at 69°C, showing a very promising reproducibility. The overhead associated with this reliable PUF design is mainly more power consumption.

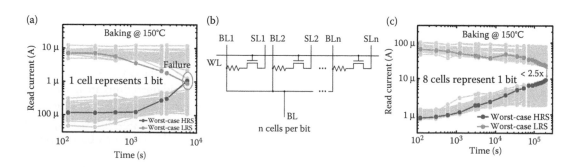

Figure 5.8 **(a) Measured retention degradation of 1 kb RRAM array with a single cell representing a PUF response bit. (b) Retention time improves with more number of cells representing a PUF response bit. (c) Measured retention degradation of 1 kb RRAM array with 8 cells representing a PUF response bit. (Adapted from R. Liu et al. *IEEE Electron Device Letters*, 36(12):1380–1383, 2015.)**

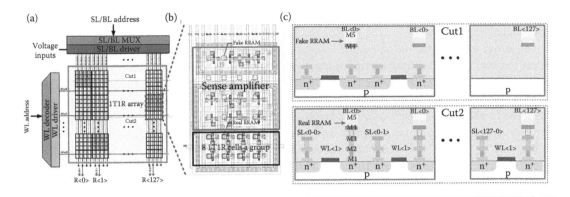

Figure 5.9 **(a) Top-level view of RRAM PUF with embedded S/A to obfuscate the adversary. (b) Cadence layout of an embedded S/A with 1T1R real RRAM cells. Fake RRAM cells are positioned on top of the S/A. If the adversary tries to invasively probe the output of the S/A, he has to remove the top-level interconnect and will destroy the RRAM cells between the interconnect layers. (c) Cross section of two cuts along the RRAM PUF showing the difference between the real RRAM contact via and the fake RRAM contact via. (Adapted from R. Liu et al.** *IEEE International Symposium on Hardware-Oriented Security and Trust,* **pp. 13–18, IEEE, McLean, VA, USA, 2016.)**

A memory-based PUF is susceptible to invasive attacks if the output of the S/A can be directly probed. Conventional memory design typically places the S/A at the edge of the array, and the adversary can easily identify the S/A's output. In order to obfuscate the adversary, it is proposed to embed the S/A within the 1T1R array and randomize the location of S/A [39], as shown in Figure 5.9a. The layout obfuscation technique is employed to embed the S/A with 8 RRAM cells in one block, as shown in Figure 5.9b. Between M4 and M5, the RRAM contact vias are uniformly placed across the array. The RRAM contact vias on top of the 1T1R are the real RRAM cells, while the RRAM contact vias on top of the S/A are fake RRAM cells. Figure 5.9c shows the cross section of the die to illustrate the difference between real RRAM cells and fake RRAM cells. Because the RRAM stack just adds a very thin (10 nm) oxide material in the contact via, from the top view the adversary cannot tell the difference between a regular contact via and an RRAM contact via. If the adversary tries to invasively probe the output of the S/A, he has to remove the top-level interconnect and may destroy the real RRAM cells between the interconnect layers. Therefore, the RRAM PUF has the "self-destructive" feature, which is highly desirable. The overhead of the proposed layout obfuscation is mainly the area.

5.3.3 RRAM PUF Based on Resistance Variability with Differential Read-Out

Y. Pang et al. experimentally demonstrated a RRAM-based PUF design with a differential read-out method [40]. The test chip architecture is same as the test chip used in Reference 35—a 128×8 1T1R RRAM array with embedded peripheral address decoding circuit. The difference is that two RRAM device structures of $TiN/TaO_x/HfO_2/TiN$ and $TiN/TaO_x/HfAl_yO_x/TiN$ are used in this work. First, all the cells in the array are SET to on-state with current target of 6 μA. Then a RESET process is performed to all the cells and a random resistance distribution of off-state is formed. To perform the differential sensing mode, two cells sitting in the same row and two adjacent columns are selected and compared to generate a binary response bit. The challenge is the address of the two adjacent columns.

In order to improve the reproducibility or reliability of PUFs response, a reliability enhancement design (RED) is employed which means after comparing a pair of RRAM cells, the cell with lower resistance is SET to on-state and the other cell is kept in off-state. This process is similar as the split process in Reference 35 but without a fixed split reference. In this way, the window of between the two adjacent cells is enlarged to mitigate the influence of reliability degradation, for example, temporal noise, retention drift, etc. The experimental results show that the intra-HD is reduced to 0% at 25°C with RED, as compared to 5% without RED. The benefit of RED is more obvious at higher temperature. The PUF with RED can maintain intra-HD at around 0% at 125°C, while intra-HD of the PUF without RED increases to 15%.

In addition, the oxide-stack engineering of RRAM structure is also employed to improve the RRAM retention and to improve RRAM PUF reliability. An extra AlO_x layer is embedded in the HfO_x stack to form the $HfAl_yO_x$ layer. Retention tests are performed on two RRAM structures of $TiN/TaO_x/HfO_2/TiN$ and $TiN/TaO_x/HfAl_yO_x/TiN$ at 150°C for 60 hours. The experimental results indicate that the $HfAl_yO_x$-based RRAM devices exhibit improved retention capability, as compared to the HfO_x-based RRAM devices due to the higher oxygen ion diffusion barrier in the $HfAl_yO_x$ layer [41].

With optimizing RRAM device structure and employing RED technique, the optimized PUF design is able to maintain the intra-HD value as low as ~1% up to 60 hours at 150°C, while the intra-HD of the PUF implemented with HfO_x-based RRAM increases to ~6% at 60 hours. This result can be translated into that the optimized PUF design with $TiN/TaO_x/HfAl_yO_x/TiN$ structured RRAM device can achieve 10-year lifetime at 81.7°C, as compared to 10-year life time at 48.8°C if $TiN/TaO_x/HfO_2/TiN$ RRAM device is used to implement the PUF design.

5.3.4 RRAM PUF Based on Resistance Variability with Digital Counting

Y. Yoshimoto et al. proposed a new response (ID)-generating method and reproducing algorithm for RRAM-based PUF to mitigate the bit error rate (BER) degradation caused by the shift of the median of the resistance distribution [42]. The RRAM device structure is $Ir/Ta_2O_5/TaO_x/TaN$, and test chips were fabricated using 40 nm process. Similar to R. Liu's work presented earlier [35], the median of the resistance distribution is obtained as the threshold (or reference) to split the cells to "0"s and "1"s. However, instead of measuring the read current of each cell to find out the median, this work proposed an architecture using a timing sense amplifier (TSA) and a resistance to time-count converter (RTC), which can digitalize the detailed resistance value information. Figure 5.10a shows the schematic of TSA and RTC, and the operating waveforms of this circuitry are shown in Figure 5.10b. The operation can be divided into two phases, precharge phase and sensing phase. SEN node is charged in the precharge phase, then it begins discharging by the BL current via RRAM cell in the sensing phase. RTC starts counting the number of CLK cycles at sensing phase, and once SEN node decays to a voltage level below VREF, Dout will become "1," leading to the termination of the counting. The lower the resistance of the RRAM cell, the larger the BL current and the faster the discharging, thereby the larger the number of counting. Thus, the RTC can sample the discharging time as a count value of the number of CLK cycles, which represents the resistance value of the RRAM cell. The median can be easily identified among those digital count values.

For a threshold (TH) fixed at the median under a certain condition, the BER increases due to the shifted median of the resistive variation distribution caused by environmental changes, for

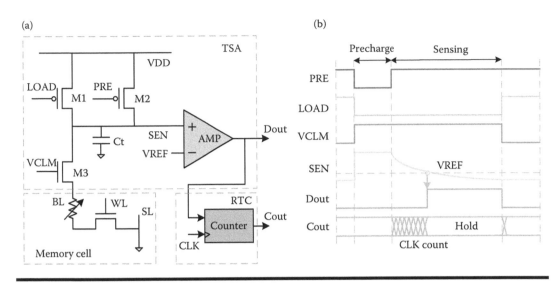

Figure 5.10 (a) Circuitry of TSA and RTC. (b) Operating waveform of TSA and RTC. (Adapted from Y. Yoshimoto et al. *IEEE Symposium on VLSI Technology*, pp. 1–2, Honolulu, HI, 2016.)

example, temperature, supply voltage, and aging degradation. Therefore, a three-step algorithm using a median detector (MD) was utilized to update the TH according to environmental changes. In the first step, the MD sequentially compares the current TH with each resistance count value, then the new median can be obtained based on the difference information acquired from the comparisons. In Step 2, the TH is updated to the new median value. In the last step, each resistance count value is compared with the new TH, thus the PUF response (ID) is generated.

Table 5.1 shows the testing results of BER of two schemes under different conditions. It is seen that with the utilization of this three-step algorithm, a significant improvement on BER is achieved compared to the fixed TH scheme. From the testing with corner conditions, the BER is <0.5% at worst, at −40°C to 125°C, and VDD±0.1 V after baking corresponding to 10 years at 25°C to 125°C as shown in Figure 5.11. The response reproduction time is more than 10^{10} at normal read voltage 0.4 V. For the uniqueness evaluation, the inter-HD and intra-HD are 49.85% and 0.19%, respectively. To sum up, this RRAM-PUF design and experiments successfully demonstrated very low BER and high uniqueness even with environmental changes, showing a high potential for embedding in IoT devices.

Table 5.1 BER Results Compared: Fixed TH and Optimized TH

Temperature	25°C	25°C	25°C	−45°C	125°C
V_{DD} variance	±0 V	+0.1 V	−0.1 V	±0 V	±0 V
Fixed TH	0%	0.21%	0.008%	0.25%	19.48%
Optimized TH	0%	0.008%	0.005%	0.008%	0.01%

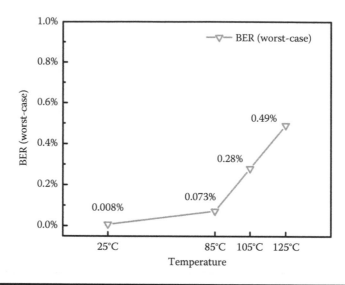

Figure 5.11 The worst BER with corner conditions: VDD±0.1 V and −40°C to 125°C versus temperature when baking corresponding to 10 years. (Adapted from Y. Yoshimoto et al. *IEEE Symposium on VLSI Technology*, pp. 1–2, Honolulu, HI, 2016.)

5.4 RRAM-Based TRNG

The random numbers generated by software or digital logic circuits (i.e., linear-feedback shift register, LFSR) have certain rules and are predictable with a given seed, thereby they are pseudo-random number generator (PRNG). TRNG generally employs the microscopic physical phenomena that generate statistically random "noise." Previous TRNG designs using thermal noise [43], soft-breakdown of gate oxides [44], or metastability [45] of circuits were not robust enough in a noisy environment. A more recent approach employed RTN in CMOS transistors as the entropy source [46]. However, it involved the von Neumann extractor to postprocess the data and thus is power inefficient. Therefore, it is attractive to investigate TRNG design using RRAM's noise or RTN. RTN is an intrinsically random phenomenon from the microscopic electron trapping/detrapping process. RRAM's conduction mechanism is trap-assisted-tunneling in the oxide, which inherently introduces RTN phenomenon [47]. RTN has been widely observed in many RRAM devices [48–51]. If there is a single dominant trap in the conduction path, RTN is observed; if there are multiple traps in the conduction path, $1/f^{\beta}$ noise is observed. The performance metrics of TRNG include randomness, robustness, and generation speed.

5.4.1 RRAM TRNG Based on RTN and Fixed Reference Comparator

C. Y. Huang et al. developed a Contact-RRAM (CR-RAM) based TRNG [52]. The RRAM cell is formed on the drain contact of a transistor, with a SiO_2 layer stacked with TiO_xN_y on top. Figure 5.12a shows the measured RTN signal of drain voltage with a fixed drain current in a 1T1R structure. The fluctuation of drain voltage is due to the RTN of the current flow through RRAM the cell. Figure 5.12b shows the circuit that consists of the RRAM cell, bias circuit, and comparator, which are all integrated on a chip using 65 nm CMOS logic process. The random numbers are generated by comparing the drain voltage with a fixed reference voltage of the voltage-mode

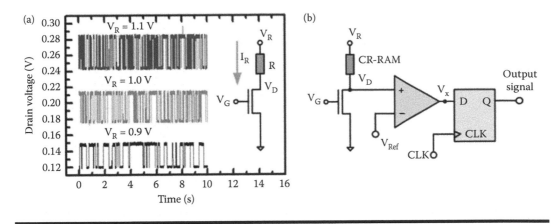

Figure 5.12 **(a) Measured RTN signal of drain voltage with a fixed drain current in a 1T1R structure. (b) A simple comparator circuit to amplify the RTN signal into the random response bit. (Adapted from C.-Y. Huang, et al. *IEEE Electron Device Letters*, 33(8):1108–1110, 2012.)**

comparator. The generated random numbers were put under a statistical test suite for validation of random numbers by the National Institute of Standards and Technology (NIST). The test results of frequency (0.088), block frequency (0.3636), spectral discrete Fourier transform (0.0755), long runs of ones (0.219), and cumulative sums (0.126/0.056) are all with a *p*-value larger than 0.01. However, the shortcoming of this design is that the random number generation speed ($\sim$kHz) is limited.

5.4.2 *RRAM TRNG Based on $1/f^\beta$ Noise and Dynamic Reference*

Z. Wei et al. developed a reliable and power-efficient RRAM TRNG using current difference in $1/f^\beta$ noise [53]. The RRAM cell comprises an Ir/Ta$_2$O$_5$/TaO$_x$/TaN stack. The test chip was fabricated with 40 nm process, similarly as the one used in RRAM PUF design [42]. Owing to its stochastic nature, RRAM filament is equivalent to a random resistance network according to the percolation model. The fluctuation of current in $1/f^\beta$ noise can be attributed to multitrap capture and emission events in the oxygen vacancies. High current indicates the empty-trap state is dominant and low current corresponds to the state with the trap being filled by an electron. Unlike a single trap involved in RTN, multiple traps contribute to $1/f^\beta$ noise. The measurement results of the current distribution and current difference (ΔI) distribution of RRAM cells suggest that the current distribution of both HRS and LRS does not follow a Gaussian distribution, which means there will be a bias in the probability of the occurrence of "1" or "0" for the TRNG that directly uses the noise current as entropy source. However, the current difference (ΔI) for both HRS and LRS follows a Gaussian distribution; therefore the difference in current is utilized as the entropy source in this design. Particularly the LRS noise is selected other than HRS due to a wider ΔI distribution of LRS. The TRNG circuit that exploits the $1/f^\beta$ noise is shown in Figure 5.13. The current value information is digitalized by TSA and RTC as illustrated in Figure 5.10 as used in RRAM PUF design [42]. Then, by the comparison between the current values of every two adjacent sampling points, the random number data can be generated. 32 Mbps random number generation throughput is achieved by parallel operation of the RRAM cells. The power efficiency is measured to be 0.04 nJ/bit. By testing with 1000 groups of 1 Mb random bit streams generated

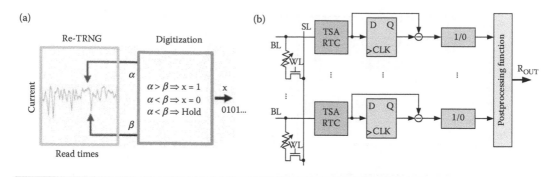

Figure 5.13 Designed circuit structure and verification of RRAM TRNG. (a) Harvest algorithm for RRAM TRNG. The resultant current difference in two adjacent sampling points is digitized as a true random number source. (b) Parallel RRAM TRNG circuit achieves 32 Mbps throughput by simultaneously generating multiple random number data. (Adapted from Z. Wei et al. *IEEE International Electron Devices Meeting*, pp. 4.8.1. San Francisco, CA, USA, 2016.)

by this RRAM TRNG using NIST SP800-22 test suite, all tests are passed across all combinations of voltages (VDD±0.1 V) and temperatures (−40°C to 125°C).

5.5 Conclusion

Hardware security has emerged as one of the most important challenges due to electronic devices penetrating every aspect of our society. TRNG and PUF are the two important primitives to assure the hardware security. RRAM as an emerging NVM has very special intrinsic randomness features, such as probabilistic switching, resistance variability, RTN, etc. These features can be exploited to design compact and low-power TRNG and PUF circuits for IoT applications. At present, several pioneering studies of RRAM-based PUF/TRNG have been carried out experimentally, showing great promises as reviewed in this chapter. More systematic evaluation of RRAM-based security primitive macro chips is necessary to fully characterize the PUF/TRNG performance and reliability metrics before they can be deployed in the field together with system-level security protocols.

Acknowledgment

This work is in part supported by NSF-CNS-1615774 and SRC Contract 2016-TS-2691.

References

1. B. Hardekopf. The Big Data Breaches of 2014. http://www.forbes.com/sites/moneybuilder/2015/01/13/the-big-data-breaches-of-2014/, 2014.
2. DHL and Cisco. Internet of Things Report. http://www.dhl.com/content/dam/Local_Images/g0/New_aboutus/innovation/DHLTrendReport_Internet_of_things.pdf, 2015.
3. M. Rostami, F. Koushanfar, and R. Karri. A primer on hardware security: Models, methods, and metrics. *Proceedings of the IEEE*, **102**(8):1283–1295, 2014.

4. V. Leest, R. S. G.-J. Maes, and P. Tuyls. Hardware intrinsic security to protect value in the mobile market. In *Information Security Solutions Europe Conference*, pp. 188–198, Wiesbaden, Germany, 2014.

5. G. E. Suh and S. Devadas. Physical unclonable functions for device authentication and secret key generation. In *ACM Design Automation Conference*, pp. 9–14, San Diego, CA, USA, 2007.

6. National Institute of Standards and Technology (NIST). Advanced Encryption Standard (AES). http://csrc.nist.gov/publications/fips/fips197/fips-197.pdf, 2001.

7. S. P. Skorobogatov. Semi-invasive attacks: A new approach to hardware security analysis, Technical Report, University of Cambridge, 2005.

8. C. Helfmeier, C. Boit, D. Nedospasov, and J.-P. Seifert. Cloning physically unclonable functions. In *IEEE International Symposium on Hardware Oriented Security and Trust*, pp. 1–6, Austin, TX, USA, 2013.

9. U. Rührmair, F. Sehnke, J. Sölter, G. Dror, and S. Devadas. Modeling attacks on physical unclonable functions. In *ACM Conference on Computer and Communications Security*, pp. 237–249, Chicago, IL, USA, 2010.

10. U. Rührmair, J. Sölter, F. Sehnke, X. Xu, A. Mahmoud, V. Stoyanova, G. Dror, J. Schmidhuber, W. Burleson, and S. Devadas. PUF modeling attacks on simulated and silicon data. *IEEE Transactions on Information Forensics and Security*, **8**(11):1876–1891, 2013.

11. X. Xu, U. Rührmair, D. Holcomb, and W. Burleson. Security evaluation and enhancement of bistable ring PUFs. In *International Workshop on Radio Frequency Identification: Security and Privacy Issues*, pages 3–16. Springer, Berlin, 2015.

12. D. Merli, D. Schuster, F. Stumpf, and G. Sigl. Side-channel analysis of PUFs and fuzzy extractors. *Trust and Trustworthy Computing*, **6740**:33–47, 2011.

13. J. Delvaux and I. Verbauwhede. Side channel modeling attacks on 65 nm arbiter PUFs exploiting CMOS device noise. In *IEEE International Symposium on Hardware-Oriented Security and Trust*, pp. 137–142, Austin, TX, USA, 2013.

14. U. Rührmair, X. Xu, J. Sölter, A. Mahmoud, M. Majzoobi, F. Koushanfar, and W. Burleson. Efficient power and timing side channels for physical unclonable functions. In *International Workshop on Cryptographic Hardware and Embedded Systems*, pages 476–492. Springer, Berlin, 2014.

15. X. Xu and W. Burleson. Hybrid side-channel/machine-learning attacks on PUFs: A new threat? In *Design, Automation & Test in Europe*, pp. 349–554, Dresden, Germany, 2014.

16. M. Majzoobi, F. Koushanfar, and M. Potkonjak. Lightweight secure PUFs. In *IEEE/ACM International Conference on Computer-Aided Design*, pp. 670–673, San Jose, CA, USA, 2008.

17. J. Guajardo, S. S. Kumar, G. J. Schrijen, and P. Tuyls. FPGA intrinsic PUFs and their use for IP protection. In *Workshop on Cryptographic Hardware and Embedded Systems*, pp. 63–80, Vienna, Austria, 2007.

18. R. Maes, P. Tuyls, and I. Verbauwhede. Intrinsic PUFs from flip-flops on reconfigurable devices. In *Benelux Workshop on Information and System Security*, pp. 1–6, Eindhoven, Netherlands, 2008.

19. Y. Dodis, L. Reyzin, and A. Smith. Fuzzy extractors: How to generate strong keys from biometrics and other noisy data. *Advances in Cryptology—Eurocrypt*, pp. 523–540, Heidelberg, Germany, 2004.

20. J. Delvaux and I. Verbauwhede. Key-recovery attacks on various RO PUF constructions via helper data manipulation. In *Design, Automation and Test in Europe*, pp. 72–77, Dresden, Germany, 2014.

21. S. Yu and P.-Y. Chen. Emerging memory technologies: Recent trends and prospects. *IEEE Solid State Circuits Magazine*, **8**(2):43–56, 2016.

22. J. Yang, D. B. Strukov, and D. R. Stewart. Memristive devices for computing. *Nature Nanotechnology*, **8**(1):13–24, 2013.

23. H.-S. P. Wong, H.-Y. Lee, S. Yu, Y.-S. Chen, Y. Wu, P.-S. Chen, B. Lee, F.T. Chen, and M.-J. Tsai. Metaloxide RRAM. *Proceedings of the IEEE*, **100**(6):1951–1970, 2012.

24. S.-S. Sheu, M. Chang, K.-F. Lin, C.-W. Wu, Y.-S. Chen, P.-F. Chiu, C.-C. Kuo, Y.-S. Yang, P.-C. Chiang, W.-P. Lin et al. A 4 Mb embedded SLC resistive-RAM macro with 7.2 ns read-write random-access time and 160 ns MLC-access capability. In *IEEE International Solid-State Circuits Conference*, pp. 200–202, San Francisco, CA, USA, 2011.

25. R. Fackenthal, M. Kitagawa, W. Otsuka, W. K. Prall, D. Mills, K. Tsutsui, J. Javanifard, K. Tedrow, T. Tsushima, Y. Shibahara et al. A 16 Gb RERAM with 200 Mb/s write and 1 Gb/s read in 27 nm

technology. In *IEEE International Solid-State Circuits Conference*, pp. 338–339. San Francisco, CA, USA, 2014.

26. T.-Y. Liu, T. Yan, R. Scheuerlein, Y. Chen, J. K. Lee, G. Balakrishnan, G. Yee, H. Zhang, A. Yap, J. Ouyang et al. A 130.7 mm2 2-layer 32 Gb RERAM memory device in 24 nm technology. In *IEEE International Solid-State Circuits Conference*, pp. 210–211, San Francisco, CA, USA, 2013.

27. A. Kawahara, R. Azuma, Y. Ikeda, K. Kawai, Y. Katoh, K. Tanabe, T. Nakamura, Y. Sumimoto, N. Yamada, N. Nakai et al. An 8 Mb multi-layered cross-point RERAM macro with 443 Mb/s write throughput. In *IEEE International Solid-State Circuits Conference*, pp. 432–433, San Francisco, CA, USA, 2012.

28. S. Yu, B. Gao, Z. Fang, H. Y. Yu, J. F. Kang, and H.-S. P. Wong. Stochastic learning in oxide binary synaptic device for neuromorphic computing. *Frontiers in Neuroscience*, 7:186, 2013.

29. A. Chen. Reconfigurable physical unclonable function based on probabilistic switching of RRAM. *IET Electronics Letters*, **51**(8):615–617, 2015.

30. S. Yu, X. Guan, and H.-S. P. Wong. On the stochastic nature of resistive switching in metal oxide RRAM: Physical modeling, Monte Carlo simulation, and experimental characterization. In *IEEE International Electron Devices Meeting*, pp. 413–416, Washington, DC, USA, 2011.

31. X. Huang, H. Wu, D. C. Sekar, S. N. Nguyen, K. Wang, and H. Qian. Optimization of CMO RRAM arrays for improved switching and data retention. In *IEEE International Memory Workshop*, pp. 1–4, Monterey, CA, USA, 2015.

32. D. Veksler, G. Bersuker, L. Vandelli, A. Padovani, L. Larcher, A. Muraviev, B. Chakrabatri, E. Vogel, D. C. Gilmer, and P. D. Kirsch. Random telegraph noise (RTN) in scaled RRAM devices. In *IEEE International Reliability Physics Symposium*, pp. MY–10, Anaheim, CA, USA, 2013.

33. C. Herder, M.-Y. Yu, F. Koushanfar, and S. Devadas. Physical unclonable functions and applications: A tutorial. *Proceedings of the IEEE*, **102**(8):1126–1141, 2014.

34. L. Zhang, X. Fong, C.-H. Chang, Z. H. Kong, and K. Roy. Feasibility study of emerging non-volatile memory based physical unclonable functions. In *IEEE International Memory Workshop*, pp. 1–4, Taipei, Taiwan, 2014.

35. R. Liu, H. Wu, Y. Pang, H. Qian, and S. Yu. Experimental characterization of physical unclonable function based on 1 kb resistive random access memory arrays. *IEEE Electron Device Letters*, **36**(12):1380–1383, 2015.

36. A. Chen. Utilizing the variability of resistive random access memory to implement reconfigurable physical unclonable functions. *IEEE Electron Device Letters*, **36**(2):138–140, 2015.

37. W. Che, J. Plusquellic, and S. Bhunia. A non-volatile memory based physically unclonable function without helper data. In *IEEE/ACM International Conference on Computer-Aided Design*, pp. 148–153, San Jose, CA, USA, 2014.

38. M.-F. Chang, A. Lee, P.-C. Chen, C. J. Lin, Y.-C. King, S.-S. Sheu, and T.-K. Ku. Challenges and circuit techniques for energy-efficient on-chip nonvolatile memory using memristive devices. *IEEE Journal of Emerging and Selected Topics in Circuits and Systems*, **5**(2):183–193, 2015.

39. R. Liu, H. Wu, Y. Pang, H. Qian, and S. Yu. A highly reliable and tamper-resistant RRAM PUF: Design and experimental validation. In *IEEE International Symposium on Hardware-Oriented Security and Trust*, pp. 13–18, IEEE, McLean, VA, USA, 2016.

40. Y. Pang, H. Wu, B. Gao, N. Deng, D. Wu, R. Liu, S. Yu, A. Chen, and H. Qian. Optimization of RRAM-based physical unclonable function with a novel differential read-out method. *IEEE Electron Device Letters*, **38**(2):168–171, 2017.

41. X. Huang, H. Wu, B. Gao, D. C. Sekar, L. Dai, M. Kellam, G. Bronner, N. Deng, and H. Qian. HfO2/Al2O3 multilayer for RRAM arrays: A technique to improve tail-bit retention. *Nanotechnology*, **27**(39):395201, 2016.

42. Y. Yoshimoto, Y. Katoh, S. Ogasahara, Z. Wei, and K. Kouno. A RERAM-based physically unclonable function with bit error rate <0.5. In *IEEE Symposium on VLSI Technology*, pp. 1–2, Honolulu, HI, 2016.

43. C. S. Petrie and J. A. Connelly. A noise based IC random number generator for applications in cryptography. *IEEE Transactions on Circuit & Systems I*, **47**(5):615–621, 2000.

44. S. Yasuda, H. Satake, T. Tanamoto, R. Ohba, K. Uchida, and S. Fujita. Physical random number generator based on MOS structure after soft breakdown. *IEEE Journal of Solid-State Circuits*, **39**(8):1375–1377, 2004.

45. C. Tokunaga, D. Blaauw, and T. Mudge. True random number generator with a metastability-based quality control. *IEEE Journal of Solid-State Circuits*, **43**(1):78–85, 2008.

46. R. Brederlow, R. Prakash, C. Paulus, and R. Thewes. A low-power true random number generator using random telegraph noise of single oxide-traps. In *IEEE International Solid-State Circuits Conference*, pp. 1666–1675, San Francisco, CA, USA, 2006.

47. J.-K. Lee, J.-W. Lee, J. Park, S.-W. Chung, J. S. Roh, S.-J. Hong, I.-W. Cho, H.-I. Kwon, and J.-H. Lee. Extraction of trap location and energy from random telegraph noise in amorphous TiOx resistance random access memories. *Applied Physics Letters*, **98**:143502, 2011.

48. S. Choi, Y. Yang, and W. Lu. Random telegraph noise and resistance switching analysis of oxide based resistive memory. *Nanoscale*, **6**:400–404, 2013.

49. D. Veksler, G. Bersuker, L. Vandelli, A. Padovani, L. Larcher, A. Muraviev, B. Chakrabarti, and E. Vogel. Random telegraph noise (RTN) in scaled RRAM devices. In *IEEE International Reliability Physics Symposium*, pp. MY–10, Anaheim, CA, USA, 2013.

50. N. Raghavan, R. Degraeve, A. Fantini, L. Goux, S. Strangio, B. Govoreanu, D. J. Wouters, G. Groeseneken, and M. Jurczak. Microscopic origin of random telegraph noise fluctuations in aggressively scaled RRAM and its impact on read disturb variability. In *IEEE International Reliability Physics Symposium*, pp. 5E-3, Anaheim, CA, USA, 2013.

51. S. Ambrogio, S. Balatti, A. Cubeta, A. Calderoni, N. Ramaswamy, and D. Ielmini. Statistical fluctuations in HfOx resistive-switching memory: Part II random telegraph noise. *IEEE Transactions on Electron Devices*, **61**(8):2920–2927, 2014.

52. C.-Y. Huang, W. C. Shen, Y.-H. Tseng, Y.-C. King, and C.-J. Lin. A contact-resistive random-access-memory-based true random number generator. *IEEE Electron Device Letters*, **33**(8):1108–1110, 2012.

53. Z. Wei, Y. Katoh, S. Ogasahara, Y. Yoshimoto, Y. Kawai, Y. Ikeda, K. Eriguchi, K. Ohmori, and S. Yoneda. True random number generator using current difference based on a fractional stochastic model in 40-nm embedded ReRAM. In *IEEE International Electron Devices Meeting*, pp. 4.8.1, San Francisco, CA, USA, 2016.

Chapter 6

Phase Change Memory and Its Applications in Hardware Security

Raihan Sayeed Khan, Nafisa Noor, Chenglu Jin, Jake Scoggin, Zachary Woods, Sadid Muneer, Aaron Ciardullo, Phuong Ha Nguyen, Ali Gokirmak, Marten van Dijk, and Helena Silva

Contents

Phase change memory (PCM) is an emerging resistive non-volatile memory technology [1]. Resistive switching memory structures are compact two-terminal devices that utilize reversible changes in resistance of a small volume of material through different mechanisms, such as magnetic switching (Magnetoresistive RAM) [2], electrothermal effects (PCM, memristors), or electrochemical effects (memristors). PCM utilizes the large electrical contrast between the highly resistive amorphous and highly conductive crystalline states in chalcogenide materials. There have been

93

significant improvements in density and scaling of PCM devices in recent years. Successful scaling down to sub-5 nm heater sizes has been reported [3]. Micron launched the first PCM-based product for mobile devices in July 2012 with endurance >10^6 cycles using 45 nm technology [4]. In recent years, IBM and Western Digital have showcased the potential of PCM as a replacement of NAND flash [5,6]. Innovative solutions to various problems that have been limiting large-scale implementation are being engineered, keeping PCM a strong competitor in the memory market [7].

This chapter discusses the physical mechanisms behind PCM technology, its unique characteristics, and how these characteristics can be put to use in hardware security applications.

6.1 Cell Structure

Typical PCM cells (e.g., mushroom cell) consist of a thin layer (~10–100 nm) of a phase change material deposited over a patterned nanoscale heater (bottom contact). The size of the bottom contact determines the volume of the active region (the minimum region that must be amorphized to effectively block conduction in the high resistance state). A metal layer is deposited on top of the phase change material which acts as the top contact (Figure 6.1a). The primary disadvantage of the mushroom cell is the large programming current required to switch the states of the PCM device, which limits the scaling of the cell selection device (e.g., transistor or diode). As a result, significant efforts focusing on reducing the programming current of PCM devices have been made. The two primary approaches taken were reduction in contact area (μ trench cell) and thermal environment optimization (confined cell, dash cell). Several modifications have been made to these basic structures for improved performance. In order to overcome lithography dependency, cross-spacer-based and pore cell structures were developed [8,9]. Planar geometries, named bridge or line cells, have also been used, but mostly for research purposes because of worse device packing density and larger voltage requirements.

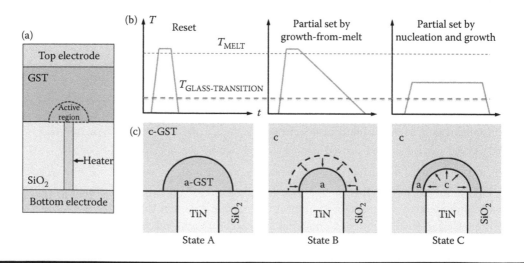

Figure 6.1   PCM mushroom cell structure (a). PCM operation (b–c).

6.2 Operation

The set and reset operations in PCM are achieved through localized self-heating via short voltage pulses in order to switch between the crystalline (low resistance) and amorphous (high resistance) states, which typically provide $\sim 10^2 - 10^4 \times$ difference in total device resistance ($k\Omega$ to $M\Omega$ range) [10]. Cells are reset (to high resistance) using short-duration high-amplitude melting pulses followed by fast cooling (Figure 6.1b (left), Figure 6.1c, State A). Set operation (going back to low resistance) can be achieved by a melting pulse followed by slower cooling (Figure 6.1b (center), Figure 6.1c, State B), or a smaller pulse, to heat the element above the crystallization temperature, with a longer duration (typically $10\sim100$ ns) (Figure 6.1b (right), Figure 6.1c, State C).

Multibit per cell storage is possible due to the large resistance ratio between the amorphous and crystalline states (also referred to as the memory window). This is achieved by partially setting an amorphous cell or partially resetting a crystalline cell to intermediate resistance values. PCM devices can be cycled $>10^{11}$ times (a significant improvement compared to conventional flash memory which can be cycled $\sim10^6$ times) and retain data for >10 years at CPU temperature [1].

6.3 Materials

Most phase change materials are in the forms of chalcogenide glasses, which are glasses that contain one or more chalcogens (sulfur, selenium, and tellurium, excluding oxygen) [11]. Common chalcogenide glasses used in electronic and optical media comprise InSe, SbSe, SbTe, InSbSe, GeSbTe, InSbTe, GbSbTeSe, AgInSbTe, and AgInSbSeTe [12]. The electrical switching phenomena occurring in these chalcogenide glasses was first discovered in the 1960s which led to the proposal of using these materials in electronic memory devices [13]. However, owing to relatively slow switching speeds between states and high power consumption, this memory technology fell behind other electronic memory technologies such as flash. It was not until the discovery of fast recrystallizing materials for optical storage in the 1980s that interest on chalcogenides was renewed [14,15]. This triggered the discovery of pseudo-binary alloys such as $Ge_2Sb_2Te_5$ (GST-225) which has become the most studied PCM material for electronic memory to date.

The most important parameters for phase change materials to be used in memory devices are crystallization and melting temperatures, as well as crystallization time and stability. These parameters determine power, speed, endurance, and stability of the devices and can be optimized for a specific application by changing the relative compositions of the chalcogenide compound. For example, high-speed memory operation requires low crystallization temperature (T_x). However, lower crystallization temperature results in lower data retention. In some security applications, low T_x may be desirable as the data would self-erase if desoldering was attempted. Precoded (ROM) applications, on the other hand, require the memory cells to withstand high temperatures of solder-reflow ($\sim260°C$) [7,16]. Higher T_x can be achieved by nitrogen doping [16].

Endurance characteristics are also affected by the composition of the phase change material. PCM needs to function for $>10^6$ cycles in order to replace flash, and for $>10^{16}$ cycles in order to replace DRAM [10]. Reactively sputtered and nitrogen-doped GST can improve endurance by three orders of magnitude or more [10,17]. However, manufacturing techniques and specific compositions used in industry are typically confidential. Failure modes of PCM are usually either stuck in a high-resistive amorphous state or stuck in a low-resistive crystalline state. Elemental segregation and void formation are believed to be the main causes of these failures [10]. Voids often form over the bottom electrode contact (hottest point) and are related to the changes in mass density between different phases. Elemental segregation is caused by electromigration under high current densities. For GST, Sb tends to migrate more than Ge or Te causing Sb-rich regions which have lower crystallization temperature [18,19].

6.4 Modeling

Reliable models of phase change devices play a vital role in the design and development of the technology as fabrication is expensive and time-consuming. After the models are validated for accuracy and precision, they can be used to predict the behavior of proposed devices and design better performing devices. Models can be used to optimize device performance according to any chosen parameter (e.g., power consumption, switching speed, reliability, density, and interactions with other circuit elements). Different types of models are currently available to study and analyze devices, each with unique advantages and disadvantages.

Compact models are the simplest models used for phase change devices. Generally, a compact model attempts to emulate the $I–V$ characteristics of the phase change device. It can be difficult to create an accurate model of the electrical behavior of these devices because the electrical properties of the material depend on many variables, including operation temperature, crystalline state, electric field, time, and history effects. To overcome these difficulties, compact models generally consist of three main components: electrical, thermal, and phase change [20–22]. The electrical component of the compact model calculates the current through the phase change layer of the device as a function of the applied voltage and current state of the material. There are multiple models proposed to construct this component, but most include multiple terms to account for transport both before and after field-dependent threshold switching [20]. The state of the material is then calculated in the thermal and phase change components of the model. The internal temperature of the device is calculated with simple heat transfer equations with Joule heating and used as an input for temperature-dependent resistivity and phase change components. The current crystalline state of the material may be determined with the calculated temperature profile or temperature at active sites (places where phase change takes place). All compact models are based on simplifications of the crystallization process, and generally follow Johnson–Mehl–Avrami–Kolmogorov (JMAK) Arrhenius relationships to calculate crystal fraction, and the stochastic nature of nucleation is not considered. The crystallinity of the device is then used in resistance calculations in the electrical component of the model. In general, compact models are easy to simulate as they use simple equations for each component and are useful for circuit-level modeling. Applications of compact models in device and waveform design are also possible, as the thermal and phase change components are dependent on geometry [22] and voltage parameters [20,23,24].

Classical nucleation theory uses thermodynamic properties to model crystallization dynamics. The energy associated with a grain is approximated as the sum of a positive component (associated with the surface area of the grain) and a negative component (associated with the volume of the grain):

$$\Delta G(r) = 4\pi r^2 \sigma - \frac{4}{3}\pi r^3 \Delta g \tag{6.1}$$

where $\Delta G(r)$ is the free energy of a crystal with radius r, σ is the surface tension between the amorphous and crystalline phases, and Δg is the energy difference per unit volume between the amorphous and crystalline phases. There is a critical grain size at the maximum of ΔG: crystal grains smaller than the critical size can reduce their energy by shrinking, while crystal grains larger than the critical size reduce their energy by growing (Figure 6.2). While it is energetically unfavorable for subcritical nuclei to form and grow, thermal energy in the system makes it possible. In a material with no subcritical nuclei (i.e., no atoms in the material are associated with a crystal), subcritical nuclei form and grow due to thermal energy until a steady-state Boltzmann distribution is reached. The experimentally observed incubation time (time before steady-state crystallization begins) is captured by classical nucleation theory as the time for this steady-state subcritical nuclei distribution to form [25]. σ and Δg can be approximated from material viscosity and the heat of fusion at melt. Kalb uses classical nucleation theory to extract nucleation and growth parameters from experimental data of $Ge_xSb_yTe_z$ compounds and $Ag_5In_5Sb_{60}Te_{30}$ (AIST) [26,27]. Burr models crystallization in GST by tracking a large 3D matrix of GST atoms with probabilistic association and dissociation rate equations based on classical nucleation theory and extracts temperature-dependent nucleation and growth rates [28]. Nucleation and growth rates extracted from classical nucleation theory can then be used in less computationally expensive models (e.g., JMAK), but typically at the expense of physical relevance and accuracy.

JMAK models describe crystallization in a material based on nucleation and growth rates. They rely on several assumptions to be accurate, notably that nucleation occurs at a steady-state rate and that growth of a crystal is independent of the crystal size. Both assumptions do not hold during typical operating conditions of PCM devices; hence, JMAK models may not be appropriate for their modeling. JMAK models can accurately predict crystallization in bulk phase change thin films, where crystallization occurs in the steady-state regime [25].

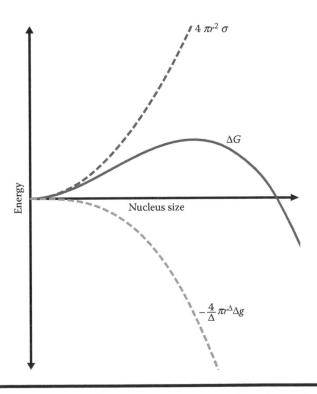

Figure 6.2 A crystal grain can reduce its energy by growing, but only after it reaches a certain size.

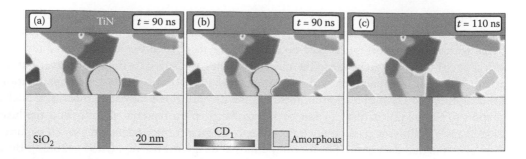

Figure 6.3 **Simulated evolution of crystal growth (CD) in the amorphous region of a mushroom cell during a set operation. Results are from a differential equation model based on classical nucleation and growth rates.**

The crystallization and grain boundary migration processes taking place during crystallization have been modeled with phase-field methods to track the orientation of individual grains. These models rely on the thermodynamic concept that atoms ordered in a lattice have lower energies than stochastically arranged, disordered atoms. Using differential equations to track the evolution of a crystal order parameter, phase-field models simulate the growth of grains along interfacial gradients [29–33]. These models provide accurate crystallization simulations and allow for anisotropic grain growth and grain boundary migration to minimize the total free energy, useful in studying the crystallization kinetics of phase change materials and predicting this behavior at any temperature. However, they are not coupled with electrothermal models to allow for simulation of device operation, which limits their applications to device design.

In our work, we combine the mathematical concepts of phase-field models and classical nucleation and growth physics to gain the advantages of both approaches. Nucleation and growth rates derived from classical nucleation and growth theory [28] are implemented in a single rate equation similar to those solved by phase-field models with finite element analysis to track local crystallinity in a device. This model retains the computational simplicity of phase-field models as well as physical accuracy from nucleation and growth theory in a finite element framework that can be coupled with existing electrothermal models [34]. It can also be used to accurately model the simultaneous heating, current conduction, and crystallization processes occurring in phase change devices (Figure 6.3) to enable design of devices with improved performance.

6.5 Scalability

Performance metrics for memory devices include read/write/erase power, read/write/erase time, data retention time, and endurance. The power required to operate PCM devices scales with the device size; smaller devices mean smaller areas being amorphized/crystallized. Crystallization time (the limiting time factor in writing to a device) also scales with the device size. Smaller devices require less total growth in growth-dominated crystallization, and nucleation rates increase as the surface-area-to-volume ratio increases in heterogeneous nucleation-dominated materials [35]. Data retention at low temperatures is limited by the amorphous to crystalline transformation rate, as the crystalline state is more energetically favorable and all devices tend to crystallize with time. Smaller devices therefore have worse retention, but devices with bottom electrode diameter ~20–40 nm have shown >10 year retention at 220°C [36]. Different degrees of nonvolatility are required for different applications such as flash or DRAM replacement.

6.6 Thermoelectrics

In the presence of a temperature gradient in a material, carriers diffuse, creating a potential difference; this effect is known as the Seebeck effect. The open-circuit potential (ΔV) is related to the temperature difference (ΔT) by [37]

$$\Delta V = S\Delta T \tag{6.2}$$

where S is the Seebeck coefficient. On the other hand, heat is generated or absorbed if an electric current is flown through a junction made of two different materials; this effect is known as the Peltier effect. The Peltier heat at the junction is given by [34]

$$Q_{Peltier} = -J\Delta\left(\pi\right) = -J\Delta\left(ST\right) \tag{6.3}$$

where π is the Peltier coefficient, J is the current density, and T is the temperature.

If both a temperature gradient and an electric current are present in a conductor, the heat exchange depends on the gradient of the temperature-dependent Seebeck coefficient and this effect is known as the Thomson effect. The Thomson heat is expressed as [34]

$$Q_{Thomson} = -T\bar{J}.\nabla\left(S\right) \tag{6.4}$$

These three effects are collectively known as thermoelectric effects (TE) and refer to the coupling between electronic and thermal transport in materials and devices.

PCMs experience extremely high temperature gradients (~50 K/nm) during the set and reset operations [34]. These extreme thermal gradients give rise to pronounced TE [38] that impact the operation of PCM cells considerably [39]. The first report on TE on PCM was made by Castro et al. [39] in 2007, where they experimentally observed asymmetric amorphization of PCM dog bone cells and T-cells. For devices with an asymmetric structure (e.g., T-cell or mushroom cell), the amorphization volume becomes polarity dependent and one polarity requires lower power than the other. Suh et al. utilized TE to design high-efficiency ultra-low-power nanoscale PCM devices [40]. A recent detailed experimental and simulation study on GST mushroom cells shows that polarity-dependent heating caused by TE impacts all the thermally induced phenomena such as melting, crystallization, ion migration, and holding of a particular state (set/reset) in the same way: one polarity results in larger power required for device operation [41]. Finite element modeling on PCM pore cells [42], dog bone cells [43], and mushroom cells [34] also predicts the effect of TE on the polarity-dependent operation of the devices. Figure 6.4 shows example results of finite element reset simulations of a GST mushroom cell. The positive polarity (current flow from the top of the device to the bottom) requires 1.5 times less current to achieve the same level of resistance contrast compared to the negative polarity.

To incorporate TE within the finite element models in an effective media approximation, the current continuity equation and the heat transport equation are solved self-consistently [34]

$$\nabla.\bar{J} = -\nabla.\left(\sigma\left(\nabla V + S\nabla T\right)\right) = 0 \tag{6.5}$$

$$\rho C_p\frac{dT}{dt} - \nabla.\left(k\nabla T\right) = \frac{\bar{J}.\bar{J}}{\sigma} - T\bar{J}.\nabla S \tag{6.6}$$

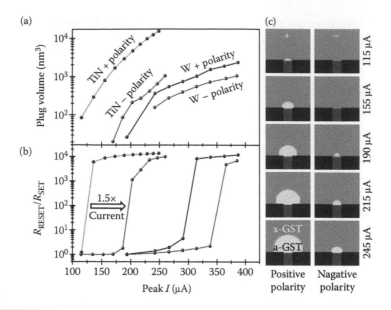

Figure 6.4 **Amorphous plug volume after reset operation (a) and final resistance contrast with respect to peak reset current for a GST mushroom cell for both TiN and W heater (b). Cross-sectional conductivity map of a mushroom cell showing the final conductivity for cells with TiN heater (c). Amorphous regions are shown in light gray and crystalline regions in dark gray. (Reprinted with permission from A. Faraclas et al. *IEEE Transactions on Electron Devices,* 61(2):372–378, 2014.)**

where σ is the electrical conductivity, V is the electric potential, ρ is the mass density, and C_P is the heat capacity. Temperature-induced diffusion current $-(\sigma S \nabla T)$ in Equation 6.5 and Thomson heat source $-T \vec{J}.\nabla S$ in Equation 6.6 describe the thermoelectric contributions. Peltier heat (Equation 6.3) is added on the boundaries as a separate heat source.

The asymmetric heating can also be understood in terms of generation–transport–recombination (GTR) of minority carriers in semiconductors at elevated temperatures [38]. When a current carrying conductor experiences a large thermal gradient ($\gtrsim$~1 K/nm) and the temperature is high enough for considerable minority carrier generation, the large numbers of thermally generated electron–hole pairs in the hottest region (*generation*) are separated and transported by drift and diffusion (*transport*), and recombine in colder regions, releasing heat (*recombination*) at these locations and giving out the asymmetric heating profile.

TE play a significant role in the operation of PCM devices and must be accounted for in design, optimization, and scaling of such devices. The impact of TE will become even stronger as devices are scaled to smaller dimensions because of the increased current density and thermal confinement leading to even more extreme thermal gradients [44].

6.7 Resistance Drift and Variabilities

As the metastable amorphous material crystallizes, the resistance shows an initial upward drift followed by a downward drift over time. Depending on the initial amorphization level and temperature, the entire spontaneous phase transition can take place over a period of time, from a

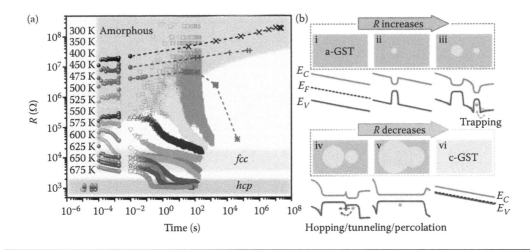

Figure 6.5 **Measurement results of resistance drift and crystallization over time. (a) Resistances calculated from the high-speed (solid symbols) and long-duration DC baseline measurements (open symbols) for individual devices. (b) Schematic Illustration of the resistance increase over time due to the resistance drift mechanism via nucleation (i and ii), capture of free holes and distortion of the potential profile (iii) and the succeeding decrease of resistance as a consequence of growth of the crystalline nuclei, initiation of percolation transport (iv–vi) and crystallization [45,46]. *fcc* (face-centered cubic) and *hcp* (hexagonal close-packed) are two existing crystalline forms of GST.**

few microseconds (Figures 6.5a and 6.6) to years, impacting data retention and mixing of the levels in multilevel cell storage [45,46]. The upward resistance drift is observed from both amorphous and fcc states and is a major reliability concern in PCM devices. The steady resistance increase with time follows a power law equation:

$$R = R_0\left(\frac{t}{t_0}\right)^n \tag{6.7}$$

where R is the resistance at time t, t is the time since amorphization, R_0 and t_0 are constants, and n is the drift exponent which is the slope of the bilogarithmic R–t plot [47]. Upward resistance drift has been reported to initiate as soon as 30 ns after the resetting operation [48]. Figure 6.5a shows our high-speed electrical measurements of long-term resistance drift of PCM line cells, which delineate the temperature dependence of the amorphous-to-crystalline phase transition from 104 μs after amorphization pulse. Whereas at room temperature it takes ~13 months to observe the turnaround in resistance drift, at ~400 K, it is observed after only ~100 s. At ~675 K, the upward drift is presumably too fast to be captured in these measurements and crystallization to *hcp* is complete after ~200 ms [45,46].

The physical origin of the upward resistance drift is not well understood yet. The current explanation of this drift is related to structural relaxation of the amorphous material, which is a thermally activated process of atomistic-level rearrangement of the disordered amorphous network [47]. During this process, annihilation of the structural defects (vacancies, distorted and dangling bonds) is believed to occur in order to achieve a more stable amorphous state. Since Poole–Frenkel hopping is considered to be the dominant conduction mechanism in the amorphous state, the reduction of the available localized states for carrier hopping is understood to give rise to a steady increase

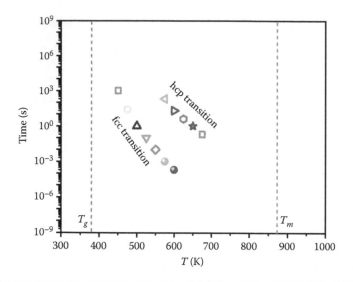

Figure 6.6 **Measurement results of amorphous-to-crystalline phase transition times as function of temperature [46]. T_g and T_m are the glass transition and melting temperatures.**

in amorphous resistance [47]. A widening of the optical amorphous bandgap has been correlated with the resistance increase and supports this hypothesis [49]. A structural relaxation process alone, however, does not explain the turnaround at maximum resistance and rapid reduction in resistance afterward.

Our alternative hypothesis is that the crystallization process is initiated immediately after amorphization by nucleating seed crystallites, and results in the initial upward and later downward resistance drift as the material relaxes toward the stable *hcp* phase [45,46,50–57]. The mechanical strain induced by these crystallites creates defects and increases the bandgap of amorphous GST. Charges can be temporarily trapped into these defects and surface states at amorphous–crystalline boundaries. As the nuclei continue to grow, the crystalline islands start to act as bulk *fcc* degenerate semiconductors and form potential wells that capture free carriers (Figure 6.5b$_{\text{i} - \text{ii}}$). Charge trapping by the nuclei results in a decrease in conductivity of the surrounding amorphous material leading to increasing resistance as nucleation and trapping progress. When the number and size of grains are sufficient to initiate percolation transport, the resistance starts decreasing [28,34,45,46,58,59] (Figure 6.5b$_{\text{iv} - \text{vi}}$).

In the relaxation model, the increase in the upward resistance drift exponent with temperature is attributed to the thermal activation of the structural relaxation process [47,60] and the faster resistance decrease is explained by both larger nucleation and growth rates at elevated temperature [28]. According to our continuous crystallization model, both upward and downward drifts increase with temperature due to the increased nucleation and growth rates (Figure 6.6) [45,46].

6.7.1 Upward Resistance Drift and Its Variability

The upward resistance drift is described by the characteristic drift exponent (n) [47]. The drift exponent is a function of temperature (Figure 6.5a) [45–47], read current [47], and amorphous resistance level [48]. The amorphous resistance is expected to exhibit stronger upward resistance

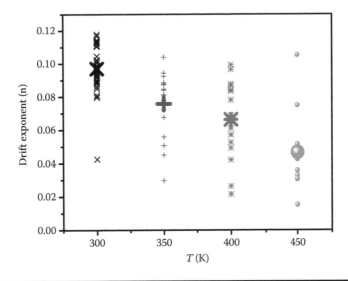

Figure 6.7 **Measured values of drift exponent and its variability as a function of temperature.** (Adapted from F. Dirisaglik. **High-Temperature Electrical Characterization of Ge₂Sb₂Te₅ Phase Change Memory Devices.** *Doctoral dissertations*, 577, University of Connecticut, 2014.)

drift (i.e., larger n or steeper slope in the $\log(R)$–$\log(t)$ plot) at lower temperature, lower read current, and higher amorphous resistance levels [48]. A high read current causes localized heat in the cell and thus affects the cell properties in a similar way as increasing the temperature [61].

Other factors also affect the drift exponents as cells with the same initial amorphous resistance values have been observed to drift with variable drift exponents. The upward resistance drift variability has been ascribed to different amorphous structures formed after the random melt-quenched reset process and shown to increase with higher amorphous resistance [48]. The variability of the drift exponent increases at higher temperature levels (Figure 6.7) [46] and at higher amorphous resistance [48].

6.7.2 Downward Resistance Drift and Its Variability

Spontaneous crystallization of PCM devices exhibits cycle-to-cycle (for a single cell) and device-to-device (in an array) stochastic variations [58,62]. Since the downward resistance drift is described by both nucleation and growth of the crystallites inside amorphous volume by Ielmini et al., the random space configuration of the nuclei and the resulting percolation patterns are attributed for the erratic resistance evolution over time [58]. The increase of the statistical spread and decrease of data retention time has been reported to result from several factors:

1. *Geometrical parameters*: Smaller amorphous volumes have shorter data retention times because the same number of nucleation events have a greater effect on crystallization. In addition, a few nucleation events within a smaller amorphous region result in an increased statistical spread of cell resistance [58]. From our drift experiments on PCM line cells of various dimensions (different lengths and widths yet same thickness), we have observed that the decrease of resistance after reaching the maximum value is slower in wider line cells

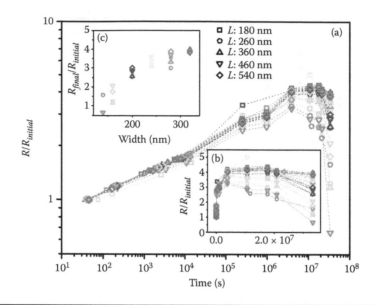

Figure 6.8 Experimental result of dimension-dependent phase transition of GST line cells [46]. Normalized resistance ($R/R_{initial}$) as a function of time at 300 K in log (a) and linear (b) scales. ($R_{final}/R_{initial}$) values as a function of device width for various lengths (c).

(Figure 6.8) [46,63]. The longer time needed for the growth of nuclei to reach the percolation threshold may be a reason for the slower downward resistance drift in wider structures.

2. *Environmental parameters*:

   a. *Temperature*: Owing to the accelerated growth of the crystallites in an amorphous region at higher temperatures, the data retention time goes down (Figure 6.1a) while the statistical spread increases [64]. For example, at 250°C, a Ga–Sb–Ge-based PCM has been reported to have a retention time of only 300 hours [36].

   b. *Read current*: As expected, higher read currents are also reported to perturb the cells' state and result in data loss by accelerating the phase transition process; this phenomenon is referred to as read disturb [41,61].

   c. *Thermal cross-talk*: Programming a cell can also cause unintentional heating of neighboring cells in an array due to thermal cross-talk. Longer pulse durations and repeated programming of cells at a smaller lithographic pitch are reported to accelerate the data loss of the adjacent bits; this phenomenon is referred to as program disturb [61].

6.8 Programming Variability

PCM cells with the same cell geometry and material composition experiencing the same reset pulse are likely to show different amorphous resistance values. The variability in programming to the amorphous state has been explained by the random disordered structures formed after the melt-quenching process of reset operation [48]. Programming variability is observed for both set and reset operations in cell-to-cell in an array and cycle-to-cycle in single cell [65]. Figure 6.9 shows

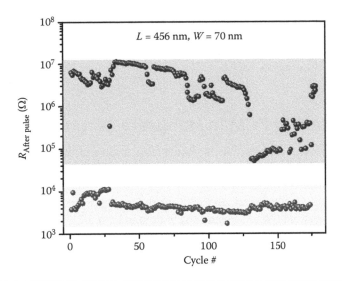

Figure 6.9 **Measurement result of a cycling operation of the GST line cell (length: 456 nm, width: 70 nm) [46]. The cycling operation consists of reset, read, set, read sequences. Reset pulses of 9 V and 100 ns and set pulses of 5 V and 1 μs resulted in variabilities on different cycles both in the high- and low-resistance states (highlighted as dark gray and light gray areas, respectively).**

an example of this variability, observed for a single GST line cell repeatedly cycled with the same set and reset pulses [46].

6.9 Noise

Noise is typically undesired in electronic devices, especially for multibit storage, but certain properties of noise like bistable fluctuation can be useful for certain applications in hardware security. Both crystalline and amorphous states display characteristic $1/f$ behavior (Flicker noise), which can be explained by the superposition of multiple single Lorentzian ($1/f^2$) contributions [66]. However, μ trench cells programmed into intermediate states ($\sim$600 kΩ) have shown resistance fluctuations between two distinct steps as a function of time in the power spectral density (PSD) in frequency domain at room temperature, resembling random telegraph noise (RTN) [67]. These phenomena can be explained by the presence of localized states caused by structural defects in amorphous GST. The distributed pool–Frenkel (DPF) mechanism assumes the emission activation energy for these states to be random [68].

Once originated, RTN can be affected by voltage and temperature [67]. When a voltage is applied, the energy of one state changes with respect to the other, changing the transition time between states and thus the characteristic frequency (f_P). It has been reported in Reference 67 that, as the voltage is changed from negative to positive, the characteristic frequency increases, resulting in a lower characteristic time t_p. The temperature (T) changes f_p of RTN as well. As the temperature is increased, the characteristic frequency increases to a certain point after which RTN is usually not observed, likely being buried in larger fluctuations.

RTN has been used to produce the true random number generator (TRNG) in the literature [69]. So the presence of RTN in PCM shows promise for PCM-based TRNG in the future. However, certain issues, such as resistance drift and operating temperature, must be accounted for while designing TRNG using PCM.

6.10 Application of PCM in Hardware Security

Variabilities arising from uncontrollable nanoscale fabrication and inherent physics are major concerns for nanodevice reliability in the digital circuits and emerging memory technologies. However, this feature can be utilized in the hardware security systems as physical unclonable functions (PUF). PUFs generate unique volatile digital keys without the need for tamper-sensing mechanisms, saving area and power overhead [70]. Conventional commercialized PUFs utilize the process variation in complementary metal oxide semiconductor (CMOS) fabrication technology to generate the secret key. As devices are scaled to smaller and smaller dimensions, the increased variability stemming from process variations can be utilized [70]. PUFs based on emerging nanodevices, such as PCM [71–73], spin-transfer torque magnetic random access memory (STT-MRAM), resistive random access memory (RRAM or memristor), and carbon nanotube field effect transistors (CNFETs), have been proposed. Nanodevice-based PUFs are small, lightweight, less power-hungry and CMOS compatible, and can be integrated in cross bar architecture with high density and low cost. Moreover, PUFs based on emerging memory technologies can benefit from nonvolatility, increased programming sensitivity, cycle-to-cycle variations, ability to reprogram (because of the high endurance), long-term stability (due to high data retention time), and multilevel cell (MLC) operation [70]. In PCM, the unique melt-quenched amorphous structure formed during every reset process (both in the cycle-to-cycle and cell-to-cell cases), the amorphous resistance evolution over time (i.e., resistance drift), and the crystalline grain distribution variability allow a promising platform for PUF applications.

Erasable and Reconfigurable PUFs

A PUF is a physical device that takes input challenges and generates random-looking output responses, where this mapping between inputs and outputs is created by random uncontrollable manufacturing process variations [74,75]. Thus, it is not possible to physically reproduce a PUF which has exactly the same behavior (i.e., can generate same challenge–response pairs [CRPs]) as another one.

Owing to these unique properties, PUFs have been suggested to be used in many different applications. For example, they can be used to generate secret keys on the device when needed, without storing the keys in any nonvolatile memory [76]. PUFs can also be used for identification and authentication [77]. Before the authentication starts, the manufacturer collects a large amount of CRPs. The PUF is then shipped to a customer and the customer needs to prove that he/she has the PUF; the manufacturer sends a challenge to the customer and asks for its response. If the replied response matches with the response stored in the system, the manufacturer concludes that this customer has this PUF.

PUFs have also been proposed to construct cryptographic protocols, for example, Key Agreement (KA), Oblivious Transfer (OT), and Bit Commitment (BC) [78,79]. Figure 6.10 describes the operation of a simplified KA protocol (for a complete protocol, please refer to Reference 79). The initial state of this protocol is that the two parties, Alice and Bob, do not have a shared

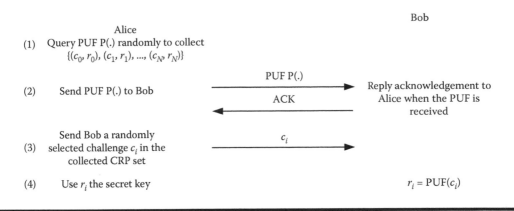

Figure 6.10   Simplified PUF-based Key Agreement protocol.

secret key. The goal of a KA protocol is to have a shared secret key between Alice and Bob after some rounds of communications over a public authenticated communication channel. Notice that in a PUF-based KA, we need another channel to transmit the PUF itself physically. To start the protocol, Alice, who has the PUF initially, measures a set of CRPs of this PUF $\{(c_0,r_0),(c_1,r_1),\ldots,(c_N,r_N)\}$. Alice then sends this PUF to Bob. After receiving it, Bob replies to Alice with an acknowledgment; then Alice randomly selects one challenge c_i out of all the collected challenges and sends it to Bob. Bob measures the response $r_i = \mathrm{PUF}(c_i)$. Therefore, Alice and Bob share the same secret r_i. The protocol is secure so far, but what happens after the protocol execution also matters. If Bob just discards this PUF after using it, and an adversary Eve gets this PUF, Eve can just query this PUF with challenge c_i, as c_i is transmitted over a public channel, and get the shared secret r_i. This violates the security requirement of a KA protocol, so this security issue, usually called PUF reuse model, should be addressed in a PUF-based KA protocol [80,81]. It is even proved that with a PUF reuse model, it is impossible for a stateless PUF to construct a secure KA, OT, and BC [82].

Definition 6.1.

In order to prevent the PUF reuse model, one has to erase a selected CRP individually in such a way that no one is able to get the response of this challenge afterward, even those in possession of the PUF. We cite the definition of erasable PUFs in Reference 83.

Specification 1 (ERASABLE PUFS). An ERASABLE PUF is a strong PUF with a unique operation: *erasure* $\mathcal{E}()$. For a given challenge $\hat{c}$ of P, $\mathcal{E}()$ transforms P into P' with the following properties:

- P' and P have the same set of challenges.
- For any challenge $c \neq \hat{c}$, $r_{(P',c)} = r_{(P,c)}$.
- For a given P' and $c = \hat{c}$, the adversary cannot determine $r_{(P',c)}$ with a probability that is much better than random guessing.

In Reference 71, the authors introduced the reconfigurable PUFs, which are formally defined below.

Specification 2 (Reconfigurable PUFS). A RECONFIGURABLE PUF is a strong PUF with a unique operation: *reconfiguration* $\mathcal{R}()$. $\mathcal{R}()$ transforms P into P' with the following properties:

- P' and P have the same set of challenges.
- Given P' and a polynomial set of CRPs collected from P', it is impossible to determine any $r_{(P,c)}$ with a probability that is substantially better than random guessing.
- Given P and a polynomial set of CRPs collected from P, it is impossible to determine any $r_{(P',c)}$ with a probability that is substantially better than random guessing.

Clearly, we can also have a partially reconfigurable PUF, in that every reconfiguration operation affects a subset of all the CRPs, but more than one CRP.

Note that we strictly require that for an erasable PUF each erasure operation can only erase one selected CRP without affecting any other CRPs, because the other CRPs may still be needed for the other protocol executions. Since each CRP should be able to be erased individually, and the challenge space of the PUF should not be so small that it can be exhaustively read out, it is very difficult to design an erasable PUF.

Implementation

A general way to implement an erasable PUF or a reconfigurable PUF is to implement it logically as an additional interface. For erasable PUFs, the interface needs to record the history of all the used challenges and how many times each of them has been queried. In addition, this interface should block any number of further evaluations of a challenge which has already been queried for a certain number of times [84]. For reconfigurable PUFs, the interface can be implemented as a reconfigurable input/output network around a strong PUF. Thus, if the input/output network is updated, the behavior of this PUF system (underlying PUF and the input/output network) can be considered as a completely new PUF [85]. Note that it is very important to make sure that the reconfiguration cannot be reversed back; otherwise, the attacker will be able to reverse the reconfiguration process and measure the CRPs from the PUF before reconfiguration.

However, a logical implementation of either erasable PUFs or reconfigurable PUFs has its drawback. Since they all require an additional digital interface, this interface will not be very sensitive to an invasive attack. If the adversary is able to bypass this interface using an invasive attack, all the protections are compromised.

As discussed earlier, some unique features of nanoscale emerging devices, such as programming variability of PCM discussed in Section 6.8, can be used to implement physically erasable/reconfigurable PUFs.

(a) Physically Erasable PUFs

A physically erasable PUF can be built, for example, using the structure of a Super High Information Content (SHIC) PUF [86]. The SHIC PUF exploits the crystallization process of polycrystalline silicon to amplify small variations present in the system to larger variations [86–88].

In the physically erasable SHIC PUF [83], an aluminum-induced layer exchange (ALILE) process is used with aluminum deposited on a-Si films. Crystallization during isothermal annealing results in polycrystalline films with p-type conduction [89], and creates a random, highly disordered material made of crystallized silicon grains (Si) and aluminum (Al). It is a relatively simple fabrication process with a small number of steps and inexpensive materials.

To read out the information in the structure, a crossbar architecture is used. It consists of two sets of parallel wires, arranged orthogonally to each other, below and above the structure, similar to the bit line and word line in a memory structure. Each crossing of the crossbar array acts as a p-n diode due to the p-type film on an n-type wafer. The current through the structure can be read out by applying a voltage at two chosen crossbar wires, bit and word lines, which selects only one crossing in the crossbar array. Owing to the random nature of the material crystallization process, the diodes show current–voltage curves which are very irregular and unique. As shown in Reference 87, information extracted from each crossing can provide at least three reliable bits. The SHIC PUF is considered a strong PUF as it is very difficult for an adversary to read out all the CRPs, due to the high information density in crossbar architecture and a slow reading interface [86].

In order to erase a response for a given challenge, the bit and word lines as represented by the challenge are chosen. A short voltage pulse applied to the diode in reverse bias destroys it and prevents the individual information from leaking to the outside world because after this operation all current–voltage curves are very similar in shape. Each erasure operation only erases one CRP and leaves all the other CRPs unchanged, because one crossing corresponds to only one CRP in the SHIC PUF structure.

Although the erasability is realized in the physically erasable PUF proposed in Reference 83, it still has one limitation. Since the erasure operation destroys the crossing used to generate a particular CRP permanently, it can never be used again. So the problem remains on how to design a physically erasable PUF, which can securely erase a selected CRP and still be able to reuse the same physical structure for creating a new CRP.

(b) Physically Reconfigurable PUFs
Kursawe et al. introduced the concept of a reconfigurable PUF (rPUF) [71] based on the reprogramming capability of PCM. In this paper, the intentionally uncontrolled programming strategies result in random resistance levels and these MLC resistance levels are precisely read. Reprogramming the cells in the same uncontrolled programming strategy reconfigures the PUFs. The unpredictability and uncontrollability of the challenge–response behavior of the original PUF are updated while preserving all the security properties [71].

Zhang et al. used an imprecisely controlled current regulator (ICCR) to demonstrate the uncontrolled programming scheme of Kursawe et al. with a single programming pulse with varying pulse parameters [72]. The ICCR consists of two CMOS circuits: one controls the amplitude of the programming current pulse with current mirrors, and the other adjusts the programming current pulse width using delay chains. Both of these auxiliary circuits depend on the CMOS process variations for producing the nondeterministic programming pulse, which is applied to the PCM cells for programming into a random state. The challenge of this PUF is the addresses of two selected PCM cells whose programmed resistance values are compared to generate one bit response (0 or 1). By using the error correction code (ECC) and a cryptographic hash function (i.e., fuzzy extractor), a random and reliable cryptographic key can be generated from the raw responses. The additional CMOS-based ICCR circuitry increases the power consumption and area overhead, but the use of the dense PCM crossbar array results in an overall footprint advantage. On the other hand, the reprogramming operation adds further power requirement [72].

Experimental evaluations with 180 nm PCM technology node were later presented, also by Zhang et al. [73]. In order to make the PUF resistant to a physical attack (where an adversary has physical access to the device and can measure the CRPs), two ways to refresh PCM cells have been proposed: *periodic refresh* that reprograms PCM cells after a certain time interval and *frequency-based refresh* which is carried out after a certain number of CRP evaluations [73]. An alternative programming approach has been demonstrated using an iterative pulsing scheme with increasing amplitudes to reach a target resistance level. Different cells use different numbers of pulses to reach the same target resistance based on process variations.

Similar to PCM, memristors, another emerging memory technology, show significant programming variability features as well, which can be exploited to create physically reconfigurable PUFs [70,90–92].

References

1. H. Wong, S. Raoux, S. Kim, J. Liang, J. Reifenberg, B. Rajendran, M. Asheghi, and K. Goodson. Phase change memory. *Proceedings of the IEEE*, **98**(12):2201–2227, 2010.
2. B. N. Engel, J. Akerman, B. Butcher, R. W. Dave, M. DeHerrera, M. Durlam, G. Grynkewich, J. Janesky, S. V. Pietambaram, and N. D. Rizzo. A 4-Mb toggle MRAM based on a novel bit and switching method. *IEEE Transactions on Magnetics*, **41**(1):132–136, 2005.
3. F. Xiong, A. Liao, and E. Pop. Inducing chalcogenide phase change with ultra-narrow carbon nanotube heaters. *Applied Physics Letters*, **95**(24):243103, 2009.
4. Micron. Micron Announces Availability of Phase Change Memory for Mobile Devices, 2012. [Online; accessed May 1, 2017]. http://investors.micron.com/releasedetail.cfm?releaseid=692563
5. IBM. IBM Demonstrates Next-Gen Phase-Change Memory Thats Up to 275 Times Faster Than Your SSD, 2016. [Online; accessed May 1, 2017]. https://www.extremetech.com/extreme/182096-ibm-demonstrates-next-gen-phase-change-memory-thats-up-to-275-times-faster-than-your-ssd
6. HGST. HGST Research Demonstrates Breakthrough Persistent Memory Fabric at Flash Memory Summit 2015, 2015. [Online; accessed May 1, 2017]. https://www.hgst.com/company/media-room/press-releases/HGST-to-Demo-InMemory-Flash-Fabric-and-Lead-Discussions
7. G. W. Burr, M. J. Brightsky, A. Sebastian, H. Y. Cheng, J. Y. Wu et al. Recent progress in phase-change memory technology. *IEEE Journal on Emerging and Selected Topics in Circuits and Systems*, **PP**(99):1–17, 2016.
8. W. Chen, C. Lee, D. Chao, Y. Chen, F. Chen et al. A novel cross-spacer phase change memory with ultra-small lithography independent contact area. In *Electron Devices Meeting, 2007. IEDM 2007. IEEE International*, pages 319–322. IEEE, New York, NY, 2007.
9. M. Breitwisch, T. Nirschl, C. Chen, Y. Zhu, M. Lee et al. Novel lithography-independent pore phase change memory. In *VLSI Technology, 2007 IEEE Symposium on*, pages 100–101. IEEE, New York, NY, 2007.
10. S. Raoux, F. Xiong, M. Wuttig, and E. Pop. Phase change materials and phase change memory. *MRS Bulletin*, **39**(08):703–710, 2014.
11. K. J. Buschow, R. W. Cahn, M. C. Flemings, B. Ilschner, E. J. Kramer, and S. Mahajan, *Encyclopedia of Materials—Science and Technology*, Vol. **1–11**, Elsevier, Amsterdam, New York, 2001.
12. K. Yasuda and K. Kurokawa. Multi-layered optical disc, January 28, 2003. US Patent 6,511,788.
13. S. R. Ovshinsky. Reversible electrical switching phenomena in disordered structures. *Physical Review Letters*, **21**(20):1450–1453, 1968.
14. N. Yamada, E. Ohno, K. Nishiuchi, N. Akahira, and M. Takao. Rapid-phase transitions of GeTe-Sb_2Te_3 pseudobinary amorphous thin films for an optical disk memory. *Journal of Applied Physics*, **69**(5):2849–2856, 1991.

15. J. Tominaga, T. Kikukawa, M. Takahashi, and R. Phillips. Structure of the optical phase change memory alloy, Ag–V–In–Sb–Te, determined by optical spectroscopy and electron diffraction. *Journal of Applied Physics*, **82**(7):3214–3218, 1997.

16. H. Cheng, J. Wu, R. Cheek, S. Raoux, M. BrightSky et al. A thermally robust phase change memory by engineering the Ge/N concentration in $(Ge, N)_x Sb_y Te_z$ phase change material. In *Electron Devices Meeting (IEDM), 2012 IEEE International*, pages 31–1. IEEE, New York, NY, 2012.

17. H.-Y. Cheng, M. Brightsky, S. Raoux, C. Chen, P. Du et al. Atomic-level engineering of phase change material for novel fast-switching and high-endurance PCM for storage class memory application. In *Electron Devices Meeting (IEDM), 2013 IEEE International*, pages 30–6. IEEE, New York, NY, 2013.

18. S. Raoux, R. M. Shelby, J. Jordan-Sweet, B. Munoz, M. Salinga, Y.-C. Chen, Y.-H. Shih, E.-K. Lai, and M.-H. Lee. Phase change materials and their application to random access memory technology. *Microelectronic Engineering*, **85**(12):2330–2333, 2008.

19. J. Kalb, M. Wuttig, and F. Spaepen. Calorimetric measurements of structural relaxation and glass transition temperatures in sputtered films of amorphous Te alloys used for phase change recording. *Journal of Materials Research*, **22**(03):748–754, 2007.

20. K. Sonoda, A. Sakai, M. Moniwa, K. Ishikawa, O. Tsuchiya, and Y. Inoue. A compact model of phase-change memory based on rate equations of crystallization and amorphization. *IEEE Transactions on Electron Devices*, **55**(7):1672–1681, 2008.

21. D. Ventrice, P. Fantini, A. Redaelli, A. Pirovano, A. Benvenuti, and F. Pellizzer. A phase change memory compact model for multilevel applications. *IEEE Electron Device Letters*, **28**(11):973–975, 2007.

22. I.-R. Chen and E. Pop. Compact thermal model for vertical nanowire phase-change memory cells. *IEEE Transactions on Electron Devices*, **98**(12):2201–2227, 2009.

23. E. Covi, A. Kiouseloglou, A. Cabrini, and G. Torelli. Compact model for phase change memory cells. In *Ph.D. Research in Microelectronics and Electronics (PRIME), 2014 10th Conference on*, pages 1–4. IEEE, New York, NY, 2014.

24. Y. Chen, S. Member, K. C. Kwong, X. Lin, Z. Song, and M. Chan. 3-D resistance model for phase-change memory cell. *IEEE Transactions on Electron Devices*, **61**(12):4098–4104, 2014.

25. S. Senkader and C. D. Wright. Models for phase-change of $Ge_2 Sb_2 Te_5$ in optical and electrical memory devices. *Journal of Applied Physics*, **95**(2):504–511, 2004.

26. J. A. Kalb and F. Spaepen. Atomic force microscopy measurements of crystal nucleation and growth rates in thin films of amorphous Te alloys. *Applied Physics Letters*, **84**(25):5240, 2004.

27. J. A. Kalb, F. Spaepen, and M. Wuttig. Kinetics of crystal nucleation in undercooled droplets of Sb- and Te-based alloys used for phase change recording. *Journal of Applied Physics*, **98**(5):054910, 2005.

28. G. W. Burr, P. Tchoulfian, T. Topuria, C. Nyffeler, K. Virwani, A. Padilla, R. M. Shelby, M. Eskandari, B. Jackson, and B.-S. Lee. Observation and modeling of polycrystalline grain formation in $Ge_2 Sb_2 Te_5$. *Journal of Applied Physics*, **111**(10):104308, 2012.

29. C. Krill III and L.-Q. Chen. Computer simulation of 3-D grain growth using a phase-field model. *Acta Materialia*, **50**(12):3059–3075, 2002.

30. M. T. Lusk. A phase-field paradigm for grain growth and recrystallization. *Proceedings of the Royal Society A: Mathematical, Physical and Engineering Sciences*, **455**(1982):677–700, 1999.

31. H. Xu, R. Matkar, and T. Kyu. Phase-field modeling on morphological landscape of isotactic polystyrene single crystals. *Physical Review E—Statistical, Nonlinear, and Soft Matter Physics*, **72**(1):011804, 2005.

32. T. Kyu, R. Mehta, and H. Chiu. Spatiotemporal growth of faceted and curved single crystals. *Physical Review. E, Statistical Physics, Plasmas, Fluids, and Related Interdisciplinary Topics*, **61**(4 Pt B):4161–70, 2000.

33. K. R. Elder, M. Katakowski, M. Haataja, and M. Grant. Modeling elasticity in crystal growth. *Physical Review Letters*, **88**(24):2457011–2457014, 2002.

34. A. Faraclas, G. Bakan, L. Adnane, F. Dirisaglik, N. E. Williams, A. Gokirmak, and H. Silva. Modeling of thermoelectric effects in phase change memory cells. *IEEE Transactions on Electron Devices*, **61**(2):372–378, 2014.

35. S. H. Lee, Y. Jung, and R. Agarwal. Highly scalable non-volatile and ultra-low-power phase-change nanowire memory. *Nature Nanotechnology*, **2**(10):626–630, 2007.

36. H. Cheng, W. Chien, M. BrightSky, Y. Ho, Y. Zhu et al. Novel fast-switching and high-data retention phase-change memory based on new Ga-Sb-Ge material. In *Electron Devices Meeting (IEDM), 2015 IEEE International*, pages 3–5. IEEE, New York, NY, 2015.

37. S. Raoux and M. Wuttig, editors. *Phase Change Materials: Science and Applications*. Springer, US, 2009.

38. G. Bakan, N. Khan, H. Silva, and A. Gokirmak. High-temperature thermoelectric transport at small scales: Thermal generation, transport and recombination of minority carriers. *Scientific Reports*, **3**, 2013.

39. D. T. Castro, L. Goux, G. Hurkx, K. Attenborough, R. Delhougne et al. Evidence of the thermo-electric Thomson effect and influence on the program conditions and cell optimization in phase-change memory cells. In *Electron Devices Meeting, 2007. IEDM 2007. IEEE International*, pages 315–318. IEEE, New York, NY, 2007.

40. D.-S. Suh, C. Kim, K. H. Kim, Y.-S. Kang, T.-Y. Lee et al. Thermoelectric heating of $Ge_2Sb_2Te_5$ in phase change memory devices. *Applied Physics Letters*, **96**(12):123115, 2010.

41. N. Ciocchini and D. Ielmini. Pulse-induced crystallization in phase-change memories under set and disturb conditions. *IEEE Transactions on Electron Devices*, **62**(3):847–854, 2015.

42. A. Padilla, G. Burr, K. Virwani, A. Debunne, C. Rettner et al. Voltage polarity effects in GST-based phase change memory: Physical origins and implications. In *Electron Devices Meeting (IEDM), 2010 IEEE International*, pages 29–4. IEEE, New York, NY, 2010.

43. F. Dirisaglik, G. Bakan, A. Gokirmak, and H. Silva. Modeling of thermoelectric effects in phase change memory cells. *2011 International Semiconductor Device Research Symposium (ISDRS)*, **61**(2):1–2, 2011.

44. J. Lee, M. Asheghi, and K. E. Goodson. Impact of thermoelectric phenomena on phase-change memory performance metrics and scaling. *Nanotechnology*, **23**(20):205201, 2012.

45. F. Dirisaglik, G. Bakan, Z. Jurado, S. Muneer, M. Akbulut et al. High speed, high temperature electrical characterization of phase change materials: Metastable phases, crystallization dynamics, and resistance drift. *Nanoscale*, **7**(40):16625–16630, 2015.

46. F. Dirisaglik. High-Temperature Electrical Characterization of $Ge_2Sb_2Te_5$ Phase Change Memory Devices. *Doctoral dissertations*, 577, University of Connecticut, 2014.

47. D. Ielmini, D. Sharma, S. Lavizzari, and A. Lacaita. Physical mechanism and temperature acceleration of relaxation effects in phase-change memory cells. In *Reliability Physics Symposium, 2008. IRPS 2008. IEEE International*, pages 597–603. IEEE, New York, NY, 2008.

48. M. Boniardi, D. Ielmini, S. Lavizzari, A. L. Lacaita, A. Redaelli, and A. Pirovano. Statistics of resistance drift due to structural relaxation in phase-change memory arrays. *IEEE Transactions on Electron Devices*, **57**(10):2690–2696, 2010.

49. P. Fantini, S. Brazzelli, E. Cazzini, and A. Mani. Band gap widening with time induced by structural relaxation in amorphous $Ge_2Sb_2Te_5$ films. *Applied Physics Letters*, **100**(1):013505, 2012.

50. J. Rarey, L. Zhang, R. Nowak, F. Dirisaglik, Kadir Cil, Yu Zhu, Chung Lam, A. Gokirmak, and H. Silva. Temperature dependent crystallization times of $Ge_2Sb_2Te_5$ nanostructures. In *Materials Research Society Fall Meeting*, Boston, USA, pages FF4.35, 2012.

51. F. Dirisaglik, J. Rarey, K. Cil, S. Muneer, L. Zhang, Y. Zhu, C. Lam, A. Gokirmak, and H. Silva. Metastable electrical resistivity of amorphous $Ge_2Sb_2Te_5$ at elevated temperatures. In *Materials Research Society Spring Meeting*, pages EE5.03, San Francisco, CA, USA, 2013.

52. F. Dirisaglik, J. Rarey, K. Cil, S. Muneer, L. Zhang, Y. Zhu, C. Lam, A. Gokirmak, and H. Silva, Crystallization times of $Ge_2Sb_2Te_5$ nanostructures as a function of temperature. *Materials Research Society Spring Meeting*, San Francisco, California, pages EE2.04, 2013.

53. F. Dirisaglik, G. Bakan, S. Muneer, K. Cil, L. Sullivan et al. High temperature electrical characterization of phase change material: $Ge_2Sb_2Te_5$. In *Materials Research Society Fall Meeting*, Vol. **01**, pages SS21, Boston, Massachusetts, 2013.

54. F. Dirisaglik, G. Bakan, Z. Jurado, L. Sullivan, S. Muneer et al. High temperature electrical characterization of meta-stable phases and crystallization dynamics of $Ge_2Sb_2Te_5$. In *Materials Research Society Fall Meeting 2014*, pages HH5, Vol. **06**, Boston, Massachusetts, 2014.

55. F. Dirisaglik, K. Cil, M. Wennberg, A. King, M. Akbulut, Y. Zhu, C. Lam, A. Gokirmak, and H. Silva. Crystallization times of $Ge_2Sb_2Te_5$ nanostructures as a function of temperature. *Bulletin of the American Physical Society*, **57**, 2012. http://meetings.aps.org/link/BAPS.2012.MAR.J23.12

56. K. C. Faruk Dirisaglik, J. Rarey, L. Zhang, R. Nowak, Y. Zhu, C. Lam, A. Gokirmak, H. Silva, Metastable electrical resistivity of amorphous, crystalline, and liquid $Ge_2Sb_2Te_5$ measurements using nanosecond pulses on patterned $Ge_2Sb_2Te_5$ nanowires. In *Materials Research Society Fall Meeting*, pages FF4.34, Boston, Massachusetts, 2012.

57. L. Sullivan, Z. Jurado, F. Dirisaglik, G. Bakan, M. Akbulut, Y. Zhu, C. Lam, H. Silva, and A. Gokirmak. Resistance drift in nanoscale amorphous $Ge_2Sb_2Te_5$ line-cell structures. In *Materials Research Society Fall Meeting*, pages SS19, Vol. **93**, Boston, Massachusetts, 2013.

58. U. Russo, D. Ielmini, A. Redaelli, and A. L. Lacaita. Intrinsic data retention in nanoscaled phase-change memories Part I: Monte Carlo model for crystallization and percolation. *IEEE Transactions on Electron Devices*, **53**(12):3032–3039, 2006.

59. S. Fischer, C. Osorio, N. Williams, S. Ayas, H. Silva, and A. Gokirmak. Percolation transport and filament formation in nanocrystalline silicon nanowires. *Journal of Applied Physics*, **113**(16):164902, 2013.

60. D. Ielmini, S. Lavizzari, D. Sharma, and A. Lacaita. Temperature acceleration of structural relaxation in amorphous $Ge_2Sb_2Te_5$. *Applied Physics Letters*, **92**(19):193511, 2008.

61. A. Pirovano, A. Redaelli, F. Pellizzer, F. Ottogalli, M. Tosi, D. Ielmini, A. L. Lacaita, and R. Bez. Reliability study of phase-change nonvolatile memories. *IEEE Transactions on Device and Materials Reliability*, **4**(3):422–427, 2004.

62. B. Gleixner, A. Pirovano, J. Sarkar, F. Ottogalli, E. Tortorelli, M. Tosi, and R. Bez. Data retention characterization of phase-change memory arrays. In *Reliability Physics Symposium, 2007. Proceedings of the 45th Annual IEEE International*, pages 542–546. IEEE, New York, NY, 2007.

63. N. Noor, R. S. Khan, S. Muneer, L. Adnane, R. Ramadan et al. Short and long time resistance drift measurement in intermediate states of $Ge_2Sb_2Te_5$ phase change memory line cells. In *Material Research Society Spring Meeting*, page ED11.6.03, Phoenix, Arizona, 2017.

64. A. Redaelli, D. Ielmini, U. Russo, and A. L. Lacaita. Intrinsic data retention in nanoscaled phase-change memories Part II: Statistical analysis and prediction of failure time. *IEEE Transactions on Electron Devices*, **53**(12):3040–3046, 2006.

65. M. Rizzi, N. Ciocchini, A. Montefiori, M. Ferro, P. Fantini, A. L. Lacaita, and D. Ielmini. Cell-to-cell and cycle-to-cycle retention statistics in phase-change memory arrays. *IEEE Transactions on Electron Devices*, **62**(7):2205–2211, 2015.

66. G. Betti Beneventi, A. Calderoni, P. Fantini, L. Larcher, and P. Pavan. Analytical model for low-frequency noise in amorphous chalcogenide-based phase-change memory devices. *Journal of Applied Physics*, **106**(5):054506, 2009.

67. D. Fugazza, D. Ielmini, S. Lavizzari, and A. L. Lacaita. Random telegraph signal noise in phase change memory devices. In *2010 IEEE International Reliability Physics Symposium*, pages 743–749, Anaheim, CA, USA, 2010.

68. D. Fugazza, D. Ielmini, S. Lavizzari, and A. L. Lacaita. Distributed-Poole–Frenkel modeling of anomalous resistance scaling and fluctuations in phase-change memory (PCM) devices. In *Technical Digest—International Electron Devices Meeting, IEDM*, pages 1–4. Baltimore, MD, USA, 2009.

69. R. Brederlow, R. Prakash, C. Paulus, and R. Thewes. A low-power true random number generator using random telegraph noise of single oxide-traps. In *IEEE International Solid-State Circuit Conference*, pages 1666–1675, San Francisco, CA, USA, 2006.

70. Y. Gao, D. C. Ranasinghe, S. F. Al-Sarawi, O. Kavehei, and D. Abbott. Emerging physical unclonable functions with nanotechnology. *IEEE Access*, **4**:61–80, 2016.

71. K. Kursawe, A.-R. Sadeghi, D. Schellekens, B. Skoric, and P. Tuyls. Reconfigurable physical unclonable functions-enabling technology for tamper-resistant storage. In *Hardware-Oriented Security and Trust, 2009. HOST'09. IEEE International Workshop on*, pages 22–29. IEEE, New York, NY, 2009.

72. L. Zhang, Z. H. Kong, and C.-H. Chang. PCKgen: A phase change memory based cryptographic key generator. In *Circuits and Systems (ISCAS), 2013 IEEE International Symposium on*, pages 1444–1447. IEEE, New York, NY, 2013.

73. L. Zhang, Z. H. Kong, C.-H. Chang, A. Cabrini, and G. Torelli. Exploiting process variations and programming sensitivity of phase change memory for reconfigurable physical unclonable functions. *IEEE Transactions on Information Forensics and Security*, **9**(6):921–932, 2014.

74. B. Gassend, D. Clarke, M. Van Dijk, and S. Devadas. Silicon physical random functions. In *Proceedings of the 9th ACM Conference on Computer and Communications Security*, pages 148–160. ACM, New York, NY, USA, 2002.

75. R. Pappu, B. Recht, J. Taylor, and N. Gershenfeld. Physical one-way functions. *Science*, **297**(5589):2026–2030, 2002.

76. D. Lim, J. W. Lee, B. Gassend, G. E. Suh, M. Van Dijk, and S. Devadas. Extracting secret keys from integrated circuits. *IEEE Transactions on Very Large Scale Integration (VLSI) Systems*, **13**(10):1200–1205, 2005.

77. J. W. Lee, D. Lim, B. Gassend, G. E. Suh, M. Van Dijk, and S. Devadas. A technique to build a secret key in integrated circuits for identification and authentication applications. In *VLSI Circuits, 2004. Digest of Technical Papers. 2004 Symposium on*, pages 176–179. IEEE, New York, NY, 2004.

78. R. Ostrovsky, A. Scafuro, I. Visconti, and A. Wadia. Universally composable secure computation with (malicious) physically uncloneable functions. In *Annual International Conference on the Theory and Applications of Cryptographic Techniques*, pages 702–718. Springer, Berlin, 2013.

79. C. Brzuska, M. Fischlin, H. Schröder, and S. Katzenbeisser. Physically uncloneable functions in the universal composition framework. In *Annual Cryptology Conference*, pages 51–70. Springer, Berlin, 2011.

80. U. Rührmair and M. van Dijk. PUFs in security protocols: Attack models and security evaluations. In *Security and Privacy (SP), 2013 IEEE Symposium on*, pages 286–300. IEEE, New York, NY, 2013.

81. M. van Dijk and U. Ruhrmair. Protocol attacks on advanced PUF protocols and countermeasures. In *Design, Automation and Test in Europe Conference and Exhibition (DATE), 2014*, pages 1–6. IEEE, New York, NY, 2014.

82. M. van Dijk and U. Rührmair. Physical unclonable functions in cryptographic protocols: Security proofs and impossibility results. *IACR Cryptology ePrint Archive*, **2012**:228, 2012.

83. U. Rührmair, C. Jaeger, and M. Algasinger. An attack on PUF-based session key exchange and a hardware-based countermeasure: Erasable PUFs. In *International Conference on Financial Cryptography and Data Security*, pages 190–204. Springer, Berlin, 2011.

84. C. Jin, X. Xu, W. P. Burleson, U. Rührmair, and M. van Dijk. PlayPUF: Programmable logically erasable PUFs for forward and backward secure key management. *IACR Cryptology ePrint Archive*, **2015**:1052, 2015.

85. S. Katzenbeisser, Ü. Kocabaş, V. Van Der Leest, A.-R. Sadeghi, G.-J. Schrijen, and C. Wachsmann. Recyclable PUFs: Logically reconfigurable PUFs. *Journal of Cryptographic Engineering*, **1**(3):177–186, 2011.

86. U. Rührmair, C. Jaeger, M. Bator, M. Stutzmann, P. Lugli, and G. Csaba. Applications of high-capacity crossbar memories in cryptography. *IEEE Transactions on Nanotechnology*, **10**(3):489–498, 2011.

87. U. Rührmair, C. Jaeger, C. Hilgers, M. Algasinger, G. Csaba, and M. Stutzmann. Security applications of diodes with unique current–voltage characteristics. In *International Conference on Financial Cryptography and Data Security*, pages 328–335. Springer, Berlin, 2010.

88. C. Jaeger, M. Algasinger, U. Rührmair, G. Csaba, and M. Stutzmann. Random pn-junctions for physical cryptography. *Applied Physics Letters*, **96**(17):172103, 2010.

89. T. Antesberger, C. Jaeger, M. Scholz, and M. Stutzmann. Structural and electronic properties of ultra-thin polycrystalline Si layers on glass prepared by aluminum-induced layer exchange. *Applied Physics Letters*, **91**(20):201909, 2007.

90. A. Chen. Reconfigurable physical uncloneable function based on probabilistic switching of RRAM. *Electronics Letters*, **51**(8):615–617, 2015.

91. A. Chen. Utilizing the variability of resistive random access memory to implement reconfigurable physical unclonable functions. *IEEE Electron Device Letters*, **36**(2):138–140, 2015.

92. Y. Gao, D. C. Ranasinghe, S. F. Al-Sarawi, O. Kavehei, and D. Abbott, Memristive crypto primitive for building highly secure physical unclonable functions. Scientific Reports, **5**, 2015.

Chapter 7

Spin-Transfer-Torque RAM and Domain Wall Memory Devices

Rekha Govindaraj, Mohammad Nasim Imtiaz Khan, and Swaroop Ghosh

Contents

In today's highly integrated circuits and systems, satisfying the functionality, frequency, and thermal design power (TDP) requirements is not adequate. It is essential to ensure the security and privacy of the overall system. The contemporary business model involves the *untrusted* third party in every step of the integrated circuit (IC) manufacturing process—from design to synthesis and layout all the way to fabrication and packaging. The trend of integrating third-party intellectual property (IP) blocks into the design makes the problem more complex. Broadly, the attacks on hardware could fall under:

■ *Malicious modifications*: The hardware Trojans can be inserted in the ICs, which causes malfunctioning of IC or leak information for instance.
■ *Cloning/fake IC*: The adversary can imitate the design, fabricate, and sell at a lower price, which lowers the market for the genuine IC.
■ *Hacking/eavesdropping*: The adversary eavesdrops on the communication channel to crack the secret key for malicious intent.
■ *Side-channel attacks*: Side channels, for example, current and voltage, are monitored to extract the secret information from the device.
■ *Reverse engineering*: IC design details are revealed by peeling off the layers of the fabrication process using chemicals and mechanical methods, which in turn reveal the secret design information.
■ *IC recycling*: Unused or barely used ICs are recycled from older PCBs and sold at a reduced price compared to genuine new ICs from the original manufacturer.

Furthermore, it is worth mentioning that security, trust, and authentication of an electronic system are intertwined with each other. Such an untrusted design environment results in infected hardware, which in turn necessitates the authentication of the ICs in the end product. Hardware security primitives such as hardware encryption engines, physically unclonable functions (PUFs), true random number generators (TRNGs), recycling sensors, and tamper detection sensors provide promising solutions to the security threats such as hardware Trojan insertion, IC recycling, chip cloning, data snooping, and side-channel attacks. Furthermore, these primitives are energy-efficient and incur low area/design overhead. Table 7.1 summarizes the key requirements of hardware security primitives along with the respective features of spintronics technology.

It should be noted that CMOS-based circuits in security applications have demonstrated the problems of area and power overhead. Further, they are sensitive to environmental fluctuations and have limited randomness and entropy offered by the silicon substrate. The emerging technologies such as magnetic and spintronic have shown promises in bringing an abundance of entropy and physical randomness. Unique identification keys can be generated by extracting spatial, temporal

Table 7.1 Hardware Security Primitives, Key Requirements, and Properties Offered by Spintronics

Security Primitive	Key Requirements	Features Offered by Spintronics
Recycling sensor	Low process variation and high sensitivity to usage	DW nucleation
PUF	High process variation nonlinearity	Stochastic DW motion in rough nanowire nonlinearity
TRNG	High entropy	Noise sensitivity of magnetization stochastic dynamics
Encryption	Recursive shift multiplication addition	Shift-based computation
Miscellaneous	Sensitivity to ambient parameters	Sensitivity to magnetic field temperature

Source: S. Ghosh. *Proceedings of the IEEE*, 104(10):1864–1893, 2016.

randomness, and inherent entropy in a magnetic system using custom-designed harvesting circuits. Furthermore, these technologies have also demonstrated robustness, speed, and orders of magnitude energy efficiency compared to their CMOS counterparts [2–4].

The experimental results on magnetic tunnel junctions (MTJ), domain wall memory (DWM), spin valves, etc. have created enormous interest in spin-based computations. Most importantly, the current-induced modulation of magnetization dynamics discovered in MTJ and DWM have opened new avenues toward energy-efficient memory technology along with logic design. Mechanisms in spin-transfer-torque (STT) devices, created by the interactions between injected current and local magnetizations, offer new sources of entropy. The entropy is further increased by the thermally activated electrons in the material. Besides, the magnetic systems are also sensitive to physical randomness (due to process variation), and the magnetization dynamics is typically nonlinear in nature. For instance, DW motion in the rough nanowire makes it resistant to modeling-based attacks that are prevalent in CMOS-based security primitives [3]. Shift-based access and energy-efficient computation are the unique features, which lead to the easy acceptance of spintronic devices for primitives such as TRNG, secure key generation in encryption engines, PUF, and so on. Figure 7.1a and b captures the sources of entropy and randomness possessed by spintronic systems such as MTJ (Figure 7.1a) and DWM (Figure 7.1b) and which is further discussed in Section 7.1. Although spintronic technology is an excellent choice for the hardware security primitives, the regular spintronic circuits and memory may be prone to carefully engineered attacks. Most of the spintronic devices are essentially susceptible to ambient parameters such as magnetic field, temperature, x-ray, and laser heating. Therefore, the basic dependency of spintronic memory technology on these ambient parameters can be exploited by an adversary for low-cost data tampering easily (Figure 7.2). Furthermore, the nonvolatility of spintronic devices keeps the data intact in chip memory even after powering down the system. The persistent data may allow the adversary to steal sensitive information like cryptographic keys or the password. Therefore, the circuits (specifically memory) designed using spintronics introduce additional security challenges that were not present in their volatile memory counterparts such as static RAM (SRAM) and embedded dynamic RAM (eDRAM) [5].

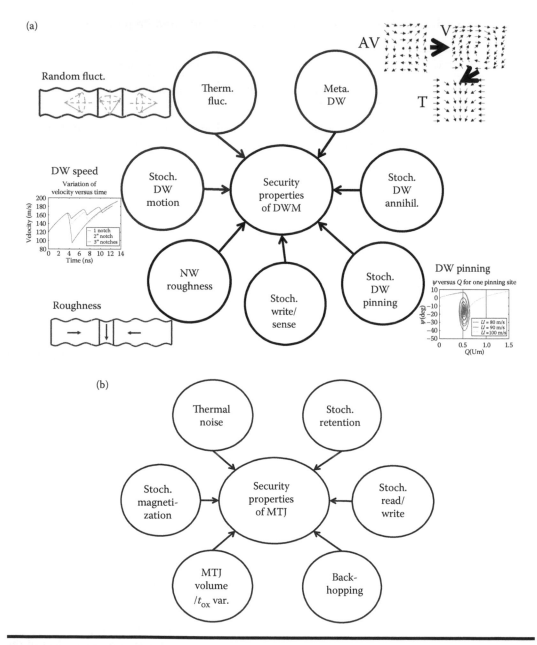

Figure 7.1 Sources of entropy and randomness in spintronic systems such as (a) MTJ and (b) DWM. (Adapted from S. Ghosh. *Proceedings of the IEEE*, 104(10):1864–1893, 2016.)

7.1 Spintronic Elements and Security Properties

In this section, different spintronic elements and their security properties are discussed. These security properties can be exploited to realize different security primitives.

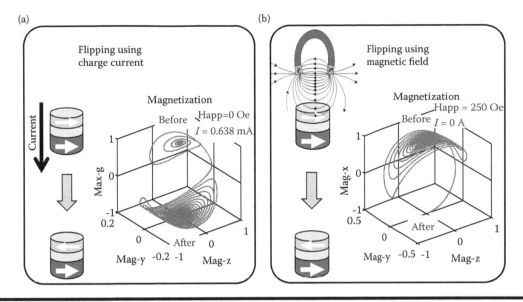

Figure 7.2 **(a) Flipping of the MTJ free layer due to STT (Happ = 0 Oe, *I* = 0.638 mA) and (b) due to an external magnetic field (Happ = 260 Oe, *I* = 0). The plots are obtained by solving the Landau-Lifshitz-Gilbert (LLG). (Adapted from S. Ghosh.** *Proceedings of the IEEE*, **104(10):1864– 1893, 2016; L. Landau and E. Lifshitz.** *Physikalische Zeitschrift der Sowjetunion*, **8(153):101–114, 1935.)**

7.1.1 Magnetic Tunnel Junctions

7.1.1.1 Technology

MTJ contains a free and a pinned magnetic layer separated by a thin tunneling oxide layer (a schematic is shown in Figure 7.3a). The equivalent resistance of the MTJ stack is high (low) if the free layer magnetic orientation is antiparallel (parallel) to that of the fixed layer. Conventionally, the high equivalent resistance is considered as data 1 and low equivalent resistance is considered as data 0. The magnetic orientation of the MTJ free layer can be changed from parallel (P) to antiparallel (AP) (or vice versa) to that of fixed layer by either magnetic field-driven or current-driven techniques. The magnetic field-driven MTJ is the basis for magneto-resistive random access memory (MRAM) technology [7], which is promising due to high-density, low standby power, and high-speed operation. On the other hand, STT magnetic random access memory (STT-RAM) [8] is an energy-efficient variant of MRAM where the switching of magnetization is based on spin-polarized current. Figure 7.3a and b shows the schematic of MRAM and STT-RAM bit-cell, respectively.

In MRAM, MTJ lies between a pair of write lines named digit-line and bit-line. These lines are arranged at right angles to each other, parallel to the cell plane, and one above and one below the cell. An induced magnetic field is created by passing current through the lines. The induced magnetic field exerts a torque on the free layer magnetic orientation causing it to flip. Therefore, the direction of write current determines the polarity of the torque and thus determines writing 0 or 1. The isolation (access) transistor is kept off during write. However, during read, the access transistor is turned on, and a voltage is applied across the cell to sense the equivalent resistance. It should be noted that the read current is unidirectional. In STT-RAM, each cell has one MTJ and

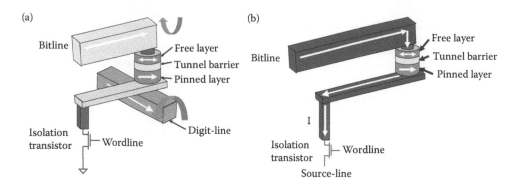

Figure 7.3 Schematic of (a) MRAM and (b) STT-RAM. (Adapted from S. Ghosh. *Proceedings of the IEEE*, 104(10):1864–1893, 2016.)

one access transistor in series. The write operation is done by turning ON the access transistor and injecting current from the source-line to the bit-line or vice versa. However, the read operation of STT-RAM is similar to that of MRAM. The dynamics of free layer magnetization for both MRAM and STT-RAM is governed by the LLG equation [6,9,10] as follows:

$$
\frac{\partial \overrightarrow{m}}{\partial t} = -\gamma \overrightarrow{m} \times (\overrightarrow{H_{eff}} + \underbrace{\overrightarrow{h_{st}}}_{stochastic}) - \alpha\gamma \overrightarrow{m} \times [\overrightarrow{m} \times (\overrightarrow{H_{eff}} + \underbrace{\overrightarrow{h_{st}}}_{stochastic})]
$$

$$
+ \underbrace{\frac{I_s \hbar G(\psi)}{2e} \overrightarrow{m} \times (\overrightarrow{m} \times \overrightarrow{e_p})}_{STT} \tag{7.1}
$$

where $\overrightarrow{m}$ is unit vectors representing the local magnetic moment, α represents the Gilbert damping parameter, γ is the gyromagnetic ratio, $\overrightarrow{h_{st}}$ is the field due to stochastic noise, I_s is the spin current, $G(\psi)$ is the transmission coefficient, $\hbar$ is the reduced Planck constant, e is the charge of the electron, and $\overrightarrow{e_p}$ is the unit vector along the fixed layer magnetization. In the above expression, $\overrightarrow{H_{eff}}$ is the effective field given by $\overrightarrow{H_{eff}} = \overrightarrow{H_a} + \overrightarrow{H_k} + \overrightarrow{H_d} + \overrightarrow{H_{ex}}$, where $\overrightarrow{H_a}$ is the applied field, $\overrightarrow{H_k}$ is the anisotropy field, $\overrightarrow{H_d}$ is the demagnetization field, and $\overrightarrow{H_{ex}}$ is the exchange field. The retention time of the MTJ, that is, the time between which the free layer magnetization tends to flip is given by $T_{ret} = t_0 e^{\Delta}$ where t_0 is attempt time ($\sim$1 ns), stability factor $\Delta = K_u V / k_B T$ where K_u is the magneto-crystalline anisotropy, V is the volume of the MTJ free layer, T is the operating temperature, and k_B is the Boltzmann constant [11]. By injecting a current (I) through the MTJ having a critical current of I_{co} (where the direction of the current flips the bit), the retention time can be altered as follows [12]:

$$
\Delta = \frac{K_u V}{k_B T} \left(1 - \frac{I}{I_{co}}\right) \tag{7.2}
$$

Note that Equations 7.1 and 7.2 are crucial to understanding the factors that can influence the magnetization dynamics and retention time of MTJ. These factors can be exploited by the designers to design high-quality security primitives (Section 7.2), whereas the same can be exploited by the hackers to tamper with the circuit functionality (Section 7.1).

7.1.1.2 Security Properties

The security-specific properties of MTJ are summarized in Figure 7.1b. The properties that can be leveraged to realize security primitives are described briefly.

Chaotic magnetization: The dynamics of the magnetic orientation of the MTJ free layer is chaotic, especially at the border of P and AP states, namely, the bifurcation point. It can be noted that chaos is deterministic for a given initial point. However, the behavior of the chaotic system is very sensitive to the initial point, which makes it unpredictable, especially when the initial point contains variation [13]. This feature makes chaos a suitable property for hardware security.

Statistical read and write failures [14–16]: The MTJ critical current is a function of stability factor (Δ), which in turn is a function of free layer volume (2). Therefore, owing to process variation, each MTJ, in an array with specific target design, can have different Δ. Higher Δ improves the robustness of MTJ to read disturb failure. However, higher Δ also means a higher critical write current, that is, higher write latency and therefore higher probability of write failures. The converse is true for the lower Δ. Therefore, process variations can result in statistical variation in read/write failure rates which can be exploited for the PUF design.

Statistical and stochastic retention: As explained earlier, the MTJ retention time is a function of Δ (higher increases the retention time). Therefore, the retention time is statistical under process variation [14] and stochastic in nature as it is a function of thermal noise and environmental conditions also. The precession of free layer magnetic orientation is also stochastic (a function of damping, effective field, current, and thermal noise), which results in variation in MTJ resistance both in P and AP states. Therefore, the stochastic nature of retention time can be leveraged to design PUF and TRNG.

Back-hopping: It has been experimentally shown that the free layer magnetization can flip back and forth (known as the back-hopping phenomena) under high bias across the MTJ [17]. Back-hopping is one of the crucial challenges for applicability of large-scale STT-RAM arrays [18]. However, owing to the highly inherent entropic response, back-hopping can be potentially useful for random number generation. The back-hopping switching probability function for AP to P switching with initial condition of $P_1(t = 0) = 0$ is given by [17]

$$P_1 = \frac{\gamma_1}{\gamma_1 + \gamma_2}(1 - e^{-(\gamma_1 + \gamma_2)t}) \quad \text{and} \quad \gamma_{1,2} = \gamma_0 e^{\left(-\frac{c}{k_B T}(H_k \mp H)^2(1 \mp (V/V_c))\right)} \tag{7.3}$$

where $CH_k^2 = E_0$ is the free layer shape anisotropy, V_c is the spin-torque switching threshold at zero temperature, and $\gamma_0 = 10^9$ Hz is the attempt frequency.

7.1.2 Magnetic Nanowire in DWM

7.1.2.1 Technology

DWM is a promising memory technology as it can store multiple bits per cell [19–22] (Figure 7.4). In addition, it provides low standby power, nonvolatility, fast access time, high endurance, and high retention time. DWM consists of three components: (i) write head, (ii) read head, and (iii) magnetic nanowire (NW).

The write and read heads of DWM are similar to conventional MTJs, while the NW holds the bits in the form of magnetic polarity. The formation of DWs takes place at the interface of two distinct magnetic polarities or domains. The reversal of magnetic orientation of the domain

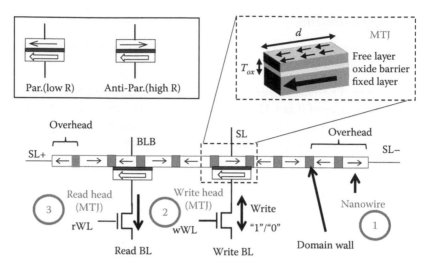

SL - Select line, BL - Bit Line, rWL - read Word Line, BLB - Bit Line complement

Figure 7.4 Schematic of DWM. (Adapted from S. Ghosh. *Proceedings of the IEEE*, 104(10): 1864–1893, 2016.)

is essentially controlled by DWs. The prospect of current-induced motion of DWs [23–29] in the ferromagnetic films has created significant interest for high-density memory application where bits are stored analogous to the hard disk [30]. The DWs can be shifted forward and backward by injecting charge current from left-shift and right-shift contacts. This causes the NW to operate as a shift register. The new domains are injected by first pushing charge current through the shift contacts to move the bits in lockstep until the desired bit is under the write head. Next, spin-polarized current is injected through the write head. To do that, the write MTJ is turned ON (by asserting wWL) and wBL and SL are biased to pass a current from SL to BL or BL to SL to write 0 or 1, respectively. During read, the desired bit is brought under the read head using a shift operation, and then sensing the resistance of the MTJ formed by the new bit (after the DW crosses the read head) using rBL and rWL. The key mechanism is the exchange interaction between itinerant electrons with the local magnetization and the resulting transfer of spin torque to push the DWs. DWM is a dynamical system, and the magnetization dynamics is governed by the LLG equation [9, 10]. The modified LLG for DW with the stochastic magnetic field is given by

$$\frac{\partial \vec{m}}{\partial t} = -\gamma \, \vec{m} \times (\overrightarrow{H_{eff}} + \underbrace{\vec{h}_{st}}_{stochastic}) - \alpha \vec{m} \times \frac{\partial \vec{m}}{\partial t} - u(\vec{J}.\nabla)\vec{m} + \beta u \vec{m} \times (\vec{J}.\nabla)\vec{m} \quad (7.4)$$

where $\vec{m}$ and $\vec{J}$ are unit vectors representing local magnetic moments and current flow. α, β, and γ represent the Gilbert damping parameter, the nonadiabatic spin transfer term, and gyromagnetic ratio, respectively. The effective field is represented by $\overrightarrow{H_{eff}} = -(1/\mu_0 M_s)(\delta w/\delta \vec{m})$ and field due to stochastic noise is $\vec{h}_{st}$. The parameter u is the STT parameter and it is proportional to the current density J, the spin polarization P, and is given by $u = \mu_B JP/eM_s$, where M_s is the saturation magnetization, w is the energy density, μ_B is the Bohr magnetron, and e is the charge of the electron. In the next section, security properties of DWM are presented. Although the discussion is limited to DWM, it should be noted that several other flavors of spintronic memory technologies have also been proposed in different literatures. Some examples include DWM with single DW, spintronic memristor, magnetic quantum cellular automata (QCA), spin gain transistor, spin Hall effect (SHE) device, and so on [31]. In theory, these devices could also be explored from a security standpoint.

7.1.2.2 Security Properties

Besides entropy, the DWM possesses several microscopic and macroscopic properties as described below (Figure 7.1a).

7.1.2.2.1 Microscopic Properties

Chaotic dynamics: The likelihood of chaos appearance during domain wall motion under electrical current has been studied in References 32–36. Bifurcation analysis and the existence of a positive Lyapunov parameter for certain values of the damping constant indicate the presence of chaos in DW motion. Furthermore, process variation and ambient temperature increase the degree of chaos.

Stochastic DW motion (speed and polarity): The speed of DW depends on the type of wall, spatial location of notches (which is stochastic in space), and the magnitude/frequency/pulse of the applied shift current. The phase between a notch and the pulse arrival time is a stochastic process in the time domain. The stochastic nature of notch location with respect to shift pulse is presented in Figure 7.5. A DW with the same initial velocity simulated with two different shift pulse characteristics (with the same average value) moves with different velocities. The DW speed and polarity are also related to the type of wall—antivortex (AV), vortex (V), and transverse (T). The AV wall is typically metastable and possesses bidirectional motion. Once converted to V or T, it shows an increase in speed and unidirectionality. Therefore, DW velocity is stochastic in nature.

Stochastic DW pinning: The DW moves smoothly if the NW is free of roughness (notches). However, process variation-induced edge roughness can reduce the velocity of DW that may result in eventual pinning. Therefore, pinning of DW is a stochastic process and depends on surface roughness (magnitude and spatial location) as well as injected shift current and magnetization dynamics. The depinning is also a stochastic process and depends on injected current magnitude, frequency, and environmental conditions. Figure 7.5b represents the stochastic nature of pinning due to notch location, DW speed, and shift pulse. Figure 7.5c shows that an out-of-sync pulse may degrade the DW speed and lead to pinning.

Stochastic DW annihilation: Two DWs can annihilate each other due to oscillatory motion (under the influence of injected shift current), slight difference in their velocities (due to the stochastic nature of DW motion), and metastability of the walls and resulting change in polarity of DW motion.

Nonvolatility and retention time: The DWs retain their state in the absence of external assistance. The retention time is a function of the thermal stability of the MTJ, which in turn depends on process variation and ambient parameters like temperature and the external magnetic field. Therefore, the retention time is also stochastic in nature.

7.1.2.2.2 Macroscopic Properties

Initialization and resetting: NW is free of DWs before first access, and initially it is magnetized in a preferred direction determined by the balance of exchange and anisotropy energies. To populate new information in the NW, DWs are nucleated using the write head by injecting sufficient current

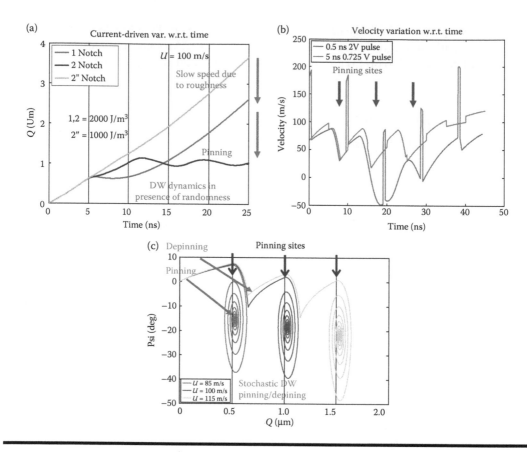

Figure 7.5 (a) DW dynamics in the presence of physical roughness induced slowdown and eventual pinning; (b) stochastic motion of DW. A misaligned shift pulse reduces velocity; and (c) stochastic pinning of DWs with respect to three different shift currents. (Adapted from A. S. Iyengar et al. *IEEE Journal on Emerging and Selected Topics in Circuits and Systems,* **5(1):40–50, 2015.)**

in the orthogonal direction to flip the local magnetization of the free layer. The NW can be flushed out by simply injecting current through shift contacts and moving the bits out.

Magnetic polarity-dependent retention: The external magnetic field significantly affects the retention time of MTJ (in turn the retention time of the DWM cell). Some bits with a lower retention time can be employed to detect a magnetic field-based attack as they will flip earlier compared to normal bits.

Bipolar DW nucleation: The nucleation of DW in the NW is bipolar in nature. The current polarity (through writing MTJ) determines the type of DW (head-to-head or tail-to-tail).

Multiple domains/NW: The NW can hold multiple domains or information bits by nucleating new DWs through writing MTJ and shifting them in the NW similar to shift register. The limit of bits per NW is set by the NW dimensions.

Serial access and bipolar shifting: In contrast to conventional magnetic devices, DWM stores multiple bits of information. The group of DWs is shifted together by injecting current. The bits in the NW can be shifted in both directions by changing the current polarity.

Miscellaneous properties: DWM provides an opportunity to exploit multiple sense points (read heads) along the NW for continuous collection of entropy and randomness. The security properties of MTJ and microscopic and macroscopic properties of DWM presented above make spintronics suitable for many hardware primitives such as PUF, TRNG, hardware encryption engine, and tamper detection sensors (such as magnetic/thermal attack) described next.

7.2 Spintronic Security Primitives

This section presents the design of spintronic hardware security primitives implemented by spintronic elements and interesting features offered by them.

7.2.1 *Physically Unclonable Function*

7.2.1.1 *DWM PUF*

7.2.1.1.1 Design and Operation

In References 2 and 3, the physical randomness in the DWM is exploited to generate a PUF response to a given challenge. A relay PUF is designed with multiple stages of parallel NWs [2]. A conventional muxing circuit between each consecutive stage is introduced to toggle the paths and create new challenges. Furthermore, a higher number of stages also provide a higher degree of randomness in the signature. An arbiter block is placed at the end to compare the arrival times of the respective DWs. The operation of relay-PUF has three stages:

■ *Challenge*: The relay-PUF, compared to conventional PUFs, provides extra degrees of freedom to choose challenges by varying input parameters like shift pulse voltage, pulse width, and pulse frequency. This increases the total number of challenges with low area overhead. It is shown that with 48 stages and 20 PM/PW settings, the total number of challenges is 10^{19}. Therefore, with 10^{19} challenges, it will take approximately 10 years to decode the response by an adversary, making the PUF attack-resistant.

■ *DW nucleation and relay race*: To generate a PUF response, the DWs in all the NWs are first nucleated by applying a pulsed current, for which the write word-line (wWL) is asserted, as shown in Figure 7.6a. Next, to trigger the DW race, the shift signal of stage-1 is activated. Then the read head is activated by pulsing the read word-line (rWL). When a change in equivalent resistance is sensed by the read head (by sensing the change in magnetization), the shifting of the stage is stopped. Unlike an inverter chain, where the transition propagates from one stage to another, the DW propagation vanishes once it reaches the NW end. To enable seamless propagation of the DW, in anticipation of the arrival of the DW after the nucleation stage, the read head is kept asserted. Once the read head detects the arrival of the DW (i.e., the DW reaches the end of NW), the shift signal of the following stage is fired and thus relays the DW information to the next stage. The mux select signal determines whether the upper or lower DW will be fired in the following stage.

■ *Response*: The response of the relay-PUF (0 or 1) is determined by an arbiter block. The arbiter block compares the arrival times of DWs that are in parallel NWs and generates an output according to the earliest DW arrival. The switching of paths, in association with shift pulse width, duration, and frequency, provides several degrees of randomness in the race condition. As the physical roughness varies from NW to NW, the DWs will race with different speeds, and the response will vary between chips. This leads to the desired inter-die and intra-die hamming distance.

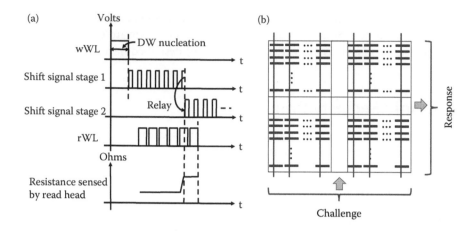

Figure 7.6 **(a) Timing diagram showing the write and read word-lines and the shift signals for each stage and the resistance sensed with respect to time. As soon as a change in the equivalent resistance is sensed by the read head (by sensing the magnetization change), the shifting of the stage is stopped. (b) Schematic of a memory-PUF. (Adapted from A. S. Iyengar et al. *IEEE Journal on Emerging and Selected Topics in Circuits and Systems*, 5(1):40–50, 2015.)**

In addition to the relay-PUF, a memory-PUF is also proposed [2] where the entire memory bank is used to obtain the authentication key. A race is employed to characterize the state of each NW in the array. The DWs winning the race are set to 1, whereas the others are set to 0. Thus, the random physical roughness in NWs is mapped to the random initialization of the array. Since the physical randomness is set during fabrication, the reliability (reproducibility) of the design is excellent for ideal temperature and voltage range. Owing to zero standby leakage of the bit-cell, this PUF is shown to be low-power compared to the SRAM PUF. The schematic of the memory-PUF is shown in Figure 7.6b.

7.2.1.1.2 Evaluation of DWM PUF

The DWM PUFs are evaluated with respect to different quality metrics such as strength, randomness, and repeatability. The performance evaluation of the DWM PUF of Reference 2 is described below:

■ *Strength*: The DWM PUF employs shift current pulse magnitude, pulse width, and pulse frequency as a set of challenges in addition to the conventional ones such as mux switching (for relay-PUF) and row address (for memory-PUF). Therefore, the relay-PUF could be categorized as a strong PUF, whereas the memory-PUF could be categorized as a weak PUF. The outcome of the race is highly randomized due to the process variation (varies from NW to NW) and the random location of the notches (both spatially and temporally). Furthermore, it has been shown that DW propagation velocity is strongly dependent on the pulse characteristics. Therefore, shift pulse could also be employed as a challenge. The nonlinear dynamics of the DW also make the PUF resilient to modeling and machine learning attack [3].

■ *Randomness and stability*: The DW dynamics in the NW is solved by using stochastic 1D-LLG [37]. For a 6-stage PUF operating at 25°C and 0.25 V, the inter-die average HD is found to be 45%. For intra-die HD, the PUF response is compared by considering two extreme operating temperatures −10°C and 90°C, and supply voltage variations of ±10%. A long tail in the distribution of intra-die HD is obtained due to sensitive bits that are highly susceptible toward ambient temperature and voltage fluctuations. In order to ensure low intra-die variation, additional techniques have been suggested in Reference 2 such as (i) temporal redundancy where the response of the bit is observed at different time instances, and the response with majority is used as the final output and (ii) error correction circuitry such as Von Neuman corrector [38] and run length encoding [30] to fix the unstable bits. An average of 25% separation between the inter-die and the intra-die variation is observed for relay-PUF. This shows good randomness and stability of the design. For HD analysis of memory-PUF, employed in Reference 2, the notch dimensions for the inter-die process variations are varied according to a Gaussian distribution. The operating voltage of the PUF is determined by ensuring an approximately equal distribution of 1's and 0's. It is presented that at the shifting pulse voltage of 0.25V, roughly 59% of the total DWs win the race (i.e., the bits are 1's). Therefore, the requirement of sensing the arrival time could be relaxed, and sensing could be performed after a fixed time. The average inter-die HD of this PUF is found to be 50%. An average of 45% separation between the inter-die and the intra-die HD is observed for memory-PUF.

■ *Area and power*: It has been shown in Reference 2 that the DW memory-PUF is 10x more power-efficient than the SRAM PUF. The footprint is found to be lower by an order of magnitude.

7.2.1.2 STT-RAM and MRAM PUF

In this section, various STT-RAM and MRAM PUFs are reviewed. These PUFs exploit different spintronic security properties to realize high-performance PUFs.

7.2.1.2.1 PUF-1

Reference 39 proposes an STT-RAM PUF that exploits the randomly initialized magnetic orientation of the MTJ free layer to generate a PUF response. During the registration phase, the technique compares two STT-RAM bits that are in two complementary rows for generating the response. If the bits are initialized to the same value during the comparison, the technique relies on the noise and the sense amplifier offset to decide the response. Repeatability is ensured by writing back the corresponding complementary values to the STT-RAM bits. Furthermore, a fuzzy extractor is used to enhance the quality of the PUF response. It should be noted that the random initialization of the MTJs makes the PUF response highly entropic. On the other hand, its nonvolatility after write-back preserves the PUF response over multiple accesses and voltage and temperature fluctuations. The entropy attained by the PUF is 0.985 [39]. Furthermore, the PUF ensures a bit error rate (BER) of $\sim 10^{-6}$ from retention and read/write errors after write-back. In Reference 40, the performance of PUF has been improved using the bit alteration phenomenon in MTJ devices incorporating multi-bit per cell. The basic idea is that, in a 2T2MTJ cell, the resistance of the first MTJ can be higher than that of the other one when both of them are in the parallel state. Furthermore, in the antiparallel state (both MTJ), the resistance of the first MTJ can be lower that of the other one. This leads to a reconfigurable response. It has been shown that 1.48 bits can be generated from each secret bit (SB) cell and the equivalent bit capacity can be further improved to approximately ≈2 by employing a hash function. The high reliability of the proposed PUF [40] greatly lowers the burden of ECC. Furthermore, it has also been shown that the response-bit map of the STT-MRAM PUF can be dynamically refreshed when it is required so that predicting the response-bits generated from the PUF becomes even more difficult. It is also reported that this scheme is superior in area (≥11x smaller in area/bit) and energy consumption (≥2x smaller in energy/bit) compared to the conventional PUFs [40]. However, the simulation result shows that only 11.4% of the cells can show the bit alteration phenomenon due to the strong correlation between the cell resistances in the parallel and antiparallel states. This strong correlation is created by different relevant parameters like area, Vth, etc. and limits the reconfigurable response.

7.2.1.2.2 PUF-2

Another MRAM PUF is proposed in Reference 41 which employs the random initialization of the MTJ exploiting physical variations in the MTJ. Intrinsic physical variations of MTJ create a random tilt of the energy barrier as shown in Figure 7.7a and b. The distribution of the tilt angle is Gaussian. Therefore, the magnetic orientation of the MTJ free layer is prone to prefer a certain initial position much similar to the SRAM PUF. The proposed technique first destabilizes the magnetic orientation of the MTJ free layer to the hard axis and releases it to settle to its preferred state. Exercising NIST benchmarks [42] on the PUF response demonstrate an intra-die HD of 0.0225 and an entropy of 0.99. To increase the tilt angle variation and enhance the stability of the PUF, different techniques such as decreasing the aspect ratio at constant volume and increasing the volume at a constant aspect ratio have been proposed.

7.2.1.2.3 PUF-3

In Reference 43, a PUF, namely, err-PUF is proposed based on the cell error rate distribution of STT-RAM. A generated stable fingerprint based on a novel concept called error-rate differential pair (EDP) is used rather than using the error rate distribution directly. The technique does not need modification of the read/write circuits. It has been shown that the two cells of an EDP have considerably different error rates even with the environmental variation [43]. The BER of the same STT-RAM array under the error-least-state (the best case with the lowest error rate) and error-most-state (the worst case with the highest error rate) needs to be considered. To be an EDP pair, the difference of the total number of errors in N round of test for the corresponding two cells

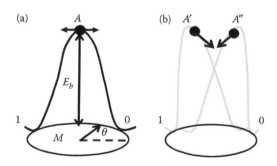

Figure 7.7 Energy landscape of MTJ for (a) ideal geometry and (b) random physical variations of MTJ causes the magnetization at location A to develop a preferential initial state. (Adapted from S. Ghosh. *Proceedings of the IEEE*, 104(10):1864–1893, 2016.)

should be equal to or greater than N in all cases. In the enrollment phase, the challenge–response pairs (CRPs) for a PUF is determined, and the information is saved in a safe database. In the evaluation phase, the response to a given challenge is calculated and compared with reference data for verification. The proposed PUF can achieve a mean intra-HD of 7.76 with a variance of 7.29. For inter-HD, the mean value is 60.56 and the variance is 32.31.

7.2.1.2.4 PUF-4

In Reference 44, a PUF is proposed, exploiting the high variability and uncontrollability of (i) MTJ resistance in an antiparallel state and (ii) the transistor threshold. First, all cells, including reference cells are written to the antiparallel state. The reference cells are read, and the current through the cells are averaged to get a reference current, I_{ref}. Now, each active cell is read, and if the read current, $I > I_{ref}$, the sense amplifier interprets the stored data as "0." However, if the read current, $I < I_{ref}$, the sense amplifier interprets the stored data as "1." The output of the sense amplifier is stored as the PUF value. The fabrication-induced variability guarantees unpredictability and unclonability. Since the randomness is set by fabrication, with constant operating voltage and temperature, the PUF value is reproducible (i.e., PUF is reliable). However, temperature variation, stochastic thermal noise, and any external magnetic field will lead to a poor reliability of the design.

7.2.1.2.5 PUF-5

In Reference 45, an MTJ-PUF is proposed based on intrinsic properties of spin transfer switching (STS). STS is measured and characterized experimentally, and a method to extract the PUF signature is presented. Owing to process variation and extrinsic properties of junction resistance, etc., each measured MTJ shows different switching voltage for both switching cases, parallel to antiparallel and antiparallel to parallel.

For PUF extraction, at first, all cells are reset to the initial state with parallel orientation. Next, a specific voltage, VPUF is applied to the MTJs to induce switching with a 50% probability for the majority of the MTJs. Owing to the stochastic switching nature of MTJ, a random distribution of parallel and antiparallel states is achieved across the array. Now, every MTJ is read by the PUF extraction circuit, and they are categorized into three groups: (i) much less than 50% (white); (ii) around 50% (gray); and (iii) much more than 50% (black). The result is stored, and the array is reset. For a better reliability, the extraction operation is repeated multiple times to extract white and black bits and discard gray bits. Finally, the black bits are chosen for the PUF signature. Since this PUF exploits stochastic STS, it is technically impossible to make a clone. However, a different performance metric and comparison of this PUF to others are yet to be analyzed.

7.2.1.2.6 PUF-6

In Reference 46, a buffer-free memory-based PUF (BF-MPUF) is proposed. This PUF can be realized using any emerging NVM technologies like STT-RAM, Phase Charge Memory (PCM), resistive RAM (RRAM), etc. and it can produce random keys without disturbing the data already stored in the memory. This technique does not require buffer storage and an additional write-back operation circuit like conventional SRAM-based PUF as it utilizes the nonvolatility of NVMs. Therefore, the design incurs a lower power and area overhead compared to SRAM PUFs. For memory mode, first a voltage is applied to the memory cell, and the current I_{dat} is measured. Then the measured current is compared with a reference current, $I_{ref} = (I_H + I_L)/2$, where I_H and I_L

are the reference currents of the antiparallel and parallel states, respectively. The polarity of this comparison is output as a digital bit. However, for the PUF mode, at first the cells are checked to determine the current state, and I_{ref} is set to I_H if the cell stores 1 (antiparallel); otherwise I_{ref} is set to I_L. Therefore, both parallel and antiparallel states are exploited to generate responses according to the current state of the NVM without disturbing its state. It has been shown that this design is resistant to possible leakage or side-channel attacks. The corresponding BER is 4%, and energy/bit is 0.001 pJ.

The performance of a PUF is determined mainly by reliability, uniqueness, and randomness. Reliability is the measure of the dependency of the PUF response to the intra-chip parameter variations such as voltage and temperature. The reliability of a PUF can be measured by the intra-die HD, which should be ideally 0% for all the possible challenges of a PUF for all responses. Uniqueness in the PUF response enables the identification of different chips uniquely. Uniqueness is measured by the inter-die HD. An inter-die HD of 50% indicates the desired (ideal) uniqueness of the PUF response. Randomness is measure by entropy [39]. Ideally, the entropy should be close to 1. The comparison of the different PUFs described in this section is summarized in Table 7.2.

7.2.1.3 Design Challenges

The stability of STT-RAM and MRAM PUF during normal operation can be affected by some factors such as thermal noise, read disturb (bit flip) due to multiple reads, write failure, tampering, external magnetic field, etc. These factors can significantly affect the overall performance of the PUFs.

- *Thermal noise*: Thermal noise can lower the retention time of the MTJ significantly. The effect is stronger at a higher temperature. Therefore, the PUF response will differ from registration value due to thermal noise resulting in poor intra-HD.
- *Read disturb*: The content of a bit-cell (magnetic orientation of the MTJ free layer) can accidentally change during a read operation, which is known as read disturb. Although the read current is significantly (5–10 times) lower than the MTJ critical write current, it still introduces a disturbance to the cell. Furthermore, multiple consecutive reads of a bit can lead to read disturb (i.e., undesirable bit flip). This will result in poor intra-HD. It should be noted that as the read current is unidirectional, the flip can only happen in one direction, that is, either from parallel to antiparallel or the other way around. Read disturb failures occur due to the increased current drivability of the access transistor or decreased critical current of the MTJ. This may be the result of process variations or thermal noise effects.
- *Write failure*: If the PUF involves a write operation, for example, write-back in Reference 39, failure to write the desired value can cause poor robustness. Write failures occur if the MTJ state does not change during a write operation as targeted. This happens due to the decreased current drivability of the access transistor or increased MTJ critical current due to process variations or thermal effects. It should be noted that the requirement of low write failure (high current drivability of the access transistor and low MTJ critical current) leads to high read disturb and vice versa.
- *Reliability/endurance*: A multiple write operation can lower the lifetime of the MTJ (due to oxide breakdown). This results in a bit that could be stuck at 0 or 1, causing poor robustness.
- *Tampering and side-channel attacks*: Temperature and magnetic field can be employed by an adversary to write or modulate the state of the PUF array. The objective of the attacker could be to gain insights for modeling the PUF responses and/or to bypass the authentication.

Table 7.2 Performance Comparison of Different STT-RAM/MRAM PUFs

PUF	Reliability	Uniqueness	Randomness	BER	Area (MTJ Contact Area)	Energy/Bit
PUF-1 [39]	–	50.1%	0.985	6.6×10^{-6} (200–400 K) Vdd (±10%)	$40 \times 116\,\mathrm{nm}^2$	–
PUF-2 [41]	0.0225	47%	0.99	–	$6.74\,\mu m^2$ (64 bit)	–
PUF-3 [43]	Mean 0.0767; Variance 0.0729	Mean 60.56%; Variance 32.3%	–	–	$50 \times 130\,\mathrm{nm}^2$	2.42 pJ
PUF-4 [44]	–	–	–	–	–	–
PUF-5 [45]	–	–	–	–	–	–
PUF-6 [46]	–	49.89%	0.95	6.60×10^{-6} (with ECC)	$45 \times 116\,\mathrm{nm}^2$	0.001 pJ

It has been noted that the effect of magnetic tampering is expected to be low due to the inherent resilience of the scaled STT-RAM from the magnetic field. However, the temperature could be used to tamper with the retention time of the MTJ which hampers the PUF performance [47].

7.2.2 Encryption Engines

Encryption engines can be realized by exploiting DW properties such as shift-based access and dependence of MTJ resistance on the relative orientation of the free layer and fixed layer. Advance encryption standard (AES) [48] is a standard encryption algorithm that has been investigated in Reference 49 using DWM. Since shift and XOR operation is inherently easier to realize with DWM, its serial access architecture is suitable to implement AES. Furthermore, superior energy efficiency, entropy, and density of DWM-AES are promising for encryption engines. Each AES step is mapped to a corresponding DWM operation. The basic building block is a 2-input XOR gate that is realized by shifting the input bits in two nanowires that are built on top of each other. To implement the AES operation, the state matrix (SM) is first implemented in the DWM array. Each byte of SM is written across eight nanowires to enable a cycle-by-cycle AES operation. The following approach is adopted to perform the AES steps using DWM:

- *SubByte*: In this step, each byte of SM is replaced using the same substitution function. A DW-based look-up table (LUT) is used to save leakage power of the conventional SRAM-based LUT.
- *ShiftRows*: This operation rotates each row cyclically to the left by the amount equal to the row number. To mimic cyclic rotation in the nanowire, redundant bits are employed in a DW nanowire where the bits are repeated. Therefore, simple left-shifting of bits mimics the rotation operation.
- *MixColumns*: This step maps each column of the SM to a new column by multiplying it with a matrix containing numbers 1, 2, and 3. Since a shift operation is natural in DWM, multiplication is achieved by a shift and addition operation. To implement addition, a DW-XOR gate is employed.
- *AddRoundKey*: In this step, the SM is XORed with the round key. DW-XOR is utilized in this step. The DWM AES implementation [49] consumes 24 pJ/bit and provides a peak bandwidth of 5.6 GB/s. It is shown to be significantly more efficient than CMOS and CMOS/molecular (CMOL) memristive implementation.

7.2.2.1 Design Challenges

The functionality of DWM AES can be affected by the following factors:

- *Process variations*: Process variation in the magnetic nanowire can create surface roughness, which in turn affects the shift operation. Similarly, variation in the read/write head, such as oxide thickness, surface area, TMR, and saturation magnetization, can affect the read/write operation. The variations can also alter the energy barrier, lowering the retention time of the read/write head. These result in degradation of the robustness of the DWM AES encryption engine.
- *Read/write/shift/retention failures*: Process variation and thermal noise can cause read and write failures during the AES operation. The shift failure during shift-rows and mix-columns can

also result in wrong computation. The volatility of the bits due to poor retention will also cause functional failures during AES computation.

- *Reliability/endurance*: A multiple write operation can lower the lifetime of the MTJ, resulting in a bit that could be stuck at 0 or 1.
- *Side-channel attacks*: Temperature and magnetic field can be employed by an adversary to write or modulate the state of the DWM LUT and/or affect other operations. The objective of the attacker could be to weaken the security. More research is required in this direction to understand the above challenges and develop countermeasures.

7.2.3 True Random Number Generator

In this section, several TRNGs employed in different literatures are presented. These TRNGs are realized by exploiting different inherent security properties of spintronics.

7.2.3.1 TRNG-1

In Reference 50, a TRNG is proposed based on the spintronic device. The key idea is to first reset the MTJ to an antiparallel state, and next excite the magnetic orientation of the MTJ free layer to the bifurcation point by applying a current pulse. Since this point is at very high energy and not a stable point, the magnetization settles in a random state (either a parallel or antiparallel state) due to thermal noise (Figure 7.8). To improve the randomness of the response and kill the correlation among bits, they are XORed with each other. Although promising, the reset pulse is detrimental to MTJ reliability. Furthermore, the sharing of a reset and sense circuit makes MTJ susceptible to read disturb.

7.2.3.2 TRNG-2

In Reference 44, a TRNG is proposed by exploiting MTJ stochastic switching and using the optimal pulse width/amplitude to control the MTJ switching with a 50% probability. The final state of the MTJ (i.e., parallel or antiparallel) solely depends on the internal thermal agitation. This leads to an unbiased output bit. First, the nominal value of write time and write current is determined for the nominal MTJ design with a 50% switching probability. Next, the SET-PROGRAM-READ operation is performed for N cycles. If the number of 1's among total bits is less than 50%, the SET-PROGRAM-READ operation is performed again for another N cycles with increased write time; if the number of 1's is higher than 50%, the operation is repeated with decreased write time.

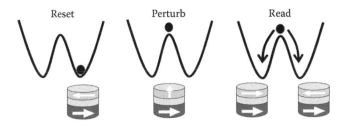

Figure 7.8 Operating principle of TRNG using MTJ. (Adapted from S. Ghosh. *Proceedings of the IEEE*, 104(10):1864–1893, 2016.)

The process is repeated until the desired bit-string length is achieved. A preliminary worst-case analysis is proposed to make the resulting bit-stream unbiased toward one of the logic states.

7.2.3.3 TRNG-3

A conditional perturb technique is proposed in Reference 51, which avoids the usage of a reset pulse by applying an optimal pulse and bringing the MTJ to a 50% switching probability contour. Therefore, a high-quality key generation is realized at a lower energy and faster rate. Furthermore, elimination of a reset pulse also prolongs the MTJ lifetime.

7.2.3.4 TRNG-4

A complementary polarizer STT MTJ (CPMTJ) structure is proposed to enhance the randomness of generated bits [52]. The cell consists of a single free layer, a tunneling oxide layer, and two complementary polarized pinned layers. Owing to the presence of a positive feedback loop that stabilizes the free layer magnetization during sensing, the randomness of this CPMTJ-based on-chip spin dice (CPSD) is preserved. It has been shown that sequential access of an array of CPSD may be used to improve the throughput of random number generation since the CPSD footprint is small. Furthermore, it has been shown that if the frequency of random switching events is sufficiently high, the CPSD state may be randomized using thermal fluctuations only. This eliminates the need for reset and programming operations. Therefore, the technique may be an energy-efficient on-chip TRNG. However, further analysis like randomness, area overhead, the impact of process variation, etc. needs to be evaluated.

7.2.3.5 TRNG-5

The precession of the MTJ free layer is also employed to generate a random number [53]. The current pulse width is applied and the duration is adjusted to cause the free layer precession that settles to a random state.

7.2.3.6 TRNG-6

In Reference 54, a current is passed through the MTJ, the magnitude of which is in between the read current and write current. The current magnitude is adjusted to make the switching probability equal for 0's and 1's. The random bit is extracted and processed further for key generation.

7.2.3.7 TRNG-7

In Reference 55, the MTJ is disturbed using DC current, and the random value is sensed and processed using an entropy extractor. A tamper detection unit is also designed by monitoring a run of 0's or 1's in the random number generated from the MTJ array.

7.2.3.8 TRNG-8

In Reference 56, an MRAM-based random number generator (RNG) is presented using an error-correcting code (ECC) as a postprocessing circuit. The technique achieves 50% switching probability with an adjustment of the applied voltage and the estimation of the balance of the number of 0's and 1's. It has been experimentally shown that the error-correcting capability of ECC, $t \leq 2$ is enough for a very low failure rate of randomness. The power consumption of MTJ for this implementation of RNG is 0.05 mW/bit. Few other MTJ-based TRNGs have also been proposed using spin-injection current in Reference 57.

7.2.3.9 Design Challenges

The operation of STT-RAM/MRAM TRNG can be affected by factors such as thermal noise, read/write failure, endurance issue, tampering and side-channel attack, etc. A brief description of how these factors influence the STT-RAM/MRAM TRNG operation is given below:

- *Thermal noise*: Thermal noise can lower the retention time of the MTJ. This, on top of the process variation-induced poor retention of certain bits, makes the response predictable. Therefore, the entropy of the TRNG can be significantly lowered.
- *Read failure*: Read failure refers to the case when wrong data are being read from a memory cell. The read operation can fail due to the poor TMR/sense margin. This weakens the TRNG since the response of certain bits could be predictable.
- *Write failure*: The TRNG that involves a write operation (e.g., RESET in References 50 and 51, stochastic switching in Reference 44) can experience failure to write the desired value resulting in degraded entropy.
- *Reliability/endurance*: As mentioned earlier, the periodic write operation can lower the lifetime of the MTJ, resulting in a bit that could be stuck at 0 or 1. This will degrade the TRNG entropy.
- *Tampering and side-channel attacks*: Temperature, magnetic field, and other side channels can be employed by an adversary to cause a write/read failure or to write the bits to a preferred state. The objective of the attacker could be to gain clues about the key and intermediate data to weaken or crack the authentication. For instance, the adversary can apply an external magnetic field and bias the TRNG to a certain bit polarity (either 0 or 1) by changing the magnetic orientation of the MTJ free layer by applying an external magnetic field.

7.3 Fundamental Security Vulnerabilities

Although spintronic devices are very promising to hardware security primitives, they themselves can be subjected to security threats. This section presents the fundamental security vulnerabilities present in spintronic devices that an adversary can exploit to tamper with the content or to cause the read/write failure. Although the discussion is focused on STT-RAM, similar attacks are also feasible on DWM and MRAM.

7.3.1 Sensitivities

Sensitivity to the external magnetic field: In STT-RAM, the write operation is done using an STT term (for low power consumption), and the external applied field H_a is kept zero (Equation 7.1). However, the external magnetic field can also be used to toggle the magnetization in the absence of a charge current (Figure 7.2). It should also be noted that magnetic field-based toggling is the foundation of MRAM [7]. Therefore, a strong-enough external magnetic field acting opposite to

Table 7.3 Temperature Dependency of MTJ Parameters for Vulnerability Analysis

Parameters	Model	Definitions
Retention [58]	$\tau = \tau_0 e^\Delta$, where $\Delta = \dfrac{H_k M_s(T) V}{2 k_B T}$	H_k: anisotropy field; $M_s(T)$: saturation magnetization; V: free layer volume
Saturation magnetization [59, 60] (M_s) [58, 59]	$M_s(T) = M_{s0} \left(\dfrac{T}{T_c} \right)^\beta$	M_{s0}: saturation magnetization at 0 K; T_c: Curie temperature; β: material-dependent constant
Polarization (P) [61]	$P(T) = P_0 \left(1 - \alpha_{sp} T^{\frac{3}{2}} \right)$	P_0: polarization at 0 K; α_{sp}: geometric constant
Conductance (G) [60]	$G(\theta) = G_T (1 + P^2 \cos\theta) + G_{SI0} T^{\frac{4}{3}}$	$G_T (G_{SI0})$: conductance due to direct elastic tunneling (imperfection effect); θ: tilt angle
$TMR(T) = \dfrac{TMR_0(T)}{1 + \left(\dfrac{V}{V_0} \right)^2}$ [62]	$TMR_0(T) = \dfrac{2 P_0^2 (1 - \alpha_{sp} T^{\frac{3}{2}})^2}{1 - P_0^2 (1 - \alpha_{sp} T^{\frac{3}{2}})^2 + \dfrac{G_{SI}(T)}{G_T(T)}}$	V_0: voltage at which TMR is halved

Source: S. Ghosh. *Proceedings of the IEEE*, 104(10):1864–1893, 2016.

the charge current (i.e., STT term) can prevent bit flipping during a write operation (leading to a write failure). The attacker can exploit this extra knob to corrupt the stored bit/prevent writing the bit. Both a permanent magnet, as well as an electromagnet, could be used for tampering by the adversary [5]. A similar issue persists for the read/write heads and magnetic nanowire of the DWM where the data can be tampered with using the external magnetic field.

Sensitivity to temperature: Different magnetic parameters of MTJ are functions of ambient temperature. Table 7.3 shows the relation between those parameters and temperature. It is evident that temperature modulation manifests itself in terms of functionality (read/write speed) and retention. Therefore, the adversary can employ this knob to tamper with the functionality or data persistence for information theft. The DWM heads have similar sensitivity to temperature.

Other tampering knobs: Localized laser-induced heating has also been employed for magnetization reversal as an alternative means to perform efficient writes [63,64]. A knowledgeable adversary can exploit this knob to tamper with the bits (to cause functional failures) or steal the information. X-ray, radio frequency, and mechanical stress can also affect the magnetization dynamics of MTJ (in STT-RAM, MRAM, and the read/write heads of DWM) and they can be exploited for tampering.

7.3.2 Prospects of Other Emerging Technologies

Besides spintronics, other emerging technologies such as memristor, PCM, and RRAM have also been explored from the security perspective due to the presence of noise and randomness such as one-time electroforming, random filament formation, and resistance variation [33]. The design of PUF using memristors [65–68], Phase charge RAM (PCRAM) [69], and RRAM [70,71] has been proposed to exploit the process variation. RRAM technology is also employed to resist differential power attack (DPA) [72]. In PCRAM, limited write endurance is known as a potential weakness that can be exploited for tampering. Techniques such as randomized address mapping [73], DRAM buffer [74], and incremental encryption [75] are proposed to address this concern. In summary, other emerging technologies have also demonstrated significant potential to aid in securing the future systems. Therefore, a hybrid system with a fusion of multiple emerging technologies can benefit significantly from the unique and complementary security features offered by these individual technologies.

7.4 Summary and Discussions

Spintronic technology is appealing for hardware security due to the presence of noise, randomness, and chaos as well as its advantages in memory and logic applications. Hardware security primitives need to be designed to fully exploit these properties as an understanding of these unique properties for security application becomes more mature. Recent research is focused toward designing security primitives such as TRNG and PUF by using devices like MTJ and DW nanowire and exploiting the properties discussed in this chapter. Understanding the properties of spintronic and DW-based devices and their implications in designing a secure system brings huge benefit to the hardware security community. Security vulnerabilities of spintronic and DW-based devices are also highlighted. Further research directed toward exploring new policies and methodologies can benefit the commercialization of this promising technology.

Acknowledgments

The author acknowledges the help from LOGICS lab students at The Pennsylvania State University and the University of South Florida and funding support in part by the National Science Foundation (NSF) grant CNS-1441757, Semiconductor Research Corporation (SRC) grant 2727.001, and DARPA Young Faculty Award # D15AP00089.

References

1. S. Ghosh. Spintronics and security: Prospects, vulnerabilities, attack models, and preventions. *Proceedings of the IEEE*, **104**(10):1864–1893, 2016.
2. A. S. Iyengar, S. Ghosh, and K. Ramclam. Domain wall magnets for embedded memory and hardware security. *IEEE Journal on Emerging and Selected Topics in Circuits and Systems*, **5**(1):40–50, 2015.
3. A. Iyengar, S. Ghosh, K. Ramclam, J.-W. Jang, and C.-W. Lin. Spintronic PUFs for security, trust, and authentication. *ACM Journal on Emerging Technologies in Computing Systems (JETC)*, **13**(1):4, 2016.
4. S. Ghosh and R. Govindaraj. Spintronics for associative computation and hardware security. In *Circuits and Systems (MWSCAS), 2015 IEEE 58th International Midwest Symposium on*, pages 1–4. IEEE, New York, NY, 2015.
5. J.-W. Jang, J. Park, S. Ghosh, and S. Bhunia. Self-correcting STTRAM under magnetic field attacks. In *Design Automation Conference (DAC), 2015 52nd ACM/EDAC/IEEE*, pages 1–6. IEEE, New York, NY, 2015.
6. L. Landau and E. Lifshitz. On the theory of the dispersion of magnetic permeability in ferromagnetic bodies. *Physikalische Zeitschrift der Sowjetunion*, **8**(153):101–114, 1935.

7. N. Rizzo, D. Houssameddine, J. Janesky et al. A fully functional 64 Mb DDR3 ST-MRAM built on 90 nm CMOS technology. *IEEE Transactions on Magnetics*, **49**(7):4441–4446, 2013.

8. M. H. Kryder and C. S. Kim. After hard drives what comes next? *IEEE Transactions on Magnetics*, **45**(10):3406–3413, 2009.

9. J. Zhang, P. M. Levy, S. Zhang, and V. Antropov. Identification of transverse spin currents in noncollinear magnetic structures. *Physical Review Letters*, **93**(25):256602, 2004.

10. A. Thiaville and Y. Nakatani. Domain-wall dynamics in nanowires and nanostrips. In *Spin Dynamics in Confined Magnetic Structures III*, pages 161–205. Springer, Berlin, 2006.

11. M. N. I. Khan, A. S. Iyengar, and S. Ghosh. Novel magnetic burn-in for retention testing of STTRAM. In *2017 Design, Automation & Test in Europe Conference & Exhibition (DATE)*, pages 666–669. IEEE, New York, NY, 2017.

12. T. Shinjo. *Nanomagnetism and Spintronics*. Chapter 3. Elsevier, Amsterdam, 1 edition, 2013.

13. C. Werndl. What are the new implications of chaos for unpredictability? *The British Journal for the Philosophy of Science*, **60**(1):195–220, 2009.

14. H. Naeimi, C. Augustine, A. Raychowdhury, S.-L. Lu, and J. Tschanz. STTRAM scaling and retention failure. *Intel Technology Journal*, **17**(1):54–75, 2013.

15. R. Bishnoi, M. Ebrahimi, F. Oboril, and M. B. Tahoori. Read disturb fault detection in STT-MRAM. In *Test Conference (ITC), 2014 IEEE International*, pages 1–7. IEEE, New York, NY, 2014.

16. Y. Ran, W. Kang, Y. Zhang, J.-O. Klein, and W. Zhao. Read disturbance issue for nanoscale STT-MRAM. In *Non-Volatile Memory System and Applications Symposium (NVMSA), 2015 IEEE*, pages 1–6. IEEE, New York, NY, 2015.

17. J. Sun, M. Gaidis, G. Hu, E. OSullivan, S. Brown, J. Nowak, P. Trouilloud, and D. Worledge. High-bias backhopping in nanosecond time-domain spin-torque switches of MgO-based magnetic tunnel junctions. *Journal of Applied Physics*, **105**(7):07D109, 2009.

18. SGMI Research Themes & Subjects. http://www.samsung.com/global/business/semiconductor/html/news-events/file/SGMI_Request_for_Proposal.pdf.

19. S. S. Parkin, M. Hayashi, and L. Thomas. Magnetic domain-wall racetrack memory. *Science*, **320**(5873):190–194, 2008.

20. A. Annunziata, M. Gaidis, L. Thomas et al. Racetrack memory cell array with integrated magnetic tunnel junction readout. In *Electron Devices Meeting (IEDM), 2011 IEEE International*, pages 24–3. IEEE, New York, NY, 2011.

21. S. Ghosh. Design methodologies for high density domain wall memory. In *Proceedings of the 2013 IEEE/ACM International Symposium on Nanoscale Architectures*, pages 30–31. IEEE Press, New York, NY, 2013.

22. S. Ghosh. Path to a terabyte of on-chip memory for petabit per second bandwidth with <5 watts of power. In *Proceedings of the 50th Annual Design Automation Conference*, page 145. ACM, New York, NY, 2013.

23. L. Berger. Exchange interaction between ferromagnetic domain wall and electric current in very thin metallic films. *Journal of Applied Physics*, **55**(6):1954–1956, 1984.

24. L. Berger. Motion of a magnetic domain wall traversed by fast-rising current pulses. *Journal of Applied Physics*, **71**(6):2721–2726, 1992.

25. P. Freitas and L. Berger. Observation of S-D exchange force between domain walls and electric current in very thin permalloy films. *Journal of Applied Physics*, **57**(4):1266–1269, 1985.

26. C.-Y. Hung and L. Berger. Exchange forces between domain wall and electric current in permalloy films of variable thickness. *Journal of Applied Physics*, **63**(8):4276–4278, 1988.

27. C.-Y. Hung, L. Berger, and C. Shih. Observation of a current-induced force on bloch lines in Ni-Fe thin films. *Journal of Applied Physics*, **67**(9):5941–5943, 1990.

28. E. Salhi and L. Berger. Current-induced displacements of bloch walls in Ni-Fe films of thickness 120–740 nm. *Journal of Applied Physics*, **76**(8):4787–4792, 1994.

29. M. Hayashi. *Current Driven Dynamics of Magnetic Domain Walls in Permalloy Nanowires*. Stanford University, California, 2007.

30. S. X. Wang and A. M. Taratorin. *Magnetic Information Storage Technology: A Volume in the Electromagnetism Series*. Academic Press, San Diego, 1999.

31. D. Nikonov, G. Bourianoff, and P. Gargini. Taxonomy of spintronics (a zoo of devices), 2006.

32. D. G. Hermann and J.-P. Nguenang. Chaos appearance during domain wall motion under electronic transfer in nanomagnets. *World Journal of Condensed Matter Physics*, **3**(3):136–143, 2013.

33. H. Okuno. Chaos and energy loss of nonlinear domain wall motion. *Journal of Applied Physics*, **81**(8):5233–5235, 1997.

34. Z. Li, J. He, and S. Zhang. Magnetization instability driven by spin torques. *Journal of Applied Physics*, **97**(10):10C703, 2005.

35. R. Hertel, W. Wulfhekel, and J. Kirschner. Domain-wall induced phase shifts in spin waves. *Physical Review Letters*, **93**(25):257202, 2004.

36. F.-X. Hu, B.-G. Shen, and J.-R. Sun. Magnetic entropy change in Ni 51.5 Mn 22.7 Ga 25.8 alloy. *Applied Physics Letters*, **76**(23):3460–3462, 2000.

37. A. Iyengar and S. Ghosh. Modeling and analysis of domain wall dynamics for robust and low-power embedded memory. In *Proceedings of the 51st Annual Design Automation Conference*, pages 1–6. ACM, New York, NY, 2014.

38. B. Jun and P. Kocher. The Intel random number generator. http://www.cryptography.com/intelRNG.pdf, 1999.

39. L. Zhang, X. Fong, C.-H. Chang, Z. H. Kong, and K. Roy. Highly reliable memory-based physical unclonable function using spin-transfer torque MRAM. In *Circuits and Systems (ISCAS), 2014 IEEE International Symposium on*, pages 2169–2172. IEEE, New York, NY, 2014.

40. L. Zhang, X. Fong, C.-H. Chang, Z. H. Kong, and K. Roy. Highly reliable spin-transfer torque magnetic RAM-based physical unclonable function with multi-response-bits per cell. *IEEE Transactions on Information Forensics and Security*, **10**(8):1630–1642, 2015.

41. J. Das, K. Scott, S. Rajaram, D. Burgett, and S. Bhanja. MRAM PUF: A novel geometry based magnetic PUF with integrated CMOS. *IEEE Transactions on Nanotechnology*, **14**(3):436–443, 2015.

42. A. Rukhin, J. Soto, J. Nechvatal et al. A statistical test suite for the validation of random number generators and pseudo random number generators for cryptographic applications, 1997.

43. X. Zhang, G. Sun, Y. Zhang, Y. Chen, H. Li, W. Wen, and J. Di. A novel PUF based on cell error rate distribution of STT-RAM. In *Design Automation Conference (ASP-DAC), 2016 21st Asia and South Pacific*, pages 342–347. IEEE, New York, NY, 2016.

44. E. I. Vatajelu, G. Di Natale, and P. Prinetto. Security primitives (PUF and TRNG) with STT-MRAM. In *VLSI Test Symposium (VTS), 2016 IEEE 34th*, pages 1–4. IEEE, New York, NY, 2016.

45. T. Marukame, T. Tanamoto, and Y. Mitani. Extracting physically unclonable function from spin transfer switching characteristics in magnetic tunnel junctions. *IEEE Transactions on Magnetics*, **50**(11):1–4, 2014.

46. L. Zhang, X. Fong, C.-H. Chang, Z. H. Kong, and K. Roy. Optimizating emerging nonvolatile memories for dual-mode applications: Data storage and key generator. *IEEE Transactions on Computer-Aided Design of Integrated Circuits and Systems*, **34**(7):1176–1187, 2015.

47. N. Rathi, S. Ghosh, A. Iyengar, and H. Naeimi. Data privacy in non-volatile cache: Challenges, attack models and solutions. In *Design Automation Conference (ASP-DAC), 2016 21st Asia and South Pacific*, pages 348–353. IEEE, New York, NY, 2016.

48. J. Daemen and V. Rijmen. *The Design of Rijndael: AES—The Advanced Encryption Standard*. Springer Science & Business Media, 2013.

49. Y. Wang, H. Yu, D. Sylvester, and P. Kong. Energy efficient in-memory AES encryption based on nonvolatile domain-wall nanowire. In *Design, Automation and Test in Europe Conference and Exhibition (DATE), 2014*, pages 1–4. IEEE, New York, NY, 2014.

50. A. Fukushima, T. Seki, K. Yakushiji, H. Kubota, H. Imamura, S. Yuasa, and K. Ando. Spin dice: A scalable truly random number generator based on spintronics. *Applied Physics Express*, **7**(8):083001, 2014.

51. W. H. Choi, Y. Lv, J. Kim, A. Deshpande, G. Kang, J.-P. Wang, and C. H. Kim. A magnetic tunnel junction based true random number generator with conditional perturb and real-time output probability tracking. In *Electron Devices Meeting (IEDM), 2014 IEEE International*, pages 12–5. IEEE, New York, NY, 2014.

52. X. Fong, M.-C. Chen, and K. Roy. Generating true random numbers using on-chip complementary polarizer spin-transfer torque magnetic tunnel junctions. In *Device Research Conference (DRC), 2014 72nd Annual*, pages 103–104. IEEE, New York, NY, 2014.

53. T. Weeks, Y. Lu, and X. Wang. Magnetic precession based true random number generator, January 6, 2009. U.S. Patent App. 12/349,354.

54. X. Zhu, W. Wu, D. M. Jacobson, S. H. Kang, and K. H. Yuen. Magnetic tunnel junction based random number generator, August 18, 2015. U.S. Patent 9,110,746.

55. K. Lee, T. Kim, X. Zhu, D. M. Jacobson, R. S. Madala, W. Wu, J. P. Kim, and S. H. Kang. Magnetic tunnel junction based random number generator, October 15, 2012. U.S. Patent App. 13/651,954.

56. T. Tanamoto, N. Shimomura, S. Ikegawa, M. Matsumoto, S. Fujita, and H. Yoda. High-speed magnetoresistive random-access memory random number generator using error-correcting code. *Japanese Journal of Applied Physics*, **50**(4S):04DM01, 2011.

57. Y. Oishi, Y. Higo, H. Kano, M. Hosomi, H. Ohmori, K. Yamane, and K. Bessho. Random number generating device, random number generating method, and security chip, January 8, 2013. U.S. Patent 8,351,603.

58. A. Nigam, C. W. Smullen, V. Mohan, E. Chen, S. Gurumurthi, and M. R. Stan, Delivering on the promise of universal memory for spin-transfer torque RAM (STT-RAM). In *Low Power Electronics and Design (ISLPED) 2011 International Symposium on*, pages 121–126. IEEE, New York, NY, 2011.

59. P. Weiss. L'hypothèse du champ moléculaire et la propriété ferromagnétique. *Journal of Theoretical and Applied Physics*, **6**(1):661–690. 1907.

60. A. Raghunathan, Y. Melikhov, J. E. Snyder, and D. Jiles. Modeling the temperature dependence of hysteresis based on Jiles–Atherton theory. *IEEE Transactions on Magnetics*, **45**(10):3954–3957, 2009.

61. C. H. Shang, J. Nowak, R. Jansen, and J. S. Moodera. Temperature dependence of magnetoresistance and surface magnetization in ferromagnetic tunnel junctions. *Physical Review B*, **58**(6):R2917, 1998.

62. Y. Lu, X. Li, G. Xiao, R. Altman, W. Gallagher, A. Marley, K. Roche, and S. Parkin. Bias voltage and temperature dependence of magnetotunneling effect. *Journal of Applied Physics*, **83**(11):6515–6517, 1998.

63. W. Lin, M. Hehn, L. Chaput, B. Negulescu, S. Andrieu, F. Montaigne, and S. Mangin. Giant spin-dependent thermoelectric effect in magnetic tunnel junctions. *Nature Communications*, **3**:744, 2012.

64. Z. Al Azim, X. Fong, T. Ostler, R. Chantrell, and K. Roy. Laser induced magnetization reversal for detection in optical interconnects. *IEEE Electron Device Letters*, **35**(12):1317–1319, 2014.

65. G. S. Rose, N. McDonald, L.-K. Yan, and B. Wysocki. A write-time based memristive PUF for hardware security applications. In *Proceedings of the International Conference on Computer-Aided Design*, pages 830–833. IEEE Press, New York, NY, 2013.

66. J. Rajendran, R. Karri, J. B. Wendt, M. Potkonjak, N. R. McDonald, G. S. Rose, and B. T. Wysocki. Nanoelectronic solutions for hardware security. *IACR Cryptology ePrint Archive*, **2012**:575, 2012.

67. G. S. Rose, N. McDonald, L.-K. Yan, B. Wysocki, and K. Xu. Foundations of memristor based PUF architectures. In *Nanoscale Architectures (NANOARCH), 2013 IEEE/ACM International Symposium on*, pages 52–57. IEEE, New York, NY, 2013.

68. G. S. Rose, D. Kudithipudi, G. Khedkar, N. McDonald, B. Wysocki, and L.-K. Yan. Nanoelectronics and hardware security. In *Network Science and Cybersecurity*, pages 105–123. Springer, Berlin, 2014.

69. L. Zhang, Z. H. Kong, C.-H. Chang, A. Cabrini, and G. Torelli. Exploiting process variations and programming sensitivity of phase change memory for reconfigurable physical unclonable functions. *IEEE Transactions on Information Forensics and Security*, **9**(6):921–932, 2014.

70. P.-Y. Chen, R. Fang, R. Liu, C. Chakrabarti, Y. Cao, and S. Yu. Exploiting resistive cross-point array for compact design of physical unclonable function. In *Hardware Oriented Security and Trust (HOST), 2015 IEEE International Symposium on*, pages 26–31. IEEE, New York, NY, 2015.

71. R. Govindaraj and S. Ghosh. A strong arbiter PUF using resistive RAM within 1T-1R memory architecture. In *Computer Design (ICCD), 2016 IEEE 34th International Conference on*, pages 141–148. IEEE, New York, NY, 2016.

72. G. Khedkar and D. Kudithipudi. RRAM motifs for mitigating differential power analysis attacks (DPA). In *VLSI (ISVLSI), 2012 IEEE Computer Society Annual Symposium on*, pages 88–93. IEEE, New York, NY, 2012.

73. M. K. Qureshi, J. Karidis, M. Franceschini, V. Srinivasan, L. Lastras, and B. Abali. Enhancing lifetime and security of PCM-based main memory with start-gap wear leveling. In *Proceedings of the 42nd Annual IEEE/ACM International Symposium on Microarchitecture*, pages 14–23. ACM, New York, NY, 2009.

74. N. H. Seong, D. H. Woo, and H.-H. S. Lee. Security refresh: Prevent malicious wear-out and increase durability for phase-change memory with dynamically randomized address mapping. *ACM SIGARCH Computer Architecture News*, **38**(3):383–394, 2010.

75. S. Chhabra and Y. Solihin. i-NVMM: A secure non-volatile main memory system with incremental encryption. In *Computer Architecture (ISCA), 2011 38th Annual International Symposium on*, pages 177–188. IEEE, New York, NY, 2011.

Chapter 8

Polarity-Controllable Silicon NanoWire FET-Based Security

Yu Bi, Pierre-Emmanuel Gaillardon, X. Sharon Hu,
Michael Niemier, Jiann-Shiun Yuan, and Yier Jin

Contents

The emergence of hardware Trojans has largely reshaped the traditional view that the hardware layer can be blindly trusted. Hardware Trojans, which are often in the form of maliciously inserted circuitry, may impact the original design by data leakage or circuit malfunction. Hardware counterfeiting and IP piracy are the other two serious issues costing the U.S. economy more than $200 billion annually [1]. In order to address such threats, various hardware Trojan detection methods and hardware metering methods have been developed [2–6]. Besides circuit-level security solutions, cybersecurity researchers also rely on layered security protection approaches and have developed various methods to protect the higher abstraction layer through security enhancement at the lower abstraction layer. Through this chain, cybersecurity protection schemes have been pushed downward from virtual machine to hypervisor [7]. Following this trend, new methods are under development through which the hardware infrastructure is modified to directly support sophisticated security policies so that the system-level protection scheme will be more efficient [8].

It is a rather common practice to think of dedicated hardware primitives that support the various security applications in the multiple layers of the system hierarchy. Physical unclonable functions (PUFs) to produce unique IDs, power regulators to hinder power analysis attacks, or encryption hardware accelerators are examples of these special hardware that only find applications in the security context. A large amount of research and experimentation has been carried out on the design of these primitives based on the currently prevailing CMOS technology. However, the security provided by these primitives comes at the cost of large overheads mostly in terms of power, delay, and area.

The development of emerging technologies provides hardware security researchers with opportunities to utilize some of the otherwise unusable properties of emerging technologies in security applications. Originally developed as alternatives to CMOS technology to overcome the scaling limit, emerging technologies also demonstrated their unique features, which, besides improving circuit performance, can simplify circuit structure for security purposes such as IP protection and Trojan detection [9,10]. While traditional metrics, such as power, delay, etc., are the major criteria to evaluate the merits of emerging devices, in this chapter, we will include the security consideration in the overall performance measurements to fully compare the emerging devices with CMOS technology. Considering the large amount of emerging device models, including graphene transistors, atomic switches, memristors, MOTT FET, spin FET, nanomagnetic and all-spin logic, spin wave devices, OST-RAM, magnetoresistive random-access memory (MRAM), spintronic devices, etc. [11], two fundamental questions have recently been raised related to their applications in the hardware security domain: (1) *Can emerging technology provide a more efficient hardware infrastructure than CMOS technology in countering hardware Trojans and IP piracy?* (2) *What properties should the emerging technology-based hardware infrastructure provide so that software-level protection schemes can be better supported?*

While most work with emerging technologies for security purposes to date has been with implementations like PUFs [12], PUFs essentially leverage device-to-device process variation. In some sense, this suggests that noisier devices are more useful. Besides these efforts, we present a collection of design concepts that leverage the unique properties of emerging technologies, other than relying on noisy devices, for IP protection and hardware attack prevention. Specifically, the chapter considers one of the emerging technologies: silicon NanoWire (SiNW) FETs [13], and makes the following contributions. To assist IP protection, we introduce SiNW FET-based camouflaging layout and polymorphic gates to help obfuscate layouts and netlists. Preliminary experimental results and hardware infrastructure designs are provided. Simulation results demonstrate that these emerging technologies outperform CMOS in area and power, while maintaining the same qualitative level of security.

8.1 Silicon NanoWire FET

In several nanoscale FET devices (45 nm and below), the superposition of n-type and p-type carriers is observable under normal bias conditions. The phenomenon, called ambipolarity, exists in various materials such as silicon [14], carbon nanotubes [15], and graphene [16]. Through the control of this ambipolarity, we can adjust the device polarity during the postdeployment stage. Transistors with a controllable polarity have already been experimentally fabricated in several novel technologies, such as carbon nanotubes [17], graphene [18], and SiNWs [19,20]. Given an additional gate, the operation of these FETs is enabled by the regulation of Schottky barriers at the source/drain junctions. An example of an emerging device considered in this chapter is a vertically stacked SiNW FET, featuring two Gate-All-Around (GAA) electrodes [13]. Figure 8.1 shows the three-dimensional (3D) structure of the SiNW FET. Vertically stacked GAA SiNWs represent a natural evolution of FinFET structures, providing better electrostatic control over the channel and, consequently, superior scalability properties [13].

In this device, one gate electrode, the Control Gate (CG), acts conventionally by turning on and off the device depending on the gate voltage. The other electrode, the Polarity Gate (PG), acts on the side regions of the device, in proximity to the Source/Drain (S/D) Schottky junctions, switching the device polarity dynamically between n- and p-type. The input and output voltage levels are compatible, enabling directly cascadable logic gates [13,21].

While many emerging devices demonstrate the polarity control property (SiNW FETs, graphene transistors, CNTFETs, NEM relays, etc.), we focus on SiNW FET due to their full process compatibility with the current silicon technology and their high probability of industrial transfer in the near term. In addition, both single transistors and basic logic gates for SiNW FETs have been experimentally demonstrated. Furthermore, a simple compact model is available. However, note that the techniques presented in this chapter are not limited only to this device, but rather can be applied to any other polarity-controllable transistor devices.

8.2 Silicon NanoWire FET in Hardware Security

The characteristics of SiNW FETs, as shown in Figure 8.1, prove to us that this new device is not a drop-in alternative to traditional MOSFETs. Instead, it is equipped with unique physical properties that may be leveraged by hardware security approaches to achieve various highly efficient implementations for IP protection, Trojan detection, and side-channel attack prevention. In this section, we will introduce SiNW FET-based circuit structures for hardware security applications.

8.2.1 SiNW FET-Based Camouflaging

Counterfeiting and IP piracy are among the most serious security threats to the IC industry. In order to prevent attackers from learning the circuit schematic through reverse engineering, various protection methods have been developed among which camouflaging is a popular

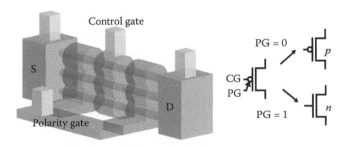

Figure 8.1 3D sketch of the SiNW FETs featuring two independent gates and theirs associated symbol. (Adapted from M. De Marchi et al. *Electron Devices Meeting (IEDM), 2012 IEEE International*, pages 8.4.1–8.4.4, December 2012.)

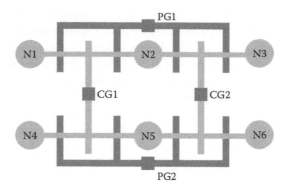

Figure 8.2 One tile layout for either an NAND or an XOR gate under different pin connections. (Adapted from P.-E. Gaillardon et al. *Philosophical Transactions of the Royal Society of London A*, 372(2012), 2014.)

solution [22–24]. This method relies on layout-level obfuscation with similar layouts for different gates. As a result, attackers cannot easily recover the circuit structure through reverse engineering [25]. However, the overhead in applying CMOS camouflaging gates can be rather high such that both power consumption and area would increase significantly for high-level protection.

8.2.1.1 *Uniqueness of the SiNW FET Layout*

As demonstrated in Reference 21, only four SiNW FETs are required to build an XOR or a NAND gate (see Figure 8.2). This one tile layout includes four SiNW FETs where circles stand for drain/source pins and bars represent the polarity gate (or control gate). A further analysis reveals that by connecting pins with different signals, the four SiNW FETs in Figure 8.2 can perform five other meaningful functions besides the NAND and XOR. A list of all these connections as well as the corresponding output functions is presented in Table 8.1. Note that the functionality of the gate is fixed postfabrication with gate signals being connected to physical terminals. After these connections, the polarity gates perform as normal input gates and no extra control circuitry is required to maintain the functionality.

8.2.1.2 *SiNW FET-Based Camouflaging Layout*

In Reference 25, a CMOS camouflaging standard cell utilizes 12 transistors and a group of contacts to achieve three logic functions. There are more contacts than normal standard cell, since some of the contacts work as dummies to camouflage the functionality of this logic cell. Different combinations of true and dummy contacts deliver three different logic functions. Certainly, the added transistors and contacts increase the area and power overhead. Compared to the 4-T NAND, 4-T NOR, and 8-T XOR gates, the area overhead of the CMOS camouflaging layout ranges from 50% to 200%.

It is not surprising that CMOS camouflaging gates consume a significantly larger area than do normal gates. Owing to the fixed polarities of both PMOS and NMOS, designers must prepare spare transistors in order to build a camouflaging gate. However, the polarity-controllable SiNW FETs, with their unique property, can help build camouflaging gates without using extra FETs.

Table 8.1   List of Possible Functions from One Tile Layout

PG1	PG2	CG1	CG2	N1	N2	N3	N4	N5	N6	Function (Y)
GND	VDD	A	B	Y	VDD	Y	GND	N/A	Y	NAND
GND	VDD	A	B	VDD	N/A	Y	Y	GND	Y	NOR
Bbar	B	A	Abar	VDD	Y	GND	GND	Y	VDD	XOR
Bbar	B	A	Abar	GND	Y	VDD	VDD	Y	GND	XNOR
Bbar	B	A	Abar	Cbar	Y	C	C	Y	Cbar	XOR3
Bbar	B	A	Abar	C	Y	Cbar	Cbar	Y	C	XNOR3
GND	VDD	A	X	X	VDD	Y	X	GND	Y	buffer

SiNW FETs, or more precisely the polarity-controllable feature, provide an ideal candidate for camouflaging gates since all these gates share the same structure with only four SiNW FETs used. In fact, the additional polarity gate is leveraged in the camouflaging gate layout to reduce the transistor count. The overhead of this SiNW-based camouflaging layout is negligible, which is mainly caused by additional insignificant dummy contacts. Following this concept, Figure 8.3 shows a more complex camouflaging gate, which can act as NAND, NOR, XOR, or XNOR given the different sets of dummy contacts. As described in Table 8.2, different connections can result in four different operations for the same input signals. Again, only four SiNW FETs are used in this camouflaging gate. Compared to the CMOS-based camouflaging gate that needs 12 transistors for a NAND-NOR-XOR gate, the proposed circuit structure can reduce two-thirds of the transistor count. However, five more contacts are used in the SiNW FET-based camouflaging gate,

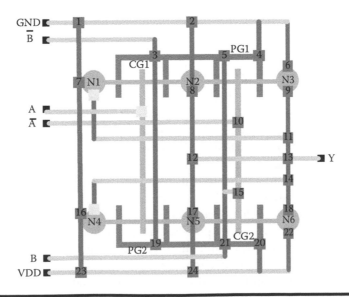

Figure 8.3   Camouflaging layout with four possible functions: NAND, NOR, XOR, or XNOR.

Table 8.2   List of True and Dummy Contacts to Realize Complex Functions for Layout in Figure 8.3

Function	Contacts	
	True	*Dummy*
NAND	1, 4, 8, 9, 11,	2, 3, 5, 6, 7, 10,
	13, 15, 16, 18, 20, 24	12, 14, 17, 19, 21, 22, 23
NOR	2, 4, 7, 9, 13,	1, 3, 5, 6, 8, 10,
	14, 15, 17, 18, 20, 23	11, 12, 16, 19, 21, 22, 24
XOR	1, 3, 6, 8, 10, 11, 12,	2, 4, 5, 7, 9, 13, 14,
	16, 17, 18, 21, 22	15, 19, 20, 23, 24
XNOR	1, 5, 6, 8, 10, 11, 12,	2, 3, 4, 7, 9, 13, 14,
	16, 17, 18, 19, 22	15, 20, 21, 23, 24

although the area overheads incurred by the extra contacts are negligible considering the transistor count reduction.

To further evaluate the security improvement, the security metric has been used to check how easily an attacker can guess the full functionality of a given design containing camouflaging gates. That is, if one camouflaging layout can achieve four functions, the chance that the attacker can retrieve the correct result is 25%. Therefore, assuming that there are N SiNW FET camouflaging layouts incorporated in the design, the attacker may have to try up to 4^N times to get the correct design layout. As a consequence, it is promising that the SiNW FET-based camouflaging layout, which has more functionality and less area consumption compared to CMOS counterparts, can offer a higher level of protection to circuit designs.

8.2.2 SiNW FET-Based Polymorphic Gates

Polymorphic electronics, which were first introduced in Reference 26, are based on the idea of having multiple functionalities built in the same cell and deciding the input-output relation by means of a controllable factor in the circuit. For instance, a polymorphic gate presented in Reference 26 would be an AND gate when the VDD is 3.3 V and function as an OR gate when VDD is lowered to 1.5 V. Such multifunctional gates would prove useful in a number of applications. Circuits that change functionality with temperature variation can find use in aerospace applications, or those that respond to VDD variation could be used to change functionality when the battery is low. Also, polymorphic electronics could prove useful in evolvable, intelligent, or self-checking hardware [27]. For security purposes, adding polymorphic gates to a digital circuit can hide the real functionality of the circuit. Since the circuit functions correctly only in a certain configuration of the control signals known to the designer, even if the adversary knows the whole netlist (including the dummy and true contacts), he or she will not be able to utilize the circuit in his or her own design. Carefully encrypting a logic in this way can ensure that it will take too long for the adversary to find the key (a vector constructed from all the morphing signals of the

Table 8.3 Summary of Developed Polymorphic Gates

Function	Morph Method	Number of Transistors	Published in
AND/OR	27/125°C Temperature	6	[29]
AND/OR/XOR	3.3/0.0/1.5 V External signal	10	[29]
AND/OR	3.3/0.0 V External signal	6	[29]
NAND/NOR/	0.0/0.9/1.1/1.8 V		
XOR/AND	External signal	11	[29]
AND/OR	1.2/3.3 V VDD	8	[29]
NAND/NOR	3.3/1.8 V VDD	6	(Fabricated) [26]
NAND/XOR	0/3.3 V External signal	9	[27]
NAND/NOR	VDD and GND interchange	4	This work

polymorphic gates) [28]. Therefore, the polymorphic gate becomes a good candidate for integrated circuits protection against IP piracy.

Traditionally, a number of CMOS-based polymorphic gates have been reported with different control methods such as temperature, VDD variation, and external signal level. A summary of the different polymorphic circuits can be seen in Table 8.3. The authors of Reference 26 designed polymorphic gates by an evolution algorithm. However, the circuits face issues during simulation as the circuit was evolved to satisfy certain constraints that do not include all aspects of a complete design. For example, the NAND/NOR polymorphic gate, based on an external signal, will experience states where the transistors have to compete over the output, causing the circuit to draw constant current through those paths. Further, since inputs may be shorted to ground or VDD during certain states, it is difficult to connect multiple stages of these gates in sequence. The circuit based on a VDD variation is the most practical solution and was fabricated [26]; however, redesigning it in newer technologies where the VDD range is limited would be a difficult task. Another promising solution presented in Reference 27 is a NAND/XOR gate controlled by a control signal using 9 transistors. The gate has a good performance even when we redesigned it in the 22 nm FinFET technology node.

8.2.2.1 SiNW FET-Based Polymorphic Gates

Here, we present a novel approach to designing polymorphic gates using polarity-controllable FETs. The ability to control the polarity of a transistor enables us to build polymorphic cells with a much less number of transistors. As shown in Figure 8.4, the basic NAND and NOR gate structure is similar for both the CMOS and the SiNW FET. The polarity control gate does not reduce the number of transistors required to implement NAND and NOR using SiNW FET technology. However, this unique property allows us to change the functionality of the gate simply by interchanging the VDD and GND. Note that interchanging the VDD and GND connections in any CMOS-based logic will produce the complement of the original function at the output but full voltage swing at the output will not be achieved due to the presence of PMOS in the pull-down

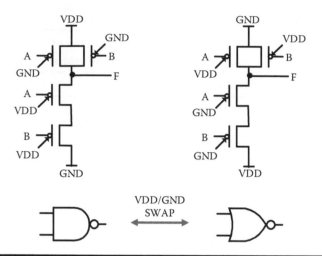

Figure 8.4 A polymorphic NAND and NOR using SiNW FET.

network or NMOS in the pull-up network. Therefore, by using this method, one can gather the VDD and GND terminals of the NAND and NOR gates in a combinational logic into a vector and construct a "logic encryption key." As opposed to the work presented in Reference 28, which adds additional XOR or XNOR gates into a logic gate to realize the logic encryption scheme and thus incurs performance overhead, this approach has zero overhead in terms of gate count and trivial wiring cost due to the switching of VDD/GND. The comparison of transistor counts for different polymorphic gates is listed in Table 8.3.

8.2.2.2 Polymorphic Logic Gates-Based Logic Locking

As mentioned, the large overhead of conventional logic locking precludes its application on real silicon chips. To further reduce the surcharge, instead of incorporating more logic gates (e.g., XOR/XNOR gates in Reference 28) for logic locking, our approach is to replace some portions of the original netlist with SiNW FET-based polymorphic logic gates.

To fully elaborate our proposed technique, the C17 benchmark circuit is adopted in Figure 8.5. The original C17 circuit consists of six NAND logic gates with five primary inputs and two primary outputs shown in Figure 8.5a. As explained in the previous section, an SiNW NAND gate can be naturally switched into an SiNW NOR gate using a polymorphic technique without any extra hardware. In this regard, we replace two original NAND gates by two polymorphic gates with two extracted locking keys in Figure 8.5b. It is important to note that the replacement does not add area overhead onto the netlist. The extracted two wires are almost negligible compared with the transistor size. We then define that when both $K1$ and $K2$ are zeros, it is original netlist with correct outputs. Otherwise, the polymorphic gate is switched to the NOR gate, resulting most likely in wrong outputs.

For instance, on applying input pattern "01000," a correct output "00" is produced for the C17 circuit. When $K1=1$ and $K2=1$, two polymorphic logic gates switch from the original NAND gates to NOR gates, consequently resulting "11" at the primary outputs. However, when one polymorphic gate is encrypted with either $K1=1$ or $K2=1$, wrong outputs "01" and "11" can be produced, respectively. With those three different key combinations, we can produce two wrong outputs. The value of Hamming distance is 50% for output "01", while HD is 100% for output "11".

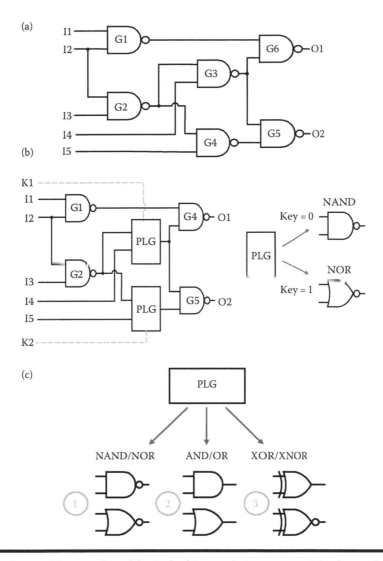

Figure 8.5 **Polymorphic gate-based logic locking technique: (a) original C17 benchmark circuit; (b) modified C17 with polymorphic gates (in this case, NAND/NOR polymorphic gates are adopted); and (c) three different polymorphic logic combinations.**

Besides the exemplified NAND/NOR polymorphic gate, the other two derivatives are also shown in Figure 8.5c. A SiNW FET-based AND gate can be reconfigured to the OR gate, while XOR can be switched to the XNOR gate. With more configurable units in the encrypted netlist, it certainly adds more complexity on discovering the locking key values. Note that we include three polymorphic gates. The detailed security evaluation will be discussed in the following section.

8.2.2.3 Experimental Results

Our experiments use combinational benchmark circuits from ISCAS'85 benchmark suites. Synopsys HSPICE is adopted for circuit-level simulation to characterize SiNW-based polymorphic gates.

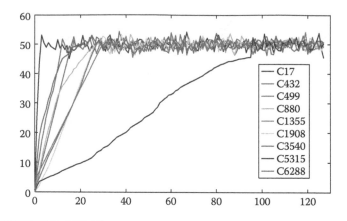

Figure 8.6   Hamming distance of ISCAS'85 benchmark circuits.

We use Java to accomplish the algorithm of the proposed logic locking technique. 1000 Random input patterns are applied to the encrypted netlist to further evaluate the Hamming distance. All benchmark circuits are synthesized using the Synopsys Design Compiler with CMOS 20 nm and SiNW 20 nm technology, respectively. The area and power overheads are retrieved accordingly.

To evaluate the security of logic locking, a Hamming distance-based metric is mostly applied [28,30]. Figure 8.6 shows the Hamming distance analysis of the ISCAS'85 benchmark circuits using our proposed algorithm. Apparently, 50% Hamming distance is achieved for all benchmark circuits. The slope of the traces implies the effectiveness of the logic locking technique. If the slope is steeper, a smaller amount of key gates are required for encryption, thereby reducing the overhead.

The majority of benchmark circuits hit the 50% mark in less than 40 key gates, except for one outlier C5315, which needs 95 key gates. Furthermore, as shown in Figure 8.6, once a design reaches 50%, its Hamming distance value does not change much even with more key gates inserted. In other words, the minimum value of key gates for achieving 50% HD is defined as the encryption threshold. The defender can intentionally increase the key gates for extra obfuscation without changing the robustness of logic locking.

Figure 8.7 shows the area overhead of all benchmark circuits with the logic locking technique. Referred to the previous work [28], we do not include the overhead of generating key bits, since it is out of scope of this work. Apparently, the polymorphic gate-based logic locking has a drastically lower area consumption than the other two techniques. When the circuit scale increases, the overhead is merely negligible for our proposed technique. It is worth noting that the C499 circuit has an almost zero area overhead, mainly because the key gate is the XOR/XNOR polymorphic gate, which is less area for SiNW FET than for CMOS.

Figure 8.8 shows the power–delay product overhead of all benchmark circuits. Except for the C499 circuit, all benchmark circuits are more favorable to NAND/NOR and AND/OR polymorphic gates. It is obvious that the polymorphic gate-based logic locking barely provokes any overhead on the power–delay product, where <1% overhead applies to every benchmark circuit. On the other hand, random and fault analysis-based logic encryption displays a considerable power–delay overhead upon original circuits, where >20% overhead occurs at the majority of benchmark circuits.

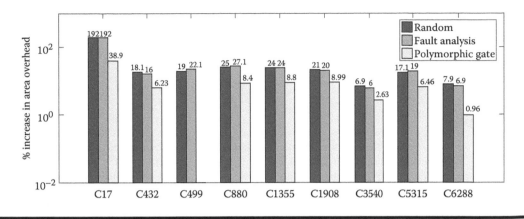

Figure 8.7 **Area overhead of random, fault analysis, and polymorphic gate-based logic locking.**

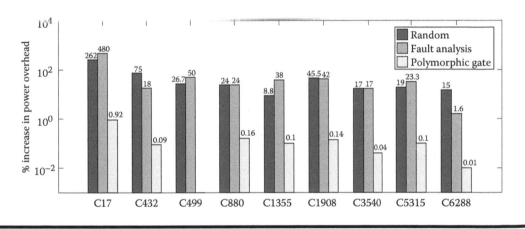

Figure 8.8 **Power–delay product overhead of random, fault analysis, and polymorphic gate-based logic locking.**

8.3 Conclusion

Emerging device technology was investigated in this chapter for its applications in the hardware security domain. Instead of simply replacing CMOS transistors with emerging devices, our work, for the first time, evaluated the unique properties of new devices in helping protect circuit designs and countering IP piracy. SiNW FETs, with their unique polarity-controllable feature, were used for the case study. Two security primitives, camouflaging layout and polymorphic gates, were fully studied and implemented by SiNW FETs. Through these examples, we demonstrated that the unique properties of emerging technologies, if used properly, can provide high-level circuit protection with extremely low-performance overhead. Besides the simulation results, as emerging technologies become more mature, measurements from fabricated devices will also be collected to verify the claim that circuit protection methods can benefit from emerging technologies.

Acknowledgments

We would like to thank Dr. Jian Zhang for providing us a compact model of SiNW FET. Dr. Gaillardon is supported by the National Science Foundation (NSF-1644592).

References

1. Jeff Hardy. Estimating the global economic and social impacts of counterfeiting and piracy. International Chamber of Commerce (ICC), 2011.
2. D. Agrawal, S. Baktir, D. Karakoyunlu, P. Rohatgi, and B. Sunar. Trojan detection using IC fingerprinting. In *IEEE Symposium on Security and Privacy*, pages 296–310, Oakland, CA, USA, 2007.
3. Y. Alkabani and F. Koushanfar. Active hardware metering for intellectual property protection and security. In *USENIX Security*, pages 291–306, 2007.
4. Y. Jin and Y. Makris. Hardware Trojan detection using path delay fingerprint. In *IEEE International Workshop on Hardware-Oriented Security and Trust*, pages 51–57, Anaheim, CA, USA, 2008.
5. M. Potkonjak, A. Nahapetian, M. Nelson, and T. Massey. Hardware Trojan horse detection using gate-level characterization. In *DAC'09: Proceedings of the 46th Annual Design Automation Conference*, pages 688–693, 2009.
6. Y. Jin, B. Yang, and Y. Makris. Cycle-accurate information assurance by proof-carrying based signal sensitivity tracing. In *IEEE International Symposium on Hardware-Oriented Security and Trust (HOST)*, pages 99–106, 2013.
7. A. Seshadri, M. Luk, N. Qu, and A. Perrig. SecVisor: A tiny hypervisor to provide lifetime kernel code integrity for commodity OSes. In *Proceedings of Twenty-First ACM SIGOPS Symposium on Operating Systems Principles, SOSP'07*, pages 335–350, Stevenson, WA, USA, 2007.
8. Y. Jin and D. Oliveira. Extended abstract: Trustworthy SOC architecture with on-demand security policies and HW-SW cooperation. In *5th Workshop on SoCs, Heterogeneous Architectures and Workloads (SHAW-5)*, Orlando, FL, USA, 2014.
9. Y. Bi, P.-E. Gaillardon, X. Hu, M. Niemier, J.-S. Yuan, and Y. Jin. Leveraging emerging technology for hardware security—Case study on silicon nanowire FETs and graphene SymFETs. In *Test Symposium (ATS), 2014 IEEE 23rd Asian*, pages 342–347, Hangzhou, China, Nov. 2014.
10. Y. Bi, K. Shamsi, J.-S. Yuan, P.-E. Gaillardon, G. D. Micheli, X. Yin, X. S. Hu, M. Niemier, and Y. Jin. Emerging technology-based design of primitives for hardware security. *Journal on Emerging Technologies in Computing Systems*, 13(1):3:1–3:19, 2016.
11. International Technology Roadmap for Semiconductors. Semiconductor Industry Association (SIA). 2013.
12. A. Iyengar, K. Ramclam, and S. Ghosh. DWM-PUF: A low-overhead, memory-based security primitive. In *Hardware-Oriented Security and Trust (HOST), 2014 IEEE International Symposium on*, pages 154–159, Arlington, VA, USA, 2014.
13. M. De Marchi, D. Sacchetto, S. Frache, J. Zhang, P.-E. Gaillardon, Y. Leblebici, and G. De Micheli. Polarity control in double-gate, gate-all-around vertically stacked silicon nanowire FETs. In *Electron Devices Meeting (IEDM), 2012 IEEE International*, pages 8.4.1–8.4.4, San Francisco, CA, USA, December 2012.
14. A. Colli, S. Pisana, A. Fasoli, J. Robertson, and A. C. Ferrari. Electronic transport in ambipolar silicon nanowires. *Physica Status Solidi (b)*, 244(11):4161–4164, 2007.
15. R. Martel, V. Derycke, C. Lavoie, J. Appenzeller, K. K. Chan, J. Tersoff, and P. Avouris. Ambipolar electrical transport in semiconducting single-wall carbon nanotubes. *Physical Review Letters*, 87: 256805, 2001.
16. A. K. Geim and K. S. Novoselov. The rise of graphene. *Nature Materials*, 6:183–191, 2007.
17. Y.-M. Lin, J. Appenzeller, J. Knoch, and P. Avouris. High-performance carbon nanotube field-effect transistor with tunable polarities. *Nanotechnology, IEEE Transactions on*, 4(5):481–489, 2005.

18. N. Harada, K. Yagi, S. Sato, and N. Yokoyama. A polarity-controllable graphene inverter. *Applied Physics Letters*, **96**(1):2010.

19. J. Appenzeller, J. Knoch, E. Tutuc, M. Reuter, and S. Guha. Dual-gate silicon nanowire transistors with nickel silicide contacts. In *Electron Devices Meeting, 2006. IEDM'06. International*, pages 1–4, San Francisco, CA, USA, 2006.

20. A. Heinzig, S. Slesazeck, F. Kreupl, T. Mikolajick, and W. M. Weber. Reconfigurable silicon nanowire transistors. *Nano Letters*, **12**(1):119–124, 2012.

21. P.-E. Gaillardon, S. Bobba, M. D. Marchi, D. Sacchetto, and G. D. Micheli. Nanowire systems: Technology and design. *Philosophical Transactions of the Royal Society of London A*, **372**(2012): 2014.

22. L.-W. Chow, J. Baukus, and W. Clark. U.S. Patent. Integrated circuits protected against reverse engineering and method for fabricating the same using an apparent metal contact line terminating on field oxide, 2002.

23. R. P. Cocchi, J. P. Baukus, B. J. Wang, L. W. Chow, and P. Ouyang. U.S. Patent. Building block for a secure CMOS logic cell library, 2012.

24. L. W. Chow, J. P. Baukus, B. J. Wang, and R. P. Cocchi. U.S. Patent. Camouflaging a standard cell based integrated circuit, 2012.

25. J. Rajendran, M. Sam, O. Sinanoglu, and R. Karri. Security analysis of integrated circuit camouflaging. In *Proceedings of the 2013 ACM SIGSAC Conference on Computer and Communications Security, CCS'13*, pages 709–720, Berlin, Germany, 2013.

26. A. Stoica, R. Zebulum, D. Keymeulen, M. Ferguson, and V. Duong. Taking evolutionary circuit design from experimentation to implementation: Some useful techniques and a silicon demonstration. *IEE Proceedings—Computers and Digital Techniques*, **151**(4):295–300, 2004.

27. R. Ruzicka. New polymorphic NAND/XOR gate. In *Proceedings of 7th WSEAS International Conference on Applied Computer Science*, Vol. **2007**, 192–196, Citeseer, 2007.

28. J. Rajendran, Y. Pino, O. Sinanoglu, and R. Karri. Logic encryption: A fault analysis perspective. In *Proceedings of the Conference on Design, Automation and Test in Europe*, pages 953–958. EDA Consortium, 2012.

29. A. Stoica, R. Zebulum, and D. Keymeulen. *Polymorphic Electronics*. Springer, Berlin, 2001.

30. A. Baumgarten, A. Tyagi, and J. Zambreno. Preventing IC piracy using reconfigurable logic barriers. *Design Test of Computers, IEEE*, **27**(1):66–75, 2010.

Chapter 9

Carbon-Based Novel Devices for Hardware Security

Haoting Shen, Fahim Rahman, Mark Tehranipoor, and Domenic Forte

Contents

In the past decades, different hardware security designs [1], including primitives like physical unclonable functions (PUFs) and true random number generators (TRNGs) for secret key generation and authentication, were mostly realized by integrated circuit (IC) devices based on complementary metal-oxide-semiconductor (CMOS) technologies. Since silicon has dominated the electronics industry, research on hardware security is naturally focused on silicon-based designs that are implemented by CMOS technologies. Basically, these designs exploit the properties of CMOS fabricated devices, such as randomly varying threshold voltage of CMOS field-effect transistors (FET) and hot-carrier injection resulted changes in the device performance (i.e., aging) [2], for security applications.

However, existing CMOS technologies are slowly saturating in development, while new attack models and vulnerabilities are continuously emerging. Meanwhile, with the fast development of Internet of things (IoT), novel devices with unique properties (compacted, low-cost, flexible, energy efficient, etc.) are highly desired. Facing these challenges, many designs based on novel nanomaterials instead of traditional silicon, such as graphene, carbon nanotubes, phase change memory, memristors, and spintronic devices, have been proposed for security applications [3]. Some of them are adaptable to standard CMOS technologies, and some can be prepared via 2D or 3D printing technology. Among these materials, carbon-based ones (graphene and carbon nanotubes) come in a variety of forms with dramatic physical and electronic properties, providing many special advantages for security applications in numerous scenarios. In this chapter, we will focus on carbon-based designs, briefly introduce the materials, describe the material features that can be leveraged for security, elaborate several typical security hardware designs based on graphene/carbon nanotubes, and highlight future research directions.

9.1 Carbon Nanotubes and Graphene

Carbon is one of the most common element in a human's life. Organic materials, including a human's body, are built up based on chains of carbon atoms. For many years, our knowledge about pure carbon matter had been limited to graphite and diamond, until a carbon nanotube was synthesized by Iijima [4] for the first time in a lab. Since then, researchers have made rapid progress in the understanding of unique properties of carbon nanotubes. In 2004, graphene was also obtained by Geim and colleagues [5] in their lab after being predicted by theory for many years. These carbon nanotubes and graphene do not only provide a good platform for fundamental physics research but also offer exciting opportunities for emerging electronic devices. The carbon-based devices were considered as alternatives to continue the trend set by Moore's law in the nanoscale regime, as well as to enhance the functionality of the traditional processing unit by integrating digital with nonlogic components such as analog circuitry and sensors. Although with current technologies, carbon nanotubes and graphene cannot be used as a satisfying replacement of CMOS logic in the silicon platform, they surely provide potential solutions for many nonlogic applications [6–8].

Compared to conventional silicon-based designs, the main electronic advantages from carbon nanotubes and graphene arise from their special physical structures and associated energy band structures. Graphene is a thin carbon sheet made of a single atomic layer. The carbon atoms in graphene are bonded in sp^2 configuration of a honeycomb hexagonal lattice structure. An isolated flat large graphene can be considered as one carbon layer in graphite, with carbon atoms aligned in the honeycomb structure, as shown in Figure 9.1. Quantization of the electronic states in graphene results in a zero gap between the valence band and conduction band on an energy band diagram, which makes graphene to be semimetallic. For a graphene sheet with a finite size such as a nanoribbon, depending on the width and the edges (e.g., zig-zag or armchair in Figure 9.1), the energy band structure may be modified and graphene can be semiconducting or metallic. Therefore, it is possible to use graphene as a channel material to fabricate FETs.

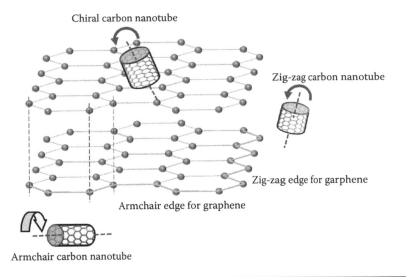

Chiral carbon nanotube

Zig-zag carbon nanotube

Zig-zag edge for garphene

Armchair edge for graphene

Armchair carbon nanotube

Figure 9.1 **In graphite, carbon atoms are arranged in layers. In each layer, the atoms are positioned in a honeycomb hexagonal structure. Graphene is actually one single layer of carbon atoms from graphite. The edge of graphene can be "armchair (the thick on bottom)," "zig-zag (the thick edge on right side)," or between these two. Carbon nanotubes can be considered as tubes formed by "rolling up" single or multiple "carbon sheets." The axis along which the tube is rolled can be along "armchair," "zig-zag," or between them, as well.**

For carbon nanotubes, they can be considered as a seamless cylinder by "rolling up" one sheet or multiple sheets of graphene along an axis (zig-zag, armchair, or between them, as shown in Figure 9.1). According to the number of graphene sheets, the nanotubes can be categorized into single-wall carbon nanotubes (SWCNTs), double-wall carbon nanotubes (DWCNTs), or multiwall carbon nanotubes (MWCNTs). The electronic states in a carbon nanotube are quantized in the circumferential direction, as determined by the periodic boundary condition around the circumference of the nanotube. As a result, carbon nanotubes can also behave as metallic or semiconducting, according to the diameter, the number of walls, and the orientation (zig-zag, armchair, or between them) of the axis along which the nanotubes are rolled up. The unique energy band structure also results in equal effective masses of electrons and holes via 1D ballistic transportation in carbon nanotubes [7]. An FET based on carbon nanotubes thus requires a low electric field in comparison to conventional silicon FETs, offering opportunities for high-speed and ultra-low power logic and RF applications.

Besides the electronic properties, graphene and carbon nanotubes also possess many other fascinating features, including a large specific surface area, flexibility, light weight, transparency, and sturdiness. In addition, different cost-efficient ways to mass-produce these carbon-based materials have been reported, such as arc discharge [9], liquid-phase exfoliation of graphite [10], and chemical vapor deposition (CVD) [11]. Once the materials are synthesized, they can be easily patterned by traditional photolithography to be integrated into CMOS devices [12–14]. They can also be readily prepared as ink for printing to print out the devices on numerous substrates [15,16]. All of these features make graphene and carbon nanotubes promising candidates for both CMOS and IoT applications.

Here, we highlight the features of carbon-based materials that can be lucrative for hardware security applications.

- *Metallic/semiconducting behavior:* As discussed above, the special energy band structures in graphene and carbon nanotubes make it possible for the fabricated device to present either metallic or semiconducting behavior. For instance, the bandgap energy of carbon nanotubes may vary widely due to the process variation and mismatch in the tube diameter [17]. Consequently, the performance of FETs with carbon nanotubes as channel materials may vary in terms of the device electrical properties, such as threshold voltage and saturation current density, based on the inherent characteristics.
- *Variability:* Transistors with different architectures have been proposed with graphene nanoribbon or carbon nanotubes as channel materials (Figure 9.2a and b) to achieve high charge carrier mobility [7,18]. Since the properties of such FETs significantly depend on the carbon-based channel materials, including the electrical property (e.g., semiconducting or metallic), length and patterning, drain/source contact, ribbon or tube numbers and placements, and many other factors, there are numerous inherent variability sources, which are mainly manufacturing process dependent.
- *Channel sensitivity:* Both graphene and carbon nanotubes are highly sensitive to external stimulations, which can cause abnormal variations in device performance for regular logic operation. Such stimulation may arise from different environmental factors, including operation conditions (e.g., temperature, supply voltage), channel contamination, surface absorption, photon absorption (i.e., exposure to light), and so on. The effects resulting from these environmental factors can be translated into digital signals. Although the sensitivity makes it challenging to obtain good control over the channel quality during large-scale logic device fabrication, it is beneficial for various nanoscale sensor applications. Micro-electro-mechanical systems (MEMS) and nano-electro-mechanical systems (NEMS)

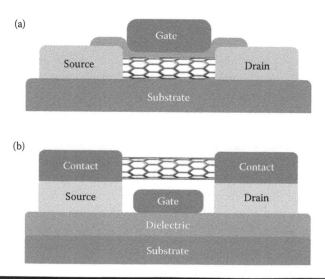

Figure 9.2   A carbon nanotube can be used for channel material in field-effect transistors. The nanotube can be placed directly on a substrate and covered by the gate (a), or be suspended between the source and drain contacts and above the gate (b).

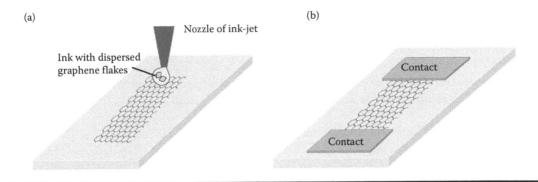

Figure 9.3   Graphene ink with dispersed graphene micro/nanoflakes is printed on a substrate (a). Diverse substrates, such as a wafer, glass, and flexible ones (e.g., soft plastic), are applicable. Contacts can be then coated for connection (b).

architectures involving graphene and carbon nanotubes structures can also be employed for many applications beyond traditional logic devices [6,19,20].

■ *Flexibility, printability, and transparency:* Graphene sheets can be dispersed into various solutions, prepared as ink, and ready for large-scale printing. Given the graphene-based ink, printers can create transparent and functional electrical circuits on different substrates with an appropriately designed interface. As shown in Figure 9.3a and b, a simple structure of a single transistor is printed using printable graphene via ink-jet printing [20]. The printed graphene serves as the channel material and provides a similar functionality as that of a traditional CMOS transistor.

9.2 Hardware Security Preliminaries

We have seen many inherent distinct features from carbon-based nano devices, which are not typically presented in conventional CMOS devices. They can be used to develop security primitives like PUFs with the inherent variability of the devices. These devices can also be designed for supply chain security with printed circuitry, for anti-physical tampering and anti-reverse engineering with transistor-level sensing mechanisms. However, most of the proposed carbon-based devices so far are not specifically designed for hardware security applications. There are more potentials for security waiting to be exploited from these devices. To better describe carbon-based merging devices for hardware security, we will briefly review the mechanisms of some hardware security preliminaries that can be related to carbon nanotube and graphene devices.

9.2.1 Physical Unclonable Function

A PUF device is used to generate specific responses upon given challenges in a cryptographically secure way. This function is realized by making use of uncontrollable physical variations introduced during the fabrication of devices. For example, two transistors with the same structure are fabricated in one die, through the same processing. However, variations in parameters, such as carrier doping density, device size, and oxide layer thickness, are inevitable. Hence, upon the same challenge, the responses from these two transistors will be slightly different. Such differences can be different time delays, different threshold voltages, different current densities, etc. Logic signals "0" and "1" can be easily obtained by comparing the responses and be used as generated keys or identities for security applications. Since such physical device variations are random and cannot be controlled, they are considered as physically unclonable. In other words, the random physical variations are the fundamental of a PUF device. Basically, we want a PUF device to generate response upon a given challenge in such a way as to satisfy requirements, including:

- *Randomness:* The response is difficult to be predicted without the PUF device.
- *Uniqueness:* The response to a given challenge generated by one PUF device is unique and different from other PUF devices.
- *Reliability:* The response to a given challenge generated by one PUF device is always the same.

On standard CMOS PUF devices, the physical variations are usually quite limited, resulting in slight differences between compared signals. In this situation, the fluctuation of supply voltage and environmental factors such as temperature [2,21,22], and aging [22–24] as well, may disturb the signal and lead to unreliable PUF device performance [2]. To deal with this issue on regular CMOS devices, researchers have introduced error-correcting codes (ECCs) with novel architectures and algorithms [25–29]. However, the ECCs usually require high area and power overhead, limiting the application of PUF devices in many scenarios [2,30]. Compared to conventional CMOS processing, carbon-based nano devices come with tremendous random variations that can be leveraged for PUF devices.

9.2.2 Anticounterfeit

Currently, counterfeit ICs have become a serious threat given the globalized industry. Counterfeit ICs include cloned, overproduced, recycled, remarked, and defective ones. By manufacturing and selling cloned and overproduced counterfeit ICs, adversaries illegally take profit from legitimate chip designers, while recycled, remarked, and defective devices and systems pose higher risks, especially if they are used for critical infrastructures like military, financial, public transportation, and health-care systems. Besides the IC industry, anticounterfeit is also important for food and pharmaceutical markets. It is obvious that outdated food and fake drugs can cause severe damage to public health. The countermeasures to counterfeits are generally based on mechanisms, including identification, detection, and prevention.

- *Identification* can be implemented by various methods. One of the most common is bar coding. However, it can be easily reproduced and used on counterfeit products. To ensure that the ID is difficult or even impossible to be cloned, PUF-based IDs are good candidates [31,32].
- *Detection* includes physical inspection or electrical characterization to check any defects. For instance, in a nondestructive way, x-ray tomography can be used to scan PCBs and a scanning electron microscope (SEM) can be used to reveal trivial surface clues left from remaking by sanding. One requirement for detection is that a golden sample is necessary for comparison, which is, however, not always available.
- *Prevention methods* usually involve the design of sensors to detect device usage in the field [33], metering techniques to prevent unauthorized production [34], or configurable transistor/connections to ensure that the authorization can be only issued by the original

designer [35,36]. Since the mechanisms behind sensing, metering, and configuration are quite different, each solution typically only takes care of one type of concerns. Even with the latest technology, to put all the solutions in one device will result in a substantial overhead cost.

We should also keep in mind that applications for different scenarios have a different emphasis. For example, for foods that are typically cheaper compared to IC chips, the anticounterfeit design focuses more on cost-efficient and fast examination. For food and pharmaceutical products, being nontoxic and safe to the human body are also essential. Thus, different materials should be carefully considered when the anticounterfeit solution is designed for food and drugs.

9.2.3 Antiphysical Tampering and Protection from Hardware Reverse Engineering

Although the purpose of tampering is to bypass authentications or protections to get sensitive data stored in devices, and the purpose of reverse engineering is to understand the structure and/or fabrication processing of devices, physical tampering and hardware reverse engineering typically involve some similar preparing steps, including grinding, polishing, and decapsulation, delayering, imaging, and microprobing of IC chips. During these preparations, the devices may be exposed to light, go through mechanical vibration, absorb air, etc. Sensors that can detect these changes can be used for the protection against tampering attacks or reverse engineering. They can be classified into two categories [37,38]: passive evident designs and active resistant/responsive designs.

- *Evident designs* allow the authorized user to check if a device has been physically tampered with using mechanical, electrical, and/or optical instruments. Though it does not stop the attacks and the adversaries can still get the sensitive data, it can warn the users so that the tampered devices/data (such as keys) can be replaced in time.
- *Active designs* provide an elevated level of security as take actions, such as erase secret key or change connections, on the detection of unauthorized physical accesses. Compared to the evident design, the resistant/responsive designs usually need extra energy to take the actions, which makes it challenging.

9.3 Proposed Designs for Hardware Security Applications

9.3.1 PUF Based on Carbon Nanotube FETs

During the synthesis, a lack of chirality control on the carbon nanotube structure yields the synthesized carbon nanotubes can be either metallic or semiconducting in a nondeterministic way. On the basis of this phenomenon, Choden Konigsmark et al. proposed to use FETs with carbon nanotubes (CNFETs) and designed a PUF device built from CNFETs [39]. As shown in Figure 9.4, a pair of CNFETs that share the same gate voltage was used as one parallel element. Multiple parallel elements are connected in series, providing symmetric current paths. Based on the gate voltages applied (i.e., input), CNFETs are set as on or off states. Since the off-current for semiconducting carbon nanotubes is considerably lower than that for metallic carbon nanotubes, the characteristic variation between carbon nanotubes can present distinguishable, but random, states. By comparing the currents from the symmetric paths, one output bit can be generated. The SPICE-based

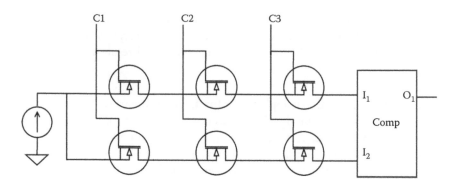

Figure 9.4 **Transistors based on carbon nanotubes are parallelly connected in series. Depending on the challenges (C1, C2, etc.), transistors are set as on or off. By comparing the current flow through two paths, 1-bit PUF output is generated.**

simulation was also performed in the study. The simulation results showed that CNPUF achieved higher reliability against environmental variations and increased resistance against modeling attacks [40–43]. The authors claimed that CNPUF had considerable power and energy reduction as well.

However, there are several barriers that need to be overcome. For example, proper and reliable CNFET models that incorporate the stochastic nature, the impact of environmental variations, and aging are still lacking. In addition, further investigation is still necessary to answer how to place the mass-produced carbon nanotubes on a substrate for the FET fabrication and whether the fabrication is CMOS adaptable.

9.3.2 PUF Based on Carbon Nanotube in Crossbar Structure

Besides the FET design, carbon nanotubes can also be used to provide the interconnection layer to a crossbar structure, as illustrated in Figure 9.5 [44]. Successful fabrication of such a device was reported by Hu and his colleagues in 2016. They first prepared a substrate with a trench patterned

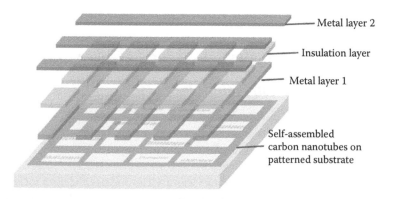

Figure 9.5 **Carbon nanotubes are randomly placed on a substrate surface with trenches patterned, serving as the interconnection between metal layers in a crossbar structure. According to whether a nanotube is filled into one trench, the corresponding read-out signal will be "1" or "0."**

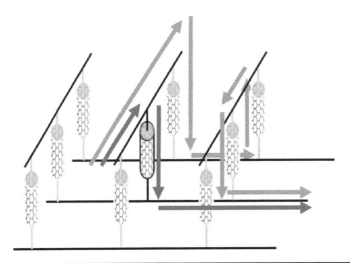

Figure 9.6 Ideally, the current should only go through the selected element in the crossbar, following the dark arrows. However, it is possible that there is a sneak current going through other elements, for example, following the light arrows, and giving an incorrect readout.

on a properly treated surface [45]. Then, commercially available carbon nanotubes (Hanhwa Nanotech) were dispersed in water with a surface-active dispersing agent. Drops of carbon nanotube solution were then dropped down onto the surface of the substrate. Owing to ion exchange, the nanotubes were positioned in trenches with good alignment. After that, metal layer 1, insulation photoresist layer, and metal layer 2 were deposited on the surface to complete the crossbar structure.

In such an architecture, a node is connected (output 1) if there is a nanotube in the trench. Otherwise, it is disconnected (output 0). The experimental results show that the nanotube positioning depends on the width of the trench. By controlling the width of the trench, the randomness of the 2D carbon nanotube arrays can be maximized, where the number of connected units was close to the number of disconnected ones. Considering that the carbon nanotubes contain both semiconducting and metallic ones, the crossbar PUF device can be upgraded from a binary bit system to a ternary bit system by properly setting threshold values.

It is worth mentioning that in a simple crossbar structure, sneaking current can be an issue for I–V measurement and output generation, as shown in Figure 9.6, where the current flows through not only the selected node but also the neighbor nodes, resulting in an incorrect read-out [46]. For the example we give here, the contact between the metal layer and carbon nanotubes are more like a metal–semiconductor contact. Therefore, the metal–carbon nanotube–metal structure works as transistors and thus inhibits the sneak path problem. A gate voltage was applied through the substrate to control the current.

9.3.3 RF Fingerprinting Using Carbon Nanotubes

Carbon nanotubes have also been introduced by a research group from Germany for radio-frequency (RF) fingerprinting [47]. The researcher designed a 12-cm-diameter brass cylindrical cavity filled with different materials to produce RF fingerprints [48], as shown in Figure 9.7. Here, it is a mixture of commercially available semiconducting carbon nanotubes (Baytubes C150P, grown via CVD, from Bayer Material Science) and plythiourethane (PTU, dielectric polymer,

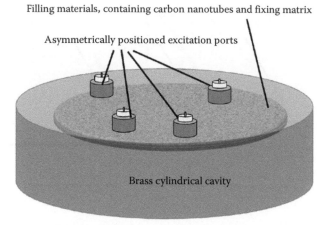

Figure 9.7   Carbon nanotubes are used for RF fingerprintings.

serving as a fixing matrix to fix the nanotubes). The cavity was excited over a wide band range (from 1 to 15 GHz) by four coaxial connectors, which were positioned in an asymmetric way. Owing to the random position and dimensions of the carbon nanotube, the RF signal generated by such a device should be able to generate unclonable functions. Aging test with a time gap of 16 weeks revealed that aging was negligible over such a period. The device was also tested under different temperatures, from −20°C to 50°C. The results showed that the phase component of the resonance RF signal shifts in a slight but consistent way along the temperature changes. On the other hand, considering that this device design was proposed for a PUF, it is necessary to fabricate more devices in future for other PUF metrics, especially the uniqueness that is important for identification applications, as well.

9.3.4 *Graphene-Based Printable Electronics*

For widespread application, mass production of graphene can be synthesized by CVD [49], sublimation of Si atoms by heat treatment of silicon carbide [50], segregation from metal substrates [51,52], and liquid-phase exfoliation [10,53]. Once graphene is obtained, it can be dispersed in solutions, serving as ink for printing. Dispersing agent and mild sonication may be used to avoid agglomeration of graphene flakes in the solution. The preparation of graphene inks can be generally classified into two categories. One is dispersing graphene in solvents like *N*-methylpyrrolidone (NMP) without a binder [20], and the other is using a binder such as ethyl cellulose [54,55]. The binder-free ink typically can be processed at a low temperature (<100°C) but offers comparably lower conductivity, while the ink with a binder can provide higher conductivity through reduced graphene oxide (RGO) but requires elevated-temperature (>250°C) annealing to decompose the insulating binder material.

Many graphene-based printed electronics have been reported in the past decades. For example, a group from the University of Cambridge presented graphene-based thin-film transistors with mobilities up to $95 \, cm^2 \, V^{-1} \, s^{-1}$ and transmittance up to 80% [20]. They ultrasonicated commercially available graphene flakes in solution for several hours, ultracentrifuged decanted dispersions, and filtered the solution to remove flakes larger than $1 \, \mu m$ to prevent clogging at the printer nozzle. To maintain a stable dispersion, NMP was chosen as the solution because its

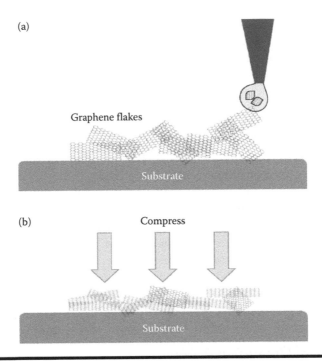

Figure 9.8 **Binder-free graphene ink is printed on substrate (a) and compressed (b) to achieve high conductivity.**

surface energy is close to that of graphene. The as-prepared graphene ink was used as the channel material for FETs, printed by Epson Stylus 1500 ink-jet printer. A S020049 cartridge was used for the printing, with a constant nitrogen flow on Si/SiO_2 substrate. Chromium–gold pads were then defined as source and drain, as shown in Figure 9.3, completing the FET structure.

Another group from the University of Manchester printed RF identification antenna using dispersed graphene nanoflakes in solvent as the ink [56]. According to their testing, the printed antenna provided practically acceptable return loss, gain, bandwidth, and radiation patterns. To obtain the printable graphene antenna with satisfying conductivity while keeping the printing processing at low temperature (100°C). According to their testing, the printed antenna provided practically acceptable return loss, gain, bandwidth, and radiation patterns. To obtain the printable graphene antenna with satisfying conductivity while keeping the printing processing at low temperature (100°C), the group used binder-free graphene ink and compressed the printed graphene to increase the conductivity via an increase in the density of graphene nanoflakes in the printed laminate, as illustrated in Figure 9.8a and b.

In summary, with graphene inks, electronic components can be printed on the top of an insulating material, such as the IC package material. Such printable electronics exhibit high potential in hardware security applications, especially in electronic supply chain security. The major advantage of printable electronic devices over traditional logic devices is that the circuit does not need to be fabricated in the die during the CMOS manufacturing processing. This enables the intellectual property owners to print circuits on the chip package after the chips are returned from the untrusted foundry. The printed circuit can generate digital fingerprints for identification and tracking to ensure the security of the product in the supply chain. It can also potentially make a counterfeit and tamper evident architecture since polishing of the package for recycled and remarked chips, or delaying, will destroy the printed circuit on the package surface. For hardware security, a key concern of such printable electronics is designing the interface and supporting circuits and architectures so that they can be properly integrated into CMOS IC circuitry. Further details in this area are still under investigation.

9.3.5 Carbon-Based Nanosensors

The electrical properties of carbon-based nanomaterials (i.e., graphene and carbon nanotubes) are found to be sensitive to some environmental factor (pressure, light, etc.) changes applied on the materials. On the basis of these phenomena, a large variety of sensors and MEMS/NEMS-based actuator using graphene and carbon nanotubes have been reported [57,58]. Such sensors and actuators can be used to create shielding around the critical components in chips, such as secure data bus and key storage memory, to protect the device from physical tampering, eavesdropping [59], and reverse engineering, as long as the attacks introduce specific environmental changes to the sensor, which occur in most instances of invasive/semi-invasive attacks. Typical environmental factors that carbon-based emerging devices can be sensitive to include mechanical pressure, light exposure, and gas absorption.

9.3.5.1 Mechanical Pressure Sensors

Researchers from Switzerland [58] connected an individual single-wall carbon nanotube to the fixed chromium/gold contacts and suspended it from the substrate. A cantilever was also placed above the suspended carbon nanotube. The concept of such a mechanical pressure (force) nanosensor in NEMS architecture is illustrated in Figure 9.9. With an external out-of-plane force applied by an atomic force microscope (AFM) tip on the cantilever, the researchers deflected the carbon nanotube and successfully measured the corresponding resistance change in the nanotube. Considering that to perform mechanical delayering and polishing, which is widely used during

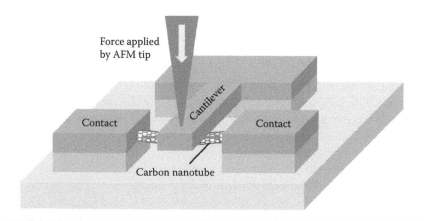

Figure 9.9   To fabricate the proposed mechanical pressure sensor, one single carbon nanotube is suspended between contacts, with the cantilever above. For performance testing, force is applied on the cantilever via the AFM tip. The pressure signal is detected by measuring the change of current that goes through the nanotube.

invasive attacks, applying force/pressure is necessary, such pressure sensors can be used in a chip to detect the force while delayering and polishing.

9.3.5.2 Optical Sensors

Imaging is one of the essential steps in invasive/semi-invasive attacks. Although for modern very-large-scale integrated (VLSI) circuits, the components are so small (<100 nm) that electron microscopes are necessary to depict the details, optical microscopy is still needed to provide information on a larger scale (from centimeters to 100 nm). Otherwise, it can easily take months for electron microscopy to finish all the imaging work on a typical IC chip while most of the details revealed are not of interest. For optical imaging, a light source (photons) is required and thus optical sensors can be used to combat such attacks. Owing to the unique energy band structure, graphene is able to absorb light over a broad wavelength range and hence attracts large interest in optical sensor applications. Researchers from Singapore and China introduced electron trapping centers and created a band gap in graphene through band structure engineering to improve the device sensitivity to photons. By coating the graphene with a titanium thin film followed by chemical wet etching, a graphene quantum-dot-like array structure was formed in graphene-based FET channels, providing improved photon sensitivity over a broad light wavelength range.

As a security component in ICs, the optical sensors will trigger an alert flag if the device is exposed to light while delayering, milling, or probing. With efficient energy harvesting, though difficult, it is also possible to erase secret data stored in memories. To attack a cryptographic module wrapped by such sensors without any loss of data will thus become difficult.

9.3.5.3 Chemical Sensors

Attributed to the large surface offered by carbon nanotube and graphene, the influence of chemical/biochemical materials absorption on the surface on material properties is more significant than that on conventional materials. On this basis, researchers have proposed several chemical and biochemical sensors using carbon nanotube and graphene to detect chemical/biochemical signals. For example, Dai and his colleagues demonstrated hysteresis caused by water molecules in carbon nanotube FETs on silicon oxide, by exposing the carbon nanotube to the ambient environment [60]. Even in dry air, which contains much fewer water molecules, the hysteresis was still observed. In addition, the absorbed water molecules were not completely released even after putting the sensor back into the vacuum environment, which meant the hysteresis was still observed. Since water molecules almost always exist in the ambient air, such a sensor can be used against invasive physical attacks like delayering. The sensor should be fabricated in a vacuum cavity in IC chips, sealed by packaging materials. Once physical attacks are performed and the sealing package is broken, the sensor is exposed to air and triggers alerts.

9.4 Challenges and the Road Ahead

Currently, the major challenges regarding graphene and carbon nanotube electronics are reliable device performance and the integration with regular CMOS circuitry for high processing yield. The mass production of carbon nanotubes has been achieved by many different methods, including arc-discharge, laser ablation, and various CVD methods [61]; however, the products are mixed with diverse chiralities and usually present both semiconducting and metallic tubes. Although the nanotubes can be purified via approaches such as column chromatography [44], variations in carbon nanotube properties (diameter, length, defects, threshold voltage, etc.) are still considerable. Such variations can be lucrative for some hardware security applications (e.g., PUFs), but can be an issue for other applications by lowering the yield in device fabrication. For example, with large length variation, a carbon nanotube can be too short to reach both source and drain contacts in an FET, and thus leads to a device failure. Furthermore, approaches [45] for dense directional placement of individual carbon nanotubes on a substrate have been developed, but whether the processing can be integrated into standard CMOS processing requires further investigation. For graphene, a major barrier remains as to how to induce a proper energy band gap to use as a digital switch, which in turn compromises the materials carrier mobility. Fortunately, with the development of technology in the nanoscale regime, advanced equipment like FIB (e.g., Orion NanoFab - Helium Ion Microscope, Zeiss) that can operate in the sub-10 nm region makes it possible to put such a circuitry or sensor device in places for selective and critical applications.

To date, we have discussed the unique features of carbon-based emerging nano devices. We have noted that many of the conceptions and designs presented in this chapter and related literature are still in the stage of the prototype demonstration and need to be integrated as part of a security-enabling system. Many designs are proposed for logic, memory, or sensor devices, rather than from the point of view of hardware security. Therefore, there is a lot of potential from the graphene and carbon nanotube devices to be leveraged for hardware-oriented security by modifying and optimizing current designs.

9.5 Conclusion

In this chapter, we first introduce that carbon-based emerging nano devices, including graphene ones and carbon nanotube ones. Such devices exhibit novel properties that are unique from existing regular CMOS devices, which makes them promising for hardware security applications. Following that, we briefly describe the novel graphene and carbon nanotube materials and highlight the features that may be uniquely useful for security applications. After a quick review of the mechanism of several hardware security primitives of interest, we give various proposed hardware designs based on graphene and carbon nanotubes that can be used for security. We also discussed the barriers we need to overcome to bring these emerging designs into mature products.

Acknowledgment

This project was supported in part by an Air Force Office of Scientific Research (AFOSR) MURI Grant under award number FA9550-14-1-0351 and by the National Science Foundation under Grant 1603475, Grant 1603483, and Grant 1603483.

References

1. M. Tehranipoor and C. Wang. *Introduction to Hardware Security and Trust.* Springer Publishing Company, New York, 2011.
2. T. Rahman, D. Forte, J. Fahrny, and M. Tehranipoor. ARO-PUF: An aging-resistant ring oscillator PUF design. In *Proceedings of the Conference on Design, Automation & Test in Europe*, page 69. European Design and Automation Association, Leuven, Belgium, 2014.

3. J. Rajendran, R. Karri, J. B. Wendt, M. Potkonjak, N. McDonald, G. S. Rose, and B. Wysocki. Nano meets security: Exploring nanoelectronic devices for security applications. *Proceedings of the IEEE*, **103**(5):829–849, 2015.

4. S. Iijima, P. Ajayan, and T. Ichihashi. Growth model for carbon nanotubes. *Physical Review Letters*, **69**(21):3100, 1992.

5. K. S. Novoselov, A. K. Geim, S. V. Morozov, D. Jiang, Y. Zhang, S. V. Dubonos, I. V. Grigorieva, and A. A. Firsov. Electric field effect in atomically thin carbon films. *Science*, **306**(5696):666–669, 2004.

6. R. H. Baughman, A. A. Zakhidov, and W. A. De Heer. Carbon nanotubes—The route toward applications. *Science*, **297**(5582):787–792, 2002.

7. A. Chen, J. Hutchby, V. Zhirnov, G. Bourianoff, editors. *Emerging Nanoelectronic Devices*. John Wiley & Sons Ltd, Chichester, United Kingdom, December 2014.

8. K. S. Novoselov, V. Fal, L. Colombo, P. Gellert, M. Schwab et al. A roadmap for graphene. *Nature*, **490**(7419):192–200, 2012.

9. Z. Shi, Y. Lian, X. Zhou, Z. Gu, Y. Zhang, S. Iijima, L. Zhou, K. T. Yue, and S. Zhang. Mass-production of single-wall carbon nanotubes by arc discharge method. *Carbon*, **37**(9):1449–1453, 1999.

10. Y. Hernandez, V. Nicolosi, M. Lotya, F. M. Blighe, Z. Sun et al. High-yield production of graphene by liquid-phase exfoliation of graphite. *Nature Nanotechnology*, **3**(9):563–568, 2008.

11. M. Kumar and Y. Ando. Chemical vapor deposition of carbon nanotubes: A review on growth mechanism and mass production. *Journal of Nanoscience and Nanotechnology*, **10**(6):3739–3758, 2010.

12. M. C. Lemme, T. J. Echtermeyer, M. Baus, and H. Kurz. A graphene field-effect device. *IEEE Electron Device Letters*, **28**(4):282–284, 2007.

13. M. Y. Han, B. Özyilmaz, Y. Zhang, and P. Kim. Energy band-gap engineering of graphene nanoribbons. *Physical Review Letters*, **98**(20):206805, 2007.

14. X. Chen, D. Akinwande, K.-J. Lee, G. F. Close, S. Yasuda, B. C. Paul, S. Fujita, J. Kong, and H.-S. P. Wong. Fully integrated graphene and carbon nanotube interconnects for gigahertz high-speed CMOS electronics. *IEEE Transactions on Electron Devices*, **57**(11):3137–3143, 2010.

15. K. Kordás, T. Mustonen, Tóth G., H. Jantunen, M. Lajunen, C. Soldano, S. Talapatra, S. Kar, R. Vajtai, and P. M. Ajayan. Inkjet printing of electrically conductive patterns of carbon nanotubes. *Small*, **2**(8–9):1021–1025, 2006.

16. L. Huang, Y. Huang, J. Liang, X. Wan, and Y. Chen. Graphene-based conducting inks for direct inkjet printing of flexible conductive patterns and their applications in electric circuits and chemical sensors. *Nano Research*, **4**(7):675–684, 2011.

17. M. Anantram and F. Leonard. Physics of carbon nanotube electronic devices. *Reports on Progress in Physics*, **69**(3):507, 2006.

18. R. Vargas-Bernal and G. Herrera-Pérez, Carbon nanotube-and graphene based devices, circuits and sensors for VLSI design, in VLSI design. E. Tlelo-Cuautle and S. X.-D. Tan, editors, page 41, InTech, Rijeka, Croatia, 2012.

19. B. Zhang and T. Cui. An ultrasensitive and low-cost graphene sensor based on layer-by-layer nano self-assembly. *Applied Physics Letters*, **98**(7):073116, 2011.

20. F. Torrisi, T. Hasan, W. Wu, Z. Sun, A. Lombardo et al. Inkjet-printed graphene electronics. *ACS Nano*, **6**(4):2992–3006, 2012.

21. L. Lin, S. Srivathsa, D. K. Krishnappa, P. Shabadi, and W. Burleson. Design and validation of arbiter-based PUFs for sub-45-nm low-power security applications. *IEEE Transactions on Information Forensics and Security*, **7**(4):1394–1403, 2012.

22. X. Xu, W. Burleson, and D. E. Holcomb. Using statistical models to improve the reliability of delay-based PUFs. In *VLSI (ISVLSI), 2016 IEEE Computer Society Annual Symposium on*, pages 547–552. IEEE, New York, NY, 2016.

23. S. Han, J. Choung, B.-S. Kim, B. H. Lee, H. Choi, and J. Kim. Statistical aging analysis with process variation consideration. In *Proceedings of the International Conference on Computer-Aided Design*, pages 412–419. IEEE Press, New York, NY, 2011.

24. M. Agarwal, V. Balakrishnan, A. Bhuyan, K. Kim, B. C. Paul, W. Wang, B. Yang, Y. Cao, and S. Mitra. Optimized circuit failure prediction for aging: Practicality and promise. In *Test Conference, 2008. ITC 2008. IEEE International*, pages 1–10. IEEE, New York, NY, 2008.

25. X. Xu and D. Holcomb. A clockless sequential PUF with autonomous majority voting. In *Great Lakes Symposium on VLSI, 2016 International*, pages 27–32. IEEE, New York, NY, 2016.

26. J. Delvaux, D. Gu, D. Schellekens, and I. Verbauwhede. Helper data algorithms for PUF-based key generation: Overview and analysis. *IEEE Transactions on Computer-Aided Design of Integrated Circuits and Systems*, **34**(6):889–902, 2015.

27. X. Xu and D. E. Holcomb. Reliable PUF design using failure patterns from time-controlled power gating. In *Defect and Fault Tolerance in VLSI and Nanotechnology Systems (DFT), 2016 IEEE International Symposium on*, pages 135–140. IEEE, New York, NY, 2016.

28. X. Xu, A. Rahmati, D. E. Holcomb, K. Fu, and W. Burleson. Reliable physical unclonable functions using data retention voltage of SRAM cells. *IEEE Transactions on Computer-Aided Design of Integrated Circuits and Systems*, **34**(6):903–914, 2015.

29. X. Xu, V. Suresh, R. Kumar, and W. Burleson. Post-silicon validation and calibration of hardware security primitives. In *VLSI (ISVLSI), 2014 IEEE Computer Society Annual Symposium on*, pages 29–34. IEEE, New York, NY, 2014.

30. M. Bhargava and K. Mai. An efficient reliable PUF-based cryptographic key generator in 65 nm CMOS. In *Proceedings of the Conference on Design, Automation & Test in Europe*, page 70. European Design and Automation Association, Leuven, Belgium, 2014.

31. S. Devadas, E. Suh, S. Paral, R. Sowell, T. Ziola, and V. Khandelwal. Design and implementation of PUF-based "unclonable" RFID ICS for anti-counterfeiting and security applications. In *RFID, 2008 IEEE International Conference on*, pages 58–64. IEEE, New York, NY, 2008.

32. K. Yang, D. Forte, and M. M. Tehranipoor. UCR: An unclonable chipless RFID tag. In *Hardware Oriented Security and Trust (HOST), 2016 IEEE International Symposium on*, pages 7–12. IEEE, New York, NY, 2016.

33. U. Guin, X. Zhang, D. Forte, and M. Tehranipoor. Low-cost on-chip structures for combating die and IC recycling. In *Proceedings of the 51st Annual Design Automation Conference*, pages 1–6. ACM, New York, NY, 2014.

34. Y. Alkabani and F. Koushanfar. Active hardware metering for intellectual property protection and security. In *USENIX Security*, pages 291–306. Boston MA, USA, 2007.

35. U. Guin, D. DiMase, and M. Tehranipoor. Counterfeit integrated circuits: Detection, avoidance, and the challenges ahead. *Journal of Electronic Testing*, **30**(1):9–23, 2014.

36. R. S. Chakraborty and S. Bhunia. Harpoon: An obfuscation-based SOC design methodology for hardware protection. *IEEE Transactions on Computer-Aided Design of Integrated Circuits and Systems*, **28**(10):1493–1502, 2009.

37. S. P. Skorobogatov, *Semi-invasive attacks: A new approach to hardware security analysis*. PhD thesis, Citeseer, 2005.

38. K. Lemke. Embedded security: Physical protection against tampering attacks. In *Embedded Security in Cars*, pages 207–217. Springer, Berlin, 2006.

39. S. C. Konigsmark, L. K. Hwang, D. Chen, and M. D. Wong. CNPUF: A carbon nanotube-based physically unclonable function for secure low-energy hardware design. In *Design Automation Conference (ASP-DAC), 2014 19th Asia and South Pacific*, pages 73–78. IEEE, New York, NY, 2014.

40. X. Xu, U. Rührmair, D. E. Holcomb, and W. Burleson. Security evaluation and enhancement of bistable ring PUFs. In *International Workshop on Radio Frequency Identification: Security and Privacy Issues*, pages 3–16. Springer, Berlin, 2015.

41. X. Xu and W. Burleson. Hybrid side-channel/machine-learning attacks on PUFs: A new threat? In *Proceedings of the Conference on Design, Automation & Test in Europe*, page 349. European Design and Automation Association, Leuven, Belgium, 2014.

42. U. Rührmair, X. Xu, J. Sölter, A. Mahmoud, M. Majzoobi, F. Koushanfar, and W. Burleson. Efficient power and timing side channels for physical unclonable functions. In *International Workshop on Cryptographic Hardware and Embedded Systems*, pages 476–492. Springer, Berlin, 2014.

43. U. Rührmair, J. Sölter, F. Sehnke, X. Xu, A. Mahmoud, V. Stoyanova, G. Dror, J. Schmidhuber, W. Burleson, and S. Devadas. PUF modeling attacks on simulated and silicon data. *IEEE Transactions on Information Forensics and Security*, **8**(11):1876–1891, 2013.
44. Z. Hu, J. M. M. L. Comeras, H. Park, J. Tang, A. Afzali, G. S. Tulevski, J. B. Hannon, M. Liehr, and S.-J. Han. Physically unclonable cryptographic primitives using self-assembled carbon nanotubes. *Nature Nanotechnology*, **11**(6):559–565, 2016.
45. H. Park, A. Afzali, S.-J. Han, G. S. Tulevski, A. D. Franklin, J. Tersoff, J. B. Hannon, and W. Haensch. High-density integration of carbon nanotubes via chemical self-assembly. *Nature Nanotechnology*, **7**(12):787–791, 2012.
46. E. Linn, R. Rosezin, C. Kügeler, and R. Waser. Complementary resistive switches for passive nanocrossbar memories. *Nature Materials*, **9**(5):403–406, 2010.
47. M. Kheir, H. Kreft, and R. Knöchel. UWB on-chip fingerprinting and identification using carbon nanotubes. In *Ultra-WideBand (ICUWB), 2014 IEEE International Conference on*, pages 462–466. IEEE, New York, NY, 2014.
48. M. Kheir, H. Kreft, and R. Knöchel. A novel RF fingerprinting approach for hardware integrated security. *Journal of Information Security and Applications*, **19**(2):143–148, 2014.
49. A. Reina, X. Jia, J. Ho, D. Nezich, H. Son, V. Bulovic, M. S. Dresselhaus, and J. Kong. Large area, few-layer graphene films on arbitrary substrates by chemical vapor deposition. *Nano Letters*, **9**(1):30–35, 2008.
50. K. V. Emtsev, A. Bostwick, K. Horn, J. Jobst, G. L. Kellogg et al. Towards wafer-size graphene layers by atmospheric pressure graphitization of silicon carbide. *Nature Materials*, **8**(3):203–207, 2009.
51. Q. Yu, J. Lian, S. Siriponglert, H. Li, Y. P. Chen, and S.-S. Pei. Graphene segregated on Ni surfaces and transferred to insulators. *Applied Physics Letters*, **93**(11):113103, 2008.
52. X. Li, W. Cai, J. An, S. Kim, J. Nah et al. Large-area synthesis of high-quality and uniform graphene films on copper foils. *Science*, **324**(5932):1312–1314, 2009.
53. M. Lotya, Y. Hernandez, P. J. King, R. J. Smith, V. Nicolosi et al. Liquid phase production of graphene by exfoliation of graphite in surfactant/water solutions. *Journal of the American Chemical Society*, **131**(10):3611–3620, 2009.
54. D. Zhang, X. Li, H. Li, S. Chen, Z. Sun, X. Yin, and S. Huang. Graphene-based counter electrode for dye-sensitized solar cells. *Carbon*, **49**(15):5382–5388, 2011.
55. J. Li, F. Ye, S. Vaziri, M. Muhammed, M. C. Lemme, and M. Östling. Efficient inkjet printing of graphene. *Advanced Materials*, **25**(29):3985–3992, 2013.
56. X. Huang, T. Leng, X. Zhang, J. C. Chen, K. H. Chang, A. K. Geim, K. S. Novoselov, and Z. Hu. Binder-free highly conductive graphene laminate for low cost printed radio frequency applications. *Applied Physics Letters*, **106**(20):203105, 2015.
57. Y. Che, H. Chen, H. Gui, J. Liu, B. Liu, and C. Zhou. Review of carbon nanotube nanoelectronics and macroelectronics. *Semiconductor Science and Technology*, **29**(7):073001, 2014.
58. C. Hierold, A. Jungen, C. Stampfer, and T. Helbling. Nano electromechanical sensors based on carbon nanotubes. *Sensors and Actuators A: Physical*, **136**(1):51–61, 2007.
59. D. Shahrjerdi, J. Rajendran, S. Garg, F. Koushanfar, and R. Karri. Shielding and securing integrated circuits with sensors. In *Proceedings of the 2014 IEEE/ACM International Conference on Computer-Aided Design*, pages 170–174, 2014.
60. W. Kim, A. Javey, O. Vermesh, Q. Wang, Y. Li, and H. Dai. Hysteresis caused by water molecules in carbon nanotube field-effect transistors. *Nano Letters*, **3**(2):193–198, 2003.
61. Q. Zhang, J.-Q. Huang, M.-Q. Zhao, W.-Z. Qian, and F. Wei. Carbon nanotube mass production: Principles and processes. *ChemSusChem*, **4**(7):864–889, 2011.

EMERGING TECHNOLOGIES AND ARCHITECTURES

11

EMERGING
TECHNOLOGIES AND
ARCHITECTURE

Chapter 10

Composition of Physical Unclonable Functions: From Device to Architecture

Fahim Rahman, Atul Prasad Deb Nath, Swarup Bhunia, Domenic Forte, and Mark Tehranipoor

Contents

Hardware security has become an increasing concern in today's world, where securing only software and protocols has become insufficient. More than a decade of research in this area has yielded many security primitives and applications to aid different aspects of hardware security [1]. This includes primitives such as physical unclonable functions (PUFs) and true random number generators (TRNGs) for cryptographic key generation and resisting emerging threats such as IC piracy and counterfeiting.

PUFs exploit the intrinsic process variation in ICs to generate unique challenge–response pairs (CRPs). The physical variability or entropy of the device and system is extracted and translated into *unpredictable but repeatable* bit strings by PUFs. A PUF generates responses or keys by leveraging inherent physical variations from manufacturing processes as identical (by design and lithography) architectures produced using the same fabrication process ideally generate different CRPs due to the existence of small but nondeterministic variations in the manufacturing process [2,3]. Distinctive properties of PUFs, such as uniqueness, unclonability, and reliability, are crucial in generating fingerprinting surface in multifarious security applications, including secure authentication, remote identification, cryptographic key generation, detecting counterfeit products, etc. [4–6]. Over the past decade, several design approaches have been taken to realize the intrinsic variation in ICs into digital form, making PUFs more convenient for application in digital electronics. Nano-CMOS logic and memory-based PUFs have been prevalent in the domain of hardware security primitives to date. Emerging nonvolatile memory-based PUF technologies, however, are getting increased attention in recent times as the stochastic and statistical behaviors of these memories are being exploited and implemented for hardware security applications [7,8]. It is an undeniable fact that selecting proper devices and architectural compositions for building high-quality PUFs is of utmost importance and carries the most significance in harvesting and extracting entropy from devices and architectures across different technologies. Consequently, the design and implementation of efficient PUFs requires a comprehensive study of the sources of variation in devices and the proper methodologies to extract the randomness in all levels of abstractions, including architectures and systems.

In this chapter, we provide an overview of the critical factors of PUF composition and how these features vary from devices to architectures. We first highlight some of the state-of-the-art nanoelectronic logic and memory devices and their promising properties that can facilitate the design of unique and robust PUFs. Our discussion continues, especially focusing on CMOS logic devices showing how to leverage the device's intrinsic properties and features, and how we can utilize different compositions for quality enhancement of PUFs and thwart different PUF-related attacks and vulnerabilities. Finally, we highlight the composition of PUFs in emerging nanoelectronic memory domains and analyze how different devices and designs offer lucrative security opportunities.

10.1 Exploiting Device Properties for PUF Applications

In the course of time, semiconductor technology has evolved at an enormous rate, trying to keep up with Moore's law [9], with most of the growth being manifested in traditional logic and memory technologies where the cost per transistor holds the driving key [10]. However, other key components of IC technologies are various high-speed RF transistors, analog devices, and multiple sensors and biocomponents, which actually increase, and also diversify, the capability of electronic systems to provide enhanced performance, and hence help to maintain the advancement trend following Moore's law from a slightly different perspective. Thus, one can say that the researchers are looking at two possible domains [11]—*More Moore* and *More than Moore* domains.

More Moore suggests how the logic and memory devices evolve following the traditional Moore's law by maintaining a reduced feature size for each technology node as it advances to the next stage, thereby increasing (doubling) the device count in a chip with possible speed enhancement and power reduction. To date, the Si-MOSFETs, from planar bulk-CMOSFETs to 3D FinFETs, have been the backbone of this domain and it is predicted to show domination for another decade or so [10]. On the other hand, *More than Moore* focuses on enhancing performance and functionality by integrating digital logic with analog modules and sensors. In the recent technological trend, a computing system is represented as the product of rather a holistic approach that combines digital and analog devices and sensor-based systems to facilitate features like ultra-low-power operation, high-volume data storage, high-quality image capture in mobile, and Internet of things (IoT) applications. An efficient integration of such high-speed and high-performance nonlogic components with the logic platform allows the overall system to perform better, and eventually comply with Moore's law in terms of cost and performance as depicted in Figure 10.1.

With the advancement in these two domains, there have been tremendous developments of CMOS logic devices (e.g., feature size potentially being reduced to sub-10 nm [12]) and non-CMOS emerging devices, especially in the memory domain. The rapid progress is leading the conventional data processing and storage systems to more compact, low-power, and low-cost operation modes. Nonvolatile memory devices, such as *memristors, resistive random access memory* (RRAM), *phase change memory* (PCM), and spintronic memory devices, for example, *spin-torque-transfer-RAM* (STT-RAM), are promising technologies in the emerging memory

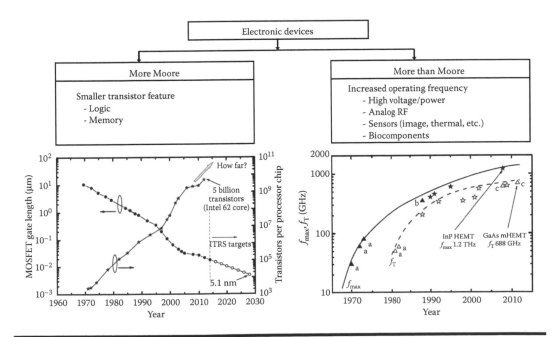

Figure 10.1 **Trends in semiconductor technology in "More Moore" and "More than Moore" domains. (Adapted from A. Chen et al.** *Emerging Nanoelectronic Devices.* **John Wiley & Sons, Chichester, 2014.)**

domain. All these nanoelectronic devices tend to show interesting, if not advantageous, properties that can open up possibilities of various security-oriented applications. For example, the device that inherently possesses a significant amount of physical process variation (maybe due to the lack of maturity in the manufacturing process) can be considered as a lucrative element for a PUF or a TRNG-like hardware security primitive. Similarly, devices sensitive to runtime and environmental variations can be used as sensors that can detect hardware tampering attacks. In Figure 10.2, we point out some of the interesting properties of these devices, namely, nano-CMOS, PCM, memristors, RRAM, MRAM, and STT-RAM devices, that can be suitably leveraged for designing PUFs.

Logic/ memory device	Manufacturing variability sources	Exploitable feature	Reliability factors
Nano-CMOS	• Geometric variation (patterning—W, L) • Random dopant fluctuation (RDF) • Line edge roughness (LER) • Oxide thickness (T_{ox}) fluctuation • Interface defect and traps (ITC) • Polysilicon/metal gate granularity (MGG)	• Path delay deviation ($\Delta\tau_{Delay}$) due to threshold voltage and mobility variation • Transistor on current variation (ΔI_{ON}) • Off-state leakage current variation (ΔI_{Leak})	• Power supply noise and temperature variation • Degradation due to aging (BTI, HCI, TDDB, EM)
PCM	• Geometric variation (GST layer thickness and bottom electrode contact diameter) • Cell resistance (R_{cell}) • Write/read strength (required minimum reset current) • Write current magnitude (I_{write})	• Cell variability—stochastic resistance variation per cell • Programming sensitivity—variation in resistance level due to the nature of applied pulses	• Power supply noise and temperature variation • Resistance drift • Poor endurance and retention
Memristor and RRAM	• Variability in dope and undoped region length • Device thickness and cross-sectional area • Stochasticity in doped and undoped resistance	• Stochastic switching mechanism and intrinsic variability of devices • Resistance variability due to applied voltage pulse duration	• Power supply noise and temperature variation • Moderate endurance and retention • Read disturbance
MRAM and STTRAM	• Geometric variation in free layer volume • Spin-torque switching • Threshold voltage (V_c) • Thermal stability (Δ) • Critical switching current	• Read current variation • Metastability of free layer magnetization • Variation in thermal energy • Back-hopping	• Temperature • External EM field • High endurance and retention

Figure 10.2 **Device-intrinsic variability sources and exploitable features for PUF application.**

It should be noted that these advanced devices are not necessarily designed for such PUF-based security applications; rather, the primary focus of such devices is the suitability for traditional (high) performance-oriented reliable logic and memory application. Hence, some of the properties exploitable for PUFs may not actually be available in a more mature technology, or may not be considered a "good" property in the first place [13]. An in-depth discussion on the issue is also depicted. This chapter, however, excludes the introduction of an elaborate segment on the topic due to limited scope and space scarcity.

Nevertheless, the key point of exploiting various promising properties of emerging nanoelectronic devices for PUFs is to leverage the features from individual devices and translate these to circuit and architectural levels of abstraction. The primary focus of the process is capturing the features with ease and maximizing the security benefits without any loss of performance of the overall system. Hence, the composition of a primitive as PUF seeks more in-depth attention. Without a comprehensive understanding of the composition of these emerging devices, it is difficult to extract the significant measures of PUF quality metrics such as uniqueness, randomness, and, most importantly, reliability. In the following sections, we focus on how various devices with different architectural compositions can lead to superior designs of PUFs.

10.2 Composition of Physical Unclonable Functions with CMOS Devices

There is no doubt that the CMOS transistors dominate the logic and volatile random access memory domain to date. Therefore, most of the hardware-oriented security primitives, such as PUFs and TRNGs, highly rely on traditional CMOS-based architectures. However, not all inherent properties of CMOS devices are suitable for hardware security-oriented applications. For example, for a mature CMOS technology node, the manufacturing process variation is minimal, which leads to lower entropy for a PUF or TRNG application. In this section, we focus on some architectural compositions based on CMOS devices that exploit inherent device properties for maximizing security features in the context of PUFs.

For simplicity, we confine our discussion to the common delay-based PUFs, namely, the arbiter PUF and ring oscillator (RO) PUF. First, we consider how the manufacturing process variation in each device is efficiently translated into some logical value. Then we explore design variations that can be resilient against producing erroneous output due to aging and can thwart machine learning attacks on strong arbiter PUFs. However, this discussion can be extended to other common CMOS-device-based PUFs, for example, SRAM-PUFs [14], DRV-PUFs [15], Flip-flop PUFs [16], and current-based PUFs [17], without loss of generality.

10.2.1 Sources of Process-Induced Variability

Since the feature sizes of CMOS technologies are approaching the fundamental dimensions, the issues of process variation are being pronounced more often due to their adverse impacts on device performance. However, process variations are considered the silver lining in the domain of hardware security—more specifically, for PUFs. Random process-induced variability in CMOS devices is deemed as an abundant source of extractable entropy for hardware-oriented security primitives. Irrespective of the type of functionality, such as logic, memory, or current-based applications, all CMOS-based PUFs are solely dependent on the intrinsic unclonable characteristics of the devices, either directly or indirectly. Furthermore, the quality of existing PUFs is evaluated based on the amount of extractable entropy, that is, randomness, from the source to output bits. A higher amount of entropy signifies a better capability of generating a unique set of challenge and response pairs and thwarts attacks based on modeling and clonability. The classification of PUFs is also defined by the entropy space. For instance, strong PUFs are usually the ones with higher CRPs; thus, they offer higher entropy and have a greater capability of CRP generation.

The process variation in CMOS-based devices mostly arises during the fabrication stage. However, some variations can occur in different phases of the device life cycle as well. Minute variations in physical properties of transistors lead to quantifiable changes in the electrical properties of the devices and result in variability in their operation [18]. For instance, the voltage mismatches between the transistors of an SRAM cell caused by process variations exhibit a metastable behavior of the SRAM cell at the start-up condition. This behavior can be utilized to design the SRAM-based PUF or TRNG [14]. Figure 10.2 provides a brief overview of the device intrinsic manufacturing variability sources, both physical parameters and their electrical manifestations, that lead to unpredictable behavior of nano-CMOS devices (as well as other emerging nonvolatile memory devices). This stochastic nature of operation is further exploited as distinctive features of PUFs.

10.2.2 Entropy Extraction and Quality Enhancement of Delay-Based PUFs

By definition, a PUF can generate bit-streams by leveraging inherent physical variations of the devices coming from the manufacturing processes. A delay-based PUF hence translates these minute but nondeterministic physical variations into path delay since the deviation in the physical parameters can vary the strength of the transistors and, in turn, the time required to propagate a signal through a specific path. An arbiter PUF (as shown in Figure 10.3) utilizes the path delay

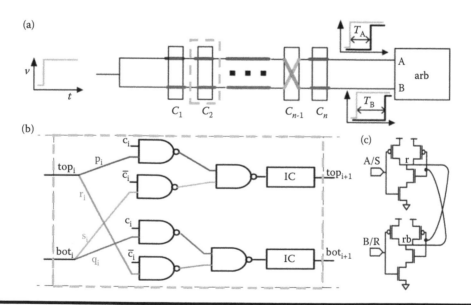

Figure 10.3 (a) Arbiter PUF architecture. (b) NAND-based delay stage. (c) S-R latch-based arbiter with very low bias. (Collected from L. Lin et al. *IEEE Transactions on Information Forensics and Security*, 7(4):1394–1403, 2012.)

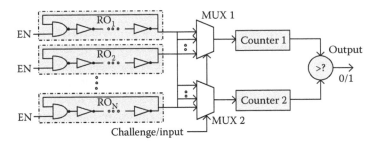

Figure 10.4 Conventional RO PUF.

variation between two design-wise identical paths (selected with the input challenge bits) due to the existing process variation within the active (i.e., transistors) and passive (i.e., interconnects) components lying in the path [3,19]. Similarly, an RO PUF (as shown in Figure 10.4) utilizes a set of identical ring oscillators that oscillate in similar but slightly different frequencies as a result of the same process variation [4]. Comparing these minute path delay (or frequency) variations, these PUFs can produce different digital signatures (or responses) based on the input selections (i.e., challenges).

For a delay-based PUF, it is crucial that the minute delay difference coming from the process variation is properly extracted, that is, manufacturing variation is translated to delay variation, with minimal loss of information for maximizing the entropy. To characterize the propagation delay of CMOS transistors, we consider the generalized inverter delay given as [20]

$$t_P = \frac{\alpha C_L}{\mu C_{ox}(W/L)V_{supply}} \tag{10.1}$$

where C_L is the effective load capacitance for the given path (e.g., a next-stage inverter), W/L is the transistor sizing ratio, μ is the mobility, C_{ox} is the effective gate capacitance, V_{supply} is the supply power, and α is given by

$$\alpha = 2 \left/ \left[\frac{7}{4} - \frac{3|V_t|}{V_{supply}} + \left(\frac{V_t}{V_{supply}} \right)^2 \right] \right. \tag{10.2}$$

where V_t is the transistor threshold voltage.

As shown in Figure 10.2, nondeterministic manufacturing process variation causes deviation in a transistor's physical length (L), width (W), oxide thickness (t_{ox}), as well as associated electrical parameters such as mobility (μ) and threshold voltage (V_t). In addition, the load capacitance (C_L) from the next stage plays a crucial role since the physical parameters of the next-stage logic gate also vary due to the process variation. Hence, the interdevice propagation delay variation can be expressed as a function of all these affecting physical and electrical parameters of Equations 10.1 and 10.2, given as

$$t_{P,interdevice} = f(t_{P,nom}, \Delta L, \Delta W, \Delta t_{ox}, \Delta V_t) \tag{10.3}$$

where $t_{P,nom}$ is the nominal propagation delay for the particular gate for a given technology node and $\Delta(\cdot)$ denotes the deviation due to the manufacturing process variation.

To leverage the maximum benefit of the manufacturing process variation for unclonability, one traditional approach for designing the PUF is to use minimum-sized logic gates (e.g., using minimum-sized NAND or multiplexer blocks for the composition of the arbiter PUF and inverter chains for the composition of the RO PUF). However, this approach is not necessarily always suited for generating a reliable key under different runtime/environmental variations and especially under aging. Another key element of these delay-based PUFs is that the design should be identical to avoid any deterministic bias or mismatch. However, the decision-making circuits (i.e., the arbiter for an arbiter PUF or the counter and comparator module for an RO PUF) tend to have a certain bias and coarse resolution that make the final output nonuniform and less unique (measured by the inter-PUF hamming distance). Researchers have proposed a few techniques where such bias can be minimized to improve statistical variability [21]. However, very few of those concentrate on solving this problem from a gate or circuit-level point of view where different composition techniques for designing the delay/inverter blocks of delay-based PUFs are taken into consideration. Lin et al. [19] suggested that the decision-making arbiter block of an arbiter PUF should be an identically designed SR latch, instead of a tristate latch, to enhance the uniqueness (i.e., exhibit the least amount of bias) of the PUF since the former has approximately zero bias for choosing 0/1 when the signal arrives. The given SR latch comprises cross-coupled NAND gates as shown in Figure 10.3c. In this case, both "r" and "rb" nodes are pulled high at the initial phase and the rising edge of the incoming signal pulls down the respective internal node. The cross-coupling of the NAND gate ensures that only one competing transition will win and, as stated previously, the identical symmetric design ensures that both signals are free from systematic bias. Capovilla et al. [22] suggested that one can improve the statistical variability of an arbiter PUF by *carefully* choosing the combinational logic gates from the foundry given the standard cell libraries and exploit the design parameters so that the gate type/driver, which maximizes the gate delay variance, would result in maximum entropy. The study suggests that the *L/W* ratio dominates the path delay deviation (as shown in Equations 10.1 and 10.3). Similarly, an unbalanced arbiter greatly reduces the statistical variability of the final output by introducing bias. A recent study by Harkle et al. [23] proposed custom-sized structures for a reduced noise sensitivity in the arbiter PUF. This work targets the modification of the sizings of the delay elements and switching elements both in the delay path and the arbiter. The results show that the width of the arbiter's NMOS transistors shows considerable impact on capturing the intrinsic manufacturing variability with an increased width producing a reduced bias. A similar design also reduces the transient (i.e., runtime) noises coming from the power supply and temperature variations. However, none of these studies have provided any aging-related performance analysis.

10.2.3 Aging-Resilient PUF Designs

It is crucial that a PUF maintains its qualities, such as uniqueness, randomness, and robustness/reliability, as close as possible to the ideal ones throughout its lifetime. Systematic process variation may create slightly biased output, reducing uniqueness and randomness, whereas high random process variation increases these qualities. More importantly, *environmental/runtime (temporal) variations*, such as power supply and temperature variations, as well as *aging and wear-out mechanisms*, lead to PUF performance degradation and reliability issues. For example, runtime variations have a negative, though temporary, effect on the analog behavior (such as drain current, delay, leakage current, etc.) of CMOS transistors by impacting the bias point, threshold voltage (V_{th}), mobility (μ), and other critical parameters, respectively, thus making the PUF performance less robust [18,19,24]. *Aging*, on the other hand, causes permanent degradation of the critical

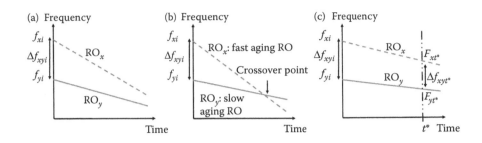

Figure 10.5 Bitflip due to frequency degradation in RO pair. (a) ROs with moderate degradation (stable pair). (b) ROs with high degradation (unstable pair). (c) ROs with negligible degradation (highly stable pair). (Adapted from M. T. Rahman et al. *IEEE Transactions on Emerging Topics in Computing***, 4(3):335–348, 2016.)**

parameters due to *bias temperature instability* (BTI), *hot carrier injection* (HCI), *time-dependent dielectric breakdown* (TDDB), and *electromigration* (EM), and, therefore, significantly degrades the PUF reliability over time. Some PUFs may produce up to 25% error in generated key due to aging, making it unsuitable for cryptographic applications [25].

To understand why a PUF generates an erroneous response, we revisit the conventional RO PUF shown in Figure 10.4, and consider the frequency profile of a randomly selected RO pair shown in Figure 10.5 [25]. For the given RO pair, if the frequency of RO_x ring oscillator (f_{xi}) is greater than that of RO_y (f_{yi}), then "1" (otherwise "0") is generated as a response (Figure 10.5a). However, it fails to generate a reliable (i.e., same as before) response if a crossover happens (i.e., $f_{xi} < f_{yi}$ after possible frequency degradation due to environmental variation and aging) (Figure 10.5b). For maintaining maximum reliability, the two frequencies should never cross each other, maintaining a minimum frequency difference (i.e., frequency threshold (Δf_{th})) to compensate counter resolution if necessary, till the end of the operational lifetime t* (Figure 10.5c). Other PUF structures, such as arbiter PUFs, also suffer from similar reliability issues. Since it is crucial for a PUF to maintain reliable (i.e., error-free) response, researchers have proposed different techniques to minimize such errors discussed as follows.

10.2.3.1 Bootstrapping with Error Correction Code

A common solution for ensuring reliability is to use schemes such as the error-correcting code (ECC) with PUF. ECC can generate reliable PUF output up to a certain margin despite the presence of noise [26]. However, it relies on helper data that may partially reveal the secret key and potentially compromise the PUF [27,28]. Most ECC schemes require redundant gates and an additional decoding unit. Thus, ECC requires a large area, power, and timing overheads, making it impractical in resource-constrained applications.

10.2.3.2 Aging-Resistant Architecture

Rahman et al. proposed NBTI and HCI-aware aging-resistant ARO PUF architecture as shown in Figure 10.6a [25]. This design has additional pull-up and pass transistors within the conventional RO PUF architecture to reduce possible aging degradation. It has two modes of operation. In the oscillatory mode (i.e., enabled, $EN = 1$, $\overline{EN} = 0$), it performs the regular PUF operation (Figure

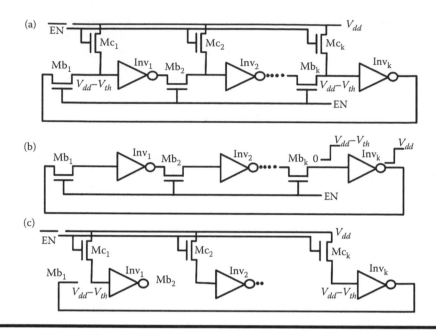

Figure 10.6 (a) Aging-resistant RO (ARO). (b) Oscillatory mode. (c) Nonoscillatory mode. (Adapted from M. T. Rahman et al. *IEEE Transactions on Emerging Topics in Computing*, 4(3):335–348, 2016.)

10.6b). It suffers from the unavoidable AC stress in this mode; however, since the PUF activation time in the field is negligible, we can consider the degradation to be minimal. In the nonoscillatory mode, when $EN = 0$ (Figure 10.6c), it removes the DC stress for PMOS transistors as it ties them to V_{dd} to eliminate NBTI. It also breaks the RO chain and removes the AC (oscillatory) stress to eliminate HCI. So, this design successfully minimizes aging degradation due to NBTI and HCI by eliminating stress when the PUF is not active.

The ARO PUF shows a promising result in terms of higher reliability (lower error) and lower-frequency degradation. Figure 10.7 shows a simulated frequency degradation profile for 5 and 10 years of operational lifetime. Table 10.1 shows that ARO PUF produces less error due to aging compared to RO PUF. However, as it is seen, this architecture is suitable for ASIC implementation only since reconfigurable platforms, such as FPGAs, do not always contain architectural modules that may provide protections against aging stress. It should also be noted that the composition of the devices in the ARO structure can be further modified by varying gate sizes and low-/high-threshold transistors without hurting the logical behavior of the PUF.

10.2.3.3 Reliable RO Pair Formation

Typically, the bitflip in RO PUF occurs due to a high mismatch in the frequency degradation rate in different ROs from environmental variations and aging. However, the degradation speed also depends on systematic and random variations and other manufacturing-related parameters. Since randomly formed RO pairs do not show any predictive correlation with such systematic and other variations within their elements, such a formation scheme tends to fail to achieve high reliability. Rahman et al. [29] proposed a reliable pair formation scheme, called *RePa*, that can achieve up to

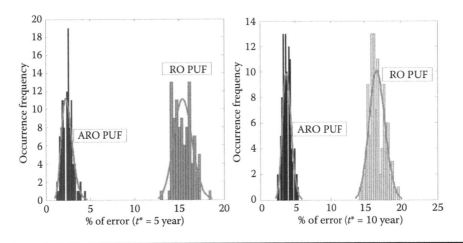

Figure 10.7 Percentage of error after 5 and 10 years of operation for ARO PUF and RO PUF under the same stress condition. (Adapted from M. T. Rahman et al. *IEEE Transactions on Emerging Topics in Computing*, 4(3):335–348, 2016.)

Table 10.1 Average Error (%) for ARO PUF and RO PUF

Year	ARO PUF (%)	RO PUF (%)
2.5	1.5781	10.3602
5	2.4316	11.4690
7.5	3.1680	12.1970
10	3.8320	12.7632

100% reliability, that is, zero error, by making selective pairing among the ROs. Using a predictive aging/voltage-based degradation profile, it sorts all ROs in an RO PUF to find the most suitable pairs to probabilistically offer zero bitflip and does the PUF registration accordingly. The authors in Reference 29 predict the aging degradation using V_{dd} variation because both simulation and silicon data suggest that the degradation trend (rate/slope) for V_{dd} variation shows strong correlation to degradation rate for aging, as shown in Table 10.2. This potentially eliminates the need for a slow and costly burn-in test for aging prediction since the required data for pair formation now can be collected during the electrical testing phase. Table 10.3 also shows RePa's effectiveness, which is up to 100%, for a given frequency threshold (Δf_{th}).

10.2.4 Thwarting Modeling Attacks for Strong PUFs

Strong PUFs, by definition, are capable of producing an exponential number of CRPs, making it extremely suitable for authentication and identification-oriented protocols. However, such a large possible CRP set makes strong PUFs potentially vulnerable to machine-learning-assisted modeling attacks [30]. In general, modeling attacks on strong PUFs start with an adversary getting hold of a subset of all CRPs of the PUF under attack. Using this CRP subset, the adversary

Table 10.2   Correlation of V_{dd} Variation versus Aging Degradation

| | HSPICE Simulation | | | Silicon Result | |
| | Correlation Coefficient (ρ) | | | Correlation Coefficient (ρ) | |
Stress (Year)	Average	Worst	Stress (Hour)	Average	Worst
2.5	0.54	0.4	7	0.41	0.37
5	0.57	0.44	14	0.46	0.41
7.5	0.61	0.45	21	0.51	0.44
10	0.67	0.49	28	0.54	0.47

Source: Adapted from M. T. Rahman et al. *Computer Design (ICCD), 2015 33rd IEEE International Conference on,* pages 415–418. IEEE, New York, NY, 2015.

tries to derive a numerical model to correctly predict the PUF's responses to additional arbitrary challenges. Researchers have launched multiple machine learning (ML) technique-based modeling attacks on the traditional arbiter PUF, an ideal example of strong PUFs, and their successes have led to necessary modifications, resulting in several relatively more attack-resilient compositions of the traditional arbiter PUF [31].

The basic numerical model of a traditional arbiter PUF is based on the fact that its functionality can be expressed by an additive linear delay model. The overall delays of the signals that are propagating through multiple paths of the delay stages can be expressed as the sum of the delays in the stages and associated interconnects [30,31]. The output of an arbiter PUF is then determined by the sign of the final delay difference, assuming that the arbiter has ideally zero bias. This simple, yet powerful, model thus leads to the creation of a two-class classification technique based on a linear-delay-based hyperplane trained with the collected/leaked CRP subset by the adversary.

As it is seen, the resiliency of the arbiter PUF is questionable due to its simple linear-delay-based modeling. Researchers have proposed several techniques to strengthen the modeling attack resiliency of the traditional arbiter PUF by introducing *nonlinearity* into the architecture. One such example is the XOR arbiter PUF [4] as given in Figure 10.8. The composition of this PUF contains multiple individual arbiter PUFs in parallel. Each of the arbiter PUFs has the same number of delay stages and is fed with same challenges. The output of the individual arbiter PUFs is XORed in

Table 10.3   Effectiveness of RePa on RO PUF against Aging

| | HSPICE Simulation | | Silicon Result | |
Frequency Threshold (Δf_{th})	Required ROs (Average)	Error (Average) (%)	Required ROs (Average)	Error (Average) (%)
0 MHz	1×	1.25	1×	0.96
$0.5 * \Delta f_{th_{min}}$	1.52×	0.41	1.7×	0.16
$\Delta f_{th_{min}}$	1.82×	0	1.94×	0

Source: Adapted from M. T. Rahman et al. *Computer Design (ICCD), 2015 33rd IEEE International Conference on,* pages 415–418. IEEE, New York, NY, 2015.

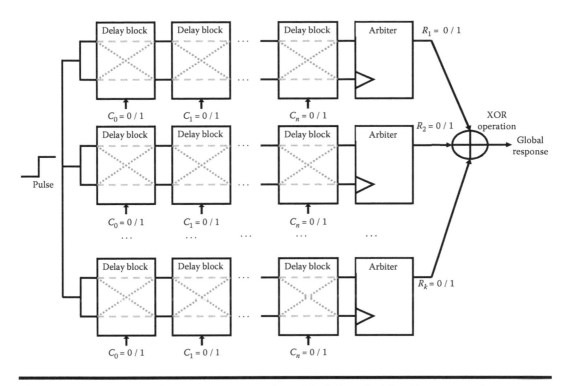

Figure 10.8 **Schematic of an XOR PUF. It consists of *k*-chains of *n*-bit arbiter PUFs. The responses of all arbiters are XORed together to generate the final binary response.**

order to produce a final response. Since the final response here depends on the XORed outputs of multiple arbiter PUFs, it contains a good amount of nonlinearity to resist simple machine learning attacks.

Nonlinearity of arbiter PUF can also be increased by introducing feedforward connections into the delay path, as shown in the simple feedforward arbiter PUF structure in Figure 10.9 [31]. This structure utilizes the "unknown" generated challenges within the PUF architecture where the intrinsically generated challenges are fed to the forthcoming delay blocks. Hence, the path switching of the delay stages connected to the "feedforward loop" depends on the behavior of the

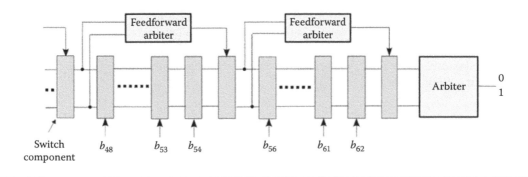

Figure 10.9 **Structure of a feedforward arbiter PUF. (Adapted from D. Lim et al. *IEEE Transactions on Very Large Scale Integration (VLSI) Systems*, 13(10):1200–1205, 2005.)**

Table 10.4 Modeling Accuracy of Traditional Arbiter PUF, XOR Arbiter PUF, and Feedforward Arbiter PUF Using Simulated CRPs

PUF Type	ML Method	Prediction Rate (%)	Required CRPs	Training Time
Traditional arbiter PUF	Logistic regression	99.9	39,200	2.10 seconds
XOR arbiter PUF (#XOR = 4)	Logistic regression	99.9	24,000	2:52 hours
Feedforward arbiter PUF (#FF Loop = 6)	Evolution strategies	99.11	50,000	3.15 hours

Source: Adapted from U. Rührmair et al. *IEEE Transactions on Information Forensics and Security*, 8(11):1876–1891, 2013.

Note: Each PUF has 128 stages.

previous stages and can be modeled as a function of the delay differences accumulated in earlier delay stages of the PUF. Such dependency creates a nondistinguishable functional model for the arbiter PUF. As a result, the feedforward arbiter PUF shows resiliency against machine learning attacks that utilize linearly separable or differentiable models. Also, the designer can choose the number of feedforward loops and connection points as necessary, making the attack model more complicated.

However, both such variant compositions of arbiter PUF are not absolutely resilient from modeling attacks. Hospodar et al. [32] and Ruhrmair et al. [30] presented exhaustive attack results on different compositions of arbiter PUFs. It is shown that both the traditional arbiter PUF and XOR arbiter PUF can be easily modeled to a very high accuracy (e.g., ~99%) using popular machine learning techniques such as *Logistic Regression* at the cost of modeling time. Ruhrmair et al. [30,33] also showed that machine learning techniques that use nonlinear classifications such as *Evolution Strategies* can be used to correctly predict the CRP set of a given feedforward arbiter PUF to a high accuracy. Table 10.4 shows some significant modeling results for the aforementioned PUFs.

Researchers have further expanded the modeling attack scenario on the delay-based strong PUFs. Delvaux et al. [34] presented a fault-injection-oriented modeling attack using the repeatability imperfections of PUF responses as a side channel information for modeling. The response evaluation faults are triggered via environmental changes. Side channel information like power and timing data can be exploited for launching an efficient modeling attack that can break the PUF within hours [35,36]. So, there is no doubt that the current PUF structures, especially for the delay-based strong PUFs, need rigorous improvements in terms of physical composition to provide superior attack resiliency.

10.2.5 PUF Composition for Emerging Applications

In addition to traditional key-based cryptographic applications, researchers have proposed several emerging security applications, such as *virtual proofs of reality*, that utilize the inherent characteristics of the PUF [37]. The idea of virtual proof (VP) is based on the underlying fact that there should be ways to verify the correctness and authenticity of the digital data obtained from tangible physical system properties or processes between two communicating parties, that is, prover and verifier, located at a distance without using any secret key-based classical mechanisms. Since classical keys are deemed vulnerable to physical and malware-based attack techniques, the avoidance of the keys might lead to safer, cost-effective, and compact designs of modern cryptographic hardware. The example of VPs, based on witness objects (WOs) such as temperature variant ICs, disordered optical scattering media, and quantum systems, can be novel protocols that successfully verify the temperature, relative position of objects, or destruction of specific physical objects.

As for proof-of-concept experimentation, the authors employed ICs for the VPs of temperature, and optical systems for VPs of relative distance, colocality, and destruction. Several novel variants of PUFs can be exploited in this regard. For example, the temperature proof can be obtained by CMOS-based bistable ring PUF where the high temperature sensitivity is advantageously exploited. To verify the VP of distance and destruction claims, one can employ variants of optical PUF.

The significance of the work lies in its difference from conventional approaches. These virtual proof mechanisms do not necessarily utilize the traditional PUF key generation concepts where the CRPs are required to maintain some significant properties (e.g., CRPs need to be "robust" across all temperature/voltage corners). For example, the virtual proof of temperature, in fact, utilizes the high error rate occurring in the CRPs at different temperature corners to obtain temperature-dependent CRPs (or signatures) that allow the verifier or the authenticator to obtain temperature information. For such a specific application, the underlying PUF composition would rather be tailored to be highly impacted by the temperature, as opposed to traditional robust PUFs. Exploiting the active components such as transistor features, and variations in logic cells, should lead to such PUF designs targeting particular emerging applications.

10.3 Composition of Physical Unclonable Functions with Emerging Memory Devices

CMOS-based memories, that is, DRAM, SRAM, and flash memory, have been the primary option for storing temporary and permanent data in the majority of the computing systems to date. However, the bottleneck in system performance due to the memory wall and the speed difference in logic and memory are major obstacles in existing systems. This has evidently led to several emerging memory devices such as PCM, resistive random access memory (RRAM), and spintronic memory devices such as spin-torque-transfer random access memory (STT-RAM) [38,39]. Though high-performance and reliable computing has always been the driving factor for memory technologies, security issues have been emphasized over recent years due to the present trend in consumer electronics. Since the contemporary electronic market is getting inclined toward mobile, more interconnected, and data-centric applications suitable for devices similar to IoT, memory types (both CMOS-based and emerging NVMs) with suitable functionalities in hardware security applications are deemed as promising technology enablers in the semiconductor industry. Apart from being used as storage space, memory systems show unique characteristics suitable for hardware security applications and can introduce the notion of security-oriented architecture to the technology developers [39].

Memory-based security primitives are highly anticipated as these eliminate the necessity of additional or dedicated circuitry in a computing system for authentication and secure operation purposes, reducing area and computational overhead in an order of magnitude [14]. Researchers have proposed several hardware security primitives, with a majority being PUFs, over the past decade as discussed in the following sections.

10.3.1 Composition of PCM-Based PUF

10.3.1.1 Sources of Process-Induced Variability

PCM is one of the emerging NVMs that operate through a reversible transition between the low-resistance phase (crystalline phase) and high-resistance phase (amorphous phase) that can be controlled through "set/reset" current pulses with *predefined* magnitude and pulse duration [40]. Consequently, the resistance of the PCM cells varies randomly during this programming process, that is, based on the set/reset current pulse as shown in Figure 10.2. Also, manufacturing process variation affects the physical dimensions as well as the strength of PCM cells, consequently inducing a stochastic nature in the electrical properties. Cell geometry features (such as GST layer thickness, heater thickness, bottom electrode contact diameter, etc.) and the electrical and thermal conductivities of the GST and heater material are prominent factors responsible for the process variations [41]. The inherent randomness originating from the cell geometry and other structural and characteristic variations, and the different types of dynamics exhibited by PCM cells, make them well suited for cryptographic measures, especially for PUF applications. Some of the interesting properties for hardware-oriented security application are listed in Figure 10.2.

10.3.1.2 PCM PUF Designs

The process variation and programming sensitivity of PCM can be exploited to implement PCM-based PUFs. A novel design for generating cryptographic keys via reconfigurable PUF based on PCM cells is proposed by Zhang et al. [42]. Here, the authors have used the variations between PCM cells in an array to generate keys as shown in Figure 10.10. PCM PUF is designed by exploiting traditional crossbar architecture and the individual PCM cells or a set of cells in the crossbar array can be programmed with a predefined pulse to extract a unique response. Although all the cells can be programmed with the exactly same pulse, the generated read-out value (i.e., analog in nature before any comparative sensing) will be unique from cell to cell within the same circuit, and also across different circuits, due to the stochastic nature of the PCM cell. Owing to the nonvolatile nature of the cell, the same unique response can be regenerated considering an ideal noise-free scenario. It should be noted that the composition of PCM PUF would result into a "weak" PUF due to the traditional crossbar architecture, that is, the PCM PUF would have a small number of CRPs unless the memory access mechanism is designed to perform a random and nonlinear

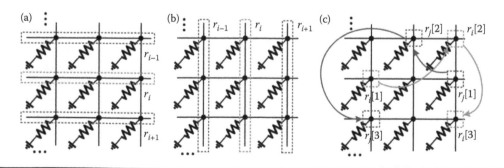

Figure 10.10 A crossbar architecture for PCM CRP generation: (a) horizontal, (b) vertical, and (c) random challenge selection. (Adapted from L. Zhang et al. *IEEE Transactions on Information Forensics and Security*, 9(6):921–932, 2014.)

access technique. Also, the produced signatures may require further postprocessing to be exploited as standard CRPs.

The generation of a unique signature from the PCM crossbar architecture can be further extended by varying the cell resistance distribution using programming pulse modification [7]. Additionally, the multilevel cell operation of a PCM cell has been exploited to generate unique signatures as a PUF in Reference 43.

10.3.2 Composition of Memristor and RRAM-Based PUF

10.3.2.1 Sources of Process-Induced Variability

Similar to PCM, it is possible to exploit the write mechanism of memristors and RRAMs and extract random cell behavior influenced by process variations for potential PUF applications. Since these devices have a larger resistance window, one can exploit the uncertainty in the logic state from the undefined region between high and low states. For memristors, such analog resistance variability and associated memory write/read time depends on the cell structure and dimensions, such as device thickness, that can be leveraged as an entropy source due to manufacturing process variation. Additionally, the source of entropy in RRAMs originates from intrinsic features such as oxide thickness and defect density, and these can very well be exploited for PUF functionalities.

10.3.2.2 Memristor and RRAM-PUF Designs

The effect of process variability in memristor cell operation is exploited in Reference 44 to develop a write-time-based memristive PUF cell. Here, the time for the write operation is set to the minimum value required to switch the cell from high-resistance state to low-resistance state. Hence, generating a probability of the output logic being "1" is raised to 50% and vice versa. Researchers have also proposed RRAM-based PUFs that utilize the traditional crossbar memory architecture [45]. This composition improves the accuracy of split references using dummy cells that eventually reduces the offset by decreasing the transistor size of the split sense amplifier (S/A).

10.3.3 Composition of MRAM and STT-RAM-Based PUF

10.3.3.1 Sources of Process-Induced Variability

Spintronic devices, such as STT-RAM and MRAM, also offer novel opportunities for hardware security applications as they exhibit phenomena such as chaotic magnetization, statistical read/write failures, stochastic retention failure, and back-hopping as depicted in Figure 10.2 [38]. The chaotic and random dynamics of the free layer of the magnetic tunnel junction (MJT) is exploited by researchers to develop hardware security primitives such as PUFs [8,46]. Additionally, the statistical and stochastic nature of read-write failures, back-hopping, and retention times can also be exploited to develop novel Spintronic circuit-based PUFs and TRNGs [47]. The compatibility of such spintronic devices with silicon substrate makes these a potential candidate for complementing existing CMOS-based security primitives.

10.3.3.2 MRAM and STT-RAM PUF Designs

Physical variation-dependent MPAM-PUF is proposed by Das et al. [46]. The authors exploited the random tilt generated in the energy barrier of MTJs due to manufacturing process variations and extracted the randomness to generate PUF responses. Since the distribution of tilt angle is Gaussian in nature, the free layer orientation of the MTJs is inclined to a certain initial value similar to the behavior of the SRAM PUF. Additional proposed techniques like gradual decrement of aspect ratio at constant volume and increment of volume at constant ratio enhance the variation in tilt angle and obtain more stable PUF output.

The random initialization of magnetic state in the free layer in STT-RAMs is exploited for PUF design in Reference 8. Here, the responses are generated during the registration phase by comparing the STT-RAM bits of complementary rows. Noise and sense amplifier offsets are utilized to produce response bits in the case of comparison bits which are initialized with similar values. The repeatability of bit generation is ensured by writing the values at MTJs. The write-back is employed to preserve the responses for multiple accesses as well as to prevent bitflips due to voltage and temperature variations. However, the authors employed a fuzzy extractor to maintain and enhance the quality of PUF output.

10.4 Conclusion

We provide an overview of the composition of PUFs over the varying range of devices to architecture level. The discussion signifies the importance of nanoelectronic device properties in designing and implementing robust PUFs. The security features at different levels of abstraction depict several untapped sources of entropy. Harnessing these tremendous entropy sources will create novel opportunities and applications for hardware security primitives, especially PUFs. Apart from nano-CMOS-based logic devices, the memory domain is also emerging as a promising alternative for hardware-oriented security measures and application. The stochastic characteristics and mechanism of emerging NVMs can be a potential technology enabler in the field of hardware security.

Acknowledgment

This project was supported in part by an Air Force Office of Scientific Research (AFOSR) MURI Grant under award number FA9550-14-1-0351 and by the National Science Foundation under Grant 1603475, Grant 1603483, and Grant 1603483.

References

1. M. Tehranipoor and C. Wang. *Introduction to Hardware Security and Trust*. Springer Science & Business Media, New York, 2011.
2. R. Pappu, B. Recht, J. Taylor, and N. Gershenfeld. Physical one-way functions. *Science*, **297**(5589): 2026–2030, 2002.
3. B. Gassend, D. Clarke, M. Van Dijk, and S. Devadas. Silicon physical random functions. In *Proceedings of the 9th ACM Conference on Computer and Communications Security*, pages 148–160. ACM, New York, NY, 2002.
4. G. E. Suh and S. Devadas. Physical unclonable functions for device authentication and secret key generation. In *Proceedings of the 44th Annual Design Automation Conference*, pages 9–14. ACM, New York, NY, 2007.
5. M. Majzoobi, A. Elnably, and F. Koushanfar. FPGA time-bounded unclonable authentication. In *International Workshop on Information Hiding*, pages 1–16. Springer, Berlin, 2010.
6. J. Guajardo, B. Škorić, P. Tuyls, S. S. Kumar, T. Bel, A. H. Blom, and G.-J. Schrijen. Anti-counterfeiting, key distribution, and key storage in an ambient world via physical unclonable functions. *Information Systems Frontiers*, **11**(1):19–41, 2009.

7. L. Zhang, Z. H. Kong, C.-H. Chang, A. Cabrini, and G. Torelli. Exploiting process variations and programming sensitivity of phase change memory for reconfigurable physical unclonable functions. *IEEE Transactions on Information Forensics and Security*, **9**(6):921–932, 2014.

8. L. Zhang, X. Fong, C.-H. Chang, Z. H. Kong, and K. Roy. Highly reliable memory-based physical unclonable function using spin-transfer torque MRAM. In *Circuits and Systems (ISCAS), 2014 IEEE International Symposium on*, pages 2169–2172. IEEE, New York, NY, 2014.

9. G. Moore. Cramming more components onto integrated circuits, *Electronics*, **38**:114–117, 1965.

10. S. I. Association et al. International Technology Roadmap for Semiconductor (ITRS) Report 2013, 2013.

11. A. Chen, J. Hutchby, V. Zhirnov, and G. Bourianoff. *Emerging Nanoelectronic Devices*. John Wiley & Sons, Chichester, 2014.

12. Samsung Group, Samsung Starts Industry's First Mass Production of System-on-Chip with 10-Nanometer FinFET Technology, 2016. Available at: https://news.samsung.com/global/samsung-starts-industrys-first-mass-production-of-system-on-chip-with-10-nanometer-finfet-technology

13. F. Rahman, D. Forte, and M. M. Tehranipoor. Reliability vs. security: Challenges and opportunities for developing reliable and secure integrated circuits. In *Reliability Physics Symposium (IRPS), 2016 IEEE International*, pages 4C–6. IEEE, New York, NY, 2016.

14. D. E. Holcomb, W. P. Burleson, and K. Fu. Power-up SRAM state as an identifying fingerprint and source of true random numbers. *IEEE Transactions on Computers*, **58**(9):1198–1210, 2009.

15. X. Xu, A. Rahmati, D. E. Holcomb, K. Fu, and W. Burleson. Reliable physical unclonable functions using data retention voltage of SRAM cells. *IEEE Transactions on Computer-Aided Design of Integrated Circuits and Systems*, **34**(6):903–914, 2015.

16. X. Xu and D. E. Holcomb. Reliable PUF design using failure patterns from time-controlled power gating. In *Defect and Fault Tolerance in VLSI and Nanotechnology Systems (DFT), 2016 IEEE International Symposium on*, pages 135–140. IEEE, New York, NY, 2016.

17. M. Majzoobi, G. Ghiaasi, F. Koushanfar, and S. R. Nassif. Ultra-low power current-based PUF. In *Circuits and Systems (ISCAS), 2011 IEEE International Symposium on*, pages 2071–2074. IEEE, New York, NY, 2011.

18. A. Maiti, V. Gunreddy, and P. Schaumont. A systematic method to evaluate and compare the performance of physical unclonable functions. In *Embedded Systems Design with FPGAs*, pages 245–267. Springer, Berlin, 2013.

19. L. Lin, S. Srivathsa, D. K. Krishnappa, P. Shabadi, and W. Burleson. Design and validation of arbiter-based PUFs for sub-45-nm low-power security applications. *IEEE Transactions on Information Forensics and Security*, **7**(4):1394–1403, 2012.

20. A. S. Sedra and K. C. Smith. *Microelectronic Circuits*. Vol. **1**. Oxford University Press, New York, 1998.

21. Y. Lao and K. K. Parhi. Statistical analysis of MUX-based physical unclonable functions. *IEEE Transactions on Computer-Aided Design of Integrated Circuits and Systems*, **33**(5):649–662, 2014.

22. J. Capovilla, M. Cortes, and G. Araujo. Improving the statistical variability of delay-based physical unclonable functions. In *Proceedings of the 28th Symposium on Integrated Circuits and Systems Design*, page 41. ACM, New York, NY, 2015.

23. A. Herkle, M. Schuster, J. Becker, and M. Ortmanns. Enhanced arbiter PUFs using custom sized structures for reduced noise sensitivity. In *Electronics, Circuits and Systems (ICECS), 2016 IEEE International Conference on*, pages 568–571. IEEE, New York, NY, 2016.

24. X. Xu, W. Burleson, and D. E. Holcomb. Using statistical models to improve the reliability of delay-based PUFs. In *VLSI (ISVLSI), 2016 IEEE Computer Society Annual Symposium on*, pages 547–552. IEEE, New York, NY, 2016.

25. M. T. Rahman, F. Rahman, D. Forte, and M. Tehranipoor. An aging-resistant RO PUF for reliable key generation. *IEEE Transactions on Emerging Topics in Computing*, **4**(3):335–348, 2016.

26. M.-D. M. Yu and S. Devadas. Secure and robust error correction for physical unclonable functions. *IEEE Design & Test of Computers*, **27**(1):48–65, 2010.

27. J. Delvaux and I. Verbauwhede. Attacking PUF-based pattern matching key generators via helper data manipulation. In *Cryptographers Track at the RSA Conference*, pages 106–131. Springer, Berlin, 2014.

28. X. Xu and D. Holcomb. A clockless sequential PUF with autonomous majority voting. In *Great Lakes Symposium on VLSI, 2016 International*, pages 27–32. IEEE, New York, NY, 2016.

29. M. T. Rahman, D. Forte, F. Rahman, and M. Tehranipoor. A pair selection algorithm for robust RO PUF against environmental variations and aging. In *Computer Design (ICCD), 2015 33rd IEEE International Conference on*, pages 415–418. IEEE, New York, NY, 2015.

30. U. Rührmair, J. Sölter, F. Sehnke, X. Xu, A. Mahmoud, V. Stoyanova, G. Dror, J. Schmidhuber, W. Burleson, and S. Devadas. PUF modeling attacks on simulated and silicon data. *IEEE Transactions on Information Forensics and Security*, **8**(11):1876–1891, 2013.

31. D. Lim, J. W. Lee, B. Gassend, G. E. Suh, M. Van Dijk, and S. Devadas. Extracting secret keys from integrated circuits. *IEEE Transactions on Very Large Scale Integration (VLSI) Systems*, **13**(10):1200–1205, 2005.

32. G. Hospodar, R. Maes, and I. Verbauwhede. Machine learning attacks on 65 nm arbiter PUFs: Accurate modeling poses strict bounds on usability. In *Information Forensics and Security (WIFS), 2012 IEEE International Workshop on*, pages 37–42. IEEE, New York, NY, 2012.

33. X. Xu, U. Rührmair, D. E. Holcomb, and W. Burleson. Security evaluation and enhancement of bistable ring PUFs. In *International Workshop on Radio Frequency Identification: Security and Privacy Issues*, pages 3–16. Springer, Berlin, 2015.

34. J. Delvaux and I. Verbauwhede. Side channel modeling attacks on 65 nm arbiter PUFs exploiting CMOS device noise. In *Hardware-Oriented Security and Trust (HOST), 2013 IEEE International Symposium on*, pages 137–142. IEEE, New York, NY, 2013.

35. X. Xu and W. Burleson. Hybrid side-channel/machine-learning attacks on PUFs: A new threat? In *Proceedings of the Conference on Design, Automation & Test in Europe*, page 349. European Design and Automation Association, Leuven, Belgium, 2014.

36. U. Rührmair, X. Xu, J. Sölter, A. Mahmoud, M. Majzoobi, F. Koushanfar, and W. Burleson. Efficient power and timing side channels for physical unclonable functions. In *International Workshop on Cryptographic Hardware and Embedded Systems*, pages 476–492. Springer, Berlin, 2014.

37. U. Rührmair, J. Martinez-Hurtado, X. Xu, C. Kraeh, C. Hilgers, D. Kononchuk, J. J. Finley, and W. P. Burleson. Virtual proofs of reality and their physical implementation. In *Security and Privacy (SP), 2015 IEEE Symposium on*, pages 70–85. IEEE, New York, NY, 2015.

38. J. S. Meena, S. M. Sze, U. Chand, and T.-Y. Tseng. Overview of emerging nonvolatile memory technologies. *Nanoscale Research Letters*, **9**(1):526, 2014.

39. A. Chen. Emerging nonvolatile memory (NVM) technologies. In *Solid State Device Research Conference (ESSDERC), 2015 45th European*, pages 109–113. IEEE, New York, NY, 2015.

40. H.-S. P. Wong, S. Raoux, S. Kim, J. Liang, J. P. Reifenberg, B. Rajendran, M. Asheghi, and K. E. Goodson. Phase change memory. *Proceedings of the IEEE*, **98**(12):2201–2227, 2010.

41. W. Zhang and T. Li. Characterizing and mitigating the impact of process variations on phase change based memory systems. In *Proceedings of the 42nd Annual IEEE/ACM International Symposium on Microarchitecture*, pages 2–13. ACM, New York, NY, 2009.

42. L. Zhang, Z. H. Kong, and C.-H. Chang. PCKGen: A phase change memory based cryptographic key generator. In *Circuits and Systems (ISCAS), 2013 IEEE International Symposium on*, pages 1444–1447. IEEE, New York, NY, 2013.

43. K. Kursawe, A.-R. Sadeghi, D. Schellekens, B. Skoric, and P. Tuyls. Reconfigurable physical unclonable functions-enabling technology for tamper-resistant storage. In *Hardware-Oriented Security and Trust, 2009. HOST'09. IEEE International Workshop on*, pages 22–29. IEEE, New York, NY, 2009.

44. G. S. Rose, N. McDonald, L.-K. Yan, and B. Wysocki. A write-time based memristive PUF for hardware security applications. In *Proceedings of the International Conference on Computer-Aided Design*, pages 830–833. IEEE Press, New York, NY, 2013.

45. R. Liu, H. Wu, Y. Pang, H. Qian, and S. Yu. A highly reliable and tamper-resistant RRAM PUF: Design and experimental validation. In *Hardware Oriented Security and Trust (HOST), 2016 IEEE International Symposium on*, pages 13–18. IEEE, New York, NY, 2016.

46. J. Das, K. Scott, S. Rajaram, D. Burgett, and S. Bhanja. MRAM PUF: A novel geometry based magnetic PUF with integrated CMOS. *IEEE Transactions on Nanotechnology*, **14**(3):436–443, 2015.

47. S. Ghosh. Spintronics and security: Prospects, vulnerabilities, attack models, and preventions. *Proceedings of the IEEE*, **104**(10):1864–1893, 2016.

Chapter 11

Security in Emerging Fabrication Technologies

Yuntao Liu, Yang Xie, and Ankur Srivastava

Contents

In this chapter, we explore the opportunities to improve the security in integrated circuit (IC) fabrication brought by emerging fabrication technologies including double patterning lithography (DPL) and three-dimensional (3D) integration. The chapter first investigates how DPL can help thwart the attacks from an untrusted employee in a foundry under the trusted foundry and untrusted employee (TFUE) model. Almost all the previous studies on the security vulnerabilities of IC supply chain label foundries as either untrusted or trusted. To thwart the foundry attacks such as Trojan insertion, IC piracy, etc., multiple countermeasures have been proposed, including obfuscation-, split manufacturing-, and postfabrication editing-based approaches [1–5]. Among these technologies, obfuscation-based approaches suffer from significant area and performance overhead, split manufacturing requires either a trusted foundry, which is expensive to maintain or 3D/2.5D integration technology, and postfabrication editing must be done on a chip-by-chip basis and suffers from low efficiency. In contrast to the above approaches that look at the IC supply chain security issues from the designer's perspective, the TFUE model tries to secure IC manufacturing from the foundry's side. In real world cases, the foundries are usually legally and financially obliged to provide trusted fabrication service. However, no matter the foundry is conventionally considered as trusted or untrusted, there can be rogue employees. We will review the fundamentals of DPL and introduce a customized DPL flow to defend the untrusted employee attacks.

In the second half of this chapter, we investigate the security opportunities and challenges in 3D integration. In a 3D IC, multiple 2D ICs are stacked together to form a single IC. Compared to connecting multiple chips using off-chip connection, 3D integration has huge advantages: it requires much smaller area, and the communication within a 3D IC is much faster than the communication between different chips. In addition to the great advances in performance, 3D integration technology unlocks new opportunities as well. For example, by having each die of the 3D IC fabricated in a different foundry, the chance that the design can be counterfeited is greatly reduced. However, 3D IC also introduces new security vulnerabilities. For example, the stacked structure will limit our physical access to the lower layers of the chip, thereby imposing difficulties to detect counterfeiting and side-channel attacks.

11.1 Security Opportunities by DPL

11.1.1 Fundamentals of DPL

In this section, we present a brief introduction to DPL. In a lithography step, the minimum distance between two features (i.e., polygons in the layout) is physically constrained, and we call this distance the *minimum feature spacing*, denoted as λ. The technology node of IC fabrication has scaled down to a point where the minimum feature spacing λ cannot provide enough resolution. To address this issue, DPL technology has been developed. DPL decomposes the layout into two sublayouts and process each of these sublayouts in an independent production line. How a sublayout is processed in its production line is similar to how an entire layout is processed without DPL: the layout will be edited to ensure compatibility with the foundry's process. These edits, however, should not change the functionality of the design. After editing, each sublayout is converted to a mask. Finally, in the lithography stage, there are two lithography steps, each using one mask converted from one of the sublayouts. Then, the fabricated chip will look like the original layout.

In order for DPL to work, each sublayout should be such that the distance between adjacent features on this sublayout is at least λ. In general, the process of layout decomposition consists of layout fracturing, graph construction, node splitting, and graph update. We illustrate the steps in

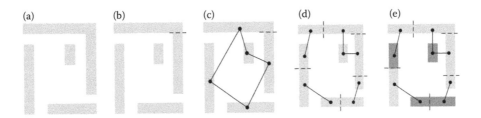

Figure 11.1 The steps of layout decomposition: (a) the original layout, (b) layout fracturing, (c) graph construction, (d) node splitting, and (e) color assignment.

Figure 11.1. The layout of VLSI is composed of features, and each feature is a rectilinear polygon. In the layout fracturing step, all the features are partitioned into rectangles. For example, in Figure 11.1a, the upper right feature is not a rectangle, so it should be fractured into rectangles. The dashed line in Figure 11.1b shows one possible way to partition that feature. We then build the *conflict graph*. Let us consider each rectangle in the layout as a node, and add an edge between a pair of nodes if the distance between their corresponding rectangles is smaller than λ, as shown in Figure 11.1c. Due to the way that the conflict graph is constructed, any two rectangles that are connected with an edge in the conflict graph cannot be assigned to the same sublayout. The layout decomposition problem now becomes a node coloring problem: we need to color the nodes in the conflict graph with two colors, subject to that adjacent nodes should have opposite colors. Therefore, if there exists an odd-length cycle in the conflict graph, there will be no feasible solution to the node coloring problem; that is, there is a conflict. For instance, as shown in Figure 11.1c, there is a five-node cycle in the conflict graph, and there is no way to color these nodes with two colors and let each pair of adjacent nodes have opposite colors. To resolve this issue, we need to split at least one of these rectangles to break the cycle. Figure 11.1d shows the possible ways to split the nodes. One feasible way of color assignment is shown in Figure 11.1e.

The node coloring problem is often formulated as an integer linear programming (ILP) problem. Existing ILP-based approaches focus on improving the yield of chips, and the following criteria are usually included in the objective function:

1. Penalizing design rule violations
2. Reducing the number of stitches, that is, avoiding color change within the same polygon
3. Other factors that may help to improve the yield

For greater details about DPL, we refer the interested readers to Reference 6.

11.1.2 TFUE: The Trusted Foundry and Untrusted Employee Model

In this section, we introduce the TFUE model [7]. We will discuss the reasons that this model is more realistic than the conventional assumption that a foundry is either completely trusted or completely untrusted. We argue that the owner and machinery of the foundry are trusted and that the untrustworthiness is actually due to the employees.

TFUE is realistic for the following reasons:

1. Every foundry wants larger market share. In order to achieve this, even the foundries that are conventionally assumed untrusted, including offshore foundries, want designers to believe

that their fabrication is trustworthy. Undermining or counterfeiting the chip designs massively at the foundry level is very risky: if this is noticed by the designer, the foundry will not only face legal and financial troubles but also lose business in the future. Therefore, the foundries will have secure setup in their machinery and enforce certain security policies. For example, a certain level of security clearance may be required for an employee to access the layout of the design. These can be reviewed by the designer and/or licensed by a third party. The process line of a foundry can, therefore, be trusted even if the foundry is conventionally assumed as untrusted.

2. Although some foundries are conventionally assumed as trusted, it does not necessarily mean that every employee of the foundry is trusted. There can be rogue employees who are bought by the foundry's or the designer's competitors. If such employees get access to the layout, there is a risk that the design will be undermined or stolen. In this case, even a conventionally trusted foundry will perform like an untrusted foundry.

Due to the above two reasons, we argue that the employees are the source of untrustworthiness in a foundry, and we no longer classify the foundries as trusted or untrusted. Instead, we will take TFUE as our primary assumption throughout this chapter, and the threaten model and countermeasures in the context of DPL will be presented in the following sections. In the next section, we will investigate how an untrusted employee of the foundry can threat the IC supply chain security even with the foundry's secure machinery and security policies in place, and we will also explore the opportunities brought by DPL to thwart these threats.

11.1.3 Threat Model and Countermeasure under TFUE

11.1.3.1 Threat Model

We consider the threats and countermeasures in the context that the foundry uses DPL to fabricate the chip. The layout obtained from the designer is decomposed into two sublayouts in the secure machinery of the foundry with automated tools. The two sublayouts are then processed in two independent production lines by two mutually exclusive sets of employees. The independent production lines do not share any information, nor can the employees communicate during work. Each of the sublayouts is edited in its production line to ensure manufacturability and converted into a mask after editing is finished. It is the employees in the production line who actually edit the sublayout and the employee can be an attacker.

In this context, we make the following assumptions about the attacker:

■ The attacker who is an employee of the foundry work in one of the independent production lines, and his or her knowledge about the design is limited to the sublayout processed by that line.
■ The attacker works alone and do not communicate with other employees.
■ The attacker is supposed to edit the sublayout to improve its manufacturability. However, he or she can actually make any change to the layout.
■ The attacker may also steal the sublayout and try to recover the original layout and counterfeit the chip design.

The attack model is illustrated in Figure 11.2.

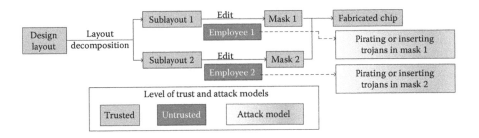

Figure 11.2 The attack model in the context of DPL under TFUE.

11.1.3.2 *Countermeasure Formulation*

In order to insert Trojans into the circuit or counterfeit the IC design, the attacker needs to have some perception of the original layout based on the inspection on the sublayout. We will define a metric of distance between two layout images. Based on the intuition that each sublayout looks as "different" as possible from the original layout, we propose a variant of layout decomposition algorithm such that the minimum distance between the original layout and each sublayout is maximized.

Before we start any mathematical derivation, let us specify the convention of notations used here. We use lower case to denote scalars and vectors, and capital case to denote matrices. For example, x is a scalar, $\mathbf{x}$ is a vector, and X is a matrix. The indices of vectors and matrices are denoted by lower scripts.

In this section, we follow the layout decomposition process specified in Section 11.1.1 up to the node splitting step, and we assume that the design rule check process performed by the designer has made sure that there will not be unresolvable coloring conflicts. We consider the layout as a binary image, where a pixel value is 1 if it is on a feature, and 0 otherwise. Similarly, each rectangle obtained by the layout fracturing and node splitting process can also be viewed as a binary image (of the size of the original layout). A comprehensive list of the symbols that are used in the derivation is in Table 11.1, and the symbols are also explained when they are used in the equations.

We consider the distance between two binary images in the frequency domain instead of pixel values. To do so, we transform the original layout using 2D Fourier transform (2D-FFT):

$$F_{\mu v} = \frac{1}{wl} \sum_{x=1}^{w} \sum_{y=1}^{l} I_{xy} e^{-2\pi j\left(\frac{x\mu}{w} + \frac{yv}{l}\right)}$$

Let F^0, F^1, and F^2 be the 2D-FFT coefficient matrices of the original layout, the first sublayout, and the second sublayout, respectively. Similar to the 1D-FFT, the 2D-FFT is also linear, that is,

$$F^0 = F^1 + F^2$$

This equation also holds elementwise, that is, $F^0_{ij} = F^1_{ij} + F^2_{ij}$ for any $i,j = 1, \ldots, p$. As a layout or sublayout is composed of multiple rectangles, its 2D-FFT coefficient matrix is also equal to the

Table 11.1 Symbols Used in the Derivation of Our DPL Approach

Symbol and Domain	Meaning
$\lambda \in \mathbb{R}_{++}$	The minimum feature spacing
n	The number of rectangles in the layout
$\mathbf{G=(V,E)}$	The conflict graph
$\mathbf{V}=\{c_k\|k=1,\ldots,n\}$	The set of nodes (rectangles) in the conflict graph
$\mathbf{E}$	$\{(c_u,c_v)\|$ the distance between c_u and $c_v \leq \lambda\}$
$p \in \mathbb{Z}_{++}$	The number of elements in each row and column of the Fourier coefficient matrices
$F^l \in \mathbb{C}^{p\times p}, l=0,1,2$	The Fourier coefficient matrix of the FFT of the layout, with $l=0,1,2$ corresponding to the original layout, the first sublayout, and the second sublayout, respectively
$s_l, l=1,2$	The distance between the original layout and sublayout l
$\mathbf{x} \in \{0,1\}^n$	The vector indicating the sublayout that each rectangle belongs to, where $\mathbf{x}_k=1$ if rectangle c_k is assigned to the first sublayout, and $\mathbf{x}_k=0$ if c_k is assigned to the second sublayout
$\bar{\mathbf{x}} \in \{0,1\}^n = \mathbf{1-x}$	
$A^l, l=0,1,2$	The real parts of F^l
$\tilde{A}^k, k=1,\ldots,n$	The real parts of $\tilde{F}^k$
$B^l, l=0,1,2$	The imaginary parts of F^l
$\tilde{B}^k, k=1,\ldots,n$	The imaginary parts of $\tilde{F}^k$
$\alpha^{(ij)} \in \mathbb{R}^n$	$\alpha^{(ij)} = \left(\tilde{A}^1_{ij}, \tilde{A}^2_{ij}, \ldots, \tilde{A}^n_{ij}\right)^T$
$\beta^{(ij)} \in \mathbb{R}^n$	$\beta^{(ij)} = \left(\tilde{B}^1_{ij}, \tilde{B}^2_{ij}, \ldots, \tilde{B}^n_{ij}\right)^T$

summation of the 2D-FFT coefficient matrices of the rectangles that compose it, that is,

$$F^0_{ij} = \sum_{k=1}^n \tilde{F}^k_{ij}, \quad F^1_{ij} = \sum_{k=1}^n \mathbf{x}_k \tilde{F}^k_{ij}, \quad \text{and} \quad F^2_{ij} = \sum_{k=1}^n \bar{\mathbf{x}}_k \tilde{F}^k_{ij}$$

The distance between two binary images in the frequency domain is defined as the RMS difference of their Fourier coefficient matrices:

$$s_l = \sqrt{\frac{1}{p^2} \sum_{i=1}^p \sum_{j=1}^p |F^0_{ij} - F^l_{ij}|^2} \tag{11.1}$$

where $l=1,2$. As we mentioned above, the distance between a sublayout and the original layout is a measure of the difficulty for the attacker. The larger the distance is, the more difficult it is to attack. Therefore, we want to partition the layout in such a way that no matter which sublayout the attacker is assigned to work on, the attacker always has a great amount of difficulty to attack. In this sense, the objective is to maximize the smaller among the two distances between each sublayout and the original layout (i.e., s_1 and s_2):

$$\max_{\mathbf{x}\in\{0,1\}^n} \min\{s_1, s_2\}$$

This can be simplified with some algebra to an equivalent form

$$\max_{\mathbf{x}\in\{0,1\}^n} \min\left\{ \sum_{i=1}^{p}\sum_{j=1}^{p}|F_{ij}^2|^2, \sum_{i=1}^{p}\sum_{j=1}^{p}|F_{ij}^1|^2 \right\} \tag{11.2}$$

Note that each Fourier coefficient is a complex number, and we have the relationship between the magnitude of the complex number and its real and imaginary parts as $|F_{ij}^l|^2 = (A_{ij}^l)^2 + (B_{ij}^l)^2$ for $l = 0, 1, 2$, where A_{ij}^l and B_{ij}^l are the real and imaginary parts of F_{ij}^l, respectively. The real and imaginary parts of Fourier coefficients also individually satisfies linearity:

$$A_{ij}^1 = \sum_{k=1}^{n}\tilde{A}_{ij}^k\mathbf{x}_k = \alpha^{(ij)T}\mathbf{x}, \quad A_{ij}^2 = \sum_{k=1}^{n}\tilde{A}_{ij}^k\bar{\mathbf{x}}_k = \alpha^{(ij)T}\bar{\mathbf{x}}$$

$$B_{ij}^1 = \sum_{k=1}^{n}\tilde{B}_{ij}^k\mathbf{x}_k = \beta^{(ij)T}\mathbf{x}, \quad B_{ij}^2 = \sum_{k=1}^{n}\tilde{B}_{ij}^k\bar{\mathbf{x}}_k = \beta^{(ij)T}\bar{\mathbf{x}}$$

where $\alpha^{(ij)} = (\tilde{A}_{ij}^1, \tilde{A}_{ij}^2, \ldots, \tilde{A}_{ij}^n)^T$ and $\beta^{(ij)} = (\tilde{B}_{ij}^1, \tilde{B}_{ij}^2, \ldots, \tilde{B}_{ij}^n)^T$. The above expressions give us the real and imaginary parts of each 2D-FFT coefficients in each sublayout. Recall that in Equation 11.2, what we need is the square of each coefficient. To obtain the quantities needed in Equation 11.2, we have

$$\sum_{i=1}^{p}\sum_{j=1}^{p}|F_{ij}^1|^2 = \sum_{i=1}^{p}\sum_{j=1}^{p}(A_{ij}^1)^2 + (B_{ij}^1)^2 = \mathbf{x}^T\left(\sum_{i=1}^{p}\sum_{j=1}^{p}\alpha^{(ij)}\alpha^{(ij)T} + \beta^{(ij)}\beta^{(ij)T}\right)\mathbf{x} = \mathbf{x}^T Q\mathbf{x}$$

where

$$Q = \sum_{i=1}^{p}\sum_{j=1}^{p}\alpha^{(ij)}\alpha^{(ij)T} + \beta^{(ij)}\beta^{(ij)T} \tag{11.3}$$

For the same reason,

$$\sum_{i=1}^{p}\sum_{j=1}^{p}|F_{ij}^2|^2 = \bar{\mathbf{x}}^T Q\bar{\mathbf{x}}$$

Now we have transformed Equation 11.2 into an integer quadratic programming (IQP) problem:

$$\max_{\mathbf{x}\in\{0,1\}^n} \min\{\mathbf{x}^T Q\mathbf{x}, \bar{\mathbf{x}}^T Q\bar{\mathbf{x}}\}$$

$$\text{subject to } \bar{\mathbf{x}} = \mathbf{1} - \mathbf{x} \tag{11.4}$$

$$\mathbf{x}_i + \mathbf{x}_j = 1 \text{ if } (c_i, c_j) \in \mathbf{E}$$

This problem is very difficult to solve for two reasons. First, the domain of $\mathbf{x}$ is $\{0,1\}^n$, and an integer problem is hard to solve in general. Second, even if we relax the domain of $\mathbf{x}$ to be continuous, we still have a problem. By Equation 11.3 we know that $Q \succ 0$, then $\mathbf{x}^T Q \mathbf{x}$ and $\bar{\mathbf{x}}^T Q \bar{\mathbf{x}}$ are convex functions of $\mathbf{x}$, and in general, the pointwise minimum of two convex functions is neither convex nor concave!

Fortunately, there is a good approximation. We discover that almost all the nonzero elements of Q are concentrated on the diagonal, and Q is very sparse off-diagonal. In fact, only less than 1% of the off-diagonal elements are nonzero for any benchmarks. Therefore, ignoring the off-diagonal elements is not likely to result in significant error. Keep in mind that each element in $\mathbf{x}$ is either 0 or 1, therefore, when we ignore the off-diagonal elements of Q, we can have the following approximation:

$$\mathbf{x}^T Q \mathbf{x} \approx \mathbf{x}^T \text{diag}(Q_{11}, \ldots, Q_{nn})\mathbf{x} = \mathbf{d}^T \mathbf{x}$$

where

$$\mathbf{d} = (Q_{11}, \ldots, Q_{nn})^T$$

The problem in Equation 11.4 can be then approximately transformed into

$$\max_{\mathbf{x} \in \{0,1\}^n} \min\{\mathbf{d}^T \mathbf{x}, \mathbf{d}^T \bar{\mathbf{x}}\}$$
$$\text{subject to } \bar{\mathbf{x}} = \mathbf{1} - \mathbf{x} \tag{11.5}$$
$$\mathbf{x}_i + \mathbf{x}_j = 1 \text{ if } (c_i, c_j) \in \mathbf{E}$$

The problem in Equation 11.5 is a well-studied ILP problem, and there exists many efficient heuristic algorithms that can get good solutions in practice.

11.1.4 Experimental Setup and Results

The experiments that simulate the countermeasure introduced in the last section are conducted, and their results are presented in this section. It can be shown that the distance between a sublayout and the original layout defined in Equation 11.1 can also be expressed as

$$s_1 = \frac{1}{p}\sqrt{\mathbf{x}^T Q \mathbf{x}} \quad \text{and} \quad s_2 = \frac{1}{p}\sqrt{\bar{\mathbf{x}}^T Q \bar{\mathbf{x}}}$$

If our approximation is reasonable, we should have

$$s_1^2 + s_2^2 \approx \frac{1}{p}(\mathbf{x} + \bar{\mathbf{x}})^T \mathbf{d} = \frac{1}{p}\mathbf{1}^T \mathbf{d} \approx \frac{1}{p}\mathbf{1}^T Q\mathbf{1}$$

Therefore, to verify our approximation, we define s_{max} as

$$s_{max} = \frac{1}{p}\sqrt{\mathbf{1}^T Q\mathbf{1}}$$

If we find that $s_1^2 + s_2^2 \approx s_{max}^2$, we can be confident about the approximated ILP we formulate.

We evaluate our approach on five benchmarks ranging up to 5000+ polygons and 8000+ polygons in the original layout and record s_1^2, s_2^2, and s_{max}^2 as well as the run time for solving problem (11.5).

Table 11.2   Experimental Results on the Countermeasure

	Benchmark		Distances			Run Time (s)
	Polygons	Rectangles	s_1^2	s_2^2	s_{max}^2	Model 1
1	200	425	461	425	883	1.174
2	510	870	669	609	1272	2.004
3	990	1596	792	734	1558	4.807
4	1989	3094	1143	1167	2313	20.26
5	5081	8398	2257	2089	4339	348.0

The data in Table 11.2 shows that the values of s_1^2 and s_2^2 that we obtain based on the solution to Equation 11.5 are close to each other and add up approximately to s_{max}^2. This indicates that our approximated ILP problem (11.5) approximates the original problem (11.4) well. As $s_1^2 + s_2^2$ is a fixed value (s_{max}^2), having them close to each other means that the smaller between them is maximized, and therefore we maximize the attacker's difficulty in inserting Trojan into the design and/or pirating the design when he or she has access to only one sublayout. The outcome using an illustrative benchmark is shown in Figure 11.3.

11.1.5 Summary and Discussion

In this part of the chapter, we explored how DPL can enhance the security of IC supply chain under the TFUE model. Based on the state-of-the-art layout decomposition algorithm, we developed our version of layout decomposition algorithm which takes security into consideration. With DPL and the secure machinery and security policies of the foundry in place, it is essentially hard for the attacker to insert Trojan or counterfeit the original design. Our contribution includes introducing the TFUE model and proposing a customized layout decomposition algorithm that maximizes the attacker's difficulty.

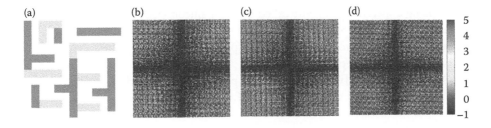

Figure 11.3   Layout decomposition result of an illustrative benchmark: (a) layout decomposition result with dark color being the first sublayout and shallower color being the second sublayout; (b) the 2D-FFt of the original layout; (c) the 2D-FFT of the first sublayout; and (d) the 2D-FFT of the second sublayout and color bar. The magnitude decreases from top to bottom. Note that the reader may need an electronic version to read (b), (c), and (d).

11.2 Security in 3D Integration Technology

Technology scaling that shrinks the physical feature size of transistors has long been an effective approach to improve chip performance. However, due to the physical limit of transistor miniaturization, the advance of technology scaling is gradually slowing down. This obstacle motivates the development of 3D integration technology.

3D integration is a technology that vertically integrates multiple 2D dies to create a high device-density chip named 3D IC [8]. This emerging technology improves chip performance in various aspects. Firstly, the vertical stacking structure reduces interconnect wirelength because two distant devices in a conventional 2D design can now be placed vertically close to each other and connected with a shorter connection. The reduction in wirelength scales down interconnect power and delay, which can be leveraged by implementing a more highly connected architecture such as the high-bandwidth memory-on-chip architecture [9]. Secondly, since multiple dies are integrated, the device density is increased and more functions can be implemented in a single chip. More importantly, 3D ICs allow heterogeneous integration, which enables different layers to be fabricated using diverse materials and technologies.

3D integration not only improves chip performance but also unlocks new opportunities to thwart various security threats. At the same time, it presents new security vulnerabilities that do not exist in conventional 2D ICs [10–12]. In this section, we provide a comprehensive survey on existing work of 3D IC-based security. We highlight the unique advantages of 3D ICs that could be leveraged to improve chips' security. Also, we discuss security vulnerabilities in 3D ICs and investigate potential solutions.

11.2.1 3D Integration

3D integration is a technology that vertically integrates multiple layers of devices and metals to create a single high-performance chip, referred to as 3D IC. Based on the integration technology, 3D IC can be classified into three types: *stacked 3D ICs* [13], *monolithic 3D ICs* [14], and *interposer-based 3D IC (or 2.5D IC)* [15], as shown in Figure 11.4. Here we first introduce and compare three types of 3D ICs.

11.2.1.1 Stacked 3D IC

Stacked 3D IC, as shown in Figure 11.4a, is fabricated by stacking multiple 2D dies and interconnecting them using a special type of wire called through-silicon-vias (TSVs). TSV is typically made of copper or tungsten. It can be used for signal communication, thermal conducting, and power delivery. The fabrication of stacked 3D ICs can exploit existing 2D IC fabrication processes. Each 2D die is firstly fabricated independently as before. After that, multiple dies are aligned and bonded together to form the 3D IC. Two key fabrication processes in the stacked 3D IC fabrication flow are TSV manufacturing [16] and die stacking [17].

11.2.1.2 Monolithic 3D IC

Different from the stacked 3D IC, monolithic 3D IC (as shown in Figure 11.4b) grows multiple device layers vertically on the same substrate in a serial order, so it does not require alignment, thinning, and bonding. Different device layers are separated using interlayer dielectric (ILD). The vertical connections through ILD in monolithic 3D ICs are nanoscale monolithic interlayer vias

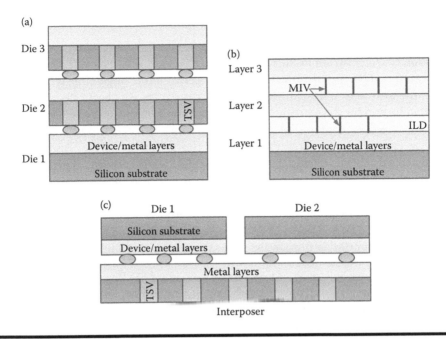

Figure 11.4   Three types of 3D ICs: (a) stacked 3D IC, (b) monolithic 3D IC, and (c) interposer-based 3D IC (2.5D IC).

(MIVs). Nanoscale MIV has much smaller size and thus has smaller parasitic capacitance than micron-scale TSV. Therefore, monolithic 3D integration can achieve more fine-grained inter-layer integration. For example, monolithic 3D IC can support transistor-level integration [18], which means that transistors in a gate can be placed in two separate layers and connected vertically using MIVs. However, the fabrication of monolithic 3D ICs faces various challenges and thus requires novel fabrication technologies, which are different from existing 2D IC fabrication technologies [19].

11.2.1.3 Interposer-Based 3D IC (2.5D IC)

Interposer-based 3D IC (or 2.5D IC) is a variant of 3D ICs, as shown in Figure 11.4c. In 2.5D ICs, multiple dies are placed side-by-side and stacked on a silicon interposer using fine-pitch micro-bumps. The interposer contains chip-scale wires and TSVs for inter-dies and external connections. Although 2.5D ICs might not obtain similar performance gain as 3D ICs, it possesses various advantages. Firstly, since the dies of 2.5D ICs do not need to have TSVs, their design and fabrication will be easier compared to TSV-penetrated stacked 3D ICs. Secondly, because the dies are not stacked, thermal dissipation problem in 2.5D ICs is less severe compared to 3D ICs. Various large-scale commercial 2.5D IC products have been developed such as Xilinx Virtex 2000 T FPGA [20], while commercial 3D IC products are still being developed.

11.2.2 Security Advantages of 3D ICs

In this section, we summarize the unique security advantages in 3D ICs and highlight new opportunities to leverage these advantages to improve hardware security.

11.2.2.1 Split Fabrication

The fabrication flow of 3D ICs provides inherent support for split fabrication, a technique for protecting outsourced IC design from piracy and counterfeiting. In 3D ICs, different dies/interposer can be fabricated in different foundries and then integrated into a single chip. Therefore, a 3D IC can be split into two tiers: a trusted tier and an untrusted tier, which can be fabricated in separate foundries. To prevent the untrusted foundry from accessing the complete design, the trusted tier can be fabricated in a trusted foundry while the untrusted tier is outsourced for advanced semiconductor technology. The final integration is also performed in the trusted foundry. This security-oriented fabrication scheme is referred to as *3D split fabrication*. With 3D split fabrication, the untrusted foundry does not have access to the trusted tier, hence it cannot pirate or counterfeit the complete IC design.

3D split fabrication can be implemented in different ways. A designer can decide which portion to be fabricated in the trusted foundry as the trusted tier. The following summarizes different split fabrication schemes proposed in previous work for three types of 3D ICs.

- *Stacked 3D IC*: Two split fabrication schemes for stacked 3D ICs were discussed in Tezzaron and Valamehr et al. [21,22]. In one way, the trusted foundry is responsible for fabricating a portion of device layers and performing the final integration. By doing so, the attacker in the untrusted foundry can obtain only partial netlist information from the incomplete outsourced portion of the IC design. In another way, all device layers are outsourced to the untrusted foundry, but the final integration is done in the trusted foundry. By doing so, the vertical connections between dies are kept secret.
- *Monolithic 3D IC*: With the development of monolithic 3D integration, split fabrication scheme based on this technology has been investigated. Yang et al. [23] proposed a split fabrication based on monolithic 3D integration and VeSFET devices. The authors assume that the monolithic 3D chip is fabricated in two untrusted foundries and they are not working together. One foundry fabricates all the VeSFET devices and the majority of interconnects on one side of the VeSFETs, while the other foundry fabricates the remaining small portion of interconnects on the other side of the VeSFETs.
- *2.5D IC*: Two split fabrication schemes based on 2.5D ICs have been proposed. Imeson et al. [5] proposed to fabricate the silicon interposer of a 2.5D IC in the trusted foundry as the trusted tier while outsourcing the dies to offshore foundries as the untrusted tier. The final integration is implemented in the trusted foundry to maintain the secrecy of interconnections in the interposer. Since the trusted tier (an interposer) contains only metal wires, its can be fabricated at a trusted foundry with less advanced semiconductor technology to reduce the overall fabrication cost. Gu et al. [11] proposed a split fabrication for 2.5D IC with an active interposer. The active interposer can contain wires and transistors thus providing better security for 2.5D split fabrication.

Split fabrication based on 3D/2.5D ICs provides a new way to obfuscate or hide critical components of an IC design to improve its security against untrusted fabrication foundries. The following summarizes existing work on 3D/2.5D split fabrication.

3D/2.5D split fabrication provides new opportunities to obfuscate the outsourced IC designs so as to prevent them from piracy, counterfeiting, and malicious modifications (hardware Trojans). To fully exploit this technique for obfuscation, various design methodologies have been proposed. Xie et al. [3,24,25] proposed secure partitioning and placement algorithms for 2.5D split fabrication to defend piracy and counterfeiting. Imeson et al. [5] proposed a heuristic wire-lifting algorithms for

2.5D split fabrication to prevent an attacker from identifying a specific location for hardware Trojan insertion. To make split fabrication secure against both piracy and hardware Trojan, Yang et al. [23] proposed a secure split fabrication for VeSFET-based monolithic 3D IC. The proposed monolithic 3D split fabrication scheme utilizes the two-side accessibility property of VeSFETs. Corresponding security-aware design methodologies, which consist of partitioning, transistor hiding, and hardware Trojan detection scan path design, have also been investigated.

Besides circuit obfuscation, 3D/2.5D split fabrication can also be used to protect security-critical circuits from being tampered by placing them inside the trusted tier. The security-critical circuits could be cryptographic modules [26] or hardware Trojan detection circuits such as on-chip transient current sensors [27], execution monitor [28], and built-in-self-authentication (BISA) block [29]. In addition, the trusted tier could be built as a control plane, which can detect and handle abnormal behavior in the untrusted tier (an untrusted computation plane) [22,26,30–32].

11.2.2.2 Stacking Structure

The stacking structure of 3D ICs can be leveraged to defend invasion attack (such as reverse-engineering) and noninvasion attack (such as side-channel attacks). When multiple layers of devices are stacked together, valuable hardware components can be placed in an internal layer that is surrounded by firmly stacked substrates, which improves the security against both attacks.

The stacking structure of 3D IC makes the 3D chip physically more difficult to be reverse-engineered [21,22]. Since the thick and tough substrates are difficult to be etched evenly [21], delayering the 3D IC becomes challenging. Also, microscopy and imaging will be complicated by the existence of extra layers, bonding materials, and many layers of vertical and horizontal interconnections. Moreover, probing internal signals will be difficult because all active devices and internal wires can be encapsulated soundly inside the substrates. The only exposure to the adversary is the primary I/O pins. Therefore, to prevent reverse-engineering, valuable hardware components can be placed in an internal layer inside firmly stacked substrates.

3D stacking also offers a natural defense against various types of side-channel attacks, which exploit power [33,34], timing [35,36], electromagnetic (EM) emission [37–39], and fault analysis [40] to extract secret information from hardware systems. By placing the vulnerable tier (e.g., memory) in the lower layer, the layers above it will act as a shield. This shield can be used to prevent the side-channel attacks in two ways. Firstly, the shield adds extra noise to the side-channel since it is composed of multiple high-density device layers. In other words, the signal-to-noise ratio for a side-channel is reduced, so it will be much harder for attackers to capture the targeted signal [26]. In order to extract useful side-channel signals, the attackers need to observe significantly more signal traces, thereby making the attack much harder, even impossible. Techniques that use 3D stacking to shield thermal side-channel [11,41] and timing side-channel [42] have been proposed. Secondly, the shield based on 3D stacking can also protect the vulnerable tier from fault injection. For instance, Zhang and Li [43] utilized 3D technology to protect security-sensitive hardware from high-energy partials by concealing them in the inner layers of a 3D chip.

11.2.2.3 Heterogeneous Integration

For 3D integration, multiple layers based on different materials and technologies can be integrated together to form a highly integrated system. This process is referred to as 3D heterogeneous integration. With 3D heterogeneous integration, security primitives that are based on special materials or emerging technologies might be integrated with conventional CMOS-based circuit components to form a high-performance and secure chip. For example, Khedkar and Kudithipudi [44] proposed to integrate resistive RAM (RRAM) into the system to mitigate DPA attacks. In addition, 3D heterogeneous integration of analog circuits and digital circuits offers opportunities for developing high-performance defense and security systems [45].

11.2.2.4 Performance Gain

With the performance improvement in 3D ICs, security techniques that were once considered impractical due to high performance overhead are now becoming feasible. In Reference 42, a 3D IC-based cache random-eviction technique was proposed to mitigate cache-based timing side-channel attacks. The authors concluded that with 3D integration, the performance overhead for implementing a secure cache eviction policy is reduced from 25% (for 2D CPU and off-chip memory architecture) to about 0% (for 3D memory-on-chip architecture). Memory authentication is another security technique that could result in high performance overhead ($6\times$ bandwidth overhead) [46]. As discussed in Reference 11, 3D IC-based processing-in-memory (3D-PIM) can be leveraged to offset the performance overhead of memory authentication. As 3D-PIM can offer $80\times$ more bandwidth [47], the performance degradation for the memory security can be compensated by using 3D-PIM technology. In addition, Gu et al. [11] concluded that fine-grain monolithic 3D integration can significantly reduce the overhead for camouflaged standard cells, which are used to defend IC reverse-engineering attack.

11.2.3 Security Vulnerabilities of 3D ICs

The security vulnerabilities of 3D IC stem from three aspects: new attack targets, limited detection accesses, and complex test flow.

11.2.3.1 New Attack Targets

To support 3D integration, new components that do not exist in traditional 2D IC designs are now required in 3D IC designs. Take TSV as an example. Since TSVs are important components that are massively used for signal communication and power/clock/thermal delivery, a malicious foundry can target the TSV and introduce TSV defects during fabrication in order to compromise the chip's performance and reliability. However, weak defects in TSVs are normally difficult to be tested [48] so it will be challenging to detect malicious modifications to TSVs. Similarly, attackers can also target the interposer of 2.5D ICs and the MIVs of monolithic 3D ICs, which are new contents in a 3D/2.5D IC design. Also, common problems in 3D ICs such as poor thermal dissipation, power delivery, and reliability could be exploited by attackers during fabrication. Overall, attackers have new design space to insert and hide hardware Trojans [10].

11.2.3.2 Limited Detection Accesses

Due to the stacking structure and high integration density, the detection accesses (including test accesses and side-channel accesses) of 3D ICs are limited, which increase the difficulty of detecting counterfeit components and hardware Trojans. For test accesses [48], the probing of micro-bump of a die is challenging since current probes (with minimum pitch size 50 µm) is unable to directly access the fine-pitch micro-bumps (20 µm). Also, testing internal signals in 3D chips requires new design-for-test (DfT) architectures for 3D ICs. For side-channel accesses, due to the stacking structure and high device-density nature of 3D ICs, the signal-to-noise ratio for a side-channel is normally small. This increases the difficulty for detecting hardware Trojans through side-channels. When the side-channel signal of Trojan is immersed in noise, differentiating Trojan-free from Trojan-active ICs becomes difficult.

11.2.3.3 Complex Test Flow

The test flow for 3D ICs becomes more complex since more potential intermediate tests are needed in order to guarantee the security of the whole chip. A 3D IC may contain 2D dies, which is composed of functional modules that are provided by third-party IP vendors. Besides, each die may be fabricated by different foundries. The complicated global supply chain introduces new chances for attackers to insert inauthentic (counterfeit or maliciously modified) designs to compromise the performance and security of the whole chip. With split fabrication scheme, as discussed earlier, the design of a trusted and effective 3D IC test flow becomes even more challenging.

11.2.4 Summary and Discussion

In this part, we provide a comprehensive survey on 3D IC-based security. While 3D integration is initially developed to improve chip performance, it has presented new opportunities to improve hardware security in different aspects. With the development of 3D integration technology and corresponding security-aware design methodologies, future 3D chip designer can leverage its security advantages in an early stage to improve the chip security.

11.3 Conclusion

In this chapter, we investigate the role that new nano-manufacturing technologies can play in enhancing IC supply chain security. In the first half, the TFUE model, the model of a trusted foundry and untrusted employees, is introduced. Under TFUE, an attack model is considered, and a corresponding countermeasure enabled by DPL is also proposed. It is shown that our customized DPL can effectively obfuscate the original layout and prevent possible Trojan insertion and design piracy conducted by an untrusted employee. In the second half, we investigated how the unique architecture of 3D IC can be utilized to mitigate supply chain and side-channel attacks. The security challenges due to the 3D structure are also addressed. In conclusion, although emerging nano-manufacturing technologies are originally introduced to build faster and smaller chips, they bring new opportunities and challenges in security as well. In general, the opportunities are more significant, and both the designer and the foundry can utilize these emerging technologies to improve the security of IC supply chain.

References

1. J. A. Roy, F. Koushanfar, and I. L. Markov. Epic: Ending piracy of integrated circuits. In *Proceedings of the Conference on Design, Automation and Test in Europe*, pages 1069–1074. ACM, New York, NY, 2008.
2. J. Rajendran, Y. Pino, O. Sinanoglu, and R. Karri. Logic encryption: A fault analysis perspective. In *Proceedings of the Conference on Design, Automation and Test in Europe*, pages 953–958. EDA Consortium, 2012.

3. Y. Xie, C. Bao, and A. Srivastava. Security-aware design flow for 2.5 D IC technology. In *Proceedings of the 5th International Workshop on Trustworthy Embedded Devices*, pages 31–38. ACM, New York, NY, 2015.

4. B. Shakya, N. Asadizanjani, D. Forte, and M. Tehranipoor. Chip editor: Leveraging circuit edit for logic obfuscation and trusted fabrication. In *Proceedings of the 35th International Conference on Computer-Aided Design*, page 30. ACM, New York, NY, 2016.

5. F. Imeson, A. Emtenan, S. Garg, and M. Tripunitara. Securing computer hardware using 3D integrated circuit (IC) technology and split manufacturing for obfuscation. In *22nd USENIX Security Symposium (USENIX Security 13)*, pages 495–510, Washington, DC, 2013.

6. A. B. Kahng, C.-H. Park, X. Xu, and H. Yao. Layout decomposition approaches for double patterning lithography. *IEEE Transactions on Computer-Aided Design of Integrated Circuits and Systems*, **29**(6):939–952, 2010.

7. Y. Liu, C. Bao, Y. Xie, and A. Srivastava. Introducing TFUE: The trusted foundry and untrusted employee model in IC supply chain security. In *2017 IEEE International Symposium on Circuits and Systems*, pages 1–4. IEEE, New York, NY, 2017.

8. T. Lu, C. Serafy, Z. Yang, S. Samal, S. K. Lim, and A. Srivastava. TSV-based 3D ICs: Design methods and tools. *IEEE Transactions on Computer-Aided Design of Integrated Circuits and Systems*, **PP**(99):1–1, 2017. doi:10.1109/TCAD.2017.2666604

9. P. Garrou, C. Bower, and P. Ramm. *Handbook of 3D Integration: Volume 1—Technology and Applications of 3D Integrated Circuits*. John Wiley & Sons, 2011.

10. J. Dofe, Q. Yu, H. Wang, and E. Salman. Hardware security threats and potential countermeasures in emerging 3D ICs. In *2016 International Great Lakes Symposium on VLSI*, pages 69–74. IEEE, New York, NY, 2016.

11. P. Gu, S. Li, D. Stow, R. Barnes, L. Liu, Y. Xie, and E. Kursun. Leveraging 3D technologies for hardware security: Opportunities and challenges. In *Proceedings of the 26th Edition on Great Lakes Symposium on VLSI*, pages 347–352. ACM, New York, NY, 2016.

12. Y. Xie, C. Bao, C. Serafy, T. Lu, A. Srivastava, and M. Tehranipoor. Security and vulnerability implications of 3D ICs. *IEEE Transactions on Multi-Scale Computing Systems*, **2**(2):108–122, 2016.

13. Y. Xie, J. Cong, and S. S. Sapatnekar. *Three-Dimensional Integrated Circuit Design*. Springer, Berlin, 2010.

14. S. Bobba, A. Chakraborty, O. Thomas, P. Batude, V. F. Pavlidis, and G. De Micheli. Performance analysis of 3-D monolithic integrated circuits. In *2010 IEEE International 3D Systems Integration Conference (3DIC)*, pages 1–4. IEEE, New York, NY, 2010.

15. Y. Deng and W. P. Maly. Interconnect characteristics of 2.5-D system integration scheme. In *Proceedings of the 2001 International Symposium on Physical Design*, pages 171–175. ACM, New York, NY, 2001.

16. M. Puech, J.-M. Thevenoud, J. Gruffat, N. Launay, N. Arnal, and P. Godinat. Fabrication of 3D packaging TSV using DRIE. In *Symposium on Design, Test, Integration and Packaging of MEMS/MOEMS, 2008*, pages 109–114. IEEE, New York, NY, 2008.

17. W. R. Davis, J. Wilson, S. Mick, J. Xu, H. Hua, C. Mineo, A. M. Sule, M. Steer, and P. D. Franzon. Demystifying 3D ICs: The pros and cons of going vertical. *IEEE Design & Test of Computers*, **22**(6):498–510, 2005.

18. S. A. Panth, K. Samadi, Y. Du, and S. K. Lim. Design and cad methodologies for low power gate-level monolithic 3D ICs. In *Proceedings of the 2014 International Symposium on Low Power Electronics and Design*, pages 171–176. ACM, New York, NY, 2014.

19. P. Batude, M. Vinet, A. Pouydebasque, C. Le Royer, B. Previtali, C. Tabone, J.-M. Hartmann, L. Sanchez, L. Baud, V. Carron et al. 3D monolithic integration. In *2011 IEEE International Symposium on Circuits and Systems (ISCAS)*, pages 2233–2236. IEEE, New York, NY, 2011.

20. K. Saban. Xilinx stacked silicon interconnect technology delivers breakthrough FPGA capacity, bandwidth, and power efficiency. *Xilinx, White Paper*, 2011.

21. Tezzaron. 3D-ICs and integrated circuit security. http://www.tezzaron.com/about/papers/3D-ICs_and_Integrated_Circuit_Security.pdf, 2008.

22. J. Valamehr, T. Sherwood, R. Kastner, D. Marangoni-Simonsen, T. Huffmire, C. Irvine, and T. Levin. A 3-D split manufacturing approach to trustworthy system development. *IEEE Transactions on Computer-Aided Design of Integrated Circuits and Systems*, **32**(4):611–615, 2013.

23. P.-L. Yang and M. Marek-Sadowska. Making split-fabrication more secure. In *2016 IEEE/ACM International Conference on Computer-Aided Design (ICCAD)*, pages 1–8. IEEE, New York, NY, 2016.

24. Y. Xie, C. Bao, and A. Srivastava. 3D/2.5D IC-based obfuscation. In *Hardware Protection through Obfuscation*, pages 291–314. Springer, Berlin, 2017.

25. Y. Xie, C. Bao, Y. Liu, and A. Srivastava. 2.5 D/3D integration technologies for circuit obfuscation. In *2016 17th International Workshop on Microprocessor and SOC Test and Verification (MTV)*, pages 39–44. IEEE, New York, NY, 2016.

26. J. Valamehr, T. Huffmire, C. Irvine, R. Kastner, Ç. K. Koç, T. Levin, and T. Sherwood. A qualitative security analysis of a new class of 3-D integrated crypto co-processors. In *Cryptography and Security: From Theory to Applications*, pages 364–382. Springer, Berlin, 2012.

27. S. Narasimhan, W. Yueh, X. Wang, S. Mukhopadhyay, and S. Bhunia. Improving IC security against Trojan attacks through integration of security monitors. *IEEE Design & Test of Computers*, **29**(5):37–46, 2012.

28. M. Bilzor. 3D execution monitor (3D-EM): Using 3D circuits to detect hardware malicious inclusions in general purpose processors. In *Proceedings of the 6th International Conference on Information Warfare and Security*, page 288. Academic Conferences Limited, 2011.

29. K. Xiao and M. Tehranipoor. BISA: Built-in self-authentication for preventing hardware Trojan insertion. In *2013 IEEE International Symposium on Hardware-Oriented Security and Trust (HOST)*, pages 45–50. IEEE, New York, NY, 2013.

30. S. Mysore, B. Agrawal, N. Srivastava, S.-C. Lin, K. Banerjee, and T. Sherwood. Introspective 3D chips. In *ACM SIGOPS Operating Systems Review*, Vol. **40**, pages 264–273. ACM, New York, NY, 2006.

31. J. Valamehr, M. Tiwari, T. Sherwood, R. Kastner, T. Huffmire, C. Irvine, and T. Levin. Hardware assistance for trustworthy systems through 3-D integration. In *Proceedings of the 26th Annual Computer Security Applications Conference*, pages 199–210. ACM, New York, NY, 2010.

32. T. Huffmire, T. Levin, M. Bilzor, C. E. Irvine, J. Valamehr, M. Tiwari, T. Sherwood, and R. Kastner. Hardware trust implications of 3-D integration. In *Proceedings of the 5th Workshop on Embedded Systems Security*, page 1. ACM, New York, NY, 2010.

33. E. Brier, C. Clavier, and F. Olivier. Correlation power analysis with a leakage model. In *Cryptographic Hardware and Embedded Systems—CHES 2004*, pages 16–29. Springer, Berlin, 2004.

34. P. Kocher, J. Jaffe, and B. Jun. Differential power analysis. In *Advances in Cryptology CRYPTO99*, pages 388–397. Springer, Berlin, 1999.

35. D. J. Bernstein. Cache-timing attacks on AES, 2005.

36. D. Brumley and D. Boneh. Remote timing attacks are practical. *Computer Networks*, **48**(5):701–716, 2005.

37. D. Agrawal, B. Archambeault, J. R. Rao, and P. Rohatgi. The EM sidechannel(s). In *Cryptographic Hardware and Embedded Systems—CHES 2002*, pages 29–45. Springer, Berlin, 2003.

38. K. Gandolfi, C. Mourtel, and F. Olivier. Electromagnetic analysis: Concrete results. In *Cryptographic Hardware and Embedded Systems—CHES 2001*, pages 251–261. Springer, Berlin, 2001.

39. Quisquater J.-J. and D. Samyde. Electromagnetic analysis (EMA): Measures and counter-measures for smart cards. In *Smart Card Programming and Security*, pages 200–210. Springer, Berlin, 2001.

40. A. Barenghi, L. Breveglieri, I. Koren, and D. Naccache. Fault injection attacks on cryptographic devices: Theory, practice, and countermeasures. *Proceedings of the IEEE*, **100**(11):3056–3076, 2012.

41. P. Gu, D. Stow, R. Barnes, E. Kursun, and Y. Xie. Thermal-aware 3D design for side-channel information leakage. In *2016 IEEE 34th International Conference on Computer Design (ICCD)*, pages 520–527. IEEE, New York, NY, 2016.

42. C. Bao and A. Srivastava. 3D integration: New opportunities in defense against cache-timing side-channel attacks. In *2015 33rd IEEE International Conference on Computer Design (ICCD)*, pages 8–15. IEEE, New York, NY, 2015.

43. W. Zhang and T. Li. Microarchitecture soft error vulnerability characterization and mitigation under 3D integration technology. In *Proceedings of the 41st Annual IEEE/ACM International Symposium on Microarchitecture*, pages 435–446. IEEE Computer Society, New York, NY, 2008.

44. G. Khedkar and D. Kudithipudi. RRAM motifs for mitigating differential power analysis attacks (DPA). In *2012 IEEE Computer Society Annual Symposium on VLSI (ISVLSI)*, pages 88–93. IEEE, New York, NY, 2012.

45. S. Bhansali, G. H. Chapman, E. G. Friedman, Y. Ismail, P. Mukund, D. Tebbe, and V. K. Jain. 3D heterogeneous sensor system on a chip for defense and security applications. In *Defense and Security*, pages 413–424. International Society for Optics and Photonics, 2004.

46. C. Yan, D. Englender, M. Prvulovic, B. Rogers, and Y. Solihin. Improving cost, performance, and security of memory encryption and authentication. In *ACM SIGARCH Computer Architecture News*, Vol. **34**, 179–190. IEEE Computer Society, New York, NY, 2006.

47. J. Ahn, S. Hong, S. Yoo, O. Mutlu, and K. Choi. A scalable processing-in-memory accelerator for parallel graph processing. In *2015 ACM/IEEE 42nd Annual International Symposium on Computer Architecture (ISCA)*, pages 105–117. IEEE, New York, NY, 2015.

48. E. J. Marinissen. Challenges and emerging solutions in testing TSV-based 2 1/2D-and 3D-stacked ICs. In *Proceedings of the Conference on Design, Automation and Test in Europe*, pages 1277–1282. EDA Consortium, 2012.

Chapter 12

Nanoscale Memory Architectures for Neuromorphic Computing

Chaofei Yang, Hai Li, and Yiran Chen

Contents

On one hand, machine learning has been widely used in data processing to help users understand the underlying property of the data [1]. As a popular type of machine learning model, neural network [2] processes input data by multiplying them with layers of weighted connections. Many embedded hardware engines, including field-programmable gate array (FPGA) and system-on-chip (SoC), have been developed to implement neural networks with high speed and efficiency, for example, Qualcomm's cognitive computing platform [3].

On the other hand, memristor has been discovered as a device whose resistance depends on the history of the voltage applied across it. The similarity between the programmable resistance state of memristors and the variable weight connection in neural networks simplifies the structure of circuit realization of a neural network. The compact structure, high energy-efficiency, and low power consumption of memristor-based learning systems greatly improve the data scale and computation capacity of learning applications in embedded systems [4].

Running learning models on an embedded device, though advantageous because of reduced processing times and high energy-efficiency, introduces security challenges. The learning model is exposed to the risk of being attacked by malicious users who have physical access to the device. Consider the following scenario. Assume there is a drone carrying an image processing system, which is being used for its navigation and guidance systems. This system implements the proprietary learning algorithms on a memristor-based neuromorphic computing system (MNCS). If the drone is captured by an unauthorized third party, say, an attacker, he or she may apply inputs to the system, observe the outputs, and learn the proprietary algorithm implemented by the system [5]. Consequently, he or she can design a pirated system.

In this chapter, we demonstrate how an attacker can learn and replicate the proprietary algorithm. Our analysis is independent of the learning model (e.g., support vector machine [SVM] [6], random forest [7], K-nearest neighbors [8]). We then propose a secure MNCS design to thwart such replication attacks by leveraging memristors obsolescence effect. A naive implementation of this idea will incur performance overhead. Hence, we develop device-, circuit-, and architectural-level techniques to balance security and performance overhead. Experimental results show that our design provides better usability as well as resilience to replication attack of the MNCS, without increasing calibration overhead.

Previously, memristor devices were used to build security primitives such as physical unclonable functions [9], public physical unclonable functions [10], and motifs to prevent side-channel attacks [11]. Here, we focus on using them to prevent replication attacks on MNCS, which none of these primitives can thwart.

This chapter presents the following:

1. The security threats faced by neuromorphic computing systems, specifically the replication attack.
2. A cross-layer approach for security. We leverage properties across device, circuit, and architectural levels to design this system, making a trade-off between security, usability, and overhead.
3. Experimenting on different benchmarks (image, faults, digit, MNIST) using various models (SVM, K-nearest neighbors, random forest, and feedforward neural network), analyzing the impacts of dataset complexity and model selection.

12.1 Preliminary

12.1.1 Memristors

Predicted by Chua [12], memristor is the fourth fundamental circuit element defining the relation between magnetic flux (ϕ) and electrical charge (q) as $d\Phi = Mdq$. The resistance (memristance) state of a memristor can be programmed by applying current or voltage [13]. In 2008, HP Lab first reported their discovery of a nanoscale memristor based on TiO_2 thin-film devices [14].

Figure 12.1 depicts an ion-migration filament model of HfOx memristors [15]. An HfOx layer is sandwiched between two metal electrodes. During the *reset* process, the memristor switches from low resistance state (LRS) to high resistance state (HRS). The oxygen ions migrate from the electrode/oxide interface and recombine with the oxygen vacancies. A partially ruptured conductive filament region with high resistance per unit length (R_{off}) and a conductive filament region with low resistance per unit length (R_{on}) are formed; during the *set* process, the memristor switches from HRS to LRS as the ruptured conductive filament region shrinks. The resistance of many types of memristors can be programmed to an arbitrary value (e.g., multilevel states) by applying a current or voltage with proper pulse width or magnitude. In many cases, the memristor resistance changes only when the applied voltage is above a threshold, for example, V_{wrth}.

The obsolescence effect of a memristor denotes the fact that the resistance of the device will gradually change after being programmed. This obsolescence effect has two major contributors: (1) the intrinsic retention property of the device [16] and (2) the read-induced change in resistance. Retention property denotes that the resistance of a programmed memristor continuously shifts to HRS without any applied voltage. This type of resistance change is hard to control since it is related to the material relaxing mechanism. The read-induced change is depicted in Figure 12.2 where a memristor is constantly stimulated by short minor voltage pulses, and its resistance change (reflected by the sensed current) is recorded every second. This experiment is to mimic the impact of the small sensing signal applied to the memristor during read operations. It shows that the memristor resistance keeps increasing with stimulation. Therefore, the obsolescence rate (i.e., changing

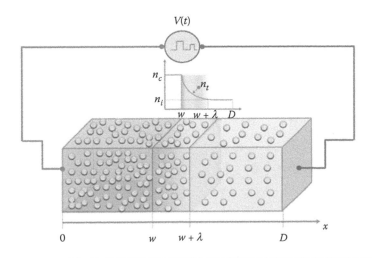

Figure 12.1   Conceptual view of a metal-oxide memristor. (Adapted from L. Zhang et al. *Applied Physics Letters*, 102(15):1–4, 2013.)

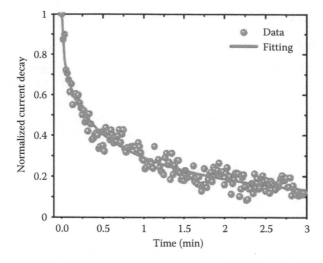

Figure 12.2 Memristor obsolescence effect when sensing pulses are applied. (Adapted from T. Chang, S.-H. Jo, and W. Lu. *ACS Nano,* **5(9):7669–7676, 2011.)**

rate of its resistance) can be controlled by choosing the amplitude and duration of the sensing current/voltage. In general, the resistance change of a memristor in a memristor-based hardware is a continuous procedure that can be described as $\Delta R = f(v,t)$. Here, v and t are the sensing voltages and operation time of the memristor-based hardware, respectively.

12.1.2 Memristor-Based Learning Systems

We define a learning system as the hardware specifically designed to accelerate neural network or machine learning algorithms. Figure 12.3a depicts a conceptual overview of a neural network that can be directly mapped onto a learning system. Here, two layers of neurons are fully connected by one layer of synapses. The output neurons collect the information from the input neurons through a network of weighted synaptic connections and process them with an activation function.

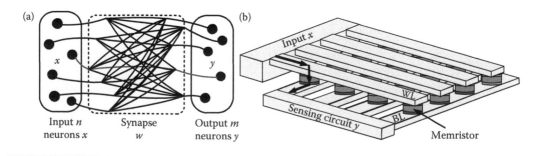

Figure 12.3 (a) Overview of a neural network. (Adapted from M. Hu et al. *Proceedings of the 49th Annual Design Automation Conference,* **pages 498–503. ACM, New York, NY, 2012.) (b) Computing core (memristor crossbar structure) in an MNCS. (Adapted from B. Liu et al.** *IEEE/ACM International Conference on Computer-Aided Design,* **pages 63–70, 2014.)**

In general, the relationship between the input vector x and the output vector y is described by Hu et al. [17]: $y_n = f(x_m \cdot W_{m \times n})$, where the connection weight matrix $W_{m \times n}$ denotes the synaptic strengths between the two layers of neurons.

Figure 12.3b shows a memristor crossbar structure that consists of two sets of nanowires running perpendicular to one another [19]. A memristor is sandwiched by two nanowires at each crosspoint. Because of its structural similarity, the memristor crossbar can efficiently execute matrix-vector multiplications [18]. For a multilayer neural network, several memristor crossbars can be connected to match the network topology [20].

In "testing" operations of a memristor-based learning system, x is represented as a vector of voltage signals applied to the word lines (WLs) of the memristor crossbar while the bit lines (BLs) are grounded. The current sensed from the bottom of each BL will be converted to output voltage vector y by a sensing circuit. In a real implementation, the matrix $W_{m \times n}$ is often implemented by two memristor crossbars, which represent the positive and negative elements of $W_{m \times n}$, respectively. In "training" operations, the resistance states of the memristors are programmed to represent the $W_{m \times n}$, while the value of the states are trained off-line.

12.2 Thwarting Learning Attacks

12.2.1 Target System

An MNCS consists of the following two proprietary information:

- *Training data* denotes the sample set used for training the MNCS. Each sample normally contains a vector of features and a label. The feature vector serves as the input of the learning model, and the label describes a property.
- *Learning model* denotes the model that has been trained for the proprietary application using the training data. It includes two parts: (1) the model info, say, the type (e.g., Hopfield or naive Bayes models) and the topology, and (2) the model parameters, for example, the weight on each synapse.

Without losing generality, we assume the function of the original learning model $g(w,x)$ is data classification, which can be described as

$$g(w, x = p(y = y_i | w, x), \quad i = 1, \ldots, n \tag{12.1}$$

Here, w is a vector of the parameters of the original model, x is the input vector of features, and y_i is the ith target class that a sample can be assigned to. The probability function $p(y = y_i | w$ is defined by the structure of the original model, for example, a neural network. After the training completes, the original model $g(w,x)$ is ready to classify new evaluating data.

12.2.2 Protocol

Figure 12.4 shows a conceptual view of the concerned embedded system and its usage model. A proprietary (classification) algorithm is running on the hardware, for example, an MNCS. The model is first trained for an application, and then the drone can submit the collected data for processing (evaluating), for example, pattern recognition or classification.

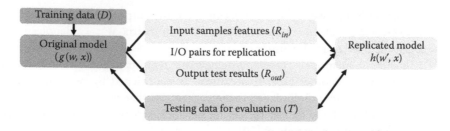

Figure 12.4 Training and replication process of the learning model. (Adapted from B. Liu et al. *Proceedings of the 52nd Annual Design Automation Conference,* **page 95. ACM, New York, NY, 2015.)**

The drone with the learning system executes the following protocol:

1. Initially, the MNCS is not trained, and hence it does not implement the proprietary algorithm.
2. The drone requests the base station for the training samples.
3. After authenticating the drone, the base station establishes a secure session with the drone using conventional cryptographic protocols.
4. The base station encrypts the training set and sends to the secure session.
5. The drone decrypts the encrypted training set and trains MNCS to implement the proprietary algorithm.
6. The MNCS executes proprietary algorithm N times, after which the weights erase due to memristor's obsolescence effect.
7. After applying N I/O pairs, repeat Steps 2 through 6.

12.2.3 Threat Model

We assume that the attacker has the following capabilities:

- The attacker can apply inputs (e.g., images, body data from patients, fingerprints) to the originally trained model and obtain the corresponding outputs without any constraints, that is, being granted with the same privilege as a normal user or being able to physically get access to it.
- The attacker does not have access to the original training set.
- The attacker has no knowledge about the parameters of the original model.
- The attacker can reverse engineer to understand the hardware implementation of the system.

The objective of the attacker is to replicate the function of the original model $g(\boldsymbol{w},\boldsymbol{x})$ by constructing a new model $h(\boldsymbol{w'},\boldsymbol{x})$, such that the $h(\boldsymbol{w'},\boldsymbol{x}) = g(\boldsymbol{w},\boldsymbol{x})$. To achieve this goal, an attacker can perform the following attacks:

1. *Eavesdropping attack.* An attacker can listen to the communication channel to obtain the training set. This attack is not possible, because the training set is encrypted and sent across the channel, as stated in Step 3 of the protocol.

2. *Spoofing attack.* An attacker can impersonate as a drone and request for the training set from the base station. This attack is not possible, because the base station authenticates the drone before sending the training set, as stated in Step 3 of the protocol.

3. *Probing attack.* An attacker can probe the memristors and can try to learn the stored weights [22]. Since he or she already has the structure of the MNCS through reverse engineering, in addition to the weights, he or she can replicate the proprietary algorithm. This attack is not possible, because memristors are highly dense and can be compactly stacked in 3D structure, making them difficult to probe without physically damaging the neighborhood devices. Besides, countermeasures can be used to prevent probing attack [23].

4. *Chosen-input attack.* An attacker can apply inputs of his or her choice, observe the corresponding outputs, and infer the weights. In this proposal, we focus on this attack and thwart it using the obsolescence effect of the memristor in the MNCS.

12.2.4 Chosen-Input Attack

In this proposal, we use D_{in} to denote the inputs chosen by the attacker to the MNCS. D_{out} is the output of the MNCS. $[D_{in}, D_{out}]$ construct I/O pairs. Here, the length of D_{in}, that is, the number of inputs chosen by the attacker, and the length of Dout and $[D_{in}, D_{out}]$ are the same, say, m, which is decided by the attacker.

Since the attacker has no knowledge about the type of the original model, he or she needs to select a learning model as a starting point for *model replication.* After the I/O pairs are constructed and the replicated model type is selected, the attacker starts to use the I/O pairs to train the replicated model; since the I/O pairs are generated from the original model, the function of the replicate model will gradually approach to that of the original model.

Since the attacker does not know the model implemented by the MNCS, an arbitrary model is selected. Besides the original model (e.g., neural network [2]), we could also use another model (e.g., SVM [6]) as the replicated model to learn the function of the original model. In addition, it has been proved that although the selection of learning model is crucial for replication efficiency and accuracy, it is not necessary to select the same model type as the one of the original model [21].

Security metric. The performance of the MNCS is evaluated by their accuracy, which is defined as

$$\text{Accuracy} = \frac{\text{Number of true positives}}{\text{Number of all evaluating samples}} \quad (12.2)$$

Here, the number of true positives is the number of predictions that match the ground-truth labels. In this proposal, we use accuracy as the security metric to quantify the effectiveness of our attack.

To demonstrate the effect of different learning models on accuracy, we use MNIST dataset as an example [24]. MNIST is a handwritten digit dataset, which is widely used in machine learning field and various image processing training. The system implements the target application using SVM [6] model. Other candidate learning models include SVM [6], random forest [7], and K-nearest neighbors [8]. The attacker does not know which of the four learning models is being implemented in the system.

As we mentioned in Section 12.2.2, the attack models take the I/O pairs from our system model as their training data. The SVM model (normal model) trained by original training labels is also evaluated for comparison. Experimental results can be found in Figure 12.5. The replicated model based on SVM has a rate of increase in accuracy similar to that of the original model. Even

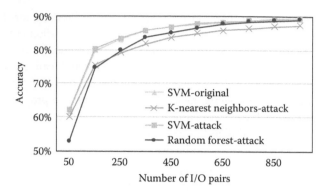

Figure 12.5 Comparison of learning model between the original model and various other learning models and parameters.

if the replication attack uses other learning models, the rate of increase in accuracy with respect to I/O pairs is similar. And, their accuracies both approach to the normal model (90%) after applying 1000 I/O pairs.

This experiment shows that the model replication attack is feasible and even if the replication model is different from the original model (SVM, in this case), it still can achieve a good enough accuracy. Thus, the proposed defense mechanism should prevent the attacker from learning the algorithm, irrespective of the underlying learning model.

12.3 Secure MNCS Design

12.3.1 Device Level: Memristors

While one can use different types of devices such as phase-change memories, RRAM, etc. [25], we use memristors because of their following attractive properties:

1. Memristors are highly dense and can be stacked in 3D structure, which makes them extremely difficult for physical attacks.
2. Memristors are energy efficient.
3. Memristors are programmable for online training.

In this proposal, we adopt the memristor model from the work of Miao et al. [26]. The memristance can be expressed as Equation 12.3, where α is the relative doping front position which ranges from 0 to 1. It can be obtained by solving the differential equation of velocity:

$$\alpha(t) = \frac{R_H - \sqrt{R_H{}^2 - 2 \cdot (R_H - R_L) \cdot (A + B)}}{R_H - R_L} \tag{12.3}$$

where $A = \mu_v \cdot R_L/h^2 \cdot \int_{t_0}^{t} V(t)\,dt$ and $B = R_H \cdot \alpha_0 + 1/2 \cdot (R_H - R_L) \cdot \alpha_0{}^2$, with α_0 being the initial condition of α. Assuming $t_0 = 0$ and $\alpha_0 = 0.3$ and substituting A and B into α and then to

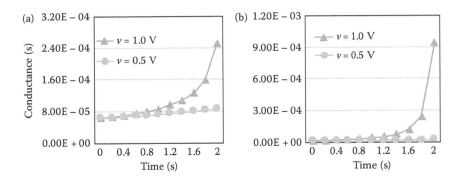

Figure 12.6   **Memristor model: (a) conductance and (b) derivative of conductance.**

$M(\alpha)$, we obtain

$$M(t) = \sqrt{R_H{}^2 - 2 \cdot (R_H - R_L) \cdot \left(\mu_v \cdot \frac{R_L}{h^2} \cdot v \cdot t + 0.255 \cdot R_H + 0.045 \cdot R_L \right)} \qquad (12.4)$$

By using the ideal memristor parameters ($h = 50$ nm, $R_H = 16$ kΩ, $R_L = 100\,\Omega$, $\mu_v = 10^{-14}$ m^2 S^{-1} V^{-1} [26]), we can have a simplified memristor model as (using conductance form)

$$G(t) = 3.5 \cdot 10^{-4} \cdot (32 - 15 \cdot v \cdot t)^{-0.5} \qquad (12.5)$$

and corresponding derivative as

$$\frac{dG(t)}{dt} = 2.7 \cdot 10^{-3} \cdot (32 - 15 \cdot v \cdot t)^{-1.5} \qquad (12.6)$$

The conductance change over time can be found in Figure 12.6. Voltages of 1.0 and 0.5 V are applied to the same memristor, respectively, for experiment. An observation is that the curve has a relatively flat portion, which we can utilize to have a linear degradation speed, for example, applying smaller sensing voltages or decreasing the duration of voltage pulses.

12.3.2 Circuit Level

12.3.2.1 Naive Design Linear Degradation

Figure 12.7 depicts an overview of the MNCS structure. Since the elements in the weight matrix W of a neural network can be either positive or negative but the conductances of memristors can be only positive, we split W into two matrices A and B as

$$a_{ij} = \begin{cases} w_{ij}, & \text{if } w_{ij} > 0 \\ 0, & \text{if } w_{ij} <= 0 \end{cases} \qquad (12.7)$$

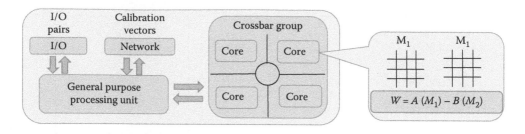

Figure 12.7   Overview of MNCS structure.

$$b_{ij} = \begin{cases} 0, & \text{if } w_{ij} > 0 \\ w_{ij}, & \text{if } w_{ij} <= 0 \end{cases} \tag{12.8}$$

Here we denote the elements in W. Matrices A and B are represented using one memristor crossbar for each (M_1 and M_2, respectively) where the conductance of every memristor $g > 0$. Then we have

$$y_n = f(x_m \cdot A_{m \times n} - x_m \cdot B_{m \times n}) \tag{12.9}$$

For simplicity, here we assume the conductance change of memristors follows Equation 12.5. In naive design, same inputs are applied to both A and B during computation. If the change of A and B denotes to ΔA and ΔB, then the change of W can be expressed as $\Delta W = \Delta A - \Delta B$. According to Equations 12.6 through 12.8, we have

$$\Delta W = sign(W) \cdot dG(v, t) \cdot input \tag{12.10}$$

Here $sign()$ is sign function, $dG(v,t)$ can be adjusted by adjusting v and t, and *input* is target application specific.

As the conductance of the crossbar changes upon applying an input, the accuracy of the system degrades over time, which means the function of the model implemented by the system is gradually changing. In order to control this property, we propose to apply random voltage pulses to all memristors for each I/O pair, so that the conductance can change linearly and evenly, across all memristors.

In order to guarantee stable, correct outputs for authenticated users, a calibration mechanism must be applied to such a system with forgetting property. A naive way to calibrate is to refresh the crossbars with initial conductance states periodically, using the protocol listed in Section 12.2.2.

12.3.2.2 Revised Design Nonlinear Degradation

When the accuracy of MNCS is high, it offers a better service quality to normal users, but aids the attacker in learning the proprietary algorithm better as he or she can obtain outputs with higher accuracy. Degradation of accuracy prevents an attacker from accurately learning the model, but also reduces the accuracy for a normal user. In order to solve the above dilemma, in this proposal, we propose to design an MNCS that has a very nonlinear degradation in accuracy (Figure 12.8b).

Consider a classification application as an example. On applying inputs, the classification accuracy degrades. The rate of degradation is slow initially so as to provide accurate outputs for the authorized user. The degradation then sharply accelerates when the number of test operations

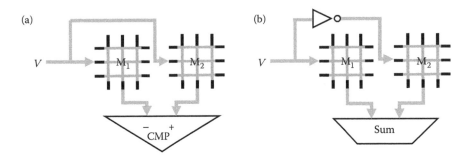

Figure 12.8 Comparison of two proposed designs: (a) naive design with positive voltages applied on both crossbars and (b) revised design with negative voltages applied on second crossbar.

exceeds a threshold to prevent the attacker from replicating the model by obtained sufficient number of I/O pairs.

We design the system by manipulating the input voltages applied on the memristor crossbar. In the naive design, only positive inputs are applied to memristor crossbars M_1 and M_2, and the result from M_2 will be deducted from the result of M_1 in the postprocessing logic. In such a design, the conductances of the memristors in both M_1 and M_2 are changing in the same direction. In our revised design (see Figure 12.8), the inverted negative inputs are applied to M_2 while the inputs to M_1 are still kept positive. The result of M_2, hence, needs to be added on the top of the result of M_1. The conductances of the memristors in M_1 and M_2 are now changing in the opposite directions, and the weight changing function will change from Equation 12.10 to

$$\Delta W = dG(v, t) \cdot input \tag{12.11}$$

Figure 12.9 shows the weight change difference between naive and revised designs. For naive design, because of the sign function, positive weights are changing to higher values, and negative weights are changing to lower values. For revised design, everything is changing to higher value.

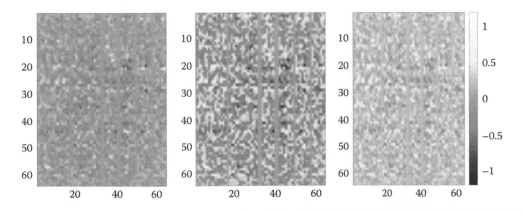

Figure 12.9 Weight change in MNCS: (a) original weight matrix, (b) weight matrix in naive design post degradation, and (c) weight matrix after revised design post degradation.

Changes in weight are represented by the shade in Figure 12.9, which follows our expectation according to Equations 12.10 and 12.11.

The revised design with negative inputs demonstrates a stronger nonlinearity than the naive design when the number of test operations increases. Hence, we prefer to use the revised design over the naive design. The comparison results will be shown in Section 12.4.

12.3.2.3 Architectural Level: Depth of Neural Network

Increasing the depth of neural network is another way to increase the nonlinearity of the MNCS. For example, neural network has intrinsic nonlinearity that arises from the error diffusion across different layers. Considering a normal feedforward network with one hidden layer, we have

$$y = f_2(f_1(x \cdot W_1) \cdot W_2)) \tag{12.12}$$

Here $f_i(i=1,2)$ are the transfer functions, W_1 is the weight matrix between input layer and hidden layer, W_2 is the weight matrix between hidden layer and output layer, x is the input, and y is the output. Hence, the partial derivative of y respect to W_1 is

$$\frac{\partial y}{\partial W_1} = \frac{\partial f_2}{df_1} \cdot \frac{\partial f_1}{\partial W_1} = f_2'(f_1(x \cdot W_1) \cdot W_2) \cdot W_2 \cdot f_1'(x \cdot W_1) \cdot W_1 \tag{12.13}$$

For simplicity, we assume the second transfer function f_2 is a linear function. Then, the derivative can be rewritten as

$$\frac{\partial y}{\partial W_1} = W_2 \cdot f_1'(x \cdot W_1) \cdot W_1 \tag{12.14}$$

The partial derivative of $\partial y / \partial W_1$ respect to W_1 has a high degree (larger than 1) because the transfer function is usually a nonlinear function, for example, hyperbolic tangent, which explains why neural network has intrinsic nonlinearity property.

Similar to the back-propagation method, the errors generated from the weight matrix at the first layer will pass onto all the subsequent layers, and affect the accuracy. The deeper the network is, the greater the influence introduced by the errors will be. Similar conclusion can be drawn for the matrices at other layers. By carefully selecting the depth of the neural network used in the original model, we are able to control the nonlinearity of the degradation curve of the accuracy (service quality).

12.4 Results

In this section, we will demonstrate the effectiveness of our proposed MNCS design. In Section 12.4.1, we will depict the obsolescence effect of memristor devices and its relationship to the accuracy of the system. The proposed revised design, which has nonlinear degradation, will be shown in Section 12.4.3 with comparison with the naive design, which has linear degradation. In Section 12.4.4, we will show security advantages provided by the revised design. In the experiments, we choose two benchmarks from UCI machine learning repository [27] (image segmentation [Image], steel plates faults [Faults])—and one benchmark from scikit-learn [28] (handwritten digits [Digit] and popular digit classification data set MNIST [24]). All the details of the data sets

Table 12.1   Summary of Benchmarks

	Training Samples #	Evaluating Samples #	Attributes #	Class #
Image	1500	810	19	7
Faults	1500	441	27	7
Digit	500	300	64	10
MNIST	50,000	10,000	784	10

are listed in Table 12.1. These are all representative classification tasks that can be realized on memristor-based devices.

12.4.1 Number of I/O Pairs versus Degradation in Accuracy

To evaluate the impact of obsolescence effect on the accuracy of the MNCS, we simulate the degradation in accuracy of MNCS due to the obsolescence effect of memristors when running different benchmarks. The memristor crossbar is configured to implement a neural network with two hidden layers for all benchmarks. Each layer has 64 neurons.

12.4.2 Circuit Level

The simulation results are summarized in Figure 12.10. Here, we take *Digit* for example, as the curves for all three benchmarks have very similar trend. X-axis denotes the number of I/O pairs. The left y-axis denotes the error rate of the system while the right y-axis denotes the normalized summed absolute changes of weights (NSCW) due to memristor obsolescence. We define the error rate and NSCW as

$$\text{Error rate} = \frac{1}{n} \sum_{i=1}^{n} \text{if}(\boldsymbol{y}_i == \boldsymbol{t}_i) \qquad (12.15)$$

$$\text{NSCW} = \frac{\sum_{i,j} |w_{ij} - w'_{ij}|}{\sum_{i,j} |w_{ij}|} \qquad (12.16)$$

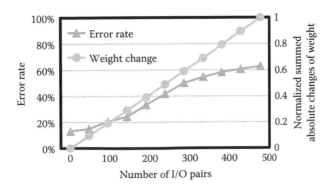

Figure 12.10   The relation between weight change and system degradation.

where y_i denotes the classification result, t_i denotes the target result, n denotes the size of I/O pairs, and $w_i j$ is the element of weight matrices in neural network. As the weight change increases, the error rate increases from less than 20% to over 60% gradually due to the obsolescence effect of the memristors.

12.4.3 Linear versus Nonlinear Degradation

To provide better usability and increase protection against replication attack, we compare the naive design and revised design. Naive design has a linear degradation model, leading to slower degradation. An attacker can apply more I/O pairs with more accuracy and can thus learn the proprietary algorithm. Revised design has a nonlinear degradation model that degrades faster than the linear one. Experimental results of the comparison between naive and revised designs are summarized in Figure 12.10, where x-axis represents the number of I/O pairs and y-axis shows the mean square error (MSE) and error rate, respectively. o_i denotes the final output obtained from the last layer of the network:

$$\text{MSE} = \frac{1}{n} \sum_{i=1}^{n} |o_i - t_i|^2 \tag{12.17}$$

The y-axis of the figure is in logarithmic scale for better view. MSE is the absolute difference between target results and classification results, so it has a smooth monotonous curve. Error rate does not necessarily linearly depend on the system degradation, so the curve may contain many inflection points, which is caused by uncertainty in real classification task.

As we can see in Figure 12.11, the degradation curve of the revised design is highly nonlinear with respect to the naive design. The low error rate region at the beginning provides the usability for normal users, and the rapidly increasing portion guarantees the protection of the model. Take Digit as an example. As we can see in Figure 12.11a, the error rate of revised design keeps below 20% before obtaining 100 I/O pairs, and it increases to over 70% between 100 and 200 I/O

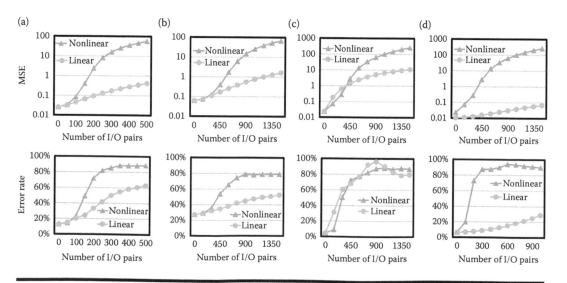

Figure 12.11 Comparison between naive and revised designs using MSE and error rate: (a) Digit, (b) Faults, (c) Image, and (d) MNIST.

Table 12.2 Nonlinearity Index of MSE and Error Rate between Naive and Revised Designs

		Digit	*Faults*	*Image*	*MNIST*
MSE	Naive	0.0320	0.0509	0.0294	0.0401
	Revised	0.1015	0.1303	0.1010	0.0814
Error rate	Naive	0.0250	0.0122	0.0243	0.0322
	Revised	0.0923	0.0762	0.0954	0.0546

pairs. At the same time, the error rate of naive design increases from below 20% to 60% gradually through the whole process without showing significant nonlinearity.

We also quantitatively analyze the nonlinearity using the correlation coefficient:

$$r = \frac{\sum(x - \bar{x})(y - \bar{y})}{\sqrt{\sum(x - \bar{x})^2} \cdot \sqrt{\sum(y - \bar{y})^2}} \tag{12.18}$$

where x denotes the evaluating operations and y denotes evaluation index, that is, error rate or MSE. $r \in (0,1)$ of which 1 represents high linearity and 0 represents high nonlinearity. Then, we define the nonlinearity index as $1 - r$. We take the curve from initial error rate to 60% of its maximum into consideration, because that is the part reflecting the change in first-order derivative. The result is shown in Table 12.2. We can notice that the nonlinearity index of the revised design is much higher than that of the naive design. The average increase in degradation rate for MSE is 179.93% and for error rate is 288.99%.

The influence of network depth on the nonlinearity is also investigated. We choose different neural networks with 1, 2, and 3 hidden layers to run on all the benchmarks. As shown in Figure 12.12, we take Digit as an example. The x- and y-axes are normalized to 0–1, respectively, for better observation of nonlinearity. The nonlinearity indexes are 0.809, 0.897, and 0.971 for 1 layer, 2 layers, and 3 layers, respectively. The result confirms with our discussion in Section 12.3.2.3: the nonlinearity in degradation increases with the depth of neural network. Another similar observation is that if the number of neurons in each layer is larger, the error rate increase is faster. This is shown in Figure 12.11d. The first weight matrix of *MNIST* is "784×64," which is

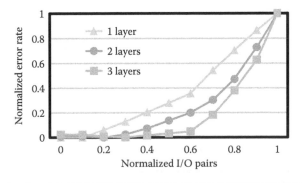

Figure 12.12 Impact of network depth, varying from one hidden layer to three hidden layers.

much larger than other data sets. The error rate increase in revised design is significant compared with that in linear one, with almost the same summed absolute changes of weights. This means that revised design does not introduce much extra overhead. Detailed discussion can be found in Section 12.4.6.

12.4.4 Accuracy of Replicated Model

In this section, we will show the effectiveness of our proposed design on preventing replication attack. The effectiveness is evaluated by determining the highest accuracy that can be achieved by a replicated model. Lower accuracy means the system has better resiliency against replication attack.

Figure 12.13 summarizes the results of comparison, where x-axis is the I/O pairs and y-axis is the accuracy. The model chosen for replication is the model with the best accuracy, for example, SVM for *digit* and random forest for *faults*. Other models include K-nearest neighbors and feedforward neural network. We compare the accuracy of three systems: original system without forgetting property, system with naive design, and system with revised design.

In the simulation, we assume the best-case scenario for an attacker: all the I/O pairs chosen by attackers are the same as the one in the original training samples. If there is another set of I/O pairs that can provide the same or better accuracy, the designer would have used it. Hence, this is the best-case scenario for the attacker. We now show that even for these chosen inputs, an attacker cannot obtain the correct outputs due to the obsolescence effect of the system.

The accuracy of system after degradation is similar to the one before degradation, during the initial phases, because this period belongs to the low error rate region as we can observe from

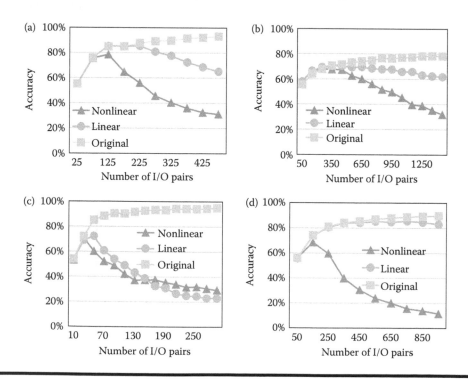

Figure 12.13 Replication accuracy comparison between naive and revised designs: (a) Digit, (b) Faults, (c) Image, and (d) MNIST.

the curve in Figure 12.11. The degradation rate remains low. The accuracy of both revised and naive designs then drops, while the accuracy of original model increases. The accuracy of naive design drops more slowly than that of the revised design. We also observe that the highest accuracy of revised design is always lower than that of naive design. For example, in Figure 12.13a, the maximum accuracy of revised design is 78.5%, compared to the maximum of naive design, which is 85.4%, let alone the fast decreasing part after the maximum. In a nutshell, the proposed revised design is more resilient to replication attack.

12.4.5 Robustness Analysis: Effect of Process Variation

In this section, we evaluate the impact of memristor process variation on its area and thickness [29]. We can safely assume the memristor conductance follows a Gaussian distribution in general. Comparison result experimented on digit is shown in Figure 12.14. Initial memristor process variation is applied to both designs with different standard deviations σ. Consider the revised design as an example. The initial error rate increases from 13% to 16% and 18%, with $\sigma = 0, 1$, and 2, respectively. However, both error rates tend to be the same as they approach the maxima. The nonlinearity index is also calculated for each case, which is our most interested index. Results are marked in orange in Figure 12.14. The overall nonlinearity change is not much, which even increases a little bit as σ increases for revised design.

The results show that our designs are robust against memristor process variation, since the nonlinearity does not change much with different standard deviations. The only thing affected

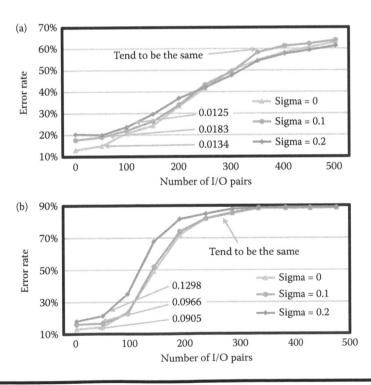

Figure 12.14 **System degradation with different memristor process variation: (a) naive design and (b) revised design.**

is the initial error rate, which is higher when variation is larger. Techniques enhancing training robustness, for example, variation-aware training, can be used to solve this issue [30], in which the impact of device variation is compensated.

12.4.6 Calibration Overhead

The cost of every calibration operation discussed in Section 12.3.2 can be measured by $\sum_{i,j} |w_{ij} - w'_{ij}|$, which is the summed discrepancy between the changed conductance and the fully trained conductance of the memristors.

$$OH_{cal} = \frac{T_{cal}}{T_{eval} + T_{cal}} \tag{12.19}$$

Each operation cycle of our proposed secured MNCS consists of two periods, that is, evaluating operations and system calibration. To evaluate the calibration time overhead, we used Equation 12.19 to quantitatively measure the percentage of calibration time T_{cal} cost of the overall time cost of one operation cycle $T_{eval} + T_{cal}$. T_{cal}, and T_{eval} can be further described as

$$T_{eval} = \frac{N_{eval}}{f_{eval}} = \frac{g(\epsilon)}{f_{eval}} \tag{12.20}$$

$$T_{cal} = \sum t_{cal} |w_{ij} - wij'| \tag{12.21}$$

Here, ϵ is error rate threshold (system needs calibration when error rate approaches ϵ) and $g(\epsilon)$ is the number of test operations that can be performed when the system is required to maintain error rate lower than ϵ. f_{eval} is the frequency of evaluating operations, and $t_{cal} |w_{ij} - w_{ij}'|$ denotes the unit time to calibrate w_{ij} from w_{ij}'.

For example, in revised design of Figure 12.11a, if we set ϵ to 20%, when error rate increases from original 13% to ϵ, only 100 I/O pairs can be applied before the calibration. A comparison of the overhead between naive and revised designs can be found in Table 12.3. Here, T means the difference between error rate when calibration is needed and original error rate. In the above case, $T = 7\%$. Our result shows that revised design does not involve a larger calibration cost than does the naive one. This is because the conductance changing speed is almost the same for both designs as indicated by Equations 12.10 and 12.11. The calibration cost depends only on the initial weight distribution.

Table 12.3 Comparison of Calibration Overhead (%)

Digit	Naive	28.05	28.14	28.30
	Revised	29.15	29.09	29.24
Faults	Naive	9.28	9.28	9.40
	Revised	9.22	9.24	9.26
Image	Naive	50.65	50.36	50.54
	Revised	50.53	50.49	50.66
MNIST	Naive	18.66	18.77	18.94
	Revised	19.67	19.67	19.67

12.5 Conclusion

In this work, we propose a design for MNCS to prevent attackers from learning the function of the model behind the system. We propose a cross-layer approach device, circuit, and architectural levels to thwart this attack. Experimental results show that our design provides better usability as well as security against replication attack. Compared to the naive design, revised design has a higher nonlinearity index, 179.93% increase on MSE and 288.99% on error rate. In this work, we assume that the attacker tries to learn the system using I/O pairs. Hence, we propose to defense against this attack. However, an attacker can also perform side-channel attacks to learn the proprietary algorithm. Our future work aims to use the low-power properties of memristors to protect against such attacks.

References

1. Y. LeCun, Y. Bengio, and G. Hinton. Deep learning. *Nature*, **521**(7553):436–444, 2015.
2. F. Rosenblatt. The perceptron: A probabilistic model for information storage and organization in the brain. *Psychological review*, **65**(6):386, 1958.
3. S. Kumar. Introducing Qualcomm zeroth processors: Brain-inspired computing, 2013.
4. M. Hu, H. Li, Q. Wu, and G. S. Rose. Hardware realization of BSB recall function using memristor crossbar arrays. In *Proceedings of the 49th Annual Design Automation Conference*, pages 498–503. ACM, New York, NY, 2012.
5. B. Lendon. Iran says it built copy of captured US drone, 2014.
6. C. Cortes and V. Vapnik. Support-vector networks. *Machine Learning*, **20**(3):273–297, 1995.
7. T. K. Ho. Random decision forests. In *Proceedings of the Third International Conference on Document Analysis and Recognition*, Vol. **1**, pages 278–282. IEEE, New York, NY, 1995.
8. N. S. Altman. An introduction to kernel and nearest-neighbor nonparametric regression. *The American Statistician*, **46**(3):175–185, 1992.
9. A. Mazady, M. T. Rahman, D. Forte, and M. Anwar. Memristor PUFA security primitive: Theory and experiment. *IEEE Journal on Emerging and Selected Topics in Circuits and Systems*, **5**(2):222–229, 2015.
10. J. Rajendran, G. S. Rose, R. Karri, and M. Potkonjak. Nano-PPUF: A memristor-based security primitive. In *IEEE Computer Society Annual Symposium on VLSI*, pages 84–87. IEEE, New York, NY, 2012.
11. G. Khedkar, C. Donahue, and D. Kudithipudi. Towards leakage resiliency: Memristor-based AES design for differential power attack mitigation. In *SPIE Sensing Technology+Applications*, pages 911907–911907. International Society for Optics and Photonics, 2014.
12. L. O. Chua. Memristor—The missing circuit element. *IEEE Transactions on Circuit Theory*, **18**(5):507–519, 1971.
13. V. Erokhin and M. P. Fontana. Electrochemically controlled polymeric device: A memristor (and more) found two years ago. *Physics*, 2008. AxXiv: 0807.033.
14. D. B. Strukov, G. S. Snider, D. R. Stewart, and R. S. Williams. The missing memristor found. *Nature*, **453**(7191):80–83, 2008.
15. L. Zhang, Z. Chen, J. J. Yang, B. Wysocki, N. McDonald, and Y. Chen. A compact modeling of TiO_2-TiO_{2-x} memristor. *Applied Physics Letters*, **102**(15):1–4, 2013.
16. T. Chang, S.-H. Jo, and W. Lu. Short-term memory to long-term memory transition in a nanoscale memristor. *ACS Nano*, **5**(9):7669–7676, 2011.
17. M. Hu, H. Li, Y. Chen, Q. Wu, and G. S. Rose. BSB training scheme implementation on memristor-based circuit. In *IEEE Computational Intelligence for Security and Defense Applications*, pages 80–87, Singapore, 2013.
18. B. Liu, H. Li, Y. Chen, X. Li, T. Huang, Q. Wu, and M. Barnell. Reduction and IR-drop compensations techniques for reliable neuromorphic computing systems. In *IEEE/ACM International Conference on Computer-Aided Design*, pages 63–70, San Jose, California, 2014.

19. H. Manem, J. Rajendran, and G. S. Rose. Design considerations for multilevel CMOS/nano memristive memory. *Journal of Emerging Technologies in Computing Systems*, **8**(1):1–22, 2012.
20. B. Liu, M. Hu, H. Li, Z.-H. Mao, Y. Chen, T. Huang, and W. Zhang. Digital-assisted noise-eliminating training for memristor crossbar-based analog neuromorphic computing engine. In *ACM/EDAC/IEEE Design Automation Conference*, pages 1–6, Austin, Texas, 2013.
21. B. Liu, C. Wu, H. Li, Y. Chen, Q. Wu, M. Barnell, and Q. Qiu. Cloning your mind: Security challenges in cognitive system designs and their solutions. In *Proceedings of the 52nd Annual Design Automation Conference*, page 95. ACM, New York, NY, 2015.
22. C. Helfmeier, D. Nedospasov, C. Tarnovsky, J. S. Krissler, C. Boit, and J.-P. Seifert. Breaking and entering through the silicon. In *Proceedings of the 2013 ACM SIGSAC Conference on Computer & Communications Security*, pages 733–744. ACM, New York, NY, 2013.
23. S. Kannan, N. Karimi, O. Sinanoglu, and R. Karri. Security vulnerabilities of emerging nonvolatile main memories and countermeasures. *IEEE Transactions on Computer-Aided Design of Integrated Circuits and Systems*, **34**(1):2–15, 2015.
24. Y. LeCun, L. Bottou, Y. Bengio, and P. Haffner. Gradient-based learning applied to document recognition. *Proceedings of the IEEE*, **86**(11):2278–2324, 1998.
25. D. Kuzum, S. Yu, and H. P. Wong. Synaptic electronics: Materials, devices and applications. *Nanotechnology*, **24**(38):382001, 2013.
26. M. Hu, H. Li, and R. E. Pino. Fast statistical model of TiO_2 thin-film memristor and design implication. In *Proceedings of the International Conference on Computer-Aided Design*, pages 345–352. IEEE Press, New York, NY, 2011.
27. A. Asuncion and D. Newman. UCI machine learning repository, 2007. http://www.ics.uci.edu/~mlearn/MLRepository.html
28. F. Pedregosa, G. Varoquaux, A. Gramfort, V. Michel, B. Thirion, O. Grisel, M. Blondel, P. Prettenhofer, R. Weiss, V. Dubourg et al. Scikit-learn: Machine learning in python. *Journal of Machine Learning Research*, **12**(Oct):2825–2830, 2011.
29. D. Niu, Y. Chen, C. Xu, and Y. Xie. Impact of process variations on emerging memristor. In *Proceedings of the 47th ACM/IEEE Design Automation Conference*, pages 877–882. IEEE, New York, NY, 2010.
30. B. Liu, H. Li, Y. Chen, X. Li, Q. Wu, and T. Huang. Vortex: Variation-aware training for memristor x-bar. In *Proceedings of the 52nd Annual Design Automation Conference*, page 15. ACM, New York, NY, 2015.

Chapter 13

Leveraging Circuit Edit for Low-Volume Trusted Nanometer Fabrication

Bicky Shakya, Xiaolin Xu, Navid Asadizanjani,
Mark Tehranipoor, and Domenic Forte

Contents

With the rising costs of building and maintaining high-end foundries, the semiconductor industry has steadily shifted to a horizontal business model, in which integrated circuits (ICs) at state-of-the-art nodes are fabricated offshore. While this off-shoring strategy makes sense from an economical perspective and drastically reduces time to market, it has raised serious concerns for semiconductor intellectual property (IP) protection. In order to fabricate ICs, a design house has to hand over the entire design to the foundry and in most cases, even the test stimuli and responses needed to verify the IC functionality. As a result, the foundry has complete access to the entire design, potentially leading to threats such as overproduction, cloning, IP infringement, and even hardware Trojan insertion. Such concerns are especially alarming for entities such as the government, military, and in other scenarios where IP protection is of paramount concern.

In this chapter, we review a recently proposed technique that leverages circuit-edit technology to support design obfuscation and trusted fabrication [1]. In this technique, a design house performs gate-level manipulation to its final design in order to obfuscate its functionality. This obfuscated design (in layout form) is then sent to an untrusted foundry for fabrication followed by structural testing. Upon the return of the die or wafers, the design house uses circuit edit to revert the design to its intended functionality. Compared with prior approaches for protecting designs against untrusted foundries, the approach introduces negligible area overhead for gate-level obfuscation. Further, since manufacturing and testing is performed at the foundry, the technique lowers the cost for the design house, as it only needs to maintain a moderate-cost circuit-edit system to de-obfuscate the chip. The shortcoming of such an approach is that it is limited to low-volume production since circuit edit can be performed only on a chip-by-chip basis. Nonetheless, it is well suited for critical applications (e.g., military and/or government, IP owners with high margins and small markets, etc.), where volume production is much less of a concern than IP protection. Further, low-volume ICs produced for such applications are usually manufactured using electron-beam lithography, which do not require expensive masks but suffer from extremely low throughput. The proposed circuit edit-based technique could compete with such approaches for ensuring trusted fabrication.

13.1 Threats

In the past, the entire semiconductor production flow used to be "horizontal," that is, specification, design, test, manufacturing, and packaging were all done under one roof (or at least onshore) at trusted facilities. However, as production costs continue to sky rocket with advancing transistor nodes, many foundries have steadily moved offshore, in order to reduce costs and time-to-market. This has also led to the emergence of "fabless" semiconductor companies, who design their ICs onshore but delegate fabrication to "pure-play" semiconductor foundries who are often located in different corners of the globe. While such a market strategy immensely helps in low-cost and high-volume production of commercial ICs (e.g., consumer system-on-chips, microprocessors, etc.), it has created an issue for application scenarios where trust and security of ICs are of paramount concern. Due to the gradual disappearance of advanced and trusted onshore foundries, entities such as the government, military, aerospace and defense industries, etc. are limited to relying on older, onshore nodes for producing ICs that need to be integrated into critical applications. Further, such applications usually require low-volume production, and maintaining multibillion dollar foundries to sustain such volume usually makes little to no economical sense.

When an untrusted foundry is relied upon, several threats are possible. Some of the pertinent ones are outlined as follows:

1. *IP Theft:* A design house usually passes on its design in the form of a GDSII or layout file to the foundry for fabrication. Since layout files are provided, the foundry has a "white-box" view of the design, that is, all the IP cores and logic blocks are in plain-sight of the foundry. Since the foundries also usually provide the design house with a process design kit, it is trivial for them to go from layout to a gate-level view of the design. Once the gate-level representation of the design is obtained, foundries can simulate and test the design at their own will. Moreover, they would also be able to sell illegal copies of the extracted IP cores (in the form of "firm IPs") to unauthorized parties interested in them. They could also sell the extracted layout as is, in the form of hard IPs. These parties would then be able to incorporate the illegitimately obtained IP cores/designs into their own products (provided that they understand their functionality) to produce clones, or use them to perform intelligence analysis (in the case of government ICs/IPs). We refer to these kinds of threats as "IP theft."

2. *IC Overproduction:* A foundry with limited design expertise could also sell manufactured and tested ICs to unauthorized parties, who may then incorporate these ICs into their own systems. Such a practice of producing ICs in excess of the contracted amount and selling them is termed as "overproduction."

3. *Malicious Modifications:* Since foundries have a white-box view of the design, they could also insert additional logic or modify pre-existing ones to implement malicious functionality. Such modifications, usually referred to as "hardware Trojans," could be as small as a few gates and can bring about effects such as denial of service and reduced reliability [2]. While it is possible to implement such Trojans with limited understanding of the design (e.g., by tampering with the clock distribution network, power supply lines, etc.), an untrusted foundry could be more interested in bringing about targeted effects (such as using rare nodes in the circuit to trigger a Trojan, impacting critical registers, etc.). For such attacks, the foundry would want to have a better understanding of the design. Since they possess the layout (and thus, netlist) of the functional design, it becomes possible (and feasible) for them to employ reverse engineering techniques [3].

Thus, there is an inherent dilemma in producing state-of-the-art ICs for critical applications in today's globalized semiconductor industry. While advanced nodes are always desired for better performance and enabling newer applications, they come at the cost of reduced trust and security. Due to this, there is a need for technologies that can allow designers to use state-of-the-art foundries and at the same time to address the threats of piracy and/or malicious modifications, all while incurring minimal design overhead.

13.2 Related Work

A plethora of techniques have been recently proposed in order to counter the aforementioned threat of IP piracy, overproduction, and hardware Trojans. A brief discussion of these techniques is provided below, along with a comparison against circuit edit-based obfuscation techniques in terms of cost and security.

13.2.1 Logic Locking

Logic locking techniques rely on "key gates" that are embedded into the design at the gate level. These key gates are usually extra XOR/XNOR/MUX gates that are inserted at special nets in the

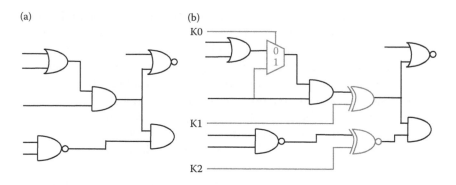

Figure 13.1 **(a) Original netlist. (b) Logic encrypted netlist with MUX, XOR, and XNOR key gates (K0, K1, and K2 are the key inputs).**

circuit and are driven by key inputs, as shown in Figure 13.1. When the correct key values are provided by an external memory into the key inputs, the circuit behaves as normal. However, if the wrong key values are provided, the key gates produce logical inversions (i.e., faults) in the circuit that corrupt its outputs. This prevents any unauthorized party who does not possess the key from using the circuit.

A variety of logic locking techniques have been proposed over the years. Most of these techniques focus on maximizing the impact of the wrong key value with a minimum number of key gates [4]. To achieve this, key gates are inserted into the netlist with metrics such as 50% Hamming distance (i.e., roughly half of the output bits need to be different between the unlocked and the locked netlist, so that the locked circuit output appears random) [5]. Another metric is fault impact, according to which key gates are inserted such that faults introduced by wrong key values propagate to the primary output [6]. At the same time, some competing metrics/techniques have also been proposed in order to secure logic encryption against recently introduced Boolean-satisfiability attacks [7]. In these techniques, the impact of the wrong key values on the circuit is minimized. This is done in order to prevent an attacker from using known-good input–output responses to quickly rule out a large number of wrong keys (thereby removing the need for brute-force attacks on the key). In addition, metering protocols for locking/unlocking chips, keeping track of the number of unlocked chips and securely transmitting the key between the design house, foundry, and assembly have also been introduced [8–10].

However, the security of all these various locking techniques rely on the secrecy of the key. Since the foundry has a white-box understanding of the circuit, the key gates could potentially be removed. In addition, techniques to resolve the correct key value given a finite number of correct input–output observations have also been proposed [5,7]. Further, conflicting techniques for logic encryption exist (e.g., those that focus on corrupting the functionality and others that try to minimize the same) and it is not known whether a good trade-off exists between these two objectives. In contrast to such locking techniques, the proposed circuit edit-based obfuscation approach is inherently "keyless." Its security lies in the inability of the attacker to find out the gates and wires used for obfuscation (as opposed to locking techniques where the point of attack, i.e., key gates are abundantly clear). In addition, the need for key management schemes (e.g., Rivest-Shamir-Adleman [RSA] public key cryptosystem, in case chips need to be activated at the foundry) is also removed.

13.2.2 Split Manufacturing

Split manufacturing enables the splitting of the fabrication process between an untrusted and a trusted foundry. In this design flow, the untrusted foundry fabricates the front-end-of-line (FEOL) layers, which include the transistor and lower metal layers (Figure 13.2). Since these are the most expensive steps in the fabrication process, a design house can use the untrusted state-of-the-art foundry to fabricate these layers at low cost. After FEOL fabrication, the incomplete design is returned to the design house where the back-end-of-line (BEOL) metal layers (i.e., higher metal layers used for routing) are fabricated and the IC is completed. Since BEOL fabrication does not require advanced lithographic capabilities, the design house can maintain (or access) trusted onshore fabs to complete its design. In addition, 3D IC technologies can also be used to enable split manufacturing, where the BEOL metal layer stack is fabricated in a trusted facility and TSVs are used to bond the BEOL stack with the untrusted FEOL stack [11].

Split manufacturing prevents the untrusted foundry from engaging in IP/IC piracy, over-production, and Trojan insertion, as they only have an incomplete view of the design (i.e., interconnections between gates are missing). However, it still requires the design house to have access to a foundry for completing the BEOL layers, which leads to increased costs. Alignment mismatch between the FEOL/BEOL stack and inability to test the design at the foundry may also lead to yield issues. It has also been shown that securely partitioning a design (i.e., making sure the FEOL layer gives no information about connections in the BEOL layer) leads to increased power, delay, and area overheads [11]. In contrast, circuit edit-based obfuscation techniques allow the design to be structurally tested (i.e., diagnosed for manufacturing defects) at the foundry, leading to improved yield. Further, FIB systems used to perform the circuit edit are much lower in cost, compared to lithographic and mask equipment that are required for fabricating the BEOL layers.

A comparison between logic encryption, split manufacturing, and circuit edit-based obfuscation technique is shown in Figure 13.3. We can see that circuit edit-based obfuscation is suited for secure low-volume and relatively low-cost fabrication. However, for high-volume production, split manufacturing and logic encryption are preferred, albeit at the cost of high design overhead, need for trusted BEOL foundry (for split manufacturing), and key management/security (for logic

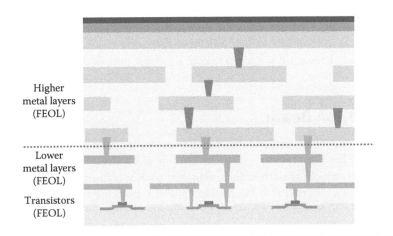

Figure 13.2 Split manufacturing enables FEOL fabrication at untrusted foundry and BEOL fabrication at trusted foundry.

	Split manufacturing	Logic encryption	Circuit edit obfuscation
Protection against untrusted foundry	✓	✓	✓
Low area overhead	✗	Possibly	✓
Low performance overhead	Possibly	Possibly	Possibly
(Structural) testability at foundry	✗	✓	✓
Low cost for design house	✗	✓	✓
Minor change to design flow (pre-foundry)	✗	✓	✓
Minor change (post-foundry)	✗	✓	Possibly
SoC applicability	✓	✓	✓
No key management required + resistance to key/key gate-based attacks	✓	✗	✓
Security in supply chain	✗	Possibly	✗
High-volume production possible	✓	✓	✗

Figure 13.3 Comparison between split manufacturing, logic encryption, and circuit edit-based obfuscation. *"Possibly"* implies that the respective technique could be adapted for the given feature, but needs further exploration.

encryption). While none of the existing work have applied the techniques to system-on-chip (SoC) designs (i.e., a single die with multiple IP cores), they could potentially be applicable. For logic encryption and circuit edit-based obfuscation, further work is required to look into distribution of key gates/gate-level modifications between different IP cores. The row with *"Minor change to design flow (Pre-Foundry)"* relates to the level of design modification required to use the obfuscation technique. In this regard, split manufacturing requires netlist and layout-level partitioning (which is nontrivial for large designs). On the other hand, logic encryption and circuit edit-based obfuscation both require only minor gate-level changes. The row with *"Minor change (Post-Foundry)"* relates to the difficulty in producing the final functional chip once the chip arrives at the trusted design house. In this regard, logic encryption is the most convenient of the three techniques, as it only requires loading of the correct key values. Spit manufacturing requires costly BEOL fabrication, and circuit edit-based obfuscation requires cheaper although time-consuming circuit edit.

13.3 Focused-Ion Beam

In this section, we introduce focused-ion beam systems, their basic modes of operation, and focused-ion beam (FIB)-based circuit edit. FIB systems use a stream of ions (positively or negatively charged atoms), which are derived from elements such as gallium (Ga), neon (Ne), or helium (He). These elements are heated to a liquid state, and the resulting ions are electrically dispersed onto the sample [12]. These ions can be used for three operations:

■ *Imaging:* FIB-based imaging relies on low-current ion beams, which produce secondary electrons on hitting the sample. These secondary electrons (as well as sputtered ions) are collected and used to image the sample with sub-10-nm resolution.

- *Milling:* FIB-based milling relies on high beam currents. Heavy ions such as Ga^+ are bombarded onto the sample, which causes a significant amount of sputtering and thus removal of material from the sample surface. In order to speed up the rate of etching, various gases such as XeF_2, Cl_2, I_2, H_2O (depending on the ion used and the material to be removed) are introduced into the FIB chamber. These gases adsorb to the materials on the sample's surface and form volatile compounds (which evaporate away) and nonvolatile compounds (which are sputtered away) on impact with ions. Such a gas-assisted FIB etching scheme is desirable for milling away large amounts of materials and also selectively removing materials (e.g., insulators or metal).
- *Deposition:* FIBs can also be used for depositing materials such as metals and insulators onto samples. These metals/insulators are introduced as gaseous *precursor* compounds (e.g., $W(CO)_6$ for tungsten, $(MeCp)PtMe_3$ for platinum) into the FIB chamber. They are then adsorbed onto the sample surface in the same way as the assistive gases used in milling. However, on impact with ions, the precursors dissociate into nonvolatile components such as tungsten (W) or platinum (Pt), which are then deposited onto the sample surface.

13.3.1 FIB-Based Circuit Edit

Due to the increasing complexity of ICs today, it is difficult to completely verify the functionality of a design in the electronic design automation (EDA) stage. More often than not, after the first silicon run, designers find the need to modify connections and also bypass cells that become defective after fabrication. They might also find the need to change transistor characteristics (e.g., threshold voltage) or modify connections to change the implemented logic. Due to the enormous time and cost involved with developing a new mask set, designers leverage FIBs as well as design-for-debug features such as spare cells in order to "fix" ICs in a matter of hours and thus reduce development time/cost. Further, due to the all-in-one functionality of FIBs (simultaneous imaging, milling, and deposition), it has become the tool of choice for post-silicon debug in the semiconductor industry.

13.3.1.1 Front and Backside Edits

As can be seen in Figure 13.4, circuit edit can either be performed from the frontside (shown on the top) or backside of ICs (shown on the bottom). Frontside FIB edits trench through the upper metal layers of the ICs in order to make net-to-net contact. With increasing number of metal layers in modern designs, frontside edits are very difficult to perform, as there might not be a clear milling and deposition route to a target metal line. Further, the top metal lines are usually thick power, ground, or clock lines, which make frontside FIB access even more difficult.

Backside FIB edits are more common in the industry today [13], especially with the advent of flip-chip packaging (i.e., the die is mounted after flipping, so that bulk silicon faces up instead of the metal layers). The main advantage with backside FIB edits is that it is possible to make contacts with almost all gate pins [14], either by accessing the lower metal layers or by directly reaching the silicide contact in the source/drain region of transistors. There is also a low probability of breaking or making inadvertent contact with other metal interconnects, which often happens in frontside edits due to the poor aspect ratio of the FIB-milled via or holes. Sub-10 nm milling/deposition using helium/neon/gallium-ion FIBs [15] have also made backside FIB edits more precise and

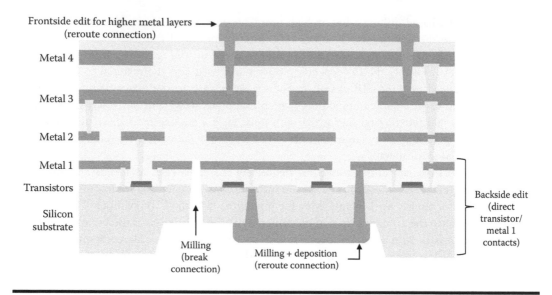

Figure 13.4   Front and backside circuit edit on ICs.

feasible. Further, infrared (IR) imaging techniques allow the nondestructive imaging of transistor regions through the bulk silicon. This kind of imaging capability, along with CAD design overlay (i.e., superimposing layout of the design on top of the IR image) makes it possible for precise backside navigation.

13.3.1.2 Substrate Thinning and Trenching for Backside Edits

In order to make gate-level contacts and edits from the backside, the thick bulk silicon has to first be trenched. In order to do this effectively, the most common approach is to first perform global wafer polishing down to $\approx 100\,\mu m$ (using plasma etching, laser ablation or regular mechanical polishing) and then, use FIB (along with reactive chemicals such as XeF_2) for local milling till the active/metal layers are precisely reached. The global thinning, followed by FIB etching, helps to speed up the trenching process, as FIB trenching alone is time-consuming and expensive for full-thickness silicon wafers. For example, let us consider the silicon removal rate of $30\,\mu m^3/min$, of the FIB system in Reference 13 (without any chemical assistance, which is the worst-case and with 1 nA beam current). Assuming a via aspect ratio of 10:1 and the shape of the via as a truncated square pyramid ($2500\,nm^2$ base area, $250{,}000\,nm^2$ top area), the FIB system would take ≈ 18.5 seconds to mill away and create one $100\,\mu m$-deep trench in silicon, compared to ≈ 2.15 minutes for a full-thickness trench that is $700\,\mu m$ in depth. However, note that polishing and thinning of the silicon substrate could lead to reliability issues (such as die cracking, chipping). Therefore, there is a trade-off between reducing FIB milling time by globally thinning the substrate and increasing the probability of chip failure due to reduced mechanical reliability from thinning. Nonetheless, it should be noted that wafers/dies are routinely thinned to $<100\,\mu m$ today for advanced packaging techniques such as 2.5D/3D ICs (for backside metallization). Therefore, a careful choice of die thickness and desired FIB milling time can be made.

13.3.1.3 Metal Deposition

After the milling operation, metals such as tungsten (W, preferred due to lower resistivity) or platinum (Pt) can be deposited by the FIB system (via FIB-induced chemical vapor deposition) in the trench and along the backside plane as wires, in order to connect the contacted node to other parts of the circuit. Typical deposition time for tungsten wires is about 120–240 s for a wire length of 25 µm (at 20 pA beam current) [16]. While deposition times are definitely longer, an issue with these wires and trenches is that their resistivity is much higher than pure tungsten, ranging anywhere from 50 to 250 $\mu\Omega \cdot$ cm, compared to 5.6 $\mu\Omega \cdot$ cm for pure tungsten [16,17]. This is because the materials to be deposited are introduced in the form of precursor compounds. When these precursors decompose on exposure to ions, several other nonvolatile materials (such as carbon, gallium ions, oxygen, carbon) are deposited as residues, along with the intended deposition material (Pt, W). One side-effect of such contamination is an increased resistivity of the the interconnects/vias that have been created by circuit edit. In terms of circuit performance, this means that any metal traces created during circuit edit are going to impact circuit delay. In order to keep the amount of high-resistivity tungsten low, one can use regular chemical vapor deposition (CVD)-based tungsten deposition to fill the FIB trenches (followed by chemical mechanical planarization). Tungsten deposited by CVD is much purer and of the same resistance as any tungsten via in a circuit. Unfortunately, the backside wires connecting the trenches still have to be deposited by FIB-induced CVD, which could potentially impact delay and needs to be taken into account.

13.4 Overall Manufacturing Flow

The overall design flow for circuit edit-based obfuscation is shown in Figure 13.5 and described as follows.

1. The flow starts with a synthesized netlist (i.e., netlist generated from register transfer level or behavioral code), which is first put through the obfuscation analysis steps described in Section 13.5. Since we perform our changes at the gate level, our approach is agnostic to the overall function of the circuit and can be generally applied to all types of logic circuit. The output of the obfuscation analysis is a list of suitable nets for modification.

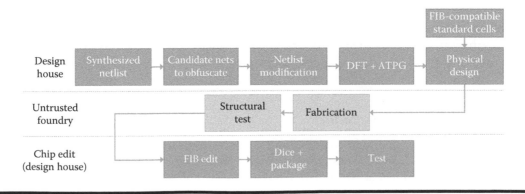

Figure 13.5 Proposed design flow.

2. These selected nets (and the adjoining gates) are then modified by the obfuscation techniques described in Section 13.5.2 until a specified area, effort, and/or security threshold are met.

3. Automatic test pattern generation (ATPG) tools are then used to generate test patterns for the resultant netlist. The test patterns produced by the ATPG tool are able to detect various types of structural faults that may be produced in the final manufactured chip (e.g., gate connections shorted to VDD/GND leading to "stuck-at" gates, shorting of wires or "bridging" faults). It is important to note that these patterns are independent of the functionality of the chip, due to which the tests conducted with ATPG patterns are called "structural tests." The design house is able to generate these test patterns and provide them to the untrusted foundry for die/wafer-level structural tests.

4. Next, physical design of the obfuscated netlist is performed by place and route tools with a standard cell library, which is a collection of predesigned logic gates such as inverters, AND, OR, flip-flops, etc. In this step, special standard cells (described in Section 13.5.3) are added to the standard cell library and used for the gates that were affected by the obfuscation. These standard cells feature contact and cut pads that are sized up to accommodate FIB-based circuit edit and subsequent "de-obfuscation" of the circuit. Note that since the foundry would readily be able to identify these cells as possible obfuscation points, each added cell should be masked by other pre-existing gates (i.e., dummies) that are also modified with the same type of layout.

5. The resulting GDSII file is handed over to the foundry which fabricates the design and performs structural tests in order to identify faulty chips. If flip-chip packaging is adopted and the foundry offers packaging services, the chips can also be packaged.

6. After fabrication and/or packaging, the chips arrive back at the design house where they undergo circuit edit. The exact obfuscation points are identified by CAD overlay and IR imaging, and the necessary cutting and rerouting operations are performed.

7. Finally, the chips are packaged (if they arrive in wafer-form from the foundry) and thoroughly re-tested (burn-in, functional, structural, etc.) before they are ready for deployment.

13.5 Obfuscation Flow

Any kind of digital design can usually be separated into two components: (i) the controller and (ii) the datapath. The datapath usually consists of arithmetic circuits whereas the controller unit consists of finite-state machines and logic in order to control the inputs and states of elements in the datapath. In terms of IP protection, we are mainly concerned with the controller unit, which contains a designer's trade secrets and is worth protecting. In this section, we discuss gate-level changes that can be implemented by the design house/designer on such controller units for circuit edit–enabled obfuscation. These changes are discussed in terms of two aspects: (i) the location of the changes and (ii) the type of changes to make, given the location.

13.5.1 Obfuscation Location

Several criteria can be adopted in order to find suitable locations for obfuscation. The goal of such criteria would be to identify the minimum number of nets in a design which can be obfuscated to maximize the effect of logical errors. This ensures that the untrusted foundry is unable to pirate the design or reverse engineer the IP to extract its high-level behavior. Some suitable metrics are discussed below.

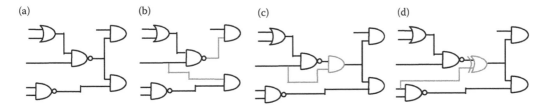

Figure 13.6 Modifications made to netlist for obfuscation. (a) Original design, (b) wire rerouting, (c) AND gate insertion, and (d) XOR gate insertion.

■ *Fanout*: Injecting a faulty value at a high fanout net can cause those faulty values to propagate to multiple nodes in a circuit. Further, these faulty values could propagate to (multiple) primary outputs, leading to erroneous output signals. If multiple flip-flops appear in the fanout cone of the net, it could also significantly distort the functionality of the FSM implemented by the design.

■ *Observability:* In VLSI testing, observability refers to the ease of discerning a logical value at an internal circuit node through one of the circuit outputs (primary outputs or scan flip-flops/pseudo outputs) and thus gives a numerical measure on the testability of the node. In other words, it tells us how likely it is for us to observe an activated fault at an internal net through the circuit outputs. Conversely, for obfuscation, this means that choosing nets or nodes with high observability will make it more likely for the faulty values to propagate and appear at the circuit outputs. Although there are numerous measures for observability, the SCOAP (Sandia Controllability/Observability Analysis Program) approach proposed in Reference 18 is the most widely used. SCOAP assigns a maximum observability of "1" to the output ports. It then statically calculates the observability (1 to ∞, where ∞ is least observable) for every node by backtracking the output observability all the way to the inputs. During backtracking, preformulated gate observability equations are used to calculate the observability values in linear time [19].

■ *Hamming Distance:* Another metric that could be used for net selection is Hamming distance (HD). Given the golden design, one can make a change to the netlist and monitor how many output bits get corrupted for a given input vector. The best set of nodes would then be the ones that lead to a 50% HD between the outputs of the obfuscated design and the original design. This 50% HD implies that two circuits are only as similar as random chance. HD figures can be approximated by gate-level simulations. However, they take longer to calculate than SCOAP figures (which are vectorless/static).

A designer may then apply one or a combination of these metrics in order to rank circuit nets and use them for obfuscation. One way to perform this ranking would be to assign a score S_i for each net i in the design. This score can be calculated as a weighted sum of the metrics discussed above for each net, and the weights can be adjusted based on the circuit under consideration. After score calculation, these nodes can be ranked and nets with a score $S_i > \lambda$, where λ is a preset threshold, can be selected for obfuscation.

13.5.2 Obfuscation Modifications

After identifying the suitable nets for obfuscation, the goal of the designer is to introduce gate-level changes that can achieve two goals: (i) to corrupt (or invert) the correct logic value at the chosen locations and (ii) to reduce FIB cost and time during de-obfuscation. Several changes such as the ones shown in Figure 13.6 could be made. However, two of such gate-level changes are described in detail below.

13.5.2.1 Gate Insertion

The general idea in this approach is as follows. Consider a two-input AND gate that is inserted into a selected net (i.e., a net selected by the criteria set forth in Section 13.5.1). During obfuscation in the design house, one input of the added gate is tied to the selected net, whereas the other input is tied to another net k in a circuit (the features for this net will be explained below). After fabrication, the design house uses circuit edit to do the following:

- Disconnect k by FIB milling.
- Reroute the connection k so that the gate now behaves as a buffer. For an AND gate, the net k could be connected to VDD and for an OR gate, the net could be connected to GND. If an XOR gate is used, the net k would be tied to GND.

Algorithm 13.1 Gate Insertion

1:   **for** each net $i = 1 : num(\mathrm{N} \in \{S_i > \lambda\}$ **do**
2:       Get $P_i(0)$, $P_i(1)$
3:       **if** $P_i(1) > P_i(0)$
4:           insert m-input AND
5:       **else**
6:           insert m-input OR
7:       **end if**
8:       Place gates
9:   **end for**
10: **for** each net $i = 1 : num(N \in \{S_i > \lambda\})$ **do**
11:       **for** $j = 1 : num(m{-}1)$ **do**
12:           Evaluate Bool A for $net(j)$
13:               Bool A =
14:                   $Distance|net(k_j) - net(i)| < \alpha$ &&
15:                   $net(k_j) \in \{CTR(i) > \gamma\}$ &&
16:                   $FO(k_j) < max(FO)$ &&
17:                   $net(k_j) \notin FO_{cone}(net_i)$;
18:           If $A = 1$, Return $net(k_j)$
19:       **end for**
20:       NetArray = $[net(k_1), \ldots, net(k_{m-1})]$
21:       Connect $net(1), \ldots, net(m{-}1)$ to $IN(1), \ldots, IN(m{-}1)$
22:       Connect $net(i)$ to $IN(m)$
23: **end for**

This gate-insertion and edit technique is also shown in Figure 13.7. Although this is one possible approach to revert the logical impact of the added gate, it is also possible to cut out all the

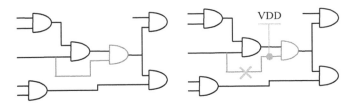

Figure 13.7   Reverting effect of inserted gate by circuit edit.

pins of the added gate and reroute the net from the added gate's sink to source. However, two key problems arise. First, floating gates are more likely to suffer from static discharge. Unlike spare gates inserted into isolated regions in a layout, these gates will be right along logic paths. Second, a rerouting operation on a two-input gate will require FIB milling at three points/pins to disconnect the gate completely, as opposed to just one point in the buffered approach. As described in Section 13.3, each milling operation takes time and when multiple such operations need to be performed, it is essential that they be kept to a minimum. Yet another option would be to entirely mill out the inserted gate, and replace the gate with FIB-deposited metal. Again, this would lead to increased time, as the FIB would have to mill through several hundred μm^2 of transistor area. Therefore, from the standpoint of minimizing FIB processing time, the rerouting and buffering approach would work the best.

Algorithm 13.1 describes the procedure for determining the type and structure of the gate inserted using the techniques described in Reference 1 (note that other approaches could also be used). The first step in this process is to analyze the "static probability" of each net and then accordingly, insert an AND/OR gate (Lines 1–9). Signal probability for a node is defined as the proportion of time for which the node is at logic "1" ($P(1)$) or "0" ($P(0)$). Intuitively, such probabilities should be obtained by gate-level simulations (which requires input vectors) and monitoring of the exact time for which each net is at a particular logic value. However, such simulations are often undesirable for large designs as they can be slow and the accuracy varies as a function of the number of input vectors applied. Therefore, static (i.e., vectorless) probability techniques are preferred. These techniques assume a signal probability of 0.5 at the primary inputs (i.e., assuming each input is independent and equally likely to be at "1" or "0"). These probabilities are then propagated throughout the circuit. Each time a logic gate is encountered, the output signal probability is calculated as a function of the type of logic gate (and its truth table) and the probability of the inputs. For example, a two-input AND gate with $P(1) = P(0) = 0.5$ for each of the two inputs gets an output static probability of $P(1) = 0.25$. Note that such techniques assume the independence of signals and there might be cases where nets in a circuit might be correlated. For example, when two nets derived from a single net reconverge into a gate, the probability is calculated by considering the two net probabilities independently. However, they are clearly correlated and need to be calculated by using conditional probabilities. Unfortunately, this increases the complexity of calculation and misses the main motivation behind using static probabilities: speed and scalability. Therefore, there is a trade-off between using exact techniques (e.g., static probability with correlation) that suffer from complexity issues and approximate techniques (such as static probability assuming signal independence) that are less accurate but extremely scalable.

After this step, the gate-inserted netlist goes through full placement, that is, place-and-route tools are used to spatially position the standard cells. This step is necessary because the additional net that feeds into the gate will be cut during circuit edit. If this net is derived from the output of a gate that is far away, the wire-length penalty increases, that is, the net will obstruct the routing of other nets in the design and lead to increased wire length. More importantly, the chance of cross-coupling with other nets in the wire is also increased. The distance of the inserted gate to another gate whose output pin is the net k is then calculated (Line 14). This is possible because the gates are now physically placed and their coordinates on a die are known. The distance measure can simply be the Euclidean distance between the coordinates of the two gates. If the wire length for k is less than α (a predetermined wire length threshold), the net k is accepted (Line 14). Otherwise, other candidate nets are evaluated. Apart from the distance, Lines 15–17 list down other features required for the net k, which are described below.

- *Controllability:* Contrary to observability, controllability is a numerical measure which indicates how easy (or difficult) it is to set the logical value of a circuit node to either "1" (CTR-1) or "0" (CTR-0). A controllability value of "1" is set to all the primary inputs (most controllable), which are then propagated all the way to the outputs to compute the controllability of each internal circuit net. In the scenario here, if an AND gate is chosen for insertion, CTR-0 of net k should be high, as this can ensure that net i with $P(1) \gg P(0)$ is inverted to a faulty value of logic "0." The converse is true for a net i with $P(1) \ll P(0)$, where net k should have high CTR-1.
- *Fanout:* Net k should be derived from the output pin of another gate. It needs to be made sure that the increase in fanout of the gate does not violate the fanout specifications provided in the technology/standard cell library (Line 16). Otherwise, delay penalties might occur, and moreover, such violations could be easily identifiable.
- *Fanout Cone:* Since we are deriving net k from another net in the circuit, it needs to be made sure that net k does not fall in the combinational fanout cone of net i (Line 17). Otherwise, forbidden feedback loops are created, which constitute a design rule violation and can be easily identified by the foundry on inspecting the extracted netlist.

13.5.2.2 Wire Rerouting

With circuit edit, another possible modification that can be made is wire rerouting. An example of such a technique is shown in Figure 13.8, where nets Y_A and Y_C have been swapped during obfuscation. In order to choose suitable nets for swapping, static probability and S_i (as described in Section 13.5.1) are utilized in Reference 1, along with the following steps.

1. A pair of nodes with $S_i > \lambda$ (score threshold) is randomly selected and paired. For example, in Figure 13.8, nodes Y_B and Y_D are two such nodes.
2. One of the n-input pins of each of the driving gates (here, B and D) are selected (say, pins R and S).
3. The static probabilities of the two selected pair of pins/nets are evaluated in the form of $P_{diff} = |P_R(1) - P_S(1)|$.
4. If $P_{diff} > (0.5 + \delta)$, the two pairs of pins are accepted for swapping.

Here, δ is the parameter that determines how different the two static probability figures must be. Since these are probabilities and not exact logic values, it makes sense to keep δ high in order to ensure the probabilities of the selected nets are as different as possible. Conversely, a higher δ (depending on the circuit) might also rule out many pin-pairs, reducing the number of pin candidates for swapping. Also, note that if the net Y_A has fanout >1, the input pin of gate B can be connected to net Y_C without having to reroute net Y_A.

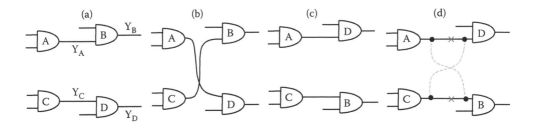

Figure 13.8   Reverting effect of a wire-swap operation by circuit edit. (a) Original design, (b) wire swapping, (c) design after wire swapping, and (d) design after circuit edit to revert wire swap.

Similar to the gate-insertion approach, another constraint beyond δ for the pin-swapping operation is the resulting wire length that must be traced out by an FIB in order to recreate the original connections. In Figure 13.8d, we can see that gates (A, B) and (C, D) must be kept physically close to decrease the high-resistivity FIB interconnect. However, since we have swapped the connections at the gate level, a place-and-route tool will instead keep these gate pairs far apart in order to reduce wire length (Figure 13.8c). In order to mitigate this, one possible option is to force the place-and-route tool to keep these two gate pairs inside a set polygon in the layout. However, this is likely very upsetting for routing congestion when these two gate pairs are far apart in the first place. Instead, in an approach similar to gate insertion, we first place the gates at the layout level, derive the exact coordinates of the corresponding cells, and during pin swapping, select gate pairs (in Figure 13.8, gates A and C) whose distance is constrained by a predefined threshold α (same as in Algorithm 13.1). Note that once the wire swapping is done, the previously generated placement information is discarded and the gates are placed again, letting the P&R tool perform its wire-length minimization placement. As will be clear in Section 13.6, this is important to prevent the foundry from using this distance as a clue against the designer.

Lastly, critical path nets are avoided for wire swapping, as the connection between the gates after circuit edit would be high-resistivity tungsten wires. For the noncritical nets on which pin swapping is applied, the RC delay penalty can be minimized by FIB-level techniques. First, the resistivity of the deposited tungsten (W) through the FIB system must be determined, since this can vary depending on the precursor and choice of ion (He, Ga, Ne) used in the FIB. If the resistivity of FIB-deposited W is determined to be $50\,\mu\Omega$ cm (compared to copper's, which is $1.72\,\mu\Omega$ cm), it can be inferred that in order to maintain the same RC delay characteristics, the cross-section area of the FIB-deposited W must be scaled up by a factor of ≈ 30. While this may seem a lot, routing is being done with the FIB on the backside of the silicon, where the area available is high and FIB-deposited interconnect density is low (since there would be <100 such changes). Another option to aid delay constraints at the gate level is to increase the width of the gate that drives the FIB-deposited net so that delay is unaffected.

In comparison to the gate-insertion approach, the wire rerouting/pin-swapping approach is likely to cause very low overhead to the latency of the design. Further, any area overhead from adding extra gates is also avoided, and with the pre-placement strategy, wire-congestion is also reduced. Unfortunately, in order to make the edit operations feasible, all four gates in the circuit need to be placed with the modified standard cells described in Section 13.5.3. During edit, as seen in Figure 13.8d, two cut points and four contact points are needed for each wire-swap operation, resulting in six FIB milling points, which is significantly higher than the gate-insertion approach which requires only one cut and contact operation with the FIB, with just one milling point. However, if the selected net has a fanout of more than 1, one cut point and two contact points will be required, resulting in three milling points.

13.5.3 Layout

As shown in Figures 13.7 and 13.8, circuit edit is utilized to disconnect and reroute nets in the fabricated IC. While backside FIB operations on older nodes (>90 nm) are easier due to the increased dimensions of the cells and interconnects, circuit-edit operations on newer nodes are much more challenging. While the editing procedure can be highly dependent on the FIB system resolution and the operator, layout-level assistance is definitely needed, especially at advanced nodes. Similar to physical-design-for-debug features proposed in Reference 20, an example of such a modification in an inverter layout is shown in Figure 13.9. In these "FIB-compatible" cells, every input as well as output pin (i.e., pins A,Y in Figure 13.9) has a contact and cut point, created by laterally extending the metal contacts.

It should also be noted that every FIB system has an aspect ratio for the trenches it creates; that is, the FIB trenches are not perfectly cylindrical or square, but rather appear conical or similar to a square frustum. This means that if we assume an aspect ratio of 10:1 (which is common in most FIB systems) and the hole created on the bulk silicon backside is $500 \times 500 \, \text{nm}^2$, the hole created on milling to the metal contacts would then be $50 \times 50 \, \text{nm}^2$. Therefore, it is necessary to create isolated spaces around these contact/cut points, which are at least as big as the size of the hole that can be created by the FIB on the silicon backside surface. Doing this ensures that as the FIB mills from the bulk silicon through to metal 1 (the gate-contact metal layer), no other regions of the transistor (e.g., the active regions) fall in the way of the trench and get accidentally milled/damaged. While such simple layout-level changes aid in post-fabrication edit, they will create unavoidable area overhead on a per-cell basis (in terms of cell width). Routing congestion will be less of a concern as the contact/cut pads are made from Metal 1 and do not affect the routing path for higher metal layers.

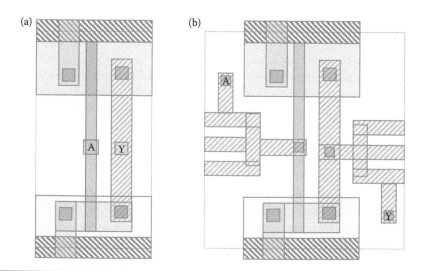

Figure 13.9 (a) Inverter layout. (b) Layout widened to accommodate probe/cut points.

13.6 Vulnerabilities

A direct consequence of the fact that we have incorporated special layouts for the added gates is that a foundry would be able to identify these gates, since it possesses both the layout and gate-level information of the design. Therefore, it is necessary to replace existing cells in the design with FIB-compatible layouts so that dummies are created. The security from adding such dummies are evaluated as follows.

- *Gate Insertion:* In order to mask the added gates, the modified layouts need to be applied to other cells in the circuit layout. A conservative approach would be to apply these layouts to all AND/OR gates in the circuit whose output pins (and the adjoining net) have a $S_i > \lambda$. Note that S_i will have changed in the obfuscated design as observability values will be affected due to gate addition. Due to this, the foundry would need to use their own chosen S_i' as well as λ', distance parameter α', and the number of gates inserted n' (all of which are parameters used in Algorithm 13.1) to work their way back from the design house's obfuscation flow. After isolating N nets based on these parameters and also assuming n' gates are inserted, the probability of correctly identifying the gates would then be

$$P = \frac{1}{\binom{N+n''}{n'}} \tag{13.1}$$

- *Wire Swapping:* Similar to the gate-insertion approach, the wire-swapping technique also requires the use of "dummy" cells, that is, other gates in the circuit will have to be modified with FIB-compatible standard cells. However, the advantage with the wire-swapping approach is that we are not limited to modifying only the same type of gates that were inserted. Since wire swapping can take place among any pair of gates, a judicious amount of gates (meeting the criteria set forth in Section 13.5.2.2) can be modified throughout the circuit. From the foundry's perspective, the complexity of attack is much more difficult because the correct gate pairs are replaced by the P&R tool, and since they do not share a connection (after obfuscation), they would be placed far apart from each other while only being limited by the distance parameter α. Thus, the foundry would have to pick his or her own distance parameter α' (see Section 13.5.2.2) and then try to randomly connect two FIB-compatible cells (after, of course, picking their own S_i'). Numerically, this can be expressed as

$$P = \frac{1}{\binom{N+n'}{n'} \cdot \prod\limits_{i=1}^{n'} \binom{K+k}{k}} \tag{13.2}$$

Here, $K + k$ stands for the total number of candidate gates that the attacker identifies for each swap operation and k refers to number of gates whose pins need to be swapped correctly among those $K + k$ choices. Note that these values will change based on the distance parameter α and the number of dummy cells K in the region set by α and whose probability values satisfy the criteria set forth in Section 13.5.2.2.

It is clear from these expressions that even inserting one dummy for every inserted gate/swapped wire makes it infeasible for the foundry to identify what changes were made during obfuscation. However, note that this is assuming a purely random choice-based attack. If attackers had a sense of the original functionality of the design (e.g., a set of known-good input–output observations for the design), they would not have to resort to brute-force/random guessing. They could conduct a Boolean-satisfiability-based attack (similar to Reference 7) and iteratively weed out the incorrectly identified dummy gates/wires. Such an attack scenario is feasible for ICs meant to be distributed in the open market. However, for tightly controlled supply chains, where the only stage that needs to be outsourced is fabrication, such issues are less of a concern. Future work could focus on potential new attacks that do not require such golden input–output but can still be used to de-obfuscate an obfuscated IC.

13.7 Assessing Obfuscation Strength

In Section 13.5, various techniques for performing gate-level obfuscation were introduced. It is also important to quantitatively assess how these modifications affect the original design. An effective obfuscation scheme would make the functionality of the obfuscated design very different from the original one. One method of checking this is to perform a simple equivalence check between the final obfuscated netlist and the original netlist. Equivalence checking tools (e.g., Synopsys Formality) can be used to see how many circuit nodes in the obfuscated netlist are functionally different from the original netlist. Here, functional difference implies that the equivalence checking tool is able to generate a *counter-example* (i.e., a pattern that generates conflicting results) for (pseudo) circuit outputs. Therefore, such outputs (i.e., flip-flop or primary outputs) can be labeled as "failed" in the obfuscated netlist. Numerically, this mismatch (percentage verification failure) can be calculated as

$$\frac{\text{No. of failing points}}{\text{No. of failing points} + \text{No. of passing points}} * 100\% \qquad (13.3)$$

Naturally, a good obfuscation scheme should maximize the number of such failing outputs (and therefore, percentage verification failure) with minimal number of changes. Further, minimal changes (i.e., minimal number of gate insertions and wire swaps) are desirable as these directly relate to FIB processing time.

13.8 Performance and Reliability of Circuit-Edited Chips

Although circuit edit-based obfuscation makes trusted low-volume fabrication possible, there is a potential concern regarding the performance and reliability of circuit-edited chips. Often, semiconductor companies perform circuit edit only on initial tape-outs (e.g., prototype chips) and perform post-silicon characterization on those edited chips. There has been some work on understanding the effect of FIBs on circuit performance. The work in Reference 21 showed that trenching through the backside till the n-well regions (about 1–2 μm below the active region) showed little to no performance change for the frequency of ring oscillators (ROs) fabricated in 0.12 μm technology. Milling deeper till the shallow trench isolation (STI) regions (≈0.35 μm below the active region) showed minor performance change (<10% change in RO frequency). They found that unintended thinning of the STI region and Ga ion damage on the surface of the STI region set up a leakage current path for the transistors in the RO, causing the slight performance drop. The authors also outlined several other factors such as change in device geometry and Ga ion/secondary electron implantation, which could all change the threshold voltage of the devices after circuit edit and affect performance. Some performance impacts from backside thinning and trenching were also explored in Reference 22, where they found no significant shift in I–V characteristics of 0.18 μm NMOS/PMOS transistors. Another study was performed for flash memory devices with frontside edits in Reference 23. In the study, the authors found no threshold voltage (V_t) shift for milling but a temporary 400 mV V_t shift when tungsten was deposited. The shift was recovered on reprogramming of the flash memory. Similar kinds of experimental study for monitoring device/circuit performance are required on the layout structures explained in Section 13.5.3, especially as milling through the backside cuts through the STI region of the cells.

While there is some work on performance-related aspects of FIB edited circuits, there is little work on the long-term reliability of the same. The work in Reference 24 conducted stress tests on structures (e.g., vias, metal strips) made with FIB-deposited tungsten. They reported that such FIB-deposited structures did not show any signs of degradation (i.e., resistance was stable) throughout the 1000+ hour stress test at >125°C. The work in Reference 25 conducted an exhaustive study of burn-in tests on FIB-exposed components such as floating gate transistors, ring oscillators, CMOS operational amplifiers, and bipolar devices. The structures were subjected to up to 2000 hours of burn-in at 125°. They concluded that FIB editing and exposure to Ga+ ions (at doses in excess of $10\,nC/\mu m^2$) had very little long-term impact on the characteristics of the structures (e.g., frequency for ring oscillator, offset output for op-amp, drain current of a 0.8 μm NMOS transistor). Further, most of the slight degradations were almost completely recovered after thermal and UV (ultra-violet) annealing. This is because annealing helps the devices to recover from charges trapped in the oxide layer due to charge accumulation during FIB exposure. Similar positive results for annealing-based recovery have also been reported in Reference 26. However, it should be noted that these studies were conducted on much older technologies, and with frontside edits. Reliability effects arising from backside edits on the kinds of layout structures described in Section 13.5.3 and at advanced nodes need to be explored in more detail.

13.9 Conclusion

In this chapter, we reviewed circuit-edit techniques as a tool for logic obfuscation. We described a complete design flow and discussed about metrics and techniques for ensuring that the obfuscated design produces a significant amount of verification failures and thus deters the foundry from engaging in overproduction and IP/IC piracy. While we only considered digital circuits, circuit edit-based obfuscation could potentially be applied to all types of circuit, including analog and mixed signal, although with a different set of metrics than those introduced here. Future work could be focused on evaluating the reliability of ICs produced after circuit edit and speeding up FIB processing time.

Acknowledgment

This work was supported in part by an Air Force Office of Scientific Research (AFOSR) MURI grant under award number FA9550-14-1-0351.

References

1. B. Shakya, N. Asadizanjani, D. Forte, and M. Tehranipoor. Chip editor: Leveraging circuit edit for logic obfuscation and trusted fabrication. In *Proceedings of the 35th International Conference on Computer-Aided Design*, page 30. ACM, New York, NY, 2016.

2. M. Tehranipoor and F. Koushanfar. A survey of hardware trojan taxonomy and detection. *IEEE Design & Test of Computers*, **27**(1):10–12, 2010.

3. T. Meade, S. Zhang, and Y. Jin. Netlist reverse engineering for high-level functionality reconstruction. In *2016 21st Asia and South Pacific Design Automation Conference (ASP-DAC)*, pages 655–660. IEEE, New York, NY, 2016.

4. A. Baumgarten, A. Tyagi, and J. Zambreno. Preventing IC piracy using reconfigurable logic barriers. *IEEE Design & Test of Computers*, **27**(1):66–75, 2010.

5. J. Rajendran, Y. Pino, O. Sinanoglu, and R. Karri. Security analysis of logic obfuscation. In *2012 49th ACM/EDAC/IEEE Design Automation Conference (DAC)*, pages 83–89, San Francisco, CA, June, 2012.

6. J. Rajendran, O. Sinanoglu, Y. Pino, and R. Karri. Logic encryption: A fault analysis perspective. In *Proceedings of the Conference on Design, Automation and Test in Europe*, DATE '12, pages 953–958. EDA Consortium, San Jose, CA, 2012.

7. P. Subramanyan, S. Ray, and S. Malik. Evaluating the security of logic encryption algorithms. In *2015 IEEE International Symposium on Hardware Oriented Security and Trust (HOST)*, pages 137–143, Washington, D.C., May, 2015.

8. G. K. Contreras, M. T. Rahman, and M. Tehranipoor. Secure split-test for preventing IC piracy by untrusted foundry and assembly. In *2013 IEEE International Symposium on Defect and Fault Tolerance in VLSI and Nanotechnology Systems (DFTS)*, pages 196–203, New York, Oct, 2013.

9. F. Koushanfar and G. Qu. Hardware metering. In *Proceedings of the 38th Annual Design Automation Conference*, DAC '01, pages 490–493. ACM, New York, NY, 2001.

10. J. A. Roy, F. Koushanfar, and I. L. Markov. Epic: Ending piracy of integrated circuits. In *Proceedings of the Conference on Design, Automation and Test in Europe*, DATE '08, pages 1069–1074. ACM, New York, NY, 2008.

11. F. Imeson, A. Emtenan, S. Garg, and M. V. Tripunitara. Securing computer hardware using 3D integrated circuit (IC) technology and split manufacturing for obfuscation. In *Proceedings of the 22Nd USENIX Conference on Security*, SEC'13, pages 495–510. USENIX Association, Berkeley, CA, 2013.

12. S. Reyntjens and R. Puers. A review of focused ion beam applications in microsystem technology. *Journal of Micromechanics and Microengineering*, **11**(4):287, 2001.

13. R. H. Livengood, P. Winer, and V. R. Rao. Application of advanced micromachining techniques for the characterization and debug of high performance microprocessors. *Journal of Vacuum Science & Technology B*, **17**(1):40–43, 1999.

14. R. Schlangen, P. Sadewater, U. Kerst, and C. Boit. Contact to contacts or silicide by use of backside FIB circuit edit allowing to approach every active circuit node. *Microelectronics Reliability*, **46**(9):1498–1503, 2006.

15. H. Wu, D. Ferranti, and L. Stern. Precise nanofabrication with multiple ion beams for advanced circuit edit. *Microelectronics Reliability*, **54**(9):1779–1784, 2014.

16. M. Prestigiacomo, F. Bedu, F. Jandard, D. Tonneau, H. Dallaporta, L. Roussel, and P. Sudraud. Purification and crystallization of tungsten wires fabricated by focused-ion-beam-induced deposition. *Applied Physics Letters*, **86**(19):192112, 2005.

17. Y. Drezner, D. Fishman, Y. Greenzweig, and A. Raveh. Characterization of damage induced by FIB etch and tungsten deposition in high aspect ratio vias. *Journal of Vacuum Science & Technology B*, **29**(1):011026, 2011.

18. L. H. Goldstein and E. L. Thigpen. SCOAP: Sandia controllability/observability analysis program. In *Proceedings of the 17th Design Automation Conference*, DAC '80, pages 190–196. ACM, New York, NY, 1980.

19. M. Bushnell and V. Agrawal. *Essentials of Electronic Testing for Digital, Memory and Mixed-Signal VLSI Circuits*, Vol. **17**. Springer Science & Business Media, 2004.

20. J. Giacobbe. Physical design for debug: Insurance policy for ICs. In *Proceedings of the 2013 ACM International Symposium on International Symposium on Physical Design*, ISPD '13, page 122. ACM, New York, NY, USA, 2013.

21. R. Schlangen, U. Kerst, A. Kabakow, and C. Boit. Electrical performance evaluation of FIB edited circuits through chip backside exposing shallow trench isolations. *Microelectronics Reliability*, **45**(9–11):1544–1549, 2005.

22. R. K. Jain, T. Malik, T. Lundquist, Q. Wang, R. Schlangen, U. Kerst, and C. Boit. Effects of backside circuit edit on transistor characteristics. In *ISTFA 2007 Proceedings of the 33rd International Symposium for Testing and Failure Analysis*, page 29. ASM International, 2007.

23. J. C. Yeoh, K. Chong, A. R. Khairizam, M. M. I. Sim, M. C. Lee, and S. Li. Threshold voltage shift in FIB circuit edit of embedded flash device. In *2010 17th IEEE International Symposium on the Physical and Failure Analysis of Integrated Circuits*, pages 1–4, Singapore, July, 2010.

24. M. Zaragoza, J. Zhang, and M. Abramo. Reliability test results for W FIB interconnect structures. In *1999 IEEE International Integrated Reliability Workshop Final Report (Cat. No. 99TH8460)*, pages 14–19, Lake Tahoe, California, 1999.

25. R. Desplats, J. C. Courrege, B. Benteo, N. Antoniou, and D. Monforte. Reliability of bipolar and MOS circuits after FIB modification. In *International Symposium for Testing and Failure Analysis*, pages 289–298, ASM International; 1998, 2001.

26. K. Chen, T. Chatterjee, J. Parker, T. Henderson, R. Martin, and H. Edwards. Recovery of shifted MOS parameters induced by focused ion beam exposure. *IEEE Transactions on Device and Materials Reliability*, **3**(4):202–206, 2003.

Chapter 14

BIST for Online Evaluation of PUFs and TRNGs

Siam U. Hussain, Mehrdad Majzoobi, and Farinaz Koushanfar

Contents

The Internet of things (IoT) is a fast evolving paradigm where remotely identifiable physical objects form an active network and are able to operate independently without external control. With these *smart* devices automatically connecting to each other and exchanging private and sensitive data, the potential for malicious attacks greatly increases. As a result, it is widely accepted that the most challenging aspect of IoT will be to ensure security and privacy. Moreover, due to potentially large scale of the network and dynamic communication among the devices, scalability is also expected to be a critical issue. This demands self-management, adaptability to situations, and autonomic capabilities of the devices involved [1]. Therefore, a compact security solution that can maintain integrity and stability on its own is vital to ensure the integrity of an IoT system.

One of the primary properties of any IoT device is a "unique identifier" [1]. A compact embedded identifier with a small footprint and energy budget is ideal for IoT as a large number of devices will operate in passive mode with limited source of power. Therefore, hardware-based security is well suited for IoT protocols and algorithms [2]. They are also naturally more resistant to physical and side-channel attacks. These facts make physical unclonable functions (PUFs) a promising enabler for generation of inherent and indelible device identifiers for IoT security solutions.

PUF is a (partially) disordered physical system: when interrogated by a challenge (or input, stimulus), it generates a unique device response (or output). The response depends on the incident challenge, specific physical disorder, and PUF structure. It is common to call an input and its corresponding output a *challenge–response pair (CRP)*. PUFs have been established as an efficient embedded identification primitive over the last decade. Identifying and authenticating individual entities among a large variety of physical devices as demanded by IoT protocol is a challenge. Classic identification methods including serial numbers on-chip/package and ID storage in nonvolatile memory are subject to attacks such as removal and remarking. Unclonable marking on the device's integrated circuits (ICs) is important in that it can enable a low-overhead identification, fingerprinting, and authentication for a wide range of devices [3].

However, environmental factors, aging, or attacks from the adversary may deteriorate PUF performance and thereby cause delays, and more importantly, security threats. Therefore, they cannot guarantee a fully stand-alone solution as the root-of-trust of IoT entities without a careful analysis.

As shown several times in practice, when the random PUF response values are not exactly random, catastrophic security failures occur. For example, several analysis and attacks on PUF have highlighted the need for appending input or output transformations for safeguarding purposes [4–7]. Moreover, as devices connect and share automatically in IoT, stability of the response over a wide range of operational conditions is essential to ensure seamless operation.

To date, there have been very few work on the evaluation of usability (stability or repeatability) and security (unpredictability or randomness) properties of PUFs. A comprehensive methodology to test the security of PUFs was first introduced in Reference 8. Their method was based on testing the randomness of the responses or conditional probability of responses (or a transformation of them) given the challenges, for example, properties of the probability distributions. Later research efforts [9–11] have defined a more formal set of properties to evaluate PUFs. However, their primary focus was the evaluation of different PUF designs rather than real-time monitoring of specific PUF instances. Moreover, to the best of our knowledge, all of the existing PUF assessment methods rely on software-based evaluation of outputs or CRPs.

In this chapter, we introduce the first methodology for online hardware-based assessment of the robust generation of streams of truly random (unpredictable) PUF responses that are unique to each device. Two main characteristics of PUF are evaluated by the built-in-self-test (BIST) scheme: stability and unpredictability. These evaluations can reveal the operational, structural, and environmental fluctuations in the PUF behavior that may be caused by variations, aging, or attacks. To demonstrate this BIST scheme, we analyze the PUF presented in Reference 4.

The continuous and online monitoring of PUF characteristics yields several advantages including (i) detection of changes/attacks during the PUF operation, (ii) providing an on-the-fly measure of confidence on the randomness/robustness of the CRPs, (iii) ensuring PUF stability by validating CRPs before adding them to library, (iv) reporting the exact conditions in the local PUF test site for a more granular debugging, and (v) enabling active online adjustment and improvements of the PUF operations.

True random number generator (TRNG) is another important cryptographic primitive that shares overlapping properties and often have structural similarities with PUFs. The integrity of any secure system depends largely on the proper functioning of these units. True random numbers are needed for encryption keys, nonces, padding bits, and many more applications. Software approaches to generate random numbers, called pseudorandom number generators (PRNG), are widely adopted and are suitable for most applications. However, they are susceptible to attacks as their outputs are deterministic functions of the seed, which carries all its entropy. Therefore, hardware-based mechanism to extract randomness from physical phenomena is required for cryptographic applications [12]. As data privacy is one of the key requirements of IoT framework, it can benefit from high-entropy TRNGs.

A number of studies have focused on online evaluation of TRNGs [13–15]. However, a limitation common to all these studies is that they deal only with the statistical properties of the output bit sequence of the TRNG. While these tests are important, complete security of the TRNG cannot be assured without evaluating its internal structure and the health of its entropy source [16]. BSI's standard AIS-31 [17] takes the construction of the TRNG into account during evaluation. NIST's recommendation for the entropy sources used for random bit generation [18] also puts large emphasis on the quality of the entropy source and suggests several tests to evaluate it. Evaluating the internal health of TRNGs exclusively requires online tests, as offline tests would reveal the internal bit sequence which may facilitate modeling attacks.

To the best of our knowledge, two studies have previously addressed the online evaluation of internal health of TRNGs. The work in Reference 19 presented a method to measure jitters that help evaluate oscillator-based TRNG. Moreover, Reference 20 presented on-the-fly tests for evaluating nonideal TRNGs where the generated internal bit sequences are not independent and identically distributed (IID). We propose the first BIST scheme that evaluates both the internal health of the entropy source of an ideal TRNG and the statistical properties of its final output and is not limited to any specific design. As a demonstration, this scheme is used to evaluate two TRNG designs: metastability-based TRNG presented in Reference 21 and ring oscillator-based TRNG presented in Reference 22.

For the BIST scheme to be usable, we have to make sure that the TRNGs and PUFs pass the tests in normal conditions and the BIST is able to detect when they deviate from this natural behavior. Therefore, we propose improvements to some of these designs to make them pass these comprehensive tests. We also show how the BIST scheme can help make the calibration of the PUF automated. In addition to these, we present a scheme to safeguard the BIST result bits against malicious interceptions.

The highlights of this chapter are as follows.

■ First BIST scheme for comprehensive online assessment of TRNGs and PUFs (in hardware)
■ Online evaluations of the internal structure of TRNGs as well as the quality of the entropy source, along with tests for the statistical soundness of the output sequence
■ Quantitative online analysis of both PUF stability and its security (unpredictability)
■ A simple but effective scheme to safeguard the BIST results bit against malicious interceptions
■ Development of low-overhead control circuitry for saving the test results for further analysis
■ Evaluation of a number of TRNG and PUF designs along with suggestions for improvements so that they pass the extensive tests performed by the BIST scheme
■ Proof-of-concept FPGA implementation that demonstrates the effectiveness, practicability, and reasonable overhead of the proposed architecture

14.1 Background

In this section, we discuss the basic properties of TRNGs and PUF along with some of their most efficient realizations on FPGA. We also discuss the properties of ideal TRNG and PUFs and the standard tests performed to evaluate those properties.

14.1.1 True Random Number Generator

True random numbers harness randomness from natural phenomena like thermal noise, shot noise, clock jitter, circuit metastability, etc. The two primary components of a TRNG are the entropy source and a mechanism to convert the entropy to random bit stream. Both components are equally important for generating unpredictable and statistically sound random bits. This work focuses on TRNGs implemented on FPGA. We first discuss a number of TRNG implementations, followed by the properties of a good TRNG.

14.1.1.1 Current TRNG Implementations

FPGA has been a popular platform for designing TRNGs because of its reconfigurability and fast time to market. Several approaches to generate random numbers in FPGA have been reported in the literature. We discuss a few examples here.

Sunar et al. introduced a TRNG that sourced randomness from the jitter produced by ring oscillators [23]. They combined the output of several identical ROs with an XOR gate based on the statistical assumption that the combined spectrum of all the ROs would be filled with jitter. This is the most widely explored method to extract entropy in FPGAs. One important improvement was proposed by Wold et al. in Reference 22 where they inserted a D flip-flop after each ring to reduce the switching activity at the XOR input.

Cherkaoui et al. replaced the ROs in Sunar's model with self-timed rings that provide a number of jittery synchronized signals having the same period and a constant mean phase difference between them [24]. By adjusting the time lapse to the jitter magnitude of one stage, it can be ensured that the full spectrum will be filled by jitters without any statistical assumption.

In the method proposed by Hisashi et al. [25], randomness is produced by tying the S and R inputs of an SR latch together to force metastability. The routing between S and R is critical in this design in order to reduce bias.

In the TRNG proposed by Majzoobi et al. in Reference 26, a flip-flop is forced to metastable state by equalizing the signal arrival times at clock and data inputs using programmable delay lines (PDLs). The PDLs were realized by controlling the propagation delay inside Look Up Tables (LUT). They introduced a feedback mechanism to adjust the delay to ensure that metastability is sustained.

We evaluate the TRNGs proposed in References 22 and 26 using our proposed BIST scheme to demonstrate its effectiveness.

14.1.1.2 Evaluation Criteria for TRNG

All the TRNG designs discussed in the previous section require combining a number of TRNG units to produce enough entropy. For example, in Ring Oscillator (RO) based TRNG, each unit comprises one RO and one flip-flop to capture the bit. We refer to the bit sequence generated by each individual unit as the *internal bit sequence*. These sequences are XORed to generate the final output sequence, which we refer to as the *external bit sequence*. The evaluation criteria common to both TRNG and PRNG is the statistical quality of the external bit sequence. Several batteries of randomness test are available for this purpose as discussed in Section 14.1.3. However, two additional features need to be evaluated for TRNGs.

One important part of the security proof of TRNGs is that the internal bit sequences are IID. However, due to increased power line noise or intentionally injected noise, the sequences produced by these units may become correlated, which might in turn facilitate an attacker. To ensure that a TRNG is cryptographically secure, the distribution of the bits generated by its composing units needs constant monitoring on their independence.

The second feature that needs to be evaluated is the level of entropy generated by each of the units. A fall in entropy level in any of the units is an indicator of an active attack or imminent failure of the TRNG. Most TRNGs employ postprocessing techniques to improve the statistical quality of the generated bit sequence. However, these techniques do not add to the entropy of the system. So the entropy level should be measured based on the raw data before any postprocessing is applied.

14.1.2 Physical Unclonable Function

The key idea behind physical unclonable function (PUF) is exploitation of inherent and naturally occurring physical disorder (fingerprint) of the device as its unique signature, for example, silicon manufacturing variations. A PUF is a function whose output (response) depends on both the applied input (challenge) and the unique physical properties of the hardware where it resides. The challenge and response together form one CRP.

There are two broad categories of PUFs: weak PUF and strong PUF [27]. Weak PUFs allow only a limited number of CRPs and it is assumed that their responses are not accessible by adversaries. On the other hand, strong PUFs support a large number of CRPs. This ensures that even if an adversary has access to a large subset of CRPs, it cannot predict the yet unknown ones. Note that although our BIST scheme is applicable to both weak and strong PUFs, without a loss of generality, in this chapter we focus on strong PUF testing. Since a weak PUF differs only with strong PUF in the number of possible responses, evaluation of weak PUF randomness is simpler since it is confined to the small space of responses.

14.1.2.1 Current PUF Implementations

A number of different realizations of the strong PUFs have been reported to date. In an *arbiter PUF* [28,29], two electrical pulses race simultaneously through two paths consisting of several stages. The exact paths are determined by the challenge vector. After the last stage, an arbiter, usually a latch or flip-flop, determines which signal has arrived first and generates a binary response based on that. In Reference 30, the responses from several arbiter PUF stages were XORed to generate the PUF response. A *lightweight secure PUF* [4] has a similar structure, but the input challenge is passed through a complicated mapping to increase security against modeling attacks. *Ring Oscillator PUFs* exploit the specific and unique delay caused by fabrication variation of oscillators [30]. We evaluate an improved version of the lightweight secure PUF presented in Reference 4 with our BIST scheme. To implement the FPGA PUF, we use the comprehensive methodology introduced in References 21 and 31.

14.1.2.2 Evaluation Criteria for PUF

To make sure that a PUF is secure and reliable, it must possess the following properties [8]:

- *Unpredictability:* This property ensures the uniqueness of the PUF behavior, that is, the CRPs. For the PUF to be truly unpredictable, two conditions need to be met: first, the response bits from the PUF should be completely random; and second, the transition of the response bit should be completely uncorrelated with the transition of one or more bits of the challenge vector. The second condition ensures that the response from the PUF cannot be predicted based on known CRPs.
- *Stability:* In a strict sense, for a PUF to be used as an identification circuitry, it must always generate the same response when excited by the same challenge vector. Since PUFs use physical components and are inherently noisy, this criterion is difficult to meet precisely. But the stability shall be present in a majority of the output bits to ensure usability.

One question that may arise is the need for online testing of PUFs. One may argue that PUFs can be evaluated offline for their randomness property during the initial testing phase; since CRPs need to be stable, there is no need for further online tests. This argument has at least two ramifications: (i) since the CRPs have to be robust, the protocols have to work even if the response bits change up to a certain percentage (typically 20% in current generations of PUFs). One could seriously bias the bits within this high percentage of robustness (e.g., by changing the temperature) to facilitate machine learning attacks [5]. (ii) One may use the side-channel information at various operational points to break the PUF security as demonstrated by the work in References 7, 32, and 33. Adapting the randomness tests for online PUF evaluations would detect these scenarios and could even provide a sensing mechanism to avoid such attacks and thus improve the robustness of PUFs.

For more information about the PUF, its properties, and recent directions, we refer the interested readers to comprehensive articles on this topic [27,34].

14.1.3 Standard Randomness Tests

Several standard test suites such as NIST [35], DIEHARD [36], FIPS [37] have been designed for evaluating the statistical quality of the bit sequence generated by Random Number Generators (RNG). NIST published recommendations for the design of entropy sources and the tests for the validation of these sources [18]. They also published documents with recommendations for deterministic algorithms to produce pseudorandom values from an entropy source [38] and on how to combine these two mechanisms to generate a good quality TRNG [39]. BSI (Bundesamt fr Sicherheit in der Informationstechnik) have also established evaluation standards for both PRNG (AIS-20 [40]) and TRNG (AIS-31 [17]).

The batteries of randomness tests were originally designed to evaluate the performance of the RNGs. As discussed above, randomness of the response bits of PUF is mandatory to ensure that the PUF cannot be modeled as a deterministic process. Here, besides evaluating TRNGs, we utilize the standard randomness test suite to evaluate the unpredictability of PUF response.

14.2 Architecture of the BIST Scheme

The BIST scheme for both TRNG and PUF is developed such that it can be used either independently or together, in which case it can share a large portion of the resources. For the sake of clarity, we describe the architecture of the two schemes separately. The exact implementation details of the BIST is outlined in Section 14.3.

We would like to mention that this BIST scheme is for real-time monitoring of TRNG and PUF instances during their operation. Initially, any new PUF or TRNG design has to undergo rigorous test to verify its effectiveness and security. Many of these tests are too complex to be performed in real time. Moreover, as already explained, their primary purpose is to evaluate designs not an individual instance of PUF or TRNG. However, even if a design passes these initial evaluations, these structures are unstable and unpredictable by nature and may exhibit short time dip in performance for inexplicable reasons. Active attacks may also create security threats. The purpose of the proposed BIST scheme is to maintain the security of the system in such scenarios.

14.2.1 Architecture of TRNG Evaluation Scheme

As mentioned in Section 14.1, most TRNG implementations employ multiple units and XOR the generated sequences to get a good quality random sequence. While it is important to monitor the quality of the final output, monitoring the health of the internal units is even more important to ensure the integrity of the TRNG and to predict a possible failure. Therefore, we perform tests on both internal and external bit sequences of TRNGs. Figure 14.1 shows an overview of the architecture of the TRNG evaluation scheme.

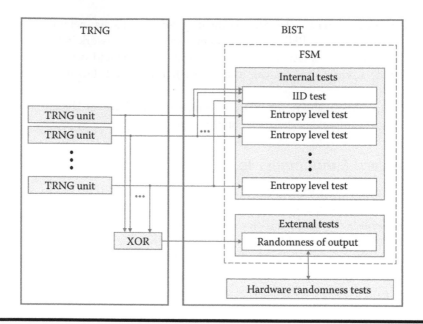

Figure 14.1   Architecture of the TRNG evaluation scheme.

14.2.1.1 Test on External Bit Sequence

This test evaluates the quality of the final output sequence (after XOR operation). It incorporates seven tests from the NIST battery of randomness test [35]:

1. Frequency
2. Block frequency
3. Runs
4. Longest run of ones
5. Nonoverlapping template matching
6. Overlapping template matching
7. Cumulative sums

The test module resides on the same chip as the TRNG. Each test operates on a block of random bits and outputs one for success and zero for failure.

14.2.1.2 Test on Internal Bit Sequence

We perform test on internal bit sequences to check

1. Whether or not the bit sequences from each unit are IID
2. The level of entropy generated by each unit

14.2.1.2.1 IID Test

The NIST recommended test for IID in Reference 18 requires complex calculation and most importantly a large amount of data to be stored on chip. While this test is essential at the initial evaluation of the TRNG design, it is not suitable for online test. We utilize the Wald–Wolfowitz runs test [41] to determine whether the bit sequences produced by different TRNG units are IID or not. Unlike the runs test in Reference 35, which needs the frequency test to be passed as a precondition, the Wald–Wolfowitz runs test does not put any condition on the frequency of "1" or "0" bits. Internal sequences almost always fail the frequency test (verified by offline testing). An error signal is generated if the IID test fails.

14.2.1.2.2 Entropy Level Test

We employ a simplified version of the procedure described in Reference 18 to estimate the level of entropy generated by each of the TRNG units. A warning signal is generated if the entropy level drops below a certain threshold in one or two of the units and an error signal is generated if that happens in more than two units.

14.2.2 *Architecture of PUF Evaluation Scheme*

The PUF evaluation scheme is much more complex than that for TRNG. It evaluates the PUF under test based on the two major properties described earlier: unpredictability and stability. The overall architecture of scheme is shown in Figure 14.2. The finite-state machine (FSM) controls the aforementioned two test sets, each of which consists of three tests that shall be described in Sections 14.2.2.1 and 14.2.2.2, respectively. The BIST generates the challenges as appropriate for each test. In addition to outputting L-bit challenges to the PUF input, the BIST output also includes the appropriate R-bit PUF tuning parameter. The input to the BIST block is the PUF response. The randomness tests are performed by the block denoted as "hardware randomness

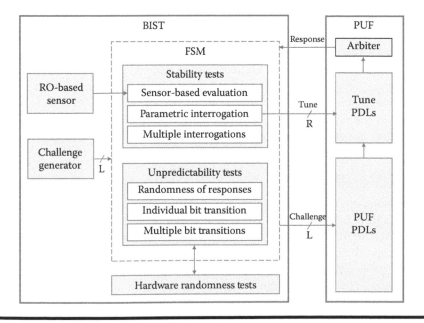

Figure 14.2   Architecture of the PUF evaluation scheme.

tests," which is shared with the TRNG evaluation scheme. There is also a random challenge generation component.

14.2.2.1 Unpredictability Test

The unpredictability tests check the randomness of the response from the PUF. It uses the same randomness test module that is used to test the TRNG as described in Section 14.2.1.1. Unpredictability is evaluated with the three following tests, denoted by UT1, UT2, and UT3, respectively.

14.2.2.1.1 UT1: Randomness of Response(s)

In each round of this test, the PUF is excited with a set of random challenges and the corresponding response bits are fed to the NIST module. The test is repeated for several hundred rounds, and the result bits are added up to calculate the average success rate over the multiple test rounds.

14.2.2.1.2 UT2: Effect of Individual Bit Transition

This test checks whether an output bit transition is correlated with the transition of any particular challenge bits. First, the PUF is excited with an L-bit random challenge vector. The PUF is then interrogated by the same vector with only the ith bit inverted $i \in \{1,2,\ldots,L\}$. The XOR of the response bits for these two challenges (differing in one bit) is applied to the test module. For an unpredictable PUF, the transition in the response must be completely arbitrary (i.e., uncorrelated with the input bit change). Thus, the XOR of the two response bits must pass the randomness tests. This test is performed several hundred times for each value of i ($i = 1,2,\ldots,L$) and the success rate is reported as a function of the inverted bit index, i.

14.2.2.1.3 UT3: Effect of Multiple Bit Transitions

This test checks for the correlation between the response bit transition and transition of one or more challenge bits. First, the PUF is excited with an L-bit random challenge vector. The PUF is then interrogated by a similar vector where h bits are inverted. Thus, the Hamming distance between these two challenge vectors is h, where $h \in \{1,2,\ldots,L\}$. The XOR of the responses in these two cases is fed to the randomness test module. This test is performed several hundred times for each value of h and the success rate is reported as a function of the Hamming distance, h.

14.2.2.2 Stability Tests

The PUF operation is very sensitive to the silicon, environmental, and operational conditions. One way to ensure stability of the responses is to comprehend these conditions and their impact of the responses and then stratify the results for each situation. Hardware-based sensors are very useful for this purpose and they form our first stability testing method.

The second proposed methodology for stability testing utilizes multiple evaluations of the same input. A simple consensus method can be used for combining the results of multiple tests and enhance the stability. The third and last stability testing method is based on changing the parameter(s) affecting the stability and then check the impact on the response.

14.2.2.2.1 ST1: Sensor-Based Evaluation

The most impactful conditions on the PUF operation are those that change the randomness (entropy) of the circuit output. Some of the conditions that could affect the PUF behavior include light, magnetic field, IC aging, and on-chip voltage and temperature. A good BIST for PUF shall include sensors that comprehend these conditions. Perhaps the simplest and most widely suggested/used sensors for on-chip sensing of the process variation, temperature, and aging are the architectures based on ring oscillators (ROs). In particular, the RO-based sensors exploit the temperature dependence of the threshold voltage and carrier mobility of CMOS transistors that in turn affect the frequency of an RO.

14.2.2.2.2 ST2: Multiple Interrogations

To test whether the PUF is able to reproduce the same response, the multiple interrogation method excites the PUF with the same challenge vector several times and computes a consensus of the response bits to the repeated challenges. This simple method was suggested and used in Reference 31 for lowering the error in the responses. The FPGA prototype of this method demonstrated that even a small number of repetitions could improve the response stability as the width of the transition region gets narrower and more statistics is gathered.

14.2.2.2.3 ST3: Active Parametric Interrogation

The PUF randomness is typically converted to a digital binary format using a metastable component, for example, an arbiter. A set of parameters, in combination with the challenge vector, drive the point of operation of this metastable part. For certain challenges, small change in this random parameter may potentially alter its operating point and change the corresponding response. In parametric interrogation, this parameter is altered in deterministic steps around its expected value and the resulting response is observed.

In the parametric interrogation for arbiter-based PUF suggested in Reference 31, a programmable delay line is used to change the delay difference between the two arbiter inputs. If the response remains unchanged at both a positive and a negative delay differences, the response is stable and the incident challenge is marked as a *robust challenge*. Otherwise, the challenge is advised to be removed from the CRP library.

14.2.3 Protecting Result Bits

A possible location of attack is the output bits from the BIST scheme. If an attacker can intercept one or more of the output bits and force them to output "1," the user will not be able to detect any attack on the PUF or TRNG. To protect the BIST from such attacks, we provide a 16-bit checksum, which incorporates the output bits from all the unpredictability tests and IID test (statistical tests that provide *pass/fail* results). The user can form the checksum from the external output bits and periodically match it with the checksum provided by the BIST to verify the integrity of the output bits. We assume that an attacker is able to force the output bits only to a certain constant (in this case "1"). Since the other tests like entropy level test provide quantitative results, such protection is not required for them.

14.3 BIST System Description

In Figures 14.1 and 14.2, the architecture of TRNG and PUF evaluation schemes is depicted separately for the sake of clarity. In the actual implementation, the hardware randomness test module, which constitutes a large portion of the BIST, is shared between the two schemes. In our design, the TRNG is monitored continuously while the PUF evaluation is done periodically. The TRNG evaluation is paused during the unpredictability test of PUF.

Along with the implementation of the BIST, we also describe the TRNGs and PUF under test for better understanding of the scheme and to make sense of the overhead estimation. We evaluated two TRNGs: the one based on ROs [22,23] and the one based on metastability [26]. The PUF under test is a delay-based strong PUF proposed in Reference 21. It also incorporates the input and interconnect networks introduced by the lightweight secure PUF in Reference 4. The output network is just an XOR mapping with a Q-bit input and a 1-bit output.

The BIST module resides on the same chip as the PUF and/or TRNG and is able to run its tests automatically. At the end of this section, we report the resource utilized by each of the modules in Table 14.1.

14.3.1 TRNG Implementation

14.3.1.1 RO-Based TRNG

We evaluate the RO-based TRNG proposed by Wold et al. in Reference 22. In this TRNG, randomness is extracted from the jitter present in the oscillating pulse of an RO. The pulse from each RO is sampled with a flip-flop to generate the bit stream. We used 16 ROs, each comprising of 3 inverters. The bit streams from the 16 units are combined with a 5-stage XOR network to produce the final output.

14.3.1.2 Metastability-Based TRNG

In this TRNG, a flip-flop is forced to metastable state by equalizing the signal arrival times at the clock and D inputs. The propagation path to these inputs is controlled by a feedback system through PDL. A PDL [21,31] is composed of LUTs where the logical output depends on only one of the inputs and other inputs act as *don't cares*. These *don't care* inputs control the signal propagation path, and consequently, the delay through the LUTs.

Operation of this TRNG depends on the delicate balance between the signal arrival times at clock and data input, which makes it very sensitive to the routing within the PDLs (see Section 14.1.1.1). As the peripheral circuitry becomes more complex, they affect the routing and at some point the routing of the two lines become so different that the feedback system is not able to compensate for that and the TRNG starts producing constants. To solve this issue, we implemented hard macros for the PDLs and instantiated the same hard macro for both PDLs. In this way, they are exactly symmetric except for the routing of clock to input and output to the flip-flop. Besides solving the issue of the peripheral circuit effect, it reduces the required number of LUTs in each PDL to only 8 instead of 64 in the original design. The original design employed only one TRNG unit, and it required complex postprocessing to ensure that the generated sequence passes the statistical tests. As our implementation requires fewer LUTs, we were able to have several units and XOR their outputs to have a good quality random sequence.

Table 14.1   Overhead Estimation

Component	Register/LUT	Latency[a]	Power (mw)	Parameters
RO-based TRNG	36/123		8.50	$P=3, Q=16$
PDL-based TRNG	104/560		40.42	$P=8, Q=8$
PUF with peripheral circuitry	28/3454		175.66	$L=64, R=16, Q=16$
Randomness test module				
1. Frequency	–	1	–	$n=20,000$
2. Block frequency	32/50	2	1.13	$N=100, M=200$
3. Runs	64/138	2	0.17	$n=20,000$
4. Longest run of ones	149/307	2	0.79	$N=16, M=8$
5. N.O. template matching	30/35	2	0.63	$N=8, M-256$
6. Overlapping template matching	273/268	68	3.38	$N=1000, M=1023$
7. Cumulative sums	77/136	2	1.80	$n=20,000$
IID test	71/63	3	20.00	$n=16,384$
Entropy estimator	713/1193	$3Q(=24)$	40.01	$W=2, N=10,000, Q=8$
Challenge generator	144/492		6.14	
RO sensor	8/14		0.00	
FSM	182/618		37.58	

Note: *P*, no. of elements (inverters/PDLs) in each TRNG unit; *Q*, no. of parallel units in TRNG/PUF; *L*, length of the challenge vector o PUF; *R*, length of the tune block of PUF; *n*, length of each test sequence; *N*, no. of blocks in each test sequence (if applicable); *M*, length of each of each block (if applicable); $n=M \times N$ (if applicable); *W*, word size.

[a] Maximum no. of clock cycles between the last bit of the test sequence is generated and the result is valid.

14.3.2 *PUF Implementation*

We evaluate a delay-based PUF using the BIST scheme. The principles of the delay-based PUF were first introduced by Gassend et al. in Reference 29. In this PUF, generating one output bit requires a step signal to travel through two parallel paths composed of multiple segments that are connected by a series of 2-input/ 2-output switches. Each switch has a selector bit, which decides whether it is configured as a cross or straight connector. The path segments are designed to have the same nominal delays, but their actual timings differ slightly due to manufacturing process variations. The difference between the top and bottom path delays are compared by an arbiter that

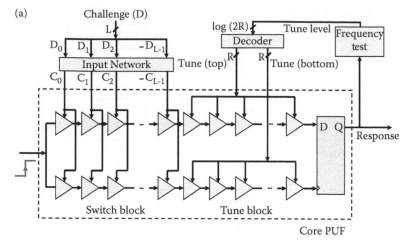

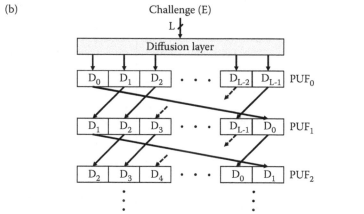

Figure 14.3 Structure of the PDL-based PUF: (a) structure of one PUF unit and (b) arrangement of the parallel PUF units.

generates the response accordingly (e.g., response is "1" if top path is faster). The PUF challenges act as the selector bits of the switches.

In our implementation, the PUF structure has two main components: the core PUF unit presented in Reference 21 and the peripheral circuitry to enhance PUF security presented in Reference 4. Moreover, we propose an automated calibration of the PUF using the BIST scheme and also propose improvement to the peripheral circuitry to make sure the PUF passes the comprehensive tests by the BIST.

The PUF circuit is shown in Figure 14.3. To increase the unpredictability (randomness) in the PUF response and make it more secure, responses from $Q(=16)$ parallel PUFs are XORed (similar to TRNG structure). We refer to each parallel PUF (before XOR) as one PUF unit, which is shown in Figure 14.3a. The arrangement of these units is shown in Figure 14.3b.

14.3.2.1 Core Unit of PUF

The switches of the delay-based PUF are realized by the PDL, which are described in Section 14.3.1.2. (The triangular elements represent the LUTs of PDL in Figure 14.3a.) The path with a larger delay is equivalent to the cross connector in the switch and the the path with shorter delay is equivalent to the straight connector. As in the implementation of the TRNG, the PDLs are designed as hard macros to minimize bias due to routing asymmetry.

PDLs are also used in the tuning block that minimizes the bias in path delays. The tuning block inserts extra delays into either the top or bottom path based on their selector inputs to compensate for the delay bias caused by the routing asymmetry. The selectors of the top and bottom PDLs in each tuning block are controlled independently while a single selector bit drives both corresponding LUTs in each PDL in the switch block.

Each of the Q PUF units consists of L switches and R tuning blocks. In our implementation, we use $L = 64$, $R = 16$, and $Q = 16$.

14.3.2.2 Calibration

The PUF goes through a calibration phase at the start of its operation where optimum tune levels for each PUF unit are set to minimize the delay bias. In Reference 21, a set of 64,000 CRPs were collected for each PUF unit at each tune level. Then, the tune level at which the mean of the responses was closest to half was chosen as the optimum one for that unit. However, the collection of so many CRPs ($64,000 \times R \times Q$) makes the calibration process tedious and time consuming. Moreover, it would require reading the response from each PUF unit while during regular operation only the XORed response is read.

Since the BIST scheme holds a random challenge generator (Section 14.3.3.4) for performing the tests, we also use this for generating the challenges for the calibration process. The responses from each PUF unit are read inside the FSM (see Section 14.3.3.7), and it sets the tune level automatically following the process described above. The decoder then sets tune (top) and tune (bottom) such that their Hamming distance is equal to the tune level.

14.3.2.3 Peripheral Circuitry

The peripheral circuitry adds security to the PUF by using input/output transformations that thwart active attacks. Its first three components were part of the original design in Reference 4. This design passes the first unpredictability test (UT1) described in Section 14.2.2.1. However, the success rates for UT2 and UT3 were close to zero. To solve this, we added a diffusion layer in front of the interconnect network.

14.3.2.3.1 Input Network

The input network transforms the challenge by a function satisfying the strict avalanche criterion (SAC). A function is said to satisfy SAC if, whenever a single input bit is complemented, each of the output bits changes with a probability of 0.5. The transformation used in our implementation is

$$c_{(N+i+1)/2} = d_i, \quad \text{for } i = 1 \tag{14.1}$$

$$c_{(i+1)/2} = d_i \oplus d_{i+1}, \quad \text{for } i = 1, 3, 5, \ldots, N-1 \tag{14.2}$$

$$c_{(N+i+2)/2} = d_i \oplus d_{i+1}, \quad \text{for } i = 2, 4, 6, \ldots, N-2, \tag{14.3}$$

where d is the input to the input network and c is the output that is fed to the PUF.

14.3.2.3.2 Output Network

In our implementation, the output network is a Q-bit XOR gate implemented by LUTs. As explained in Reference 42, XOR operation reduces the bias present in a set of random sequences if they are independent and uncorrelated.

14.3.2.3.3 Interconnect Network

If an adversary knows the structure of the input network, he or she would be able to compute its inverse and pass the challenge through it to nullify the security effect of the input network. To thwart this, the challenge is transformed through the interconnect network as shown in Figure 14.3b. With this network present, the inverse of each of the Q input networks is distinct, and it is not possible to bypass more than one of them.

14.3.2.3.4 Diffusion Layer

The purpose of the diffusion layer is to make sure that the probability of flip in the response bit is close to half when one or more bits at any position in the challenge vector is flipped. The second and third unpredictability tests in Section 14.2.2.1 check for correlations of the flip in response bit with flips in a single and multiple challenge bits, respectively. With only the above three elements of the peripheral circuitry which were proposed in Reference 4, the success rate for these two tests are close to zero. The possible reasons are either (a) the effect of few bits on the response bit is not enough, so the response never flips or (b) the effect is very strong, so it always flips.

As a remedy to both of the above causes, the diffusion layer distributes the effect of a flip in a single bit in its input, E over multiple bits in output, D. This layer is essentially a multiplication by a constant matrix similar to Advanced Encryption Standard (AES) [43]. The 64-bit challenge vector is divided into sixteen 4-bit numbers and these sixteen numbers are arranged as a 4×4 matrix. This matrix is then multiplied by another 4×4 constant 2-bit matrix with rank (number of independent rows) of 3. Higher rank of the matrix results in more diffusion. However, to ensure that this diffusion layer cannot be bypassed by placing its inverse matrix in front, we chose a matrix with determinant of zero. Therefore, the highest possible rank is 3.

Figure 14.4 shows the relation between the number of flipped bits in output (F_E) and number of flipped bits in input (F_D) for input length ($L = 64$). For $F_E = 1$, $F_D \approx 9$. Initially, F_D increases with increase in F_E. However, as F_E increases more, F_D asymptotically reaches 32 ($= L/2$). This trend works against both the causes mentioned before and makes sure the PUF passes UT2 and UT3.

In our implementation platform, Virtex 6, the delay through the diffusion layer is about 4 ns while delay through the core PUF is about 160 ns. Therefore, the delay caused by the diffusion layer is negligible.

14.3.3 BIST Scheme

The BIST architecture incorporates a randomness testing module, IID test module, entropy estimation module, a challenge generator, an RO-based sensor, and an FSM which controls the flow of all the tests.

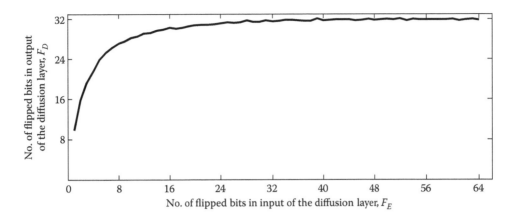

Figure 14.4 **Average number of flipped bits in output (F_D) versus number of flipped bits in input (F_E) of diffusion layer for input length ($L = 64$).**

14.3.3.1 Randomness Test Module

The randomness test module incorporates seven tests from the NIST test suite [35] listed in Section 14.2.1.1. These tests involve complex mathematical functions like *complementary error function (erfc)* and *incomplete gamma function (igamc)* that are unsuitable for hardware implementation. In our implementation, we adopt the simplifications suggested in Reference 14. Equations 14.5 and 14.6 show the general form of simplifications on the *erfc* and *igamc* functions respectively.

$$P\_value = erfc(x)$$
$$P\_value > \alpha => x < erfcinv(\alpha) \tag{14.4}$$

$$P\_value = igamc(a, x)$$
$$P\_value > \alpha => x < igamcinv(a, (1 - \alpha)) \tag{14.5}$$

Here, x is a function of a counter value and the input sequence length n; a is a function of the number of blocks N; and α is the Type I error probability. For a constant set of n, N, and α, one can use the above equations to set conditions on the counter value. The counter accumulates the respective test metric. For details of each test implementations, please refer to Reference 14.

In Reference 35, the frequency test is noted as a prerequisite to the runs test and Reference 14 utilizes this fact to simplify the runs test implementation. Therefore, we do not implement the frequency test separately. Note that a recent work in Reference 15 presents more optimization by sharing resources among these tests. This scheme can be seamlessly incorporated in our design.

14.3.3.2 IID Test

We implement the Wald–Wolfowitz runs test to evaluate the independence of the distribution of bit sequences produced by different TRNG units. It requires three counters to count the number of bits, number of ones, and number of runs: one multiplier which is time shared for computations of the mean and variance of the distribution and two comparators to generate the final result. The test sequence is generated by cyclically taking one bit from each TRNG unit. If there are Q units and the bit produced by the ith unit at cycle c is $b_i(c)$, the test sequence is $[b_0(c), b_1(c), \ldots, b_Q(c), b_0(c+Q), b_1(c+Q), \ldots]$. Since Q internal bits are generated in each clock cycle, the Q-bit vector is read in cycle c and the vectors for the next Q clock cycles are ignored so that this test runs at the same clock as other parts of the design. The runs test depends on the relation between the consecutive bits in the test sequence. The inconsistency in filling this sequence takes place only once in Q bits while all other consecutive bits are generated at the same instance. Moreover, the probability that distribution will change within this time period should be very low. Therefore, the resultant error should be negligible.

14.3.3.3 Entropy Estimation

To estimate the level of entropy, we follow the procedure provided in Reference 18. The equation for lower level of entropy bound (E) is given by

$$
E = \min \left\{ W, -\log_2 \left(\frac{1}{N} \left(C_{max} + 2.3 \sqrt{C_{max} \left(1 - \frac{C_{max}}{N} \right)} \right) \right) \right\} \tag{14.6}
$$

where the test sequence is generated by grouping W bits of the input sequence, C_{max} is the number of occurrence of the most common element in the test sequence, and N is the length of the test sequence.

Precise calculation of entropy would require operations like square root or logarithm, which are costly in resource and time. While this is important during initial evaluation of an entropy source, for an online test estimating the level of entropy up to certain precision is sufficient. Our implementation provides the entropy level of each TRNG unit in a scale of 0–7. Figure 14.5 shows the entropy as a function of C_{max} for $W = 2$ and $N = 10,000$. The minimum entropy associated with each level is shown in the left y-axis.

Implementation of this simplified entropy estimation scheme requires four counters to count the occurrence of the four 2-bit words (for $W = 2$), six comparators to determine C_{max}, and eight comparators to determine the entropy level. There need to be one estimator for each of the TRNG units. In our implementation, entropy estimation of the ith unit is started at ith clock cycle so that the two comparators are shared between the entropy estimators for all the units. Only the resource used by the counters is proportional to the number of TRNG units, Q.

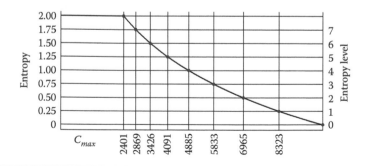

Figure 14.5 Entropy level versus C_{max} for $W = 2$ and $N = 10,000$.

14.3.3.4 Challenge Generator

To perform one round of tests described in Sections 14.2.2.1 and 14.2.2.2, several gigabytes of random challenge vectors are required. To generate these challenge vectors, we implement an on-chip TRNG. We adopt the implementation suggested by Wold et al. in Reference 22. It generates random numbers at a 132-Mbits/sec rate. In this particular implementation, generating a single bit response requires a 64-bit challenge. We concatenate the outputs from four TRNGs to generate one challenge vector.

14.3.3.5 RO-Based Sensor

Zick et al. presented a compact RO-based sensor for online measurements of variations in delay [44]. We incorporate that design in the BIST-PUF to monitor the stability of the delay-based PUF. This sensor consists of an RO and a frequency counter.

14.3.3.6 Parametric and Multiple Interrogation Schemes

In actual implementation, this scheme resides inside the PUF module. It needs two additional signals: an input signal, GEN/AUTH which indicates if the challenge is applied for CRP generation or authentication, and an output signal RESP_VALID, which indicates if the applied challenge passed ST3: Active Parametric Interrogation (Section 14.2.2.2). During CRP generation, the challenge is applied V times at each of the following three settings of the tune level of the PUF: (i) extra delay on top path, (ii) extra delay on bottom path, and (iii) similar delays. The response from each excitation is summed up. If the final sum is close to either 3V or 0, the RESP_VALID signal is set to "1," which indicates that challenge is robust. Otherwise, it is set to "0," which indicates to the user to mark the challenge as unstable and discard it from the CRP table. During authentication, only the robust challenges are applied and the tune levels are set to its optimal condition required to ensure unpredictability.

We employ two multiple interrogation schemes: one is incorporated in the PUF structure to generate the response by voting and the other is part of the BIST scheme to assess the stability of the PUF. In the first one, the challenge is applied T_1 times and the responses from each excitation are summed. The *final* response is set as the Most Significant Bit (MSB) of the sum, which means the response is "1" if $sum > (T_1 - 1)/2$, and "0" otherwise. As we show in the evaluation, PUF stability is greatly enhanced by employing both parametric and multiple interrogation schemes during CRP generation. The second multiple interrogation scheme, which is part of the BIST, sums up these *final* responses for T_2 times. If this sum S_R is close to either T_2 or 0, the response is stable. On the other hand, if S_R is close to $T_2/2$, the response is unstable.

14.3.3.7 Finite-State Machine

The FSM is designed to control the tests described in Section 14.2. The tests for TRNG evaluation are relatively simpler. The FSM reads the test results and sums them up for several hundred instances and reports the mean success rate. Our design provides both instantaneous results for real-time monitoring and cumulative results over several hundred rounds of testing. The cumulative results are stored in a memory block and can be later read to have a full assessment of the TRNG performance using a more comprehensive data. The BIST scheme also sets up error/warning signals when the success rate goes below a certain level.

The PUF requires complex control elements to perform complete evaluation. The unpredictability tests require the randomness test module, which it shares with the TRNG evaluation scheme. To optimize the area, we designed the FSM such that it performs the three unpredictability tests on the PUF sequentially using the same module. The random challenge vectors from the challenge generator are read by the FSM, which performs the necessary manipulations on them as required by the tests UT2 and UT3 (Section 14.2.2.1). The responses from the PUF are sent to the test module via the FSM. Similar to TRNG evaluation scheme, both cumulative and instantaneous results are available. The FSM also generates the checksum from the output bits that provide instantaneous results as explained in Section 14.2.3.

Our sensor-based evaluation reads the delay measurement data from the RO sensor and saves it for future reference. For the multiple interrogation test, the tuning parameters are set to the optimum values. The same challenge is applied 100 times, and the sum of the responses is stored in the memory. A sum close to either 0 or 100 indicates a stable PUF. This test is done entirely inside the FSM without using any external module. The active parametric interrogation test is performed inside the PUF module as explained in the previous section.

14.3.4 Overhead Estimation

We implement the BIST scheme on a Xilinx Virtex 6 FPGA. The resource used by different components of the BIST scheme is reported in Table 14.1. These numbers are functions of different parameters, for example, number of inverters/PDLs in the TRNG, the test sequence length, block size, or maximum latency in the test module. Therefore, the parameters used in our implementation are also reported.

As mentioned in Section 14.2, the randomness test module is required to test both PUF and TRNG. IID test and entropy estimator are used to test only TRNG, and challenge generator and RO sensor are used only for PUF. All these components together use only 2% of the total resource available in Virtex 6.

We also report the estimated power usage of each component. The power is estimated with XPower Analyzer [45] from Xilinx. Note that the reported power estimation is for the case when the BIST is running. However, the BIST need not run continuously. Instead, it can be run at certain intervals to ensure safe operation.

14.4 Evaluation

We evaluated two TRNG designs, namely, the TRNG based on ring oscillators [22] and TRNG based on metastability [26], and one PUF design, namely, the PUF based on PDL [21]. Here, we present selected evaluation results. Type I error rate α is set to 0.05 for all the statistical tests.

14.4.1 Evaluation of TRNGs

14.4.1.1 Evaluation of Metastability-Based TRNG

The estimated entropy level of different units and mean success rate for the seven NIST tests at different temperatures are plotted in Figure 14.6a and b, respectively. The mean entropy of all the units is also shown. Even though the entropy level of the units fluctuates widely, the mean entropy level follows that of unit 1 as its value is higher than the others. At around $-6°C$, there is a dip in

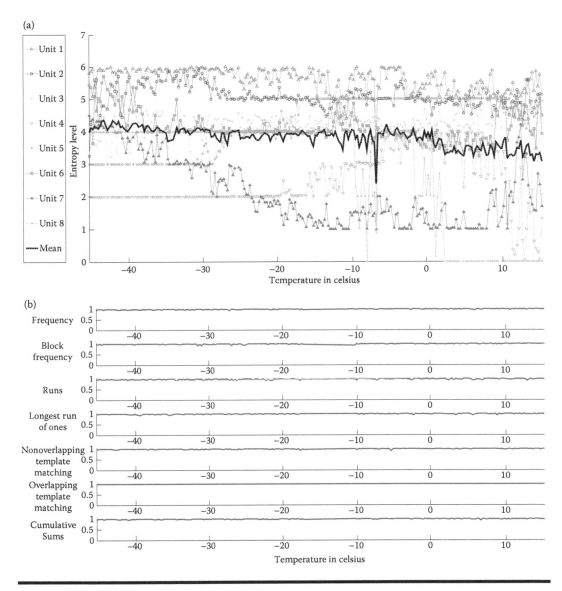

Figure 14.6 Evaluation result for metastability-based TRNG: (a) estimated entropy level of different units and (b) mean success rate of the output sequence in NIST tests.

the entropy level, which also manifests itself in the success rates of the NIST tests. As mentioned in Section 14.3.3.7, each test is performed 250 times and the mean success rate is reported. Moreover, each test is performed on a sequence of several thousand bits. Therefore, the dip in the curves shows that the TRNG produced low-quality output for a long sequence.

One important fact to notice is that while the entropy level of most of the units either remains similar or increases (units 4 and 5) with temperature, the entropy level of units 7 and 8 decreases, which is contrary to the general concept that entropy should increase with temperature. This fact validates the importance of online tests as it shows that theoretical concepts do not always hold during TRNG operation.

Note that the reported results are selected from many observations. For most of the cases, the observations conform to the theoretical concepts. However, we present these particular observations to demonstrate that TRNGs may exhibit inexplicable behavior at times due to their physical nature and therefore real-time monitoring of its performance is crucial to ensure proper operation.

14.4.1.2 Evaluation of RO-Based TRNG

The evaluation results for RO-based TRNG are shown in Figure 14.7. Note that to improve readability, entropy level of only half of the units is plotted. The entropy levels remain relatively more stable as compared to the previous one. The entropy levels either remain similar or increase with temperature.

14.4.2 Evaluation of Unpredictability of PUF

The results of the three unpredictability tests described in Section 14.2.2.1 are shown in Figure 14.8 for two different temperatures: $-5°C$ and $33°C$. Although the success rates for these tests are reduced slightly at lower temperature, the difference is negligible. Note that the original design presented in Reference 4 does not include the diffusion layer without which the PUF passes only UT1 but fails UT2 and UT3.

14.4.3 Evaluation of Stability of PUF

As mentioned in Section 14.3.3.6, we include both multiple interrogation (ST2) and parametric interrogation (ST3) schemes in the CRP generation process to enhance stability of the PUF responses. We also include ST2 in the BIST scheme to assess the improvements provided by these two tests. We assess the stability of PUF in the following three cases:

1. CRP is generated without any validation: the challenge is applied only once and the response is recorded.
2. CRP is generated after validation by ST2: challenge is applied several times and the response is generated by vote.
3. CRP is generated after validation by both ST2 and ST3: challenge is first validated by active parametric interrogation and then the response is generated by vote.

Figure 14.9 shows the results of ST2: Multiple Interrogation Test for the above three cases. As explained in Section 14.3.3.6, this test sums up the PUF responses for T_2 times. The stability in the plot is calculated as $2max(S_R, T_2 - S_R)/T_2$. For S_R close to either T_2 or 0, stability is close to 1. For S_R close to $T_2/2$, stability is close to 0. We see from the plot that applying ST2 in Case 2 greatly enhances the stability of the PUF as compared to Case 1. However, the most stable responses are generated in Case 3 where both ST2 and ST3 are applied.

14.5 Related Work

There have been a few studies on online hardware evaluation of TRNGs. Four tests (frequency test, poker test, run test, long run test) from FIPS 140–2 [37] were implemented on FPGA for hardware-based online testing of randomness in Reference 13. They evaluate two TRNG designs

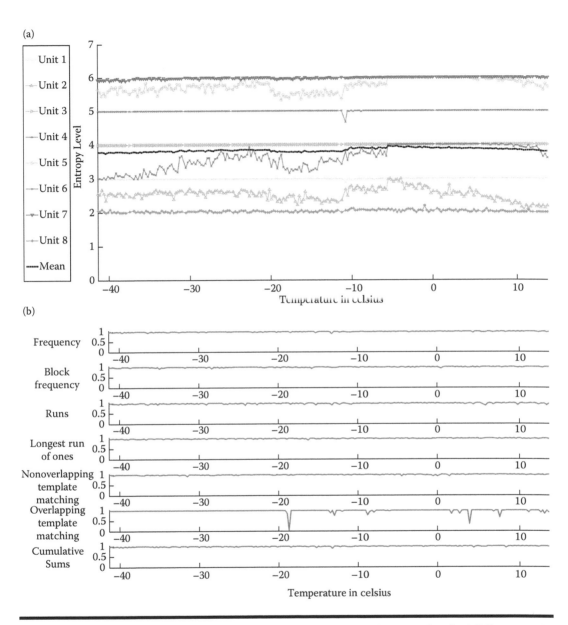

Figure 14.7 **Evaluation result for RO-based TRNG: (a) estimated entropy level of different units and (b) mean success rate of the output sequence in NIST tests.**

presented in References 46 and 47 based on those four tests. In Reference 14, 8 tests out of 15 NIST randomness tests were simplified for constant test sequence length and implemented in hardware (FPGA). Reference 15 implemented 9 tests from the NIST suite for on-the-fly testing of TRNGs. While operations like counting ones and zeros, finding the maximal longest run of the same value and keeping track of a random walk were implemented in hardware, all other operations including addition, multiplication, etc. were performed in an on-chip processor. The latter two work focus only on the implementation of the tests; they do not provide any TRNG evaluation results.

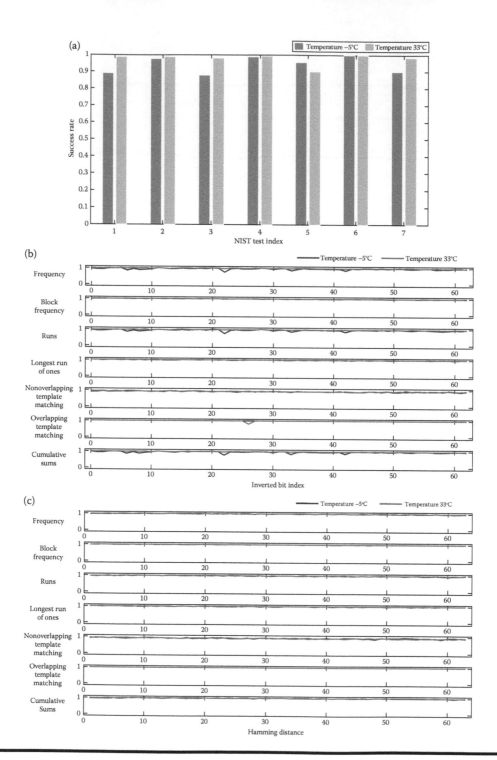

Figure 14.8 Evaluation of unpredictability of PUF at −5°C and 33°C: **(a) result of UT1: randomness of response; (b) result of UT2: effect of individual bit transition; and (c) result of UT2: effect of multiple bit transitions.**

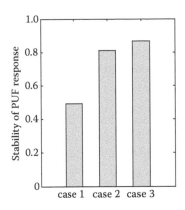

Figure 14.9   Evaluation of PUF stability for three different CRP generation methods.

All the work described above is on testing the output bit sequence of ideal TRNGs. Unlike our BIST scheme, they do not test its internal health. A method to assess the internal health of an oscillator-based TRNG by measuring the jitter was proposed in Reference 19. The work in Reference 20 present an online scheme for evaluating the internal health of nonideal TRNGs with non-IID internal sequences. Our BIST scheme tests both the output bits sequence and internal health and is generally applicable to any ideal TRNG design.

The work on the testing of security and stability of PUF is rather limited. The seminal work by Majzoobi et al. introduced the first formal methodology to test the security of strong PUFs in Reference 8. Four different tests are proposed: (i) predictability, (ii) collision, (iii) sensitivity, and (iv) reverse-engineering. Predictability test identifies the difficulty of correctly calculating or predicting the PUF output for a given input. Collision assessment studies how often two PUFs produce same outputs for an incident challenge. Sensitivity test ensures that the amount of process variation is sufficient for a PUF to remain stable when the operational, structural, and environmental conditions change. Reverse-engineering test determines the hardness of characterizing the PUF circuit component. These offline, software-based tests were important because they paved the way for understanding the PUF attack surface. They also enabled suggestions for novel input and output transformations for safeguarding the PUFs against attacks [4,48].

Our BIST scheme adapts the predictability tests from Reference 8 for the tests described in Section 14.2.2.1. However, the predictability tests were based on examining the probability of the output bit values and transitions, which is equivalent to the frequency test from NIST. We employ six more tests from NIST battery for a more comprehensive evaluation of unpredictability. The BIST scheme also includes the sensitivity tests for ST2 and ST3 described in Section 14.2.2.2. Besides a way to measure the stability, they are also made a part of the CRP generation process by online implementation. It greatly enhanced the stability of the PUF response.

The work by Hori et al. [10] and Maiti et al. [11] presented testing methodologies for quantitative analysis of different PUF designs. Maiti et al., besides defining their own parameters, analyzed the parameters proposed by several other work including Reference 10 to determine any redundancy and defined a compact set of seven parameters: uniformity, reliability, steadiness, uniqueness, diffuseness, bit-aliasing, and probability of misidentification.

The measurement of uniformity is equivalent to the frequency test, which is one of the seven standard randomness test included in our BIST scheme. Steadiness, a measure of stability, is similar to what we measure in the second stability test (ST2) described in Section 14.2.2.2. In both cases, a challenge is applied multiple times, and the bias of the response bit towards either "0" or "1" is measured (more biased means more stable, irrespective of the direction). To measure reliability, the responses to the same challenge are compared to the reference response. This requires saving the reference response on the chip, which would create security threat. Therefore, this parameter is not suitable for online test.

The collision and reverse-engineering test from Reference 8 and the last four parameters from Reference [11] are different ways to measure the similarity (or dissimilarity) of two or more instances of PUFs. While these parameters are important for evaluating a PUF design, the BIST scheme proposed in this work is designed for real-time monitoring of a single PUF instance, the design of which has already passed the initial evaluation. So these parameters are not relevant to our current work.

Evaluation of the weak PUF has been the subject of a number of earlier publications. Armknecht et al. provided theoretical analysis on robustness, physical unclonability, and unpredictability properties of weak PUFs in Reference 9. Leest et al. used software-based Hamming weight test, inter-class uniqueness test, context tree weighting test, and NIST randomness tests to evaluate the randomness and entropy [49]. Cortez et al. tried to increase the fault coverage of physical faults, like stuck-at-fault, of fuzzy extractor (FE), which is the main component of weak PUFs, and proposed a secure BIST scheme to perform the fault tests [50].

To the best of our knowledge, BIST-PUF [51] is the first online and hardware-based testing methodology that includes higher-order NIST randomness tests (other than the frequency test) and is applicable to all PUF families (weak and strong).

14.6 Conclusion and Future Directions

This paper presents a BIST scheme for online evaluation of PUFs and TRNGs. This is the first online hardware evaluation scheme for PUFs. The rising importance of PUF and its applications in several security and cryptography methodologies highlight the need for analysis and evaluation of the PUF input–output behavior. The IoT platform especially needs PUF with self-test capability to ensure seamless and secure operation as a large number of devices operate autonomously in a complex framework. The BIST structure is designed to evaluate two main properties of PUFs, namely, *unpredictability* and *stability*. The unpredictability tests investigate the randomness of the response bits and the correlation between the transitions of response bit and challenge bits. The stability tests study the CRP behavior and the chip conditions in three distinct ways, namely, sensor-based, parametric interrogation, and multiple interrogations.

While a number of studies have dealt with online evaluation of TRNGs, all of them were concerned with only testing statistical quality of the TRNG output. Even though these tests are important, monitoring the internal health of the TRNG is more crucial to ensure its integrity. Our BIST scheme is the first online test that, besides evaluating the output bit sequence, continuously monitors the internal health of ideal TRNGs and application of which is not limited to any specific TRNG design.

Other than the testing components, the BIST architecture also includes a low-overhead control circuitry and memory for saving the test results. Proof-of-concept implementation on FPGA demonstrated an overhead which is reasonable in terms of the percentage of the total used area of FPGA. We also provide evaluation results for a number of TRNG and PUF designs.

Going forward, there is a lot of room for continuing along the lines of research suggested in this work. A natural extension is working on built-in-self-repair mechanisms that use the test results from the BIST scheme for on-the-fly improvement of randomness (entropy) and robustness (stability). A simple instance of such an improvement is provided by the stability tests: multiple interrogation and active parametric interrogation. The metastability-based TRNG also employs a feedback mechanism, which is essentially the frequency test from NIST or Diehard. Development of more complex repair methodologies is desirable.

Another important direction is development of new tests that can evaluate the susceptibility of TRNGs and PUFs to specific attacks. Devising attacks and countermeasures for modeling/reverse-engineering of PUFs is an active area of research [5,7,27,32,34,52]. Yet, another possibility is to devise more efficient and compact tests for evaluations of PUF stability and robustness. While this paper focuses on strong PUF testing that is also applicable to several weak PUFs, it is interesting to extend the devised methodologies by applying them to other families of PUF such as public PUF [53], processor-based strong PUFs that use aging for response tuning [54], or the FPGA-based time-bounded PUFs that utilize the concept of erasability [55].

Acknowledgments

This work was supported in parts by an Office of Naval Research grant (ONR-R17460), National Science Foundation grants (CNS-1059416 and CCF-1116858), and Air Force Office of Scientific Research grant under Multidisciplinary Research Program of the University Research Initiative (FA9550-14-1-0351).

References

1. D. Miorandi, S. Sicari, F. De Pellegrini, and I. Chlamtac. Internet of things: Vision, applications and research challenges. *Ad Hoc Networks*, **10**(7):1497–1516, 2012.
2. T. Xu, J. B. Wendt, and M. Potkonjak. Security of IoT systems: Design challenges and opportunities. In *IEEE/ACM International Conference on Computer-Aided Design*, pages 417–423, San Jose, CA, 2014.
3. M. Rostami, F. Koushanfar, and R. Karri. A primer on hardware security: Models, methods, and metrics. *Proceedings of the IEEE*, **102**(8):1283–1295, 2014.
4. M. Majzoobi, F. Koushanfar, and M. Potkonjak. Lightweight secure PUFs. In *IEEE/ACM International Conference on Computer-Aided Design*, pages 670–673, San Jose, CA, 2008.
5. U. Rührmair, F. Sehnke, J. Sölter, G. Dror, S. Devadas, and J. Schmidhuber. Modeling attacks on physical unclonable functions. In *CCS*, pages 237–249. ACM, New York, NY, 2010.
6. U. Rührmair, J. Sölter, F. Sehnke, X. Xu, A. Mahmoud, V. Stoyanova, G. Dror, J. Schmidhuber, W. Burleson, and S. Devadas. PUF modeling attacks on simulated and silicon data. *IEEE Transactions on Information Forensics and Security*, **8**(11):1876–1891, 2013.
7. U. Rührmair, X. Xu, J. Sölter, A. Mahmoud, M. Majzoobi, F. Koushanfar, and W. Burleson. Efficient power and timing side channels for physical unclonable functions. In *CHES*, pages 476–492. Springer, Berlin, 2014.
8. M. Majzoobi, F. Koushanfar, and M. Potkonjak. Testing techniques for hardware security. In *IEEE International Test Conference*, pages 1–10, Santa Clara, CA, 2008.
9. F. Armknecht, R. Maes, A. Sadeghi, O.-X. Standaert, and C. Wachsmann. A formalization of the security features of physical functions. In *IEEE Security & Privacy (Oakland)*, pages 397–412, Oakland, CA, 2011.
10. Y. Hori, T. Yoshida, T. Katashita, and A. Satoh. Quantitative and statistical performance evaluation of arbiter physical unclonable functions on FPGAs. In *ReConFig*, pages 298–303. IEEE, New York, NY, 2010.

11. A. Maiti, V. Gunreddy, and P. Schaumont. A systematic method to evaluate and compare the performance of physical unclonable functions. In *Embedded Systems Design with FPGAs*, pages 245–267. Springer, Berlin, 2013.

12. X. Xu, V. Suresh, R. Kumar, and W. Burleson. Post-silicon validation and calibration of hardware security primitives. In *2014 IEEE Computer Society Annual Symposium on VLSI (ISVLSI)*, pages 29–34. IEEE, New York, NY, 2014.

13. R. Santoro, O. Sentieys, and S. Roy. On-line monitoring of random number generators for embedded security. In *IEEE International Symposium on Circuits and Systems*, pages 3050–3053, Taipei, Taiwan, 2009.

14. F. Veljkovic, V. Rožic, and I. Verbauwhede. Low-cost implementations of on-the-fly tests for random number generators. In *Design, Automation Test in Europe Conference & Exhibition*, pages 959–964, Dresden, Germany, 2012.

15. B. Yang, V. Rožic, N. Mentens, W. Dehaene, and I. Verbauwhede. Embedded HW/SW platform for on-the-fly testing of true random number generators. In *Proceedings of the 2015 Design, Automation & Test in Europe Conference & Exhibition*, pages 345–350, Grenoble, France, 2015.

16. W. Schindler and W. Killmann. Evaluation criteria for true (physical) random number generators used in cryptographic applications. In *CHES*, pages 431–449. Springer, Berlin, 2012.

17. W. Killmann and W. Schindler. A proposal for: Functionality classes for random number generators. AIS, 2011.

18. E. Barker and J. Kelsey. Recommendation for the Entropy Sources Used for Random Bit Generation. Draft NIST Special Publication, 2012.

19. V. Fischer and D. Lubicz. Embedded evaluation of randomness in oscillator based elementary TRNG. In *Cryptographic Hardware and Embedded Systems*, pages 527–543. Springer, Berlin, 2014.

20. B. Yang, V. Rožic, N. Mentens, and I. Verbauwhede. On-the-fly tests for non-ideal true random number generators. In *IEEE International Symposium on Circuits and Systems*, pages 2017–2020, Lisbon, Portugal, 2015.

21. M. Majzoobi, F. Koushanfar, and S. Devadas. FPGA PUF using programmable delay lines. In *IEEE International Workshop on Information Forensics and Security*, pages 1–6, Seattle, WA, 2010.

22. K. Wold and C. H. Tan. Analysis and enhancement of random number generator in FPGA based on oscillator rings. *International Journal of Reconfigurable Computing*, **2009**:4, 2009.

23. B. Sunar, W. J. Martin, and D. R. Stinson. A provably secure true random number generator with built-in tolerance to active attacks. *IEEE Transactions on Computers*, **56**(1):109–119, 2007.

24. A. Cherkaoui, V. Fischer, A. Aubert, and L. Fesquet. A self-timed ring based true random number generator. In *IEEE 19th International Symposium on Asynchronous Circuits and Systems*, pages 99–106, New York, 2013.

25. H. Hisashi and S. Ichikawa. FPGA implementation of metastability-based true random number generator. *IEICE Transactions on Information and Systems*, **95**(2):426–436, 2012.

26. M. Majzoobi, F. Koushanfar, and S. Devadas. FPGA-based true random number generation using circuit metastability with adaptive feedback control. In *Springer Workshop on Cryptographic Hardware and Embedded Systems*, pages 17–32, Berlin, Germany, 2011.

27. U. Ruhrmair, S. Devadas, and F. Koushanfar. *Security Based on Physical Unclonability and Disorder*. Springer, Berlin, 2011.

28. J. W. Lee, D. Lim, B. Gassend, G. E. Suh, M. Van Dijk, and S. Devadas. A technique to build a secret key in integrated circuits for identification and authentication applications. In *Symposium on VLSI*, pages 176–179. IEEE, New York, NY, 2004.

29. B. Gassend, D. Clarke, M. van Dijk, and S. Devadas. Silicon physical random functions. In *CCS*, pages 148–160, 2002.

30. G. E. Suh and S. Devadas. Physical unclonable functions for device authentication and secret key generation. In *Design Automation Conference*, pages 9–14. ACM, New York, NY, 2007.

31. M. Majzoobi, A. Kharaya, F. Koushanfar, and S. Devadas. Automated Design, Implementation, and Evaluation of Arbiter-based PUF on FPGA using Programmable Delay Lines. Cryptology ePrint Archive, Report 2014/710, 2014.

32. A. Mahmoud, U. Rührmair, M. Majzoobi, and F. Koushanfar. Combined Modeling and Side Channel Attacks on Strong PUFs. Cryptology ePrint Archive, Report 2013/632, 2013.

33. X. Xu and W. Burleson. Hybrid side-channel/machine-learning attacks on PUFs: A new threat? In *Proceedings of the Conference on Design, Automation & Test in Europe*, page 349. European Design and Automation Association, 2014.

34. M. Rostami, J. B. Wendt, M. Potkonjak, and F. Koushanfar. Quo vadis, PUF? Trends and challenges of emerging physical-disorder based security. In *Design, Automation Test in Europe Conference Exhibition*, pages 1–6, Grenoble, France, 2014.

35. A. Rukhin, J. Soto, J. Nechvatal, M. Smid, and E. Barker. A Statistical Test Suite for Random and Pseudorandom Number Generators for Cryptographic Applications. Technical Report 800–22, NIST, 2001.

36. G. Marsaglia. The marsaglia random number cdrom including the diehard battery of tests of randomness, 1995. http://www.stat.fsu.edu/pub/diehard, 2008

37. FIPS PUB 140-2: Security requirements for cryptographic modules. National Institute of Standards and Technology, 2001.

38. E. B. Barker and J. M. Kelsey. *Recommendation for Random Bit Generator (RBG) Constructions*. US Department of Commerce, NIST, 2012.

39. E. B. Barker and J. M. Kelsey. *Recommendation for Random Number Generation Using Deterministic Random Bit Generators (Revised)*. US Department of Commerce, NIST, 2007.

40. W. Schindler. Functionality classes and evaluation methodology for deterministic random number generators. In *Anwendungshinweise and Interpretation (AIS)*, pp. 5–11, 1999.

41. A. Wald and J. Wolfowitz. On a test whether two samples are from the same population. *The Annals of Mathematical Statistics*, **11**(2):147–162, 1940.

42. R. B. Davies. Exclusive or (XOR) and hardware random number generators, Tech. report. http://www.robertnz.net/pdf/xor2.pdf, 2002.

43. Advanced Encryption Standard (AES), Federal information processing standards publication 197.441 (2001).

44. K. M. Zick and J. P. Hayes. On-line sensing for healthier FPGA systems. In *FPGA*, pages 239–248, 2010.

45. Analyzing Power Consumption, Tech. report. https://www.xilinx.com/support/documentation/sw_manuals/xilinx11/pp_p_process_xpower_analyzer.htm, 2015.

46. D. Schellekens, B. Preneel, and I. Verbauwhede. FPGA vendor agnostic true random number generator. In *International Conference on Field Programmable Logic and Applications, 2006 (FPL '06)*. Madrid, Spain.

47. V. Fischer and M. Drutarovský. True random number generator embedded in reconfigurable hardware. In *Cryptographic Hardware and Embedded Systems-CHES 2002*. Springer, Berlin.

48. M. Majzoobi, F. Koushanfar, and M. Potkonjak. Techniques for design and implementation of secure reconfigurable PUFs. *ACM Transactions on Reconfigurable Technologies and Systems (TRETS)*, **2**(1):5:1–5:33, 2009.

49. V. van der Leest, G.-J. Schrijen, H. Handschuh, and P. Tuyls. Hardware intrinsic security from D flip-flops. In *STC*, pages 53–62. ACM, New York, NY, 2010.

50. M. Cortez, G. Roelofs, S. Hamdioui, and G. Di Natale. Testing PUF-based secure key storage circuits. In *Design, Automation Test in Europe Conference Exhibition*, pages 1–6, Grenoble, France, 2014.

51. S. U. Hussain, S. Yellapantula, M. Majzoobi, and F. Koushanfar. Bist-PUF: Online, hardware-based evaluation of physically unclonable circuit identifiers. In *IEEE/ACM International Conference on Computer-Aided Design*, pages 162–169, New York, 2014.

52. X. Xu, U. Rührmair, D. E. Holcomb, and W. Burleson. Security evaluation and enhancement of bistable ring PUFs. In *International Workshop on Radio Frequency Identification: Security and Privacy Issues*, pages 3–16. Springer, Berlin, 2015.

53. M. Potkonjak and V. Goudar. Public physical unclonable functions. *Proceedings of the IEEE*, **102**(8):1142–1156, 2014.

54. J. Kong and F. Koushanfar. Processor-based strong physical unclonable functions with aging-based response tuning. *IEEE Transactions on Emerging Topics in Computing*, **2**(1):16–29, 2014.

55. M. Majzoobi and F. Koushanfar. Time-Bounded Authentication of FPGAs. *IEEE Transactions on Information Forensics and Security (TIFS)*, **6**(3–2):1123–1135, 2011.

Chapter 15

Digital Microfluidic Biochip Security

Jack Tang, Mohamed Ibrahim, Krishnendu Chakrabarty, and Ramesh Karri

Contents

Digital microfluidics refers to the manipulation of small, discrete quantities of fluids [1,2]. This paradigm runs counter to older, more established microfluidic design methods, which rely on continuous flow channels driven by micropumps and controlled by microvalves [3,4]. The discrete nature of digital microfluidics lends itself nicely to design automation techniques; many methods for high-level synthesis [5], design-for-test [6], and error recovery [7,8] have been demonstrated, leading to increased ease-of-use, throughput and reliability. Digital microfluidic biochips (DMFBs) have thus emerged as one of the most promising techniques for realizing the lab-on-a-chip.

Contemporaneously, computer security threats have broadened in their sophistication and scope. The proliferation of microcontrollers equipped with sensors and actuators in an expansive array of applications—that is, the "Internet-of-Things" [9] and cyberphysical systems [10,11]—is causing alarm among the security research community. Automobiles [12], power grids [13], and industrial control systems [14] are all hackable. Horizontal hardware supply chains provide ample opportunities for insertion of malicious circuits and intellectual property crimes [15–17]. Given the many proposed applications of DMFBs along with their cyberphysical nature, it is imperative that researchers tackle security in the context of digital microfluidics. To that end, we provide a brief background on digital microfluidic technology and explore the many emerging threats and countermeasures being investigated today.

15.1 Background

Digital microfluidics is a general term; any technology with the ability to manipulate droplets discretely can be considered to be a type of digital microfluidics [1]. Several techniques have emerged over the years and are now commonly employed in practical applications such as DNA sequencing [18] and single-cell analysis [19]. Here, we describe some of the most important developments in digital microfluidics that are relevant to our discussion on security.

15.1.1 Structure and Operation

A typical DMFB is illustrated in Figure 15.1. The biochip consists of a substrate upon which a grid of electrodes are patterned. The electrodes are coated with a thin dielectric layer and a hydrophobic layer. Fluid droplets are placed on the substrate and manipulated. The substrate can be exposed to air, or covered with ITO glass and filled with oil. Droplets are able to move from electrode to electrode through the application of suitable control voltages inducing *electrowetting-on-dielectric* (EWOD).

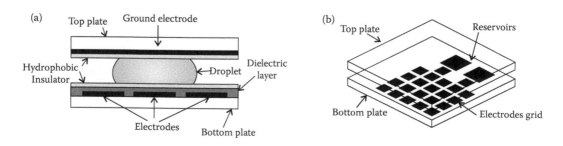

Figure 15.1 (a) Schematic side view of a digital microfluidic biochip (DMFB). (b) Patterned electrodes form a substrate over which droplets can be manipulated.

Electrowetting-on-dielectric is a phenomenon by which the contact angle between a droplet and a surface can be modulated by application of an electric field [20]. Application of a positive bias on an electrode causes the contact angle to decrease relative to the zero-bias case. As the contact angle decreases, the droplet encroaches upon any adjacent electrodes. This behavior is described by the Lipmann–Young equation

$$\cos\theta(V) = \cos\theta(0) + \frac{\varepsilon_0\varepsilon_r V^2}{2d\gamma_{LG}} \tag{15.1}$$

where d is the thickness of the substrate, ε_r is the relative permittivity of the insulating layer, γ_{LG} is the liquid–gas interfacial tension, and V is the applied voltage [21]. The cosine of the contact angle increases with the square of the voltage. Actuation voltages reported in the literature are often higher than those typically found in modern digital logic supplies, in some cases by an order of magnitude. Voltage conditioning circuitry is thus required to convert digital control signals into a form suitable for actuating droplets on a DMFB array.

Sequencing the bias voltages on neighboring electrodes allows a droplet to be transported, split, mixed, and dispensed [22]. These fundamental operations are the building blocks for more complicated protocols. While other mechanisms for realizing digital microfluidics exist, this chapter emphasizes EWOD-based DMFB technology. EWOD has been extensively targeted for novel computer-aided design techniques and cyberphysical integration, implying that security issues may exist.

15.1.2 DMFB Design Flows

A typical custom DMFB design flow is illustrated in Figure 15.2a. At the highest level, a *biocoder* is responsible for designing the protocol to be executed on the platform. The protocol describes the fluid handling operations: dispensing of samples and reagents, mixing, splitting, storage, and detection. The protocol is specified in a language such as BioCoder [23], and is analogous to the RTL description of a digital circuit in Verilog or VHDL. At the next step, the *biochip designer* is responsible for integration of all the hardware and software resources required to implement the biocoder's protocol. The *CAD tool vendor* provides a high-level synthesis toolchain which converts the protocol into a set of instructions executable by the biochip hardware. The biochip hardware is provided by the *foundry*. Once the design is completed, it may be forwarded to a *testing facility* to ensure a high yield before being shipped to the end user. The *end user* receives the completed biochip platform and may be responsible for loading of samples and reagents, operating the device, and interpreting the results. Once the biochip's useful life has been exceeded, it must be sent to a *recycling and disposal facility*.

A general-purpose DMFB design flow is illustrated in Figure 15.2b. The biochip designer integrates the protocol from the biocoder, architectural information from the DMFB vendor, and synthesizes an actuation sequence using tools from the CAD tool vendor. The completed design then passes through a testing facility and is deployed to the end user. The used biochip is then sent to a recycling and disposal facility for safe handling.

Design flows will generally follow one of the two paradigms described here, but in practice may include flows of information between various parties as a design is iteratively improved. Additionally, reconfigurability of a biochip lies on a spectrum. A hybrid approach can be taken where certain aspects of the chip architecture are dictated by the application and require a custom design, while other parts of the chip are more general purpose. Consequently, the design of these biochips will incorporate aspects of both custom and general-purpose flows.

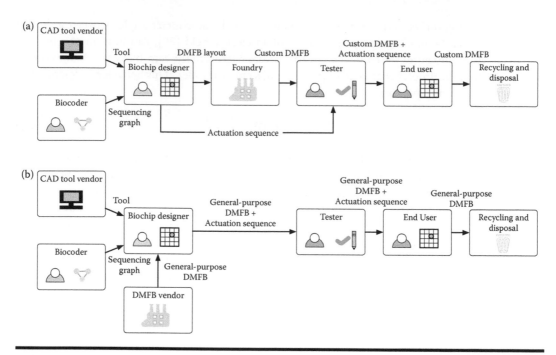

Figure 15.2 (a) Custom DMFB design flow. (b) General-purpose DMFB design flow.

15.1.3 High-Level Synthesis

The high-level synthesis flow takes the protocol specification and hardware architecture, and produces a set of actuation sequences that can be used to directly drive a DMFB. Synthesis typically consists of the following major subtasks (Figure 15.3):

1. *Sequencing graph generation.* The instructions for how to execute the protocol are converted into a sequencing graph $G = (V,E)$, where each vertex represents a fluid handling operation and an edge ($e \in E$) represents a dependency between two operations.
2. *Architectural-level synthesis.* The sequencing graph and hardware architecture description are fed to a scheduler and binder. The scheduler assigns start and stop times for each operation. In resource binding, on-chip resources for each task are assigned [24].
3. *Physical-level synthesis.* Modules, detectors, and actuators are physically placed on-chip [25]. Routing algorithms then transport droplets to the required locations prior to the start of each operation [26].

The final output consists of a sequence of bit patterns that can be directly applied to the DMFB. Other high-level synthesis techniques take a more holistic approach; instead of considering each of the scheduling/placing/routing subtasks separately, they can be cooptimized. Such an approach has been demonstrated for micro-electrode-dot-array DMFBs [27].

15.1.4 Cyberphysical Integration

A DMFB is merely a platform for droplet manipulation. Cyberphysical integration can be leveraged to form a more powerful, useful system that can dynamically reconfigure itself [7,28]. A typical

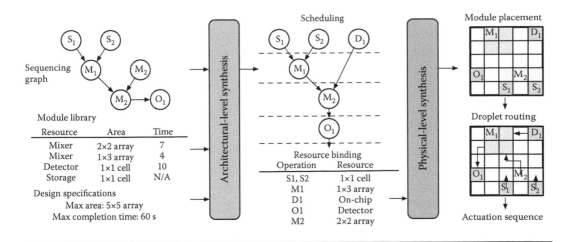

Figure 15.3 High-level synthesis of DMFB actuation sequences begins with biochip resource descriptions and a protocol converted to a sequencing graph. Architectural-level synthesis schedules operations and assigns on-chip resources. Physical-level synthesis places the modules and routes droplets.

cyberphysical DMFB system implementation is shown in Figure 15.4. Sensors such as CCD cameras and capacitive sensors can be used to detect the state of droplets on the biochip [8]. The quality and integrity of an assay is thus known to the controller, and it can be programmed to correct errors in real time. Electrodes allow fluids to be manipulated, and other actuators such as heaters can be used to further alter fluids on a biochip.

15.1.5 Error Recovery

Efficient error recovery has been a major challenge for DMFB designers due to a plethora of naturally occurring hardware faults [29]. Checkpoint-based error recovery has been proposed, which utilizes a CCD camera to sense the state of electrodes at specific times and locations (i.e., the checkpoints) and inform the DMFB controller to take corrective action [7]. CCD camera-based imaging is limited in its speed in accuracy. The camera image must be cropped to a specific location, and a template pattern matching algorithm has to be executed to determine the state [7]. Consequently,

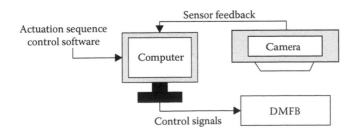

Figure 15.4 Cyberphysical integration with sensors such as CCD cameras provides intelligent fluid processing capabilities.

the placement of checkpoints in a protocol must be optimized to ensure fast and reliable operation. Fast online synthesis [30] and dictionary-based methods [28] have been devised to generate actuation sequences which compensate for errors while minimizing the number of steps that must be repeated.

15.2 DMFB Security Threats

Digital microfluidic biochip security consists of a complex relationship among threats, vulnerabilities, assets, motivations, actors, attacks, and countermeasures (Figure 15.5). Due to the cyberphysical nature of DMFBs, security threats are diverse and are related to problems encountered in both hardware and software security [31,32]. A particular security threat may be related to a combination of factors, and the relationship between each of these factors is only beginning to be explored. The remainder of this section surveys several potential threats and discusses some of the ways they can be realized.

15.2.1 Denial-of-Service

Denial-of-service (DoS) is a violation of a system's availability. In a microfluidic system, this attack can be particularly catastrophic due to their cyberphysical nature. Unlike DoS as typically encountered in computer network security, recovery from a DoS attack is not easily guaranteed due to the potential for physical damage. The samples and reagents that comprise the system can be destroyed, and may be prohibitively expensive or near impossible to replace. For instance, DNA samples used in a forensics context will be collected from a crime scene and will be available only in limited quantities. Destruction of these samples may hinder criminal proceedings. Additionally, the DMFB hardware could be damaged due to excessive wear. Below, we illustrate some DoS scenarios driven from attacks where the DMFB controller behavior is modified.

1. *Interference region violation.* Two droplets on adjacent electrodes can inadvertently merge. Synthesis routines implement an "interference region" design rule around operations to

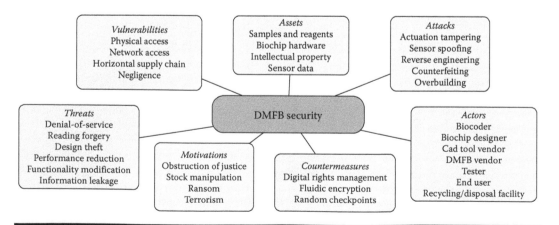

Figure 15.5 **Factors contributing to the emerging field of DMFB security. The factors listed here are not exhaustive.**

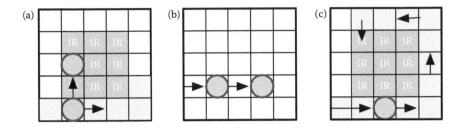

Figure 15.6 Examples of DoS attacks. (a) Encroachment upon interference regions can cause inadvertent mixing. (b) Droplets can leave residues which contaminate subsequently arriving droplets. (c) Excessive electrode wear can be achieved through inefficient routing.

prevent mixing. An attacker can easily cause DoS through routing into an interference region (Figure 15.6a).

2. *Electrode contamination.* Droplets may leave a residue behind, causing contamination of subsequently arriving droplets. Methods have been devised to optimize the routing of *wash droplets*, which clean up these residues and permit reliable operation [33] (Figure 15.6b).

3. *Excessive electrode wear.* Excessive actuation of electrodes is one of the major factors leading to device failure. An attacker could force droplets to take circuitous routes, causing unnecessary wear. Eventually the device will exhibit a premature failure. If the assay continues to execute properly in the interim, this attack can easily escape notice of the end user (Figure 15.6c).

15.2.2 *Reading Forgery*

Reading forgery is the creation of a result that may deviate from reality or the desired assay outcome. An attacker may be interested in altering the final concentration that is read back to the end user. Such an outcome can be achieved through several means, depending on where in the design flow the attacker is present and their capabilities. Sensor spoofing could be used to deceive the end user; the assay may be carried out with integrity, but the final result is misinterpreted by a malicious sensor that is inserted at an untrusted fabrication house. Or the fluid handling steps can be altered by a remote party who compromises the DMFB controller and modifies the actuation sequences.

Example: Glucose Assay—A glucose assay is a colorimetric assay used to gauge the concentration of glucose in a sample such as serum [34]. This assay has practical application in the monitoring of blood sugar levels for diabetes patients. Figure 15.7 illustrates the sequencing graph specification of the assay. It consists of four independent reaction chains. Chain 3 processes the sample, while chains 1, 2, and 4 measure reaction rates of a glucose and buffer solutions for calibration.

The glucose assay can be attacked through actuation tampering. An attacker who is able to compromise the computer system used to drive the biochip alters the actuation sequence such that an alternate protocol is realized. *Attack* 1: The sequencing graph can be modified such that a waste buffer droplet dilutes the sample droplet. The final glucose concentration reading is directly altered. *Attack* 2: Waste buffer droplets are used to dilute reaction chains 2 and 4, which alters the calibration curve. In this case, the final sample glucose concentration is correct but is interpreted incorrectly due to the altered calibration curve (Figure 15.8) [31]. These attacks illustrate how a final sensor reading can be forged through physical manipulation of fluids.

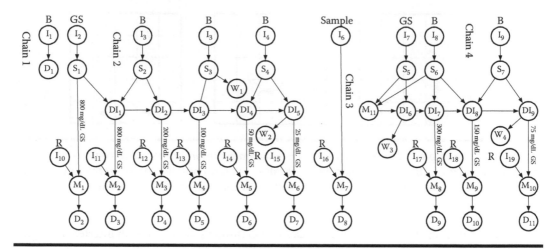

Figure 15.7 Golden assay sequencing graph. B is the 1:4 mL buffer droplet, Sample is the 0:7 mL glucose sample droplet, R is the 0:7 mL reagent droplet, GS is the 1:4 mL 800 mg/dL glucose solution droplet, and W is the waste droplet. D, DI, S, M, and I are the detection, dilution, splitting, mixing, and dispensing operations, respectively.

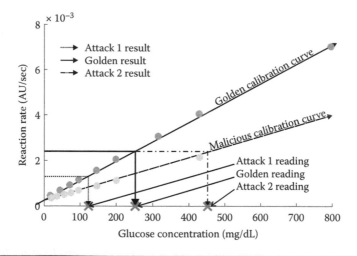

Figure 15.8 Glucose assay results are generated against a calibration curve. Attack 1 alters the sample concentration and is interpreted against the golden calibration curve. Attack 2 alters the calibration curve and leads to misinterpretation of the final result.

15.2.3 Design Theft

Design theft is a broad attack outcome encompassing many threats occurring at the manufacturing level. Currently, DMFB platforms are often fabricated in a vertically integrated process where each of the design steps are in-house and trusted. As the size, complexity, and sophistication of DMFB technology increases, it is anticipated that the design flow will begin to resemble the practice in the semiconductor industry today: a large marketplace of vendors supplying intellectual property blocks, and manufacturers each with their own specialized processes that are prohibitively expensive to bring in-house. This distributed manufacturing flow is reasonably untrusted; as the integrated circuit industry has shown, the risk of overbuilding [15], counterfeiting [35], and IP theft [36] is real and has led to a proliferation of low-quality, underpriced devices flooding the market [37,38]. DMFB designers must anticipate such supply chain security threats and incorporate measures to protect their designs [32].

15.2.4 Performance Reduction

A performance reduction in a DMFB is a more subtle form of DoS. End users have an expectation that a device will perform its intended functions, so repeated outright failures may suggest that there is a malicious cause. If the performance of a device is merely altered, an attack may be difficult to detect or distinguish from naturally occurring faults. The following performance reductions can lower the quality of service and subsequently, reduce quality of patient care in medical applications, or degrade trustworthiness in a company's product offerings.

1. *Execution time.* An attacker can slow the execution of an assay by altering the hardware actuation frequency or tampering with the actuation sequences. The result may be minor annoyance for a single assay, but in certain use cases—such as in scientific research where repeated large-scale measurements are made to gather high-quality datasets—these minor delays can be compounded and result in significant productivity declines.
2. *Lower output.* Certain classes of assay protocols are designed to produce a physical result, such as the duplication of DNA or a novel chemical reagent. An attacker can lower the efficiency of these reactions such that output is inhibited.
3. *Lower efficiency.* Resources are consumed in the execution of a protocol; power is consumed in controlling and actuating a DMFB, while fluid reagents and samples are consumed in the DMFB. An attacker can lower the efficiency of a device by unnecessarily toggling sensors and actuators, or causing excess fluids to be dispensed and wasted.

15.2.5 Functionality Modification

Functionality modification causes a DMFB to perform an action that was not specified by the system designer. Unlike DoS or performance reduction attacks, functionality modification does not preclude the normal operation of a device. Rather, the security concern is that the device does something different or superfluous to the task it was designed for. An attacker may wish to leverage excess processing capabilities to run a distributed algorithm for their own profit, such as the mining of bitcoins. Or an attacker may have identified a chemical product that can be synthesized using excess fluid resources on a biochip. Once the desired protocol is executed and the biochip is sent to a recycling and disposal facility, the attacker can harvest these unintended fluid products.

15.2.6 Information Leakage

Information leakage attacks cause some sensitive data to become known to a malicious actor. Sensitive information in a DMFB can include patient data [39] and secret keys used to lock the hardware. The information leakage problem can be as complicated as insertion of hardware Trojans [17] to communicate a sensor reading upon an activating signal. Or it may be as simple as an over-the-shoulder attack where a casual observer notices the color of a colorimetric assay and records the name of a patient on the DMFB user interface. Furthermore, the physical nature of DMFBs leaves open the possibility of data remanence attacks—where the attacker collects a discarded DMFB and performs analysis on residual fluids—and side-channel analysis [40], where physical modalities are exploited.

15.3 Emerging Attacks and Countermeasures

The catastrophic outcomes of Section 15.2 can be realized through many novel attacks. It is anticipated that many of these new attacks will arise from the unique properties of cyberphysical DMFBs, causing difficulty for defenders to effectively anticipate and identify vulnerabilities. However, designers of new defenses can also leverage these same properties. The following section surveys these emerging attacks and countermeasures.

15.3.1 Actuation Tampering

Actuation tampering refers to the deliberate modification, augmentation, or deletion of the control signals used to drive a DMFB. Actuation tampering can be used to realize DoS: droplets can be dispensed and routed to interfere with an assay. The technical means required to carry out this attack are varied and can occur at any phase of the design flow. At the design phase, a malicious CAD tool vendor may insert extraneous operations in the resulting synthesized actuation sequence. A malicious hardware vendor may insert hardware Trojans into the controller which, when triggered, activates a payload that causes unintended actuation. A remote party who has compromised the computers used to control the DMFB can alter the instructions stored in memory. And an end user can physically tamper with the hardware and inject faults—clock/power glitching, temperature stressing, and tampering with fluids are all possible [41].

15.3.1.1 Randomized Checkpoints

A cyberphysical DMFB equipped with error recovery hardware presents challenges for an attacker; the attack must be conducted in such a way as to avoid checkpoints. This provides a small measure of security. An intrusion detection system (IDS) based on randomized checkpoints has been proposed to take advantage of this observation (Figure 15.9). Without knowledge of the checkpoint locations, an attacker cannot optimize their attack to avoid detection. The effectiveness of the detection is measured as the probability that an attacker evades detection. A system designer is interested to know the minimum number of checkpoints required to attain a certain probability of evasion. Such a countermeasure will be effective against attackers outside of the design flow: end users and remote adversaries who have compromised the main DMFB controller.

Figure 15.10 illustrates the concept. At the first time step, five electrodes are randomly selected to be checkpoints. The state of these five electrodes is compared against a golden assay. At the following four time steps, no electrodes are randomly chosen. At time step 5, another five random electrodes are selected. The final time step does not contain any random electrodes. The probability of evasion is found to be

$$P(E) = \left(1 - \frac{ck}{s}\right)^L \tag{15.2}$$

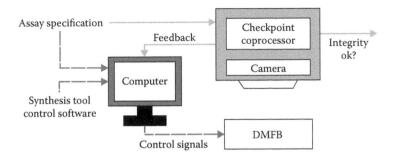

Figure 15.9 **DMFB secure coprocessor implementation. Solid lines indicate signals assumed to be trustworthy, while dotted lines are susceptible to attack.**

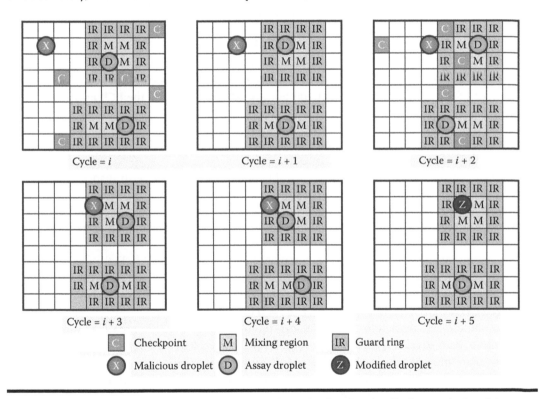

Figure 15.10 **Example assay execution with random checkpoints applied at cycle *i* and *i* + 2. In this case, *s* = 72, *k* = 5, *L* = 5. This example is a realization of the random sampling times. Assuming *c* = 0.33, then *P(E)* = 0.89.**

where c is a constant defining the probability of monitoring the biochip at any time step, k is the number of electrodes to monitor, s is the number of electrodes on the biochip, and L is the length of the malicious route. The ratio k/s is defined as the *electrode coverage ratio*.

The parameter s represents the size of the DMFB array. The parameters c and k are design parameters, which should be maximized subject to the computational and imaging capabilities of the DMFB platform. The model does not assume any particular malicious route; it only assumes that an attack exists for a certain number of cycles L. We note that the probability of evasion has an

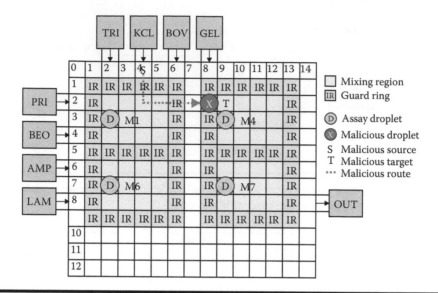

Figure 15.11 Malicious route on a general-purpose DMFB executing the PCR protocol.

exponential dependence on L, which leads to the possibility of decreasing $P(E)$ through influencing the routability of malicious droplets.

Example: Polymerase Chain Reaction—We illustrate the real-world performance of a randomized checkpoint scheme by studying the polymerase chain reaction (PCR), which is used for the amplification of DNA. We consider a general-purpose DMFB architecture executing PCR under DoS attack. Excess KCl concentration inhibits PCR [42], so an attacker could route an extra KCl droplet to cause DoS.

The route taken by our malicious attacker is shown in Figure 15.11. Eight execution cycles are required to reach the destination. Figure 15.12 illustrates how $P(E)$ varies as a function of the electrode coverage ratio for the given route. With the given constraint of $k = 20$, the electrode coverage ratio is 10.3%. This route yields $P(E) = 0.66$.

The randomized checkpoint technique can be further improved through placement of static checkpoints. If an attacker is able to learn the location of these static checkpoints, they will attempt to avoid them. However, by avoiding them their routing becomes longer and more susceptible to detection by the random checkpoints. Static checkpoint placement algorithms and its performance evaluation are discussed in Reference 43.

15.3.2 Intellectual Property Attacks

The intellectual property contained in a DMFB design consists of both the physical hardware—electronics, chip layout, fabrication processes—as well as the high-level protocol specification. These protocols require a significant investment to research and develop, and therefore companies have an interest in protecting them from theft. Beyond IP theft, other manufacturing-related attacks include overproduction and counterfeiting. These attacks present a broad array of challenges for companies looking to prevent lower cost, lower quality devices from flooding the market. In addition to design theft, IP attacks can potentially cause performance reduction, functionality modification, and information leakage.

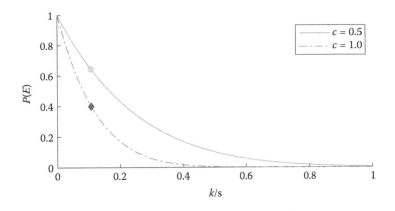

Figure 15.12 **Probability of evasion versus electrode coverage ratio for a minimal length route and a route with static checkpoints attempting to dispense KCl into M4. Probability that a given cycle is monitored c was set to 50% and 100%. The two large dots indicate operating points where the number of checkpoints is constrained to 20.**

15.3.2.1 Fluidic Encryption

Fluidic encryption is a hardware metering technique that requires the end user to apply a fluid-based secret key before use [44]. Application of the wrong key causes the assay to produce erroneous results. The secret key is known only to the biocoder and the end user. This protects the DMFB from unauthorized production and use in a distributed, untrusted supply chain.

Fluidic encryption is based upon the 2-to-1 fluidic multiplexer, which is an operation primitive originally introduced to realize built-in-self-test. Consider an imaginary protocol having two mix operations O_3 and O_5 (Figure 15.13a). Fluids dispensed from O_1 and O_2 first mix, and then mix with O_4. The output of these operations is detected at O_6. To encrypt this protocol, we can insert two fluidic multiplexers (Figure 15.13b). The original dispense operation for O_1 is replaced by the

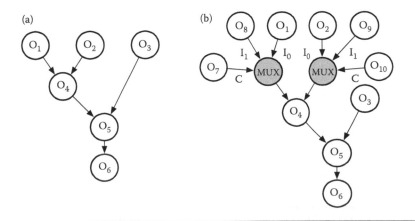

Figure 15.13 **(a) A simple example protocol represented as a sequencing graph. (b) An encrypted version of the same protocol, modified so that the original input fluids may be substituted with an alternate fluid if the correct "key" is not provided.**

fluidic multiplexer which takes a control input fluid O_7 and a secondary fluid O_8. Similarly, O_2 is replaced by a multiplexer accepting O_{10} as control, and O_9 as secondary input. The presence of a fluid at the control port chooses the fluid at input I_0, while the absence of a fluid routes fluid I_1 to the output of the multiplexer. Without the correct application of fluids at these control ports (i.e., the secret key), the protocol will function incorrectly by selecting the wrong fluids.

The fluidic encryption problem can thus be stated: given an assay protocol specification in the form of a sequencing graph G, determine the optimal number and location of fluidic multiplexers to create a related graph $G'(G \in G')$ such that an attacker cannot recover G from G' within reasonable physical constraints. The concept is analogous to logic encryption, where the problem is to place "key gates" in a digital design, but differs in several significant ways. The complexity of DMFB typical protocols and hardware is orders of magnitude lower than those encountered in VLSI design. This can both help and hinder the problem. The size of the key may be limited by the physical size of the DMFB array, potentially limiting security. On the contrary, the limited protocol size greatly limits the design space for placing key primitives.

Realization of a fluidic multiplexer can be achieved through the sequencing graph in Figure 15.14a. Two input droplets arrive at I_1 and I_2. A control fluid is input at C. The fluid is output at vertex X. R represents reference droplets, M is a mix operation, W is a waste storage operation and S is a split. Dotted lines represent a conditional route; droplets are only routed to mix with a stored droplet only if that stored droplet has half volume. If the stored droplet has full volume, it indicates that the control droplet was present. The sequencing graph in Figure 15.14b shows the result when the control fluid is present. Without the control, Figure 15.14c is realized.

Simulation results on *in vitro*, PCR and protein assays [45] demonstrate reasonable overhead; the number of electrodes required to realize the assay increases linearly with the number of multiplexers. Increasing the number of actuations decreases the operating lifetime of a DMFB due to natural wear. From a security standpoint, this is beneficial as this will provide a physical limit to brute-force attacks against the fluidic encryption scheme. Engineering the lifetime of the DMFB through selection of key sizes and dielectric layer properties will thus provide an effective defense against attackers [44].

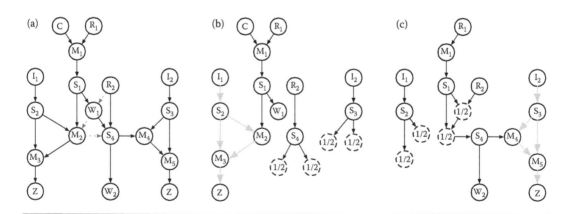

Figure 15.14　**(a) Fluidic multiplexer sequencing graph. Dotted lines are conditional transitions that require full droplet volume to proceed. (b) Realization of the sequencing graph in the presence of the control droplet. 1/2 indicates a half volume droplet. Fluid I_1 is forwarded to Z. (c) Realization in the absence of the control droplet. Fluid I_2 is forwarded to Z.**

15.3.2.2 PUF-Based FSM Locking

A digital rights management scheme based on finite-state machine (FSM) locking and physical unclonable functions (PUFs) has been proposed to prevent piracy of DMFBs [46]. The controller for a DMFB can be implemented as an FSM, where the actuation sequences are determined by the current FSM state. Locking of the FSM is accomplished through the addition of redundant states, while the PUF authenticates the device (Figure 15.15) [47].

A PUF is a hardware primitive leveraging random process variations to generate unique device fingerprints [48]. PUFs are, in theory, unclonable by even the manufacturer, and tamper-evident; any attempt to invasively probe a PUF will alter its characteristics. A PUF interacts through a challenge-response protocol: when a challenge bit string is received, a response bit string is generated. The mapping between challenge-response pairs (CRPs) is unique for each PUF instance, and can thus be used as a way to authenticate devices.

The initial state of a locked FSM is called the *verification state*, which only permits the device to be verified using a PUF. The response of the PUF is used to select state transitions. Only an authentic PUF will generate the correct response to put the FSM into the original states. A license key is XOR'ed with a subset of the PUF response bits to decide the final transitions. Such a locking scheme can be used in practice as follows:

1. The DMFB designer in conjunction with the foundry and tester enrolls the DMFB PUFs in a database.
2. Additional FSM states are added to lock the DMFB.
3. The DMFB is sold to the end user.
4. The biocoder sends a sequencing graph to the biochip designer.
5. The designer uses the database information to "encrypt" the synthesized actuation sequence from the sequencing graph.
6. The encrypted actuation sequence and license are sent to the end user and executed on hardware.

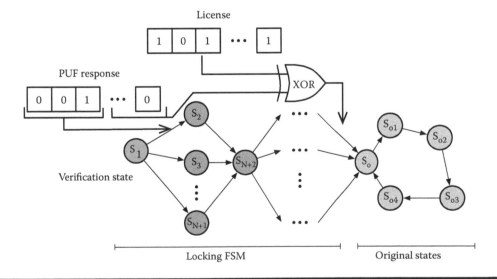

Figure 15.15 Extra states are added to lock the FSM. Transitions between states are controlled by the PUF response.

Table 15.1 Summary of DMFB Properties and Security Challenges and Opportunities

Property	Description	Security Challenges and Opportunities
Low-frequency operation	Due to physical limitations, actuation sequences are necessarily applied at relatively low frequencies, on the order of kHz or less [49].	Slow devices make monitoring easy, and can limit the scope of attacks that drastically alter execution times. Many stealthy attacks are still possible [50], and techniques may yet exist that take advantage of low speed to make executions more tamper-evident.
Visible droplet movement	Execution of assays on DMFBs are often visible with the naked eye.	Can enable technologies to monitor assay progression such as randomized checkpointing with CCD cameras [43].
Reprogrammability	General-purpose DMFBs are attractive for cost reduction by taking advantage of economies of scale.	Arbitrary droplet movement allows attackers to modify assay to cause DoS or subtle errors [31]. Explore intermediates between fully general purpose devices and application specific biochips.
Sensor feedback	A variety of sensors can be integrated onto a biochip to provide feedback on the state of the chip or to measure some property of a droplet, such as for colorimetric assays.	Depending on how sensor is integrated, the reading may be susceptible to tampering. Also, sensor reading is just a number and has no link with the source of the sample droplet. SensorPUF is promising hardware security primitive for "encrypting" readings while ensuring authenticity [51].
Relatively large scale	Loading of reagents/samples onto biochips are necessarily large to interface with the "macro" world.	Large scale makes devices easy to physically tamper with. Devices need to be designed with tamper-resistance in mind, which may occur in a macro/mechanical domain, or using sensors [52].
Low-cost fabrication	DMFBs are increasingly becoming accessible, with new low-cost techniques being developed that utilize PCBs and off-the-shelf components.	Lowering the barrier for entry also makes it easy for inauthentic devices to be fabricated, which can be substituted and lead to lower reliability, quality, or incorrect measurements. PUFs can be made at the PCB level to authenticate genuine devices [53].
High-voltage actuation	Actuation voltages used in electrowetting-on-dielectric devices are often large, in the range of hundreds of volts.	Switching high voltages necessarily produce more electromagnetic noise. This can cause leakage of information in the form of a side-channel, and may be difficult to control until operating voltages can be scaled down.

(Continued)

Table 15.1 (*Continued*) Summary of DMFB Properties and Security Challenges and Opportunities

Property	Description	Security Challenges and Opportunities
Open-source platforms	DropBot [54], UCR Static Synthesis [45,55] are among the first DMFB platforms freely available under open-source licenses.	Open-source hardware and software provides the ability to independently audit the design to see if it follows best practices or contains trojans. Adoption appears to be limited at present, and these platforms are primitive as compared to the state of the art (e.g., no error recovery).
Automation	DMFBs have a rich, established literature on design automation techniques.	A platform that is automated implies the presence of some computational ability; some portion of this computing power can be redirected for security purposes.
High-level synthesis	Assay specifications must go through a synthesis toolchain before usable actuation sequences can be applied to DMFB.	The many software layers in the synthesis toolchain, down to hardware actuation sequences presents opportunities for tampering. Encryption and obfuscation are possible candidates to protect assays from tampering, or from intellectual property theft [32, 44].
One-time use	Biochips are often designed to be single-use to prevent contamination.	Single-use biochips allows usage of weak PUFs, which are limited in the number of challenge-responses [48]. SensorPUFs also become more feasible in the single-use model [51].

The PUF-based locked FSM scheme provides protection against intellectual property theft, counterfeiting, and reverse engineering due to the requirement of a secret key. The PUF used in the scheme can be based upon the DMFB hardware itself—The Route PUF has been proposed to take advantage of natural variations in droplet volume loss during routing. The Split PUF takes advantage of unequal droplet splitting behavior, which arises from electrode characteristic variations [46].

15.4 Challenges and Opportunities

This chapter has described several emerging security threats and countermeasures targeted towards digital microfluidic systems. These preliminary works are diverse in their methods, but share a commonality in that they leverage the unique properties of cyberphysical DMFBs. We summarize some key properties of DMFBs in Table 15.1 and discuss their potential security challenges and opportunities to provide guidance for future research.

15.5 Conclusion

Digital microfluidics has become one of the most successful paradigms for realizing the lab-on-a-chip due to the wealth of computer-aided design knowledge developed over the last decade. Commercial adoption of this technology is well on its way, and continual improvements in these devices promise to revolutionize many application areas that have been hindered by slow processing times and inefficient lab processing protocols. Yet security concerns may potentially impede this progress; emerging threats can have catastrophic or even subtle consequences for end users, which could undermine trust in this new technology. New countermeasures that leverage unique properties of DMFBs are promising, and future research is encouraged to continue to exploit these properties. Security-centric design in DMFBs as it matures and becomes standardized will ensure its continued adoption and success.

References

1. K. Choi, A. H. Ng, R. Fobel, and A. R. Wheeler. Digital microfluidics. *Annual Review of Analytical Chemistry*, **5**:413–440, 2012.
2. R. B. Fair. Digital microfluidics: Is a true lab-on-a-chip possible? *Microfluidics and Nanofluidics*, **3**(3):245–281, 2007.
3. E. Verpoorte and N. F. De Rooij. Microfluidics meets MEMS. *Proceedings of the IEEE*, **91**(6):930–953, 2003.
4. T. Thorsen, S. J. Maerkl, and S. R. Quake. Microfluidic large-scale integration. *Science*, **298**(5593):580–584, 2002.
5. F. Su and K. Chakrabarty. High-level synthesis of digital microfluidic biochips. *ACM Journal on Emerging Technologies in Computing Systems*, **3**(4):1, 2008.
6. T. Xu and K. Chakrabarty. Parallel scan-like test and multiple-defect diagnosis for digital microfluidic biochips. *IEEE Transactions on Biomedical Circuits and Systems*, **1**(2):148–158, 2007.
7. Y. Luo, K. Chakrabarty, and T.-Y. Ho. Error recovery in cyberphysical digital microfluidic biochips. *IEEE Transactions on Computer-Aided Design of Integrated Circuits and Systems*, **32**(1):59–72, 2013.
8. K. Hu, M. Ibrahim, L. Chen, Z. Li, K. Chakrabarty, and R. Fair. Experimental demonstration of error recovery in an integrated cyberphysical digital-microfluidic platform. In *Proceedings of the IEEE Biomedical Circuits and Systems Conference*, pages 1–4, Atlanta, GA, 2015.
9. R. H. Weber. Internet of things—new security and privacy challenges. *Computer Law & Security Review*, **26**(1):23–30, 2010.
10. M. E. Karim and V. V. Phoha. Cyber-physical systems security. In *Applied Cyber-Physical Systems*, pages 75–83. Springer, Berlin, 2014.
11. A. Cardenas, S. Amin, B. Sinopoli, A. Giani, A. Perrig, and S. Sastry. Challenges for securing cyber physical systems. In *Workshop on Future Directions in Cyber-physical Systems Security*, page 5, Newark, NJ, 2009.
12. S. Checkoway, D. McCoy, B. Kantor, D. Anderson, H. Shacham, S. Savage, K. Koscher, A. Czeskis, F. Roesner, T. Kohno. et al. Comprehensive experimental analyses of automotive attack surfaces. In *USENIX Security Symposium*, pages 77–92, San Francisco, CA, 2011.
13. S. Sridhar, A. Hahn, and M. Govindarasu. Cyber–physical system security for the electric power grid. *Proceedings of the IEEE*, **100**(1):210–224, 2012.
14. K. Stouffer, J. Falco, and K. Scarfone. Guide to industrial control systems (ICS) security. *Special Publication (NIST SP) 800-82 Rev 2*, **800**(82):16–16, 2014.
15. M. Rostami, F. Koushanfar, and R. Karri. A primer on hardware security: Models, methods, and metrics. *Proceedings of the IEEE*, **102**(8):1283–1295, 2014.
16. J. Rajendran, O. Sinanoglu, and R. Karri. Regaining trust in VLSI design: Design-for-trust techniques. *Proceedings of the IEEE*, **102**(8):1266–1282, 2014.

17. S. Bhunia, M. S. Hsiao, M. Banga, and S. Narasimhan. Hardware Trojan attacks: Threat analysis and countermeasures. *Proceedings of the IEEE*, **102**(8):1229–1247, 2014.
18. H.-H. Shen, S.-K. Fan, C.-J. Kim, and D.-J. Yao. EWOD microfluidic systems for biomedical applications. *Microfluidics and Nanofluidics*, **16**(5):965–987, 2014.
19. M. Ibrahim, K. Chakrabarty, and U. Schlichtmann. CoSyn: Efficient single-cell analysis using a hybrid microfluidic platform. In *Proceedings of the Design, Automation and Test in Europe Conference*, pages 1673–1678, Lausanne, Switzerland, 2017.
20. W. C. Nelson and C.-J. C. Kim. Droplet actuation by electrowetting-on-dielectric (EWOD): A review. *Journal of Adhesion Science and Technology*, **26**(12–17):1747–1771, 2012.
21. F. Mugele and J.-C. Baret. Electrowetting: From basics to applications. *Journal of Physics: Condensed Matter*, **17**(28):R705, 2005.
22. S. K. Cho, H. Moon, and C.-J. Kim. Creating, transporting, cutting, and merging liquid droplets by electrowetting-based actuation for digital microfluidic circuits. *Journal of Microelectromechanical Systems*, **12**(1):70–80, 2003.
23. V. Ananthanarayanan and W. Thies. Biocoder: A programming language for standardizing and automating biology protocols. *Journal of Biological Engineering*, **4**(1):13, 2010.
24. F. Su and K. Chakrabarty. Architectural-level synthesis of digital microfluidics-based biochips. In *Proceedings of the IEEE/ACM International Conference on Computer-Aided Design*, pages 223–228. IEEE Computer Society, New York, NY, 2004.
25. F. Su and K. Chakrabarty. Unified high-level synthesis and module placement for defect-tolerant microfluidic biochips. In *Proceedings of the Design Automation Conference*, pages 825–830. ACM, New York, NY, 2005.
26. F. Su, W. Hwang, and K. Chakrabarty. Droplet routing in the synthesis of digital microfluidic biochips. In *Proceedings of the Design, Automation and Test in Europe Conference*, Vol. **1**, 1–6. IEEE, New York, NY, 2006.
27. Z. Li, K. Y.-T. Lai, P.-H. Yu, T.-Y. Ho, K. Chakrabarty, and C.-Y. Lee. High-level synthesis for microelectrode-dot-array digital microfluidic biochips. In *Proceedings of the Design Automation Conference*, page 146. ACM, New York, NY, 2016.
28. Y. Luo, K. Chakrabarty, and T.-Y. Ho. Real-time error recovery in cyberphysical digital-microfluidic biochips using a compact dictionary. *IEEE Transactions on Computer-Aided Design of Integrated Circuits and Systems*, **32**(12):1839–1852, 2013.
29. T. Xu and K. Chakrabarty. Functional testing of digital microfluidic biochips. In *Proceedings of the IEEE International Test Conference*, pages 1–10. IEEE, New York, NY, 2007.
30. D. T. Grissom and P. Brisk. Fast online synthesis of digital microfluidic biochips. *IEEE Transactions on Computer-Aided Design of Integrated Circuits and Systems*, **33**(3):356–369, 2014.
31. S. S. Ali, M. Ibrahim, O. Sinanoglu, K. Chakrabarty, and R. Karri. Security assessment of cyberphysical digital microfluidic biochips. *IEEE/ACM Transactions on Computational Biology and Bioinformatics*, **13**(3):445–458, 2016.
32. S. S. Ali, M. Ibrahim, J. Rajendran, O. Sinanoglu, and K. Chakrabarty. Supply-chain security of digital microfluidic biochips. *Computer*, **49**(8):36–43, 2016.
33. C. C.-Y. Lin and Y.-W. Chang. Cross-contamination aware design methodology for pin-constrained digital microfluidic biochips. *IEEE Transactions on Computer-Aided Design of Integrated Circuits and Systems*, **30**(6):817–828, 2011.
34. V. Srinivasan, V. K. Pamula, and R. B. Fair. Droplet-based microfluidic lab-on-a-chip for glucose detection. *Analytica Chimica Acta*, **507**(1):145–150, 2004.
35. U. Guin, K. Huang, D. DiMase, J. M. Carulli, M. Tehranipoor, and Y. Makris. Counterfeit integrated circuits: A rising threat in the global semiconductor supply chain. *Proceedings of the IEEE*, **102**(8): 1207–1228, 2014.
36. J. A. Roy, F. Koushanfar, and I. L. Markov. Ending piracy of integrated circuits. *Computer*, **43**(10): 30–38, 2010.
37. U.S.D.S.B.T.F. on High Performance Microchip Supply. *Defense Science Board Task Force on High Performance Microchip Supply*. Office of the Under Secretary of Defense for Acquisition, Technology, and Logistics, 2005.

38. M. Pecht and S. Tiku. Bogus: Electronic manufacturing and consumers confront a rising tide of counterfeit electronics. *IEEE Spectrum*, **43**(5):37–46, 2006.

39. M. Zhang, A. Raghunathan, and N. K. Jha. Trustworthiness of medical devices and body area networks. *Proceedings of the IEEE*, **102**(8):1174–1188, 2014.

40. M. Joye and F. Olivier. Side-channel analysis. In *Encyclopedia of Cryptography and Security*, pages 1198–1204. Springer, Berlin, 2011.

41. H. Bar-El, H. Choukri, D. Naccache, M. Tunstall, and C. Whelan. The sorcerer's apprentice guide to fault attacks. *Proceedings of the IEEE*, **94**(2):370–382, 2006.

42. R. Higuchi, C. Fockler, G. Dollinger, and R. Watson. Kinetic PCR analysis: Real-time monitoring of DNA amplification reactions. *Biotechnology*, **11**:1026–1030, 1993.

43. J. Tang, R. Karri, M. Ibrahim, and K. Chakrabarty. Securing digital microfluidic biochips by randomizing checkpoints. In *Proceedings of the IEEE International Test Conference*, pages 1–8. IEEE, New York, NY, 2016.

44. S. S. Ali, M. Ibrahim, O. Sinanoglu, K. Chakrabarty, and R. Karri. Microfluidic encryption of on-chip biochemical assays. In *Proceedings of the IEEE Biomedical Circuits and Systems Conference*, pages 152–155. IEEE, New York, NY, 2016.

45. D. Grissom, K. O'Neal, B. Preciado, H. Patel, R. Doherty, N. Liao, and P. Brisk. A digital microfluidic biochip synthesis framework. In *Proceedings of the IEEE/IFIP International Conference on VLSI and System-on-Chip*, pages 177–182, Santa Cruz, CA, 2012.

46. C.-W. Hsieh, Z. Li, and T.-Y. Ho. Piracy prevention of digital microfluidic biochips. In *Proceedings of the Asia and South Pacific Design Automation Conference*, pages 512–517. IEEE, New York, NY, 2017.

47. J. Zhang, Y. Lin, Y. Lyu, and G. Qu. A PUF-FSM binding scheme for FPGA IP protection and pay-per-device licensing. *IEEE Transactions on Information Forensics and Security*, **10**(6):1137–1150, 2015.

48. C. Herder, M.-D. Yu, F. Koushanfar, and S. Devadas. Physical unclonable functions and applications: A tutorial. *Proceedings of the IEEE*, **102**(8):1126–1141, 2014.

49. V. Srinivasan, V. K. Pamula, and R. B. Fair. An integrated digital microfluidic lab-on-a-chip for clinical diagnostics on human physiological fluids. *Lab on a Chip*, **4**(4):310–315, 2004.

50. S. S. Ali, M. Ibrahim, O. Sinanoglu, K. Chakrabarty, and R. Karri. Security assessment of cyberphysical digital microfluidic biochips. *IEEE/ACM Transactions Computational Biology and Bioinformatics*, **13**(3):1–14, 2015.

51. K. Rosenfeld, E. Gavas, and R. Karri. Sensor physical unclonable functions. In *Proceedings of the IEEE International Symposium on Hardware-Oriented Security and Trust*, pages 112–117. IEEE, New York, NY, 2010.

52. D. Shahrjerdi, J. Rajendran, S. Garg, F. Koushanfar, and R. Karri. Shielding and securing integrated circuits with sensors. In *Proceedings of the IEEE/ACM International Conference on Computer-Aided Design*, pages 170–174. IEEE Press, New York, NY, 2014.

53. L. Wei, C. Song, Y. Liu, J. Zhang, F. Yuan, and Q. Xu. BoardPUF: Physical unclonable functions for printed circuit board authentication. In *Proceedings of the IEEE/ACM International Conference on Computer-Aided Design*, pages 152–158. IEEE, New York, NY, 2015.

54. R. Fobel, C. Fobel, and A. R. Wheeler. DropBot: An open-source digital microfluidic control system with precise control of electrostatic driving force and instantaneous drop velocity measurement. *Applied Physics Letters*, **102**(19):193513, 2013.

55. D. Grissom, C. Curtis, S. Windh, C. Phung, N. Kumar, Z. Zimmerman, O. Kenneth, J. McDaniel, N. Liao, and P. Brisk. An open-source compiler and PCB synthesis tool for digital microfluidic biochips. *INTEGRATION, the VLSI Journal*, **51**:169–193, 2015.

Chapter 16

Nanoelectromechanical Systems Secure FPGA and Security Primitives

Philip X.-L. Feng and Swarup Bhunia

Contents

Emerging nanoscale devices with distinctive properties are poised to impact the design of secure systems in profound and unanticipated ways. First, properties of these devices (e.g., large and unpredictable variations, possibly accelerated aging, power and timing asymmetry, and nonvolatility) could lead to new attack modalities or render hitherto acceptable defenses against known attacks ineffective. Second, new defense mechanisms or drastic improvements in today's existing hardware-based security, for example, entirely new designs for random number generators (RNGs) and physical unclonable functions (PUFs), may be enabled by the unique and individually distinctive characteristics of nanoscale devices. Therefore, there is a critical need to evaluate security properties of integrated systems and explore novel secure and trusted hardware solutions in the context of nanoscale devices.

Nanoelectromechanical systems (NEMS) are distinguished by their electromechanical actuation and mechanical transition properties. They originate from the logical miniaturization steps following the so-called microelectromechanical systems, or MEMS devices. Spurred by advancements in reliably fabricating and manipulating mechanically active nanostructures, recently NEMS devices have been explored as logic building blocks, including single switches, logic gates [1–11], and nonvolatile memories [12] as well as a wide array of sensing applications [13] where physical movement or resonances of MEMS/NEMS cantilever structures are used to sense motions and other parameters. Consequently, these devices have been extensively used in accelerometer, gyro and multitude of other sensors used in diverse applications including cell phones, biomedical instruments, and military systems. NEMS devices with truly nanoscale dimensions and capability for reliable long-term (>21 billion cycles [1]) low-voltage operation have been recently demonstrated. Furthermore, NEMS are amenable for large-scale batch fabrication using the CMOS-compatible lithographic process steps [5–8]. Advancements in NEMS device design, fabrication, and characterization steps and their distinctive beneficial properties make them a promising computing as well as sensing device technology in the beyond-CMOS era.

In this chapter, we first present and analyze properties of NEMS devices with respect to security applications and investigate novel applications of NEMS devices in implementing high-quality

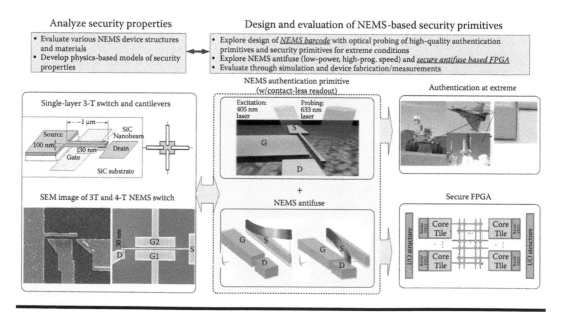

Figure 16.1 Conceptual synopsis and illustration of NEMS-enabled security primitives and their perspectives and potential impact. This vision will be enabled by comprehensive study and evaluation of security-relevant characteristics of NEMS of various geometries and dimensions and investigation on novel hardware security primitive designs using NEMS. In particular, in this chapter, we investigate NEMS antifuse design and its application in secure FPGA. We also explore designs of NEMS barcode using an array of NEMS resonators with optical readout of their resonance frequencies.

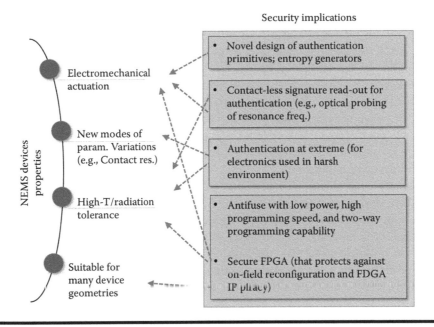

Figure 16.2 Key distinctive properties of NEMS devices, which can have significant implications in secure system design for diverse applications, particularly for applications (e.g., high-temperature) where conventional electronics would fail.

hardware security primitives with unique beneficial properties, which are difficult or impossible to achieve with alternative nanoscale devices. These security primitives can potentially serve as the backbone of hardware root-of-trust. We note that NEMS devices, when combined with judicious choice of materials and device geometries, enable the creation of security primitives/components of unique properties (Figure 16.1). Figure 16.2 illustrates these properties and their implications for enabling new hardware security features and functionalities. Key NEMS device properties, which can have profound implications in secure and trustworthy computing systems, are (1) both process-induced and temporal variability in device properties, which are amenable to various forms of measurements including optical readout; (2) ability of NEMS devices to function at extremely harsh conditions (high temperature beyond 250°C and high radiation up to 30 Mrad); (3) electromechanical actuation that may enable unprecedented defense mechanisms, for example, novel antifuses, which are robust against tampering attacks and which can be used as essential building blocks for secure field programmable gate arrays (FPGA); and (4) flexibility to easily create various device geometries and dimensions to adapt to design requirements. Extensive study of the security implications of these distinctive device properties and their roles in enabling novel security primitives/components can create new avenues of building secure and trustworthy hardware.

Security primitives that can function reliably at temperature beyond 250°C and high radiation (up to 30 Mrad) can be extremely useful in diverse applications, ranging from aerospace, automotive, energy production, geothermal explorations, and industrial systems [1–3,5,9]. For example, intelligent propulsion systems, spacecraft for Venus exploration, and active combustion control require prolonged operations of the sensors and associated circuits at temperatures exceeding 500°C. On the other hand, electronics in many automotive and industrial systems typically require operating in a temperature range of 250–350°C. Similarly, electronics for use in outer space, high-altitude flight, nuclear reactors, particle accelerators, or during nuclear accidents or nuclear warfare would require tolerating high radiation (particle radiation and high-energy electromagnetic radiation) [14]. Conventional Si-based security primitives fail to operate at such extreme condition, due to device failures resulting from excessive leakage caused by p–n junction degradation and thermionic leakage [15]. The situation is aggravated due to self-heating effect of conventional field effect transistor (FET) devices. Even though such high temperatures and radiation are not typically encountered by consumer electronics, they are unavoidable in multitude of niche applications, which include integrated sensors, electronics, and packaging capable of operating in extreme environments. These applications can essentially benefit from security primitives for secure trusted operations and data communication.

The major challenge in designing hardware-based security primitives with NEMS devices lies in understanding device behavior that can be utilized to build these primitives. Although NEMS devices of various types have been analyzed through theoretical studies as well as experimental characterization for computing and sensing applications, they mostly have *not* yet been studied with security in mind. In particular, the nature and modes of variability in NEMS devices can have profound implications in designing primitives for cryptographic applications, for example, RNGs. Similarly, electrostatic actuation mechanism of NEMS cantilever can be tailored to implement NEMS antifuses which can serve as building blocks for secure FPGA. These features are not adequately studied in previous research. Manufacturing yield and reliable long-term operations of NEMS devices are fundamental issues in circuit structures made with these devices. Judicious choice of NEMS materials as well as exploration of optimal device geometries/dimensions can greatly improve the yield and run-time reliability of these structures. Finally, device aging and other temporal variations in NEMS structures can have significant impact on the properties of security primitives. In particular, for high-temperature applications, temporal variations in device property can be a major issue. To address these issues, efforts need to be dedicated to joint explorations of NEMS materials, device structures, and circuit/architecture-level design options.

16.1 Nanoelectromechanical Building Blocks

Although security primitive design and characterization using conventional CMOS technology have been addressed by researchers and practitioners for decades, the task of leveraging the unique characteristics of emerging nanoscale devices to design secure systems is relatively new. Research efforts in this domain are sporadic, and they primarily involve study on few specific devices, namely, spintronic [16,17] and resistive devices [18,19], due in large part to availability of device data/models relevant to their security properties (e.g., variability). NEMS switch design and their possible hybridization with CMOS electronics for minimizing leakage have been widely explored in recent times [1–4]. A new class of devices, referred to as MEMFET and MEMSET, has been developed to design digital logic circuits for low-leakage low-voltage applications [20,21]. NEMS switches have also been explored for high-density nonvolatile memory design [22,23]. However, to our knowledge, comprehensive analysis of security properties of NEMS devices and design/evaluation of NEMS-based security primitives have not been addressed. A recent publication [24] reports the use of photodetector sensors or NEMS-based sensors to detect physical tampering of electronic components. This work, however, does not target building novel NEMS-based security primitives for major security applications including authentication and secure reconfigurable computing (FPGA), which are the focus of the current effort. In recent collaborative research, the authors and their coworkers have pioneered the study of SiC NEMS logic devices and have made important breakthroughs in recent years. In particular, in SiC NEMS logic switches, we have accomplished a number of highly relevant achievements with very encouraging results [1–11,25–30].

16.1.1 Abrupt Logic Switches

Figure 16.3 shows the characteristic abrupt switching behavior of NEMS logic switches. The measurement system is carefully calibrated for low-noise, high-precision measurement, capable of monitoring device operation with very low current levels (quiet switching cycles, with current from hundreds of fA to tens of nA) [5–8].

We record detailed information of device switching quietly, with on-state current sometimes even lower than the noise floor of many other measurement systems (which are thus unable to detect device switching). Such high-precision measurements allow us to extract the basic parameter of SiC NEMS logic switch operation, such as the threshold switch-on voltage V_{on}, the switch-off voltage V_{off}, the on-state drain current I_{on}, the off-state drain current I_{off}, and gate leak current I_G.

16.1.2 Long-Cycle Operations in Ambient Air and at High Temperature

We investigate SiC NEMS switch lifetime by switching the device on and off for long cycles and carefully monitoring its response [5–8]. Figure 16.4 shows $>10^4$ switching cycles recorded for a device. We measure ambient air and program resting period between cycles, simulating realistic switch operations. We also monitor the $I–V$ curve hysteresis between cycles to study the evolution of switching parameters such as V_{on}, I_{on}, and contact resistance R_{on}. SiC is one of the best materials for high-temperature electronics. We have demonstrated high-temperature operations of SiC

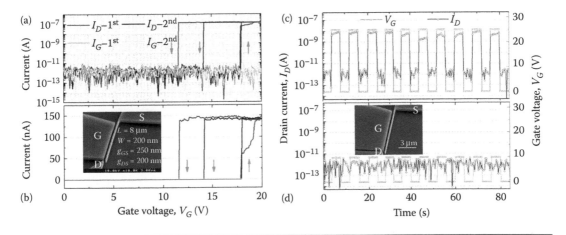

Figure 16.3 **SiC NEMS switches: a representative example of clear and repeatable switching behavior of three-terminal (3-T) SiC NEMS switches. (a,b) First two switching cycles with hysteresis, measured in another SiC NEMS switch, with currents in logarithmic scale (a) and linear scale (b), respectively. Inset of (b) is an SEM image of the actual device. (c,d) Representative data selected from a long-cycle high-precision measurement (recorded over consecutive days). (c) The waveforms show SiC NEMS switch operating multiple cycles following the applied gate voltage waveform ($V_{G,pk} > V_{on}$). (d) The clear control experiment where no mechanical switching happens at a subthreshold gate voltage ($V_{G,pk} < V_{on}$).**

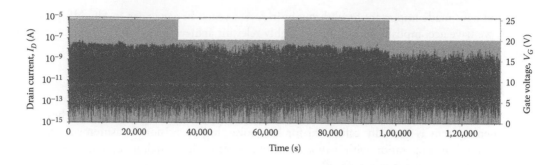

Figure 16.4 **Over 14,000 switching cycles recorded in real time over 7 consecutive days (idle time not plotted). Blue, drain current I_D; Magenta, actuation voltage.**

NEMS switches in ambient air. We observe clear, abrupt switching at 500°C with both three- and four-terminal (3-T and 4-T) devices [5,6,8].

16.1.3 Logic Circuit Implementation with NEMS Switches

Using the robust SiC NEMS switches as building blocks, we construct pure mechanical logic gates. Figure 16.5 shows the logic OR and NOR gates realized with our SiC NEMS switches. The measured data show designed logic functions in multiple cycles [8].

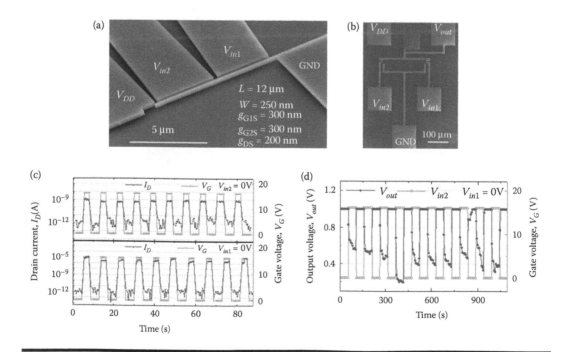

Figure 16.5 **SiC NEMS logic circuits. (a,b) Logic OR and NOR functions realized by NEMS switches, respectively. (c,d) Measured logic OR and NOR gate output with respect to the inputs.**

16.2 NEMS Antifuse for Secure FPGA

16.2.1 Antifuse and FPGA

FPGAs are integrated circuits that are prefabricated to be electrically programmed and configured in the field to serve individual users' different needs for digital circuits or systems [31]. The key feature of FPGAs compared to application specific integrated circuits (ASICs) is the reconfigurability or programmability. The FPGA is able to implement a new function on the chip after it is fabricated by the manufacturers. Because of this feature, FPGAs are often preferred in situations that call for low-volume units with lower cost and shorter time to deployment, as compared to ASICs that would normally require more time and invest to develop a prototype. However, in order to have a fully flexible circuit that can be configured to satisfy all the needs from various users, today's FPGAs are significantly larger, slower, and more power consuming than their ASIC counterparts. At the device level, the fundamental cause of these limitations lies in the structure of the FPGAs.

An FPGA typically consists of three components: programmable logic blocks that implement various logic functions, programmable routing that connects these logic functions, and I/O blocks that are connected to logic blocks through routing interconnect and make input/output of chip connection. Among the three, the programmable routing interconnect comprises almost 90% of the total chip area, and thus contributes to most of the delay, area, and power consumption. Typically, an FPGA uses 20 to over 100 interconnects per logic gate to link logic blocks [32].

Antifuses are among the commonly used interconnect devices for FPGAs. An antifuse is a one-time-programmable (OTP), two-terminal (2-T) device that has high initial resistance (e.g., open circuit) till a programming voltage changes it to low resistance in an irreversible process [32–36]. It has been extensively employed as an economical and convenient solution in complex logic ICs for improved functionality and flexibility, and thus widely used in nonvolatile memories and OTP secure FPGAs [37–40]. Compared to other FPGA programmable interconnect devices such as SRAM-controlled pass transistors [41] and EPROMs [42], antifuse interconnects offer smaller size, faster programming, lower programmed resistance and lower parasitic capacitance [43,44]. In particular, antifuse-based FPGAs offer higher security, stemming primarily from their nonvolatility [44]. It secures a design due to piracy and difficulty in determining the state of an antifuse that protects against direct physical attack [45]. Figure 16.6 presents the architecture of a commercial antifuse FPGA. The major components are core tiles, which contain the logic blocks, RAMs and data buffering for data storage, and I/O structure for data input and output. The core tiles are linked by antifuses as interconnects.

While antifuse-based FPGAs are currently among the most secure programmable devices available [45], limitations and challenges remain in high leakage power, increasing security requirements (e.g., against potential attack in the form of reprogramming), and scalability to advanced technology nodes. Many critical defense and aerospace applications drive great demands for devices with higher programming speed, lower power, increasing tolerance to radiation [46,47] and harsh environment, and higher resistance to attacks.

A conventional antifuse consists of a dielectric layer sandwiched between two electrodes as shown in Figure 16.7a. Commonly used implementations include n+ diffusion/oxide–nitride–oxide (ONO) dielectrics/poly-silicon [33,48], metal-to-metal structures [49–51], and amorphous silicon/metal structures [52,53].

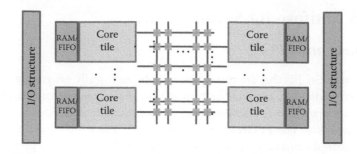

Figure 16.6   Schematic architecture of Microsemi Axcelerator antifuse FPGA. The major components include core tiles containing the logic blocks, RAMs, and data buffering for storage and I/O structure for inputs and outputs. Green squares are antifuses; FIFO stands for first-in and first-out.

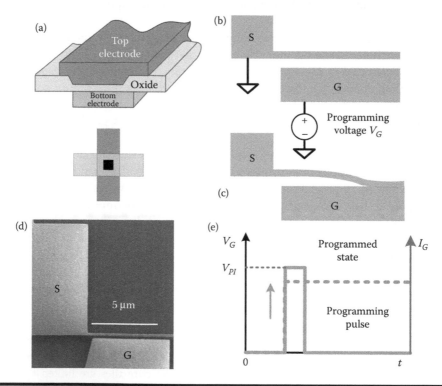

Figure 16.7   NEMS-enabled antifuse design and operation principle. (a) Conventional antifuse device structure and top view. (b) Unprogrammed NEMS antifuse and the programming scheme. (c) Programmed NEMS antifuse, with S permanently connected to G upon first programming event. (d) SEM image of an SiC NEMS antifuse. (e) Expected *I* curve (red dashed line) as we apply the gate voltage V_G (green solid line) in programming cycle. V_{PI} is the minimum programming voltage required.

16.2.2 NEMS Antifuse

Spurred by advancements in reliably fabricating and manipulating mechanically active nanostructures, recently NEMS have been explored as logic building blocks, including single switches, logic gates [8], and nonvolatile memories [12,54]. NEMS antifuses offer intrinsically strong and ideal insulation at off state with air gaps separating electrodes, instant programming via abrupt switching, low programming voltage, and robust nonvolatile programmed state. In particular, SiC NEMS exploit the outstanding thermal and mechanical properties of this technologically important material for reliable performance even in harsh environments (e.g., high temperature, radiation) [8]. Established thin-film technologies make SiC NEMS on various substrates [55]. SiC is especially suited for NEMS antifuses also thanks to its exceptional ability in carrying high current; SiC can hardly be fused even at very high current levels. In this work, we demonstrate very-low-voltage SiC NEMS antifuses for the first time and show significant enhancement in energy efficiency in FPGA designs enabled by such NEMS antifuses.

The NEMS antifuse is based on electrostatically actuated SiC nanocantilevers illustrated in Figure 16.7b and c. It is a two-terminal (2-T) device in lateral configuration, with a fixed electrode gate (G) for programming and a movable nanocantilever as source (S), separated by an air gap. At the initial (unprogrammed) state, G and S form an open circuit. A programming voltage applied between G and S actuates the device to connect G and S (i.e., to *program* the antifuse). In contrast to three-terminal (3-T) NEMS logic switches [8], in antifuses we *exploit* adhesion forces to keep G and S connected *after programming* (which must be *avoided* in three-terminal NEMS logic switches [8]).

We have studied the programming of NEMS antifuse and have compared the initial state with programmed state. The characteristics of the SiC NEMS antifuses are investigated by high-precision $I-V$ measurements using a source measurement unit (SMU) shown in Figure 16.8a.

Prior to programming, the NEMS antifuse is in its initial state, which is open, with high resistance of >10 GΩ. The current increases abruptly at $V_{PI} = 4.3$ V, showing instant programming via NEMS contact. As V_G sweeps back to 0 V, the antifuse stays connected with on-state current $I_{on} \geq 1$ μA, which is the current measurement compliance we manually set. We sweep V_G again after the programming cycle on the NEMS antifuse whose state has been changed to programmed, and observe resistive behavior from the $I-V$ curve in Figure 16.7d and e.

The NEMS antifuse can have very low programming voltage and high on/off ratios. In recent studies, our collaborative team has demonstrated NEMS antifuses with ultralow programming voltage at $V_{PI} = 1.6$ V. The nonvolatility is demonstrated as it stays connected with high I_{on} (≥ 1 μA) as V_G sweeps back to 0 V. The gate leakage observed in some of these devices is not fundamental to this type of devices, but is caused by local defects in the SiO_2 layer underneath this specific SiC device (which happens to be on top of a region of nonideal SiO_2 with defects). With good insulating layers, the devices show low programming voltages, without any measurable gate leakage.

To study the on/off ratio between unprogrammed and programmed device, we apply the same stress voltage sweep on an unprogrammed NEMS antifuse and an already programmed antifuse, and the currents are plotted in Figure 16.9. Under the same applied stress voltage, the on/off current ratio is $>10^7$, showing that NEMS antifuses provide excellent insulation when unprogrammed and stable connection after being programmed. This margin leaves a sufficient space for designers to define the on/off state using these devices in logic circuits and FPGAs.

16.2.3 NEMS Antifuse OTP FPGA

Next, we discuss antifuse-based FPGA designs and simulations using specialized software for the FPGA-based logic design, synthesis, and simulation. We first compare NEMS antifuse with conventional antifuse at single device level, then we simulate and analyze the system-level power performance in a large-scale system on an FPGA platform.

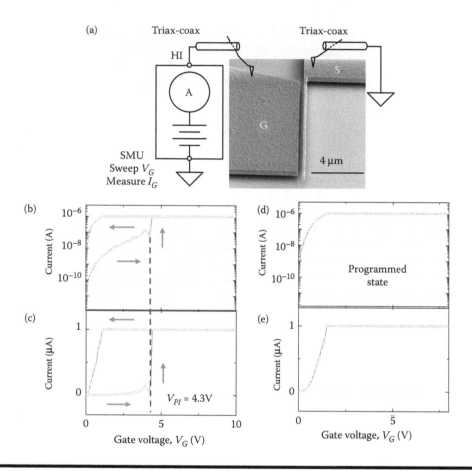

Figure 16.8 SiC NEMS antifuse programming cycles. Data show the first and second cycle of the device. (a) Schematic of the measurement system with SEM image of an NEMS antifuse. (b,c) Programming cycle of NEMS antifuse: sweeping the gate voltage V_G to above V_{PI} and back. (d,e) Apply the same sweeping gate voltages after the programming cycle, showing the connection is irreversible. Currents are plotted (b,d) in logarithmic scale and (c,e) in linear scale.

The NEMS antifuse is a promising candidate for OTP FPGA thanks to its minimal leakage power, high programming speed, and small and scalable volume. Table 16.1 summarizes the comparison of the SiC NEMS antifuses *versus* conventional antifuses at the single device level. The leakage current I_{leak} for unprogrammed antifuses is obtained at the same conditions. Both devices are tested with stress voltage of 3.6 V at 25°C. Note that for some of the antifuse devices fabricated, some leakage comes from the defects in oxide layer, which can be alleviated by using high-quality insulator in the fabrication.

NEMS antifuse has the intrinsic advantage of near-zero leakage or off-state current due to the air gaps in the device structure. The measured off-state current is as low as 10 fA, which is the noise floor of the measurement system. This indicates that the ultimate leakage or off-state current is well below this level. The programming voltage can be as low as 1.6 V and can be scaled down by scaling the actuation gaps. A <50 nm actuation gap is reported [10] with similar fabrication techniques. The active area for NEMS antifuses is estimated by including the actuation gaps, G and cantilever beam width but no connecting pads, which are only needed for accessing individual

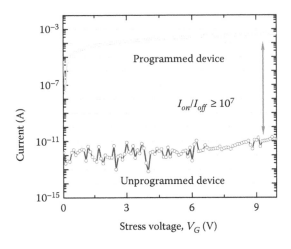

Figure 16.9 Stress voltage sweep on programmed and unprogrammed NEMS antifuse showing a large on/off ratio between programmed/unprogrammed interconnect devices.

Table 16.1 Comparison of NEMS Antifuse and Conventional Antifuse

Properties/Features	NEMS Antifuse	Conventional Antifuse
Leakage (unprogrammed)[a]	$\leq$0.1–1 pA/μm^{2}[b]	20 pA/μm^2 [49]
Program speed/time	1–300 ns/bit	50 μs/bit–50 ms/bit
Program voltage	1–10 V	5–15 V [56]
Highest current density	10^5–10^6 A/cm^2	800–10^6 A/cm^2
Operating temperature	25–500°C	25–125°C
Radiation resistance	High	Low [46]
Active area[c]	0.001–2.5 μm^2	0.4–21 μm^2 [35]
Device volume	0.01–1 μm^3	0.1–3 μm^3 [57]
Bi-directionality?	Yes	No

[a] Leakage current obtained with 3.6 V stress voltage at 25°C.
[b] Ultimate leakage current is well below the noise floor of measurement system.
[c] Active areas do not include connecting pads for both NEMS and conventional devices, for fair comparison. NEMS cantilevers can be made with dimensions of $L \times w \times t$=1 μm $\times$ 50 nm $\times$ 50 nm and smaller, with coupling gaps <50 nm [10].

devices in the characterization stage. For large network of antifuses, the pads can be eliminated to achieve large-scale integration. The device volume is calculated by multiplying the active area and the SiC film thickness.

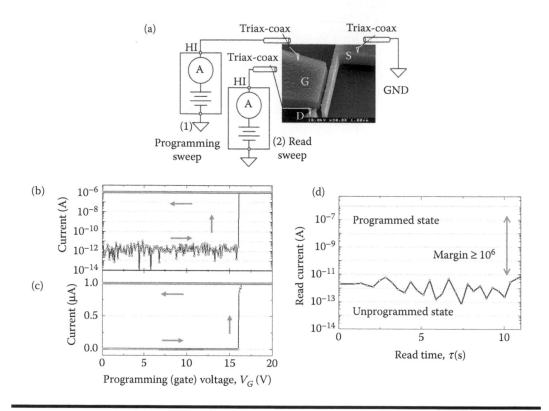

Figure 16.10 NEMS OTP memory cell. (a) Programming scheme (1) and read scheme (2). (b) and (c) Programming cycle through G with scheme (1). (d) Read sweep before/after programming cycle in showing large read margin between the programmed/unprogrammed memory cell, showing a read margin of over 6 orders of magnitude.

The growing market for products that require code storage and customized settings drives great demand for nonvolatile memory (NVM) and therefore high-density and low-power logic NVM solutions. Among them, antifuse-based OTP memories provide better compatibility with scaled CMOS process while maintaining highly reliable long-term data retention. We implement an OTP memory cell based on SiC NEMS antifuse with demonstrated writing and reading cycles (Figure 16.10) [58]. The read current margin between programmed state and unprogrammed state of the same NEMS antifuse OTP memory is measured to be more than 6 orders of magnitude, offering circuit designer a sufficient design margin when using NEMS antifuse-based OTP memory cell [58].

16.3 Resonant NEMS PUFs for Noninvasive Hardware Authentication

In parallel to the contact-mode NEMS switches and antifuses are dynamic NEMS that operate with their resonance modes. These NEMS resonators offer new suites of security-relevant characteristics that have largely not yet been explored, including resonances sensitive to external physical disturbances, multiple resonances with engineerable mode sequences and mode spacing and splitting, rich and abundant spatially resolvable multimode shapes, complex nonlinear dynamics and coupling effects, engineerable energy dissipation processes in different modes, etc. We thus envision the resonant NEMS as an entirely new platform that is essentially a multimodal, multiparameter carrier of tokens or information, and thus a unique system for enabling new unique objects (UNOs) and physically unclonable functions (PUFs). In this chapter, we first preview the principles and possibilities of demonstrating specifically designed resonant NEMS [11,59] as security primitives toward engineerable UNOs and PUFs.

16.3.1 NEMS Operating Near Resonance

To further increase the operating speed of the SiC NEMS switches to approach their intrinsic speed and study the dynamic behavior of nanocontacts, we have developed a technique to directly probe the motion of the cantilever tip with laser interferometry shown in Figure 16.11. This technique is much less destructive as no current passes through the switch during contact, and the impact force is much smaller compared to the lower speed operation. We first use a modulated laser to excite the cantilever beam to vibrate near its resonance frequency and read out the tip motion with a second laser. We also actuate the switch electrostatically while adjusting the motion amplitude and monitoring the switch closely until it makes contact with the drain. This technique allows us to actuate the switch at high speed ($\sim$2–20 MHz) with mV voltages for $>10^{10}$ cycles without failure [11].

16.3.2 NEMS Resonators as New UNOs and PUFs

As illustrated in Figure 16.11, noninvasive optical readout of simple, singly clamped NEMS cantilever beams can reveal unique signatures of these NEMS devices. These can directly serve as UNOs and PUFs. These cantilever devices can nowadays be made by routine surface micro/nanomachining and are among the simplest NEMS. Even in such simple systems [11], we have rich freedom in designing secure PUFs. For example, as shown in Figure 16.12a, the 10-μm-long cantilever has two fundamental NEMS resonances that can be very easily readout with strong signals, for both in-plane and out-of-plane modes. These modes, their characteristics (e.g., resonance frequency f_{res} values), and their splitting values can all be readily exploited and engineered as PUFs. As shown in Figure 16.12b, by varying the design parameters, we can also tune the signatures of these NEMS resonators as we desire.

16.3.3 Multimode Resonators and Their Structural Features as New UNOs and PUFs

The multimode resonances can be used to identify geometrical defects that are invisible/inaccessible to other physical probes, such as electron/optical imaging or surface scanning probes. The relative spacing between the different resonant modes is extremely sensitive to the detailed structure of the NEMS resonator, and thus can sense the slightest deviation from ideal structure. In particular, the degenerate modes (that has nominally identical frequency under perfectly symmetric geometry) will split in frequency, which gives clear indication of the asymmetry in the device structure. Further, the magnitude of frequency splitting can be used to quantify the amount of deviation from the ideal structure (Figure 16.13a) [59], and thus provides unambiguous identification of different devices.

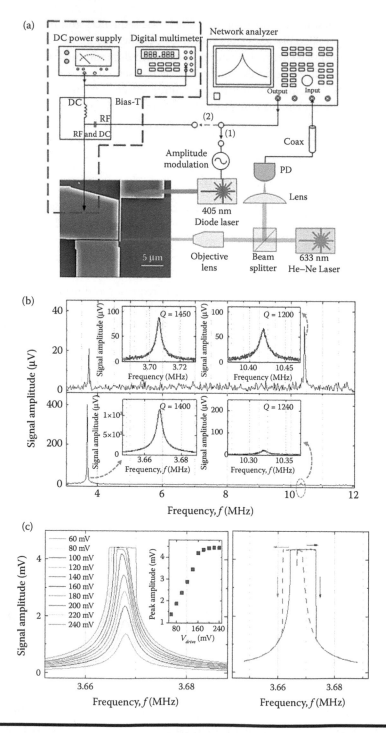

Figure 16.11 **Interrogating the dynamical behavior of the SiC NEMS contacts. (a) Schematic of the optoelectronic measurement system. (b) Measured responses from optical and electrostatic excitations. (c) Frequency-domain probing of the nanocontact dynamics, with nanocantilever tip approaching and tapping the contact (drain) electrode.**

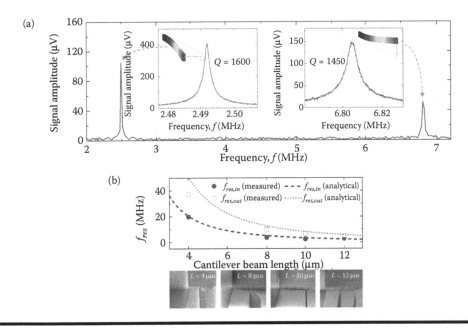

Figure 16.12 **Measured resonances from an $L\approx10\,\mu m$ SiC cantilever ($w\approx200\,nm$, $t\approx500\,nm$).** **(a) Wide-range frequency spectrum shows resonances from both in-plane ($f_{res} = 2.492\,MHz$) and out-of-plane ($f_{res} = 6.802\,MHz$) modes.** *Insets*: **Enlarged view of the two modes with illustrations of the mode shapes. (b) Effect of varying cantilever length on measured f_{res} values for both modes. The insets show the SEM images of devices with different lengths measured in preliminary study.**

The high sensitivity of the frequency ratio between the different resonant modes ensures that any tampering or disturbance to the device will be detected. Such disturbance includes, but is not limited to, adsorption of additional mass, removal of any device volume/mass [60], deformation of device, change in elastic properties (as a result of, e.g., chemical alternation), etc. The multimode nature is critical to this unique property: if only one mode is monitored, then it is possible to physically alter the device while keeping the resonance frequency unchanged. For example, additional mass may be loaded onto the resonator without affecting the resonance frequency if the location is crossed by the nodal line of that resonance mode. However, this is virtually impossible to be simultaneously true for a number of modes, and thus the added mass may not evade detection (Figure 16.13b) [60].

The multimode technique allows one to quantify device geometric details, such as asymmetries. This can enable engineered devices with intentional asymmetric design to fully explore the multimode nature of these disk resonators, with the detailed information of device geometry encoded in the measured mode shape (but invisible to other imaging techniques). One of the authors' team has systematically investigated the multimode frequency responses of NEMS resonators by adjusting their geometric parameters [60]. Therefore, our multimode technique shall provide an unprecedentedly powerful decoder of the device geometry, which can be used to encrypt information.

Due to the extremely high sensitivity of multimode resonant behavior to the many details of any given device, it is possible to identify any individual device unambiguously through its multimode

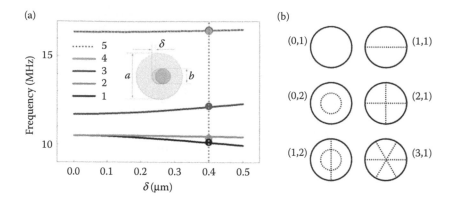

Figure 16.13 **Multimode resonances from a center-clamped circular microdisk resonator, and their dependency on engineerable structural asymmetry (e.g., here it is the slight offset of the center clamping pedestal). The inset in (a) is the top-view illustration of the device, with diameter of the microdisk, diameter of the clamping pedestal, and the offset all labeled [59]. (a) Evolution of multimode frequencies versus device asymmetry. Curves: theory. Scatters: data. Dashed line shows the device structure determined from frequency analysis. (b) Illustrations of the resonance mode shapes and node lines of different modes of a circular disk resonator.**

resonant signature. Even nominally identical structures, due to the nature of any fabrication process that does not have atomic-level control, will have nanoscale defects that are detectable through multimode resonances. Therefore, these NEMS resonant structures can serve as UNOs and PUFs, with the multimode resonance techniques providing a practical measurement and signatory readout of identity for enabling robust security.

16.4 Summary and Perspectives

In summary, we have presented the emerging opportunities and potential for employing and exploiting NEMS to realize new secure FPGA and hardware security primitives. In particular, we have reviewed the development of a new type of robust antifuse based on SiC NEMS to serve as interconnect building blocks for secure OTP FPGAs. We demonstrate the devices can have very low programming voltage, high current density, abrupt switching, small footprints, and long-term stability. New designs and dimensional scaling will further enable smaller devices with higher performance. We have also demonstrated with experiments an SiC NEMS antifuse–based OTP memory cell with separated programming and reading path and over 10^6 of current margin for reading. The unique properties and advantages of NEMS antifuses open many opportunities for designing low-power, high-security and harsh environment operable logic circuits and systems. We have also proposed the resonant NEMS as an entirely new platform that is essentially a multi-modal, multiparameter carrier of tokens or information, and thus a unique system for enabling UNOs and PUFs. With the advancement in fabrication technology, integration of the emerging NEMS devices with mainstream integrated circuit technologies is feasible and promising. We envision a bright future in realizing secure NEMS antifuse–based FPGA and other security primitives.

Acknowledgments

The authors thank NEMS teams and colleagues at Case Western Reserve University for discussions and the support from DARPA MTO (NEMS Program, under Grant No. N66001-07-2039, NBCH1090007, D11AP00292), National Science Foundation (Grant No. CCF-1116102), DTRA Basic Scientific Research Program (Grant No. HDTRA1-15-1-0039). P.X.-L.F. thanks the support from T. Keith Glennan Fellowship and from Case School of Engineering.

References

1. T.-H. Lee, S. Bhunia, and M. Mehregany. Electromechanical computing at 500C with silicon carbide. *Science*, **329**:1316–1318, 2010.
2. P. X.-L. Feng. NEMS switches: Opportunities and challenges in emerging IC technologies, In *Proceedings of the 2015 International Conference on IC Design & Technology (ICICDT'2015)*, 6 pages, Leuven, Belgium, June 1–3 (2015). DOI: 10.1109/ICICDT.2015.7165878
3. X. Wang, S. Narasimhan, and S. Bhunia. Nemtronics: Symbiotic integration of nanoelectronic and nanomechanical devices for energy efficient adaptive computing. In *Proceedings of the 7th IEEE/ACM Int. Symp. on Nanoscale Architectures (NANOARCH)*, pages 210–217, San Diego, CA, June 8–9, 2011.
4. R. S. Chakraborty, S. Paul, Y. Zhou, and S. Bhunia. Low-power hybrid CMOS-NEMS FPGA: Circuit level analysis and defect-aware mapping. *IET Computers and Digital Techniques (IETCDT)*, **3**:609–624, 2009.
5. T. He, R. Yang, S. Rajgopal, M. A. Tupta, S. Bhunia, M. Mehregany, and P. X.-L. Feng. Robust silicon carbide (SiC) nanoelectromechanical switches with long cycles in ambient and high temperature conditions. In *Proceedings of the 26th IEEE Int. Conf. on Micro Electro Mechanical Systems (MEMS'13)*, pages 516–519, Taipei, Taiwan, January 20–24, 2013.
6. T. He, R. Yang, S. Rajgopal, S. Bhunia, M. Mehregany, and P. X.-L. Feng. Dual-gate silicon carbide (SiC) lateral nanoelectromechanical switches. In *Proceedings of the 8th IEEE Int. Conf. on Nano/Micro Engineered & Molecular Systems (NEMS'13)*, pages 554–557, Suzhou, China, April 7–10, 2013.
7. T. He, V. Ranganathan, R. Yang, S. Rajgopal, S. Bhunia, M. Mehregany, and P. X.-L. Feng. Time-domain AC characterization of silicon carbide (SiC) nanoelectromechanical switches toward high-speed operations. In *Tech. Digest of 17th Int. Conf. on Solid-State Sensors and Actuators & Microsystems (Transducers'13)*, pages 669–672, Barcelona, Spain, June 16–20, 2013.
8. T. He, R. Yang, V. Ranganathan, S. Rajgopal, M. Tupta, S. Bhunia, M. Mehregany, and P. X.-L. Feng. Silicon carbide (SiC) nanoelectromechanical switches and logic gates with long cycles and robust performance in ambient air and at high temperature. In *Tech. Digest of Int. Electron Devices Meeting (IEDM'13)*, pages 108–111, Washington DC, December 9–11, 2013.
9. X. Wang, S. Narasimhan, A. Krishna, F. G. Wolff, S. Rajgopal, T.-H. Lee, M. Mehregany, and S. Bhunia. High-temperature (>500°C) reconfigurable computing using SiC NEMS switches. In *Design Automation and Test in Europe (DATE)*, pages 1–6, Grenoble, France, March 14–18, 2011.
10. X. L. Feng, M. H. Matheny, C. A. Zorman, M. Mehregany, and M. L. Roukes. Low voltage nanoelectromechanical switches based on silicon carbide nanowires. *Nano Letters*, **10**:2891–2896, 2010.
11. T. He, J. Lee, Z. Wang, and P. X.-L. Feng. Interrogating contact-mode silicon carbide (SiC) nanoelectromechanical switching dynamics by ultrasensitive laser. In *Proceedings of the 27th IEEE Int. Conf. on Micro Electro Mechanical Systems (MEMS'14)*, pages 1079–1082, San Francisco, CA, January 26–30, 2014.
12. V. Ranganathan, T. He, S. Rajgopal, M. Mehregany, P. X.-L. Feng, and S. Bhunia. Nanomechanical non-volatile memory for computing at extreme. In *Proceedings of the 2013 IEEE/ACM International Symposium on Nanoscale Architectures (NANOARCH)*, pages 44–45, New York City, NY, July 15–17, 2013.

13. Y. T. Yang, C. Callegari, X. L. Feng, K. L. Ekinci, and M. L. Roukes. Zeptogram-scale nanomechanical mass sensing. *Nano Letters*, **6**:583–586, 2006.

14. L. B. Johnson. Space Center NASA facts: Understanding space radiation. http://spaceflight.nasa.gov/spacenews/factsheets/pdfs/radiation.pdf.

15. J. S. Suehle, E. M. Vogel, P. Roitman, J. F. Conley, Jr., A. H. Johnston, B. Wang, J. B. Bernstein, and C. E. Weintraub, Jr. Observation of latent reliability degradation in ultrathin oxides after heavy-ion irradiation. *Applied Physics Letters*, **80**(7):1282–1284, 2002.

16. A. Iyengar, K. Ramclam, and S. Ghosh. DWM-PUF: A low-overhead, memory-based security primitive. In *IEEE International Symposium on Hardware-Oriented Security and Trust (HOST)*, pages 154–159, Arlington, VA, USA, May 6–7, 2014.

17. L. Zhang, X. Fong, C.-H. Chang, Z.-H. Kong, and K. Roy. Highly reliable spin-transfer torque magnetic RAM-based physical unclonable function with multi-response-bits per cell. *IEEE Transactions on Information Forensics and Security*, **10**:1630–1642, 2015.

18. P.-Y. Chen, R. Fang, R. Liu, C. Chakrabarti, Y. Cao, and S. Yu. Exploiting resistive cross-point array for compact design of physical unclonable function. In *IEEE International Symposium on Hardware-Oriented Security and Trust (HOST)*, pages 26–31 Washington, DC, USA, May 5–7, 2015.

19. G. S. Rose, N. McDonald, L.-K. Yan, and B. Wysocki. A write-time based memristive PUF for hardware security applications. In *Proceedings of IEEE/ACM International Conference on Computer-Aided Design (ICCAD'13)*, pages 830–833, San Jose, CA, USA, November 18–21, 2013.

20. K. Akarvarda, C. Eggimann, D. Tsamados, Y. Chauhan, G. Wan, A. Ionescu, R. Howe, and H.-S. Wong. Analytical modeling of the suspended-gate FET and design insights for low-power logic. *IEEE Transactions on Electron Devices*, **55**:48–59, 2008.

21. H. Kam, D. T. Lee, R. T. Howe, and T.-J. King. A new nano-electro-mechanical field effect transistor (NEMFET) design for low-power electronics. In *Technical Digest of International Electron Devices Meeting (IEDM'05)*, pages 463–466, Washington, DC, USA, December 5–7, 2005.

22. Y. Goto, S. Machida, and N. Yokoyama. Semiconductor device using MEMS switch, US Patent, No. US 7,045,843 B2, 2004 (App. No. US 2005/0067621 A1).

23. Nantero. NRAM nanotube-based/non-volatile random access memory. http://www.nantero.com/mission.html.

24. D. Shahrjerdi, J. Rajendran, S. Garg, F. Koushanfar, and R. Karri. Shielding and securing integrated circuits with sensors. In *Proceedings of IEEE/ACM International Conference on Computer-Aided Design (ICCAD'14)*, pages 170–174, San Jose, CA, USA, November 2–6, 2014.

25. X. L. Feng, M. H. Matheny, R. B. Karabalin, C. A. Zorman, M. Mehregany, and M. L. Roukes. Silicon carbide (SiC) top-down nanowire electromechanical resonators. In *Tech. Digest of the 17th Int. Conf. on Solid-State Sensors and Actuators & Microsystems (Transducers'09)*, pages 2246–2249, Denver, CO, USA, June 21–25, 2009.

26. P. X.-L. Feng, M. H. Matheny, R. B. Karabalin, and M. L. Roukes. Very low voltage, ultrafast nanoelectromechanical switches and resonant switches, US Patent, No. US 8,115,344 B2, 2012 (App. No. US 2010/0140066 A1).

27. R. Yang, T. He, C. Marcoux, P. Andreucci, L. Duraffourg, and P. X.-L. Feng. Silicon nanowire and cantilever electromechanical switches with integrated piezoresistive transducers. In *Proc. 26th IEEE Int. Conf. on Micro Electro Mechanical Systems (MEMS'13)*, pages 229–232, Taipei, Taiwan, January 20–24, 2013.

28. S. Rajgopal, T. H. Lee, P. X.-L. Feng, S. Bhunia, and M. Mehregany. Nanomanufacturing of SiC circuits nanomechanical logic and MEMS-JFET integration. In *Technical Digest of the Workshop on Technologies for Future Micro & Nano Manufacturing*, pages 183–186, Napa, CA, USA, August 8–10, 2011.

29. M. L. Roukes. Mechanical computation, redux? In *Technical Digest of International Electron Devices Meeting (IEDM'04)*, pages 539–542, San Francisco, CA, USA, December 13–15, 2004.

30. X. L. Feng, R. B. Karabalin, J. S. Aldridge, and M. L. Roukes. Nano-electro-mechanical systems (NEMS) switches, US Patent, No. US 8,258,899 B2, 2012 (App. No. US 2011/0094861 A1).

31. U. Farooq, Z. Marrakchi, and H. Mehrez. *Tree-Based Heterogeneous FPGA Architectures*. Springer, Berlin, 2012.

32. C. Hu. Interconnect devices for field programmable gate array, in *Technical Digest of International Electron Devices Meeting (IEDM'92)*, pages 591–594, San Francisco, CA, USA, December 13–16, 1992.

33. E. Hamdy, J. McCollum, S. Chen, S. Chiang, S. Eltoukhy, J. Chang, T. Speers, and A. Mohsen. Dielectric based antifuse for logic and memory ICs. In *Technical Digest of International Electron Devices Meeting (IEDM'88)*, pages 786–789, San Francisco, CA, USA, December 11–14, 1988.

34. D. Liu, K. Chen, H. Tigelaar, J. Paterson, and S. Chen. Scaled dielectric antifuse structure for field-programmable gate array applications. *IEEE Electron Device Letters*, **12**:151–153, 1991.

35. S. Wang, G. Misium, J. Camp, K. Chen, and H. Tigelaar. High performance metal/silicide antifuse. *IEEE Electron Device Letters*, **13**:471–473, 1992.

36. G. Zhang, C. Hu, P. Y. Yu, S. Chiang, S. Eltoukhy, and E. Z. Hamdy. An electro-thermal model for metal-oxide-metal antifuses. *IEEE Transactions on Electron Devices*, **42**:1548–1558, 1995.

37. F. Li, X. Yang, A. T. Meeks, J. T. Shearer, and K. Y. Le. Evaluation of SiO_2 antifuse in a 3D-OTP memory. *IEEE Transactions on Device and Materials Reliability*, **4**(3):416–421, 2004.

38. J. Kim and K. Lee. Three-transistor one-time programmable (OTP) ROM cell array using standard CMOS gate oxide antifuse. *IEEE Electron Device Letters*, **24**(9):589–591, 2003.

39. H.-K. Cha, I. Yun, J. Kim, B.-C. So, K. Chun, I. Nam, and K. Lee. A 32-KB standard CMOS antifuse one-time programmable ROM embedded in a 16-bit microcontroller. *IEEE Journal of Solid-State Circuits*, **41**(9):2115–2124, 2006.

40. H. Ito and T. Namekawa. Pure CMOS one-time programmable memory using gate-Ox anti-fuse. In *Proceedings of IEEE Custom Integrated Circuits Conference*, pages 469–472, Orlando, FL, USA, October 3–6, 2004.

41. S. Trimberger. Effects of FPGA architecture on FPGA routing. In *Proceedings of the 32nd Annual ACM/IEEE Design Automation Conference (DAC'95)*, pages 574–578, San Francisco, CA, USA, June 12–16, 1995.

42. S. Wong, H. So, J. Ou, and J. Costello. A 5000-gate CMOS EPLD with multiple logic and interconnect arrays. In *Proceedings of IEEE Custom Integrated Circuits Conference*, pages 581–584, San Diego, CA, USA, May 15–18, 1989.

43. J. Greene, E. Hamdy, and S. Beal. Antifuse field programmable gate arrays. *Proceedings of the IEEE*, **81**:1042–1056, 1993.

44. S. Chiang, R. Foruohi, W. Chen, F. Hawley, J. M. E. Hamady, and C. Hu. Antifuse structure comparison for field programmable gate arrays. In *Technical Digest of International Electron Devices Meeting (IEDM'92)*, pages 611–614, San Francisco, CA, USA, December 13–16, 1992.

45. Microsemi Corporation. Understanding Actel Antifuse Device Security. www.actel.com/documents/AntifuseSecurityWP.pdf

46. R. Katz, K. LaBel, J. J. Wang, R. Koga, S. Penzin, and O. Swift. Radiation effects on current field programmable technologies. *IEEE Transactions on Nuclear Science*, **44**(6):1945–1956, 1997.

47. R. Katz, J. J. Wang, R. Koga, K. A. LaBel, J. McCollum, R. Brown, R. A. Reed, B. Cronquist, S. Crain, T. Scott, W. Paolini, and B. Sin. Current radiation issues for programmable elements and devices. *IEEE Transactions on Nuclear Science*, **45**(6):2600–2610, 1998.

48. S. Chiang, R. Wang, J. Chen, K. Hayes, J. McCollum, E. Hamdy, and C. Hu. Oxide–nitride–oxide antifuse reliability. In *28th Annual Proceedings of the IEEE International Reliability Physics Symposium*, pages 186–192, New Orleans LA, USA, March 27–29, 1990.

49. C.-C. Shih, R. Lambertson, F. Hawley, F. Issaw, J. McCollum, E. Hamdy, H. Sakurai et al. Characterization and modeling of a highly reliable metal-to-metal antifuse for high-performance and high-density field-programmable gate arrays. In *35th Annual Proceedings of the IEEE International Reliability Physics Symposium*, pages 25–33, Denver, CO, USA, April 8–10, 1997.

50. S. S. Cohen, J. I. Raffel, and P. W. Wyatt. A novel double-metal structure for voltage-programmable links. *IEEE Electron Device Letters*, **13**:488–490, 1992.

51. J. S. Lee and Y. H. Lee. Metal-to-metal antifuse with amorphous Ti-rich barium titanate film and silicon oxide film. *Solid-State Electronics*, **43**:469–472, 1999.

52. Quick Logic. Reliability of the amorphous silicon antifuse, White Paper Rev A, 2008.

53. K. Gordon and R. Wong. Conductive filament of the programmed metal electrode amorphous silicon antifuse. In *Technical Digest of International Electron Devices Meeting (IEDM'93)*, pages 27–30, Washington, DC, USA, December 5–8, 1993.

54. K. Akarvardar and H.-S. P. Wong. Ultralow voltage crossbar nonvolatile memory based on energy-reversible NEM switches. *IEEE Electron Device Letters*, 30(6):626–628, 2009.

55. J. Trevino, X.-A. Fu, M. Mehregany, and C. A. Zorman. Low-stress, heavily-doped polycrystalline silicon carbide for MEMS applications. In *Proceedings of 18th IEEE International Conference on Micro Electro Mechanical Systems (MEMS'05)*, pages 451–454, Miami, FL, USA, January 30–February 03, 2005.

56. E. Ebrard, B. Allard, P. Candelier, and P. Waltz. Review of fuse and antifuse solutions for advanced standard CMOS technologies. *Microelectronics Journal*, 40(12):1755–1765, 2009.

57. N. Patil, D. Das, E. Scanff, and M. Pecht. Long term storage reliability of antifuse field programmable gate arrays. *Microelectronics Reliability*, 53(12):2052–2056, 2013.

58. T. He, F. Zhang, S. Bhunia, and P. X.-L. Feng. Silicon carbide (SiC) nanoelectromechanical antifuse for ultralow-power one-time-programmable (OTP) FPGA interconnects. *IEEE Journal of Electron Device Society (JEDS)*, 3(4):323–335, 2015.

59. Z. Wang, J. Lee, and P. X.-L. Feng. Spatial mapping of multimode Brownian motions in high frequency silicon carbide microdisk resonators. *Nature Communications*, 5:5158, 2014.

60. Z. Wang, J. Lee, K. He, J. Shan, and P. X.-L. Feng. Embracing structural nonidealities and asymmetries in two-dimensional nanomechanical resonators. *Scientific Report*, 4:2014, 2014.

Chapter 17

A Chaotic Logic-Based Physical Unclonable Computing System

Cory Merkel, Mesbah Uddin, and Garrett S. Rose

Contents

Hardware security issues such as integrated circuit (IC) counterfeiting, piracy, reverse engineering, and cloning have emerged as critical design considerations in the face of increasingly global approaches to IC manufacturing. From the government perspective, hardware security and trust have become even more critical given the recent loss of a true trusted fab in the United States. In the context of the proposed work, one solution to such issues is logic obfuscation [1] where key gates are strategically inserted into a logic design in order to mitigate the threat of reverse engineering. Obfuscation techniques are also important to a range of other security challenges at various abstraction layers. For deployable embedded systems, side-channel analysis (SCA) has been proven to be a viable tactic for attacking implementations of trustworthy encryption systems, including the Advanced Encryption Standard [2,3]. Several techniques exist where information leakage via a range of side channels (e.g., power signatures) can be obfuscated in such a way as to minimize the threat of an SCA attack [4]. Furthermore, at a high level, code obfuscation has emerged as an important technique for ensuring that code executing on a given system is not easily reverse engineered. Thus, there exists the need for obfuscation across all abstraction layers in the construction of deployable computer systems that handle sensitive data and code.

In recent years, the field of nanoelectronics has been explored as a new solution space for dealing with several hardware security challenges. For example, it was proposed in 2013 that metal-oxide memristive devices could be leveraged for tamper detection and in the development of physically unclonable functions (PUFs) [5]. A write-time-based memristor PUF (WTMPUF) was then designed and simulated showing how variability in several memristor device parameters could be exploited to yield a high degree of uniqueness, useful for applications such as secret key generation and metering [6]. The WTMPUF was later fabricated and tested by researchers, providing experimental validation for the idea itself [7]. Over the past couple of years, several other groups have proposed various implementations of nanoelectronic PUF circuits [8–11], showing how process variations of nanoelectronic device parameters can be exploited in the design of improved security primitives. Other examples where nanoelectronic systems have been investigated for security solutions include: nanoelectronics-based public PUFs, sneak-path encryption, nanoelectronics-based forensics, and a variety of approaches to nano-enabled tamper detection [12]. These approaches primarily utilize the high degree of parameter variations found in nanoelectronic devices coupled with the system complexity resulting directly from the high density nature of the technology. These very features (variability, uniqueness, and system complexity) are utilized in the development of the physically unclonable computing system (PUCS).

PUCS is a novel class of computer architecture where operation of all physical implementations of a given design are unique in relation to one another. While unclonable computing systems are novel in their construction, high-level behavior is assumed to follow that of the classic Von Neumann architecture. Key differentiating features of a PUCS include: (1) uniqueness across IC implementation, (2) uniqueness across op code sets, and (3) reconfigurability of op code sets.

The above attributes are enabling factors for guaranteeing obfuscation across multiple abstraction layers of a PUCS design. At the logic level, the reconfigurability requirement for the op code sets ensures that the physical design is not easily determined from the functionality. Further, the uniqueness requirements also apply to side-channel information leakage such that reverse engineering via SCA (e.g., power analysis) is likely to be unfruitful. Finally, the very existence of multiple op code sets and the uniqueness requirement thereof leads to hardware handles for code-level obfuscation.

An extreme example of building blocks of a PUCS would be any secure nonlinear computing systems, like the chaos-based computing [13]. Chaos, as described by Lorenz [14] and Rössler [15], is a deterministic, aperiodic flow of a system's state through its state space. Chaotic behavior is observed in a wide range of natural and man-made systems, from weather patterns to integrated circuits. Two key features of chaotic systems are: (1) apparently random behavior despite being deterministic and (2) high sensitivity to initial conditions. As a result, these systems are difficult to study, hard to predict, and often exhibit rapid changes in their behavior over time. A fundamental question that has been asked by Sinha et al. is whether chaotic behavior in electronic systems can be harnessed to design efficient computers [16]. To that end, a number of authors [17–19] have

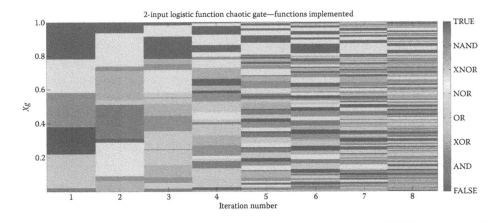

Figure 17.1 Color-coded illustration of some possible logical operations of a basic chaos logic gate. This illustrates the aperiodicity and near randomness of the occurrence of various operations relative to control parameters and the time allowed for the system to evolve.

explored the design and analysis of individual chaotic logic (CL) gates (*chaogates*) to implement CL functions. A CL function is one whose output changes chaotically over time depending on its initial inputs. Noise and fault tolerance in chaogates [20,21] have also been studied, which is of particular interest due to the high sensitivity to initial conditions and perturbations in chaotic systems. Chaotic systems from the viewpoint of hardware security have been proposed and described in previous works [22,23]. An illustration showing the complexity of the state space for several logical operations in a chaos computer is shown in Figure 17.1.

CL implementations have many potential advantages over traditional logic circuits. First, a single chaogate can be used as a universal logic gate, implementing all possible functions of its inputs. Unlike traditional reconfigurable logic (e.g., lookup table logic), the amount of additional hardware needed for a chaogate grows linearly with the number of inputs, leading to an area savings for functions with large fanin. Second, the apparent randomness of CL circuits may help to mitigate side channel attacks, such as differential power analysis. Despite these advantages, the existing work has primarily focused on individual chaogate design, making it unclear how to scale CL circuits to efficiently implement complex functions. Here, we address challenges that arise when incorporating chaogates with conventional digital logic gates into larger CL circuits. For example, one drawback of CL is that it will necessarily lead to degradation in performance compared with conventional logic. Therefore, we address the performance degradation issue by treating chaogates probabilistically as simple Bernoulli trials. We adjust the associated probabilities of success to increase the number of useful functional outputs of the CL circuit, while making sure that there is still a large number of unused, or "garbage" functions to obfuscate the useful computation. Specifically, our contributions are:

- A parameterized chaogate model
- Expressions for the probability and maximum probability of obtaining a particular logic function from a chaogate
- A deterministic sum-of-products design methodology for CL circuits
- A metaheuristic design methodology for CL circuits

17.1 Chaos-Based Logic

The concept of using chaos for computing was made concrete by Ditto, who introduced a basic construct referred to as a chaogate [17]. The gate uses a chaotic oscillator (e.g., Chuas function [25] or the logistic map) to determine the functionality of the logic gate at any given time. Consider the schematic of a one-dimensional chaogate as shown in Figure 17.2. A generic chaotic oscillator is represented by the box labeled C. The signal going into the box from the left is the initial condition, and the output signal coming from the right side of the box is the state variable. The initial condition is formed by the sum of the analog control input x_g and two digital inputs A and B, each of which are converted to an analog value by multiplication with a constant weighting factor δ. The digital output Y is generated using the comparator with a threshold x_{th}.

The logic functionality of the gate can be altered by varying the control input x_g, weighting factor δ, or the threshold x_{th}. If the chaotic oscillator is seen as a pseudorandom number generator, then x_g and δ determine the seed and x_{th} converts the analog output into a digital 0 or 1 [17].

For a generic two-input reconfigurable logic gate, there are 16 possible logic functions. However, for the one-dimensional CL gate, the input sets {0,1} and {1,0} will produce the same initial condition such that the output for these two input sets will be identical. This restriction on the outputs reduces the number of possible logic operations the gate can perform to eight. These logic functions are as follows: FALSE, AB, $A + B$, $\overline{AB}$, $\overline{A + B}$, $A \oplus B$, $\overline{A \oplus B}$, TRUE.

As an example, a simple function that has been shown to exhibit chaotic behavior is the logistic map. The logistic map is the recurrence relation associated with the logistic function, often used to model population growth. The logistic map is typically written as follows:

$$x_{n+1} = rx_n(1 - x_n), \tag{17.1}$$

where r is a positive real number and x_n is the state variable of this particular system. When the logistic map is used to represent population dynamics, r represents the combined rate for reproduction and starvation. The state variable x_n represents the ratio of the existing population to the maximum possible population for iteration n.

The logistic map is a simple system that acts as a useful example of deterministic chaos. Roughly speaking, a chaotic system is one that is very sensitive to even minute changes in initial conditions. Chaotic systems are also aperiodic in nature. These two properties combined lead to a system that is very difficult to predict without a perfect understanding of the system itself and all of its initial conditions.

CL circuits have been demonstrated in prior research as a means to providing inherent obfuscation across various abstraction layers. In Reference 24, we presented a chaos-based arithmetic

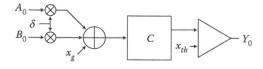

Figure 17.2   A basic 2-input chaogate leveraging a single chaotic oscillator C. (From W. L. Ditto et al. Construction of a chaotic computer chip. In, P. Longhini, and A. Palacios, editors, *Applications of Nonlinear Dynamics: Model and Design of Complex Systems*, pages 3–13. Springer, Berlin Heidelberg, 2009; G. S. Rose et al. Nanoelectronics and hardware security. In *Network Science and Cybersecurity*, pages 105–123. Springer, Berlin, 2014.)

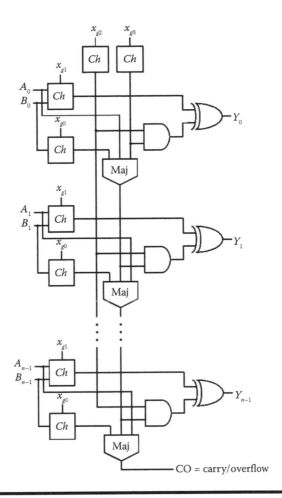

Figure 17.3   Schematic of a chaos-based ALU as presented in Reference 24.

logic unit (ALU) (illustrated in Figure 17.3) and showed how each possible operation could be implemented in a variety of unique ways, determined by control inputs x_g and iteration number n. Further, since the ALU is constructed from chaotic oscillators, no discernible pattern emerges to relate the various ways any given operation can be implemented. In Reference 23, a similar ALU constructed from 2D Chua's circuits was shown to exhibit roughly the same number of implementations (or frequencies of operation) for each operation considered.

17.2 A Parameterized Chaogate Model and Probability Analysis

We propose a simple parameterized chaogate model (Section 17.2.1), where parameters are provided to govern (i) how an initial state is created from a set of digital inputs, (ii) how the chaogates state is updated at each time step, and (iii) how a digital output is determined from the state. Furthermore, we state the particular parameterization used in this work. Then, in Section 17.2.2, we analyze the probability of a chaogate implementing different logic functions of its inputs.

17.2.1 Parameterized Chaogate Model

A simple parameterized chaogate model is shown in Figure 17.4. The chaogate inputs x_i are mapped to an initial state vector (or scalar) $s[t = 0]$ using a mapping function h. When the reset signal rs is low, the chaogate's state is set to the initial state. The t variable is the number of time steps since the reset transitioned from low to high. The duration of a time step depends on the exact implementation, and could be equal to a clock period or a differential time step dt, in the case of a continuous system. When the reset signal is high, the chaogate's state is set by the chaotic function g. Since the state may be a vector, of which each component may be analog, an output mapping function is required to produce the digital output.

A particular implementation of a chaogate is defined by specifying h, g, and ψ. For example, in Ditto's work, h is usually a scaled summation, g is governed by a Chua circuit, and ψ is a threshold function [17]. In this work, h is a linear combination of the inputs:

$$s[\Delta t = 0] = h(x_0, \ldots, x_{N1}) = \mathbf{x} \cdot \delta + x_g, \tag{17.2}$$

where δ and x_g are constants. The specific chaotic function studied as an example in this work is the logistic map:

$$s[\Delta t] = g(s[\Delta t - 1]) = 4s[\Delta t - 1](1 - s[\Delta t - 1]). \tag{17.3}$$

Here, the logistic map function is chosen instead of a Chua circuit (or any other chaotic system) because of its simplicity (scalar state) and its well-defined probabilistic behavior, which is discussed later in this section. Finally, the output function ψ is a threshold function:

$$y[\Delta t] = (s[\Delta t]) = \begin{cases} 0 : s[\Delta t] < \theta, \\ 1 : s[\Delta t] \geq \theta, \end{cases} \tag{17.4}$$

where θ is the threshold. Note that a chaogate with a vector state variable would require a dimensionality reduction to get to the (scalar) digital output.

It should be mentioned here that one may apply some useful constraints to the value of δ in Equation 17.2. In order for the chaogate to be able to implement all possible $2(2^N)$ functions of the N inputs, we have to make sure that every unique input vector maps to a unique initial state. Accordingly, it should be the case that

$$x_1 \cdot \delta = x_2 \cdot \delta \implies x_1 = x_2. \tag{17.5}$$

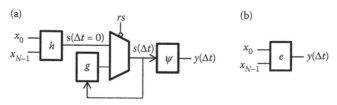

Figure 17.4 (a) Parameterized chaogate model block diagram consisting of an input mapping function *h*, a state vector *s*, a chaotic function *g*, and an output mapping function *Ψ*. (b) The equivalent "black box" representation.

Furthermore, valid initial states to the logistic map range from 0 to 1, so

$$0 < \mathbf{x} \cdot \delta + x_g < 1 \quad \forall x. \tag{17.6}$$

It is easy to show that $x_g = \frac{1}{2}$ and $\delta = [\frac{1}{4} \frac{1}{8} \dots \frac{1}{2^N}]$ will satisfy both these conditions.

17.2.2 Probability Analysis

It is important to understand the probability that a chaogate will implement a particular function after a given number of time steps. The ability to tune the probability will allow us to adjust the performance of a digital circuit built from several chaogates, which will be discussed later. Here, we treat the function implemented by the chaogate as a random variable *F*. Furthermore, the probability that a chaogate will implement a specific function *f* of its inputs is equal to the probability that the chaogates output will be 0 for every 0 in the output column of *f*'s truth table, and 1 for every 1 in the output column of *f*'s truth table:

$$\Pr(F = f) = p^k (1 - p)^{2^N - k}, \tag{17.7}$$

where $p \triangleq \Pr(y[\Delta t] = 1)$, and k is the number of 1's in f's truth table. Taking the derivative,

$$\frac{\mathrm{dPr}(F = f)}{\mathrm{d}p} = p^{k-1}(1 - p)^{2^N - k - 1}(k - 2^N p). \tag{17.8}$$

Therefore, $\Pr(F = f)$ is maximized in three ways. First, if $p = 0$ or $p = 1$, there will be a 100% probability of the outputs being either 0 or 1, meaning that the probability or the constant functions are easily maximized. The nontrivial case, where $p = k/2^N$, yields a maximum probability of

$$\Pr_{max}(F = f) = \left(\frac{k}{2^N}\right)^k \left(1 - \frac{k}{2^N}\right)^{2^N - k}. \tag{17.9}$$

The value of p is determined by the probabilistic behavior of g as well as the threshold value θ. In the case of the logistic map, the probabilistic behavior is defined by its probability density function (PDF), which is a beta distribution:

$$\Pr(s) = \frac{\Gamma(0.5 + 0.5)}{\Gamma(0.5)\Gamma(0.5)} s^{-0.5}(1 - s)^{-0.5}. \tag{17.10}$$

However, notice that it is not important for s to be a particular value. Rather, it is important for the chaogate's final output to be a particular value. Since the final output value, given by Equation17.4 is produced by a threshold function, its probability distribution will be related to the cumulative distribution function (CDF) of s, which is a regularized incomplete beta function I parameterized by θ:

$$\Pr(y[\Delta t] = 1) = p = 1 - I_\theta(0.5, 0.5). \tag{17.11}$$

Two example trajectories through the logistic map's phase space are shown in Figure 17.5a, and its PDF and complementary CDF are shown in Figure 17.5b. From a design perspective, Equation 17.11 is the most useful of all equations discussed thus far. Whether g is a logistic map,

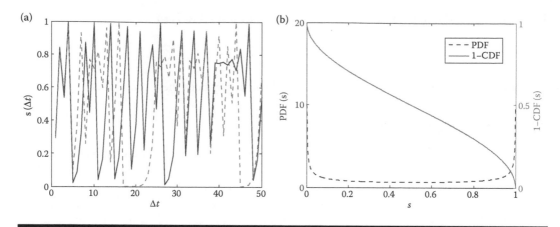

Figure 17.5 (a) State of the logistic map over time for two different initial conditions: $s[0] = 0.3$ (solid line) and $s[0] = 0.29$ (dashed line). The PDF and inverse CDF of the logistic map function are shown in (b).

a Chua circuit, or some other chaotic function, it is important to know the chaogate output probability as a function of the controllable parameters. In this case, we can tune the probability by adjusting the threshold θ.

17.3 CL Circuits

A CL circuit is composed of one or more chaogates as well as conventional digital logic gates. The function performed by a CL circuit with N inputs and M outputs after Δt time steps from its initial condition is a random variable $F[t]$ and takes a particular value f:

$$F[\Delta t] \Longleftrightarrow Y[\Delta t] = Y^f, \tag{17.12}$$

where Y is a $2^N \times M$ matrix formed by the circuit's M outputs for all possible 2^N input vectors:

$$Y[\Delta t] = \begin{bmatrix} y_{0,0}[\Delta t] & \cdots & y_{0,M-1}[\Delta t] \\ \vdots & \ddots & \vdots \\ y_{2^N-1,0}[\Delta t] & \cdots & y_{2^N-1,M-1}[\Delta t] \end{bmatrix}. \tag{17.13}$$

Similarly, Y^f is the $2^N \times M$ matrix for the Boolean function f. Furthermore,

$$\begin{aligned} Y[\Delta t] = Y^f &\Longleftrightarrow (Y_{i,j}[\Delta t] = Y^f_{i,j} \vee Y^f_{i,j} = X), \\ (i,j) &= (0,0), \dots, (2^N - 1, M - 1). \end{aligned} \tag{17.14}$$

Here, X denotes a "don't care" condition, where any circuit output is valid.

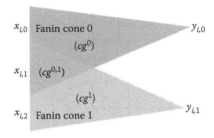

Figure 17.6 A 3-input, 2-output logic circuit, demonstrated as fanin cones from the primary inputs to the primary outputs. Each fanin cone has a set of chaogates which is unique to that fanin cone. In addition, the intersection of the fanin cones has a set of chaogates which are shared.

If every chaogate in the CL circuit drives only one output, then the probability that a CL circuit will perform a particular function f after Δt time steps is given as

$$\Pr(F = f) = \Pr\left(\bigcap_{j=0}^{M-1} y_j = y_j^f\right),\tag{17.15}$$

where y_j and y_j^f are the column vectors of Y and Y^f, respectively.

However, in more complicated circuits (Figure 17.6), a set of chaogates may belong to the fanin cones of multiple outputs. This implies that the outputs have some statistical dependence and, as a result, Equation 17.15 is no longer valid. Therefore, algorithms to calculate the output probabilities based only on the probabilities associated with each chaogate may actually be slower than the brute force method of simulating the circuit and investigating the outputs.

17.4 Design and Optimization of CL Circuits

Adopting a CL design paradigm may be beneficial in a wide spectrum of research domains, including reconfigurable logic, reliability enhancement, and hardware security. Although this work is applicable to any application domain, hardware security will be used to motivate the following discussions. The major design constraints considered in this work are functionality (the probability of a CL circuit producing a particular function), performance, and circuit size. In the context of hardware security, it is reasonable to assume that a secure system will perform a large number of garbage operations, which are not in the CL ALUs instruction set. We will also assume that the probability of all nongarbage operations should be the same. The two methods of tuning the probability of a specific CL ALU operation are modifying the CL circuit and tuning the chaogate thresholds within a CL circuit. Here, we start with the latter.

17.4.1 Threshold Tuning

Consider the CL ALU slice design shown in Figure 17.7. Chaogate C0 will produce any Boolean function of its input with a probability given by Equation 17.15, which will pass to the output y_0

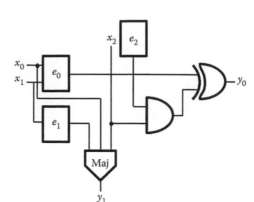

Figure 17.7   CL ALU slice design capable of performing AND, NAND, OR, NOR, XOR, XNOR, ADD, and SUB operations.

if chaogate C2's output is 0. Therefore, the slice design can implement bitwise functions. Furthermore, when C0 implements an XOR function and C2's output is "1," y_0 is a 3-bit XOR function of the inputs. Finally, y_1 will be a carry or borrow function when C1 implements a buffer or inversion function, respectively. Therefore, the CL ALU slice can implement the set of functions $NG = \{\text{AND,NAND,OR,NOR,XOR,XNOR,ADD,SUB}\}$. Other functions are also possible, but will be considered garbage.

It is not obvious how the thresholds of each chaogate should be set to tune the probability of each function. Here, we examine three potential methods. First, since the circuit structure is known, we can write a system of equations that relate the probability of each chaogate outputting a 1 and the desired probabilities of the circuit implementing each function. We will assume that we want the probability of each function in NG to be 0.01, or 12.5% of the nongarbage functions. Therefore, the system of equations is

$$
\begin{aligned}
(1 - p_2)(1 - p_0)^3 p_0 - 0.01 &= 0, \\
(1 - p_2)(1 - p_0)p_0^3 - 0.01 &= 0, \\
(1 - p_2)(1 - p_0)^2 p_0^2 - 0.01 &= 0, \\
p_2(1 - p_1)p_1(1 - p_0)^2 p_0^2 - 0.01 &= 0.
\end{aligned}
\tag{17.16}
$$

The least-squares solution is obtained numerically as $p_0 = 0.5$, $p_1 = 0.74$, and $p_2 = 0.84$. Using Equation 17.11 to find the corresponding thresholds yields $\theta_0 = 0.5$, $\theta_1 = 0.16$, and $\theta_2 = 0.06$. Figure 17.8a and b shows the probabilities of different operations when each chaogate threshold is 0.5, and when the thresholds are set as discussed above, respectively, validating the method.

17.4.2 Sum-of-Products Design Method

One drawback of the design shown in Figure 17.7 is that one of the chaogates has two inputs. In Equation 17.9, it is apparent that the maximum probability for a particular function drops off exponentially with the number of chaogate inputs. That is why the probability of each operation (Figure 17.8) is relatively small compared to the probability of a garbage operation. In the case where each operation has a probability of 0.01, the ALU may have to wait 100 cycles to perform

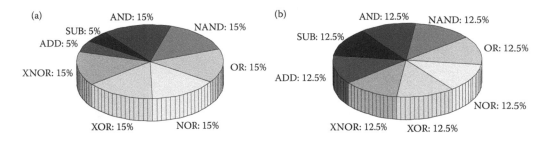

Figure 17.8 Operation probabilities of nongarbage functions (a) before and (b) after tuning the chaogates' probabilities.

any specific nongarbage operation, which would create a large performance degradation. Notice that when $N = 0$ and $k = 0$ in Equation 17.9, the maximum probability is 1. In other words, we can create a circuit with larger probabilities of nongarbage operations by only using chaotic oscillators (zero-input chaogates) and combinational logic. The design process is as follows:

1. Create a sum-of-products circuit that concatenates each nongarbage operation that needs to be implemented.
2. Assign each nongarbage operation to a control state. The size of the state vector should be at least $\log_2 (NG + G)$, where NG and G are the sizes of the nongarbage and garbage operation sets, respectively. Furthermore, there should be a control circuit with a number of zero-input chaogates equal to the size of the state vector.
3. Create a system of nonlinear equations relating the probabilities of each chaogate to the probability of each control stage.
4. Solve the system and set each chaogate's threshold according to the desired output probability, as well as its CDF.
5. Finally, add logic to turn off appropriate product terms for each control state.

This process is easily demonstrated with an example. Suppose that we want a circuit that will implement an AND function with a probability of 10%, an OR function with a probability of 20%, and an XOR function with a probability of 30%. Furthermore, we want five different garbage states, with no constraints on their relative probabilities. Therefore, we need a state vector of size $\log_2(3 + 5) = 3$, and there will be three chaogates in the control circuit, with probabilities p_0, p_1, and p_2. We assign the state 001 to the AND function, 111 to the OR function, and 110 to the XOR function. Accordingly, the system of equations is:

$$(1 - p_2)(1 - p_1)p_0 - 0.1 = 0,$$
$$p_2 p_1 p_0 - 0.2 = 0, \tag{17.17}$$
$$p_2 p_1 (1 - p_0) - 0.3 = 0.$$

The system is solved numerically, with the additional constraint that each probability should be between 0 and 1. An approximate solution is $p_0 = 0.41$, $p_1 = 0.7$, and $p_2 = 0.7$. The resulting circuit and probability pie chart are shown in Figure 17.9. The AND gates probability is 6% lower than the target of probability. However, this can be improved by assigning each of the three nongarbage operations to different states, such as 000, 001, and 010.

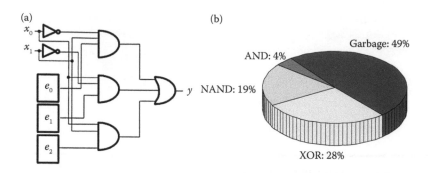

Figure 17.9 **(a) Sum-of-products design approach and relative and (b) relative probabilities.**

17.5 Metaheuristic Design Approach

Although the sum-of-products design method discussed above is deterministic and well structured, it may not be scalable. The size and power consumption of each chaogate motivates us to look for solutions that limit the number of chaogates present, while still allowing probability tuning and probabilities large enough for good performance. Since the design space of CL circuits is very large and multi-modal, the use of a metaheuristic design approach is proposed. Specifically, the use of an evolutionary algorithm (EA) is investigated here to define both the structure and the chaogate thresholds of a CL circuit. The following subsections discuss the details of the algorithms, including the fitness function, genetic representation.

17.5.1 Fitness Function

When designing an algorithm to automatically find the circuit structure and the chaogate thresholds for a given operation probability distribution, it may be easier to ignore the first assumption. Furthermore, a practical system will undergo a finite maybe even small number of iterations. In that case, where the gradient of the search space is unknown, it makes sense to use a metaheuristic search algorithm. Two algorithms are tested here: an EA and simulated annealing. For both these, the first step is to define a fitness, or energy function, which will measure how close the probability of a particular function is to a target probability Pr_{target}. In this work, we use a Gaussian function:

$$fit_i = \exp\left(-\frac{[Pr(F - f)]^2}{2\sigma^2}\right). \tag{17.18}$$

The fitness will reach a maximum value of 1.0, when $Pr(F = f_i) = Pr_{target}$, and asymptotically approaches zero as $Pr(F = f_i)$ moves away from the target probability. The σ parameter controls the fitness functions decay rate near its maximum and can be used as a tolerance control when searching for the maximum fitness. The fitness of a set of chaogate thresholds for a CL ALU implementing each function in NG with a given probability is the product of the individual fitness terms:

$$fit = \prod_i fit_i. \tag{17.19}$$

17.5.2 *Representation*

In this algorithm, each circuit is represented as a matrix, with a maximum number of gates defined by the number of matrix rows. The first column of each row is the type of gate. So far, only 2-input gates are considered. However, the algorithm could easily be modified to allow gates with a heterogeneous number of inputs. The second and third columns are the gate inputs, which may be primary inputs or outputs of other gates. The fourth column indicates whether or not the output of a particular gate is a primary output, and which output it is. Finally, the fifth column is the threshold value for chaogates, indicated as CG2. The scheme is shown in Figure 17.10 for an example circuit.

The matrix circuit representation has a couple of implications for which types of circuits can be evolved. First, each row in the matrix corresponds to a gate and is assigned to a unique output node. Therefore, a single node cannot have multiple drivers. However, it can be noticed that there is nothing preventing a circuit from having a feedback loop. Although feedback loops are not typically wanted in these circuits, removing this constraint allows the EA to more easily explore the design space. Finally, allowing the primary outputs to be moved around allows the creation of composite functions, where one output is a function of another one.

The EA used here includes tournament selection, probabilistic crossover, probabilistic mutation, elitism, and 100% replacement of the previous population. The evolved CL is shown in Figure 17.11. Crossover is achieved by taking the matrix representation of two circuits and then swapping a random subset of their rows. Furthermore, the mutation operators that can be applied are listed in Table 17.1.

We applied the EA to a simple design problem, where within 100 iterations, we wanted a CL circuit which had a 0.5 probability of being an AND gate. It is interesting to note that the theoretical probability of the circuit performing an AND function is 0.25. However, using Equation 17.19

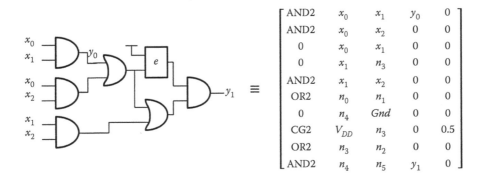

$$
\equiv
\begin{bmatrix}
\text{AND2} & x_0 & x_1 & y_0 & 0 \\
\text{AND2} & x_0 & x_2 & 0 & 0 \\
0 & x_0 & x_1 & 0 & 0 \\
0 & x_1 & n_3 & 0 & 0 \\
\text{AND2} & x_1 & x_2 & 0 & 0 \\
\text{OR2} & n_0 & n_1 & 0 & 0 \\
0 & n_4 & Gnd & 0 & 0 \\
\text{CG2} & V_{DD} & n_3 & 0 & 0.5 \\
\text{OR2} & n_3 & n_2 & 0 & 0 \\
\text{AND2} & n_4 & n_5 & y_1 & 0
\end{bmatrix}
$$

Figure 17.10   CL circuit (left) and its chromosomal representation (right).

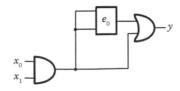

Figure 17.11   CL circuit evolved using the proposed EA.

Table 17.1   Mutation Operators

Mutation	Effect on CL Circuit
Change first component of randomly chosen row vector to a randomly chosen element in G	Changes function of logic gate
Change second or third component of randomly chosen row vector to randomly chosen element in N	Change the input to a logic gate
Assign zero to first component of randomly chosen row vector	Removes a gate
Change randomly chosen row vector with first component equal to zero to a randomly chosen element in G	Adds a gate
Permute fourth column	Change output nodes
Change fifth column of row with "CG2" as first element	Change a chaogate threshold

the error was determined to be ≈ 0.01, indicating that the simulated probability is very close to the target of 0.5. The discrepancy between the theoretical and simulated probabilities lies in the fact that we only simulated for 100 iterations, and within those 100 iterations the chaogate's probability was skewed away from its theoretical value, given in Equation 17.11. This is a demonstration of the utility of the metaheuristic design approach, especially when we are targeting specific probabilities within a small number of cycles.

17.6 Conclusions and Future Directions

Chaotic computing is a promising research domain with a broad application spectrum, including hardware security, reconfigurable logic, and neuromorphic computing. We explored the design space of CL circuits and proposed methods for tuning the probabilities of achieving particular functions. Results indicate that metaheuristic approaches may be effective at designing CL circuits, especially when a small number of runtime iterations are considered. We also presented several avenues for future work, including reduction of the number of chaogates in a CL circuit and selection of robust input to initial state mapping functions. In this chapter, however, we specifically focused on the security aspects of chaos-based systems. As mentioned earlier, there exists an opportunity of implementing multiple op code sets using the same hardware because of the morphing nature of chaogates. Having same hardware for different implementations also indicates a similar or almost same amount of energy consumption across different operations. Therefore, the difficulty for an adversary to mount an SCA-based attack or layout reverse engineering attack would be much higher. Thus, chaotic circuits pave the way for a secure and unique computing system, namely PUCS.

There are a lot of things to consider while designing and building this PUCS system with chaotic circuits. A major bottleneck in the CL design paradigm is the size of the chaogate. Typically, these are analog circuits, with capacitive and inductive elements (especially in the case of the Chua circuit), which require a significant amount silicon real estate. Therefore, reducing the number of chaogates or the size of individual chaogates is critical. The latter may be achieved through clever circuit designs with emerging nanotechnologies and will be discussed in future. The former is more

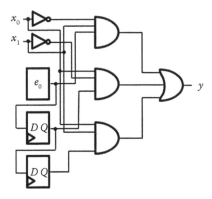

Figure 17.12 Single chaogate and shift register circuit derived from the sum-of-products design method.

tangible in the short term by considering parts of a CL circuit have chaogates with identical inputs. For example, the sum-of-products design method described in Section 17.4.2 will yield circuits with several 0-input chaogates. We can replace that set of chaogates with a single chaogate and a shift register, as shown in Figure 17.12. By delaying a single chaogates output, we can create one or more new chaotic bit streams which are independent [26]. Since the state space of a single chaotic element is huge, it could be useful to build a secure computing system with exponential number of different op code sets with virtually the same circuit configuration. As being completely analog circuits, how chaogates performs in a real hardware with inherent process variations and added probing circuitries are yet to be explored. Analysis of the op code implementations, uniqueness of op code sets and energy consumption, and delay analysis of the whole system are also some of the works that are left to be done in near future.

Acknowledgments

The authors would like to thank Lok Yan, Bryant Wysocki, and Nathan McDonald of the Air Force Research Laboratory for interesting discussions on this topic. This work was supported by the Air Force Office of Scientific Research under award numbers LRIR-13RI05COR and FA9550-16-1-0301.

The material and results presented in this paper have been CLEARED (Distribution A) for public release, unlimited distribution by AFRL, case number 88ABW-2017-2375. Any opinions, findings, and conclusions or recommendations expressed in this material are those of the author and do not necessarily reflect the views of AFRL or its contractors.

References

1. J. Rajendran, H. Zhang, C. Zhang, G. S. Rose, Y. Pino, O. Sinanoglu, and R. Karri. Fault analysis-based logic encryption. *IEEE Transactions on Computers*, **64**(2):410–424, 2015.
2. P. Kocher, J. Jaffe, and B. Jun. Differential power analysis. In *Annual International Cryptology Conference*, pages 388–397, Springer, Berlin, 1999.
3. M.-L. Akkar and C. Giraud. *An Implementation of DES and AES, Secure against Some Attacks*, pages 309–318. Springer, Berlin, Heidelberg, 2001.

4. G. Khedkar, D. Kudithipudi, and G. S. Rose. Power profile obfuscation using nanoscale memristive devices to counter dpa attacks. *IEEE Transactions on Nanotechnology*, **14**(1):26–35, 2015.

5. G. S. Rose, N. McDonald, L. Yan, B. Wysocki, and K. Xu. Foundations of memristor based PUF architectures. In *Proceedings of the IEEE/ACM International Symposium on Nanoscale Architectures (NANOARCH)*, pages 52–57, New York, July 2013.

6. G. S. Rose, N. McDonald, L. Yan, and B. Wysocki. A write-time based memristive PUF for hardware security applications. In *Proceedings of the IEEE/ACM International Conference on Computer-Aided Design (ICCAD)*, pages 830–833, San Jose, CA, November 2013.

7. A. Mazady, H. Manem, M. Rahman, D. Forte, and M. Anwar. Memristor PUF – a security primitive: Theory and experiment. *IEEE Journal on Emerging and Selected Topics in Circuits and Systems*, **5**(8):222–229, 2015.

8. P. Koeberl, U. Kocabas, and A.-R. Sadeghi. Memristor PUFs: A new generation of memory-based physically unclonable functions. In *Design, Automation & Test in Europe Conference & Exhibition (DATE)*, pages 428–431, Grenoble, France, March 2013.

9. O. Kavehei, C. Hosung, D. Ranasinghe, and S. Skafidas. mrPUF: A Memristive Device based Physical Unclonable Function. *ArXiv e-prints*, February 2013.

10. W. Che, J. Plusquellic, and S. Bhunia. A non-volatile memory based physically unclonable function without helper data. In *Proceedings of the 2014 IEEE/ACM International Conference on Computer-Aided Design*, pages 148–153, San Jose, CA, 2014.

11. Y. Gao, D. C. Ranasinghe, S. F. Al-Sarawi, O. Kavehei, and D. Abbott. Memristive crypto primitive for building highly secure physical unclonable functions. *Scientific Reports*, **5**: 1–11, 2015.

12. J. Rajendran, R. Karri, J. B. Wendt, M. Potkonjak, N. R. McDonald, G. S. Rose, and B. T. Wysocki. Nanoelectronic solutions for hardware security. *IACR Cryptology ePrint Archive*, **2012**: 575, 2012.

13. W. L. Ditto, K. Murali, and S. Sinha. Chaos computing: Ideas and implementations. *Philosophical Transactions of the Royal Society of London A: Mathematical, Physical and Engineering Sciences*, **366**(1865):653–664, 2008.

14. E. Lorenz. Deterministic nonperiodic flow. *Journal of the Atmospheric Sciences*, **20**:130–141, 1963.

15. O. E. Rössler. An equation for continuous chaos. *Physics Letters A*, **57**(5):397–398, 1976.

16. S. Sinha and W. Ditto. Dynamics based computation. *Physical Review Letters*, **81**(10):2156–2159, 1998.

17. W. L. Ditto, K. Murali, and S. Sinha. Construction of a chaotic computer chip. In P. Longhini, and A. Palacios, editors, *Applications of Nonlinear Dynamics: Model and Design of Complex Systems*, pages 3–13. Springer, Berlin, Heidelberg, 2009.

18. M. R. M. Rizk, A.-M. A. Nasser, E.-S. A. El-Badawy, and E. Abou-Bakr. A new approach for obtaining all logic gates using chuascircuit with fixed input/output levels. In *Japan–Egypt Conference on Electronics, Communications and Computers (JEC-ECC)*, pages 12–17, Alexandria, Egypt, March, 2012.

19. T. Munakata, S. Sinha, and W. L. Ditto. Chaos computing: Implementation of fundamental logic gates by chaotic elements. *IEEE Transactions on Circuits Systems I*, **49**(11):1629–1633, 2002.

20. M. R. Jahed-Motlagh, B. Kia, W. L. Ditto, and S. Sinha. Fault tolerance and detection in chaotic computers. *International Journal of Bifurcation and Chaos*, **17**(06):1955–1968, 2007.

21. B. Kia, A. Dari, W. L. Ditto, and M. L. Spano. Unstable periodic orbits and noise in chaos computing. *Chaos*, **21**(4): 047520, 2011.

22. G. S. Rose. A chaos-based arithmetic logic unit and implications for obfuscation. In *IEEE Computer Society Annual Symposium on VLSI*, pages 54–58, Tampa, FL, July 2014.

23. J. Bohl, L. K. Yan, and G. S. Rose. A two-dimensional chaotic logic gate for improved computer security. In *IEEE International Midwest Symposium on Circuits and Systems (MWSCAS)*, pages 1–4, Fort Collins, CO, August, 2015.

24. G. S. Rose, D. Kudithipudi, G. Khedkar, N. McDonald, B. Wysocki, and L.-K. Yan. Nanoelectronics and hardware security. In R. E. Pino, editor, *Network Science and Cybersecurity*, pages 105–123, Springer, Berlin, 2014.

25. L. O. Chua and G. N. Lin. Canonical realization of Chua's circuit family. *IEEE Transactions on Circuits and Systems*, **37**(7):885–902, 1990.

26. B. D. Brown and H. C. Card. Stochastic neural computation. I. Computational elements. *IEEE Transactions on Computers*, **50**(9):891–905, 2001.

Chapter 18

Security from Sneak Paths in Crossbar Memory Architectures

Md. Badruddoja Majumder, Mesbah Uddin, and
Garrett S. Rose

Contents

The crossbar array is an attractive nanoelectronic structure due to its high-density integration of nanoscale devices. A nanoelectronic resistive crossbar memory array is a popular emerging technology for future memory architectures. Due to the small size of nanoelectronic devices and also the density advantages of crossbars, larger memory can be integrated within a smaller area as compared to other existing technologies. However, one of the major deterrents for this architecture is the existence of sneak path currents. Sneak paths are undesired current paths in a crossbar of passive memory elements. Sneak path current causes unselected devices to be written erroneously, which is a severe reliability issue [1,2]. A number of design modifications have been proposed to mitigate write problems that arise from sneak paths. Most mitigation techniques are based on controlling the voltage applied to the selected row and column such that unselected memory cells do not observe enough voltage to change the resistive state. Sneak paths also affect the read operation in a crossbar because the output current is not only a function of the selected device but also a function of the unselected ones [3,4]. The effect of sneak paths on reading with respect to crossbar sizes has been studied extensively in the literature with various solutions being proposed to mitigate the effect. The most prominent architecture for mitigating the sneak path issue in nanoelectronic memory uses a selector device, transistor (1T1R) or rectifying device, diode (1D1R) to restrict current flow only through the selected cell.

Along with the problems associated with sneak paths in crossbar structure, researchers have also proposed how to leverage them for a number of hardware-based security applications. These applications constitute low overhead alternatives for traditional security primitives, especially in highly resource constrained applications from the perspective of area, power, and delay. As crossbar architectures are mainly used as memory, these security applications are all memory based. Among these applications are sneak path-based encryption for memory data, memory testing based on sneak path currents, and tag generation from memory data for integrity checking [5–7]. Security applications for memory data in traditional way are facilitated by completely separate hardware such as an encryption engine, hash functions, etc. On the contrary, sneak path-based security applications use the memory itself for the security application such as an encryption and integrity checking, thus saving extra hardware. At the same time, a sneak path-based method is also lightweight in terms of processing time and power consumption.

18.1 Resistive Crossbar Arrays

The crossbar is a well-known structure useful for resistive nanoelectronic memory architectures. In a crossbar-based architecture, horizontal and vertical nanowires form a grid-like structure. Resistive memory cells are placed at the crosspoints of the rows and columns. Figure 18.1 shows such a crossbar structure. The crossbar enables very large scale integration for high-density memory. The row lines and column lines of the crossbar are connected with row and column decoders, respectively. Row and column decoders enable the addressing and read–write operation of the memory. When a particular address is applied to the memory, the row and column decoders select the corresponding row and column of the crossbar. The resistive memory element at a given crosspoint, such as memristor, exhibits a hysteresis current–voltage characteristic. For set and reset operations of an addressed memory cell, a positive and negative voltage are applied to the corresponding row and column, respectively. On the other hand, for reading an addressed memory cell, a nondestructive voltage that does not alter the resistance level of the memory cell is applied across it, and the current flowing through the cell is sampled with a sensing circuitry to determine the stored state of the memory.

Addressing only the particular memory cell is not achievable in a resistive crossbar memory architecture due to the passive nature of resistive memory. When a memory cell is addressed for writing or reading, due to the sneak path current through other unaddressed memory cells, the cells in that path are also affected by the same writing or reading method.

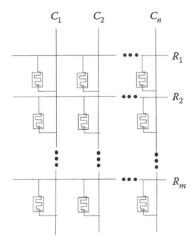

Figure 18.1   Crossbar resistive memory architecture.

18.2 Sneak Path

Sneak path current is a common feature and challenge of resistive crossbar memory architectures. Figure 18.2 illustrates sneak path currents in a simple 2×2 crossbar example. Here, R_0 is the addressed memory cell and the series path connecting R_1, R_2, and R_3 is the sneak path. For proper functionality of the memory, when a cell is addressed for writing, all other unaddressed cells should be unaffected. Otherwise, a memory cell would be undesirably overwritten due to a write operation to another memory cell. Similarly, during a read operation, memory cells in the sneak path also contribute to the reading from an addressed memory cells. Thus, it is clearly a concern for reliable write and read operation of crossbar memory architecture. The following sections will elaborate on the write and read disturbance resulting from sneak path currents.

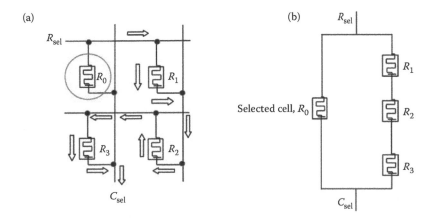

Figure 18.2   (a) sneak paths in a 2×2 crossbar. (b) Simplified circuit for illustrating sneak path.

18.2.1 Write Disturbance

To write a memory cell in the crossbar, a write voltage is applied across the selected cell. The write voltage must be greater than the minimum amount of voltage required to switch the resistive state of the memory cell and also needs to be applied for a minimum period of time. Due to sneak paths, current flow is not only confined to the selected cell but also to unselected cells. A memory cell among the unselected cells has the chance of being overwritten if a voltage greater than the switching threshold is applied for a sufficient amount of time. The mechanism for write disturbance of unselected memory cells depends on the write scheme followed in the crossbar. There are different methods for writing to a crossbar memory. Here, we discuss the write disturbance in a resistive crossbar memory according to a few different write methods.

18.2.1.1 Write Method 1

In this method, the write voltage is applied to the selected memory cells and all unselected rows and columns are left floating [1]. In Figure 18.2, we see that when R_0 is selected for writing, write voltage (V_W) is applied across it. The same voltage (V_W) appears across the series combination of R_1, R_2, and R_3. Let us inspect the possible cases here.

Figure 18.3 shows a 4×4 crossbar array to further explain the write disturbance due to sneak paths. If we examine the circuit, there are a number of ways a sneak path can be formed. Each sneak path consists of an odd number of memory cells such as 3, 5, 7, and so on. In this architecture, the write voltage, V_w, appears across each of the sneak paths. The case where only one cell is OFF

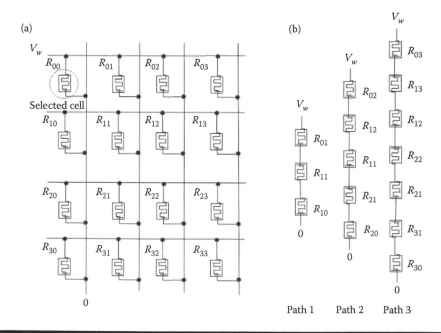

Figure 18.3 (a) Write method by applying write pulse (V_w) across selected cells and keeping all unselected rows and columns floating. (b) Sneak path consisting of three cells, five cells, and seven cells in the crossbar shown in (a).

among all other cells in the sneak path, that one OFF cell is most likely to be affected by the write operation of the selected cells. In this case, due to a negligible drop across the ON cells in sneak path, most of the write voltage, V_w, will appear across the cells which are OFF. If the write operation to the selected cell is a SET, the only OFF memory cell in the sneak path would be also SET due to having nearly V_w across it. If the number of memory cells in the sneak path is large, then the drop across the ON memory cells would not be negligible anymore, which would reduce the chance for write disturbance. Therefore, sneak paths that contain a large number of memory cells are less likely to be affected by the SET write operation. It can also be inferred that the write disturbance is only due to the SET operation. The condition for a memory cell in the sneak path to get sufficient write voltage is only that cell is in the OFF state and all others in the same path is in the ON state. However, the memory cell that gets the write voltage, V_w, is already in the OFF state and cannot be affected by reset operation.

18.2.1.2 Write Method 2

In this method, the write voltage, V_w, is applied across the selected cell and all unselected rows and columns are grounded. Figure 18.4a illustrates this method of writing. For example, during SET operation, V_w is applied to the selected row and the selected column is grounded. In this method, all cells in the selected row and unselected column, which are also known as half selected cells, get the full write voltage, V_w, across them. Write disturbance is most dominant in this write method. The number of cells that are affected by this method are the number of columns in the crossbar. Unlike write method 1, this method is susceptible to both the SET and RESET write operation.

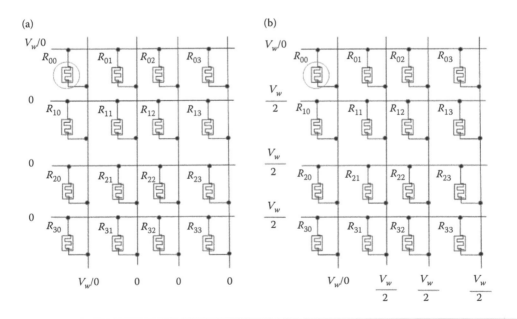

Figure 18.4 **(a) Writing by applying write voltage across the selected cells and keeping all unselected rows and columns grounded. (b) Writing by applying write voltage across the selected cells and applying half of the write voltage to all unselected rows and columns.**

18.2.1.3 Write Method 3

In this method, during a write operation, V_w is applied across the selected memory cell by applying V_w and 0 to the selected row and column, respectively, for the SET operation and vice versa for the RESET. A half write voltage, $V_w/2$, is applied to all unselected rows and columns. Figure 18.4b illustrates this method where all half selected cells between selected row and unselected column get a voltage of $V_w/2$ across them. Now the likeliness of those cells to be overwritten depends on the parameters such as the margin between the write voltage used in the write process and minimum write voltage needed for a cell to be switched. If $V_w/2$ is greater than the minimum voltage required for the write operation, the half selected cells are likely to be overwritten during any write to the selected memory cell. Even if the voltage across half selected cells is not large enough to alter the resistance level fully from ON (OFF) to OFF (ON) state with every write because of the write pulse width, subsequent write disturbance in the same direction has a high chance of eventually overwriting the unselected cells.

18.2.2 Read Disturbances

Sneak path currents contribute to the total current that flows through the sensing circuit and thus affects the the reading of a selected cell in the crossbar. It can be easily inferred that current that flows through any sneak path is dependent on the resistance value of the memory cells in that path. Therefore, sneak path currents follow a statistical distribution based on the distributions of the memory contents. The crossbar array shown in Figure 18.5a can be represented as a parallel combination of the selected cell resistance and equivalent resistance of the all other unselected cells. The equivalent circuit is shown in Figure 18.5b. The total current read is the summation of both the currents flowing into the selected cells and the sneak paths. With an increase in crossbar size, the number of sneak paths increases and sneak path current becomes larger too. Due to this

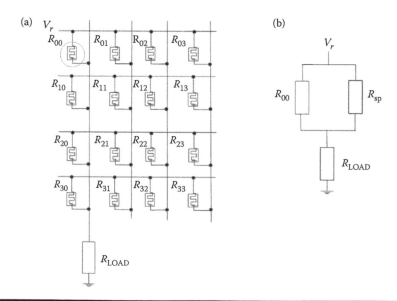

Figure 18.5 (a) Reading a selected cell by keeping all unselected rows and columns floating. (b) Equivalent circuit showing sneak path equivalent resistance.

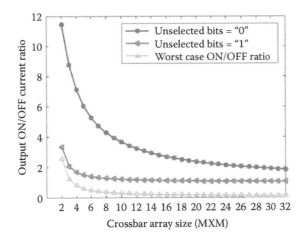

Figure 18.6 **Output current ratio for selected cells being "1" and "0." Two curves shows the case where all unselected bits are "0" and "1," respectively. Third curve shows the worst case considering the unselected bits "1" for the selected bit "0" and vice versa.**

larger sneak path current, a memory cell in an OFF state may be read as ON and thus affects the reliability of a read operation. In other words, the noise margin of the read operation becomes narrower. After a certain point, the output voltage distribution curves due to the ON and OFF state of the selected cells overlap. Figure 18.6 shows the ON/OFF current ratio in a crossbar for three different cases: considering unselected cells to "1," "0," and the worst case where unselected cells are "0" for selected cell "1" and vice versa. Results indicate that ON/OFF current ratio decreases with crossbar size and the ON/OFF current ratio becomes lower as we take the measurement by considering unselected cells as "1," "0," and the worst case, respectively.

18.3 Practical Crossbar Memory Architecture

A number of methods have been proposed by researchers to overcome problems associated with sneak paths in crossbar resistive memory. The main motives of these methods are to restrict the current flow into the selected memory cell only. One of the approaches used for this purpose consists of using a diode in series with each memory cell. The memory structure used in this approach is known as one-diode one-resistor (1D1R) memory [8,9]. Another method is to use a transistor in series with each resistive memory cell. This is known as one-transistor one-resistor (1T1R) architecture [4,9].

18.3.1 1D1R Structure

In this memory architecture, each memory cell consists of the resistive memory element and a diode that makes the name 1-diode 1-resistor (1D1R). Figure 18.7 shows a 1D1R crossbar memory architecture. Since diode is a rectifying device, it allows the current to flow only in one direction, which makes this architecture suitable only for unipolar resistive switching devices. However, assuming a unipolar switching device, this architecture reduces the sneak path affect on writing and reading operation in a crossbar resistive memory.

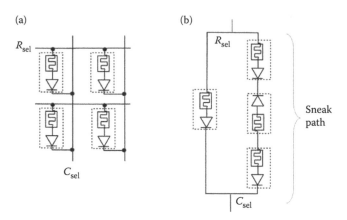

Figure 18.7   (a) 1D1R architecture for crossbar resistive memory. (b) Simplified circuit showing how reverse biased diodes prevent current flow in any direction in the sneak path.

Figure 18.7b shows the sneak path in a 2×2 1D1R crossbar array where the path consists of three memory cells in series. The first and last cells are connected in the same polarity where the middle one is in the opposite polarity. As a result, there are no conducting paths for unselected memory cells. We described in an earlier section that there are a number of ways sneak path currents may exist in a generalized crossbar array where each consists of a stack of an odd number of memory cells. In that stack, diodes of first and last cells are connected in the same polarity and the rest of the cells are connected as back-to-back pairs. Current cannot flow in a path where diodes are connected in a back-to-back manner because of the reverse bias. As a result, most of the write voltage will be dropped across the diodes and the memory element in the sneak path will not have sufficient voltage for switching. The back-to-back diode arrangement in sneak paths prevents current flow in any direction. The 1D1R structure thus significantly reduces the reliability concern of read method due to sneak paths in crossbar-based memory.

18.3.2 1T1R Structure

In this memory architecture, every memory cell comprises one transistor and one resistive memory element. Current flowing through the channel of a transistor can be controlled by its gate terminal. Therefore, it can be used to control the current flow through the two terminal passive memory element, which is incapable of controlling its current flow itself as it has no independent third terminal. Figure 18.8 shows the structure of a 1T1R memory cell. The transistor gates are connected with the word lines (WLs). For each cell, a source/drain terminal is connected with the bit line (BL) while the other is connected with the passive memory element. The other end of the memory element is connected with lines named as load lines (LLs).

During a write operation, a memory cell is addressed by selecting the corresponding WL and BL in the crossbar. Selected WLs are driven by enough voltage to turn on the transistor. For writing "1" to the memory cell, BLs and LLs are driven with write voltage, and V_w and 0 and vice versa for writing "0."

For reading a selected cell, a read voltage is applied to the BL and the corresponding LLs are connected with load resistors to sense the voltage resulting from the stored ON or OFF states of the selected memory elements.

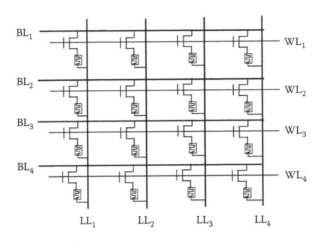

Figure 18.8 1T1R crossbar architecture.

Let us explain how this architecture helps to prevent write disturbance with a 2 × 2 1T1R crossbar array shown in Figure 18.9. When memory cell M_0 is selected for writing by driving V_w across the selected bit lines and load lines, the stack of three other memory cells M_1, M_2, and M_3 also gets the same voltage. However, the access transistors of M_2 and M_3 are not enabled since their corresponding WLs are not selected. The resistance of these transistors would be high enough that most of the write voltage V_w would be dropped across them. None of the memory elements in the sneak path will get sufficient voltage to be overwritten by the write operation of the selected cells.

Similarly, during a read operation, every sneak path will be disabled by corresponding unselected transistors, which makes the equivalent resistance of the sneak paths higher and thus reduces the current flow by a significant amount. If the select transistors are all turned on, then the sneak paths will again exist as they would in a resistive crossbar.

Investigating the properties of sneak path, during a write, a selected cell affects the unselected cell in the sneak path. On the other hand, during a read, the selected cell is disturbed by the other unselected cells in the sneak path. The most important observation here is that sneak path

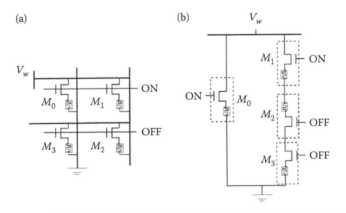

Figure 18.9 (a) 1T1R architecture for a 2 × 2 crossbar resistive memory. (b) Simplified circuit illustrating how sneak path currents are restricted only to the selected memory cells.

interference is dependent on the combination of memory data in unselected cells. Different combinations of data in the unselected cells result in different interference during write and read. This data dependency of the sneak path read and write can be leveraged for various security applications for memory such as data encryption, fault testing, data integrity check, etc.

18.4 Sneak Path Data Encryption

Resistive crossbar memory is a potential technology for nonvolatile main memory of a computer system. Memory has been the most attractive target for attack on any computing system. As computer memory stores different confidential information, encryption or obfuscation of memory data is an important security requirement. We can leverage sneak path write disturbance for encrypting data stored in a crossbar resistive memory as proposed by Kannan et al. [6]. The sneak path encryption technique we describe here considers a crossbar resistive memory capable of storing 2 bits per memory cell.

When a memory cell is selected for writing by applying a voltage across it, unselected memory cells can also get a nonnegligible voltage across them. This voltage is dependent on the combination of data stored in unselected memory cells. By applying a voltage pulse across the selected cell, we can change the resistive state of some other cells in the sneak path. Considering 1T1R structure, we can limit the sneak paths to a limited area around the selected cells. Thus, by gradually selecting a memory cell for writing along with enabling a subset of sneak paths around it, we can encrypt the whole memory. The targeted cell is termed as the point of encryption (POE) and the set of memory cells in the enabled portion of sneak path is termed as polyomino [6].

Figure 18.10 illustrates a crossbar showing a selected memory cell working as the POE and a set of unselected memory cells as polyomino. The whole sneak path-based encryption and decryption mechanism is illustrated in Figure 18.11 with an example plain text and four processing steps. A pseudo-random number generator (PRNG) is used to randomly generate the sequence of voltage

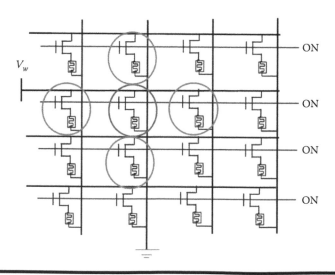

Figure 18.10   Example of selected cells as POE and few unselected cells as polyomino in a 1T1R resistive crossbar memory structure.

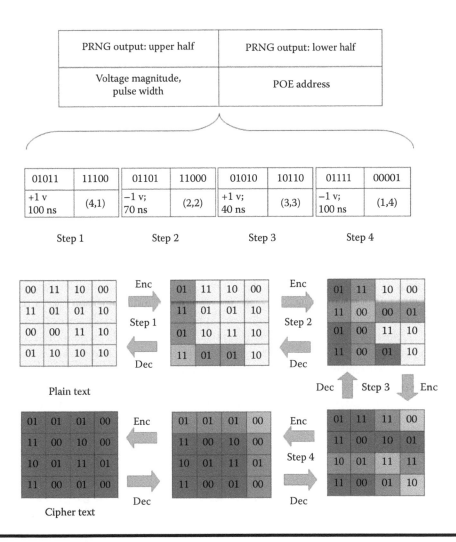

Figure 18.11 **Sneak Path encryption and decryption steps. PRNG output is mapped to a POR address and a voltage pulse information. Highlighted cells and intersection of them represent polyomino and the POE, respectively.**

pulses and a target address location in the memory for applying the pulse. Applying random voltage pulses to a number of randomly selected POE each with overlapping polyominos encrypts the whole memory. The seed of the PRNG works as the encryption key. The output of PRNG is divided into two halves: one half determines the voltage pulse to be applied to POE and another determines the address for the POE. The half of the PRNG that determines the voltage pulse is fed into a look-up table (LUT) mapping that random number into a pulse magnitude and duration for the applied voltage. Similarly, other half of the PRNG is fed into another LUT that maps it into an address location for the POE.

The polyominos for each POE is selected based on minimizing the total number of POE while fulfilling the criteria such as that (i) two polyomino should not have exactly same POE, (ii) no memory cell should be used twice as a POE, and (iii) the overlap between memory cells in polyominos should be minimized.

For decryption, the random sequence for selecting the POEs is reversed. The magnitude of the applied voltage is reversed too. However, the pulse width may be slightly different because of the hysteresis nature of the resistive switching device such as memristors. Hysteresis nature causes the device to take a different path for switching from low to high resistive states and high to low resistive states. Another factor that affects the decryption is that we can just control the applied voltage to the POE while voltage appearing across the each memory cell in the polyomino depends on the resistive states of other memory cells in the same set. The resistive states of the memory cells in the polyomino changes after encryption. Therefore, simply applying an opposite voltage to POE does not guarantee to write memory cells to the desired resistance level. However, by analyzing the crossbar circuit, proper voltage range that can take resistance value within the desired memory state can be figured out and hence reliability of the decryption process can be ensured.

18.5 Sneak Path Memory Testing

Sneak path currents can also be leveraged for a faster and more energy efficient memory testing technique for resistive crossbars proposed by Kannan et al. [5]. Physical defects cause different types of faults in memory. There are a number of faults that can potentially occur in memory such as stuck-at 0(1), deep 0(1) fault, slow write, etc. [10]. In stuck-at faults, a memory cell is stuck at a particular resistance level and does not change with applied voltage. For example, in a stuck-at 0 fault, the memory cell remains in the high-resistance state irrespective of the stimulation applied. Similarly, in a stuck-at 1 fault, the memory cell remains in the low-resistance state. Deep 0 or 1 fault occurs when the high-resistance limit of a memory cell increases and low resistance limit decreases. During deep 0 faults, the memory cell has a resistance R, such that $R_{OFF} + \Delta R > R > R_{OFF}$.

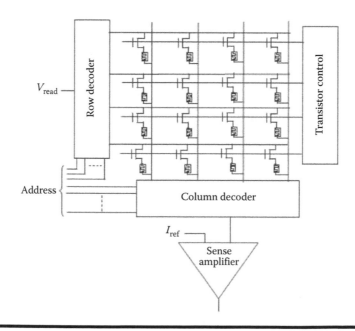

Circuit for sneak path memory testing. Region of detection is controlled by the transistor control block.

Similarly, during a deep 1 fault, $R_{ON} + \Delta R < R < R_{ON}$. Now, if the deep 0 faulty memory cell is written to "1" using the usual write pulse, it will not reach the resistance level required for memory state "1" and causes a fault. Similarly, a faulty deep 1 memory cell cannot reach the required level of resistance when attempted for writing a "0" to it. Slow write fault occurs when the rate of change in resistance level during the write process decreases and the memory cell does not switch to desired state.

Traditional memory testing is an exhaustive method which requires each memory cell to be tested individually. This method is very time consuming. As we already know that due to sneak paths in a crossbar resistive memory, current read from a selected memory element is corrupted by the other unselected memory cells around it. The read value of the output current essentially reflects the resistive state of all memory cells in the crossbar. We can leverage this idea for a more faster memory testing approach where by reading a memory cell in the presence of sneak path we can detect whether there is a faulty cell in the memory. Since the current is a function of the resistive state of all memory cells in the crossbar, we can detect any fault by comparing the read current to its ideal value corresponding to the case where there was no fault. However, there are few concerns for this technique to be feasible. The deviation of read current due to a fault must be large enough to be detected by the comparator. It can easily be inferred that with the increase of crossbar size the sensitivity of read current to individual memory cell reduces. Therefore, the total number of unselected cells in the sneak path must be restricted during testing process. Considering an 1T1R structure, we can enable or disable memory cells to be included in the sneak path by controlling the corresponding transistor of 1T1R memory cell. Memory cells that are enabled during the read of memory for test purpose is termed as the region of detection (ROD).

To detect a stuck-at 0 fault, all memory cells in an ROD are written to 1. The read current is compared with a reference current. The reference current is chosen such that if a there is a fault in any of the memory cells within the ROD the read value will be less than the reference value and the read current will be greater than the reference if no fault occurs. Similarly, during a stuck-at 1 fault, all cells are written to 0 and a selected cell within the ROD is read. The read current will be higher than the reference value if there is a fault and lower if no fault within the ROD.

Deep 0(1) faults are similar to slow write faults. Deep 0(1) faults are sensitized in a particular memory cell by applying the write pulse for a longer time than usual. An opposite write pulse is applied then with an usual pulse width. As the resistance level of the memory cell remains in a deep region, the usual pulse width cannot pull it to the required resistance level for having a normal operation. Instead, the memory cell gives a faulty reading. During a deep 0 fault, the output read current will be less than the reference value and vice versa for a deep 1 fault. Thus, different faults can be tested by calibrating the comparator with appropriate reference value corresponding to the type of fault under test.

18.6 Sneak Path Integrity Checking

Sneak paths can also be leveraged for integrity checking of the data stored in a resistive crossbar memory. When sneak paths are enabled in a 1T1R memory by keeping the corresponding transistors on, current flowing through a selected column is dependent on every memory cell in the crossbar. This current is a representation of the data stored in the crossbar memory, which is also termed as a data tag. To store more information in the tag, multiple columns can be selected for reading. Figure 18.12 shows such a tag generation scheme, which has been proposed in Reference 7.

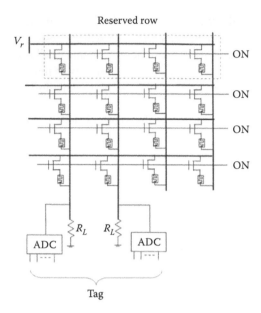

Figure 18.12 Sneak path tag generation pulse. Reserved row is shown by encircling with a dotted rectangular box.

A voltage is applied to a crossbar row, and multiple columns are selected for reading while sneak paths are enabled. A sense resistor is used with each selected column to sample the current flowing through it. The voltage across the sense resistor in each selected column is converted to a multibit digital value with an analog to digital converter (ADC).

A crossbar resistive network is such that change in the selected memory cell is significantly dominant over each unselected cells individually. In other words, sneak path tag generation is biased toward the selected cell. However, a secure tag generation system is supposed to be unbiased to all data bits. Otherwise, adversaries would try to modify the bits in which the tag is less dependent and remain unnoticed. A method is proposed to overcome this bias where the selected row for tag generation is not a part of regular memory data. Rather, it is a row of reserved memory cells used only for tag generation. During every write to the memory, memory cells in the reserved row are reconfigured with random bits. In this way, contents in the reserved row also become unpredictable by the adversaries.

As the crossbar becomes larger, dependency of the tag on individual memory cells decreases. Therefore, sneak path tag generation cannot be applied to an infinitely large crossbar. Instead, the crossbar is divided into multiple sections for tag generation. Figure 18.13 shows the sectioning of a crossbar for tag generation. Though the sections are physically connected with each other, they can be electrically isolated by disabling the corresponding transistor lines in the 1T1R memory. The sections are enabled sequentially for tag generation and the same reserved row is used for all sections. Tags generated from multiple sections can be combined together by XORing so that more memory data can be represented by fewer tag bits.

Using this tag generation mechanism, integrity of the data stored in the memory can be verified. This mechanism considers any unauthorized modification of memory data by an adversary as the violation of integrity. No fault diagnosis or error checking is considered as integrity checking with

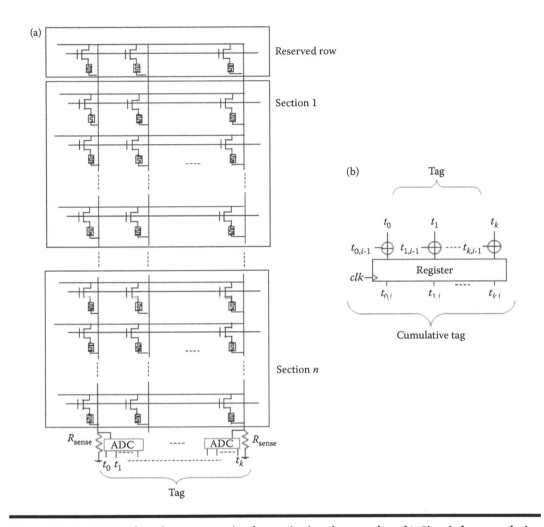

Figure 18.13 **(a) Sneak path tag generation by sectioning the crossbar. (b) Circuit for cumulative tag generation by combining tag from different sections.**

this sneak path integrity checking mechanism. Fault diagnosis is covered in sneak path testing described in the previous section.

When data are written to the memory, the reserved row is configured with new random bits as well. After that, tags are generated sequentially from each section using the same reserved row and stored in registers. Finally, all tags from all sections are XORed to generate the overall tags. The final tag is stored to a secure location to be used as a reference for detecting any unauthorized modification of memory data.

Before reading from memory, the tag is regenerated and compared against the reference tag which was stored during the previous write operation. Tag regeneration is performed in the same way the tag is generated except the reserved row is not changed during tag regeneration. If the regenerated tag matches with the reference tag, memory data are taken as untampered. Otherwise, an exception is raised indicating that unauthorized modification was performed in memory data.

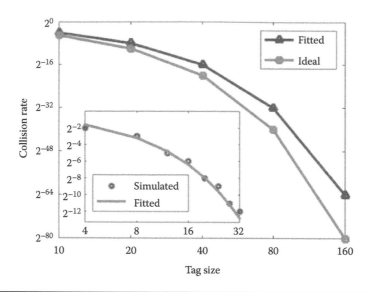

Figure 18.14   Collision rate versus different tag size for ideal data and extrapolated best fit of simulated data. Simulated data and the best fit for a tag size up to 32 bits are shown in the inset.

The security of this integrity checking protocol is measured in terms of collision resistance. Figure 18.14 shows the comparison between collision resistance of the sneak path integrity checking protocol and the one based on ideal hash function. Results suggest that to obtain the same security as an ideal integrity checking protocol provides, sneak path-based one requires 25% more tag bits. However, since the sneak path integrity checking protocol uses the memory itself for tag computation and therefore requires very little extra hardware, reaching the required level of security with significantly less implementation overhead is realistic.

18.7 Conclusion

Sneak path has been an intriguing area of research in nanoelectronic circuit design. It has been treated a troublesome issue which obstructs using the benefit of nanoelectronic crossbar architecture due to the interference among selected and unselected memory cells. The most practical solutions to sneak path issue is to use selector device with the passive resistive devices in the crossbar memory architecture which is known as 1T1R architecture. This architecture facilitates selecting each memory cell individually without interference from unselected cells. However, this comes with an overhead of area which reduces the high density benefit of crossbar architecture to some extent. Though different other architectures have been proposed without using a selector device as a mitigation technique for sneak paths, none of them have proven to be a general purpose and cost-effective solution yet. Therefore, sneak path mitigation without a selector device is still an open area for research. Besides, sneak path has been used for lightweight memory-based security applications such as encryption, integrity checking, fault testing, etc. These applications also show the possibility of nano-enabled in-memory computation, which will open new computing architecture where computer memory serves the purpose of both storage and processing units.

Acknowledgments

This material is based upon the work supported by the Air Force Office of Scientific Research under award number FA9550-16-1-0301. Any opinions, finding, and conclusions or recommendations expressed in this material are those of the authors and do not necessarily reflect the views of the United States Air Force.

References

1. Y. Cassuto, S. Kvatinsky, and E. Yaakobi. Write sneak-path constraints avoiding disturbs in memristor crossbar arrays. In *2016 IEEE International Symposium on Information Theory (ISIT)*, pages 950–954. IEEE, New York, NY, 2016.
2. A. Ghofrani, M. A. Lastras-Montaño, and K.-T. Cheng. Towards data reliable crossbar-based memristive memories. In *2013 IEEE International Test Conference (ITC)*, pages 1–10. IEEE, New York, NY, 2013.
3. G. S. Rose, Y. Yao, J. M. Tour, A. C. Cabe, N. Gergel-Hackett, N. Majumdar, J. C. Bean, L. R. Harriott, and M. R. Stan. Designing CMOS/molecular memories while considering device parameter variations. *ACM Journal on Emerging Technologies in Computing Systems (JETC)*, 3(1):3, 2007.
4. S. Kim, J. Zhou, and W. D. Lu. Crossbar RRAM arrays: Selector device requirements during write operation. *IEEE Transactions on Electron Devices*, 61(8):2820–2826, 2014.
5. S. Kannan, J. Rajendran, R. Karri, and O. Sinanoglu. Sneak-path testing of crossbar-based nonvolatile random access memories. *IEEE Transactions on Nanotechnology*, 12(3):413–426, 2013.
6. S. Kannan, N. Karimi, O. Sinanoglu, and R. Karri. Security vulnerabilities of emerging nonvolatile main memories and countermeasures. *IEEE Transactions on Computer-Aided Design of Integrated Circuits and Systems*, 34(1):2–15, 2015.
7. M. B. Majumder, M. Uddin, G. S. Rose, and J. Rajendran. Sneak path enabled authentication for memristive crossbar memories. In *IEEE Asian Hardware-Oriented Security and Trust (AsianHOST)*, pages 1–6. IEEE, New York, NY, 2016.
8. M.-J. Lee, Y. Park, B.-S. Kang, S.-E. Ahn, C. Lee, K. Kim, W. Xianyu, G. Stefanovich, J.-H. Lee, S.-J. Chung et al. 2-stack 1D-1R cross-point structure with oxide diodes as switch elements for high density resistance RAM applications. In *IEEE International Electron Devices Meeting, 2007. IEDM 2007*, pages 771–774. IEEE, New York, NY, 2007.
9. H. Manem, J. Rajendran, and G. S. Rose. Design considerations for multilevel CMOS/nano memristive memory. *ACM Journal on Emerging Technologies in Computing Systems (JETC)*, 8(1):6, 2012.
10. Y.-X. Chen and J.-F. Li. Fault modeling and testing of 1T1R memristor memories. In *2015 IEEE 33rd VLSI Test Symposium (VTS)*, pages 1–6. IEEE, New York, NY, 2015.

Acknowledgments

This research was all operated work supported in the part by Office of Scientific Research under contract numbers FA9550-15-1-0501. Any opinions, findings, and conclusions or recommendations expressed in this material are those of the author(s) and do not necessarily reflect the views of the U.S. Air Force.

Index

9 780367 572624